Daily Life through World History in Primary Documents

Daily Life through World History in Primary Documents
Lawrence Morris, General Editor

Volume 1: *The Ancient World*
David Matz

Volume 2: *The Middle Ages and Renaissance*
Lawrence Morris

Volume 3: *The Modern World*
David M. Borgmeyer and Rebecca Ayako Bennette

3 THE MODERN WORLD

Daily Life through World History in Primary Documents

Lawrence Morris
GENERAL EDITOR

David M. Borgmeyer and Rebecca Ayako Bennette
VOLUME EDITORS

GREENWOOD PRESS
Westport, Connecticut • London

Library of Congress Cataloging-in-Publication Data

Daily life through world history in primary documents / Lawrence Morris, general editor.

p. cm.

Includes bibliographical references and index.

ISBN: 978–0–313–33898–4 (set : alk. paper)

ISBN: 978–0–313–33899–1 (v. 1 : alk. paper)

ISBN: 978–0–313–33900–4 (v. 2 : alk. paper)

ISBN: 978–0–313–33901–1 (v. 3 : alk. paper)

1. Civilization—History—Sources. 2. Manners and customs—History—Sources. 3. Social history—Sources. I. Morris, Lawrence, 1972–

CB69.D35 2009

909—dc22 2008008925

British Library Cataloguing in Publication Data is available.

Library of Congress Catalog Card Number: 2008008925

ISBN: 978–0–313–33898–4 (set)

978–0–313–33899–1 (vol. 1)

978–0–313–33900–4 (vol. 2)

978–0–313–33901–1 (vol. 3)

First published in 2009

Greenwood Press, 88 Post Road West, Westport, CT 06881

An imprint of Greenwood Publishing Group, Inc.

www.greenwood.com

Printed in the United States of America

The paper used in this book complies with the Permanent Paper Standard issued by the National Information Standards Organization (Z39.48–1984).

10 9 8 7 6 5 4 3 2 1

To E.F.B. and D.H.B.
To James

CONTENTS

PART III ECONOMIC LIFE

PART IV INTELLECTUAL LIFE

SET INTRODUCTION

What time we leave work; the food we eat for dinner; how we spend our free time—these small, almost mundane details, can shape our lives as powerfully as who is the president or what battles are being fought in a far-distant country. In fact, we often judge major events—wars, legislation, trade deals—by how those events affect our everyday lives. If trade negotiations mean that we can purchase more goods for less money, we may very well support the negotiations: we will be able to eat out more, see more movies, buy more books. If the negotiations mean that we lose our jobs—resulting in skipped meals, bankruptcy, and ulcers caused by stress—we are likely to be much more critical. How an event impacts our daily life frequently determines how we view that event. Daily life, in other words, is very important and always has been.

The study of daily life therefore enables us to examine the cultural norms, concerns, and priorities of societies across time. We learn the vital importance of maritime trade for the citizens of medieval Barcelona, for example, when we examine the detailed law codes by which they carefully regulated the rights and responsibilities of ships' captains and merchants. We understand more deeply the pervasive role of religious ritual in medieval Japan when we read about the exorcisms practiced to combat ailments that we would now consider physical, not spiritual. When we learn about the day-to-day politics of the ancient Roman Republic, we appreciate how radically different life was under the Roman Empire. When we read a letter home from a U.S. soldier fighting in Vietnam, we feel more intimately the pain of separation. By studying daily life, we get a firmer understanding of what it was like to live in a certain era and a certain place. Learning that Constantine I was emperor of Rome in A.D. 313 gives us important information, but learning about the foods prepared by a Roman peasant or how a Roman merchant traveled about on business gives us a better idea of what it was really like to live in Italy during the same time period.

Primary sources, moreover, offer a uniquely valuable way of learning about the past. Primary sources, of course, are documents or artifacts produced by the people under investigation. These sources enable us to listen directly to the voices of the past. A primary source enables us to view the past from the inside, from the point of view of a person alive at the time. Our tour guide to the culture of ancient Egypt is an ancient Egyptian. Primary sources are the ultimate historical authority—there can be no greater expert on ancient Rome than an ancient Roman or on medieval France than a medieval Frenchman or woman or on twentieth-century Africa than a modern African.

Daily Life through World History in Primary Documents, therefore, offers the reader a feast of knowledge. Packed within the covers of this important three-volume set are over 500 documents, each of which offers readers the opportunity to listen to a voice from the past (and sometimes the present) explaining that person's own culture and time. The volumes are organized chronologically as follows:

- Volume 1: *The Ancient World* contains almost 300 documents from various ancient cultures, including those of Sumeria, Egypt, Israel, China, India, Greece, and Rome, with its primary focus being upon the daily life of Greece and Rome up to roughly the sack of Rome in the fifth century A.D.
- Volume 2: *The Middle Ages and Renaissance* contains almost 130 documents from various European (e.g., Anglo-Saxon England, Renaissance Italy), Asian (e.g., Tang China, medieval Japan, Mogul India), Middle Eastern (e.g., medieval Persia, early Islamic Arabia), and Latin American (e.g., Aztec Mexico, Inca Peru, Mayan Central America) cultures spanning the period from the fifth to the seventeenth centuries.
- Volume 3: *The Modern World*, covering the birth of modern democracy in the eighteenth century up through the present day, contains over 100 documents from various world cultures, including Turkey, West Africa, India, the United States, and Russia.

At the edges of these basic divides, there is some overlap between volumes, demonstrating how each era carries on from the preceding one.

Within each volume, the myriad aspects of daily life are grouped under seven overarching categories: Domestic Life, Economic Life; Intellectual Life, Material Life, Political Life, Recreational Life, and Religious Life. These categories, which were also employed by the award-winning *Greenwood Encyclopedia of Daily Life*, allow for quick reference between all three volumes. Browsing Religious Life in all three volumes, for example, will offer a scintillating introduction to and overview of the major spiritual traditions across time. Under these shared categories, each volume then further subgroups the texts in the way most useful for the time period under discussion. Common subcategories include Women, Marriage, Children, Literature, Transportation, Medicine, Housing, Clothing, Law, Reform, Sports, and Rituals. Under "Economic Life" in Volume 2, for example, the subcategories employed highlight the important roles played by urban and rural populations, as well as the well-established practice of slavery and the increasingly important role of international trade and commerce.

The scope of *Daily Life through World History in Primary Documents* is truly global. Within these pages, we see documents from countries with such diverse histories and cultures as Japan, Italy, India, West Africa, Persia, the United States, and Central America. Browsing almost any of the subcategories will offer the reader fascinating voices from non-Western cultures. Each section, however, also includes a solid central focus on the major cultures that have shaped the Western world, including Europe and the Americas. None of these cultures exists in a vacuum, however, nor are they entirely dissimilar. Western and non-Western cultures contextualize each other and comment on the common concerns of human beings around the world. Brief analytical essays at the start of each subcategory outline the documents that follow and draw out important themes that weave throughout the documents, charting a cultural conversation that crosses time and place.

To benefit the most from the primary sources, each individual document also is preceded by an analytical introduction that explains and highlights the main features of that particular document. An author of a primary document, just like authors today, may have a bias, a limited perspective, or missing information that results in a slightly inaccurate portrayal of life in a given culture. The non-specialist reader, moreover, may not be familiar with the items and ideas discussed in a document written a thousand years ago, or in a completely different more contemporary culture. The concise analytical introductions preceding each document mitigate these difficulties by providing an expert evaluation and contextualization of the following document. The combination of primary sources and modern historical analyses of those sources offers the reader a balanced perspective and a solid grounding in the modern the study of daily life.

Part I in each volume offers a detailed historical overview of the period covered. Each volume also contains a chronology of important world events for the period covered, an appendix of brief biographies of document authors or creators, a glossary defining and describing unfamiliar names and terms encountered in the section and document introductions which are also in italics throughout the text for ease of reference, and a bibliography of sources used. Glossary terms in the text appear in italics. Many documents are also illustrated and information can be further accessed through a detailed subject index for the set.

These volumes will be used in many different ways by many different readers, including high school students, college and university undergrads, and interested general readers. Some readers will delve into one volume and browse extensively, gaining an overview of how generations in one era lived their lives. Other readers may be more interested in exploring how one realm of life—political life—for example, has changed from ancient Rome through the present day; those readers will devour the appropriate categories and subcategories from each of the three volumes. Other readers will use the sources to research and support their own written analyses, for assigned essays or for their own independent research. However the reader uses these volumes, I am confident that he or she will enjoy the experience. We have collected an amazing array of intriguing sources that cannot help but capture the interest and the imagination. Enjoy!

SET ACKNOWLEDGMENTS

Many people have made working on *Daily Life through World History in Primary Documents* rewarding. First of all, the volume editors David Matz, Rebecca Ayako Bennette, and David Borgmeyer have created interesting and illuminating conversations between the plethora of texts included in their volumes—daily life comes alive in their pages. Dr. William McCarthy also helped to get the project rolling in its early stages. All the editors at Greenwood, and most especially Mariah Gumpert and John Wagner, have supported and encouraged us from day one. I thank Joyce Salisbury in particular for first awakening my interest in the study of daily life. Agus, ar ndóigh, gabhaim buíochas ar leith le mo bhean chéile, Amy, agus le mo chlann, a bhí foighneach agus tuisceanach nuair a bhuailinn an doras amach go dtí an oifig arís eile i ndiaidh an dinnéir chun beagáinín tuil-leadh a scríobh. Tá cuid díobh féin istigh san obair seo; go gcúití Dia leo é.

ACKNOWLEDGMENTS

First, I would like to thank Lawrence Morris, David Borgmeyer, and the editors at Greenwood. I also wish to express my appreciation to those who helped me at the Middlebury College Library and at Harvard University's Widener Library. In particular I would like to acknowledge the efforts of the staff members at Middlebury College's Special Collections and at the Henry Sheldon Museum's archive. My colleagues, especially professors Stephen Snyder and Neil Waters, also provided support. Finally, I want to thank James, Clara, Molly, and Lena.

Rebecca Ayako Bennette

My gratitude first of all is to the series editor Lawrence Morris for inviting me to be a part of this project. Rebecca Bennette, my co-editor, has been a joy to work with. Mariah Gumpert and John Wagner at Greenwood have made this project easy to do and much credit goes to them.

The shortcomings of this volume are fewer because of many colleagues who were willing to answer questions, read portions of the manuscript, offer advice, suggestions, expertise, and share their own research on a host of subjects. Those whom I have not forgotten to mention are Bentley Anderson, S. J., Thomas Bird, Mary Rose Grant, Mark Konecny, Thomas Madden, Nicole Monnier, Ben Moore, Mikhail Palatnik, Jennifer Popiel, Michal Rozbicki, Frank Sciacca, Meg Sempreora, Silvana Siddali, Nicole Svobodny, and Sarah Warren.

I am very grateful to Erik Palmore and his staff at the Webster University Faculty Development Center for extraordinary efforts, to Edward Kasinec and the exceptional staff at the Slavic and Baltic Division of the New York Public Library for their support and access to their outstanding collections, to holders of private collections for their willingness to allow publication from their archives, and to the staffs of the Missouri Historical Society Archives, Emerson Library at Webster University, Olin Library at Washington University, and Pius XII Memorial Library at St. Louis University for their assistance.

Very special thanks also to Jen, James, Kate, Molly, and Lucy.

David M. Borgmeyer

ACKNOWLEDGMENTS

CHRONOLOGY

CHRONOLOGY OF SELECTED EVENTS: THE MODERN WORLD

1700–1721	Great Northern War is fought between Sweden and a coalition of states led by Russia
1701–1714	War of Spanish Succession is fought between France and a European coalition that includes Britain and the Netherlands
1702–1713	Queen Anne's War, the American phase of the War of Spanish Succession, is fought between France and Britain and their respective colonists in North America
1703	Czar Peter the Great of Russia founds St. Petersburg as the new Russian capital; serious earthquake strikes the Japanese city of Edo (later Tokyo)
1707	Death of the Mughal Emperor Aurangzeb—the Mughal Empire in India begins a long period of gradual decline; Act of Union is passed creating a political union between England and Scotland
1713–1714	Treaties of Utrecht and Rastatt are signed, thus ending the War of Spanish Succession; Philip V, the grandson of Louis XIV of France is recognized as king of Spain
1715	Death of Louis XIV of France, who is succeeded by his great-grandson Louis XV; First Jacobite Rebellion, which aims at restoring the House of Stuart to the British throne, is quelled
1718	City of New Orleans is founded by the French at the mouth of the Mississippi River
1721	Treaty of Nystad is signed ending the Great Northern War, which results in Russia supplanting Sweden as the dominant power in the Baltic region
1722	Afghans invade and conquer Iran; death of the Kangxi Emperor of the Qing Dynasty, whose 61-year reign is the longest in Chinese history
1722–1723	Russo-Persian War is triggered by Peter the Great's attempt to expand Russian influence into the Caspian Sea region
1735–1739	Russo-Turkish War is fought between Russia and the Ottoman Empire
1736	Nadir Shah, founder of the Afsharid Dynasty, becomes shah of Persia

1738–1756	Severe famine spreads across the Sahel region of northern Africa, over half the population of the trading city of Timbuktu dies as a result
1739	Nadir Shah of Persia invades the Mogul Empire of northern India and sacks Delhi
1740	Frederick the Great becomes king of the German state of Prussia
1740–1748	War of the Austrian Succession is fought in Europe
1745	Second Jacobite Rebellion fails to restore House of Stuart to the British throne
1754–1763	French and Indian War, the American phase of the Seven Years War is fought in North American between Britain and France, with each supported by their colonists in America
1755	Severe earthquake devastates Lisbon, the capital of Portugal
1756–1763	Seven Years War is fought in Europe—it eventually involves most of the powers in Europe
1757	British victory at the Battle of Plassey initiates the start of British rule in India
1760	George III succeeds his grandfather George II as king of Britain
1762	Catherine the Great succeeds to the throne of Russia
1763	Treaty of Paris ends the Seven Years War/French and Indian War—France cedes its American colonies to Britain
1769	Spanish missionaries establish the first of 21 missions in California
1770	Boston Massacre—British troops fire upon civilians in Boston
1773	Protesting a tax on tea, British colonists dressed as Indians throw a shipload of tea into Boston Harbor in what is now known as the "Boston Tea Party"
1775–1783	American Revolutionary War is fought between the American colonists and Britain
1776	British colonies in North America declare their independence, forming a new republic called the United States of America
1781	Battle of Yorktown ends the fighting during the American Revolutionary War
1783	Treaty of Paris is signed ending the American Revolutionary War and securing British recognition of American independence
1788	First European settlement in Australia established by the British in Sydney
1789	Bastille prison is stormed in Paris, signaling the start of the French Revolution; George Washington is elected the first president of the United States
1793	Louis XVI of France is executed in January and his wife, Queen Marie Antoinette, is executed in October
1793–1794	French Revolution enters the phase known as the "Reign of Terror"
1795	*Marseillaise* is adopted as the national anthem of Revolutionary France
1796	In England, Edward Jenner administers the first smallpox vaccination
1799	Napoleon Bonaparte seizes power as First Consul, essentially dictator, of France
1801	The Kingdom of Great Britain and the Kingdom of Ireland are merged to form the United Kingdom

1803	Louisiana Purchase: the United States greatly enlarges its territory by buying Louisiana from France
1804	Haiti gains independence from France to become the first black republic; Napoleon crowns himself emperor of France
1807	Britain prohibits the slave trade within British dominions
1810–1821	Mexican War for Independence: Mexico frees itself from Spanish rule
1810s–1820s	Most Spanish and Portuguese colonies in Latin America win independence from colonial rule
1812	Napoleon invades Russia, but the onset of the Russian winter brings the French army to disaster
1815	Napoleon is defeated at the Battle of Waterloo, ending the Napoleonic Wars—the former emperor is exiled to the Atlantic island of St. Helena; the Congress of Vienna redraws the map of Europe
1816–1828	Shaka establishes a powerful Zulu kingdom in southern Africa
1819	Singapore is established on the tip of the Malay Peninsula by the British East India Company
1820	American Colonization Society establishes Liberia on the west coast of Africa as a haven for freed American slaves
1824	Ludwig van Beethoven, completely deaf, conducts the first performance of his Ninth Symphony in Vienna
1827	Greece achieves independence from the Ottoman Empire
1830	The Liverpool and Manchester Railway, the first passenger railway with steam-powered locomotives, opens; Joseph Smith founds the Church of Jesus Christ of Latter-Day Saints (Mormons) in New York State
1833	Slavery is abolished throughout the British Empire
1836	Texas declares and wins independence from Mexico, becoming an independent republic
1837	Victoria becomes queen of the United Kingdom
1839–1842	First Opium War is fought between Britain and China—British victory forces China to tolerate the opium trade and to open the country to increased Western trade
1840	Signing of the Treaty of Waitangi between Britain and the Maori initiates British rule in New Zealand
1845–1849	Irish potato famine reduces the population of Ireland by almost one-quarter through death and emigration
1846–1848	Mexican-American War is fought between the United States and Mexico
1847	Mormons, led by Brigham Young, settle near Salt Lake in Utah
1848	Signing of the Treaty of Guadalupe-Hidalgo results in the Mexican cession to the United States of a large part of the modern southwestern United States; gold is discovered in California; Karl Marx publishes *The Communist Manifesto;* revolutions erupt throughout Europe
1851	The Great Exhibition opens in London in the Crystal Palace, showcasing achievements in industry and culture; *New York Times* begins publishing

1851–1865	Taiping Rebellion, a large-scale revolt against the authority of the Qing government, erupts in China
1854	U.S. Commodore Matthew Perry forces Japan to end more than 200 years of isolation
1854–1856	Crimean War is fought between Russia and a coalition consisting of Britain, France, and the Ottoman Empire
1856–1860	Second Opium War is fought between Britain and China
1857–1858	Sepoy Mutiny erupts in India, resulting in the establishment of direct British rule in place of government by the East India Company
1859	Charles Darwin publishes *On the Origin of Species*
1861	Alexander II of Russia abolishes serfdom
1861–1865	American Civil War is fought between the United States and the Confederate States
1861–1867	France intervenes in Mexico imposing a French puppet government on the Mexicans
1863	U.S. President Abraham Lincoln issues the Emancipation Proclamation freeing all slaves in Confederate territory
1865	Ratification of the Thirteenth Amendment to the Constitution abolishes slavery with the United States
1867	United States purchases Alaska from Russia; the Canadian confederation is formed
1868	Meiji Restoration ends the Japanese shogunate, a feudal military dictatorship, and formally restores power to the emperor
1869	Suez Canal opens, linking the Mediterranean and Red Seas
1870–1871	Franco-Prussian War results in the formal unification of the German Empire under the Prussian monarchy
1874	British East India Company is dissolved
1877	Great Railroad Strike in the United States is the world's first nationwide labor strike; Reconstruction ends in the United States
1879	Anglo-Zulu War is fought between Britain and the Zulus in southern Africa
1880–1881	First Boer War is fought between the British and the Boers (descendents of Dutch settlers) in South Africa
1884–1885	Berlin Conference signals the start of the "Scramble for Africa," a period of intense competition between European nations for control of colonies in Africa
1888	Slavery is abolished in Brazil
1890	Wounded Knee Massacre, the last conflict of the American Indian Wars, occurs in South Dakota
1896	First modern Olympic Games are held in Athens
1898	Spanish-American War results in the expulsion of Spain from Cuba, Puerto Rico, and the Philippines, all of which come under the control of the United States
1898–1900	Chinese Boxer Rebellion is suppressed by an eight-member international coalition

1899–1902	Second Boer War is fought between the British and the Boers in South Africa
1900	Sigmund Freud publishes *The Interpretation of Dreams*
1901	First Nobel Prizes are awarded
1903	Flight of the Wright Brothers at Kitty Hawk, North Carolina
1904–1905	Russo-Japanese War results in Japan's recognition as a world power
1905	Revolution of 1905 in Russia results in the establishment of the Russian Duma (legislature)
1906	Great earthquake destroys San Francisco
1907	Robert Baden-Powell establishes the scouting movement
1908	Henry Ford introduces the Model-T
1909	Sergei Diaghilev founds the *Ballets Russes* in Paris; establishment of the National Association for the Advancement of Colored People (NAACP) in the United States
1910	Boy Scouts established in the United States
1911	Chinese Revolution overthrows the Qing Dynasty
1912	Ocean liner *Titanic* sinks with great loss of life
1914	Formal opening of the Panama Canal
1914–1918	World War I is fought in Europe
1916	Easter Rising, an effort to end British rule in Ireland, fails in Dublin
1917	Russian Revolution leads to the overthrow of Czar Nicholas II
1918	Influenza epidemic causes many deaths worldwide
1920	Establishment of the League of Nations; women receive the right to vote in the United States
1921	Irish Free State is established
1922	Fascist leader Benito Mussolini becomes prime minister of Italy; the Union of Soviet Socialist Republics (USSR) is established
1925	Adolf Hitler publishes *Mein Kampf*
1927	American Charles Lindbergh becomes the first person to fly solo across the Atlantic Ocean
1928	Biotic penicillin is discovered
1929	New York Stock Market crashes initiating the Great Depression
1933	Nazi leader Adolf Hitler becomes chancellor of Germany
1934	Chinese communist leader Mao Zedong begins the Long March
1936	*Billboard* magazine publishes its first music hit parade
1936–1939	Spanish Civil War is fought between Republic and Nationalist forces, with the Fascist-supported Nationalists eventually winning control of Spain
1937	Japan invades China
1939–1945	World War II is fought in Europe, North Africa, Asia, and in the Pacific primarily between Great Britain, the Soviet Union, and the United States against Germany, Italy, and Japan

1941	Japanese launch a surprise attack on Pearl Harbor, Hawaii, thus initiating American involvement in World War II
1942–1943	Battle of Stalingrad between the Soviet Union and German-led coalition produces over 1.5 million casualties
1944	D-Day: Allied forces land on the beaches of German-occupied France, thus beginning the invasion of Nazi-controlled Europe
1945	United States drops two atomic bombs on Japan, thus ending World War II; United Nations is founded
1947	India achieves independence from Britain, though British India is partitioned into two states—Hindu India and Muslim Pakistan
1948	Jewish state of Israel is founded; Mohandas K. Gandhi, leader of the Indian independence movement, is assassinated
1949	Communist People's Republic of China is established; North Atlantic Treaty Organization (NATO) is established
1950–1953	Korean War is fought between a U.S.-led coalition of UN states and North Korea, back by Communist China
1952	Polio vaccine is created
1954	U.S. Supreme Court decision in *Brown v. Board of Education* declares racial segregation illegal
1957	European Economic Community is established; Soviet Union launches the *Sputnik* satellite
1959	Fidel Castro becomes dictator of Cuba
1960	First televised U.S. presidential debates between Richard Nixon and John F. Kennedy
1961	Soviets launch the first person into space
1963	American civil rights leader Dr. Martin Luther King, Jr., delivers his "I Have a Dream" speech; U.S. President John F. Kennedy is assassinated
1964	Nelson Mandela is sentenced to life in prison in South Africa
1965	United States sends ground troops into Vietnam, thus initiating the American phase of the Vietnam War
1966	Mao Zedong launches the Cultural Revolution in China
1967	Six-Day War is fought in the Middle East between Israel and neighboring Arab states
1968	Martin Luther King, Jr., is assassinated
1969	American Neil Armstrong becomes the first person to walk on the moon
1973	U.S. Supreme Court decision in *Roe v. Wade* legalizes abortion in the United States; the United States withdraws from Vietnam
1974	U.S. President Richard Nixon resigns as a result of the Watergate Scandal
1978	Election of the Polish Pope John Paul II, the first non-Italian pope since the sixteenth century

1979	Margaret Thatcher becomes the first woman prime minister of Great Britain; the Iranian Revolution overthrows the pro-Western Iranian monarchy and replaces it with an Islamic Republic; Iranian revolutionaries take hostage some 50 U.S. diplomats
1981	Personal computers are introduced by IBM; Iran releases the American hostages; first woman, Sandra Day O'Connor, is appointed to the U.S. Supreme Court
1983	Sally Ride becomes the first American woman in space
1985	Hole is discovered in the vital ozone layer of the atmosphere; serious famine strikes the African nation of Ethiopia
1986	*Challenger* space shuttle explodes, killing its seven-member crew
1989	Berlin Wall dividing East from West Berlin is torn down; Chinese anti-government protestors are massacred by government forces in China's Tiananmen Square
1990	Lech Walesa becomes the first post-Communist president of Poland
1991	Soviet Union collapses and breaks up, with many former Soviet republics declaring their independence; Cold War comes to an end; in the Gulf War, a U.S.-led coalition drives invading Iraqi forces out of Kuwait
1993	Islamic terrorists bomb the World Trade Center in New York City
1994	Nelson Mandela is elected president of a post-Apartheid South Africa; tribal genocide erupts in the African nation of Rwanda
1995	Anti-government terrorists bomb the Federal Building in Oklahoma City; Israeli Prime Minister Yitzhak Rabin is assassinated
1997	Britain returns Hong Kong to China
1998	Construction begins in orbit of the International Space Station
1999	Panama Canal passes from American to Panamanian control
2000	Disputed U.S. presidential election is decided in favor of George W. Bush
2001	Islamic terrorists destroy the World Trade Center Towers in New York City; U.S.-led coalition invades Afghanistan and overthrows the militant Islamic government of the Taliban
2003	In the Iraq War, U.S.-led coalition invades Iraq and overthrows Saddam Hussein
2004	Ten new countries join the European Union, eight of which are former Communist states
2005	NASA's *Deep Impact* probe collides, as planned, with Comet Tempel 1
2006	Former Iraqi dictator Saddam Hussein is executed
2008	Kosovo declares independence from Serbia; the Internet has over one billion users

Part I
HISTORICAL OVERVIEW

An understanding of what "modern" is might be reached through a brief example, especially since this volume seeks to explore daily life in the modern world precisely through the examples provided by a collection of primary documents. In a 1965 interview recounting the events surrounding the test of the first nuclear bomb at Las Alamos, New Mexico, in the summer of 1945, Robert Oppenheimer described his thoughts turning to a line from the Bhagavad-Gita, an ancient Hindu scripture: "I am become Death, the destroyer of worlds." Another speech by Oppenheimer is included in this volume in the section on Science in Part IV, "Intellectual Life," in which he talked at more length about the consequences of the development of nuclear power and nuclear weapons, and the role and value of science in society. However, his citation of the Bhagavad-Gita is far more often quoted and much better remembered; Oppenheimer had learned Sanskrit and read the text in its original while studying at Harvard. What is peculiar about this incident is how it points to so many elements central to understanding the modern world. Many points can be made about this simple incident that point to significant trends in the modern world, many of which are explored in this volume.

The fact that a scientist and son of a German immigrant testified in a filmed and broadcast interview about an event that occurred in western North America to the power and fear created by technological achievement in the words of an Asian religious text is revealing about many important trends in the modern world, including the dominance of the scientific worldview and rapid changes in technology; the large-scale migration and movements of peoples and the expansion of European presence and influence around the world; the continuing importance to many of religion and religiously motivated views to help make sense of a rapidly changing world; the transformation of communications media; the creation of weaponry that fundamentally changed both warfare and politics; and the international and global nature of culture, in which all cultures give to and take from others to different degrees, some for the better, and some not.

This third volume of *Daily Life through World History in Primary Documents* includes document selections that describe daily life in the more than 300 years from 1700 to the present. While this division is somewhat arbitrary, it picks up where Volume 2 leaves off and covers a period called "modern." In its most common usage, modern simply means current or up-to-date. In terms like modern conveniences, modern ideas, and modern technology, *modern* means whatever is recent or now. Modern can contrast with terms like *vintage*, *classic*, *antique*, or *old-fashioned*. In this volume, modern has a larger meaning, while the term *contemporary* is used to include the common sense of modern as "the present or immediate past," although contemporary also means "of the same period as something else" that is mentioned, even if they both are not contemporary with the present.

Defining modern can be somewhat complicated. Modern means many different things, and even varies among experts; depending on the field or area, the modern period begins at very different times. In history, modernity can start as early as the middle of the seventeenth century, or, at the latest, after the revolutions of the late eighteenth century in France and America. In visual arts, the modern period doesn't start until the late nineteenth century. Modern in terms of computer science doesn't happen until the second half of the twentieth century. Many people disagree not only as to when the modern period began, but also as to whether or not it is even still going on. Some think civilization and culture have moved into a new era or period that some call "post-modern," but there is a lack of consensus as to whether the present is still the modern period or whether we have moved into a new era that we still do not know enough about to name.

The periodicity of this book is fixed roughly by the timeline of Western cultural chronology, but it is not limited to Western cultures in its scope. This book is intended primarily for an American reader, and the United States is a predominantly, but certainly not exclusively, a Western culture. Although the focus is on modern American and European civilizations, many different cultures from every continent are included. This emphasis on a Western timeline and simultaneously global scope makes sense not only in regard to the reader's likely point of view. European and American economic, political, military, and cultural power expanded and increasingly dominated the world through much of the modern period, at one point, just before the First World War, at least nominally controlling over 80 percent of the earth's land mass. Only in the latter part of the twentieth century has Euro-American influence waned, although these civilizations remain powerful and the consequences of that expansion and contraction are very much a part of the modern world.

It has been said that a person from 1700 B.C. would understand the world of A.D. 1700 without much difficulty. Styles and languages would have changed, but technology was basically the same, changing in degree, not type. The primary sources of energy and transportation were still muscle, wind, or water. Most work was hard and done by hand. The material trappings of life were almost all made by hand from materials that had not changed much in nearly 3,500 years. Of course, some important discoveries and inventions can be pointed out, like printed books or gunpowder. However, if a person from A.D. 1700 was somehow transported only 300 years to the year 2000, he or she would find the world far more difficult to comprehend. The number and nature of changes in the modern world set it apart from previous periods in world history.

The Eighteenth Century—1700–1815

In 1700, most of the American continent was nominally claimed by Europeans, but vast portions of these territories were in fact still under the control of Native American tribes. The most complex and sophisticated Native American civilizations in Central and South America had been destroyed by the Spanish in the sixteenth century; in North American, Mississippian culture cities like Cahokia had disbanded before 1500, well before the modern period and before European contact. European activity was clustered on the Atlantic and Gulf coasts with some missionary and trading activity penetrating to the interior. However, during the eighteenth century in America, European colonies grew rapidly, putting pressure on tribes and involving them in trans-Atlantic wars and revolutions. Native American populations suffered tremendously from European diseases. After acquiring horses from the Spanish, a horse culture developed rapidly among Plains tribes, creating a new way of life in North America—one that would be extinguished in the next century.

In East Asia in this same period, the Chinese Qing Dynasty was consolidating its power, Japan had entered into a period of official isolation, and, in South Asia, the Indian subcontinent was almost entirely controlled by the Islamic *Mughal Empire*, which, like the Qing Dynasty, peaked in power during the first part of the eighteenth century. Islamic power began to wane elsewhere as well, and though the Islamic world still offered a rich and complex civilization that stretched from India to the African Atlantic coast, the Mughals were overstretched in India and the defeat of the Ottoman Turks at Vienna in 1683 marked the furthest point of Ottoman expansion into Europe. Although the *Ottoman Empire* would survive until the end of the First World War in 1918, it increasingly lost territory and power to rising European states, like the Austrian Hapsburg empire, the Russian empire, and the British empire.

In 1700, these states on the European continent were a collection of increasingly powerful and centralizing imperial nations, especially England, France, Austria, Prussia, and Russia. They were, though, with the exception of Russia, physically quite small compared to the territories of other non-European governments. Of all these European powers, the only one with a government that was not an absolute monarchy was England. Centralizing power in the hands of one person had the advantage—if the ruler was strong and effective—of making it easier to accomplish significant reforms and consolidate the power of the state to accomplish goals and solve problems. For example, *Peter the Great* of Russia built a new national capital named after himself—*St. Petersburg*—on the Baltic Sea to provide Russia with a Western orientation and new deepwater port. In Prussia, Frederick the Great used his authority to create the first professional, national army, and also to help create the first public school systems in the modern world. He saw the advantages of a population that was literate, was properly formed in virtue and religion, and had the skills to build the economy and state. On the other hand, absolutist rule was problematic in that corruption was common and if the hereditarily determined ruler was weak, it could create significant problems for the government, as in France after the death of Louis XIV in 1715. The French monarchy ended in 1792.

Of course, the *French Revolution* had many causes besides the weakness of the French king. Other political ideas were growing, not only in France, but also in America and in England, where the political experiments of the seventeenth century had also killed the king—and then restored the monarch with limited constitutional powers. Thinkers like Voltaire, Denis Diderot, the Baron de Montesquieu, Adam Smith, Thomas Jefferson, and others led an intellectual movement called the *Enlightenment* that introduced new ideas about the nature of the person and the proper relationship between individuals and governments. Ideas about constitutionalism, limited government, liberalism, and new concepts of the natural equalities of people, civil rights, and freedoms stimulated reforms and even revolutions. The *American Revolution* against English rule, begun in 1776, created the United States, while the French Revolution, begun in 1789, eventually cost King Louis XVI his head. While a small but stable democracy emerged in the United States, the French Revolution degenerated into chaos until order was restored under the authority of *Napoleon* Bonaparte, who set out to create a French Empire and rule the European continent, and he nearly succeeded. His defeat at Waterloo in 1815 marked the end of the long eighteenth century, although intellectual foment and revolutionary fervor would continue into the nineteenth century through rapid and radical social changes.

Some of the political ideals of the eighteenth century—democratic governments that draw their power from the consent of the people rather than from religious belief, hereditary privilege, or brute force; the natural and individual rights of people in society, like freedom of speech and conscience; and limitations on the powers of government—remain powerful ideas that still form notions of legitimacy and proper political arrangements today. Even totalitarian regimes today often try to adopt the trappings of democratic legitimacy.

The same interest in a rational political worldview also shaped other important ideas in the eighteenth century. The scientific method that had begun to prove very powerful in the early modern era gained increasing currency, and its application to an increasing number of spheres of human activity led to new developments in medicine and new styles and practices in art, politics, and social life. The Scientific Revolution had begun in the pre-modern world, but the eighteenth century saw many scientific discoveries and, more importantly, the increasing use of the scientific method as a tool for understanding the world on the part of a rapidly increasing number of people. The expansion of scientific reasoning to social problems did not always yield scientifically precise results, but science proved its worth as a tool for learning and knowing.

Another revolution was also taking place in the contact of Europeans with other peoples. The exploration of lands previously unknown to Europeans, followed by trade and, sometimes, missionary activity, conquest, and colonization, had begun in the early modern period, but accelerated in the modern era. In 1700, European nations were territorially smaller than Indian and Asian powers, although they were rapidly becoming global powers in the eighteenth century. At the same time, trading networks and regional political powers spread across Africa and Asia, with Europeans playing only a peripheral role. In Asia, the Qing and Mughal Empires began to weaken, while the European powers began to grow in terms of military power, population, technology, and other factors.

International trade continued to expand, and European joint-stock trading companies, such as the Dutch and *British East India* Companies, became more powerful than many nations in the eighteenth century. They acted as governments in their territories, printing money, maintaining standing armies and navies, and administering colonial possessions. Coffee, tea, sugar, chocolate, opium, tobacco, and other consumables, along with cotton, indigo, silk, and other raw materials became important commodities, as demand increased, populations grew, and industrialization began in earnest. For example, the textile industry, one of the first to industrialize and develop the factory system, increased production in England from 2.7 million yards to 70 million yards of cloth from 1760 to 1810. The ability of Asian powers to resist European intrusion gradually declined in the eighteenth century, and European control over parts of Asia increased along with global trade, creating some of the conditions that allowed for European domination in the nineteenth century and into the twentieth.

Another aspect of the eighteenth century was the dramatic expansion of the slave trade, especially for the burgeoning sugar plantations of the Caribbean, where death rates were so high for slaves that they could not maintain a population. Large numbers of Africans were transported across the Atlantic into *slavery* for colonial possessions in America and the West Indies. Not only Africans, but large numbers of European emigrated to the Americas and around the world, settling in South Africa and in smaller numbers in other colonies. For example, the non-Native American population of the American British colonies was 10 times larger in 1776 than it had been at the beginning of the eighteenth century.

The religious controversies of the preceding centuries in Europe were no longer the direct cause of such massive violence and bloodshed, but religious life remained an important element in personal identity and community life. Religion itself began to undergo transformations like the Great Awakening in colonial America, the rise of Methodism in England, the development of Pietism in German-speaking Protestant countries, and the emergence of Freemasonry as an alternative or supplement to organized religion. There were other, divisive trends in eighteenth-century religious life as well. European missionary activity continued and expanded, although it met with mixed results. Tensions between the *Roman Catholic Church* and Protestant groups remained high, while within the Catholic Church the Jansenist controversy in the first half of the century and the suppression of the Jesuits caused difficulties. Anti-Semitism shifted from a religious to a nationalist orientation, but continued across Western life, and anti-clericalism and Deism were closely associated with Enlightenment rationalism and French Revolutionary ideals.

In the arts, the eighteenth century was important as well. The forms of ballet and opera that we know today took their recognizable forms in the eighteenth century, and new musical instruments, such as the modern piano, and styles, such as the symphony, developed in the hands of composers like Wolfgang Amadeus Mozart and Ludwig van Beethoven. The remnants of pre-modern artistic styles were carried to decadent extremes in the gaudiness of the Rococo, and a revival of interest in classical antiquity—and the discovery of Pompeii in 1748—provided inspiration for new styles in literature, art, and architecture at the end of the century. In addition, private cabinets of curiosities began to evolve into modern museums, all laying the foundations for artistic revolutions in the nineteenth century.

The Nineteenth Century—1815–1914

The nineteenth century saw startling transformations around the globe. European expansion and industrial development exploded. European countries took control of most of the African continent, the British solidified control over India and colonized Australia, China was forced to open to Western trade and influence, and Japan tried to industrialize itself to compete with Western powers and begin its own territorial expansion. The United States expanded dramatically westward. The Louisiana Purchase in 1803 more than doubled the size of the United States. Other territorial acquisitions and the idea of "Manifest Destiny" stretched the United States across the American continent. European Americans and immigrants moved westward (or eastward from California) in droves, settling the whole continent and fighting and winning wars against Native American tribes so that by the beginning of the twentieth century the United States no longer had a "frontier."

Consolidation was still taking place politically in Europe. Germany and Italy emerged as nation-states. Although there were no major wars between more than two belligerents fought on the territory of mainland Europe between the end of the Napoleonic campaigns in 1815 and the outbreak of World War I in 1914, this did not mean that the nineteenth was a peaceful century. It witnessed dramatic political and military upheaval and change, but the locations and types of conflicts shifted to social unrest, rather than national wars, and to colonial conflicts fought beyond the European mainland.

Social revolutions rocked Europe in 1830, 1848, and 1870, sometimes toppling governments and prompting significant social reforms. The United States fought a *Civil War* from 1861 to 1865. Non-European peoples fought with Europeans for control of their own countries—and lost. The Chinese fought two *Opium Wars* and the Boxer Rebellion; numerous wars were fought across Africa, including the Boer War and Zulu Wars; significant other European conquests were made by the French in North Africa and by Britain, Belgium, and Germany in sub-Saharan Africa; Britain took control of Australia from the aboriginal peoples; and American Indians fought and lost Indian Wars across the American continent from the Seminoles in what is now Florida in the 1820s to the Apache in the southwest in the 1890s. On the other hand, many European possessions in the Caribbean gained independence, some, like Haiti, through slave revolts. Most of South and Central America threw off the control of the declining Spanish Empire, although the descendents of the Spanish elites retained control over the large indigenous populations, and they remained susceptible to the influence of outside nations, especially the United States, as its power waxed.

The nature of military power also changed as military technology changed. Mass produced revolvers and accurate, breech-loading rifles; improved artillery; armored steel warships; and faster transportation and effective logistics were among the changes that made for more deadly fighting forces that were also increasing in size. Non-European states and groups attempted to compete with the growing military capacities of Western nations. Some groups tried what is now known as asymmetrical warfare, engaging in guerilla tactics and avoiding pitched battles with superior forces. Others tried to adopt Western military innovations on their own, purchasing Western weapons and ships, and learning to build their own. China created a New Model Army on the Western model, and Japan had the most notable success, defeating Russia in 1904 on land and sea and embarking on its own imperial expansion in East Asia as the twentieth century began.

Another important trend in the nineteenth century was the gradual emancipation of large numbers of people. Millions of Africans had been enslaved and transported to European possessions in the Americas as well as to the United States. The slave trade was officially outlawed by most European states in the beginning of the nineteenth century, but slavery continued. Britain outlawed slavery in its possessions in 1833. France allowed slavery to continue until 1848. Slavery in the United States only ended in the bloodshed of the American Civil War in the 1860s. Not all people who were freed were African or African-heritage slaves, though. Russian peasants, who had been bound to the land and owned by the landowners, were liberated in 1861.

The changes in industrialization and transportation in the nineteenth century were also breathtaking. The *Industrial Revolution* had begun in the textile industry in England and America in the eighteenth century, but steam power, interchangeable parts, the factory system, railroads, steamboats, and steamships are just a few of the technical innovations that allowed, for example, textile producers in England to buy Indian cotton, ship it to England from India, manufacture finished clothing, ship it back to India, and still have it cost less than non-industrially produced Indian clothing. The second wave of industrialization in the second half of the century brought inexpensive steel, the internal combustion engine, electricity, petroleum products, and new sets of changes that bridged into the twentieth century, making animal power, wooden-hulled sailing ships, and transportation technologies that had been improved by degree but not type for thousands of years defunct in a matter of a few decades. The oil lamps and candles used in 1800 were essentially the same that had lit ancient Roman homes; by 1900, incandescent electric lighting was spreading across the world. In 1830, there were no more than a few dozen miles of railroad in the United States. By the end of the century, there were over 200,000 miles of track. Trade continued to grow, and, with steam-powered transport, it became much faster and more reliable. The patterns established in the eighteenth century continued in the most general terms, with industrializing countries importing raw materials and exporting finished goods, but new commodities also became increasingly important, such as coal, steel, and, later in the nineteenth century, oil, as economies shifted from agrarian to increasingly industrial.

The population of the world also increased dramatically over this period as increased production of food and cheaper production of material goods made larger families more affordable, and increased medical knowledge made for longer life spans and lower mortality rates, although the most significant gains in medical science in modern history would have to wait for the twentieth century. The shift from rural to urban population and development of an industrial working class in the most rapidly industrializing nations also brought radical social changes and people struggled to define new ways of being and relating to each other. Immigrant groups tended to remain cohesive in their new places for a generation or two, but also began to assimilate and influence their new societies and cultures. The first professional police forces and fire departments were established under state control and growing urban areas demanded new ways of maintaining law and order.

Education became a state-run institution, and some countries closed religious schools. Most industrial counties had compulsory public education by the end of the century. At the beginning, none did. As education spread and literacy increased, mass audiences from the middle classes became increasingly important as patrons for music, dance, art, and literature. Major new changes also occurred in art and literature. Poets such as Lord *Byron* and Alexander Pushkin created lasting works at the beginning of the century and great novelists emerged around the world later in the century, such as Charles Dickens, Leo *Tolstoy*, Fyodor Dostoevsky, and Victor Hugo. American arts and letters began to come of age too, with writers like Mark Twain. Opera and ballet, which had grown greatly in the eighteenth century, reached new peaks of popularity and expanding audiences as elite art forms. Writers, painters, musicians, and others began to explore the emotional side of the human experience in ways they previously had not. Nature became a central concern, and its awesome power became an inspiration for many, sometimes as a substitute Divinity for those who eschewed organized religion. The modern idea of the artist as a misunderstood, solitary genius, working on his own inspiration, was born, and creative works began to be seen often as serving as a social conscience. Experimentation in music, painting, and literature heralded radical changes in art and culture in the twentieth century, preparing for the expression of deep doubts and great hopes for the modern world.

The Twentieth and Twenty-First Centuries—1914–Present

Many of the trends of the modern period that emerged in the eighteenth and nineteenth centuries continued in the twentieth and into the twenty-first, but the European global empires and positive ideals of civilized progress that dominated the nineteenth century were irrevocably altered in the First World War that began in 1914. War was transformed by new, more destructive technologies such as machine guns, long-range artillery, airplanes, tanks, high explosives, and poison gas, changing the nature of battle and killing many more than ever before. Millions died in trench warfare and the better part of a generation of European men was killed. A total of 20 million people died, about half military and half civilian. The major combatant nations were reduced to fighting a war of attrition rather than military victory, and the numbers of casualties were shocking. In the wake of the war, the empires of Germany, Austria-Hungary, Ottoman Turkey, and Russia all fell, and the French and British empires were substantially weakened.

The terms of the peace led to world war again in less than 20 years with a similar alignment of belligerents, leading some historians to see both wars as parts of one conflict. Total deaths for the Second World War that began in 1939 amounted by some estimates to a staggering 72 million—tens of millions civilian, famine, and *Holocaust* deaths included. The Second World War was even worse than the first, with large scale civilian bombing and air wars, the use of nuclear weapons at the end of the war, combat on a truly global scale, and millions upon millions of casualties, including over 20 million from the Soviet Union alone, and 6 million Jews exterminated by the Nazis and their collaborators. The combined deaths for the wars of the first half of the twentieth century amount to over 90 million people, enough to depopulate the entire Earth around the time of the Ancient Greeks.

Of course, there were many more people in the world during the twentieth century, and continued rapid population growth is another aspect of modernity. World population more than doubled between the year 1000 and the year 1700, from roughly 300 million to over 700 million. However, between 1700 and 2000, it doubled almost 5 times to over 6 billion. What the future holds is uncertain, but it is likely to keep growing. This tremendous population growth has had important consequences for everyday life, as an ever-growing number of people have material needs and an ongoing demand for food, clothing, housing, health care, and the other trappings of modern life—if they are available. Much of the growth, especially in the twentieth century, has been in developing nations, and the pressures this growth has put on governments and societies has been significant.

The struggle for influence in these developing nations was part of the geopolitical division into "three worlds" at the end of the Second World War. A new balance of global power was dominated by the competition for hegemony on the part of two superpowers, the United States and its industrialized allies (the First World), and the Soviet Union and its satellites and dependencies (the Second World); other countries in South America, Africa, and Asia were the Third World. The superpowers were competing not only for power, but also on an ideological plane, with the United States, practicing *capitalism,* confronting the *Union of Soviet Socialist Republics* (USSR), practicing *communism.* The creation of large arsenals of nuclear weapons made the standoff even more intense, as the evolution from the *Cold War* to a Hot War might well lead to a strategic nuclear war, all but ending human life on earth. The disintegration of the Soviet Union in 1991 effectively ended this period, but nuclear proliferation is still an important global political and military issue. Many observers point to the growing economic and military power of Asian and Pacific Rim nations like China, India, South Korea, Indonesia, and Japan as defining a new stage of geopolitics that will be dominated by non-Western industrializing nations gaining on those currently with the most power, such as Europe and the United States, but also beset with overconsumption, internal dissent, aging populations, and other factors. Others see the terrorist attacks on the United States of September 11, 2001, and the related conflict between fundamentalist Islam and the West as a central issue for global political events.

Whatever the political future, the level of material comfort of those living in developed countries is vastly better than those living in other places, and the disparities of wealth, power, and opportunities is an issue that many see as a situation demanding remedy for the purposes of basic justice. At the same time, it has also launched large migrations, as people have begun moving on an unprecedented scale to places where there is more safety or opportunity, either within their own country or region, as in India and China, or around the world, sometimes to former colonial powers, such as the large number of North Africans in France, Indians and Pakistanis in England, Turks and other Middle Easterners in Germany and other European nations, Russians in America, others to small but wealthy Middle Eastern states, and Jews from around the world, but especially eastern Europe and North Africa, to Israel after its creation following World War II.

The prosperity of the twentieth century that has inspired migration has been driven by the continuation of the industrialization of countries around the world. Added to previous industrial technologies were new ones, such as the assembly line, synthetic and chemical materials, and others that have changed how much and how efficiently things can be made. Coupled with industrial growth are further huge changes in transportation and communications. There are very few places not affected by global markets, and the scale of commerce has continued to grow. A merchant vessel of the eighteenth century might displace around 1,000 tons and carry 500 tons of cargo. Just one of the largest contemporary supertankers can carry over 500,000 tons of bulk cargo—the equivalent capacity of more than 1,000 ships from the beginning of the modern era. Along with the dramatic expansion of trade, modern banking and financial institutions have also evolved, creating extremely sophisticated and interconnected global markets.

The growth of paved roads in the twentieth century parallels the growth of railways in the nineteenth century. Not including wood, cobblestone, brick, or macadam—none of which were well suited to automobiles—there were only 10 miles of paved roads in the United States in 1900, but by the end of the century, there were nearly 6 million miles of paved roadways. Cars, trucks, buses, and other vehicles have become the main means of personal transportation. At the same time, this development has been dramatically uneven. In the Democratic Republic of Congo, for example, a central African country roughly the size of Western Europe, there are fewer than 1,500 miles of paved roads.

In addition to the effect engendered by the internal combustion engine on ground transportation, there was the entirely new dimension of air travel and transportation. The first airplane flew in 1903, and by the 1930s, there were regular transatlantic commercial flights. The development of jet engines further accelerated air travel and fueled the growth of the airline industry, which operates thousands of flights daily worldwide, connecting every continent with every other, for those with the means, in a matter of hours.

Communications that were changed by telegraph and telephone in the nineteenth century were further altered in the twentieth by the development of broadcast media like radio, then television. Toward the end of the century, the phenomenal explosion of the computer based on microchip technology created an Information Revolution and the Internet. Long distance communication in 1700 was done in person, and communications were limited to the speed of sailing ships, a horseback rider, or a person on foot. Broadcast media was only the range of the human voice, a horn, a bell, or the report of a cannon. By the end of the twentieth century, billions of people around the world could simultaneously watch the same events in color and sound, and the Internet, email, and instant-messaging linked people personally around the world.

Changes in media technologies have altered the way people communicate and think, but also how they express themselves in art, literature, and music. In the nineteenth century, the invention of photography created a powerful new way to record images and impressions, one used by those interested in documentation as well as by artists. Verisimilitude (or life-likeness) ceased to be a priority in much art in the decades that followed as that task was relegated to photography, and millions of people had their pictures made, while ever fewer had their portraits painted. Art and artistic influence became increasingly global. For example, imported goods from China and Japan produced a vogue in Europe and the United States for orientalism in design and art beginning as early as the eighteenth century. Japanese woodblock prints inspired the French Impressionists, and sub-Saharan African tribal art, masks, and other objects inspired Cubists such as Pablo *Picasso*. Abstract and nonrepresentational art evolved in the late nineteenth and twentieth centuries among other trends, creating new ways of looking at the world and often offering pointed and powerful commentary on the conditions of life in the modern world. Art and literature today are evolving new forms, genres, and styles as the modern world changes. Some critics question even whether ideas about art and literature formed in the early modern period will continue to survive in the modern world.

Other changes have dramatically affected life in the twentieth century. In agriculture, the so-called Green Revolution has enabled humans to much more easily feed our own burgeoning population. Chemically or biologically engineered seeds, fertilizers, pesticides, and herbicides, combined with mechanical agricultural machinery and internal combustion tractors, have created crop yields unthinkable before the modern era. These products are sold on global markets as raw materials and food products made possible because of transportation, growth of trade, and industrial processing. Better diets have resulted for many, leading to better health and longer life, although other discoveries in medical sciences and technologies have radically altered medical care and global health, with some diseases, such as smallpox, effectively wiped out. Sterile practices, antibiotics, and discoveries in microbiology and genetics are among the many innovations of twentieth-century medicine. The field of psychology, essentially created by Sigmund Freud, has had consequences far beyond the medical professions. On the other hand, although medicine has advanced rapidly, life expectancies are higher, infant mortality rates are lower than any point in human history, and global public health programs help many without the means to help themselves, there is still much medicine cannot do, and cures for diseases such as cancer and human immunodeficiency virus (HIV) continue to elude doctors and scientists.

The contemporary world is far from a perfect place, but, by many measures, it is probably better to be alive now than at any other point in human history. A person today is more likely to be freer, healthier, and wealthier; to live longer, have a more secure, comfortable life and less work; and to have more opportunities for education, travel, and leisure. What the future of the contemporary world will be is unclear, but the achievement and failures of our modern world are recorded in the document selections that follow. The collected voices of priests and kings, housewives and factory workers, scholars and soldiers provide a fascinating account of daily life in the modern world by those who have lived it.

Part II

DOMESTIC LIFE

What exactly is domestic life? Domestic life encompasses a wide variety of different relationships and activities, primarily those between members of a household. People prepare food, eat, sleep, clothe, and take care of themselves and others, and go about daily routines. This section on domestic life does not focus on the material trappings of the everyday activities of the household, such things as the food, clothing, and the architecture and furnishing of homes; those topics are covered in the section on material life. Aside from the everyday, larger events are also a central part of domestic life, marking significant milestones, defining and celebrating relationships, and lamenting their loss. Marriages take place, children are born and come of age, and people grow old and die. How people think about the different stages of life and their domestic relationships is at least as important as the physical environment in which they live and the actual objects they use in everyday life. These relationships and what people think about them are the focus of this section.

In some places and times, there has been little or no distinction between domestic life and other aspects of life—no distinction between public and private, no society outside of clan and kinship groups. One of the important changes scholars note in the emergence of the modern world has been an increasing distinction between the private or domestic sphere of life and the public or social sphere of life.

Even if there may not have always and everywhere been a distinction between domestic and public, there is no doubt that the nuclear family or kinship group has been the basic unit of human society, and this has been so in the *modern* era also. That is not to say, however, that there have not been dramatic changes in the family and domestic life, and models of how humans arrange their households and domestic relationships continue to change. The documents in this section focus on a number of different aspects of domestic life, exploring and comparing them in different times and places in the modern world.

One focus in this section is on women and women's roles in domestic life. It is notable that although there is a section on women's roles, there is not a corresponding section specifically on men's roles. This exclusion is not a judgment that men do not have roles within the domestic environment. However, there are good reasons to include readings on women's roles rather than men's roles in a section on domestic life in the modern world.

The modern era, especially in Western cultures, saw the creation of ideals of femininity almost exclusively defined by domestic life and then subsequent challenges to those ideals. In many non-Western cultures, women were never subjected to the limitations imposed by the ideal of domestic femininity, but in some, even today, substantial restrictions still remain on the roles that women can play in society outside the household.

Childhood, another aspect of domestic life that is closely connected to the roles of women, is also covered here. Since women give birth and can nurse children, womanhood and motherhood have often been seen as overlapping or even identical. The raising and education of children are a central part of domestic life; in some cultures, raising children is seen as the purpose of life. The documents included here are not so much about what parents—either male or female—have to say about their children as much as they are about trying to capture the experience of childhood from the children's perspective.

Old age is another facet of domestic life. While many of the elderly in twenty-first-century America do not live in the same household as their adult children and grandchildren, this has not been the norm in even the recent past. The familial bonds that define domestic relationships are also often the bonds that decide who will care for the aged and how. The selections presented here recount how people are often reluctant to give up the independence and vigor they had when they were younger, and struggle to retain it, try to recapture it, to lament it, or to deny its loss.

These different categories and entries are of course not independent of each other. The subtle racism of Robert Baden-Powell's description of a Zulu charge that he compares to the rally of *Boy Scouts* (Document 6) is connected to the racial attitudes that permitted slavery to flourish in the United States, and is also related to imperialism and the disparities between childhood in the industrialized West and the difficulties faced by West African children in the middle of the last century. Some might argue that the relegation of women to limited domestic roles in the nineteenth and twentieth centuries in England and the United States are not dissimilar to the institutions of racial slavery or the mistreatment or dismissal of the elderly. There is something common, too, in the suffering of Aurangzeb in his old age (Document 8), witnessing the breakdown of his domestic life as old age leads to death, and the unhappiness of Frederick Douglass (Document 5), denied the company or care of his parents from the earliest age. Defining these connections and relationships can be challenging, but together they make up a rich and interesting picture of a central aspect of daily life—the domestic.

Women's Roles

Women's roles are often taken as a bellwether of sorts in domestic life. Some of the selections here were written to criticize the roles women played in their societies, and some of them are an endorsement of women's positions in the domestic sphere. The selections range from Louis de Jaucourt (Document 1), a progressive eighteenth-century European attempting to put the idea of marriage and husband-wife relations into historical context—and thereby challenging some of the popular ideas of his day, to a reaction against the twentieth-century suburban American housewife in a selection from Betty Friedan's groundbreaking work of American *feminism*, *The Feminine*

Mystique (Document 4). In between there is Mrs. Isabella Beeton (Document 2), whose name is synonymous with the domestic Englishwoman of the nineteenth century, and an account by Halil Halid of women's lives in Western Asia (Document 3). His description of the Turkish *Harem* in the early twentieth century records a changing but very traditional way of life in the last years of the *Ottoman Empire*.

It is also worth noting that it is not simply a matter of men's voices keeping women in the domestic sphere, and women agitating to be liberated from it. Betty Friedan is a powerful voice for change, but Isabella Beeton embraces her role in the domestic sphere, and her firm, prim prose clearly encourages other women to do the same. On the other hand, Jaucourt is a man of privilege and wealth encouraging his society to reconsider its attitudes toward marriage and the role of the wife—a reconsideration that, along with a reconsideration of many other domestic, social, and political attitudes in eighteenth-century France, would eventually lead to revolution and the loss of his class privileges and wealth, while Halil Halid's frank description of the harem is an apologetic for the near total exclusion of women from public life.

1. *The Definition of "Wife" in the* Encyclopédie

In the eighteenth century, Denis Diderot *and Jean le Rond* d'Alembert *compiled their encyclopedia in France. The* Encyclopédie *was a milestone—one of the first attempts to unify and categorize all human knowledge. In this sense, it was a project typical of the* Enlightenment, *an intellectual movement of the eighteenth century that focused on the power of human reason to order society and understand the world. Among the entries in the* Encyclopédie *was "Wife," written by Louis de Jaucourt, a French nobleman and philosophe. Jaucourt's article on "Wife" indicates that well before the rise of contemporary* feminism *and the feminist movement, both the idea of male authority within marriage and the idea of female equality in marriage were present in European culture.*

The Enlightenment was a period of great intellectual change, and the idea of male authority in marriage was not as strong or as pervasive as is often assumed. In fact, the domestic ideal of the submissive, nurturing, at-home mother is itself largely a product of the nineteenth century. Although Jaucourt admits that many civilized countries reinforced the primacy of the male in marriage, and he is not altogether opposed to such laws, Jaucourt cites a number of historic and world cultures as evidence that what is understood as the traditional arrangement was not as universal, or even as traditional, as might be thought today. He does not argue directly for the changing of these traditions and laws, but he does suggest, perhaps with a bit of understatement, that the law should make provisions for exceptions to the usual arrangement when it is suitable to the husband and wife. To Jaucourt's Enlightenment mind, the submission of a wife to her husband might be seen only as a part of civil law, not of natural law; in other words, it is a custom or convention, rather than an arrangement founded by Nature or God, and it can be questioned or altered by the judicious use of humane reason.

Wife, (Natural Law), in Latin *uxor*, female of man, considered such when she is united to him by ties of marriage. *See therefore* Marriage *and* Husband.

The supreme being having judged that it was not good for man to be alone, conceived a desire to unite him in close society with a companion, and this society is made through a voluntary accord between the parties. As this society has as its principal goal the procreation and protection of the children it produces, the father and mother of necessity devote all their energies to nourishing and properly rearing the fruits of their love up until the time when they are able to care and judge for themselves.

But although the husband and the wife have fundamentally the same interests in their marriage, it is nevertheless essential that governing authority belong to one or the other: now the affirmative right of civilized nations, the laws and the customs of Europe give this authority unanimously to the male, being the one endowed with the greatest strength of mind and body, contributing more to the common good in matters of sacred and human things; such that the woman must necessarily be subordinated to her husband and obey his orders in all domestic affairs. This is the belief of the ancient and modern jurists and the formal decision of legislators. [. . .]

However the reasons we have just listed for marital power are not without rejoinder, humanely speaking; and the character of this work allows us to boldly enunciate them.

It appears first of all that it would be difficult to demonstrate that the authority of the husband comes from nature; because this principal is contrary to the natural equality of men; and just because one is suited for commanding doesn't mean that it is actually one's right to do so: 2. man does not always have greater strength of body, wisdom, spirit or conduct than woman: 3. Scriptural precepts being established in punitive terms indicates as well that there is only a positive right. One can therefore claim that there is no other type of subordination in marital relations than that of the civil law, and as a consequence, the only things preventing change in the civil law are particular conventions, and that natural law and religion do not determine anything to the contrary.

We do not deny that in a society composed of two people, it is necessary that the deliberative laws of one or the other carry the day; and since ordinarily men are more capable than women of ably governing particular matters, it is wise to establish as a general rule that the voice of the man will carry more weight as long as the two have not made any agreement to the contrary, because general law results from human institutions, and not from natural right. In this way, a woman who knows the basis of civil law and who contracts her marriage purely and simply, has by law submitted, tacitly, to this civil law.

But if this woman, persuaded that she has more judgment and direction, or knowing that she has greater fortune or is of a higher station than that of the man

The Life & Age of Woman—Stages of Woman's Life from the Cradle to the Grave, a ca. 1849 U.S. print illustrating 11 chronological stages of virtuous womanhood. Library of Congress.

who asks her to marry him, stipulates the contrary of that which the law implies, and with the consent of this husband, should she not have, by virtue of natural law, the same power her husband has by virtue of the law of the realm? The case of a queen, who, being sovereign in her own right, marries a prince below her rank, or if she likes, one of her subjects, is enough to show that the authority of a woman over her husband, even in matters concerning the governance of the family, is not incompatible with the nature of the marital contract.

In effect, we have seen among the most civilized nations, marriages which submit the husband to the domain of the wife; we have seen a princess, heir to the realm, reserve to herself, while marrying, the sovereign power of the state. [...]

The example of England and of Muscovy make evident that women can succeed equally, both in moderate and despotic government; and if it is not against reason and nature that they rule an empire, then it seem that it is no more contradictory that they should be mistresses in a family.

When Lacedaemonian [Spartan, an ancient Greek province] marriages were ready to be consummated, the woman took the dress of a man; and it was a symbol of the equal power that she would share with her husband. On this subject we know what Gorgon, the wife of Leonidas, king of Sparta, said to a foreign woman who was extremely surprised by this equality: Don't you know, responded the queen, that we bring men into the world? In other times, even in Egypt, marriage contracts between individuals, as much as those of the king and the queen, gave authority over the husband to the wife. (Diodore de Sicile, liv. I. ch. xxvij.)

It makes no difference (because it is not a matter here of exploiting unique examples which prove too much); it makes no difference, I say, if the authority of a woman in marriage cannot exist within conventional bounds, between people of equal stature, at least let the legislature refrain from prohibiting exceptions to the law, made with the free consent of the parties.

Marriage is by its nature a contract; and as a result, in all things not expressly prohibited by natural law, the contractual engagements between the husband and the wife determine reciprocal rights.

Source: Jaucourt, Louis de. "Femme [Wife]." In *La Encyclopédie*, edited by Denis Diderot and Jean le Rond d'Alembert. Volume 6. Paris: Briasson, 1751–1777. Translated and reprinted by permission of Naomi Andrews.

2. *Isabella Beeton: The Angel of the House*

Isabella Beeton (1836–1865) originally published her Book of Household Management *in serial form in an English women's magazine, and then as a single volume in 1861. The book was a huge success. It was revised and re-revised by others and became the most famous cookbook and domestic advice manual in England for decades, and made Beeton the most recognized advocate of the nineteenth-century ideal of female* domesticity. *Beeton, herself a wife, mother, and household manager as well as an author, died in 1865 at age 28 after the birth of her fourth child.*

Although she included instructions for many different categories of servants, both male and female, including cooks, butlers, footmen, valets, and maids of all sorts, the following excerpt is taken from her instructions to the mistress of the house. Her audience comprises the aspiring middle- and upper-class wives of the prosperous professional classes created by the Industrial Revolution *and the social transformations of the nineteenth century. These women, although excluded for the most part from professional and public lives, were not the middle-class stay-at-home moms of twentieth-century America. The management of a large household and regulation of social and domestic life was a formidable task. Without many of the appliances common today, daily tasks were much more labor-intensive, and running an upper-class home required the labor of numerous servants. The household was essentially a small business, with domestic employees living and working on the premises; maintaining the house, grounds, and animals; caring for children; preparing meals for the family and themselves; and cleaning, doing laundry, and so on. Employees had to be managed, accounts kept, social calls had to be made and received, and, of course, husbands had to be kept happy, too.*

The virtues Beeton demands are a catalog of respectable feminine qualities: modesty, prudence, frugality, good temper, and propriety. Sexuality, intellect, and personal satisfaction were not emphasized. Feminine happiness was the result of faithful execution of domestic duties, making the good bourgeois wife an angel of the house. Some scholars see this domestic arrangement as simply patriarchal and oppressive, while others see it more positively as a place for the development of an independent feminine sphere, while others claim it lays the groundwork for later strides in women's roles outside the home by asserting that women are responsible and virtuous in their roles within it. Of course, not everyone shared Beeton's views or conformed to her advice; but she offers a succinct representation of what the dominant social ideal was for middle- and upper-class women of the nineteenth century in the industrializing West.

1. AS WITH THE COMMANDER OF AN ARMY, or the leader of any enterprise, so is it with the mistress of a house. Her spirit will be seen through the whole establishment; and just in proportion as she performs her duties intelligently and thoroughly, so will her domestics follow in her path. Of all those acquirements, which more particularly belong to the feminine character, there are none which take a higher rank, in our estimation, than such as enter into a knowledge of household duties; for on these are perpetually dependent the happiness, comfort, and well-being of a family. In this opinion we are borne out by the author of "The Vicar of Wakefield," who says: "The modest virgin, the prudent wife, and the careful matron, are much more serviceable in life than petticoated philosophers, blustering heroines, or virago queens. She who makes her husband and her children happy, who reclaims the one from vice and trains up the other to virtue, is a much greater character than ladies described in romances, whose whole occupation is to murder mankind with shafts from their quiver, or their eyes."

2. PURSUING THIS PICTURE, we may add, that to be a good housewife does not necessarily imply an abandonment of proper pleasures or amusing recreation; and we think it the more necessary to express this, as the performance of the duties of a mistress may, to some minds, perhaps seem to be incompatible with the enjoyment of life. Let us, however, now proceed to describe some of those home qualities and virtues which are necessary to the proper management of a Household, and then point out the plan which may be the most profitably pursued for the daily regulation of its affairs.

10. GOOD TEMPER SHOULD BE CULTIVATED by every mistress, as upon it the welfare of the household may be said to turn; indeed, its influence can hardly be over-estimated, as it has the effect of moulding the characters of those around her, and of acting most beneficially on the happiness of the domestic circle. Every head of a household should strive to be cheerful, and should never fail to show a deep interest in all that appertains to the well-being of those who claim the protection of her roof. Gentleness, not partial and temporary, but universal and regular, should pervade her conduct; for where such a spirit is habitually manifested, it not only delights her children, but makes her domestics attentive and respectful; her visitors are also pleased by it, and their happiness is increased.

12. IN PURCHASING ARTICLES OF WEARING APPAREL, whether it be a silk dress, a bonnet, shawl, or riband, it is well for the buyer to consider three things: I. That it be not too expensive for her purse. II. That its colour harmonize with her complexion, and its size and pattern with her figure. III. That its tint allow of its being worn with the other garments she possesses. The quaint Fuller observes, that the good wife is none of our dainty dames, who love to appear in a variety of suits every day new, as if a gown, like a stratagem in war, were to be used but once. But our good wife sets up a sail according to the keel of her husband's estate; and, if of high parentage, she doth not so remember what she was by birth, that she forgets what she is by match.

14. CHARITY AND BENEVOLENCE ARE DUTIES which a mistress owes to herself as well as to her fellow-creatures; and there is scarcely any income so small, but something may be spared from it, even if it be but "the widow's mite." It is to be always remembered, however, that it is the *spirit* of charity which imparts to the gift a value far beyond its actual amount, and is by far its better part.

16. A HOUSEKEEPING ACCOUNT-BOOK should invariably be kept, and kept punctually and precisely. The plan for keeping household accounts, which we should recommend, would be to make an entry, that is, write down into a daily diary every amount paid on that particular day, be it ever so small; then, at the end of the month, let these various payments be ranged under their specific heads of Butcher, Baker, &c.; and thus will be seen the proportions paid to each tradesman, and any one month's expenses may be contrasted with another. The housekeeping accounts should be balanced not less than once a month; so that you may see that the money you have in hand tallies with your account of it in your diary. Judge Haliburton never wrote truer words than when he said, "No man is rich whose expenditure exceeds his means, and no one is poor whose incomings exceed his outgoings."

When, in a large establishment, a housekeeper is kept, it will be advisable for the mistress to examine her accounts regularly. Then any increase of expenditure which may be apparent, can easily be explained, and the housekeeper will have the satisfaction of knowing whether her efforts to manage her department well and economically, have been successful.

19. THE TREATMENT OF SERVANTS is of the highest possible moment, as well to the mistress as to the domestics themselves. On the head of the house the latter will naturally fix their attention; and if they perceive that the mistress's conduct is regulated by high and correct principles, they will not fail to respect her. If, also, a benevolent desire is shown to promote their comfort, at the same time that a steady performance

of their duty is exacted, then their respect will not be unmingled with affection, and they will be still more solicitous to continue to deserve her favour.

28. IN PAYING VISITS OF FRIENDSHIP, it will not be so necessary to be guided by etiquette as in paying visits of ceremony; and if a lady be pressed by her friend to remove her shawl and bonnet, it can be done if it will not interfere with her subsequent arrangements. It is, however, requisite to call at suitable times, and to avoid staying too long, if your friend is engaged. The courtesies of society should ever be maintained, even in the domestic circle, and amongst the nearest friends. During these visits, the manners should be easy and cheerful, and the subjects of conversation such as may be readily terminated. Serious discussions or arguments are to be altogether avoided, and there is much danger and impropriety in expressing opinions of those persons and characters with whom, perhaps, there is but a slight acquaintance.

An illustration from Isabella Beeton's *The Book of Household Management*, showing kitchen maids, a parlor maid, and scullery maids; published in 1901. Courtesy of photos.com

54. SUCH ARE THE ONEROUS DUTIES which enter into the position of the mistress of a house, and such are, happily, with a slight but continued attention, of by no means difficult performance. She ought always to remember that she is the first and the last, the Alpha and the Omega in the government of her establishment; and that it is by her conduct that its whole internal policy is regulated. She is, therefore, a person of far more importance in a community than she usually thinks she is. On her pattern her daughters model themselves; by her counsels they are directed; through her virtues all are honoured;—"her children rise up and call her blessed; her husband, also, and he praiseth her." Therefore, let each mistress always remember her responsible position, never approving a mean action, nor speaking an unrefined word. Let her conduct be such that her inferiors may respect her, and such as an honourable and right-minded man may look for in his wife and the mother of his children. Let her think of the many compliments and the sincere homage that have been paid to her sex by the greatest philosophers and writers, both in ancient and modern times. Let her not forget that she has to show herself worthy of Campbell's compliment when he said,—

> "The world was sad! the garden was a wild!
> And man the hermit sigh'd, till *woman* smiled."

Let her prove herself, then, the happy companion of man, and able to take unto herself the praises of the pious prelate, Jeremy Taylor, who says,—"A good wife is Heaven's last best gift to man,—his angel and minister of graces innumerable,—his gem of many virtues,—his casket of jewels—her voice is sweet music—her smiles his brightest day;—her kiss, the guardian of his innocence;—her arms, the pale of his safety, the balm of his health, the balsam of his life;—her industry, his surest wealth;—her economy, his safest steward;—her lips, his faithful counsellors;—her bosom, the softest pillow of his cares; and her prayers, the ablest advocates of Heaven's blessings on his head."

Cherishing, then, in her breast the respected utterances of the good and the great, let the mistress of every house rise to the responsibility of its management; so that, in doing her duty to all around her, she may receive the genuine reward of respect, love, and affection!

Source: Beeton, Isabella. Mrs. *Beeton's Book of Household Management: Comprising Information for the Mistress, Housekeeper, Cook, Kitchen-Maid, Butler, Footman, Coachman, Valet, Upper and Under House-Maids, Lady's Maid, Maid-of-all-Work, Laundry-Maid, Nurse and Nurse-Maid, Monthly, Wet, and Sick-Nurses, etc. etc., Also Sanitary, Medical, and Legal Memoranda, with a History of the Origin, Properties, and Uses of All Things Connected with Home Life and Comfort*. London: S. O. Beeton, 1861.

3. The Turkish Harem in the Early Twentieth Century

In the following selection, Halil Halid, a Turkish intellectual and social activist, offers a perspective on the practice of the harem *from the last years of the* Ottoman Empire, *which would crumble in the wake of World War I (1914–1918), and become modern-day Turkey. His audience is English society, and he attempts to make the practices of the harem and* polygamy *more understandable and palatable to the* Edwardian English *mind. In the Western imagination, harems had become mysterious and exotic places of luxury, eroticism, and decadence. Because they were forbidden to most foreign observers, especially men, an understanding of what life was like for women in the harem was often thoroughly exaggerated or simply made-up. Halid tries to make a number of points, including that the term harem refers to one part of a divided domestic space and the women of a household who inhabit it. He describes a social custom in transition, with shifting attitudes on polygamy, and differing degrees of seclusion for harems. He describes differing occupations and responsibilities for women in harems depending on social status, including domestic labor and education.*

At the simplest level, a harem is a social practice that sequesters women from men in a private domestic space, whether for protection, privacy, or possession is a matter of perspective. A Turkish household was divided into public and private spaces, with outside men excluded from the private space, and women restricted in their presence and behavior in the public space. Harems at the highest levels of Ottoman society were complex social hierarchies within palace life of wives, concubines, eunuchs, children, and servants. Within the elite Harem, young women were educated to prepare themselves for marriage to officers or other aristocrats and to run harems of their own.

The typical harem Halid describes is not this type of elite level. Harems were also places for education and training of girls according to their social standing, as well as places for domestic labor. Although the Western segregation of women and men into separate spaces was not nearly so systematic and strict, the degree of regulation and rigidity of social interactions in terms of manners, dress, and sexual behavior were certainly comparable in many ways between the British for whom Halid was writing and the late Ottoman Harem.

There are many people in England whose ideas on the subject of the harem are but a confused misconception, based on what they may have heard about Eastern polygamy. In this chapter, that I may correct these mistaken conceptions, I will give some more exact information on the subject of the harem and its inmates, as well as on the position of women in Turkey in general.

Although the word harem is known and used by the people of Western Europe, the true meaning of the term is understood by but few persons in this country. As a matter of fact, many subjects concerning the East are much misunderstood in the West, just as there are certain manners and customs of Western Europe that cause prejudice in the Eastern mind. When an Englishman uses the word harem, he means thereby the numerous wives whom a man in our part of the East is supposed to shut up in his house. He, moreover, believes that every man in the Mohammedan East may marry as many women as he pleases. This idea is not only mistaken, but grotesque. There are thousands of men who would consider themselves fortunate if they could marry even a single woman; while, on the other hand, there are thousands who would be happy to get rid of the single wife they have. Any man who can manage to keep two, not to say more, wives in peace, and can cope with the requirements of each, must be an exceptionally brave person. Wives are not all religiously obedient in the East, just as all men are not tyrants. Religion, law, and custom impose upon men many duties to be discharged towards their wives. An honest man must discharge these duties, and indeed it is very difficult to find many men who are able to fulfill their obligations as husbands towards more than one wife. It has been proved that in many parts of the Ottoman empire the number of women does not exceed that of men, a fact which alone is enough to show the absurdity of the notion prevailing in England about the plurality of wives in that country. As a matter of fact, there is no law against the practice of polygamy, but the feeling of decent people condemns it. A man who is once married to a gentleman's daughter would find it no light matter to add another wife to his home circle. There are nowadays many men of Western education who marry in order to find a life companion, and they quite understand that were they so injudicious as to take another wife, they would very likely render their lives the reverse of peaceful.

After pointing out the absurdity of the notion that a man's harem is his collection of wives, I will now explain what it really is. In Mohammedan countries, where the seclusion of women is a deeply rooted and religiously observed custom, every house is divided into two separate parts. In Turkey the section of a house where the ladies reside is called the harem, and the men's portion is named the *selamlik*—that is to say, the reception-place. Though the female inmates of a house are also collectively called the harem, this does not mean that they are all the wives of the master of the house. A man's wife, his mother, his sister, his daughter, and such other women as may lawfully appear unveiled in his presence, belong to his harem.

The male members of a family who are permitted to enter the harem are the master of the house, his sons, his father, his father-in-law, and his wife's brother. In large cities such as Constantinople, Smyrna, and Adrianople, the advanced class of people may even permit their more distant relatives to enter. Those who adopt European customs may even admit their intimate friends. But in the old-fashioned families, such as form the great bulk of the population, no male relation of the master is allowed to enter the harem portion of his house after he has reached his thirteenth or fourteenth year if marriage between such male relation and the master's daughter, or other young marriageable inmates of his house, be possible. [. . .]

The life in most Turkish harems is very simple, and, if we leave out the case of the few polygamists who still remain, very peaceful and happy. The absolute authority of the husband does not interfere with the recognised privileges of the wife; while the obedience of the wife, which is regarded by more advanced women in Western Europe with such contempt, in most cases strengthens the affection and respect of the husband for her. Wives are not slaves of their husbands, as some people in this country fancy them to be. The inmates of harems live mostly indoors, but they are not entirely shut up. They go out in groups of two, three, and more to pay visits to other harems, and they receive visitors from the harems of friends and relations. Of course their gatherings are almost always unmixed, but, like the women of other countries, some of them sing and play to entertain others. Dancing has been introduced recently, but it is confined only to very advanced private families. Among the people of the old school the dancing of young ladies in the presence of others is considered shocking. At weddings and other similar festivities only hired professional women amuse the guests by dancing, and these professional dancers are not regarded as respectable. In my time, reading aloud was a favourite pastime in many harems.

The number of educated women was much less than it is now. The most learned among them used to read sacred legends, or religious tracts, or recite hymns to the other ladies, who would listen attentively for hours. I believe this social pastime is still in favour in the provinces.

Turkish women, according to their social position, have various duties to discharge. No qualities are so much sought after in an average marriageable woman as the domestic ones. In the provinces the peasant women, besides managing their humble domestic affairs, have to work in the fields, more especially when their brothers and husbands are away discharging their compulsory military service. The daughters of well-to-do people, besides attending to the business of their households, are indefatigable with their needles, and are always busy with needlework or embroidery; while the daughters of high dignitaries must, among other duties, learn what their instructors or governesses teach them.

It will be understood from the details I have given that the popular notion prevailing in this country of the harem and the life in the harem is much mistaken. Women in Turkish harems do not really pass their time lying on sofas or couches, eating sweetmeats and smoking water-pipes all day long. Of course they are as fond of sweet stuffs as most ladies of this country. But to lie down on a couch in presence of others is considered by Turkish women vulgarity of the most disgraceful kind.

Source: Halid, Halil. *Diary of a Turk*. London: Charles and Black, 1903.

4. Betty Friedan on the Suburban Housewife

There is no doubt that the role of women in society has changed from Mrs. Isabella Beeton's day (see Document 2) in the mid-nineteenth century. Most women and many men now identify themselves as feminists, though of course the term means very different things to different people. However feminism *is defined, one of the landmark pieces of feminist writing in the twentieth century was Betty Friedan's* The Feminine Mystique, *which argued that the role of the suburban housewife of mid-century America was deeply flawed and created legions of unhappy, unhealthy, unfulfilled women. "The problem that has no name" as*

Friedan called it, was a result of the feminine mystique, an emerging ideal of womanhood created not only from cultural and historical precedent (one can compare it to the domesticity of Beeton's "angel of the house"), but also a mass culture that formed notions of feminine identity almost exclusively in the role of housewife; saw marriage and childbearing as the ultimate goal of even professionally trained, educated women; and generally limited housewives' activities to volunteer work, childcare, and homemaking.

Friedan demanded a re-education of women and a re-evaluation of their roles, insisting that women form an identity separate from family and home and pursue their own ambitions and promising that it was possible to have it all—happy home, husband, children, as well as work and a fulfilling career outside the home. In the following excerpt from her book, she offers her advice on a new life plan for American women and a method to defy the feminine mystique. What Friedan wanted in large part occurred, with significant changes in women's roles and the social, economic, and cultural structures of the family. In the twenty-first century, the movement of large numbers of women into the workforce has created its own difficulties and challenges as well as new and different social problems for women. The shift away from earlier models of gender roles has met with resistance from some traditional and conservative points of view, but represents an important change in women's roles as they had been predominantly defined in the nineteenth century, a change that is now a fact of social life in most of the Western world.

When society asks so little of women, every woman has to listen to her own inner voice to find her identity in this changing world. She must create, out of her own needs and abilities, a new life plan, fitting in the love and children and home that have defined femininity in the past with the work toward a greater purpose that shapes the future. To face the problem is not to solve it. [...]

There are no easy answers, in America today; it is difficult, painful, and takes perhaps a long time for each woman to find her own answer. First, she must unequivocally say "no" to the housewife image. This does not mean, of course, that she must divorce her husband, abandon her children, give up her home. She does not have to choose between marriage and career; that was the mistaken choice of the feminine mystique. In actual fact, it is not as difficult as the feminine mystique implies, to combine marriage and motherhood and even the kind of lifelong personal purpose that once was called "career." It merely takes a new life plan—in terms of one's whole life as a woman. [...]

The second step, and perhaps the most difficult for the products of sex-directed education, is to see marriage as it really is, brushing aside the veil of over-glorification imposed by the feminine mystique. Many women I talked to felt strangely discontented with their husbands, continually irritated with their children, when they saw marriage and motherhood as the final fulfillment of their lives. But when they began to use their various abilities with a purpose of their own in society, they not only spoke of a new feeling of "aliveness" or "completeness" in themselves, but of a new, though hard to define, difference in the way they felt about their husbands and children. [...]

But a job, any job, is not the answer—in fact, it can be part of the trap. Women who do not look for jobs equal to their actual capacity, who do not let themselves develop the lifetime interests and goals which require serious education and training, who take a job at twenty or forty to "help out at home" or just to kill extra time, are walking, almost as surely as the ones who stay inside the housewife trap, to a nonexistent future.

If a job is to be the way out of the trap for a woman, it must, be a job that she can take seriously as part of a life plan, work in which she can grow as part of society. [...]

The key to the trap is, of course, education. The feminine mystique has made higher education for women seem suspect, unnecessary and even dangerous. But I think that education, and only education, has saved, and can continue to save, American women from the greater dangers of the feminine mystique.

Source: Friedan, Betty. *The Feminine Mystique*. New York: W. W. Norton and Co., 1963.

Children

For most of us, the first memories we have are of childhood and our domestic environment: parents, grandparents, siblings, our homes, and so on. The domestic environment is of obvious importance in every child's or person's life. The modern period has seen dramatic shifts in child rearing practices and the very nature of childhood. In early modern Europe, children were sometimes seen as either beast-like, or as miniature adults; there was no general idea of a unique intermediate stage of childhood.

The modern era saw the development of childhood as a discrete and important stage. That stage was cruel and difficult for Frederick Douglass and other African-American slaves in nineteenth-century America (Document 5); separated from his mother and denied by his father. Douglass lacked exactly what it was said every child needed: a nurturing mother and a protecting father. Robert Baden-Powell's description of Boy Scouting (Document 6) brings in activities of childhood outside the home, and the ways childhood was seen by states and parents as a time for training in virtue, self-reliance, and patriotism—things important not only to the individual but also to a nation and society as a whole. The precariousness of life is highlighted by the discussion of the high rate of infant mortality in West Africa (Document 7), a persistent problem in many parts of the world where childhood is decidedly dangerous. At the same time, it also offers an opportunity to see how domestic situations react to cultural influences brought by the creation of European empires in many parts of the world in the eighteenth and nineteenth centuries, and it documents the lasting consequences of imperialism and newer contemporary globalization movements.

5. Frederick Douglass: Being a Slave Child

Frederick Douglass (c. 1817–1895) was one of America's most famous African Americans. Born a slave in Maryland, he escaped to Massachusetts and spent his life speaking, traveling, and publishing for the abolition of slavery *and the rights of various oppressed groups. In this excerpt, which begins his first book, Douglass tells little of his daily life as a child, but gives a fascinating account of the endemic contradictions of slavery and the tragic effects on children and families. In a culture where maternal care was considered paramount, Douglass describes being intentionally separated from his mother by his owners. He claims his father might have been a white man, perhaps even his master, as frequently occurred.*

The description of Douglass's relationship to his mother is designed to be touching—she would at times walk 12 miles each way after work to lie down with him for a few hours before she had to leave to make it back to the fields at dawn the next day, and he never saw her in daylight. However, he also insists he was not attached to her, which makes the whole situation and her extraordinary efforts to see her child all the more tragic and ironic.

Whether Douglass's father was a white man or not, the relationship of a mixed-race slave to his father, if his or her father was the master, was even more conflicted. Douglass points out the jealousy of slave owners' wives when confronted with their husbands' illegitimate children; the need for owners to whip, beat, and even sell their own children; have siblings torture one another; separate their children from their mothers; and deprive their children of any family and the affection and support that comes with it.

Douglass raises the important issue of interracial relationships, or miscegenation, *as it was called in the nineteenth century. Such relationships were not only taboo to many whites, but also illegal in some states until 1967 when the U.S. Supreme Court overturned racial purity laws. The natural distinction between races was a staple argument of pro-slavery whites, who used pseudoscientific theories and, as Douglass mentions, biblical support to conclude that blacks were inferior to whites and were not intended by God to intermarry or have children.*

If Douglass, in fact, was a mixed-race child (he himself admitted he did not know for certain who his father was), his having a white father and black mother made Douglass in some sense at least as much white as black. The differences he points out between himself and his African ancestors indicates the changing nature of race in the United States well before the Civil War *and the resulting emancipation of all slaves in the 1860s, and race continues to be a central but changing issue in American society even today.*

I was born in Tuckahoe, near Hillsborough, and about twelve miles from Easton, in Talbot county, Maryland. I have no accurate knowledge of my age, never having seen any authentic record containing it. By far the larger part of the slaves know as little of their ages as horses know of theirs, and it is the wish of most masters within my knowledge to keep their slaves thus ignorant. I do not remember to have ever met a slave who could tell of his birthday. They seldom come nearer to it than planting-time, harvest-time, cherry-time, spring-time, or fall-time. A want of information concerning my own was a source of unhappiness to me even during childhood. The white children could tell their ages. I could not tell why I ought to be deprived of the same privilege. I was not allowed to make any inquiries of my master concerning it. He deemed all such inquiries on the part of a slave improper and impertinent, and evidence of a restless spirit. The nearest estimate I can give makes me now between twenty-seven and twenty-eight years of age. I come to this, from hearing my master say, some time during 1835, I was about seventeen years old.

My mother was named Harriet Bailey. She was the daughter of Isaac and Betsey Bailey, both colored, and quite dark. My mother was of a darker complexion than either my grandmother or grandfather.

My father was a white man. He was admitted to be such by all I ever heard speak of my parentage. The opinion was also whispered that my master was my father; but of the correctness of this opinion, I know nothing; the means of knowing was withheld from me. My mother and I were separated when I was but an infant—before I knew her as my mother. It is a common custom, in the part of Maryland from which I ran away, to part children from their mothers at a very early age. Frequently, before the child has reached its twelfth month, its mother is taken from it, and hired out on some farm a considerable distance off, and the child is placed under the care of an old woman, too old for field labor. For what this separation is done, I do not know, unless it be to hinder the development of the child's affection toward its mother, and to blunt and destroy the natural affection of the mother for the child. This is the inevitable result.

I never saw my mother, to know her as such, more than four or five times in my life; and each of these times was very short in duration, and at night. She was hired by a Mr. Stewart, who lived about twelve miles from my home. She made her journeys to see me in the night, traveling the whole distance on foot, after the performance of her day's work. She was a field hand, and a whipping is the penalty of not being in the field at sunrise, unless a slave has special permission from his or her master to the contrary—a permission which they seldom get, and one that gives to him that gives it the proud name of being a kind master. I do not recollect of ever seeing my mother by the light of day. She was with me in the night. She would lie down with me, and get me to sleep, but long before I waked she was gone. Very little communication ever took place between us. Death soon ended what little we could have while she lived, and with it her hardships and suffering. She died when I was about seven years old, on one of my master's farms, near Lee's Mill. I was not allowed to be present during her illness, at her death, or burial. She was gone long before I knew any thing about it. Never having enjoyed, to any considerable extent, her soothing presence, her tender and watchful care, I received the tidings of her death with much the same emotions I should have probably felt at the death of a stranger.

Called thus suddenly away, she left me without the slightest intimation of who my father was. The whisper that my master was my father, may or may not be true; and, true or false, it is of but little consequence to my purpose whilst the fact remains, in all its glaring odiousness, that slaveholders have ordained, and by law established, that the children of slave women shall in all cases follow the condition of their mothers; and this is done too obviously to administer to their own lusts, and make a gratification of their wicked desires profitable as well as pleasurable; for by this cunning arrangement, the slaveholder, in cases not a few, sustains to his slaves the double relation of master and father.

I know of such cases; and it is worthy of remark that such slaves invariably suffer greater hardships, and have more to contend with, than others. They are, in the first place, a constant offence to their mistress. She is ever disposed to find fault with them; they can seldom do any thing to please her; she is never better pleased

A large family of African Americans pose outside former slave quarters at Hermitage Plantation, Savannah, Georgia, 1909. Library of Congress.

than when she sees them under the lash, especially when she suspects her husband of showing to his mulatto children favors which he withholds from his black slaves. The master is frequently compelled to sell this class of his slaves, out of deference to the feelings of his white wife; and, cruel as the deed may strike any one to be, for a man to sell his own children to human flesh-mongers, it is often the dictate of humanity for him to do so; for, unless he does this, he must not only whip them himself, but must stand by and see one white son tie up his brother, of but few shades darker complexion than himself, and ply the gory lash to his naked back; and if he lisp one word of disapproval, it is set down to his parental partiality, and only makes a bad matter worse, both for himself and the slave whom he would protect and defend.

Every year brings with it multitudes of this class of slaves. It was doubtless in consequence of a knowledge of this fact, that one great statesman of the south predicted the downfall of slavery by the inevitable laws of population. Whether this prophecy is ever fulfilled or not, it is nevertheless plain that a very different-looking class of people are springing up at the south, and are now held in slavery, from those originally brought to this country from Africa; and if their increase do no other good, it will do away the force of the argument, that God cursed Ham, and therefore American slavery is right. If the lineal descendants of Ham are alone to be scripturally enslaved, it is certain that slavery at the south must soon become unscriptural; for thousands are ushered into the world, annually, who, like myself, owe their existence to white fathers, and those fathers most frequently their own masters.

Source: Douglass, Frederick. *Narrative of the Life of Frederick Douglass, an American Slave, Written by Himself*. Boston: The Anti-Slavery Office, 1845.

6. "The Most Impressive Sight": A Rally of English Boy Scouts in 1914

Sir Robert Baden-Powell (1857–1941) was a British officer and veteran of colonial wars, as well as the founder of the Scouting movement. The creation of such youth organizations is the product of nineteenth-century cultural phenomena, such as nationalism, an emphasis on self-control, and mass culture. Scouting groups encouraged nationalism, physical fitness, outdoor skills, and character growth. In the United States today, groups like the Boy Scouts, *Girl Scouts, Campfire, and others trace their roots, directly or indirectly, to Baden Powell's idea of* Scouting for Boys, *the title of his 1908 book that became one of the best sellers of the twentieth century in the English-speaking world. Of course, youth organizations promoting nationalism, citizenship development, and, sometimes military preparedness have also been used by totalitarian regimes, such as the Young Pioneers and Communist Youth League in the former* Union of Soviet Socialist Republics *or the Hitler Youth in Adolf* Hitler's *Nazi Germany.*

The following selection describes a rally of English Boy Scouts in 1914, at which King George V made an appearance, as "the most impressive sight," comparing it favorably with a moving, makeshift military funeral and a vivid account of an attack by African Zulu warriors. Of course, as the founder of Scouting, Baden-Powell may not have been objective, but personal bias notwithstanding, Baden-Powell's account reflects a concern for the importance of proper development of male youth, the value of selflessness and egalitarianism despite social and class differences, and a patriotic devotion to country that had developed throughout the nineteenth century in Western culture. Much of the worldview that gave rise to Scouting would be forever altered by the events of the twentieth century, including the First World War (1914–1918), which began the same year this article was published. Yet despite the dramatic social and cultural changes of the twentieth century, Scouting continues to have an impact on children and youth around the world. Although not immune to controversy, it remains the largest international youth movement, with over 28 million members worldwide and affiliated organizations in over 200 countries, many of which include girls as well as boys, and another 9 million members in Girl Scouts or Girl Guides groups.

It is true that in my time, I have seen many impressive sights, and not the least impressive that occurs immediately to one's mind is the scene when we stood round the grave-side of one of our bravest and best officers in the South African Campaign. It was in the dead of night, without even a glimmer of a lantern that might draw-upon us some of the shells which were flying near. There was a dark, silent crowd of men dimly seen in the starlight shuffling round the body of one who, only six short hours before, had been full of life and strength, the soul and spirit of those who were now carrying him to his grave, who had led them on to face the death which he himself had met. After they had lowered him into the hastily-prepared grave, a husky voice broke the silence and growled out, with a sob, "Well, good-bye Captain," from those around there was a murmured response in the shape of "That's it." "Hear, hear," which, though nearing the comic, was at that moment deeply pathetic, coming as it did, from hardy, rough campaigners, and was more impressive than an "amen" of a cathedral service.

Then, too, I remember being present with a great Zulu impi [regiment] about to make its attack upon an enemy's stronghold. It was an inspiring sight to see this mass of savage warriors, decked out in war-paint with the blood lust in their eyes, squatting round in a vast circle, straining eagerly to hear that chief giving them orders for the battle. It reminded one of nothing so much as a great bronze serpent, lying coiled ready to spring, for, although almost silent and motionless, there was a rhythmic heaving and sob amongst the men during the whole of their leader's address, which, together with their straining eyes and twitching muscles, showed their whole-hearted earnestness in grasping, every word that came from him, and at the same time their eagerness to be off to work his bidding. Then when the leader gave the word to go, the whole force rose as one man, for a moment in silence, and then, with a hiss from every one of the thousand mouths, which gave a keen, cruel meaning to their move, they started to run. The young warriors sped out to either flank at top speed, racing each other for the place of honour which meant first blood to the winner. Then from the dense mass in the centre there came forward, in serried ranks, the older warriors, the reserve or "chest" of the force, and as they strode forward to support the whole move, there broke out like an organ pealing the deep chorus from a thousand throats:

If we go forward we die;
If we go backward we die;
Better go forward and die.

Many other stirring scenes crowd on my memory, but in the end they revert to that great day two years ago, when, in the Great Park, under Windsor Castle the King reviewed the Boy Scouts. One of the impressive features of that day was the army of young men working earnestly and cheerfully in the cause of the Movement. At the railway station one met with familiar faces of men well known in London society, but dressed in very different uniform to their society clothes, just the khaki and cowboy hat of the Scout Army. They were doing the work of the railway staff officers, receiving trains, telling the scoutmasters what to do and the boys where to go, and getting them quickly away, ready for the immediate arrival of troop upon troop of other boys coming or returning, by rail. The work of these men, peers of the realm some of them, was of the most arduous and harassing description, since it went on hour after hour without relief and without notice, for they were working behind the scenes; but they were working away, keeping a cheery face on it and good-natured tongue the whole time, and that in itself was an impressive sight.

Then out on the great plains under the shade of the oaks was arrayed an immense crowd of thousands upon thousands of boys, all dressed alike—all the same type—all working under suppressed excitement though many of them had been travelling the whole of the previous night. Go where you would it was the same sight; after going through one enormous division of them you only realized that there were still three more similar divisions to be seen, all preparing themselves for the great moment when they were to see the King. A few hours later these same boys were all massed in solid ranks in a vast horseshoe in the open park, and facing them was a great crowd of spectators, watching and waiting for what they might do.

What struck one at that moment was the mysterious hush which seemed to pervade the whole scene where these thousands of human beings were quietly waiting for something, and ready at any moment to burst out—no one could tell quite in what direction. Expectation had reached a kind of climax when at last the King and his Staff arrived upon the scene. He had arranged that he himself should be seen by every boy—that was what they came for all these hundreds of miles. This would not be possible if they marched past him in the usual fashion where only those on the flank could see him—the only way would be for him to ride round and show himself to all. It was his own idea, and when carried out proved how truly he had fathomed the wishes of the whole of the parade. For, steady as they were in their rank. The King had not gone half-way round when the boys could no longer restrain themselves. A sudden tornado of cheers broke out where the King was—like a prairie fire, and it spread all round the

A WWI poster featuring a Boy Scout handing Lady Liberty a sword inscribed "Be prepared." Library of Congress.

great concourse in a moment so that the whole scene was a mass of cheering lads and tossing hats—their enthusiasm knew no bounds, and that no doubt, was a sight which impressed itself on all who were there.

The King himself remarked on another feature of the scene which also, in its way, impressed a thoughtful onlooker, and that was the massed body of men formed in rear of the boys. These were the scoutmasters—the men who pulled the strings—the men who did the work—the men who were behind the scenes, in the background, and had done so much to train these boys and to bring them for their Sovereign's inspection. There were men among them of every kind—young and old, rough and smooth, high and low, rich and poor—all shoulder to shoulder in one seat cause—the cause of the future generation of their country. Here was a distinguished colonel with cavalry bearing, many medals and orders on his breast. Alongside him was a pale curate of an East-end slum, brushing shoulders with an old bluejacket and a bank clerk from Canada. The same kind of thing might be seen anywhere along that wonderful line. It was an indication of what there is in our fellow-countrymen of patriotism and good will for voluntary work where it is often not suspected.

But these and many other impressive incidents were swallowed up in the great moment of the day, when then the King took his place under the Royal Standard at the saluting-point. There was a minutes dead silent pause, and then a sudden scream rent the air, and the whole mighty horseshoe of thirty thousand boys with one impulse leapt forward from either side, rushing as only boys can rush, gathering speed and force as they came, a mighty roaring torrent of humanity, screaming out rallying cries of their different patrols as they came in a whole kaleidoscopic mass of colour, with flags fluttering, hats waving, knees glinting, in the great charge when they flew in towards the King.

Then, at a sign, the whole mass suddenly stopped its rush, up went a forest of staves and hats, and higher into the skies went the shrill, screaming cheers of the boys that gripped the throats of all onlookers—"God Save the King"—that apogee of patriotic fervour in young Britain, that surge of enthusiasm to do anything that might be demanded of them in the cause of their country and King, That was the most impressive sight that I have ever seen.

Source: Baden-Powell, Sir Robert. "The Most Impressive Sight I Ever Saw: The Royal Rally of Boy Scouts at Windsor." *The Strand Magazine*, January 1914.

7. *Sister Marie-Andre du Sacre Coeur: Growing Up in West Africa*

Sister Marie-Andre du Sacre Coeur was born as Jeanne Dorge in northern France, but became a nun of the Roman Catholic Church *and missionary against the wishes of her parents after finishing a law degree and doctorate. She went to Africa, where she did work as a nurse, teacher, social worker, and missionary. She was no ordinary missionary, though. Her background, experience, and enthusiasm made her a powerful force for change, especially in the French-speaking world. She single-handedly rewrote legislation on the status of women in French colonial possessions, successfully lobbied for its adoption into law, and provided the impetus for major international reform efforts for African women. She addressed legislatures and UN bodies, and she became an international advocate for improving the status of African women.*

The following selection discusses typical life in West Africa for children in the middle of the twentieth century. The domination of Africa by European colonial powers that had controlled virtually all of Africa since the nineteenth century was beginning to wane, but the presence of European social and cultural institutions was still evident, although the degree to which European cultural penetration had taken place depended in large part on the locale, with influence in centers and cities being much stronger. Colonialism *has created a contentious legacy on the African continent, although* de-colonization *was only beginning when this text was written in the 1950s.*

Sister Marie-Andre describes daily life for children in Africa as basically good, but precarious, a life where African ways and colonial influences interact. Health care and education taken for granted in Europe and North America were not readily available to (or even necessarily trusted by) large portions of the population. In a region with an infant mortality rate of up to 60 percent, she describes parents who would not count children until they knew they would survive and children at risk of infection, disease, and malnutrition. Traditional initiation practices such as naming customs and haircutting are conducted in parallel with Christian rituals like baptism. So too, traditional toy making turns millet stalks into rifles, airplanes, and the like. Children learn their roles, values, and trades from their parents, older siblings, and extended family, and ancestor worship and kinship groups are very important and strong. There is no doubt that much has changed in Africa, but at the same time many of the issues that African children and families faced 50 years ago in Sister Marie-Andre's day are also faced today.

It is often said that the child is king in Africa. It is true that he is at home in every house in the village, that every effort is made to prevent his tears, and when they come they are quickly dried. For children are the end and purpose of African marriage, awaited and desired by the wedded couple and both their families. But in a region where the percentage of infant mortality is sometimes as high as sixty percent, the birth and care of children is also fraught with anxiety and grief.... One did not count a child until it was certain to live. [...]

Among many African people, the name given a child has great significance. In some tribes the father gives his baby a name that reflects his own sentiments at its birth. In others, the grandmother, aunt, or clan chief names the child. In some areas of Northern Ghana, the child is not named until it is two years old. Then it is dedicated to an ancestor or to a guardian spirit of the family, whom the diviner has indicated wishes, to be its protector and whose name is then given the child. Until this ceremony, it is called *Diampana*, meaning "without a name." [...]

Christians have come to feel a spiritual relationship with the patron saint whose name they receive in baptism and with all others who bear the same name. In the various countries along the West African coast, it is not unusual to come across friendship groupings or associations of persons having the same name—Association of Jeans, of Germaines and the like. [...]

In many areas, there is no special name-giving ceremony. Often, however, the child receives its name eight days after birth in the midst of family rejoicing intermingled with customary rites. Among the latter is the first cutting of the baby's hair. I was privileged to witness this in the family of some friends in Mali. The baby had been baptized Felicia in church, a name chosen by her father. But according to ancestral custom there remained the matter of cutting her hair. The house was full of guests—relatives, friends, and the one who was to perform the ceremony—all of whom had brought gifts. These consisted of millet, peanuts, combed cotton, kola nuts.

One of the women of the family held little Felicia on her lap while the ritual master snipped off her baby hair. As fast as he did so this was gathered up by another woman and laid on a strip of raveled string. She had to be extremely careful not to let the wind carry the wisps of hair away, otherwise, according to local belief, Felicia would have a headache for a very long time. To carry out this custom her mother would have to keep her baby hair hidden until the child could walk by herself. Then Felicia would take the little package of hair and throw it into a deep hole, so that the wind would never be able to reach it.

When the hair cutting ceremony was over, the women presented their gifts to Felicia's mother, dancing about her and chanting their good wishes for the baby: "May God give her health. May he give her long life!" Next, one of the older women washed the baby with warm water and soap, using a small brush made of vegetable fibers. Next she warmed shea butter in her hands over the fire and rubbed the baby with it. Meanwhile, the guests were assembling for the meal, the men on one side, the women on the other, the old women in the house. The woman who had held Felicia throughout the ritual then set her on the back of one of the little girls and wrapped her in place with a long, new white cloth. The little girl so honored took her place among the other children, the woman joined the older members in the house, and the ceremony was over. [...]

Almost every African woman nurses her baby. If she works where she cannot take him with her, she leaves bottles prepared for the hours she is away and nurses him when she gets home. The minute he cries, he is fed, "demand feeding" being an old African custom. [...]

When a child is six or eight months old he is given porridge made with water and millet or corn flour, sometimes sweetened with sugar. But the porridge does not have the necessary nutritive value, and since his mother's milk is no longer sufficient either, this is the period when malnutrition sets in. Toddlers attempt to dip into the family dish at mealtime, but the stew of meat or fish is not the most appropriate food for them since it is highly spiced and often seasoned with an abundance of pepper which their little digestive system finds difficult to handle.

Lung infections are common ailments, while ignorance of contagion is another source of danger. To a grandmother with leprosy, for example, may be left the care of small children while both parents work in the fields. Obviously there is a high rate of infant mortality—sometimes over 60 percent—especially in areas where there are no clinics or hospitals. Half of the infant deaths occur before the age of six months, most of them due to umbilical tetanus or to respiratory or gastric infections. Later, besides the usual childhood diseases like measles and whooping cough there is danger from smallpox and the inevitable malaria. Lack of environmental sanitation and pure drinking water contribute a number of parasitic diseases, further aggravated by the occasional tendency of all children to eat dirt.

Where tradition still prevails, it is believed necessary for the child's health to make him swallow some warm concoction every day. The mother brews a kind of tea of bitter herbs and then, seated on her mat, she holds the child firmly between her legs and makes him drink it all no matter how much he struggles. Then she holds him up by his feet and shakes him to lengthen him before putting him to sleep. [...]

In Africa the mother is the child's first educator, who teaches him his manners and proper behavior. Where traditional custom still prevails, his older brothers and sisters also undertake to teach him to obey them and to render them little services, so that he will recognize and respect their seniority. For example, at mealtime the youngest must never help himself before his elders and his hand must never touch theirs in the family dish. He must eat with his right hand and in silence.

Normally a child is not allowed alone outside the family circle until he is about five or six years old. Then he has the run of the village and takes refuge with one or another relative when parental punishment threatens. And like grandparents everywhere, those of the African child tend to spoil him. [...]

When a boy is six or seven years old, his father begins to take over his education. He takes him to help in the fields, and when he is a little older begins to teach him both his own trade and the customary tasks about the house and compound. The African father has a rich supply of proverbs to help mold his son's character. For example, "If the bricks say to each other, I will not stay next to you, the house will never be built." In other words, people must work together for there are many things a person working alone cannot accomplish. Crafts, such as ironwork, jewelry making, tanning, saddlery, cordwaining, shoemaking, are passed on from father to son. The healer, or medicine man, will choose a son to succeed him, teaching him the qualities of medicinal plants and how to prepare his remedies.

The African girl remains with her mother until her own marriage unless she is being brought up in the family of her future husband. In either case she is taught how to keep house and cook, and she performs a number of errands such as fetching water and wood, in addition to helping take care of her little brothers and sisters. She takes the role of "little mother" very seriously and her care of a younger child is always affectionate. She also learns to grow the ingredients for the stew, to cultivate cotton and to comb and spin it. When she is a little older she helps to brew millet or banana beer and is taught how to make soap, weave mats, or make pottery.

Source: Sacre Coeur, Sister Marie-Andre du. *The House Stands Firm: Family Life in West Africa.* Translated by Alba I. Zizzamia. Milwaukee: The Bruce Publishing Company, 1962.

Old Age

A popular saying declares that nothing is certain except death and taxes. For most, the certainty of death is preceded by the decline of physical and often mental abilities as the human body ages. This stage of life, old age, is treated differently by different groups at different times. In some cultures, the aged are revered and carefully looked after; in others, the infirmity of body and mind that comes with advancing age is seen as a liability. The diverse accounts in this section include the reflections of an emperor ruling the Muslim *Mughal Empire* in northern India in the eighteenth century (Document 8), a nineteenth-century American publisher looking forward to a quiet retirement (Document 9), an anthropologist's report on the resistance to aging in a traditional Native American culture in northern Canada (Document 10), and a recent interview on active Japanese baby boomers (Document 11). These documents reflect the diversity of responses to aging, but also mark some of the changes in the daily life of the aged in the modern period. If Aurangzeb laments the coming of death more than old age specifically, and Nathan Parker Willis looks forward to the comfortable leisure that old age can bring, the *Chipewyan* resist aging to the point of risking their lives to prove that they can avoid it, and some Japanese adopt a similar strategy of continued activity, although seemingly without the desperation of the subarctic indigenous Canadians. It is not coincidental that older people in the late twentieth and early twenty-first centuries, who are living longer, healthier lives, would have a less pessimistic view of the last part of life than those without similar expectations from earlier periods. That is not to say that there are uniform responses based on place and time: some still choose to deny aging, some choose to lament it, and some choose to embrace it. These attitudes are influenced by cultural factors, but they are not determined by them.

Often it becomes the responsibility of domestic groups to care for the older members of the family. Until recently in American culture, and still in many places, this meant primarily having the elderly live with younger family members. In contemporary society, there is an increasing trend toward separation of domestic and family groups and institutional care for the aged, as well as social problems arising from an increasing life expectancy and growing demand for medical care. Governments also have guaranteed payments and services to the aged, and whole communities are dominated by populations of older people who have relocated for better weather or other reasons. Old age, perhaps, isn't what it used to be. Different societies engage with aging and closely related dying issues in different ways. While the articles here deal more with the aging process than death, perspectives can be found in this book under "Death and Dying" in the "Religious Life" section on the importance of death, funerary practices, and beliefs in the afterlife.

8. *Letter from the Mughal Emperor Aurangzeb*

Aurangzeb (1618–1707), also known as Alamgir I, whose father built the famous Taj Mahal, was the ruler of the Mughal Empire, *which expanded Muslim control over most of the Indian subcontinent, in some ways laying the groundwork for centuries of succeeding conflict between Muslims and Hindus. He was known as a strong and pious ruler who imposed a strict version of Muslim* sharia *law and engaged in constant warfare that by his death left a larger, but less secure political dominion. The Hindi population was restive, and he predicted that the Mughal Empire would succumb to internal dissension and the increasing power of European* imperialism.

All this is part of the distant background of the following selection: Aurangzeb's letter to a friend on his own approaching death. Whether penned by an emperor or a peasant, the sentiments are broad and eloquently articulated. His mood is marked by profound regret at what he perceives as his own failures as a father and leader, pessimistic reflections on his prospect in the afterlife, and a certain resignation before his impending death. Aurangzeb sees most of his struggles as vain. What he means by God and Providence is somewhat obscured by the translation; as a devout Muslim, it is the Muslim God, Allah, to whom Aurangzeb appeals. While Muslim teaching may see the nature of an individual's afterlife as a recompense for the deeds of this life, Aurangzeb seems concerned with the course of his life not only for the impending reckoning that he believes comes with death, but also with a sense of disappointment that his days are spent, that he cannot do more, and that his strength is failing him.

He must rely on the following generation to carry on after him, and he does not seem to think they are up to the task. He does not say that he takes hope or faith with him, but, sadly, he takes only the infirmities of man out of the world with him. This sense of hopelessness and the vanity of life is certainly not unique to Aurangzeb. Sentiments such as these in advanced age and in anticipation of death can be found throughout history, and the modern era certainly is no exception.

Health to thee! My heart is near thee. Old age has arrived: weakness subdues me, and strength has forsaken all my members. I came a stranger into this world and a stranger I depart. I know nothing of myself, what I am, or for what I am destined. The instant which has passed in power hath left only sorrow behind it. I have not been the guardian and protector of the empire. My valuable time has been passed vainly. I had a guide in my own dwelling (conscience), but his glorious light was unseen by my dim sight. Life is not lasting; there is no vestige of departed breath, and all hopes for the future are lost. The fever has left me; but nothing remains of me but skin and bone... The camp and followers, helpless and frightened, are, like myself, full of alarms, restless as quicksilver. Separated from their lord, they know not if they have a master or not.

I brought nothing into this world, and, except the infirmities of man, carry nothing out. I have a dread for my salvation, and with what torments I may be punished. Though I have strong reliance on the mercies and bounties of God, yet, regarding my actions, fear will not quit me; but when I am gone reflection will not remain. Come then what may, I have launched my vessel in the waves. Though Providence will protect the camp, yet, regarding appearances, the endeavors of my sons are indispensable. Give my last prayers to my grandson, whom I cannot see, but the desire affects me. The Began [his daughter] appears afflicted; but God is the only judge of hearts. The foolish thoughts of women produce nothing but disappointment. Farewell, farewell, farewell.

Source: Elliot, Sir Henry Miers. *The History of India, as Told by Its Own Historians: The Muhammadan Period*. Edited by John Dowson. Volume 7. London: Trubner, 1867–1877.

9. Nathan Parker Willis: Aging Gracefully

The author of this selection, Nathan Parker Willis, was a successful American writer, publisher, and editor in the first half of the nineteenth century. Among his friends was Edgar Allan Poe, and it was Willis who first published Poe's famous poem, "The Raven," in 1845.

Just like Aurangzeb (see Document 8), Willis is writing to a friend about his old age, but the tone of the letter is quite different from that of Aurangzeb, who laments his failures and bitterly regrets that his life is coming to an end. Aurangzeb did not want to leave this life, while Willis, on the other hand, actually wants to look at the life of others from the outside, enjoy the company of friends, and live a quiet, slow, and peaceful retirement.

Willis is trying to convince a friend of his, a doctor, to retire to the country near his own retirement home on the Susquehanna River in upstate New York, luring him with promises of leisure and companionship. Willis wants, and is trying to convince the doctor, to grow old quietly in the company of like-minded friends. The natural environment for Willis is one of the main attractions, and he assures his friend that he is even caring for the placement of trees and shrubbery. It bears remembering that cities in the 1840s were smaller than today, but growing rapidly and becoming crowded, dirty, and more prone to disease. Retired life in the country was potentially a more pleasant and viable prospect.

Willis definitely seems to be looking forward to a life without the business and pressures of what had been his professional life, although he is not interested in giving up intellectual pursuits. Certainly neither money nor health seems to be a problem. He does not seem to have unsatisfied ambitions. He anticipates a stimulating social and intellectual life being more pleasurable without other motivations or concerns. One can imagine Willis's sentiments being shared by many, especially those to whom the modern world has been kind in terms of daily life.

...You can scarce understand, dear Doctor, with what pleasure I find this new spring in my path—the content with which I admit the conviction, that, without effort or self-denial, the mind may slake its thirst, and the heart be satisfied with but the waste of what lies so near us. I have all my life seen men grow old, tranquilly and content, but I did not think it possible that *I* should. I took pleasure only in that which required young blood to follow, and I felt that, to look backward for enjoyment, would be at best a difficult resignation.

Now, let it be no prejudice to the sincerity of my philosophy, if, as a corollary, I beg you to take a farm on the Susquehannah, and let us grow old in company. I should think Fate kinder than she passes for, if I could draw you, and one or two others whom we know and "love with knowledge," to cluster about this—certainly one of the loveliest spots in nature, and, while the river glides by unchangingly, shape ourselves to our changes with a helping sympathy. Think of it, dear Doctor! Meantime, I employ myself in my rides, selecting situations on the river banks which I think would be to yours and our friends' liking; and in the autumn, when it is time to transplant, I intend to suggest to the owners where trees might be wanted in case they ever sold, so that you will not lose even a season in your shrubbery, though you delay your decision. Why should we not renew Arcady? God Bless you. [...]

And I will allow that I can scarce write a letter to you without shaping it to the end of attracting you to the Susquehannah. At least, watch when you begin to grow old, and transplant yourself in time to take root, and then we may do as the trees do—defy the weather until we are separated. The oak, itself, if it has grown up with its kindred thick about it, will break if left standing alone; and you and I dear Doctor, have known the luxury of friends too well to bear the loneliness of an unsympathizing old age. Friends are not pebbles, lying in every path, but pearls gathered with great pain, and rare as they are precious. We spend our youth and manhood in search and proof of them, and, when Death has taken his toll, we have too few to scatter—none to throw away. I, for one, will be a miser of mine. I feel the avarice of friendship growing on me with every year—tightening my hold and extending my grasp. Who, at sixty, is rich in friends? The richest are those who have drawn this wealth of angels around them, and spent care and thought on the treasuring. Come, my Doctor! I have chosen a spot on one of the loveliest of our bright rivers. Here is all that goes to make an Arcadia, except the friendly dwellers in its shade. I will choose you a hillside, and plant your grove, that the trees, at least, shall lose no time by your delay. Set a limit to your ambition, achieve it, and come away. It is terrible to grow old amid the jostle and disrespectful hurry of a crowd. The Academy of the philosophers was *out* of Athens. You can not fancy Socrates run against, in the market-place. Respect, which grows wild in the fields, requires watching and management in the cities. Let us have an old man's Arcady—where we can slide our "slippered shoon" through groves of our own consecrating, and talk of the world as *without*—ourselves and gay philosophy within. I have strings pulling upon one or two in other lands, who, like ourselves, are not men to let Content walk unrecognized in their path. Slowly, but, I think, surely, they are drawing hitherward; and I have chosen places for *their* hearthstones, too, and shall watch, as I do for you, that the woodsman's axe cuts down no trees that would be regretted. If the cords draw well, and Death take but his tithe, my shady "Omega" will soon learn voices to which its echo will for long years be familiar, and the Owaga and Susquehannah will join waters within sight of an *old man's Utopia*.

Source: Willis, N. Parker. *Rural Letters and Other Records of Thought at Leisure Written in the Intervals of More Hurried Literary Labor*. New York: Baker and Scribner, 1849.

10. The Chipewyan Resist Aging

The Chipewyan are an indigenous society of northern Canada that has in many ways evaded the many changes brought by modernity. Snowmobiles have replaced dogsleds and Christianity has influenced native ways, but this account from the 1970s of old age among a Native American tribe living in a remote part of Canada indicates how one culture does not value old age.

The approach in this document is ethnographic. Ethnography is the science of studying ethnic groups or cultures through the systematic direct observation of their ways of life. The author is not a member of the Chipewyan, but he has lived among them and observed and interviewed them to gather information on their attitudes, culture, and ways of life in a systematic and methodical way. The result is a synthesis of Henry Sharp's observations of their beliefs on aging, not only providing information on the Chipewyan, but also showing the idea that social scientists studying cultures recognize old age as a discrete and separate category for study (gerontology) and the idea that such ethnographic studies can be and are conducted in a scientific way.

Other similar studies reveal that in some indigenous cultures, older people who are no longer able to perform the physical tasks of younger adults shift to new and different tasks, often ones that are more highly regarded—the experience that comes with age is valued. As Sharp chronicles, this is not the case among the Chipewyan—it is clear at the end of the reading that John would rather die in the wilderness than admit incapacity—and likely did.

This is in part the result of the remote and difficult environment in which the Chipewyan live. While this harshness and isolation has prevented many aspects of their culture from being destroyed by outside influences, it also has other consequences, sometimes seemingly harsh from an outside perspective.

Gender is an important element in how aging is perceived. Among humans, while men typically have greater physical strength, women generally have longer life expectancies and retain their physical capacities longer. The sex roles in Chipewyan society determine very different aging patterns for men and women. Women neither need nor have magic to sustain them in their tasks, unlike men, who rely on magic to successfully provide food through competence in hunting. Loss of magic and competence for men in old age is the loss of manhood. If a person reaches a stage of incompetence then he can be treated with contempt, and even if someone is disliked, magical competence still demands respect.

The lack of value placed on the old by the Chipewyan may have parallels to the treatment of the old in American society. While few older people feel the need to hunt caribou in the tundra until they die, there is a stigma attached to aging into incompetence, for example, being unable to continue to drive, take care of a home, or even care for oneself. Many elderly people struggle to remain independent and competent in their daily lives for as long as they can, not unlike John and other Chipewyan.

The homeland of the Chipewyan is four hundred miles beyond the northern limit of agriculture and far from the major trade routes of the Northwest Territories. As a result of their isolation, the Chipewyan did not come into extensive contact with Canadian society until after the First World War, when many Euro-Canadians came north to trap. [. . .]

For a male Chipewyan the maturation process is not marked by any dramatic change but instead involves the mastery of the skills needed to wrest a living from the harsh Canadian subarctic. Success in economic activities, especially hunting and trapping, and the display of the implements of his livelihood (dogs, more recently a snowmobile) give evidence of the underlying magical power that, as we will see, is central to the notion of male adulthood. Once a man does marry, he becomes an adult member of the community and will remain such as long as he retains and can use his skills. When he no longer has them, or is not physically able to use them, he will be considered "elderly."

MAGIC

The Chipewyan believe that competence as a man is conferred by magic. This magic derives from unsought visions in which power is given by a supernatural being. . . . Magical power . . . is the exclusive property of men. Women with supernatural power appear in myth but never in stories about real women, whether living or dead. This gives quite a different aspect to the aging process of men and women. [. . .]

An example of the respect for a man's magical power that develops as he remains active despite growing old can be shown by something my principal woman informant, Beth, said to me in the course of a conversation about a 71-year-old neighbor in the village, George. Beth had always been fond of George's wife, but she disliked George and criticized him at every opportunity. She and I were discussing the relative magic powers of several men and she remarked of George, "Look at that old man, still walking about. He must 'know something.'" This grudging respect apparently stemmed from the fact that George had recently recovered, without hospitalization, from a case of tuberculosis.

THE DIFFERENCE IN AGING FOR MEN AND WOMEN

Magical power does eventually fail, however, and the Chipewyan man either dies or deteriorates physically and becomes incompetent. Unable to hunt or trap, he is forced to rely upon his relatives for subsistence. His decline can be delayed for a time by the efforts of a healthy wife and the use of young Chipewyan obtained by temporary adoption. But when a man can no longer drive his dogs and venture into the bush alone to hunt, his days as a complete adult male are ended, and he must subsist, like a woman or a dog, on meat and fish obtained by others. The Chipewyan do not value the telling of myths and tales greatly, and there are no handicrafts or other activities to which a man can turn in compensation. . . . The situation of an old woman in Chipewyan society is quite different. Where a man has a single paramount activity—obtaining food from the bush—a woman has three: reproduction, handicrafts, and processing food. As I mentioned earlier, women do not have magic (though female midwives may use a kind of magic in performing their specialty). Unlike hunting, women's work does not involve continuous walking, violent bursts of energy, or running, so it can still be performed by women in declining physical condition. Because women's work is considered to involve the use of skills acquired through instruction and practice rather than the use of magic, women are able to remain competent adults much longer than men. Since no special powers are involved, women can cooperate in their work without any loss of face. And old women whose physical strength is waning are valued for the advice and expertise they can contribute. [. . .]

An undated photo of a family of Chipewyan just outside Alberta Canada. Library of Congress.

Elderly men are not in a position to command much influence or respect. Men's affairs are centered upon the bush rather than the village or camp. For them, the increasing confinement to the village imposed by the loss of strength with advancing age is a punishment mitigated by few compensating rewards. They are ill-inclined to become involved in the issues of moral conduct or the proposed marriages that are a mainstay of village gossip. For many men the onset of old age begins in their late forties or early fifties with lung or heart disease, and they must wage a more desperate (and dangerous) struggle to be merely "old" instead of "elderly."

A good illustration of the desperation a Chipewyan man feels when his body begins to fail with advancing age is the case of my informant Beth's husband, John. Through 1971 John was able to keep most of his sons together in a hunting unit by suppressing conflict among them and by exploiting his extensive knowledge of the bush, which made them all economically successful. His magical power was well regarded, though he had given up an active curing practice some years before. In late 1971 John had a heart attack in the bush and had to be hospitalized. He recovered from the attack, but it was discovered that he had emphysema. He refused treatment for the disease and refused to stop his heavy use of tobacco. By 1975 he was so weak that he was unable to perform any work requiring heavy exertion or endurance. As his condition worsened a split developed in his hunting unit as the eldest son attempted to take control. John moved to a different hunting area in the fall of 1975 with one son, but even he was becoming increasingly autonomous.

To compensate for his growing weakness John began to spend more time alone in the bush, avoiding the village where Beth wished him to remain because of his ill health. Beth considers John's attempts to continue his activities in the bush dangerous, and feels he must be watched and protected from himself as the attempted exertion will kill him. John is aware of this watching over him, but refuses to accept the need for it. To maintain his status, he must constantly risk his life—a risk he is more than willing to take to avoid being categorized as "elderly."

Source: Sharp, Henry. "Old Age Among the Chipewyan." Excerpts from Pamela T. Amoss and Stevan Harrell, eds. *Other Ways of Growing Old: Anthropological Perspectives*.

11. *Japan's Baby Boomers*

The end of the Second World War in 1945 was followed by a demographic event known in the United States as the Baby Boom, *when the peace and stability that followed the war resulted in an increase in the number of children born. As the members of this generation has grown up and aged, they have had a significant impact on daily social, cultural, and economic life. The post-war rebuilding of Japan also produced a dankai or "mass" generation, as well as an unprecedented economic boom, but since about 1950 the birth rate has generally been in decline, and an increasing portion of Japan's population is aging.*

In Japan and elsewhere, aging isn't necessarily what it used to be. In part as a result of the technological advances and economic prosperity of the second half of the twentieth century, state-sponsored and tax-subsidized safety nets and retirement and social services, improved health care, and many other factors, find people are living longer, in better health, and with more money, particularly in industrialized countries such as Japan. While the shift of a larger portion of the population from working to retirement will put strains on the retirement systems of many states, the lifestyles of many older people are significantly different from those of their parents' or previous generations. The following selection, from an interview in 1998 with Sezikawa Hidehiko, records attitudes toward aging that are very different from Aurangzeb's (Document 8) or Willis's (Document 9). Sezikawa was the director of the Hakuhodo Institute for Life and Living (HILL), a think tank associated with one of Japan's largest advertising agencies. Aside from being an expert in tracking demographics and predicting consumer behavior and lifestyle choices, he is also himself a member of the Baby Boomer generation.

While the selection points to the trend that many Japanese will keep working while those in other countries may not, a common element is the interest in vital, active life at a point when previous generations slowed down—or even died. Whether pursuing leisure or work, the perception has grown that for increasing numbers of people, old age has become an important and viable stage of life in its own right, which, for some, is decades long, rather than simply a short period between the decline of capacities and death.

Though many of the predictions Sezikawa made have been proven quite accurate, certainly not every 75-year-old in Japan or anywhere else is planning to buy a Harley or to climb Mount Everest—like Yuichiro Miura is famous in Japan for doing in 2008, or the other things Sezikawa anticipates. Many are not operating businesses or continuing to work at all. Many are beset by financial difficulties and declining health, and feel left out of a culture that does not value their agedness or the needs that come with it. Many in old age may find more in common with Aurangzeb's resigned bitterness or Willis's pleasant indolence than Miura's mountain-climbing exploits. At the same time, people around the globe are living longer, healthier, wealthier lives than ever before, and the daily life of old age reflects these trends.

CONVERSATION WITH SEZIKAWA HIDEHIKO, SEPTEMBER 22, 1998

JLM What has been the biggest change in the lives of Japan's elderly since the founding of HILL in 1981?

SH HILL did large-scale studies of the lifestyles of the elderly in 1986 and 1996. For both, our subjects ranged in age from 65 to 75. In 1986 we found that people had plenty of time left for long retirements and suggested that they should relax and enjoy themselves. The retired people with whom we talked understood what we were saying, but some didn't like the idea. Many of their friends had died in World War II. They knew war and, in many cases, their friends had been killed but they had survived to grow old and have time on their hands. Talk about relaxing made them feel guilty.

By 1996, very few of those people were left. More than fifty years had passed since the end of the war. Retirees had experienced the war but only as children, as victims. That is the cohort whose support made high growth possible. They were the ones people called worker bees, and they were ready to taste the honey. When we talked about how they planned to relax, there was no guilt involved.

The biggest difference, then, may be that the asceticism characteristic of the traditional Japanese culture has weakened. Today's older people have an active interest in recreation and leisure. The other big difference, of course, is that the proportion of older people in Japan's population is larger.

JLM Thinking ahead, then to 2006, what kind of changes would you expect?

SH The Baby Boomers will be retired. If the trend we saw in the difference between 1986 and 1996 continues, more people will be more concerned about what they will do with their lives and be more skilful in their choices. In 1986, the American style of "happy retirement" didn't make sense to Japan's retirees. Retirement was sad and lonely, because they didn't have work to do. By 1996, the percentage of people who wanted to retire early and were looking forward to retirement had increased. That same trend will continue. Still, however, the proportion of Japanese who would prefer to go on working will probably be high compared to other parts of the world. [. . .]

Especially in Japan, I think, people become too busy with work and families in middle age. Private life becomes very thin. [. . .]

Now elderly people, who didn't have much time for private life in middle age, are climbing mountains, riding Harleys, enjoying themselves in all sorts of ways. They're enjoying a second [youth] before going on to the next stage. People are reading novels, watching movies, listening to music, and thinking about the meaning of their lives. Like the young, this group is freed from work and had the time to think about that question.

Source: McCreery, John L. *Japanese Consumer Behavior: From Worker Bees to Wary Shoppers: An Anthropologist Reads Research by the Hakuhodo Institute of Life and Living*. Honolulu: University of Hawai'i Press, 2000.

Part III

ECONOMIC LIFE

Economics provide a powerful method for understanding how many relationships between people, businesses, institutions, and governments work. Economists study how people and groups of people behave at levels ranging from the individual to the global. There is an old saying that "money makes the world go 'round." In economic life, it certainly does. Economic activity can be divided into several different spheres, including urban, rural, trade, and migration.

Cities are centers of certain kinds of economic activities. Many goods and services are produced in cities that are not available outside of them, and historically they have been centers for commerce, manufacture, and trade. Cities serve as focal points for the movement of people and goods, and the distribution of these things. Today, for the first time in human history, the majority of people have become urban dwellers, in large part because modern agriculture has allowed far fewer people to produce enough food to feed the whole population. Friedrich Christian Weber's entry on *St. Petersburg* (Document 1) shows how a state created a city—a city that became not only a political and cultural center, but an economic center as well. The descriptions of child labor (Document 2) and slum housing (Document 3) expose the human costs and negative side of the *Industrial Revolution*, while Bruegmann (Document 4) looks at the post-industrial city in the West and compares it to earlier cities.

Rural areas are also important economic locations. The use of land for food production was the basis for most wealth before the modern era, and while that may not be the case in most places any longer, humans still need to eat! Rural locations are often where many raw materials are gathered, and rural dwellers in the *modern* period have also moved—either to new rural places, settling and starting new frontiers, or to cities to find new kinds of work. Lottie Bump's diary (Document 6) describes life on a dairy farm in rural Vermont. She and her family live in relative isolation, and their economy is about domestic self-sufficiency; her time is spent in cooking, cleaning, and manufacturing textiles for the family to use. The extremities of weather and constant work are evident, but while their lives seem hard, it is perhaps less so than the factory families in England whose children were being virtually worked to death. On the other hand, while reports by *Parliament* (Document 2) and the selection from Jacob Riis (Document 3) may document the squalor of urban life, rural life could often be miserable as well. Arthur Young, an Englishman who spent several years traveling through Europe studying agriculture, recorded his impressions of French peasants' lives (Document 5), which were often hungry and tenuous. William Razavi's account (Document 7) takes us to rural Iran in the first half of the twentieth century, as modern changes were altering the landscape of ancient *Persia*.

Trade and migration have also fundamentally affected modern daily life. In the modern world, trade has assumed a scale and efficiency unimaginable in premodern times. Adam Smith's capitalist theory (Document 8) promoted freer production and freer trade. The importance of trade is highlighted by the Revolutionary War document that lists all the things the American colonists will have to make for themselves because the war will prevent them from acquiring those items by trade (Document 9). The Chinese tea trade was a bellwether for modern global commerce. William Melrose's letters (Document 12) highlight how this trade was both advantageous and sometimes dangerous; obtaining the tea that was a staple drink in England could be risky—both economically and personally—because the Chinese restricted access and resisted European pressure—and imports of opium. As moving goods involved risks, so did moving oneself and one's family. Migration, the movement of people from one place to another, became one of the most important economic elements of all. Sometimes migration is voluntary—people move seeking a new life, or better conditions for themselves and their families, and sometimes it is not—as is the case with slavery or refugees. The entries in this section cover a scope of these places and activities. The grand gamble of the California gold rush (Document 10) contrasts with the struggle of Soviet Jews isolated in their own land to emigrate to Israel (Document 13) and the viciousness of a slave auction (Document 11).

Together, the dramatic expansion of cities, fundamental shifts in industrial production, growth in population, ballooning trade, global migrations, and the movement from country to city have been hallmarks of the modern age. Whether or not money really does make the world go around, economics are inseparable from daily life.

Urban Life

Cities have always been hubs of economic activity; they have been trading centers, markets, and places where people practice trades, manufacture goods, obtain services, and exercise power. Historically, cities require a thriving economy if they are to grow and survive. The documents in this section take a variety of views toward the relationship between economic activity and cities. The first selection on the new, purpose-built Russian city of *St. Petersburg* (Document 1) is a deviation from the usual pattern. Cities usually grow up where economic activity takes place. In the case of St. Petersburg, like such cities as Washington, D.C.; Canberra, Australia; and Brasilia, Brazil, the city's reason for existence began politically, not economically. The idea that a city could simply be built from the ground up by the state is itself something that only became possible in the modern era because only centralized states with modernizing, growing economies wielded enough resources to undertake such projects.

The Parliamentary report on child labor (Document 2) and Jacob Riis's description of slum life (Document 3) record the consequences of the transformations that cities underwent as the economic revolution of industrialization altered them and the way their inhabitants lived. While city transportation systems were not well developed and industries required large numbers of laborers who worked long hours for subsistence wages, workers and their families had to live in relatively close proximity, often in crowded, poor conditions. As reform and labor organization improved hours and pay, and mass transit and individual automobiles changed transportation, the geographic size of cities expanded and their densities declined. This latter process is discussed in the selection by Breugmann (Document 4), a modern city dweller himself, who offers a perspective on *urban sprawl* and a meditation on the vast city of today as he contemplates it from an airplane window (itself an action impossible for the other authors in this section). Breugmann attempts to put the radical changes experienced by cities in the twentieth century into context, as the populations in Europe, the United States, and elsewhere shifted from being predominantly rural to being urban or suburban.

1. St. Petersburg: Building a New Capital City

Almost one hundred years before the founding of the United States and the decision to build a city for that new nation's capital, Czar Peter the Great *of Russia decided to relocate the capital of his empire from* Moscow, *which had been its chief city for hundreds of years, to* St. Petersburg, *an entirely new city to be built from the ground up at the mouth of the Neva River where it flowed into the Baltic Sea.*

The idea of building a city to be a capital was not only undertaken in the eighteenth century by Russia and the United States, but also in the twentieth century in Brazil, whose new capital, Brasilia, was begun in 1956, and Australia, whose capital of Canberra was built from virtually nothing in 1908 at a midpoint between Melbourne and Sydney as a compromise to Australia's two largest cities.

The idea of starting a city was for Peter the Great a way to work toward the remaking of his nation as a "Westernized country" and St. Petersburg was to compete with other European capitals. Cities normally would grow up where there was an economic reason for them to exist, such as the junction of two roads or rivers, a natural harbor, or along a trade route. Peter decided to build his city in a marshy wasteland at the edge of the Arctic Circle because it provided at least partial-year access by water to Western Europe via the Baltic Sea.

Peter insisted on many Russian boyars *(i.e., nobles) moving to St. Petersburg and building stone houses. Thus, St. Petersburg became not only the center of government, but also a military, cultural, and trading center for the vast Russian Empire. Sometimes called the "Venice of the North" for the canals that crisscross the city (it was, after all, built on a swamp), today it is one of the most architecturally unified cities in the world.*

Purpose-built cities present a unique opportunity; they allow one to see what a practical realization of the ideal city looked like for a particular place and time. Planning and building cities from nothing is a feature of the modern era; in previous times, some civic centers, squares, and sections of a city were planned as the city grew, but "top-down" urban planning tactics, such as grid-style street layouts, zoning, and managed development, were not even considerations. Elements like landscape, markets, and local political maneuvering determined what got built where, without much, if any, consideration for the whole plan of the city.

This document by Friedrich Christian Weber describes the founding—in May 1703—and beginnings of St. Petersburg. Weber was a diplomat from the German state of Hanover in the service of England, and originally wrote the book in Dutch from which this account is taken. He was, however, not the lone foreigner among Russians. Peter the Great hired many Dutch and German specialists to bring their trades, knowledge, and technology to Russia. From the beginning of St. Petersburg as a military outpost to the decision to build a capital there, to a description of the houses, canals, and markets, the following excerpt gives not only an account of Peter's military and governmental purposes, but also of the immediate economic effects of his decisions and the extraordinary growth of construction, trade, and population—how a European capital city was planned and built in less than 20 years.

A
DESCRIPTION
Of the CITY of
St. *PETERSBOURG*,
With
Several Observations relating to it.

I am now going to relate many Particulars not yet mentioned, of a City which may be called a Wonder of the World, was it only in consideration of the few Years that have been employed in the raising of it.

His Czarish Majesty from his younger Years shewed a particular Inclination for Shipping and Sea-affairs. . . . when Fortune seconded his Arms so far that in the Year 1702 he took Notebourg And the Year following Nie-Schantz, a trading Town, having observed that about a German Mile further down, the River Neva forms several Islands, the conveniency of the Situation inspired him with Thoughts of building a Town there, in order to get footing in the Baltick [Sea]. The Czar being more and more pleased with the Situation of the neighboring Country, which actually is one of the most agreeable to be found in those Parts, resolved not only to build a Fortress on the River Neva, as he designed at first, but also to make his chief Dock there for building large Men of War [warships]. . . . The resolution was no sooner taken, but Orders were forthwith issued, that next Spring a great number of Men, Russians, Tartars, Cosacks, Calmucks, Finlandish and Ingrian Peasants, should be at the place to execute the Czar's Design. [. . .]

At the same time that they were going on with the Fortress, the City itself also by degrees began to be built, and to this End Numbers of People both of the Nobility and the trading Part of the Nation were ordered to come from Russia to settle at Petersbourg and to build Houses there, all which was executed with such Forwardness, that in a short time the Place swarmed with Inhabitants. The Boyars and others of the Nobility brought with them numerous Retinues and many Servants. The Merchants and Shopkeepers found their Account at this new Place, where everything was excessive dear. Many Swedes, Finlanders, and Livonians, [and] . . . All sorts of Artificers, Mechanicks, and Seamen with their Families were drawn to Petersbourg, in order to encourage Shipping and settle a Commerce by Sea. Many Labourers being Russians, Tartars, and Calmucks, having served the Time prefixed by their Sovereign, and being unwilling to return so far home, engaged with the Boyars who were building Houses every Day, and got sufficient Work to get their Bread by; some thousands of them even built houses for themselves, and settled at Petersbourg... All those Circumstances together very much contributed to the sudden peopling of Petersbourg, which now hardly yields to any in Germany as to the number of Houses and Inhabitants: For there are reckoned at this time sixty odd thousand Houses in that City. [...]

Round about the Fortress lies the City of Petersbourg, partly on the several Islands, and partly on the Continent; it is of so large an extent, that it rather resembles a Landship of many Boroughs than a City. It is a good German Mile [about four U.S. miles] long, and very near as broad. The Houses are built very close together; and as very little is left of the good and dry Ground, those People who are continually arriving to settle there, are obliged to look out for places to build on in the Morass, which renders the new Streets exceeding dirty, particularly in Spring and Autumn.

The Canals that were begun to be cut in the Year 1717, are already in such perfection, that a Man may almost at his own Door step into a Boat, and from thence be carried into the Neva, and further into the main Sea. It is a good Diversion on Holidays to see one hundred and more Sloops rowing and sailing together in Emulation of each other, which Shew is the more set off by the handsome Dress of the Watermen.

Near the Chancery stand the Russian Church of the Holy Trinity, which, next to the Cathedral and Prince Menzicoff's [Alexander Menshikov, governor of St. Petersburg 1703–1727] Church, is the largest and finest at Petersbourg. It has a sort of chime which is but indifferent, and is played with Hands every hour. Then come the Lawks [*lavki*, shops], as they call it, or the Shops which is the Market-Place, where the whole Trade of Petersbourg is carried on, and all forms of Merchandize are sold, no body being allowed to lay in or sell any Goods any where else. It is a very spacious building two Stories high of Carpenters work, covered with Pantiles [roofing tiles], having a large empty yard within.... All those Shops in both Stories are well furnished. The House is the Czar's own, to whom the Shopkeepers are obliged to pay large Rents, but no body is allowed to live in it, and for Security there are Centinels placed on the four Corners and the four Gates. [...]

Tsar Peter the Great founding the city of St Petersburg in spring of 1703. The Art Archive.

[G]oing by the Fortress one comes to the Tartarian Rag-Fair, opposite to the Crown-work [of the Fortress]. The Goods are sold there very cheap, either in open Streets, or in two Rows of Shops... Those Shops generally have most Customers, and the Throng thereabouts is such, that he who chances to come among them, ought well look to his Purse, Sword, and even Hat, and for better Security, carry them in his Hands... Behind the Rag-Fair lies the Tartarian Slaboda [suburb], inhabited by the Tartars, Turks, Calmucks, and many the like Nations, among whom there is such a variety of fine House-keeping as far exceeds the Way of Life practiced among the Inhabitants of the Out-skirts and By-lanes of Rome, Paris, or London. [...]

Wasili-Osrtrov is a large and fine Island... the first remarkable Thing on the said Island is the Prince's House... built of Stone after the Italian Manner, three Stories High, and covered with large Iron Plates painted red. It has Wings behind and before, is all vaulted underneath, and as for the rest, provided with every thing that is requisite in a fine House. It has a great number of Apartments furnished with rich Household Goods, particularly of Silver and Plate. In the middlemost Story is a spacious Hall, in which are usually kept all great Entertainments, and the Weddings of Kneeses [*kniaz*, prince or high nobleman] or Boyars.

Source: Weber, Christian. *The Present State of Russia in Two Volumes... with a Description of Petersbourg and Cronslot, And Several other Pieces relating to the Affairs of Russia*. London: W. Taylor, W. and J. Innys, and J. Osborn, 1723.

2. Child Labor in Nineteenth-Century Britain

Industrialization brought with it the potential production of far greater quantities of goods than could be produced by hand, and often better quality and lower prices. Concepts such as interchangeable parts and automation had an extraordinary impact on the lives of ordinary people. However, the factories that manufactured these goods using new techniques required workers, and these workers were often migrants from the countryside, who had been displaced as industrial technology also made agriculture more efficient. Men, women, and children were employed to work long hours at low wages under hard and even dangerous conditions in these factories. Regulation of working hours and ages happened slowly, with the English Parliament, *for example, enacting a 10-hour workday for women and children in 1847.*

The following selection contains excerpts from reports taken from workers in various English textile mills in the early 1800s. One such worker is a boy of 12 who works 13 or more hours a day, and has begun to go to school—but only on Sundays. Others are parents who describe the poor health, deplorable working conditions, and exhaustion of their working children. The child workers are given only one break for a meal per day, are sometimes beaten, and would be fired—along with the rest of their families—if they were late, sick, or complain. At the same time, the idea of child labor was not new to modern, industrial societies. In rural environments, children worked hard at agriculture along with their parents (the reason the standard academic schedule includes summers off is a vestige of the times when children were needed as a source of labor during the summer growing season and education was a luxury or privilege) as it is for the boy in this selection.

From one perspective, child labor is nothing new—it is simply Adam Smith's theory at work (see Document 8) in the emerging industrial manufacturing environment; from another perspective, it is abusive and repugnant. For many poor families, sending their children to work was the only way to survive, although it might mean that the child was slowly worked to death rather than starved to death. Some factory owners claimed to have the best interests of their workers at heart, providing such amenities as reading rooms, schools, child care, and other perquisites. While some factories did offer such things for their workers, no doubt many were more like the situations described here. The economic realities of daily life in an industrial city for working children in the nineteenth century were typically harsh and difficult.

Charles Harris, a boy working in the carding room of Mr. Oldacres's mill for spinning worsted yarn, testifies as follows:

I am twelve years old. I have been in the mill twelve months. I attend to a drawing machine. We begin at six o'clock and stop at half past seven. We don't stop work for breakfast. We do sometimes. This week we have not. Nothing has been said to me by Mr. Oldacres or the overlooker, or anybody else, about having any questions asked me. I am sure of that. The engine always stops for dinner. It works at tea time in the hot weather; and then we give over at half past seven instead of eight, which is the general time. We have generally about twelve hours and a half of it. On Saturdays we begin at six and give over at four. I get *2s. 6d.* a week [2 shillings 6 pence—roughly equivalent to $15 today]. I have a father and mother, and give them what I earn. I have worked overhours at the rate of *2d.* for three hours. I have always that for myself.

What do you do with it?

I save it for clothes sometimes. I put it into a money club for clothes. I have worked nine hours over in one week. I got for that *51/2d.* I gave it to my mother, and she made it up to *6d.* and put it into the money club. She always puts by 6d. a week from my wages for that.

Then your mother gets what you earn by the overhours, don't she?

No; I gets it for myself.

Do you work overhours or not, just as you like?

No; them as works must work....

If overhours are put on next week, shall you be glad or sorry?

It won't signify. I shall be neither glad nor sorry. Sometimes mother gives me a halfpenny to spend.

What do you do with it?

I saves it to buy shoes. Have never saved above a shilling for that; mother put more to it, and bought me a pair....

Don't you play sometimes after work's over?

Yes, sometimes.

Well, are you not sorry to lose that?

No, I don't mind about it. I am quite sure I don't. I am sometimes tired when I have been at work long hours. I am not tired now; I have been at work all day except dinner; it is now five o'clock. I am sure I had rather work as I do than lose any of my wages. I go to school of a Sunday sometimes. I went first about a month ago. I have been every Sunday since. I can only read in the alphabet yet. I mean to go regular. There is no reason why I should not. I wants to be a scholar.

The father of two children in a mill at Lenton deposed as follows:

My two sons (one ten, the other thirteen) work at Milnes's factory at Lenton. They go at half past five in the morning; don't stop at breakfast or tea time. They stop at dinner half an hour. Come home at a quarter before ten. They used to work till ten, sometimes eleven, sometimes twelve. They earn between them *6s. 2d.* per week. One of them, the eldest, worked at Wilson's for two years, at *2s. 3d.* per week. He left because the overlooker beat him and loosened a tooth for him. I complained, and they turned him away for it. They have been gone to work sixteen hours now; they will be very tired when they come home at half past nine. I have a deal of trouble to get 'em up in the morning. I have been obliged to beat 'em with a strap in their shirts, and to pinch 'em, in order to get them well awake. It made me cry to be obliged to do it.

Did you make them cry?

Yes, sometimes. They will be home soon, very tired; and you will see them.

I [i.e. the government inspector] preferred walking towards the factory to meet them. I saw the youngest only, and asked him a few questions. He said, "I'm sure I shan't stop to talk to you; I want to go home and get to bed; I must be up at half past five to-morrow morning."

A family in the same town of Lenton gave the following evidence:

The boy. I am going fourteen; my sister is eleven. I have worked in Milnes's factory two years. She goes there also. We are both in the clearing room. I think we work too long hours; I've been badly with it. We go at half past five; give over at half past nine. I am now just come home. We sometimes stay till twelve. We are obliged to work overhours. I have *4s*. a week; that is for staying from six to seven. They pay for overhours besides. I asked to come away one night lately, at eight o'clock, being ill; I was told, if I went I must not come again. I am not well now. I can seldom eat any breakfast; my appetite is very bad. I had a bad cold for a week.

Father. I believe him to be ill from being overworked. My little girl came home the other day cruelly beaten. I took her to Mr. Milnes; did not see him, but showed Mrs. Milnes the marks. I thought of taking it before a magistrate, but was advised to let it drop. They might have turned both my children away. That man's name is Blagg; he is always strapping the children. I shan't let the boy go there much longer; I shall try to apprentice him; it's killing him by inches; he falls asleep over his food at night. I saw an account of such things in the newspapers, and thought how true it was of my own children.

Mother. I have worked in the same mills myself. The same man was there then. I have seen him behave shocking to the children. He would take 'em by the hair of the head and drag 'em about the room. He has been there twelve years. There's many young ones in that hot room. There's six of 'em badly now, with bad eyes and sick headache. This boy of ours has always been delicate from a child. His appetite is very bad now; he does not eat his breakfast sometimes for two or three days together. The little girl bears it well; she is healthy. I would prefer their coming home at seven, without additional wages. The practice of working overhours has been constantly pursued at Milnes's factory.

Source: "Extracts from a Parliamentary Report on Child Labor." In *Readings in Modern European History*, edited by James Harvey Robinson and Charles A. Beard. Volume 2: *Europe Since the Congress of Vienna*. Boston: Ginn & Company, 1909.

3. *Jacob Riis: Slum Housing in New York*

Historically cities were close, crowded, and unplanned, and living conditions were potentially unhealthy and dangerous. The rapid growth of cities in the modern era exacerbated these problems on a geometric scale, with ever more people occupying less space. At the same time, practices such as trash removal, municipal sewer and water systems, police, and public health services enabled cities to accommodate larger numbers of people. Conditions for immigrants and the poor were especially bad though.

This selection offers a description of life in the slums of New York in the last part of the nineteenth century, inhabited almost exclusively by waves of European immigrants who arrived in America after the Civil War. *The author, Jacob Riis, was himself an immigrant, having arrived from Denmark to work as a carpenter in 1870. Before he became successful as a photographer and reform journalist exposing the conditions of poor immigrant populations in New York, he was one of the poor, foreign-born immigrants himself, sleeping in shabby shelters and taken to police stations. The source for the selection,* How the Other Half Lives, *was a milestone in social reform literature, and in it Riis is writing to support a case for particular changes. Besides being a social reformer, he was also one of the pioneers of flash photography, allowing him to accompany his descriptions with pictures.*

New York was certainly not the only city in the United States to have such slums; all industrial cities had neighborhoods of tenement *housing for the poor and often for the immigrant laborers who drove the* Industrial Revolution. *Those who lived there could afford nothing better, and Riis makes a clear argument that there were social, cultural, and moral consequences to the kind of existence the immigrant families lived. The neighborhoods Riis writes about at the time were some of the most densely populated in the world and there is no doubt that the circumstances in tenement neighborhoods were deplorable. Riis describes children and adults falling to their deaths trying to escape heat waves by sleeping on rooftops, and the moral threats to young men and women, who live where there is no green space and no viable alternatives to prostitution and alcohol.*

As a reformer, Riis had an obvious interest in depicting the conditions as especially bad and the population as sympathetic. He gives a depressing and one-sided account of urban life in the burgeoning industrial centers of the United States and the rest of the Western world. Riis can be credited with some real impact when How the Other Half Lives *prompted then New York Police Commissioner Theodore* Roosevelt *to undertake immediate reforms, and to a significant extent the reform efforts met with success in the long-term. The tenement-housing sections of the urban core of most cities have been demolished or redeveloped, and even though the relegation of poor and immigrant populations to less-desirable, run-down, and higher-crime neighborhoods continues today, the intensity of the crowded, hopeless, and violent tenement neighborhoods is for the most part a thing of the past—at least in industrialized and Western nations. While Riis may have been dramatic in his presentation, he provides a fascinating account of everyday urban life for hundreds of thousands in the lowest economic stratum in society, a daily life he himself had lived.*

In the dull context of life bred on the tenement-house dead level there is little to redeem it, or to calm apprehension for a society that has nothing better to offer its toilers; while the patient efforts of the lives finally attuned to it render the situation tolerable, and the very success of these efforts, serve only to bring out in stronger contrast the general gloom of the picture by showing how much farther they might have gone with half a chance. Go into any of the "respectable" tenement neighborhoods—the fact that there are not more than two saloons on the corner, nor over three or four in the block will serve as a fair guide—where live the great body of hard-working Irish and German immigrants and their descendants, who accept naturally the conditions of tenement life, because for them there is nothing else in New York; be with and among its

Jacob Riis, 1904. Library of Congress.

people until you understand their ways, their aims, and the quality of their ambitions, and unless you can content yourself with the scriptural promise that poor we shall have always with us, or with the menagerie view that, if fed, they have no cause of complaint, you shall come away agreeing with me that, humanly speaking, life there does not seem worth the living. Take at random one of these uptown tenement blocks, not of the worst nor yet of the most prosperous kind, within hail of what the newspapers would call a "fine residential section." These homes were built since the last cholera scare made people willing to listen to reason. The block is not like the one over on the East Side in which I actually lost my way once. There were thirty or forty rear houses in the heart of it, three or four on every lot, set at all sorts of angles, with odd, winding passages, or no passage at all, only "runways" for the thieves and toughs of the neighborhood. These yards are clear. There is air there, and it is about all there is. The view between brick walls outside is that of a stony street; inside, of rows of unpainted board fences, a bewildering maze of clothes-posts and lines; underfoot, a desert of brown, hard-baked soil from which every blade of grass, every stray weed, every speck of green, has been trodden out, as must inevitably be every gentle thought and aspiration above the mere wants of the body in those whose moral natures such home surroundings are to nourish. In self-defence, you know, all life eventually accommodates itself to its environment, and human life is no exception. Within the houses there is nothing to supply the want thus left unsatisfied. Tenement-houses have no aesthetic resources. If any are to be brought to bear on them, they must come from the outside. There is the common hall with doors opening softly on every landing as the strange step is heard on the stairs, the air-shaft that seems always so busy letting out foul stenches from below that it has no time to earn its name by bringing down fresh air, the squeaking pumps that hold no water, and the rent that is never less than one week's wages out of the four, quite as often half of the family earnings.

Why complete the sketch? It is drearily familiar already. Such as it is, it is the frame in which are set days, weeks, months, and years of increasing toil, just able to fill the mouth and clothe the back. Such as it is, it is the world, and all of it, to which these weary workers return nightly to feed heart and brain after wearing out the body at the bench, or in the shop. To it come the young and their restless yearnings.... These in their coarse garments—girls with the love of youth for beautiful things, with this hard life before them—who shall save them from the tempter? Down in the street the saloon, always bright and gay, gathering to itself all the cheer of the block, beckons the boys. In many such blocks the census-taker found two thousand men, women, and children, and over, who called them home....

With the first hot nights in June police dispatches, that record the killing of men and women by rolling off roofs and window-sills while asleep, announce that the time of greatest suffering among the poor is at hand. It is the hot weather, when life indoors is well-nigh unbearable with cooking, sleeping, and working, all crowded into the small rooms together, that the tenement expands, reckless of all restraint. Then a strange and picturesque life moves upon the flat roofs. In the day and early evening mothers air their babies there, the boys fly their kites from the house-tops, undismayed by police regulations, and the young men and girls court and pass the growler. In the stifling July nights, when the big barracks are like fiery furnaces, their very walls giving out absorbed heat, men and women lie in restless, sweltering rows, panting for air and sleep. Then every truck in the street, every crowded fire-escape, becomes a bedroom, infinitely preferable to any the house affords. A cooling shower on such a night is hailed as a heaven-sent blessing in a hundred thousand homes.

Life in the tenements in July and August spells death to an army of little ones whom the doctor's skill is powerless to save. When the white badge of mourning flutters from every second door, sleepless mothers walk the streets in the gray of the early dawn, trying to stir a cooling breeze to fan the brow of the sick baby. There is no sadder sight than this patient devotion striving against fearfully hopeless odds. Fifty "summer doctors," especially trained to this work, are then sent into the tenements by the Board of Health, with free advice and medicine for the poor. Devoted women follow in their track with care and nursing for the sick. Fresh-air excursions run daily out of New York on land and water; but despite all efforts the grave-diggers in Calvary work over-time, and little coffins are stacked mountains high on the deck of the Charity Commissioners' boat when it makes its semi-weekly trips to the city cemetery....

That ignorance plays its part, as well as poverty and bad hygienic surroundings, in the sacrifice of life is of course inevitable....

No doubt intemperance bears a large share of the blame for it; judging from the standpoint of the policeman perhaps the greater share....Even if it were all true, I should still load over on the tenement the heaviest responsibility. A single factor, the scandalous scarcity of water in the hot summer when the thirst of the million tenants must be quenched, if not in that in something else, has in the past years more than all other causes encouraged drunkenness among the poor. But to my mind there is a closer connection between the wages of the tenement and the vices and improvidence of those who dwell in them than, with the guilt of the tenement upon our heads, we are willing to admit even to ourselves. Weak tea with a dry crust is not a diet to nurse moral strength.

Source: Riis, Jacob. *How the Other Half Lives*. New York: Charles Scribner's Sons, 1890.

4. The Postmodern City

The conventional wisdom of the development of the city goes something like this: the increasingly crowded and concentrated nature of the city in the nineteenth and early twentieth centuries has changed as shifts in economic patterns away from industrial economies in many first-world urban environments produced in America declining urban cores and complex, though inefficient, transportation systems that allowed the spreading out of typical American life into the suburbs *and even, in recent years, into* exurbs. *Many European nations have engineered very different urban models, with cities whose centers remain viable and desirable places, with the economically disadvantaged, often immigrant, populations, unpleasant manufacturing, and other infrastructural elements relegated to the suburban margins of the city.* Urban sprawl *is a late modern American phenomenon, typical of abusive and irresponsible development. The dominance of this new type of suburban and exurban model is lamentable, since these cities are not sustainable, and they separate and isolate people, make walking or public transit impossible, inhibiting civic life and wasting huge amounts of resources and energy.*

This selection takes a very different approach. Robert Bruegmann is a city-dweller himself as well as an academic who studies urban development. Enabled by modern infrastructures and motivated by complex economic factors, modern cities are larger than ever before, but he argues that they don't have lower population densities: in other words, today's sprawl, on his account, is less a function of land misuse and more a function of larger groups of people following a pattern similar to one observable for at least several hundred years.

His description of flying over Los Angeles at dusk is very evocative of the contemporary city; its marvel is in its sheer size, not in the density or individual landmarks. In fact, it is marked more by the lack of distinguishing marks and features than anything else. The observable patterns of Los Angeles from the air are the same at the beach as they are almost 150 miles inland.

And this is not even the fullness of the city, according to Bruegmann. He also insists that we include the exurban or semi-rural fringes in looking at the city. Many decry modern suburbia, but instead he sees the suburban and exurban edges of cities as a dynamic space on a borderland between urban and rural. Whether it is at the edges of cities where change is fastest or in their very centers, economic factors play a decisive role in Bruegmann's description. His litany of the various groups and institutions who are blamed for sprawl all have predominantly economic influences; ultimately, he claims, it is ordinary individuals and families who collectively exercise the largest influence on the modern city through their ordinary, everyday choices. Whether or not one agrees with his analysis of the nature or causes of vast, sprawling cities, one must agree that they are truly some of the most marvelous works of the modern world.

In American cities, as well as in European cities after their walls came down, there were two kinds of suburban development. The first involved outward expansion all along the urban periphery, creating a pattern of yearly growth like the annual rings on a tree. Despite the fairly small numbers of inhabitants, the suburban districts for the affluent took up a great deal of this space. Usually located on the other side of town and occupying much less space per capita were modest apartment blocks for the working classes and factories for industrial production. The other kind of suburban development appeared along railroad lines radiating outward from the city, creating small commuter suburban settlements that appeared on maps like the beads on a necklace.

Finally, at the edge of the urban galaxy could often be found large exurban regions. At first, in Europe, the largest amount of this land was occupied by the large estates of the landed aristocracy. Increasingly in the nineteenth century, in both North America and Europe, successful middle-class merchants sought to emulate the aristocracy by buying property and building country houses. These properties were often located outside small villages where there were urban services and good railroad connections back to the city center.

Even those who recognize that the general trend of decentralization has been essentially similar in Europe and North America sometimes say that American cities have followed a different social pattern. For example, it is often said that the wealthy have always lived in city centers in Europe with the poor at the periphery while in North America the reverse has been true. This formulation is quite misleading. In both cases there was a vast exodus of families of all kinds from the center. The difference was how quickly each left the center and how far each went. In Paris, for example, over the course of several centuries, the wealthiest families did exactly what their counterparts did in London or in New York or Boston. They kept moving from more congested districts at the center toward less dense districts in the periphery. [...]

Contrary to the notion of many historians and sprawl reformers, suburbanization and decentralization are not peculiarly American. They have been pervasive characteristics of urban growth around the world for at least a century whenever cities have become more affluent.

One of the most remarkable things about the development of European and American cities and suburbs since the 1970s has been the way in which they seem to be converging. In part this is because an increasing number of American central cities are becoming denser while most European cities continue to decentralize. Moreover, the edges of cities everywhere, with their superhighways, supermarkets, and subdivisions, look increasingly similar, one to another. In fact, the parts of suburban Phoenix that have developed in the past ten or twenty years are actually quite comparable to the Parisian suburbs that have grown at the same time. [...]

We will end with an evening flight out of Los Angeles, that paragon of sprawl for several generations of urban reformers. Departing from LAX at dusk on a cloudless day, the plane will take off to the west, rising up sharply over the blue-black ocean, punctuated only by the faint lights of boats far below and the almost imperceptible outline of the Channel Islands, which, only slightly darker than the sky itself, loom against the horizon. As the plane banks to the south and then again to the east, the lights of the Los Angeles basin come into view.

Even for people who have seen it a hundred times before, this view can take one's breath away. Marking off a vast grid are the great arterial highways with their regular punctuation of yellowish sodium vapor lamps and the pools of colored light created by electric store signs at the major intersections. Snaking across the arterials are the dark linear voids of the river beds and the brightly lit freeways with their shimmering ribbon of white headlights and red tail lights. Between these brilliantly lit lines of motion are the darker residential neighborhoods with a fainter and more irregular block pattern. Only the streetlights flickering through the tree canopy and the occasional sweep of a car headlight turning into a driveway illuminate these territories.

Perhaps the most remarkable thing about this panorama is its size. Even at four hundred miles per hour it takes the plane a full fifteen minutes to fly from the beach at Redondo to the place where the city lights stop in the desert beyond Palm Springs.

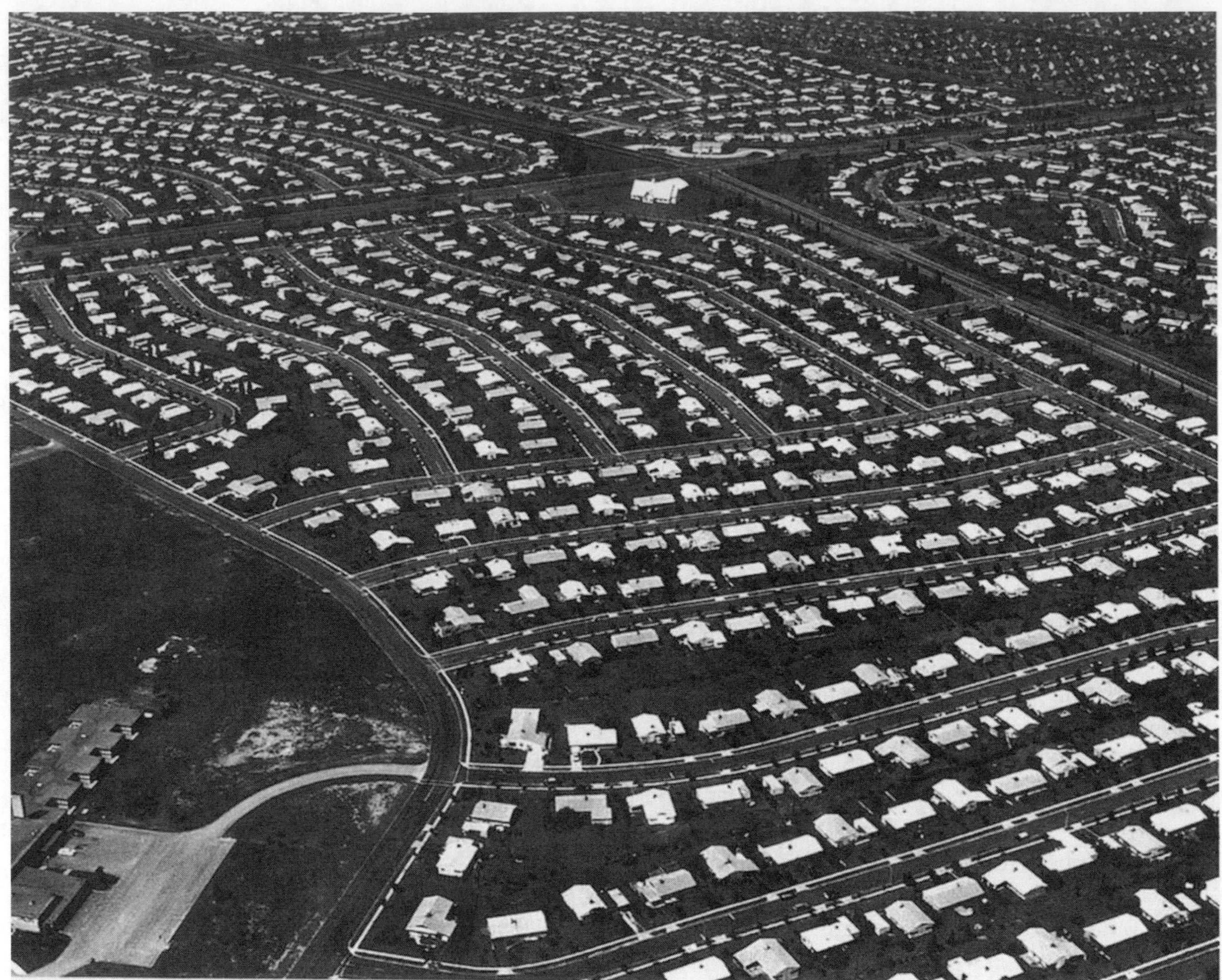

An aerial view of Levittown, Pennsylvania. Returning G.I.s made up the bulk of a huge demand for housing. The government introduced legislation that virtually guaranteed financing to residential developers and making housing loans easily available. Library of Congress.

The great city of today is so large and complex that it defies our attempts to describe, let alone to comprehend it.

Almost everyone at one time or another has pondered the question of who provided the real force, for better or for worse, behind a great urban panorama like this one. Some people will say that it happened this way because of planning, because of those individuals who imagined the grid and those who platted all of the subdivisions. Others instinctively counter that, in fact, developers, uninterested in planning but with a steadfast eye to the bottom line, had the upper hand. This in turn, will lead the next person to argue that, since the developers needed money, it was the owners of capital that pulled the strings. Then someone will come back with the thought that governmental organizations like Fannie Mae or the FHA set out the rules that guided the bankers. The urban historian then might observe that these regulations were put in place based on an analysis of what already worked in the private financial market place. Very few people seem to complete the circle by observing that what worked and what didn't in the market was, in turn, based, at least in part, on the choices of millions of individuals and families about where and how they wanted to live.

Many people, especially academics, have resisted the notion that ordinary citizens have played a major role in the creation of the great cities of the world. They would argue that the average urban family actually has few choices because these choices are so heavily controlled by vast economic, political, and social systems. The family can only buy what the merchant offers or the developer builds or the government allows. They will say that it is those with power who make all the important decisions. Of course, in one sense they are correct. Everyone is constrained by what is available to them, whether by governmental decree, the marketplace, or societal pressure. But it seems fair to say that the average family in the affluent world today has more choices available to it than a similar family in any other society or era in history. Moreover, even a little reflection will suggest that very few individuals, no matter how wealthy or powerful, have much ability to change fundamentally any large piece of our built environment on their own. Even if the wealthiest family of any large American city devoted its entire fortune to creating change, this money would not go very far unless that family was able to mobilize support from many other individuals or institutions. A billion dollars, for example, in most cities would buy only about 2,000 moderately expensive houses.

At the same time, every individual has some role in determining how the city looks and functions. If I shop at a suburban Wal-Mart rather than a downtown department store or choose to live in an apartment near the old downtown rather than in a single-family house on five acres in exurbia, these choices have an effect on urban form. If my choices are echoed by those of many other people, they can have a profound effect. More than any other human artifact in the world today, our urban areas are the result of the actions of every citizen, every group, and every institution, every day. In its immense complexity and constant change, the city—whether dense and concentrated at the core, looser and more sprawling in suburbia, or in the vast tracts of exurban penumbra that extend dozens, even hundreds, of miles into what appears to be rural land—is the grandest and most marvelous work of mankind.

Source: Bruegmann, Robert. *Sprawl: A Compact History*. Chicago: University of Chicago Press, 2006. Courtesy of University of Chicago Press and Robert Bruegmann.

Rural Life

One of the great markers of the modern era is the shift from a predominantly rural population to a predominantly urban population. At the same time, this has been a slow process and rural life continues to be crucially important both culturally and economically. Prior to the *Industrial Revolution*, land for agriculture and other resources was the primary source of wealth in society. While industrial and post-industrial economies no longer base wealth primarily on the productivity of land, without the rural and agricultural economy the world simply would not have anything to eat! If the image of the French countryside today is picturesque and idealized, Arthur Young's account (Document 5) of the poor condition of the French agricultural economy documents some of the causes of the *French Revolution*. Lottie Bump's diary (Document 6) shows the amount of labor that the rural economy and domestic household required, although she does not seem to want for things or be at all unhappy in her work. William Razavi's selection (Document 7) documents the changing face of rural Iran in the twentieth century, as modern transformations have made the rural communal and feudal lifestyle of his father and grandfather little more than memories today.

5. *Arthur Young: Poverty in Eighteenth-Century France*

Arthur Young was one of eighteenth-century England's foremost agricultural minds. A country gentleman whose own experimental attempts at practical farming were utterly unsuccessful, he nonetheless made a career of examining agricultural techniques and conditions around England and all of Western Europe. He was appointed to the new post of Director of the English Board of Agriculture in 1794. He collected and published his descriptions of his tours of France in 1787–1789, from which this selection is taken. The last tour was interrupted at the end by the outbreak of the French Revolution. *Disruptions notwithstanding, his accounts give an interesting insight into the conditions of life in the French countryside in the late eighteenth century.*

Young finds the general state of the French countryside to be poor. While the benefits of the Industrial Revolution had not yet made substantial inroads in providing cheap manufactured goods, Young notes a lack of products which were not made on the farms, such as wool, leather, and glass, which shows a lack of trade and prosperity. He is surprised at the amount of agricultural labor performed by women, the lack of advanced or efficient agricultural techniques, and the inequities of the land and tax system of the French kingdom.

Not only does Young's journal give an expert historical eyewitness account of the condition of the rural French economy at the time of the French Revolution from a foreigner's point of view, but also a look at a new approach to examining this central part of daily life in the modern period. Young was very much a man of his age; the idea of considered study of agriculture, experimentation, and comparative surveys to find the best techniques in a systematic way to improve overall agricultural productivity is a social application of scientific methodologies—the beginnings of modern agricultural sciences and business practices that have transformed the economics of rural life and the modern world.

The 22d. Poverty and poor crops in Amiens; women are now ploughing with a pair of horses to sow barley. The difference of the customs of the two nations [England and France] is in nothing more striking than in the labours of the sex; in England, it is very little that they will do in the fields except to glean and make hay; the first is a party of pilfering, and the second of pleasure: in France, they plough and fill the dung-cart. Lombardy poplars seem to have been introduced here about the same time as in England. [...]

The 10th. Cross the Dordonne by a ferry... Pass Payrac, and meet many beggars, which we had not done before. All that country, girls and women, are without shoes and stockings; and ploughmen at their work have neither sabots nor feet to their stockings. This is a poverty, that strikes at the root of national prosperity; a large consumption among the poor being of more consequence than among the rich: the wealth of a nation lies in its circulation and consumption; and the case of poor people abstaining from the use of manufactures of leather and wool ought to be considered as an evil of the first magnitude. It reminded me of the misery of Ireland. Pass Pont-de-Rondez and come to high land... Pass by several cottages, exceedingly well built, of stone and slate or tiles, yet without any glass to the windows; can a country be likely to thrive where the great object is to spare manufactures? Women picking weeds in their aprons for their cows, another sign of poverty I observed, during the whole way from Calais. [...]

The 12th. Walking up a long hill, to ease my mare, I was joined by a poor woman, who complained of the times, and that it was a sad country; demanding her reasons, she said her husband had but a morsel of land, one cow, and poor little horse, yet they had a franchar (42 lb.) of wheat, and three chickens, to pay as quit-rent to one Seigneur; and four franchar of oats, one chicken and 1 livre [French royal currency equal to about $5.50 U.S. in 1790] to pay to another, besides heavy tailles [real estate taxes] and other taxes. She had seven children, and the cow's milk helped make soup. But why, instead of a horse, do not you keep another cow? Oh, her husband could not carry his produce so well without a horse; and asses are little used in that country. It was said, at present, that something was to be done by some great folks for such poor ones, but she did not know who not how, but God send us better, car les tailles & les droits nous ecrasent [because the taxes and feudal levies are crushing us]. This woman, at no great distance, might have been taken for sixty or seventy, her figure was so bent, and face so furrowed and hardened by labour, but she said she was only twenty-eight. An Englishman who has not travelled, cannot imagine the figure made by infinitely the greater part of the countrywomen in France; it speaks, at first sight, hard and severe labour: I am inclined to think, that they work harder than the men, and this, united with more miserable labour of bringing a new race of slaves into the world, destroys absolutely all symmetry of person and every feminine appearance. To what are we to attribute this difference in the manners of the lower people in these two kingdoms? To Government.

Source: Young, Arthur. *Travels during the Years 1787, 1788 and 1789 Undertaken more Particularly with a View of Ascertaining the Cultivation, Wealth, Resources, and National Prosperity of the Kingdom of France.* Dublin: R. Cross et al., 1793.

6. Lottie Bump's Vermont Diary, 1868

Lottie Bump kept a diary, not of her travels like Arthur Young (see Document 5), but of her everyday life on a farm and in the very small town of Salisbury in rural Vermont in 1868. The extended Bump family was prominent in the area, and Lottie's husband, Samuel, though farming at the beginning of the diary, opens a school in the fall and they move into the town. Her matter-of-fact reporting of items like morning temperatures at 20 degrees below zero without central heating or indoor plumbing might seem remarkable to modern-day readers; however, her accounts of whole days spent washing or ironing or 20-hour days of sausage making give a vivid impression of daily life without modern conveniences that are taken for granted today, yet at that time would have been unthinkably luxurious. Her constant labor at cooking and baking, washing and housekeeping, a whole range of activities to make and maintain clothing, and, in the second half of the year, caring for a newborn, is relieved only by visiting friends and relatives, prayer meetings, and church.

Her husband's agricultural labor is parallel to hers but more seasonally determined: drawing wood and manure, plowing, planting, haying, and tending livestock. She doesn't even mention in her diary that she is pregnant, and offers no description of her labor or delivery—just announces that she is a mother and it went as well as could be expected. The necessary tasks of daily life are seldom interrupted. She mentions her husband going fishing once; holidays or important days are mentioned in passing, such as her birthday or wedding anniversary, and New Years Day, July Fourth, and Christmas even go unmentioned, with no descriptions of celebrations of any kind. Regardless of her mood or health, she seems to work very hard. Without all this work, the domestic economy of the Bump family could not function.

Jan. 1, 1868 (Wed.) Thermometer at 9 A.M. 36°. We did not rise until late this morning then I swept and ironed and Mother attended to other work, then by working all the evening I succeeded in making the flannel skirts and putting a waist on a cotton one. It has been a very windy snowy day but not much snow has fallen.

Jan. 6 Thermometer at 7 A.M. 22° below zero. It has been the coldest day we have had this month. We rose quite early but it was so cold that Samuel only drew one load of wood, and this afternoon he went to get the horses sharpened and did not get home until night. He received a letter from home saying Father is worse, and tomorrow he goes there. I did the washing and all the machine work to a shirt today and finished one mitten this evening.

(Jan.) 18 Thermometer at 7 A.M. 0°. We thought to rise early this morning but overslept and when we rose it was late before Samuel commenced drawing wood but he got three loads. Mr. Smith went from here this morning. I paid for a book for Mrs. George Thomas this morning. Mother and I worked on fancy work all day but Mr. Rice came here this evening, so I finished the trimming for my night-dress and sewed it on.

Saturday, February 8, 1868. Thermometer at 7 A.M. 27° below. We did not rise until late. It has been a beautiful day but very cold. The wind has been strong in the South. Mother and I had some housework to do and then I ripped up my green dress and partly ripped up a coat of Samuel's. Then cut and made him a pair of drawers and crocheted a little. Georgia is spending the night here. I have had a very severe headache all day.

Monday February 10, 1868. Thermometer at 7 A.M. 6° below. Another washing day has passed and we have finished two weeks washing. Mother has not been at all well today but she has kept hard at work. I did most of the washing and she did the other work and mopped. She has baked eleven pies since nine o'clock. We are all retiring very early. Wind strong in the south.

Sunday, March 1, 1868. Thermometer at 8 A.M. 12° below. We did not rise until very late this morning but it was considered early enough here. After breakfast we went over to Alice's and went to church with them. We staid all day and through to "Communion" which I enjoyed very much.

Saturday, March 14, 1868. Thermometer at 7 A.M. 48°. We rose quite early this morning and I helped get breakfast. Then I churned and swept my room, the stairs, hall and kitchen. Mother washed dishes, mopped and blacked the stove, but she ought not to have done it for her cold makes her about sick. I marked a great number of clothes this P.M. I made some trimming for mother's chemise and finished the trimming for my drawers. Samuel sacked his wool and took it to the depot today. He has gone to meeting tonight.

Sunday, March 15, 1868. Thermometer at 7 A.M. 42°. We rose at the usual time this morning and found it had rained during the night—but it has been very clear and warm all day. Samuel has been to church and has gone to meeting this evening, but I did not think it hardly prudent for me to go and I have had a very severe pain in one limb all day. It is three years today since we were married.

Friday, March 27, 1868. Thermometer at 6 A.M. 26°. Another day has passed and now I number 21 years of age. It has been a beautiful day. Mother and I cleaned the halls and the little bedroom this morning and then after dinner Father and Mother started for Forestdale. I finished some tatting, finished my waist, and partially embroidered Samuel's slippers. Samuel worked (drawing manure) until very late tonight.

Monday, March 30, 1868. Thermometer at 6 A.M. 20°. We rose in quite good season this morning and I went to washing. Our washing was not very large so I got done at noon. Mother whitewashed the kitchen and I helped her clean it. I am very tired tonight and have been having the heart-burn terribly. Georgia and Abbie spent a few moments here this evening.

Tuesday, March 31, 1868. Thermometer at 6 A.M. 28°. This morning when I rose I thought it looked a little like storm, but it has been a beautiful day. Samuel commenced ploughing today. Tonight he is at a school meeting. Mother and I ironed this afternoon and then I walked up to Aunt Libbie's but Marion, Olive and Delia came to our house so Samuel came for me. I have tatted a little and mended pants this evening.

Monday, April 6, 1868. Thermometer at 6 A.M. 20°. I rose early this morning and helped about breakfast and then I ironed. and I had to put some waist-bands on some night-dresses. Then I mended a few articles, and this afternoon I have been fixing hoops and I am not done yet. I have been sad today but that beautiful Psalm, "The Lord is my Shepherd I shall not want" has been with me. Georgia and Abbie are here this evening.

Tuesday, April 7, 1868. Thermometer at 6 A.M. 31°. When I rose this morning I thought it looked very much like snow and it commenced early and has snowed just all day. Samuel went to the village this morning and I went to see how Helen Hamilton got along. The girls went from here this morning. I worked a little on my hoops. Knit some and tatted some today.

Thursday, May 7, 1868. I rose quite early this morning and went to work on Henry's coat. I finished it and they came for it about nine o'clock. Then I quilted most of the day, so night finds me tired. Father went to the depot today and Samuel commenced ploughing in the meadow with his three horse team. I have been making some tatting today. Oh, when shall I get everything done that I want to get done.

Monday, May 11, 1868. Thermometer at 5 A.M. 35°. I rose early this morning and as we had only 1 week's washing to do we got all cleaned up before ten o'clock. Samuel went away a little while this morning and tagged some sheep and turned them out this afternoon. Mother and I have been quilting most of the day, but we are retiring quite early. 87 sheep.

Thursday, May 28, 1868. Thermometer at 5 A.M. 57°. I rose quite early and helped about the work this morning. Then I sewed my hat. After which Mother, Aunt Esther and I went up to uncle Cyrus'. Father went to the village and when he came home, about three o'clock, we come with him. I have made tatting most of the day. Tonight I finished a little sack. Samuel planted his corn today.

Wednesday, June 3, 1868. Thermometer at 5 A.M. 36°. It was very cold last night. I think there was a light frost on the low lands. It has been a beautiful day. Samuel, Oliver and Judson Mead went trout fishing today. Samuel enjoyed himself very much. We have a new milch cow today. The first we have had this year. I finished my little sack and my screen for the bed today beside some other sewing.

Sunday, June 14, 1868. Thermometer at 5 1/2 A.M. 57°. I did not wake until very late this morning but I was awake considerable during the night with a severe pain in my back, and that has continued to trouble me all day. I hope I shall get through my pain soon. Samuel went to church this forenoon. but I was at home. It has been a beautiful day. Miss Samson came home tonight.

Monday, June 15, 1868. Another morning finds me a mother. May God bless me in fulfilling my mission well. I had as comfortable a time as could be expected, I suppose, but I am glad it is done with and now I wish I was well, but no one knows how long it will be before I shall be well. A brave great boy. Weighs 10 pounds. Helen Boardman is here to stay with us a few days.

Sunday, July 5, 1868. Oh such a hot day as it has been. The thermometer started at 80 this morning and at half past 9 it stood at 95. It is cooler this afternoon. How much better I am than I was one week ago. Samuel has stayed at home with me all day.

Thursday, July 9, 1868. I slept well last night and rose quite early this morning and I have not lain down much during the day. Mary came over here quite early this morning and has staid all day. Samuel intended to commence haying but it has been unpleasant today so he finished his rake. I had my hair combed today.

Monday, August 10, 1868. I have helped a little today. I have washed the dishes twice and helped get breakfast and dinner, swept & c. I wish I could work as much any day. We have had no rain today and Samuel got a very large piece of grass down and part of it in the stack.

Wednesday. August 26. 1868. This morning I rose quite early and found it pleasant. Samuel got his oats into the barn and then went to East Midd[lebury]. I helped about the house until noon then I commenced my sack and got it pretty nearly done. Mother fixed one of the baby's dresses and I another today. Olive Thomas is spending the night here. There is a large fire somewhere. We can see and smell the smoke.

Friday. August 28, 1868. I rose quite early this morning and as Father and Mother concluded to go to Brandon I had all of the work to attend to. I was tired when I got it done so I rested until noon when Mrs. Walker came here, and Mrs. Scott came over here and took tea. Night finds me very tired.

Wednesday, September, 9, 1868. Samuel's school commenced today. It has been unpleasant but has not rained much. I have been busy all day but have not seemed to accomplish much. Mother has been spinning. Father is quite lame.

Saturday, September 12, 1868. I rose early and while Samuel went to the depot I packed the household goods for moving. When he got home we started right away, and tonight we are at Mr. Gibson's with all our effects in one room. The baby had his nap disturbed at noon and he has slept very little since but he has been very good. He does not feel at home and I do not either.

Sunday, September 13, 1868. There was no preaching here today but a sermon read in the morning and a prayer meeting in the afternoon and evening. Samuel attended all of these meetings and I took care of the baby. I have not enjoyed the day as well as I should of. I have read some.

Thursday, December 24, 1868. Today Mother and I have worked most of the time on Father's coat and I have been knitting again this evening. Ernest is very good. This evening I spent with Mary.

Friday, December 25. 1868. All day at Father's coat again and today I have finished a pair of socks.

Tuesday, December 29, 1868. This morning we rose at four o'clock and have had a hard day's work. Mr. Crook helped the men butcher and they got their part done early. We worked until nearly midnight and got along nicely. Got the sausage made and the mincemeat chopped, everything done that we could. Georgia and Ella came here this P.M. and Abbie is with them spending the night here.

Source: Bump, Lottie, "Diary of Lottie Bump," Unpublished manuscript, 1868. Transcription used by permission of the Henry Sheldon Museum of Vermont History, Middlebury, Vermont, and Norman and Pamela Lizotte.

7. Iran in the 1930s: Clans and Local Authority

The author of this selection, William Razavi, was born in Iran in the 1970s. He emigrated to the United States as a child with his parents who fled the regime of pro-Western monarch Mohammad Reza Pahlavi, *the second ruler of the* Pahlavi Dynasty, *in 1976, three years before the* Iranian Revolution *that overthrew the Shah's government. The account here, from a forthcoming book on life in Iran, recounts some of the details of his father's early life in rural* Lorestan *in the 1930s. Lorestan, then primarily inhabited by nomadic tribes and more settled Persian clans, is a province in the eastern part of present-day Iran geographically dominated by the Zagros Mountains and their fertile valleys. The town of Aligudarz, Seyed Razavi's hometown, was a center for the surrounding rural region, but much more a part of the rural landscape than a distinct urban environment, and 400 miles from the national capital of Tehran.*

Razavi recounts the importance of clan life and extended family connections, reflected in the economic and architectural unity of the family compound. The local economy functioned much as it had for centuries, with local inhabitants working the land in an economy driven by resident agriculture and the nomadic raising of livestock; in fact, the town's most important building was a silo, and the local cleric, Razavi's grandfather, the bank.

The self-sufficiency of the economy complements the family and political structures, allowing a substantial degree of local autonomy and resistance to outside influence—even the Shah's army. In the period after that described here, economic incentives and other events ended the nomadic herding lifestyles of the Lor and Bakhtiari tribes as well as disrupting the economic and political structures that lent stability and local opportunities to many Lorestanis, resulting in many leaving Lorestan—with Razavi, for example, ending up in Texas. The daily rural life of Lorestan in 1933, with French-studying shepherds and women concealing weapons under their chadors, was poised at an interesting junction of traditional and modern.

LORESTAN, 1933

My father, Seyed Abolhassan Razavi was born in the city of Aligudarz in the eastern part of Lorestan. His was the last generation to know a semi-feudal kind of existence out in the land. His father, Mohammad Mahdi Razavi was a cleric and jurist who commanded a certain degree of regional respect and whose role as an arbiter was important enough to be legitimized by a government that needed him more than he needed them. In fact, the writ of Reza Shah's authority was still shaky with the Lors and the Bakhtiari tribesmen who had long been accustomed to their autonomy.

Aligudarz itself was divided into quarters that belonged to certain families: Razavis in the southwest, Dabiris in the Southeast and Ashrafis, Fouladvands, Tavakkolis and others in their respective areas. Many were khan families, related back to local atabegs [Ottoman Turkish officials] and chieftains. The Razavis were seyeds, descendants of the Prophet Mohammad, and thus more mobile than the local clans. Though they had long been a part of Aligudarz they were still considered outsiders into my father's own time. "Beggar seyeds from Samarra" was how it was sometimes put. Mohammad Mahdi Razavi had actually come from Khonsar, to the east in Isfahan province. It was from there that he had set out for Tehran during the Constitutional crisis at the beginning of the twentieth century. It was there during that period that his mother was shot by bandits. And it was from Khonsar that he set out with volunteers to join the Ottomans in fighting the British during the First World War. But in the chaotic atmosphere of the aftermath of that war marauding tribesmen had looted and burned his home in Khonsar and he was later treated to the spectacle of being invited over for dinner by a friend and having tea served to him on a tray that was clearly stamped with the seal of his father Mir Seyed Ismail Razavi. Shortly after that he accepted an invitation to move west to Aligudarz where his brothers lived.

The Razavi house in Aligudarz was a prototypical large compound. It would cover something like 1/8th of the modern city of Aligudarz, maybe more. Most of this interior space was an extensive orchard that featured a variety of fruit trees and other specimens. The living quarters of the extended Razavi clan all opened into the shared interior park and it was not until the late 1940s that my father's elder brother Ibrahim put up the first wall dividing Razavi from Razavi and beginning the cycle of division and destruction of the old communal way of living.

But while my grandfather lived, the home in Aligudarz was a regional center of activity. Nomadic tribesmen following their herds would pass through and pay their respects, seeking assistance in settling disputes and often banking their money in my grandfather's trust. During the late Qajar period the only law to speak of was to be found in the homes of clerics such as Mohammad Mahdi Razavi and Reza Shah was quick to affirm many of the most prominent such people in their position with official judicial magistracies in order to solidify his own power and subordinate the local chiefs to a central authority. Typically, there would be a civil magistrate or mayor who was paired with a jurist. But the pull of local autonomy was still strong and in the late 1930s when Reza Shah attempted to forcibly disarm the tribesmen the Lors and Bakhtiari responded by storing their arms in the Razavi house. When it was learned that the Army would be raiding the house my grandmother invited the whole Ashrafi clan to dinner. At the end of the evening every Ashrafi woman carried a rifle hidden under her chador back to the Ashrafi compound right past the surrounding soldiers.

Of course, that kind of cooperation points to the connections that had long become established in Aligudarz. Razavis and Ashrafis were intermarried and close, and in some way or another all the families in Aligudarz were tied together. Rural polygamy was still common, especially for political reasons: my grandfather, for instance, had three wives.

One clear division was over language and dialect. My grandmother spoke an elegant standard Farsi [modern Persian] dialect and discouraged her children from using the local Lor dialect (at least in her presence) and didn't even approve of Khonsari, the dialect of her hometown which is almost its own distinct language.

A *dasteh* commences their mourning procession on Ashura (10th of Muharram) in 2005. *Dastehs* (groups) are often formed by local communities, mosques, husseynichs, guilds, charitable organizations, and fraternal orders (similar to the krewes of Mardi Gras). This *dasteh* is marching in North Central Tehran (Division 4) between the old U.S. Embassy, Bahar Avenue, and Shariati Avenue. Photo courtesy of William Razavi.

Agriculture was done the old-fashioned way with manual labor and hand-held sickles bringing in the staple wheat and barley crops that were the mainstay of the central Zagros valleys. The most important building in Aligudarz was the silo, which was constructed by German engineers between the wars. Men and women both worked the fields. Milking of dairy animals was the exclusive province of women, as men's hands were considered too rough for the animals. Nightblindness was common and sometimes children were given raw mullets from the underground qanats [a type of aqueduct] as a home remedy.

My father recounts that his biggest concern in childhood was always shoes. He only had one pair a year, which were made to order by a cobbler at the beginning of the fall, and summers in Aligudarz he and his friends went mostly barefoot. But then, he was luckier than most as he grew up with servants and a wet-nurse among other luxuries.

Of course, Aligudarz was not without its local flavor. While many small towns around the world could boast of showing Charlie Chaplin films projected onto sheets hanging from bridges, few of those towns could boast of shepherds who learned French in their spare time and fewer still could boast (or would boast) of students and parents forming a posse and waking up a math teacher in the middle of the night to get the answer to a particularly puzzling equation that he had given as the night's homework. But there was something of a love of learning that was the hallmark of the old Aligudarz, and which explained the success of the old families as they left town and made their mark in the rest of the country.

All of this, of course, would be disrupted by the war, the Allied occupation, and the tumultuous decades of expropriation and the destruction of local powers by the Pahlavis that would ultimately come back to haunt them. But for a brief while, in the early 1930s Aligudarz was Lorestan's Lake Wobegon and something of a Mark Twain idyll in rural Iran: that was Lorestan in 1933.

Source: Razavi, William M. "Turban Cowboy." Unpublished manuscript, 2007. Courtesy of William M. Razavi.

Trade and Migration

It might seem odd at first to link migration and trade, but they both address the movement of economic elements, in one case people, and in the other goods. In the case of slavery, of course, trade and migration were tragically the same thing. The movement of people and goods has undeniable economic and other consequences for daily life. Trade is one of the primary activities of economic life. In its simplest form, it is the center of the most basic economies—bartering one thing for another. Modern economies are of course vastly more sophisticated, and even the means of exchange—money—is itself traded as a commodity. With the movement of people and goods also comes the movement of ideas. People's daily lives are changed both by the availability of new and different goods, and by their interactions with the people who make those movements possible.

Adam Smith's description (Document 8) of entrenched interests and William Melrose's letter (Document 12) reveal the difficulties and suspicions sometimes attendant on new patterns of trade. While Europeans and Americans wanted Chinese tea, the Chinese did not want the influence of these cultures, and gladly traded while attempting to limit interaction—understandably resisting the threat of European domination and suspicious of the importation of highly addictive opium. Tradesmen and guilds also resisted new patterns. At the beginning of the modern period, trade and manufacturing in Europe were inhibited by the remnants of medieval and early modern systems. These had worked well in the past, but, as Adam Smith argued, these provided more protection for producers of goods and higher prices for consumers. At the same time, as the document from the *American Revolution* shows (Document 9), the inability to trade—as a result of the expected British embargo—could produce hardships and opportunities of its own.

The modern period also has seen some of the largest movements of people in human history. The shift, accelerated in the twentieth century, from rural to urban population is addressed previously (see Documents 1–4 under "Urban Life"), but that is not the only important trend. In 1700, there were only 250,000 Europeans or their descendents in America, while the current U.S. population recently surpassed 300,000,000. Within the huge movement of people to and across the North American continent, there are individual aspects worth noting. Slaves were brought from Africa and then they and their descendants were moved from place to place without their consent (Document 11). The migration westward, typified by the California gold rush in 1849, displaced virtually every American Indian nation in North America (Document 10).

Of course, the United States is not the only place where dramatic economic changes took place due to trade and migration, or where it has been difficult or controversial. Sometimes there is anti-immigrant sentiment on the part of people already living in a place when large numbers of non-native people move in. This has happened historically in the United States, and also in recent decades in Europe, as many African and Asian people migrate there. Sometimes people arriving is not the problem, but people leaving is. One example is the plight of Jewish "refuseniks" denied permission to leave the *Union of Soviet Socialist Republics* (USSR) (Document 13). Sometimes migration and trade are seen as a threat to local economies or economic patterns; sometimes not. Yet the movement of people and things has unquestionably helped shape the modern world, and today it goes on, unalterably a part of daily and economic life.

8. *Adam Smith: Breaking Barriers to Trade*

The Scottish philosopher and political economist Adam Smith (1723–1790) is best known for his formulation of the theory of capitalism *in his seminal text of capitalist economics, now known as* The Wealth of Nations. *He proposed the doctrine of the* invisible hand *that would move individuals to make decisions in their best economic interest, which would serve the economic interest of the nation overall. In this selection, Smith laments the restrictions placed on development of tradesmen in England by the* apprenticeship systems *of* guilds *and professional corporations. Guilds had developed in medieval Europe to assure standards, provide a system of training, and protect a profession's collective interests. In some ways similar to the labor unions of today, guilds performed similar functions in pre-industrial societies, although the guild consisted of master craftsmen who owned and operated their own businesses, rather than laborers who worked in a field or profession for others. Whether making teapots, hats, wheels, coaches, or virtually anything else, a craftsman first had to complete an apprenticeship to a master craftsman and guild member to legally be allowed to practice a trade. Apprentices often lived with the master and worked for him without pay, and were given progressively more responsible tasks until they had thoroughly learned a trade. Sometimes boys were apprenticed as early as the age of 10 or 12.*

Smith decries this system, seeing it as far more in the interest of the masters who limit competition, acquire free or cheap labor, and maximize profits. Smith argues that men can be trained in far less time than the years and years the guilds required, and the general public suffers from a system that means less competition, higher prices, inhibitions on entrepreneurship, and restrictions on pursuing one's own economic self-interest. The freedom of the individual in economic activities that Smith endorsed and promoted is connected to other thinkers who also argue for political freedom. Critics have accused Smith's laissez-faire *(French for let it be) economic theory with relying too much on a theoretical market to regulate economic outcomes, ignoring the plight of those at the bottom of the economic ladder, and legitimizing huge inequities of wealth and exploitation of the working masses. While the merits of Smith's theory will continue to be debated, there is no doubt that his ideas were immensely influential, contributed to the transformations of economic life in the* Industrial Revolution, *and stand at the beginning of the modern field of economics.*

In Sheffield no master cutler can have more than one apprentice at a time by a bylaw of the corporation. In Norfolk and Norwich no master weaver can have more than two apprentices under pain of forfeiting five pounds a month to the king. No master hatter can have more than two apprentices anywhere in England or in the English plantations, under pain of forfeiting five pounds a month, half to the king and half to him who shall sue in any court of record. Both these regulations, though they have been confirmed by a public law of the kingdom, are evidently dictated by the same corporation spirit which enacted the by-law of Sheffield. The silk weavers in London had scarce been incorporated a year when they enacted a by-law restraining any master from having more than two apprentices at a time. It required a particular act of Parliament to rescind this by-law. . . .

By the 5th of Elizabeth, commonly called the Statute of Apprenticeship, it was enacted that no persons should for the future exercise any trade, craft, or mystery at the time exercised in England, unless he had previously served to it an apprenticeship of seven years at least; and what before had been the by-law of many particular corporations became in England the general public law of all the trades carried on in the market towns. For, though the words of the statute are very general and plainly seem to include the whole kingdom, by interpretation its operation has been limited to market towns, it having been held that in country villages a person may exercise several different trades, though he has not served a seven years' apprenticeship to each, they being necessary for the conveniency of the inhabitants, and the number of people frequently not being sufficient to supply each with a particular set of hands.

By a strict interpretation of the words too, the operation of this statute has been limited to those trades which were established in England before the 5th of Elizabeth and has never been extended to such as have been introduced since that time. This limitation has given occasion to several distinctions which, considered as rules of police, appear as foolish as can be imagined. It has been adjudged, for example, that a coach maker can neither himself make nor employ journeyman to make his coach wheels, but must buy them of a master wheelwright, this latter trade having been exercised in England before the 5th of Elizabeth. But a wheelwright, though he has never served an apprenticeship to a coach maker, may either make them himself or employ journeymen to make coaches, the trade of a coach maker not being within the statute because not exercised in England at the time when it was made. The manufactures of Manchester, Birmingham, and Wolverhampton are, many of them, upon this account not within the statute, not having been exercised in England before the 5th of Elizabeth.

In France the duration of apprenticeship is different in different towns and in different trades. In Paris five years is the term required in a great number; but before any person can be qualified to exercise the trade as a master he must in many of them serve five years more as a journeyman. During this latter term he is called the companion of his master and the term is called companionship. . . .

The property which every man has in his own labor, as it is the original foundation of all other property, so it is the most sacred and inviolable. The patrimony of a poor man lies in the strength and dexterity of his hands; and to hinder him from employing his strength and dexterity in what manner he thinks proper without injury to his neighbor is a plain violation of this most sacred property. It is a manifest encroachment upon the just liberty both of the workman and of those who might be disposed to employ him. As it hinders the one from working at what he thinks proper, so it hinders the others from employing whom they think proper. To judge whether he is fit to be employed may surely be trusted to the discretion of the employers whose interest it so much concerns.

The affected anxiety of the lawgiver lest they should employ an improper person is evidently as impertinent as it is oppressive.

Long apprenticeships are altogether unnecessary. The arts which are much superior to common trades, such as those of making clocks and watches, contain no such mystery as to require a long course of instruction. The first invention of such beautiful machines, indeed, and even that of some of the instruments employed in making them, have been the work of deep thought and long time, and may justly be considered as among the happiest efforts of human ingenuity. But when both have been fairly invented and are well understood, to explain to any young man in the completest manner how to apply the instruments and how to construct the machines cannot well require more than the lessons of a few weeks—perhaps those of a few days might be sufficient. In the common mechanic trade those of a few days might certainly be sufficient. The dexterity of hands indeed even in common trades cannot be acquired without much practice and experience. But a young man would practice with much more diligence and attention if from the beginning he wrought as a journeyman, being paid in proportion to the little work which he could execute and paying in his turn for the materials which he might sometimes spoil through awkwardness and inexperience. His education would generally in this way be more effectual and always less tedious and expensive.

The master indeed would be a loser. He would lose all the wages of the apprentice which he now saves for seven years together. In the end perhaps the apprentice himself would be the loser. In a trade so easily learnt he would have more competitors and his wages when he came to be a complete workman would be less than at present. The same increase in competition would reduce the profits of the masters as well as the wages of the workmen. The trades, the crafts, the mysteries would all be losers. But the public would be a gainer, the work of all artificers coming in this way much cheaper to the market.

Source: Smith, Adam. *An Inquiry into the Nature and Causes of the Wealth of Nations*. London: W. Strahan and T. Cadell, 1776.

9. The Economics of the American Revolution, 1775

Between 1700 and 1775, the number of Europeans in the American colonies had grown to 2,500,000, an increase of 1,000 percent. In 1775, there was one American colonist for every three inhabitants of Britain, an increase from one for eight at the turn of the century, and many of these were either not English-born, nor even of English descent. In short, the American colonies had grown and changed tremendously in the decades before they declared independence from Great Britain in 1776.

The growing size and importance of the colonies gave them the confidence to assert their independence, but the trade with England and other nations that was crucial to America's economic success would be largely cut off by a war for independence. The following selection, from a 1775 resolution by the Pennsylvania Convention, anticipates the economic problems and needs likely to result from the American Revolution, *and encourages preparations to compensate. Specialized manufactured goods were often imported to the colonies, and raw materials such as whale oil, tobacco, indigo, and rice, among other items, were primary exports. It was seen as important not only for the potential future of the fledgling nation to be less reliant on trade to acquire certain goods, but also crucial for the potential war effort. In this context, the desire for the colonies to create self-sufficiency in a great many commodities expressed in this document of the Revolutionary period makes good sense both militarily and economically, but it also reveals how dependent on trade the colonies were, even in Philadelphia, the largest city in the colonies.*

Many of the items mentioned have specific military purposes: from the obvious need for iron, steel, and gunpowder for weaponry; to sheep, dyes, and wool combs to make more cloth for blankets and uniforms; to hemp for rope, flax for sails, and copper sheathing for ship bottoms. Not only goods with direct military uses were encouraged but also salt, glass, paper, millstones, printing type, and even beer were included. Even in a revolution, daily life has to go on.

PENNSYLVANIA CONVENTION

Proceedings of the Convention for the Province of Pennsylvania, held at Philadelphia, January 23, 1775, and continued by adjournments until the 28th. [...]

Resolved unanimously, That it is the most earnest wish and desire of this Convention to see harmony restored between great Britain and the Colonies; that we will exert our utmost endeavours for the attainment of that most desirable object; that it is the opinion of this body that the commercial opposition pointed out by the Continental Congress, if faithfully adhered to, will be the means of rescuing this unhappy country from the evils meditated against it. But if the humble and loyal Petition of said Congress to his most gracious Majesty, should be disregarded, and the British Administration, instead of redressing our grievances, should determine, by force, to effect a submission to the late arbitrary acts of the British Parliament; in such a situation we hold it our indispensible duty to resist such force, and at every hazard to defend the Rights and Liberties of America.

Whereas, it has been judged necessary, for the preservation of our just Rights and Liberties, to lay a restraint on our Importations; and as the freedom, happiness, and prosperity of a state greatly depend on providing within itself a supply of necessary articles necessary for subsistence, clothing, and defence, a regard for our country, as well as common prudence, call upon us to encourage Agriculture, Manufactures, and Economy; therefore, this Convention do resolve as follows:

Resolved unanimously, That from and after the first day of March next, no person or persons should use in his, her, or their families, unless in cases of necessity, and no account sell to the Butchers, or kill for the market, any Sheep under four years old; and where there is a necessity for using any Mutton in their families, it is recommended to kill such as are the least profitable to keep.

Resolved unanimously, That we recommend the setting up of Woollen Manufactures in as many different branches as possible, especially Coating, Flannel, Blankets, Rugs or Coverlids, Hosiery, and Coarse Cloths, both broad and narrow. [...]

Resolved unanimously, That each person having proper land should raise a quantity of Flax and Hemp, sufficient not only for the use of his own family, but also to spare to others on moderate terms; and that it be recommended to the Farmers to provide themselves with a sufficient quantity of Seed, for the proposed increase of the above articles of Hemp and Flax.

Resolved unanimously, As Salt is a daily and almost indispensible necessity of life, and the making of it among ourselves must be esteemed a valuable acquisition, we therefore recommend the making of it in the manner used in England and other countries; and are of the opinion it may be done with success in the interior part of the Province, where there are Salt springs, as well as on the sea-coast.

Resolved unanimously, That Saltpetre being an article of great use and consumption, we recommend the making of it, and are a farther opinion that it may be done to great advantage.

Resolved unanimously, That the necessity we maybe under for Gunpowder, especially in the Indian trade, induces us to recommend the manufacturing of that article as largely as possible, by such persons who are or may be owners of Powder Mills in this Province.

Resolved unanimously, That we recommend the manufacturing of Iron into Nails and Wire, and all other articles necessary for carrying on our Manufactures, evidently in general use, and which, of consequence, should our unhappy differences continue, will be in great demand.

Resolved unanimously, that we are of opinion the making of Steel ought to be largely prosecuted, as the demand for this article will be great.

Resolved unanimously, That we recommend the making of different kinds of Paper now in use among us, to the several Manufactures; and as the success of this branch depends on a supply of old Linen and Woollen Rags, request the people of this Province, in their respective houses, may order the necessary steps to be taken for preserving these otherwise useless articles.

Resolved unanimously, That as the consumption of Glass is greater than the Glass-Houses now established among us can supply, we recommend the setting up of other Glass-Houses, and are of the opinion they would turn out to the advantage of the proprietors.

Resolved unanimously, That whereas Wool Combs and Cards have for some time been manufactured in some of the neighboring Colonies, and are absolutely necessary for carrying on the Hosiery and Clothing business, we do recommend the establishment of such a Manufactory in this Province.

Resolved unanimously, That we also recommend the manufacturing of copper into Sheets, Bottoms, and Kettles.

Resolved unanimously, That we recommend the making of Tin Plates, as an article worthy of the attention of the people of this Province.

Resolved unanimously, That as Printing Types are now made to a considerable degree of perfection by an ingenious artist in Germantown, it is recommended to the printers to use such Types in preference to any which may hereafter be imported.

Resolved unanimously, That recommend the erecting a great number of Fulling-mills, and Mills for breaking, singling, and softening Hemp and Flax, and also the making of Grindstones in this country.

Resolved unanimously, that as the brewing of large quantities of Malt Liquors within this Province, would tend to render the consumption of Foreign Liquors less necessary, it is therefore recommended that proper attention be given to the cultivation of Barley; and that the several Brewers, both in City and Country, do encourage it by giving a reasonable and sufficient price for the same.

Resolved unanimously, That we do recommend to all the inhabitants of this Province, and do promise for ourselves in particular, to use our own Manufactures, and those of other Colonies, in preference to all others.

Resolved unanimously, That for the more speedily and effectually putting these Resolves in execution, we do earnestly recommend Societies be established in different parts, and are of the opinion that Premiums ought to be granted in the several Counties, to persons who may excel in the several branches of manufactory; and we do further engage, that we, in our separate Committees, will promote them to the utmost of our power.

Resolved unanimously, That if any Manufacturer or Vendor of Goods and Merchandises in this Province, shall take advantage of the necessities of his country, by selling his Goods or Merchandise at an unusual and extravagant profit, such person shall be considered enemy to his country, and be advertised as such by the Committees of the place where the offender dwells. [. . .]

Ordered, That the Proceedings of this Convention be sent to the Press and printed in English and German, under the direction of the President and Messrs. Jonathan B. Smith and John Benezet.

Source: Force, Peter, ed. *American Archives: Containing a Documentary History of the English Colonies of North America from the King's Message to Parliament of March 4, 1774, to the Declaration of Independence by the United States*. Volume 1. Washington, D.C., 1837.

10. *In Search of Gold in California, 1849*

The territory that is today California only became part of the United States in 1848. Mexico ceded it to the United States after the Mexican-American War. That same year, gold was discovered in northern California at a place called Sutter's Mill. Wild stories of chunks of gold lying on the ground waiting to be picked up filled many with dreams of easy riches, and they flocked to the West in droves.

Alonzo Delano was just a man like thousands of others who, enticed by the promise of gold, made the trek to California in 1849 to become miners, or forty-niners. *His account gives a vivid description of the difficulties of the journey and the men and animals that did not make it across the plains and mountains. In 1849, almost 100,000 people started the journey to California from the eastern United States or other countries, including China, Australia, and Latin America, with tens of thousands taking the overland route like Delano. By 1855, an estimated 300,000 people had immigrated to California, compared to a population of 15,000 non-Native Americans before gold was discovered.*

Delano makes virtually no mention of the inhabitants of the land who were there before the settlers, only indicating that there was some danger of attack. The rapid growth and chaotic, almost mob mentality of the miners in establishing towns and claims shows an attitude that sees the natural environment as a landscape to be exploited for wealth and has little regard for those who were there before them.

The economic consequences of the gold rush were enormous. The value of the gold taken out of the ground gave Californians the wealth to buy many things, the waves of settlers and fortune-seekers demanded goods and services, and within two years California became a state. The influx of immigrants seeking gold laid the basis for the development of transportation systems, the growth of the agricultural economy, and the immense future prosperity of the state: California's economy is now the seventh largest in the world. The gold alone could not have begun this transformation—the people who migrated were the real catalyst. Without the influx of the many forty-niners like Alonzo Delano, California could not have become, for good or ill, what it is today.

Our general rendezvous was to be at St. Joseph, on the Missouri, from which we intended to take our departure. I had engaged men, purchased cattle and a wagon, and subsequently laid in my supplies for the trip, at St. Louis. My wagon I shipped by water to St. Joseph, and sent my cattle across the country about the middle of March, [1849] to meet me at the place of rendezvous, in April....

[May 21.] Our desire to be upon the road induced us to be stirring early, and we were moving as soon as our cattle had eaten their fill, when a drive of a mile placed us upon the great thoroughfare of the gold seekers.

For miles, to the extent of vision, an animated mass of beings broke upon our view. Long trains of wagons with their white covers were moving slowly along, a multitude of horsemen were prancing on the road, companies of men were traveling on foot, and although the scene was not a gorgeous one, yet the display of banners from many wagons, and the multitude of armed men, looked as if a mighty army was on its march; and in a few moments we took our station in the line, a component part of the motley throng of gold seekers, who were leaving home and friends far behind, to encounter the peril of mountain and plain....

[June 29.] On leaving the Missouri, nearly every train was an organized company, with general regulations for mutual safety, and with a captain chosen by themselves, as a nominal head. On reaching the South Pass, we found that the great majority had either divided, or broken up entirely, making independent and helter-skelter marches towards California....

[August 10.] Reports began to reach us of hard roads ahead; that that there was no grass at the Sink, or place where the river disappears in the sands of the desert, and that from that place a desert of sand, with water but once in forty-five miles, had to be crossed. In our worn-out condition this looked discouraging, and it was with a kind of dread that we looked to the passage of the sandy plain. At the same time and indefinite tale was circulated among the emigrants, that a new road had been discovered, by which the Sacramento might be reached in a shorter distance, avoiding altogether the dreaded desert; and that there was plenty of grass and water on the route....

[August 11.]... There were a great many men daily passing, who, having worn down their cattle and mules, had abandoned their wagons, and were trying to get through as they might; but their woe-begone countenances and meagre accoutrements for such a journey, with want and excessive labor staring them in the face, excited our pity, wretched as we felt ourselves. Our own cattle had been prudently driven, and were still in good condition to perform the journey. Although our stock of provisions was getting low, we felt that under any circumstances we could get through, and notwithstanding we felt anxious, we were not discouraged....

[August 15.] . . . It was decided, finally, that we would go the northern route, although some of our company had misgivings. The younger portion being fond of adventure, were loud in favor of the road. . . .

[August 16.]. . . . Beyond us, far as we could see, was a barren waste, without a blade of grass or a drop of water for thirty miles at least. Instead of avoiding the desert, instead of the promised water, grass, and a better road, we were in fact upon a more dreary and wider waste, without either grass or water, and with a harder road before us. . . .

[August 17.] As I walked on slowly and with effort, I encountered a great many animals, perishing for want of food and water, on the desert plain. Some would be just gasping for breath, others unable to stand, would issue low moans as I came up, in a most distressing manner, showing intense agony; and still others, unable to walk, seemed to brace themselves up on their legs to prevent falling, while here and there a poor ox, or horse, just able to drag himself along, would stagger towards me with a low sound, as if begging for a drop of water. My sympathies were excited at their sufferings, yet, instead of offering them aid, I was a subject for relief myself.

High above the plain, in the direction of our road, a black, bare mountain reared its head, at the distance of fifteen miles; and ten miles this side of the plains was flat, composed of baked earth, without a sign of vegetation, and in many places covered with crustations of salt. Pits had been sunk in moist places, but the water was salt as brine, and utterly useless. . . .

The train had passed me in the night, and our cattle traveled steadily without faltering, reaching the spring about nine o'clock in the morning, after traveling nearly forty hours without food or water. If ever a cup of coffee and slice of bacon was relished by man, it was by me that morning, on arriving at the encampment a little after ten.

We found this to be an oasis in the desert. A large hot spring, nearly three rods [fifty feet] in diameter, and very deep, irrigated about twenty acres of ground—the water cooling as it ran off. . . .

[August 20.] . . . Through the day there was a constant arrival of wagons, and by night there were several hundred men together; yet we learned by a mule train that at least one hundred and fifty wagons had turned back to the first spring west of the Humboldt, on learning the dangers of crossing the desert, taking wisely the old road again. This change of route, however, did not continue long, and the rear trains, comprising a large portion of the emigration, took our route, and suffered even worse than we did. It was resolved that several trains should always travel within supporting distance of each other, so that in case of an attack from the Indians, a sufficient body of men should be together to protect themselves. . . . Reports again reached us corroborating the great loss of cattle on the desert beyond the Sink. The road was filled with dead animals, and the offensive effluvia had produced much sickness; but shortly afterward, our own portion of the desert presented the same catastrophe, and the road was lined with the dead bodies of worn out and starved animals, and their debilitated masters, in many cases, were left to struggle on foot, combating hunger, thirst and fatigue, in a desperate exertion to get through. . . .

[September 17.] . . . Ascending to the top of an inclined plain, the long-sought, long-wished-for and welcome valley of the Sacramento, lay before me, five or six miles distant. . . .

In May, 1850, a report reached the settlements that a wonderful lake had been discovered, an hundred miles back among the mountains, towards the head of the Middle Fork of Feather river, the shores of which abounded with gold, and to such an extent that it lay like pebbles on the beach. An extraordinary ferment among the people ensued, and a grand rush was made from the towns, in search of this splendid El Dorado. Stores were left to take care of themselves, business of all kinds was dropped, mules were suddenly bought up at exorbitant prices, and crowds started off to search for the golden lake.

Days passed away, when at length adventurers began to return, with disappointed looks, and their worn out and dilapidated garments showed that they had "seen some service," and it proved that, though several lakes had been discovered, the Gold Lake *par excellence* was not found. The mountains swarmed with men, exhausted and worn out with toil and hunger; mules were starved, or killed by falling from precipices. Still the search was continued over snow forty or fifty feet deep, till the highest ridge of the Sierra was passed, when the disappointed crowds began to return, without getting a glimpse of the grand *desideratum*, having had their labor for their pains. Yet this sally was not without some practical and beneficial results. The country was more perfectly explored, some rich diggings were found, and, as usual, a few among the many were benefited. A new field for enterprise was opened, and within a month, roads were made and traversed by wagons, trading posts were established, and a new mining country was opened, which really proved in the main to be rich, and had it not been for the gold-lake fever, it might have remained many months undiscovered and unoccupied....

From the mouth of Nelson's Creek to its source, men were at work in digging. Sometimes the stream was turned from its bed, and the channel worked; in other places, wing dams were thrown out, and the bed partially worked; while in some, the banks only were dug. Some of these, as is the case everywhere in the mines, paid well, some, fair wages, while many were failures. One evening, while waiting for my second supply of goods, I strolled by a deserted camp. I was attracted to the ruins of a shanty, by observing the effigy of a man standing upright in an old, torn shirt, a pair of ragged pantaloons, and boots which looked as if they had been clambering over rocks since they were made—in short, the image represented a lean, meager, worn-out and woe-begone miner, such as might daily be seen at almost every point in the upper mines. On the shirt was inscribed, in a good business hand, "My claim failed—will you pay the taxes?" (an allusion to the tax on foreigners.) Appended to the figure was a paper, bearing the following words: "Californians—Oh, Californians, look at me! Once fat and saucy as a privateersman, but now—look ye—a miserable skeleton. In a word, I am a used up man...."

Ludicrous as it may appear, it was a truthful commentary on the efforts of hundreds of poor fellows in the "golden land." This company had penetrated the mountain snows with infinite labor, in the early part of the season, enduring hardships of no ordinary character—had patiently toiled for weeks, living on the coarsest fare; had spent time and money building a dam and digging a race through rocks to drain off the water; endured wet and cold, in the chilling atmosphere of the country, and when the last stone was turned, at the very close of all this labor, they did not find a single cent to reward them for their toil and privations, and what was still more aggravating, a small, wing dam, on the very claim below them, yielded several thousand dollars. Having paid out their money, and lost their labor, they were compelled to abandon the claim, and search for other diggings, where the result might be precisely the same....

The population of Independence represented almost every State in the Union, while France, England, Ireland, Germany, and even Bohemia, had their delegates. As soon as breakfast was dispatched, all hands were engaged in digging and washing gold in the banks, or in the bed of the stream. When evening came, large fires were built, around which the miners congregated, some engrossed with thoughts of home and friends, some to talk of new discoveries, and richer diggings somewhere else; or, sometimes a subject of debate was started, and the evening was whiled away in pleasant, and often instructive, discussion, while many, for whom this kind of recreation had not excitement enough, resorted to dealing monte, on a small scale, thus either exciting or keeping up a passion for play. Some weeks were passed in this way under the clear blue sky of the mountains, and many had made respectable piles. I highly enjoyed the wild scenery, and, quite as, the wild life we were leading, for there were many accomplished and intelligent men; and a subject for amusement or debate was rarely wanting. As for ceremony or dress, it gave us no trouble: we were all alike....At length a monte dealer arrived, with a respectable bank.

A change had been gradually coming over many of our people, and for three or four days several industrious men had commenced drinking, and after the monte bank was set up, it seemed as if the long smothered fire burst forth into a flame. Labor, with few exceptions, seemed suspended, and a great many miners spent their time in riot and debauchery....The monte dealer, who, in his way was a gentleman, and honorable according to the notions of that class of men, won in two nights three thousand dollars! When he had collected his taxes on our bar, he went to Onion Valley, six miles distant, and lost in one night four thousand, exemplifying the fact, that a gambler may be rich to-day, and a beggar to-morrow....

Source: Delano, Alonzo. *Life on the Plains and Among the Diggings: Being Scenes and Adventures of an Overland Journey to California: With Particular Incidents of the Route, Mistakes, and Sufferings of the Emigrants, the Indian Tribes, the Present and the Future of the Great West.* Auburn, NY: Miller, Orton & Mulligan, 1854.

11. A Georgia Slave Auction, 1859

This excerpt, taken from Horace Greeley's New York Tribune, *an extremely popular anti-slavery newspaper, describes in precise and ironic detail the carnival atmosphere of a large slave auction in Savannah, Georgia, in 1859.* Slavery *had been legal in all the English colonies that became the United States, but was outlawed by the northern states in the early National period. Sectionalist tensions would finally lead to the secession of southern states and the American* Civil War *from 1861 to 1865, the Emancipation Proclamation in 1863, and the Thirteenth Amendment in 1865, which abolished slavery in the United States.*

As repugnant at it seems today, slavery had been an important part of life in many countries besides the United States. England outlawed the slave trade in 1807 and slavery throughout its empire in 1833. Non-racial slavery was also practiced in the modern world, but it too died out as a legal institution. The Russian Empire emancipated its serfs about the same time as the United States, in 1861, but slavery remained a part of the Turkish Ottoman Empire *until it was dissolved after the First World War in 1919.*

While the political and cultural motives and consequences of racial slavery are deep-seated, and throughout the modern era a variety of arguments were offered justifying the continued ownership of one human by another, the underlying motivation for slavery can be seen as principally economic: the owner of a slave obtains the value of the slave's labor without having to pay wages. Economists have documented the significant economic advantages of slave ownership and slavery as an institution in the antebellum American South. There is no doubt that slave labor was valuable, as the prices mentioned in this article reveal.

The injustice of the institution of slavery is on full display in this article. The excitement and bustle of the white slave traders, who fill the hotels and places of entertainment with energy and anticipation, is in sharp contrast to the slaves themselves, one of whom is described as begging a buyer to purchase him and his family to keep them together, or parading themselves to demonstrate their physical fitness or attributes. The men and women for sale are inspected, made to run, and have their teeth checked like livestock. While this article was written to encourage its audience to support the abolition of slavery in a society that still allowed it, the affect on a contemporary audience, long after slavery has ceased, is still dramatic.

The largest sale of human chattels that has ever been made in Star-Spangled America for several years took place on Wednesday and Thursday of last week, at the Race Course near the City of Savannah, Georgia. The lot consisted of four hundred and thirty-six men, women, children and infants, being that half of the negro stock remaining on the old Major Butler plantations which fell to one of the two heirs to that estate....

The sale had been advertised largely for many weeks, and as the negroes were known to be a choice lot and very desirable property, the attendance of buyers was large. The breaking up of an old family estate is so uncommon an occurrence that the affair was regarded with unusual interest throughout the South. For several days before the sale every hotel in Savannah was crowded with negro speculators from North and South Carolina, Virginia, Georgia, Alabama and Louisiana, who had been attracted hither by the prospects of making good bargains. Nothing was heard for days, in the bar-rooms and public rooms but talk of the great sale, criticisms of the business affairs of Mr. Butler, and speculations as to the probable prices the stock would bring. The office of Joseph Bryan the negro broker who had the management of the sale, was thronged every day by eager inquirers in search of information, and by some who were anxious to buy, but were uncertain as to whether their securities would prove acceptable. Little parties were made up from the various hotels every day to visit the Race-Course, distant some three miles from the city, to look over the chattels, discuss their points, and make memoranda for guidance on the day of sale. The buyers were generally of a rough breed, slangy, profane and bearish, being for the most part, from the back river and swamp plantations, where the elegancies of polite life had not perhaps developed to their fullest extent [...]

The following curiously sad scene is the type of a score of others that were enacted:

"Elisha," chattel No. 5 in the catalogue, had taken a fancy to a benevolent looking middle-aged gentleman, who was inspecting the stock, and thus used his powers of persuasion to induce the benevolent man to purchase him, with his wife, boy and girl, Molly, Israel and Sevanda, chattels Nos. 6, 7, and 8. The earnestness with which the poor fellow pressed his suit, knowing, as he did, that perhaps the happiness of his whole life depended on his success, was interesting, and the arguments he used were most pathetic. He made no appeal to the feelings of the buyer; he rested no hope on his charity and kindness, but only strove to show how well worth his dollars were the bone and blood he was entreating him to buy.

"Look at me, Mas'r; am prime rice planter; sho' you won't find a better man den me; no better on de whole plantation; not a bit old yet; do mo' work den ever; do carpenter wook, too, little; better buy me, Mas'r; I'se be good sarvant, Mas'r. Molly, too, my wife, Sa, fus rate rice hand; mos as good as me. Stan' out yer, Molly, and let the gen'lm'n see."

Molly advances, with her hands crossed on her bosom, and makes a quick short curtsy, and stands mute, looking appealingly in the benevolent man's face. But Elisha talks all the faster.

"Show mas'r yer arm Molly—good arm dat mas'r—she do a heap of work mo' with dat arm yet. Let good mas'r see yer teeth Molly—see dat mas'r, teeth all regular, all good—she'm young gal yet. Come out yer Israel, walk aroun' an' let the gen'lm'n see how spry you be"—

Then, pointing to the three-year-old girl who stood with her chubby hand to her mouth, holding on to her mother's dress, and uncertain what to make of the strange scene.

"Little Vardy's on'y a chile yet; make prime gal by-and-by. Better buy us mas'r, we'm fus' rate bargain"—and so on. But the benevolent man found where he could drive a closer bargain, and so bought somebody else....

Mr. Walsh mounted the stand and announced the terms of the sale, "one-third cash, the remainder payable in two equal annual installments, bearing interest from the day of the sale, to be secured by approved mortgage and personal security, or approved acceptances on Savannah, Ga., or Charleston, S.C. Purchasers to pay for papers." The buyers, who were present to the number of about two hundred, clustered around the platform; while the negroes, who were not likely to be immediately wanted, gathered into sad groups in the background to watch the progress of the selling in which they were so sorrowfully interested. The wind howled outside, and through the open side of the building the driving rain came pouring in; the bar downstairs ceased for a short time its brisk trade; the buyers lit fresh cigars, got ready their catalogues and pencils, and the first lot of human chattels are led upon the stand, not by a white man, but by a sleek mulatto, himself a slave, and who seems to regard the selling of his brethren, in which he so glibly assists, as a capital joke. It had been announced that the negroes would be sold in "families," that is to say, a man would not be parted from his wife, or a mother from a very young child. There is perhaps as much policy as humanity in this arrangement, for thereby many aged and unserviceable people are disposed of, who otherwise would not find a ready sale. [...]

The expression on the faces of all who stepped on the block was always the same, and told of more anguish than it is in the power of words to express. Blighted homes, crushed hopes and broken hearts was the sad story to be read in all the anxious faces.

Some of them regarded the sale with perfect indifference, never making a motion save to turn from one side to the other at the word of the dapper Mr. Bryan, that all the crowd might have a fair view of their proportions, and then, when the sale was accomplished, stepping down from the block without caring to cast even a look at the buyer, who now held all their happiness in his hands. Others, again, strained their eyes with eager glances from one buyer to another as the bidding went on, trying with earnest attention to follow the rapid voice of the auctioneer. Sometimes, two persons only would be bidding for the same chattel, all the others having resigned the contest, and then the poor creature on the block, conceiving an instantaneous preference for one of the buyers over the other, would regard the rivalry with the intensest interest, the expression of his face changing with every bid, settling into a half smile of joy if the favorite buyer persevered unto the end and secured the property, and settling down into a look of hopeless despair if the other won the victory. . . .

The auctioneer brought up Joshua's Molly and family. He announced that Molly insisted that she was lame in her left foot, and perversely would walk lame, although, for his part, he did not believe a word of it. He had caused her to be examined by an eminent physician in Savannah, which medical light had declared that Joshua's Molly was not lame, but was only shamming. However, the gentlemen must judge for themselves and bid accordingly. So Molly was put through her paces, and compelled to trot up and down along the stage, to go up and down the steps, and to exercise her feet in various ways, but always with the same result, the left foot *would* be lame. She was finally sold for $695 [about $18,000 today].

Whether she really was lame or not, no one knows but herself, but it must be remembered that to a slave a lameness, or anything that decreases his market value, is a thing to be rejoiced over. A man in the prime of life, worth $1,600 or thereabouts [over $42,000 today], can have little hope of ever being able, by any little savings of his own, to purchase his liberty. But, let him have a rupture, or lose a limb, or sustain any other injury that renders him of much less service to his owner, and reduces his value to $300 or $400, and he may hope to accumulate that sum, and eventually to purchase his liberty. Freedom without health is infinitely sweeter than health without freedom.

And so the great sale went on for two long days, during which time there were sold 429 men, women and children. There were 436 announced to be sold, but a few were detained on the plantations by sickness. . . .

The total amount of the sale foots up $303,850—the proceeds of the first day being $161,480, and of the second day $142,370. . . .

Source: "A Slave Auction," *New York Daily Tribune*, March 9, 1859.

12. *Tea for Two: The Anglo-Chinese Tea Trade*

Tea was first imported to Europe in the seventeenth century, and had become a staple drink in England by 1750. Like coffee, tobacco, cotton, sugar, and other products, tea was imported to Europe on a large scale. China, where much of the tea drunk in England was grown, had strongly resisted allowing Europeans access to the interior. Although China exported much tea, porcelain, silk, and other products from 1757 to 1842, they carefully regulated this trade through the Canton system, *by which the Chinese funneled all official trade through the port of Canton (Guangzhou), which by 1800 was the third largest city in the world. European nations also controlled the trade through powerful chartered monopoly trading companies, like the* British East India Company, *which had a larger army and navy than the United States.*

Hoping to offset the balance of trade that was favorable to the Chinese, the British began illegally importing large quantities of cheaply produced Indian opium, and the resulting addiction of a significant part of the Chinese population made it easier to gain greater influence and control. The monopoly system ended on both sides in 1842 after the Chinese defeat by Britain in the first Opium War, *which opened more Chinese ports and allowed more British companies to trade.*

William Melrose, a Scotsman whose family was in the tea trade, spent a decade in Canton trading in tea starting in 1845. Melrose's letters demonstrate his knowledge of the tea trade and the many economic factors that would go into his decisions, including the cost and quality of the tea, its quantity, the exchange rate for the notes he used to pay for the tea, the shipping cost, the supplies of various teas shipped to Britain, the demand and prices of the British tea markets, and other factors.

Melrose's letters are not all facts and figures. He offers a view of trade that is in some ways akin to debates on trade today. There is a justifiable fear, especially on the part of the Chinese, that the increased trade will bring not only wealth—exports to the West were very profitable for the Chinese, but also undesirable foreign influences and negative consequences. A business trip from Canton to Shanghai could be a risky proposition, stemming from the hostility of the Chinese populace.

Nonetheless, the scale of the trade created sophisticated international structures to regulate and facilitate the commerce in tea and other goods flowing through Chinese ports. The system of regulated trade developed by the English and Chinese in the nineteenth century is indicative of the new patterns of international commerce that would dominate much of the modern world, bringing with it liberated market forces, complex international banking systems, and improving transportation and communication systems. The trading networks helped create the colonial issues that plague much of the developing world today, but these networks also created the economic basis for modern national and international economies.

William to Mr. Simpson
Canton, 21 July 1851

I have yours of 17th and 21st May. I started for this place soon after I dispatched your last month's letters from Macao but have done nothing yet. The market is not open here yet, that is, properly opened. [...]

At Shanghai they are going ahead, 71 chops [groups of chests of the same type and quality] by last advice settled from Tls 15 to 211/2 [Tls means Taels per picul, taels were units of Chinese currency equal to one ounce of silver and piculs units of weight equal to 133 pounds]. I have seen some samples; the high priced appear to me very dear, nothing but tarry Pekoe flavour, not nearly so good as ours per Aden to Liverpool and far more tarry. I do not think they have any fine [tea] up there this year, but I will see samples and prices tomorrow and will be able to tell you more about it. I hear some of the Congous they shipped from there last year were awful trash. If low [grade] Congous come down [in price] at home and any of that low stuff get in after it, it will leave a balance on the wrong side. A good many people have gone up from here to Shanghai this year and a great many ships. They must have made good profits last year which is sending them all up there and it must have all been made on low [grade] Congou. [...]

There are very few fine chops of Congou this year, not over a dozen, a few second class and all the rest are as tarry as you could wish. If you hold the Souchongs they will come in very well yet. About 230 chops of Congou are down and nearly all tarry; and if those that are to come are as bad, and the chances are that they will be, a good two thirds of the Congou export will be tarry, say 25,000,000 pounds. Now one million or so of Souchong will hardly be known amongst it. Just think, every chop of Congou is nearly 600 to 800 chests and the most of those tarry, some of them bitter with tar. What are a few chops of (150 to 200 chests) Souchong to mix with them! [...]

[The] exchange [rate] still keeps up, 4 s. 10 d. [4 shillings and 10 pence], and most are of the opinion that it is going higher. I notice what you say about selling the bills first in case exchange may rise after the teas are bought; but it is just six of one and half a dozen of the other because you may sell your bills first and then tea may get up, and it is more subject to fluctuation than exchange is. A tael on a Tls 16 Congou makes a difference of 6%, a thing which frequently takes place, and sometimes double that, say

J. C. Heard painting of an East Indian merchantman approaching Bombay, 1850. Courtesy of Photos.com.

12%. In exchange there is seldom that change in a month; besides you must remember the risk of keeping dollars here. The Bank won't take them and all you have to depend on is some secured Chinaman, generally safe certainly, but still accidents will happen; a fire may take place and the mob plunder your treasury and a row may take place and you have to cut your lucky and leave all. You seem to think business can be done here with as much ease and security as in London or Edinburgh.

As for travelling, you must think our accommodation in that respect beats all railways. In one of your last you told me that I should have gone to Shanghai to buy a few chops of Congou which were not to be had in Canton and were to be had there, and that I was not justified in not going, no more than you would be if you got an order for a hogshead of London porter and did not go to London to execute the order in the event of it not being available in Edinburgh. So you compare a voyage to Shanghai to a ride in a railway coach to London—a voyage of 800 miles along the most dangerous coast in the world where, if you do happen to be wrecked and escape drowning, you are sure at least of being killed. Read about the crews of the *Nerbudda* and *Ann* and others. Read the China Mail about six weeks back only, about the crew of the *Larpent* on her way to Shanghai—only two men saved out of the whole crew, although all escaped shipwreck to be shot in the water, or beheaded on shore. And this you compare to starting after a comfortable supper and bottle of ale with your head well wrapped up, all ready for a nap in a railway carriage with seats as soft as a feather bed.

I wonder they do not have steamers from Hong Kong to Shanghai. They have taken off the one that used to ply and no word of another to be put on. Surely they will have one soon; the opium trade itself would pay a steamer.

Source: Melrose, William. *William Melrose in China, 1845–1855: The Letters of a Scottish Tea Merchant.* Edited by Hoh-cheung Mui and Lorna H. Mui. Edinburgh: T. and A. Constable, 1973. Courtesy of the Scottish History Society.

13. "Refusenik" Soviet Jews and Emigration

The creation of the state of Israel in 1948 prompted perhaps the largest emigration of Jews in history. Many Jews living in Arab countries and regions, such as the North African coast, left for Israel; in Europe, many Jews who survived the Holocaust *fled to Israel. Many Jews living within the* Union of Soviet Socialist Republics *(USSR), however, were not allowed to leave.*

The history of Jews within the Russian and subsequent Soviet Empire has been a difficult one. The Russian Empire was no exception to the anti-Semitism that existed across Europe. Before the Russian Revolution *of 1917, Jews were confined to a region called the Pale of Settlement, and only a certain number of Jews were given government permission to receive a higher education or live in capital cities. The Russians invented the word "pogrom," which means a violent repression focused on an ethnic or religious group, especially Jews. After the Russian Revolution, despite the Soviet government's claims to have established freedom of religion and ethnic equality in the USSR, Jews continued to be discriminated against and were often refused permission to leave.*

The following documents include a report written by Soviet authorities explaining why permission to emigrate should be denied, a letter written by a Jew in the Ukraine, *a republic of the USSR, to the Secretary-General of the United Nations (from whose hands it found its way to Soviet authorities), and a report on the problem of pro-emigration sentiment and the state's efforts to counteract it. The Soviet policy of refusing exit visas to Jews who wished to emigrate became an international issue in the 1960s and 1970s, with the term "refusenik" being coined to describe those who were not allowed to leave. A large number applied after the 1967 Arab-Israeli War, and were refused.*

Permission was often denied on the grounds that the émigré had at one time had access to sensitive or secret information, as is the case with Aleksandr Abramovich. In many cases, the information or technology possessed by would-be émigrés was insignificant, but still provided an excuse for repression. Simply applying to emigrate would often result in being dismissed from one's job and having other social and cultural pressures applied. The act of asking to leave the Soviet Union was a political and social taboo—even potentially a crime. Zionism *itself was viewed as anti-Soviet; the Soviet Union viewed culture from the point of view of economic class, not an ethnic or religious one. Since the process took months, and applications at most points in time usually were refused, trying to emigrate was a serious risk. Yet thousands did so, even from the upper levels of society, as Kapto's report points out.*

25 November 1967
Secret
To CPU CC [Communist Party of the Ukraine Central Committee]
Re No. 62/2662/01 of 6 November 1967

We hereby report that citizen Aleksandr Mikhailovich Abramovich—born in 1913, a native of the city of Novosibirsk, a Jew, citizen of the USSR, not a party member, in the past a CPSU [Communist Party of the Soviet Union] member (expelled from the party in 1959 for loss of membership card), married, in possession of a higher education, a lieutenant-colonel in the reserves—works as a construction engineer at the building material factory in Ivano-Frankovsk and lives in the city of Ivano-Frankovsk on 59 Moskovska Street, apartment no. 4. In the last three years he has been actively pursuing the goal of emigrating from the Soviet Union to Israel or to another capitalist country.

Abramovich's family is composed of four persons: Matelia Iankeleevna, wife, born in 1916 in the city of Liubash in the Minsk Oblast of the Belorussian Soviet Socialist Republic, a Jewess, works as a copy machine operator at the building material factory. Irina Aleksandrovna, daughter, born in 1939, a Moscow native, Jewess, has a technical high school education and works as a foreman at the research factory of the Scientific Research Institute of Computerized Control Equipment and lives in the city of Severo-Donetsk in the Lugansk Oblast. Elena Aleksandrovna Abramovich, born in 1948, a native of Donetsk, has a high school education and lives with her parents.

Citizen Abramovich graduated from the physics department of the University of Leningrad in 1937, after which he enlisted in the Soviet army and enrolled in the F.E. Dzerzhinskii Military Artillery Academy. After graduating he received the diploma of a military mechanical engineer of radio engineering and precision instruments.

During his entire service in the Soviet army, from 1937 to 1955, he was a lecturer on military instruments in military schools in the cities of Tula, Leningrad and Zhitomir. In addition, he worked in an industrial institute. This institute has a series of publications and patents in secret military technology of which he is the author.

Abramovich is anti-Soviet and has Zionist leanings. He calumniates Soviet reality, expresses treacherous views and is described by his colleagues as a chicanerer and a slanderer.

In 1965, 1966 and 1967 Abramovich sent almost two and a half thousand complaints and appeals to party and Soviet organs, to CPSU CC and CPU CC members, to USSR and UkSSR [Ukrainian Soviet Socialist Republic] Supreme Soviet [highest Soviet legislative body] members and to all the embassies in Moscow, in which he persistently pleaded to be given permission to emigrate from the Soviet Union. Lacking any grounds for emigrating from the Soviet Union to Israel, Abramovich presents his religious persuasions as his motive.

The Abramovich family is well-to-do. All the family members are working. They have a three-room flat and their own light motor vehicle.

Considering that Abramovich is of an anti-Soviet and nationalist disposition, is privy to military and economic secrets and may know of the location of highly classified installations on the territory of Ivano-Frankovsk Oblast, the obkom [regional committee of the Communist Party] considers his emigration, together with family members, to be out of the question.

Reply to the author of the letter was submitted
Secretary, Ivano-Frankovsk Obkom
I. Mitiura
Kharkov, 11 May 1970

...

TO UN SECRETARY-GENERAL U THANT,
TO THE REPRESENTATIVES OF THE GREAT POWERS
AT THE FOUR-POWER MEETINGS ON THE MIDDLE EAST

I understand very well that at a time when the UN is powerless to solve the problems of entire peoples, an individual person has little hope of focusing attention on his fate, even if that fate is a reflection of some of the century's great events.

Compared to those who are dying in Indochina, starving in Eastern Nigeria or languishing in prisons in numerous countries around the world, there is no great tragedy in my life. I received a higher education and I have a job and a family. Why, in my situation, should I disturb the world's conscience?

I do not expect sympathy or help from those who think that it is sufficient to guarantee a person a minimum or maximum level of material well being. I turn to you in the hope that you share the conviction that the conscience, the national sentiment and the spiritual condition of a person, no less than his life and physical freedom, deserves the attention and protection of international organizations and world opinion. I am a Jew—not a member of the Russian intelligentsia nor a Soviet citizen of Jewish origin—but a Jew first and foremost. A Jew by birth and, to a considerable degree, by upbringing and on the basis of my world view as well. [...]

Since childhood I have felt completely void of national feeling when I think of Russia and Russian history.... I am in Russia, this is Kharkov, Moscow... How did I come to be here? How was I born here? My paternal grandfather was born in Poland. My maternal grandfather was from Lithuania where they were merchants and rabbis, having originally come from Holland. I must continue on my way. My true motherland is already somewhere close by. Why are they detaining me?

I want to go to Israel. I have wanted to go there all my life, ever since I was 13 or 14, once I learned that we were Jews and that the country of Israel is our historic motherland. The conviction that we must return and revive our state was my first thought after learning of the catastrophe which befell us eighteen centuries ago and the consequent exile. There was no one around me who could have suggested such an idea, and I knew nothing about the existence of Zionism. In my mind there is no simpler or more natural idea. When the state of Israel was founded in 1948 I was 21 years old, my sole desire was to go there. [...]

I was imprisoned for ten years by a decision made in my absence by the Special Commission (a punitive organ in existence during the period of Stalin's personality cult). I was confined in special camps in Kolyma.

In 1956 I was released "due to the inexpediency of my further detention"—I was freed by a commission of the Presidum of the Supreme Soviet of the USSR. Before delivering the decision to release me, the chairman's final question to me was, "And what is your attitude now to the State of Israel?" I remarked that I would always remain faithful to the people and State of Israel. The conversation was recorded by a stenographer.

After the Six Day War, in 1968 I once again had an opportunity to confirm my allegiance to Israel in the presence of representatives of Soviet organs. In 1969 my request for an exit visa to Israel on the basis of an invitation by relatives was rejected.

I am turning to you in the hope that my yoke will be heard and that I shall be able to fulfill my life's desire. [...]

In conclusion, I want to say that my desire to leave for Israel is not in protest against Soviet life. I can affirm with all responsibility that neither in Russia nor in any other country of the world was there ever, nor could there ever be, a society for which I would be willing to reject Israel. For, "If I forget thee, O Jerusalem..."

With respect,
Elfim Haim' Spivakovskii
Krasnoznamennaia St., No.16,
Block 1, Apt. 5, Kharkov, USSR

...

REPORT OF THE UKRAINE COMMUNIST PARTY CENTRAL COMMITTEE SECRETARY, O.S. KAPTO, ON INTENSIFICATION OF THE STRUGGLE AGAINST ANTI-SOVIET ZIONIST PROPAGANDA AND PREVENTING PRO-EMIGRATION ATTITUDES AMONG A CERTAIN SECTOR OF THE REPUBLIC'S JEWISH POPULATION

A study of the implementation of the CPSU Central Committee's resolution "Measures for Further Exposure of the Reactionary Essence of International Zionism and Anti-Soviet Zionist Propaganda" and the relevant resolution of the CPU Central

Committee indicated that party committees in the republic have begun to deal more concretely with these issues and to address them more frequently at their meetings. Several organizational measures have been implemented. Commissions of the Central Committee and party obkoms that are concerned with foreign policy propaganda and the ideological struggle have begun operations. A sector has been established in the division of propaganda and agitation of the CPSU Central Committee that is entrusted with coordinating all counter-propaganda work. One official in the Department of Propaganda and Agitation of each party obkom is now specializing in problems of counter-propaganda.

In the Higher Party School of the CPU Central Committee two-year courses have been organized to train lecturers to speak on the struggle against bourgeois nationalism and Zionism. Groups of lecturers prepared to speak on this issue have been organized in the lecture sections of party obkoms and of gorkoms [city committees of the Communist Party], as well as under the auspices of the boards of the UkSSR Znanie [Knowledge] Society and its regional organizations. The training of members of these groups has been organized. An ongoing republic-wide seminar, Patriotic and internationalist education of the workers and an intensification of the struggle against international Zionism, has been established. The materials used in this seminar are being published in separate booklets for official use.

A division for a critique of the ideology and policy of bourgeois nationalism is operating at the UkSSR Academy of Sciences Institute of Social and Economic Studies of Foreign Countries. It has been resolved that from the start of the new academic year several institutes of the UkSSR Academy of Sciences and institutions of higher learning in the republic will offer graduate training to students that specialize in a critique of the ideology and policy of international Zionism.

There has been improvement in the coordination of the mass media efforts to expose subversive anti-Soviet propaganda. Republic newspapers and journals, as well as television and radio, are generating statements that address these issues on the basis of coordinated quarterly plans. Goskomizdat [Government publishing authority] has worked out a long-term plan for producing literature on the struggle against international Zionism.

At the same time, an analysis indicates that the assertiveness and, even more so, the effectiveness of counter-propaganda work remains low, and there are serious shortcomings in the way it is organized. [. . .]

The number of emigrants leaving for capitalist countries has grown in recent years. Whereas from 1970 to 1977 an average of 5,000 to 6,000 Jews left the republic annually—principally to Israel—in 1978 alone about 11,500 left. In the first half of the present year the number is close to 9,000. The greatest number of emigrants comes from the Kiev, Odessa, Chernovtsy, Transcarpathia and Lvov Oblasts: in 1978 a total of 12,500 persons left the republic, 10,500 of them coming from those areas. Over 9,000 of them went to Israel. The strongest pro-emigration sentiment is manifested by Jews employed in the spheres of commerce, consumer services, medicine, science, and culture.

In the past three years alone, 625 teachers have emigrated, including 280 from Odessa Oblast and 110 from Chernovtsy Oblast. In the past year-and-a-half over 100 applications for exit visas have been received from teachers in Odessa music schools.

In the past six years, 14 members of the UkSSR Artists Union, 40 workers of organizations supervised by the UkSSR Art Fund and eight workers of the Kiev Art Institute, including holders of Ph.D. degrees left the republic. In the past seven years, 82 persons who worked in the republic's film studios emigrated to Israel and other capitalist countries.

The number of persons leaving the country who work in the republic's medical institutes and medical institutions has increased. About 2,000 left between 1971 and July 1979; 425 left in the first six months of this year. Among those who emigrated were two persons with post-doctoral degrees, 27 with Ph.D.s, 790 with a higher education, 108 former members of the CPSU and 83 former Komsomol members. [...]

An organized effort to prepare individuals of Jewish nationality for departure abroad has been noted. They enroll in foreign language courses, acquire specialties that are in demand and so forth. For example, among the 565 individuals of Jewish nationality studying in the English division courses in Kiev, over 200 received invitations to leave for Israel or other capitalist countries. The majority of those attending do not need knowledge of a foreign language to fulfill work responsibilities. However, they present the relevant certification from their place of work, often signed by individuals who do not have the right to sign.

A. Kapto
CPU CC Secretary

Source: Khanin, Vladimir. *Documents on Ukrainian-Jewish Identity and Emigration, 1944–1990*.

Part IV
INTELLECTUAL LIFE

The intellectual aspect of daily life is both broad and vital to the human experience. Sometimes it is easy to look at the changes in the modern world and see first the material changes in technology and infrastructure, communications and computers. It is important to remember that the capacity to create all these things comes from the human mind. It is important to remember that ideas, while hard to see, have just as significant an impact on the daily lives of people as material things do.

The *modern* period witnessed the rise of new, very successful types of education at different levels, including mass public education and the evolution of the modern university. Frederick the Great's instructions (Document 1) and Amasa Moore's letters (Document 2) show both of these modern systems in their early stages. Education, though, is not synonymous with academic instruction. It includes schooling, but in its broader meaning it concerns the basic formation of a person's knowledge, as well as beliefs, customs, attitudes, conscience, and so forth. In this more general sense, education can be seen as one of the linchpins of intellectual life. J. Robert Oppenheimer (Document 7) and his fellow scientists' ability to build a nuclear weapon, Percy Bysshe Shelley's (Document 14) passionate defense of the value of poetry, and Edward *Jenner*'s (Document 9) insights into how to prevent smallpox in millions: all of these documents reflect in their own way the educations of their respective authors.

The widespread application of the scientific method is a central part of the development of modern life. Science has proven to be a dominant intellectual paradigm and a powerful tool for creating and evaluating knowledge. Montesquieu's experiments (Document 4) with sheep tongues heralded the beginning of social sciences in the Enlightenment, and Samuel Wilson's positivism (Document 5) and Frederick Winslow Taylor's (Document 6) management systems show how flexible, dynamic, and pervasive scientific methodology has become in the modern world. Medicine's achievements are based largely on the application of science-based research to medical practices, from Jenner's promotions of the first reliable vaccines in the eighteenth century to the international fight against Human Immunodeficiency Virus (HIV) in the twenty-first century.

In the world of art and literature, there have also been dramatic changes. If modern education, science, and medicine have helped shape ideas and institutions, so have the arts. The support of a wealthy patron has been displaced by the public exhibition or museum as the primary locations for the consumption of art, and art itself has been through profound changes. In a similar way, expanding literacy has created mass audiences and transformed the scope and styles of literature. William Gilpin's (Document 18) theory of the picturesque shares the basic impulses of *Romanticism* with Shelley's defense of poetry and is a far cry from Kazimir Malevich's (Document 19) radical manifesto, but all of them seek to lead society to new ways of seeing, feeling, and understanding the everyday world around us, a task that artists and writers only consciously assumed in the modern period.

In fact, critical consciousness is another hallmark of modern intellectual life, as art and literature lead contemporary culture to continually question many of the ideas and institutions it has created. Vitaly Komar and Alex Melamid (Document 20) teaching elephants to paint questions the premises of modern art; Oppenheimer is deeply concerned about the uses of atomic science; David Crystal (Document 16) warns that the dominance of several globalizing languages threatens the loss of the thousands of unique viewpoints encoded in dying languages. All the fields of intellectual life—education, art, language, literature, science, and medicine—have changed radically in the modern period and developed unique modern institutions and forms, and no account of modern daily life is complete, or even possible, without them.

Education

Education is as old as humans, but it is not the same thing as formal instruction. The oldest educational institutions in the Western world are European universities, the oldest of which trace their origins to the thirteenth, fourteenth, and fifteenth centuries. Before the modern era, primary and secondary education was the province of private tutors and religious institutions. Only in the eighteenth century did the idea of government-sponsored public education arise, and it did not become widespread for another 100 years. Even today, millions of children do not have the chance to go to school. In his instructions for education in eighteenth-century *Prussia*, the eastern German state around which modern-day Germany was formed in 1871, Frederick the Great (Document 1) offers a strict regimen for Prussian schools. Virtually every aspect of the school day, down to the smallest details, was spelled out in Frederick's regulations.

In Europe, public educational systems such as Frederick's were designed to train disciplined, informed citizens with the skills and knowledge to function in European societies. However, as Europeans spread to control large parts of Asia, Africa, and America they brought their education systems with them, along with the belief that they had an obligation not only to rule the peoples who lived in these places, but also to educate and civilize them. At the end of the nineteenth century, Mary Kingsley (Document 3) pointed out that what worked well and may have been appropriate to England, France, Germany, or the United States, did not necessarily fit so well in Africa, where education had historically been conducted in a much less formal way and created and sustained rich cultures—though cultures that were vastly different from those of Europe.

Amasa Moore's (Document 2) perspective is not that of an educator looking at the system from the outside, but of a student at a small American college who is seeing things from the inside. Less directly concerned with the merits of the educational system than the practical needs of being a part of it, Moore offers a look at the many challenges facing a young college student seeking a higher education in the early years of the American nation.

Frederick the Great wanted to assure a basic level of moral and intellectual formation for all his subjects. Kingsley critiques the attempts of missionaries and other Europeans to inculcate European ideas in colonial subjects. Moore's higher education would induct him into a class of elites with privileged knowledge and skills that would set him apart from most of the population. Globally, less than one percent of people today have a college degree, so Moore's elite status still remains, although basic and higher academic education is far more widespread. This expansion of educational systems in the modern world has been one of the many changes in education in the last 300 years, as those systems both create and reflect the changing nature of everyday life in the modern world.

1. Origins of Public Education: Frederick the Great's Regulations for Prussian Schools

When most people think of education in the modern world, they think of government-sponsored public schools supported by taxes providing universal compulsory instruction. It strikes most people as reasonable that the education of the entire population is desirable and important enough to devote a significant amount of social resources to it and to delegate this responsibility to the state. This idea, however, is very much a modern notion. Before the modern era, most instruction below the collegiate level was the province of private tutors hired by wealthier families or was provided by clergy or other religious institutions. Literacy was unusual outside the upper classes.

Many of the changes in the modern world, such as the growth of centralized state power, the development of participatory government, new ideas about the nature of humans and their relationship to the world, and developing technological and demographic changes, made public education an increasingly appealing and attractive idea. Frederick the Great, king of the German state of Prussia *from 1740 to 1786, was one of the first rulers to see the advantages of using the state's resources to create a well-trained and virtuous population. He established the first national system of public schools and wrote many of the regulations for their operation himself. The following selection is an excerpt from his instructions, issued in 1763, which strictly regimented and ordered the course of instruction. Much of the basic curricular content is still familiar today, including reading, writing, and arithmetic, with the addition of compulsory moral and religious education that was seen as at least as important as any other part of the curriculum.*

In issuing these regulations that created the first system of compulsory public schools run by a government in Europe, Frederick laid the foundations, both in conceiving the state's role in education and articulating the basic institutional structures for the modern education systems of virtually every Western and industrialized nation around the world.

General School Regulations, August 12, 1763.

We Frederick, *by the grace of God, King, etc.:*

Whereas, to our great displeasure, we have perceived that schools and the instruction of youth in the country have come to be greatly neglected, and that by the inexperience of many sacristans and schoolmasters, the young people grow up in stupidity and ignorance, it is our well considered and serious pleasure, that instruction in the country, throughout all our provinces, should be placed on a better footing, and be better organized than heretofore. For, as we earnestly strive for the true welfare of our country, and of all classes of people; now that quiet and general peace have been restored, we find it necessary and wholesome to have a good foundation laid in the schools by a rational and Christian education of the young for the fear of God and other useful ends. Therefore, by the power of our own highest motive, of our care and paternal disposition for the best good of all our subjects, we command hereby, all governors, consistories and other collegiates of our country; that they shall, on their part, contribute all they can, with affection and zeal, to maintain the following General School Regulations, and in future to arrange all things in accordance with the law to the end that ignorance, so injurious and unbecoming to Christianity, may be prevented and lessened, and the coming time may train and educate in the schools more enlightened and virtuous subjects.

Section 1. First, it is our pleasure that all our subjects, parents, guardians or masters, whose duty it is to educate the young, shall send their children to school, and those confided to their care, boys and girls, if not sooner, certainly when they reach the age of five years; and shall continue regularly to do so, and require them to go to school until they are thirteen or fourteen years old, and know not only what is necessary of Christianity, fluent reading and writing, but can give answer in everything which they learn from the school books, prescribed and approved by our consistory.

§2. Masters to whom children in Prussia, by custom are bound to render work for certain years, are seriously advised not to withdraw such children from school until they can read well, and have laid a good foundation in Christian knowledge; also made a beginning in writing, and can present a certificate from the minister and school master to this effect to the school-visitors. Parents and guardians ought much more to consider it their bounden duty that their children and wards receive sufficient instruction in the necessary branches. [...]

§12. Since the chief requisite in a good school is a competent and faithful teacher, it is our gracious and earnest will, that one and all, who have the right of appointment, shall take heed to bring only well qualified persons into office as teachers and sacristans. A schoolmaster should not only possess the necessary attainments and skill in instruction, but should be an example to the children, and not tear down by his daily life what he builds up by his teaching. He should therefore strive after godliness, and guard against everything which might give offence or temptation to parents or children. Above all things, he should endeavor to obtain a correct knowledge of God and of Christ, thereby laying a foundation to honest life and true Christianity, and feeling that they are entrusted with their office from God, as followers of the Saviour, and in it have an opportunity, by diligence and good example, not only to render the children happy in the present life, but also to prepare them for eternal blessedness. [...]

§17. The daily work of the school should begin with prayer to the Giver of all good gifts, that He will send His divine blessing on their work, and give them a heart full of tenderness and sincerity towards the children entrusted to their care, that may do willingly and without passion all that is incumbent upon them as teachers; being always reminded that they can have no influence over children, nor win their hearts without the divine assistance of Jesus, the friend of children, and of His holy spirit. During the instructions they should devoutly pray that they may not only keep their minds composed, but that God will bless their work, and to planting and watering graciously give His increase.

Teachers should also devise various means to win the confidence of young pupils, especially of the bashful and slow, and to render their task easy. To this end, they should make themselves familiar with the third part of the "*Berlin Schoolbook*," by which all the elementary branches are successfully taught. [...]

§19. The order of school shall be thus:

In the first hour of the morning they will—

First. Sing a hymn, the words being slowly pronounced by the schoolmaster, and sung by the children after him. Every month, but one hymn, designated by the clergyman, and not too long or unfamiliar, shall be learned and sung, in order that the old and young may remember the words and tune by frequent repetition. While singing, the teacher must see that all participate, and no child should be permitted to hold open the hymnbook and sing from it, but all should be required to follow him.

Second. After the hymn, a prayer shall be offered, either by the master, or one of the pupils may be allowed to read slowly and distinctly a prescribed prayer, while the rest join in silence. Then all should directly offer up a common prayer, learned by heart; and after the reading of psalm for the month by one of the pupils, the devotional exercise should close with the Lord's prayer. Any tardy children must wait at the door until the prayer is ended, in order not to disturb the others.

Third. After prayer such a portion of the catechism is explained that in every six weeks the book is gone through. In this exercise the following method should be adopted: The portion to be interpreted must be read by the children until it is familiar to most of them. Then the words and their meaning are explained, by questions and answers, and verified by passages from the Scriptures; and finally the children should be told how to apply the truth of what they hear to practical life. For little children Luther's smaller catechism should be used; for the more advanced the clergyman and schoolmaster should use the larger catechism with interpretations.

During the remaining hours of the morning, exercises in reading, spelling, and the ABCs should follow according to the proficiency of the pupils.

(1.) In the first half hour the advanced pupils read a chapter from the Old or New Testament, sometimes together, sometimes a certain portion of the class, alternating with a single pupil, as the teacher may designate to keep the order and attention of all alive.

(2.) The next half hour is devoted to spelling, either by the entire class in concert or each child alone. Sometimes a word is written on the "tafel" (*blackboard*), which all are required to spell and pronounce. During this lesson with the younger pupils the older are practiced in finding passages of Scripture or hymns in the hymnbook; or they commit to memory verses and the names of Biblical books in their succession, that they may become ready in consulting the Scriptures.

(3.) The next hour is devoted to the ABC classes, with copying on their tablets one or two letters from the larger tablet, the teacher often calling them to name the letters, or show them on their slates, while he is hearing an advanced class spell, or attending to their writing, which last is in this wise:

(1.) The larger children write during the first half of the third hour, when their work is inspected and corrected in the next half hour. That no child may be neglected, the teacher keeps a list of the scholars, who present their copy-books in succession, and he continues the next day where he left off. In this manner every child will have his book returned and corrected several times each week.

Here it should be remarked, that the left side of the copy-book should be written and corrected first, and the scholar should re-write the same exercise on the right-hand page, free of the errors pointed out by the teacher.

(2.) While the larger pupils are writing, the spelling class is to be exercised and made familiar with the rules of reading, and the powers of letters. While the larger scholars have their copies corrected, the spelling class may now and then recite their Bible-verse for the week. Towards the end of the third morning-hour, the whole school is called to prayer, after which the teacher reads the psalm or part of the hymn designated for the season, and then the pupils are quietly dismissed. The master looks to their behavior in going home, that carelessness and wickedness may not dissipate the instructions of the morning.

During the first hour of the afternoon the whole school is occupied with the teacher, and after singing some verses and reading a psalm, they are taught biblical history and the "Manual for the instruction of children in country-schools."

The second hour of the afternoon, the classes alternately learn portions of the catechism. This may be done after the method shown in the third part of the Berlin Reader, by writing down the first letters, or in the following manner:

(1.) The teacher reads repeatedly, slowly and distinctly, the portion which the children are to commit, while the pupils follow in the open book mentally. Then the children read the exercises in concert, while the middle and spelling class listen.

(2.) After this is done, the teacher reads aloud from comma to comma, while the children repeat until they know it by heart; then he proceeds with the next paragraph in the same manner, explaining the Bible phraseology of the catechism, which the children learn together. As regards the interpretation of Luther's catechism, the larger children will learn that by frequent repetition; the middle class, and the small pupils meanwhile listening attentively. After the first class has in concert repeated the lesson a few times, the teacher indicates the individuals to recite the lesson from memory, and thus he satisfies himself as to their mastery of it.

(3.) Finally each class recites its weekly Bible-verse, varying in length according to the age of the pupils. In this manner children generally learn the portions of the catechism and Christian Doctrine in their proper connection, together with their Bible-verses, a psalm and a hymn every month.

The next half hour, the larger children attend to reading, the middle class to spelling, and the lower class to their letters, as in the morning.

During the third and last hour of the afternoon, the first class shall write and cipher; while the middle class continue their spelling, and the little children the A,B,C.

On Saturday, instead of the catechism in the first hour of the morning, the children will repeat the Bible-verses, psalms and hymns they have learned, of which the teacher keeps a memorandum. Then, from week to week, he relates to them a history from the Old or New Testament, explains the same and shows its application to life and conduct.

For the older children he may use the Biblical chart, to aid them in more perfectly understanding the Holy Scriptures. After this they shall read the gospel or the epistle for the next Sunday. Next they write on their slate, of which the teacher corrects the orthography. At the conclusion of the school, the children shall be earnestly exhorted to behave well on Sunday; to be quiet and devotional at church; to listen and treasure up the word of God for their salvation.

The schoolmaster, during all the hours above designated, must be constantly with the children, and never be absent from school one hour, much less one day, without the knowledge of the pastor and the permission of his superiors, in which case he must in time provide another person to teach the school, that the young may not be neglected.

In large cities, and villages, where there is more than one class-room, it shall be reported by the inspectors and clergymen to our provincial consistory, which will regulate the order of lessons and method of instruction according to the conditions of the place.

Source: Barnard, Henry, ed. *Memoirs of Eminent Teachers and Educators with Contributions to the History of Education in Germany*. Rev. ed. Hartford, CT: Brown & Gross, 1878.

2. *College Life in Vermont in 1817*

A college education was a privilege reserved for relatively few in the eighteenth and early nineteenth centuries. In the days before financial aid programs, going to college was an expense only those who already had wealth could afford. A college education might be required for certain professions, such as lawyers, ministers, physicians, and, of course, professors, but not many others.

This selection is a previously unpublished letter from a student at Middlebury College in Middlebury, Vermont, to his father shortly after the student's arrival to begin his studies in 1817. Even though it was written nearly 200 years ago, many things are recognizable to students today: housing issues, buying books, fitting in, the underlying excitement and apprehension about being away from home, sharing with roommates, and even doing laundry. A major concern for Amasa Moore and his family, as for many students today, was money. Moore's father is evidently very concerned about costs; his son is aware he needs to account for virtually every penny he has spent—and he has spent virtually every penny his father has given him and is asking for more. He also tells stories of the happenings at school—in this case, the tragic death of one of the professors—who dies in Moore's own room.

At the same time, an American college in the late eighteenth and early nineteenth centuries was very different from a college today. Most were affiliated with religious groups and training ministers was a central task. Very few admitted women. Social life was more connected with educational life and groups like fraternities and sororities did not yet exist. Most colleges were very small by contemporary standards, with no more than a few hundred students, a handful of faculty, a small library, and limited facilities. In fact, the Philomathesian Society, a social and literary group Moore was encouraged to join, like most students at Middlebury did, had a better library than the college and existed to supplement the curriculum, rather than provide respite from its rigors. The university does not, as many do today, provide rooms or dining facilities for the students, and Moore must make his own arrangements.

Higher education in the United States and around the world has changed significantly in the modern period. Colleges and universities are much larger and more accessible, some with tens of thousands of students; have highly specialized faculty and billions of dollars in resources; and offer an immense range of degrees and training. For the students, alumni, and faculty of today, just as for Moore and his classmates and professors who went before them, education is a part of everyday life.

Middlebury Septem'r 27th 1817

Having been favored with a prosperous journey being partly settled in my room and partially initiated in this institution, I for the first time address you from Middlebury College. Not that on this account I should wish you to expect that my letters should be better composed written or more correct than they have been heretofore (because I have not yet had time to improve) but that I should give a true statement of my affairs as I was directed by Mama.

And this I will endeavor to do as near as I am able—as follows

I received $28.

Steamboat passage	$1.50
Trunk and bed portage, Supper, Lodging	$0.75
Stage passage	$2.50
Breakfast	$0.40
Tr'k and b'd portage to the College	$0.25
Total	$5.30
To Mr. Brown Cloth and trimmings	$9.50
To Room Rent	$6.00
To Books, a Greek Menora and Caesar	$2.00
To Crape for the funeral of Professor Allen	$0.12
To one Tenter box with a steel wheel	$0.75
To My share of procuring benches for our recitation room	$0.25
To getting one coat made	$4.00
Total	$27.92

All of which expenses I have conceived to have been perfectly necessary and therefore transmit them to your inspection. The Caesar & Greek Menora are the first two books which we study. One of them at the bookstore generally costs more than I gave for both—but One of the last freshman Class sold them to me. In the course of six or eight weeks Other books will be necessary.

As our lessons do not at present occupy all our time, our tutor has recommended to all of us to join the Phylomathesian society as soon as we possibly can because it has the best selection of books. Admittance is one dollar.

The price of wood here is $2 per Cord however my roommate gets the first cord or half cord.

I have inquired of a number of students what they gave for board and find the standard price to be $2.00. Professor Huff boards for that, he has now two boarders and they tell me that he does not wish to take more.

The Old Chapel of Middlebury College in Vermont. Library of Congress.

A Mr. Heart about the same distance from the College boards for the same price two dollars, he keeps several boarders and they all think it the best boarding house in town, he adapts his meal times to the convenience of his boarders who are all students and makes it a practice to have his meals in preparation at the ringing of the bells which is considered as no small convenience.

Whereas at my present boarding place I am oblieged frequently to wait an hiur for a meal, which not only puts me back in my studies but which may be the means of putting me behind in my class. It cannot be expected that at a public house where there is much company that the convenience of one student a regular boarder should be attended to.

A Stove would save much wood and much more comfortable than a fire place if you think it proper to send one. One joint of pipe and an elbow is all the pipe that is required as it must go in the fire place. I shall be obliegged to buy Soap, candles, wood, ink, quills, and paper, all of which my room mate at present supplies.

President Davis is now here, but the people are all up in arms against him, he offered to officiate in office while he remained here, his proposals were rejected by other officers.

Probably you have heard of that dreadful event which took place here on Tuesday last if not perhaps a short imperfect recital may not be uninteresting—as I have gathered it from the students.

Last Tuesday Professor Allen went on the top of the New College for the purpose of fixing some of the chimnies which smoked. To effect this he laid a plank across the college [building] from the top of one chimney to the other. He then laid a long pole which might be four or five inches through at one end and three or four at the other lengthways of the college extending from one chimney to another and a ladder was out up against the middle chimney. He then laid a board from the plank to the pole for a stageing. He placed one of his knees on the pole and the other on the board, and was in the act of nailing a board to the pole when the pole broke where there had been an augur hole boared. He fell on the roof, which is ten feet, and then slid slowly towards the edge of the roof, while in this situation he made some useless efforts to save himself and when he arrived at the edge caught hold of it and then looked to the scholars who were on the roof [rather] than at the pole which came rolling after and which instantaneaously precipitated him headlong to the ground. He struck on his head and shoulders and curled up in a heap.

The scholars descended in tumultuous haste jumping through and over the banisters from the top of the stairs to the bottom until they reached the ground. "Allen is dead" was reiterated from every tongue and thrilled through every breast with freezing horror. A general shriek from all present proclaimed to the inhabitants the misfortune. All within hearing rushed to the spot. The deepest interest, the greatest anxiety was depicted in every countenance.

Allen was taken up and conveyed to the room which I now occupy as there was no nearer bed—where he died the following night in extreme pain.

From the roof of the College to the ground is at least 40 feet and ten more to the top of the Chimney.

Professor Allen was allmost the idol of this town. But as I am unable to do him justice by recounting his merits I shall leave them for persons of better abilities to eulogize upon.

They cannot do my washing at Mr. Mattocks. Please tell Mama not to be concerned for fear that should lose my Cloaths on this account as I shall make a practice of write-ing down the number that send to be washed.

Give my love to all our family and friends
And be assured that shall ever remain
Your affectionate Son,
Amasa Moore

Source: Amasa Moore Papers. Courtesy of College Archives, Special Collections, Middlebury College.

3. Mary Kingsley: Colonialism and Education in Late Nineteenth-Century Africa

Mary Kingsley was an Englishwoman who spent several years traveling in Africa at the end of the nineteenth century. She became famous for her works describing African life and customs, her research in natural sciences, her enthusiasm for native African ways, and her controversial but well-informed criticisms of European colonial administration and education. Although she previously had never been outside of England for any significant time, she found her way to places in West Africa no European had been before, climbing mountains, canoeing up rivers, escaping crocodiles, and studying cannibalistic tribes in person.

In the following excerpt from her first book, she critiques the system of education that has been set up by various colonial powers as being impractical and misdirected. The subjects and curricula in colonial schools she sees as offering little of practical value to African students, both male and female, and in fact even doing them significant harm. While there is still an element of superiority to her tone, there is also a legitimate knowledge and respect for African cultures, customs, and institutions. She claimed that the attempts by Europeans, especially missionaries, to teach Africans using European models were having a cumulative negative effect. According to Kingsley, colonial instruction was disrupting native African educational and social systems and failing to replace them with a stable system of its own instead of bringing civilization and creating Europeanized African societies.

She does not reproach European colonialism, *nor does she seem to oppose the paternalistic attitudes toward African groups that is part of European colonization and domination, but instead she advocates European intervention and education that more directly addresses the needs of local populations and recognizes and respects the values and structures of*

African cultures and ways. Her influence in Britain was so great that some of her ideas were translated into changes in British colonial policies.

In some ways, she anticipated many of the criticisms leveled against European colonialism in the later twentieth century. Colonialism and its consequences are still central issues for Africa today, in education and many other areas. At the same time, that does not mean that pre-colonial life in Africa was utopian, or that there have been no benefits to instruction in modern European technologies, social sciences, religious beliefs, and other fields in Africa. Regardless, Kingsley's perspective raises questions about the role of education and modern life that are complex, to say the least.

It is regarded as futile to attempt to get any real hold over the children unless they are removed from the influence of the country fashions that surround them in their village homes; therefore the schools are boarding; hence the entire care of the children, including feeding and clothing, falls on the missionary.

The French government has made things harder by decreeing that the children should be taught French. It does not require that evangelistic work should be carried on in French, but that if foreign languages are taught, that language shall be French first. The general feeling of the missionaries is against this, because of the great difficulty in teaching the native this delicate and highly complex language. English, the Africans pick up sooner than any foreign language.... Indeed, I believe that if the missionary was left alone he would not teach any European language, but confine himself to using the native languages in its phonetically written-down form; because the Africans learn to read this very quickly, and the missionary can confine their reading to those books he thinks suitable for perusal by his flock—namely, the Bible, hymn-books, and Bunyan's *Holy War.*

The native does not see things in this light, and half the time comes only to learn, what he calls "sense," *i.e.* white man's ways and language, which will enable him to trade with greater advantage. Still, I think the French government is right, from what I have seen in our own possessions of the disadvantage, expense, and inconvenience of the bulk of the governed not knowing the language of their governors, both parties having therefore frequently to depend on native interpreters; and native interpreters are "deceitful above all things and desperately wicked" occasionally, and the just administration of the country under these conditions is almost impossible.

You may say, Why should not the government official learn the native language like the missionary? and I think government officials who are settled like missionaries on the Coast should do so, but if you enforced this rule in Congo Français, where the government officials fly to and fro, Mezzofantis [from Cardinal Giuseppe Mezzofanti, a famous polyglot] only need apply for appointments. Take the Gaboon district, to use the hand, but not obsolete division of the colony. This district, being the seaboard one, is where most of the dealings with the natives occur. In my small way I have met there with representatives of tribes speaking Shekani, Balungi, M'benga, M'billo, M'pongwe, Bakele, Ncomi, Igalwa, Adooma, Ajumba, and Fan, and there are plenty more. Neither are any of these tribes neatly confined to distinct districts, so that you might teach your unfortunate official one language, and then tie him down in one place, where he could use it. Certain districts have a preponderance of certain tribes, but that is all. The Fans are everywhere in the northern districts of the Ogowé: but among them, in the districts below Lembarene, you will find Igalwa and Ajumba villages, side by side, with likely enough just across the stream a Bakele one. Above Talagouga, until you get to Boué, you could get along with Fan alone; but there is no government rule that requires languages up there because, barring keeping the Ogowé open to the French flag, it is not interfered with; and then when you get up to Franceville above Boué, there is quite another group of languages, Okota, Batoke, Adooma, &c., &c., and the Middle Congo languages. To require a knowledge of all these languages would be absurd, and necessitate the multiplication of officials to an enormous extent.

But to return to the Mission Évangélique schools. This mission does not undertake technical instruction. All the training the boys get is religious and scholastic. The girls fare somewhat better, for they get in addition instruction from the mission ladies in sewing, washing, and ironing, and for the rest of it they have an uncommonly pleasant and easy time, which they most bitterly regret as past when they go to their husbands, for husbands they each of them have.

It is strange that no technical instruction is given by any government out here. All of the governments support mission schools by grants: but the natives turned out by the schools are at the best only fit for clerks, and the rest of the world seems to have got a glut of clerks already, and Africa does not want clerks yet; it wants planters—I do not say only plantation hands, for I am sure from what I have seen in Cameroons of the self-taught native planters there, that intelligent Africans could do an immense amount to develop the resources of the country. The Roman Catholic mission and Landana carries on great work in giving agricultural instruction in improved methods: but most of the other technical mission stations confine their attention to teaching carpentering, bricklaying, smith's work, tailoring, bookbinding and prints, trades which, save the two first named, Africa is not yet in urgent need to be taught.

The teaching even of sewing, washing, and ironing is a little previous. Good Mme. Jacot will weary herself for months to teach a Fan girl how to make herself a dress, and the girl will learn eagerly, and so keenly enjoy the dress when it is made that it breaks one's heart when one knows that this same girl, when her husband takes her to his village soon, in spite of the two dresses the mission gave her, will be reduced to a bit of filthy rag, which will serve her for dress, sheet, towel and dish cloth; for even were her husband willing to get her more cloth to exercise her dressmaking accomplishments on, he dare not. Men are men, and women are women all the world over; and what would his other wives, and his mother and sisters say? Then the washing and ironing are quite parlour accomplishments when your husband does not wear a shirt, and household linen is non-existent as is the case among the Fans and many other African tribes. There are other things that the women might be taught with greater advantage to them and those round them. [...]

Nothing strikes one so much, in studying the degeneration of these native tribes, as the direct effect that civilization and reformation has in hastening it. The worst enemy to the existence of the African tribe, is the one who comes to it and says:—Now you must civilize, and come to school, and leave off all those awful goings-on of yours, and settle down quietly. The tribe does so; the African is teachable and tractable; and then the ladies and some of the young men are happy and content with the excitement of

European clothes and frequent Church services; but the older men and some of the bolder young men soon get bored with these things and the, to them, irksome restraints, and they go in for too much rum, or mope themselves to death, or return to their native customs. The African treats his religion much as other men do: when he gets slightly educated, a little scientific one might say, he removes from his religion all the disagreeable parts. He promptly eliminates its equivalent Hell, represented in Fetishism by immediate and not future retribution. Then goes his rigid Sabbath-keeping, and food-restriction equivalent and he has nothing left but the agreeable portions; dances, polygamy, and so on; and it's a very bad thing for him. I only state these things so as to urge upon people at home the importance of combining technical instruction in their mission teaching which by instilling into the African mind ideas of discipline, and providing him with manual occupation, will save him from these relapses which are now the reproach of missionary effort, and the curse and degradation of the African.

Source: Kingsley, Mary H. *Travels in West Africa: Congo Français, Corisco and Cameroons*. London: Macmillan and Company, Ltd., 1897.

Science

Science has developed remarkably in the modern period. Although the scientific method was being worked out before the modern era began, the full effects of science as a way of understanding and exploring the world have become an integral part of daily life in the modern world. Science has altered how we know and describe ourselves and the world around us, and it is most often to science that people turn for real knowledge. Science, though, is a method of learning and knowing, and in many areas it has taken time for science to learn about things. Well into the modern period, ideas like substantial ether (a substance that filled in all the empty space in the universe) or abiogenesis (the propagation of life from decaying materials, such as maggots from meat, mice from hay, and so on) that have been discarded by science were still commonly held.

The field of applicability of the scientific method has only expanded in the modern period. The eighteenth-century movement called the *Enlightenment* took the method that had had such success in the beginning to describe the physical world and began to apply its method to the analysis and understanding of human society. Montesquieu (Document 4) offered an analogy between human governments and thawing sheep tongues under a microscope. While not credible today, Montesquieu's need to support his theories on politics with natural science shows that the application of the scientific method was spreading beyond its original scope. This trend is also evident with scientific management or *Taylorism* (Document 6), which attempted to apply science to industry, and give human workers a mechanical, machine-like efficiency.

For some, like Samuel Wilson (Document 5), there seemed little that science could not know, and varieties of scientific *Positivism* developed by Auguste *Comte* and others in the nineteenth and twentieth centuries became increasingly popular as new discoveries in science seemed to indicate the possibility of victory over all the mysteries of the universe and the rejection of ways of understanding the world based in faith or pure thought. The twentieth century also saw many scientists and others begin to confront the negative potential of scientific knowledge, as scientists like Albert *Einstein* and

J. Robert Oppenheimer (Document 7) not only discovered the secrets of the atom and the relationship between matter and energy, but gave humanity the capacity to destroy itself through its own scientific accomplishments. Among other factors, applications of science in the events of the twentieth century caused many to question the assumptions of the benevolent progress of science and its advances in knowledge and human capacities.

In contrast with the positivism of Wilson and others, late twentieth-century science has witnessed the introduction of some scientific acknowledgement of the limits of positive scientific knowledge, with emerging ideas like fuzzy math, chaos theory, and string theory. Some scientists and scientific ideas have sought to recognize that science may have limits in what it can know. Even if science does seem to see some limits, its potential to influence everyday life seems not yet to have reached them; science is responsible for an extraordinary amount of knowledge about the world, and the scientific method is one of the most dominant ideas in human intellectual life in the modern age.

4. Montesquieu on Sex and Sheep's Tongues

Charles de Secondat, Baron de Montesquieu, was one of the foremost political minds of the eighteenth century. His most important publication, from which this selection is taken, called The Spirit of the Laws, *is a monumental work on history, law, politics, and social theory. His work was highly influential among political thinkers of the time, including the founders of the United States; the U.S. Constitution's principle of separation of powers, for example, is directly attributable to Montesquieu's influence on James Madison and other framers. Because Montesquieu was known as a political theorist and social satirist, it might seem odd to find him included in the section on science; however, it is the connections that Montesquieu and others of his time made between scientific methods and political and social thought that make him appropriate here.*

The Enlightenment *saw an important shift in the scope of scientific thought. If, in the sixteenth and seventeenth centuries, science had emerged as a powerful method of learning and knowing about the physical universe and challenged the explanations of ancient wisdom and religious doctrines, in the eighteenth century, those same scientific methods began to be applied not only to the physical world, but also to the social world as well. In this sense, the era saw the beginning of what are today called the social sciences. Adam Smith founded modern economics; Jean-Jacques* Rousseau *laid out influential plans for the education of children. Montesquieu formulated an alternative to monarchical or despotic governments. As part of his research, he watched a frozen sheep tongue thaw under a microscope—and then wrote about politics.*

Montesquieu's experiments with microscopic examination of the surface of the tongue of a sheep might strike us as odd or distasteful, but in the 1730s the microscope was a new tool for biological research, and this was cutting-edge science. The leap that is most interesting is from the physical world to the social, and it is on full display in Montesqueieu's work. One of Montesquieu's peculiar ideas was that climate had an influence on the character of populations. He claims people from the south, where the climate is hotter, are inherently lazier, more sensual and sexually licentious, and more deceitful, cowardly, and criminal. While the proposition is rife with racial and cultural prejudices, the evidence he gathers from the observation of the surface of a sheep's tongue in colder and warmer temperatures he uses to support his theory of the activity of nervous glands of humans in accordance with eighteenth-century physiology, and the consequent effects on government, politics, law, and social life.

Certainly few people today would agree with Montesquieu that the effect of temperature on livestock tongues is evidence of the general temperament of populations in different climates, but the connections that Montesquieu tried to make are noteworthy as indicators of the beginnings of modern politics, sociology, anthropology, geography, and other social sciences.

Book XIV. Of Laws in Relation to the Nature of the Climate

1. General Idea. If it be true that the temper of the mind and the passions of the heart are extremely different in different climates, the laws ought to be in relation both to the variety of those passions and to the variety of those tempers.

2. Of the Difference of Men in different Climates. Cold air constringes the extremities of the external fibres of the body; this increases their elasticity, and favours the return of the blood from the extreme parts to the heart. It contracts those very fibres; consequently it increases also their force. On the contrary, warm air relaxes and lengthens the extremes of the fibres; of course it diminishes their force and elasticity.

People are therefore more vigorous in cold climates. Here the action of the heart and the reaction of the extremities of the fibres are better performed, the temperature of the humours is greater, the blood moves more freely towards the heart, and reciprocally the heart has more power. This superiority of strength must produce various effects; for instance, a greater boldness, that is, more courage; a greater sense of superiority, that is, less desire of revenge; a greater opinion of security, that is, more frankness, less suspicion, policy, and cunning. In short, this must be productive of very different tempers. Put a man into a close, warm place, and for the reasons above given he will feel a great faintness. If under this circumstance you propose a bold enterprise to him, I believe you will find him very little disposed towards it; his present weakness will throw him into despondency; he will be afraid of everything, being in a state of total incapacity. The inhabitants of warm countries are, like old men, timorous; the people in cold countries are, like young men, brave. If we reflect on the late wars, which are more recent in our memory, and in which we can better distinguish some particular effects that escape us at a greater distance of time, we shall find that the northern people, transplanted into southern regions, did not perform such exploits as their countrymen who, fighting in their own climate, possessed their full vigour and courage. [...]

The nerves that terminate from all parts in the cutis form each a nervous bundle; generally speaking, the whole nerve is not moved, but a very minute part. In warm climates, where the cutis is relaxed, the ends of the nerves are expanded and laid open to the weakest action of the smallest objects. In cold countries the cutis is constinged and the papillæ compressed: the miliary glands are in some measure paralytic; and the sensation does not reach the brain, except when it is very strong and proceeds from the whole nerve at once. Now, imagination, taste, sensibility, and vivacity depend on an infinite number of small sensations.

I have observed the outermost part of a sheep's tongue, where, to the naked eye, it seems covered with papillæ. On these papillæ I have discerned through a microscope small hairs, or a kind of down; between the papillæ were pyramids shaped towards the ends like pincers. Very likely these pyramids are the principal organ of taste.

I caused the half of this tongue to be frozen, and, observing it with the naked eye, I found the papillæ considerably diminished: even some rows of them were sunk into their sheath. The outermost part I examined with the microscope, and perceived no pyramids. In proportion as the frost went off, the papillæ seemed to the naked eye to rise, and with the microscope the miliary glands began to appear.

This observation confirms what I have been saying, that in cold countries the nervous glands are less expanded: they sink deeper into their sheaths, or they are sheltered from the action of external objects; consequently they have not such lively sensations.

In cold countries they have very little sensibility to pleasure; in temperate countries, they have more; in warm countries, their sensibility is exquisite. As climates are distinguished by degrees of latitude, we might distinguish them also in some measure by those of sensibility. I have been at the opera in England and in Italy, where I have seen the same pieces and the same performers: and yet the same music produces such different effects on the two nations: one is so cold and phlegmatic, and the other so lively and enraptured, that it seems almost inconceivable.

From this delicacy of organs peculiar to warm climates it follows that the soul is most sensibly moved by whatever relates to the union of the two sexes: here everything leads to this object. In northern climates scarcely has the animal part of love a power of making itself felt. In temperate climates, love, attended by a thousand appendages, endeavours to please by things that have at first the appearance, though not the reality, of this passion. In warmer climates it is liked for its own sake, it is the only cause of happiness, it is life itself.

In southern countries a machine of a delicate frame but strong sensibility resigns itself either to a love which rises and is incessantly laid in a seraglio, or to a passion which leaves women in a greater independence, and is consequently exposed to a thousand inquietudes. In northern regions a machine robust and heavy finds pleasure in whatever is apt to throw the spirits into motion, such as hunting, travelling, war, and wine. If we travel towards the north, we meet with people who have few vices, many virtues, and a great share of frankness and sincerity. If we draw near the south, we fancy ourselves entirely removed from the verge of morality; here the strongest passions are productive of all manner of crimes, each man endeavouring, let the means be what they will, to indulge his inordinate desires. In temperate climates we find the inhabitants inconstant in their manners, as well as in their vices and virtues: the climate has not a quality determinate enough to fix them.

The heat of the climate may be so excessive as to deprive the body of all vigour and strength. Then the faintness is communicated to the mind; there is no curiosity, no enterprise, no generosity of sentiment; the inclinations are all passive; indolence constitutes the utmost happiness; scarcely any punishment is so severe as mental employment; and slavery is more supportable than the force and vigour of mind necessary for human conduct.

Source: Secondat, Charles de, Baron de Montesquieu. *The Spirit of Laws*. Translated by Thomas Nugent. London: J. Nourse and P. Vaillant, 1750.

5. Samuel Wilson: Mount Ararat and Positivism

Mount Ararat, the central element in this selection, is traditionally the place where the Book of Genesis says Noah's Ark landed, and one of the highest peaks in Western Asia. In this excerpt from his book on travels in Persia, *Samuel Wilson—missionary and scholar of Islam and Persia at the end of the nineteenth and beginning of the twentieth centuries—describes his encounter with the mountain and his thoughts about it. Wilson's description comes from a point of view that is willing to relate many of the myths and legends about Ararat for their poetic beauty or rhetorical effect, but these he does not accept as real knowledge about the mountain.*

Wilson creates a contrast between pre-modern ways of knowing and modern knowledge based on scientific method and observation. The scientific revolution that began before the advent of the modern period changed the nature of knowing in the modern world. An important idea that emerged in connection with science in the nineteenth century was that of scientific positivism, most famously articulated by the French philosopher Auguste Comte, *who proposed that the scientific method was the only truly reliable way of gaining knowledge about the world. Previous modes of knowledge, like theological and metaphysical knowledge, represented preliminary steps in human knowledge and social development. Using the scientific method, the human mind could finally arrive at real, positive knowledge instead of speculation and superstition.*

The scientific impulse to learn also led to a vogue for exploring in the nineteenth century among Europeans and Americans. In the name of science and the advancement of human knowledge, scientist-explorers who brought back new observations and evidence from far-off and exotic places were admired, and Wilson admires those who conquered the mysteries of Mt. Ararat in the same way.

Whether Noah's Ark or any other story about Mt. Ararat is true or not is in some sense beside the point. While there is no doubt that scientific knowledge has greatly increased in the modern period and expanded humans' understanding of the world in which we live, Wilson's story still seems divided between the revelations of myth and story on one hand, and the compelling reality of observed, measured, and verifiable fact on the other—though this is enough evidence to affirm that science and scientific thought was an essential element in everyday life.

Proceeding further, almost the only object which could draw our attention was Ararat, which for three days was almost constantly in view. It was the last sight at night and the first in the morning. There it stood, silent, solitary, awe-inspiring, mysterious, grand. The clouds had rolled away and left it distinct in all its majestic outline and massiveness. The ages, like the clouds, have come and gone, but it remains immovable. Since the ark rested on its heights there have been movements in heaven above and on the earth beneath—earthquake, storm, and flood—but it remains, presumably, substantially the same. Like the old ocean, a thousand years sweep over it in vain. It reminded one of Napoleon's address under the shadow of the pyramids. In forty centuries what has it not seen of the rise and fall of empires and the wonderful movements of the race of Noah? He sits a king, wrapped in his snowy robes, and with a perennial crown upon his brow. Though the puppet kings of man may include him in their dominion, he scorns subjection to their sway, and even bids defiance to the king of day. However near and furiously Apollo may drive his chariot and let his horses blow their warm breath upon him, neither the fire from his eye, the heat from the wheels, nor the warm breath of the horses can cause the whiteness of his countenance to color, or tan his fair complexion. His foot may become scorched and burned, his twin brother, the Little Ararat, may lay aside his crown, by the Great Ararat, unsubdued, lifts his proud head nearer to the throne in the sky and acknowledges no allegiance. The Little Ararat is like an earthly dynasty, which for a season wears the insignia of supremacy and then must surrender them; but the Great Ararat is like God himself, whose dominion is everlasting.

Ararat is not now the mysterious and unknown mountain, the center of myths and legends and of superstitious awe among the natives, and of vague admiration and reverence from the Christian world. It is true, the popular associations still cling around it. Bryce in his work [James Bryce, "Transcaucasia and Ararat in 1876"] describing his ascent, gives an extended notice of these traditions. It was supposed to be the center of the earth. It was connected with the Chaldean worship of the stars. Upon it stood a pillar with the figure of a star. Before the birth of Christ twelve wise men were stationed by the pillar to watch for the appearing of the star in the east, which three of them followed, when it appeared, to Bethlehem.

Its summit was declared to be inaccessible, and it became almost an article of faith with the Armenians, and a firm belief among all the natives, that God would not permit it to be ascended; nor are they convinced that this has ever been done. So much stronger, observes a traveler, is prejudice than evidence. On its top were said to be the remains of the ark. Far in the distant past the monk Jacob attempted its ascent, to obtain some of the precious relics. In the midst of each attempt he was overcome with sleep, and found himself on awakening at the same point where he started. The third time an angel told him that it was forbidden man to touch the vessel in which the race had been preserved, but he gave him a piece of the ark as a reward for his perseverance. The relic is said to be still preserved in the treasury of the monastery of Etchmiadzin.

All these myths have been rudely shattered and cast in to the vortex in which the legendary lore of the nations is fast disappearing. Modern adventure and scientific investigation, which compass sea and land in the search for truth, have dispelled all these fancies, and have given us much information about this Koh-i-Nuh [Persian/Farsi name for Ararat, meaning "Noah's Mountain"]. Daring travelers, from Parrot, in 1835, to Allen and Sachtleben, the bicyclists, who waved the American flag on it July 4, 1890, have scaled its glaciers and crossed its ravines and stood upon its summit. Its altitude has been measured. Its geological structure has been critically treated by the celebrated Hermann Abich. Its great chasm on the north and east sides has a perpendicular height of four thousand feet. Its fissures and its glaciers have been described. I will not repeat the description. Its solitary position adds much to its grandeur. At Karmalou, a station directly east of the mount, we ascended to the flat roof of one of the native houses and took a long and meditative view of Ararat. Though thirty miles away, the levelness of the country and the lack of intervening objects made this appear scarcely credible. From the plain the Great Ararat rises in irregular form to the height of seventeen thousand feet above sea-level. Its line of perpetual snow is thirteenth thousand four hundred feet. The little Ararat is almost a perfect cone, thirteen thousand feet high, and, though below the level of the perpetual snow, was for a considerable distance down covered with the white winding-sheet, owing to the rigorous season. Its summit is the boundary-line of the empires of the czar, the sultan, and the shah.

Source: Wilson, S. G. *Persian Life and Customs: With Scenes and Incidents of the Residence and Travel in the Land of the Lion and the Sun*. New York: Fleming H. Revell Company, 1899.

6. *Scientific Management*

The idea of scientific management was pioneered by Frederick Winslow Taylor, a mechanical engineer by trade and an industrial experimenter, who thought to apply the scientific method to help satisfy the ambition for achieving efficiency in industrial management and production processes. The idea was called scientific management by its promoters and Taylorism *by its detractors. The following selection is not by Taylor himself, but from a compilation of sources by followers of Taylor's ideas, published the year before he died in 1915.*

Taylor's theories represent the conscious application of the scientific method to further areas of human endeavor. In addition to analyzing human society scientifically like Montesquieu (see Document 4), and exploring the natural world scientifically like Wilson (see Document 5), Taylor wanted to use science to answer questions like "What is the most efficient way for a person to perform this task?" His methods recorded dramatic successes at increasing efficiency and productivity, and his ideas became very popular, not only in capitalist nations but also in the Soviet Union, where the Communist government unevenly tried to apply Taylor's ideas to aid its drive for rapid industrialization. (See Capitalism *and* Communism *in the Glossary.)*

Central components of the scientific management system were time and motion studies, which analyzed different labor tasks and broke them down into simple component parts, which on analysis could be revised to provide the most efficient way to do a task. Taylor sought to make human functions in industrial processes more efficient by timing, classifying, and analyzing human actions as mechanical operations. He also sought to scientifically select and train workers to do certain tasks, to plan and manage tasks, and to ensure workers did their tasks the right way.

Most of the theories of scientific management are no longer used in management. They came to be criticized for carrying division of labor to an extreme and creating a dehumanizing work environment. Nonetheless, Taylor and his studies substantially changed how work was understood, performed, and managed, and elements or derivations of his theories survive in practice today—another application of science to everyday life.

As has already been intimated, the art of industrial administration was stationary for a long period of time. In spite of tremendous changes in our social, economic and industrial systems, we have been content to adapt or modify methods which originated thousands of years ago. I may liken the system of administration which obtains in most industrial plants to one of those "old homesteads" which dot our New England landscape. They started as a log cabin, to which was successively added a lean-to, a barn, a shed, an ell, an upper story, and other "modern conveniences." As a result, they are roomy—and also inconvenient. The common system of industrial administration is constructed of the surviving remains of Greek slavery, Roman Militarism, Saxon serfdom, the mediaeval guilds, and various other historical oddities, slightly altered to adapt them to the twentieth century conditions, and engrafted on one another in very much the same way as the additions to the old house. This system of management has been a growth in which each manager appropriated those developments of the past which appealed to him. Sometimes methods were adopted as a result of a carefully and properly conducted investigation, but nine times out of ten they were adopted because the manager "guessed" they were the best ones. [. . .]

Scientific management, on the other hand, has been developed by the engineer. Scientific management aims at the careful investigation of every problem of the industrial world in order to determine its best solution. It is not content to rely upon records, or upon the judgment of the most experienced workman. It brings to its aid all the resources of science. Every possible method of performing a piece of work is carefully analyzed and the best elements of all of the methods combined in order to form a new method. Having established the best methods of work, scientific management then instructs the workman how best to perform his task, and offers an incentive to do it in the prescribed manner. Scientific management is often called the "Taylor System" in honor of its foremost exponent. Scientific management is not an invention but a discovery. It is the application of the scientific method of research to the problems of the industrial world. In so far as it is concerned with the investigation of these problems, it is science and nothing else. In so far as it is concerned with the proper application of the results of these investigations, it is management and nothing else. The combination is therefore correctly termed "scientific management."

If, in the near future, it is extensively applied to all industries or even to any one industry, it will give rise to very serious political, social and economic problems as well as intensify a great many of the problems that are now pressing for a solution. It will be seen, then, that the application of scientific management in industrial administration is not only important to the factory owner, the superintendent, and the workman, but to the law maker, the citizen and, in fact, to every man, woman and child in the country. The field of industrial administration is a very great one, but we cannot appreciate the importance of a right understanding of the problems which will be raised by the extensive introduction of scientific management until we realize how this field is interrelated with our entire political and social system. [. . .]

Time study is the one element in scientific management beyond all others making possible the "transfer of skill from management to men." The nature of time study, however, is but imperfectly understood and it is therefore important to define it clearly. "Time study" consists of two broad divisions, first, analytical work, and second, constructive work.

The analytical work of time study is as follows:

(a) Divide the work of a man performing any job into simple elementary movements.
(b) Pick out all useless movements and discard them.
(c) Study, one after another, just how each of several skilled workmen makes each elementary movement, and with the aid of a stop-watch select the quickest and best method of making each elementary movement known in the trade.
(d) Describe, record and index each elementary movement, with its proper time, so that it can be quickly found.

(e) Study and record the percentage which must be added to the actual working time of a good workman to cover unavoidable delays, interruptions, and minor accidents, etc.

(f) Study and record the percentage which must be added to cover the newness of a good workman to a job, the first few times that he does it. (This percentage is quite large on jobs made up of a large number of different elements composing a long sequence infrequently repeated. This factor grows smaller, however, as the work consists of a smaller number of different elements in a sequence that is more frequently repeated.)

(g) Study and record the percentage of time that must be allowed for rest, and the intervals at which the rest must be taken, in order to offset physical fatigue.

The constructive work of time study is as follows:

(h) Add together into various groups such combinations of elementary movements as are frequently used in the same sequence in the trade, and record and index these groups so that they can be readily found.

(i) From these several records, it is comparatively easy to select the proper series of motions which should be used by a workman in making any particular article, and by summing the times of these movements, and adding proper percentage allowances, to find the proper time for doing almost any class of work.

(k) The analysis of a piece of work into its elements almost always reveals the fact that many of the conditions surrounding and accompanying the work are defective; for instance, that improper tools are used, that the machines used in connection with it need perfecting, that the sanitary conditions are bad, etc., and knowledge so obtained leads frequently to constructive work of a high order, to the standardization of tools and conditions, to the invention of superior methods and machines. It is unusual to make a study such as this of the elementary movements of the workmen in a trade.

Source: Thompson, Clarence Bertrand, ed. *Scientific Management: A Collection of the More Significant Articles Describing the Taylor System of Management*. Cambridge, MA: Harvard University Press, 1914.

7. J. Robert Oppenheimer on the Atomic Age

One of the most significant scientific discoveries of the twentieth century is the development of atomic theory, with the resulting development of nuclear weapons. The first nuclear weapons were built in 1945 by the Manhattan Project, the name for the U.S. government's secret program to build atomic weapons during the Second World War. Once the bombs were built, the decisions about whether to use them and when, where, and how were obviously not made by the scientists who built them, but by political and military authorities. The bombs built by the Manhattan Project and used against Japan in 1945 yielded the approximate destructive power of between 15,000,000 and 20,000,000 tons of TNT (15–20 kilotons) each. Today nuclear weapons can yield hundreds of times that much destructive power (devices yielding 50 megatons were tested during the Cold War*).*

J. Robert Oppenheimer was a brilliant mathematician and physicist, as well as one of the directors of the Manhattan Project. Oppenheimer and other scientists became concerned about the moral and political consequences of the applications of the science they had pioneered, and this excerpt, from a speech Oppenheimer made in 1945 to a concerned group called the Association of Los Alamos Scientists, named after the location of the Manhattan Project in Los Alamos, New Mexico, is interesting in several regards.

Oppenheimer's speech indicates how unsure many were of the consequences of the atomic age, but he does clearly understand that the power of nuclear weapons was a whole new type, not another degree, of power and that it was an epoch-making alteration of how science and the world were viewed, analogous to the Renaissance or evolution. At the same time, he is optimistic about the power of science to improve things, despite the incredible destructive power unleashed on the world by the atomic bomb. He also argues that it was impossible in a sense not to build the bomb—that science will make progress and it cannot be stopped, only directed, and should not be stopped as there is an inherent good in the knowledge it obtains.

He also understands that the destructive power of nuclear weapons will alter the state of world politics, but he still has hope for peace. In a sense, he was prescient: despite the tensions of the Cold War, the assurance of total mutual destruction with nuclear weapons kept the Soviet Union and the United States officially at peace through the rest of the twentieth century. Although many other applied nuclear technologies have also been developed, issues such as nuclear waste, the dangers of radioactivity, and the proliferation of weapons continue to make this science a controversial part of everyday life.

SPEECH TO THE ASSOCIATION OF LOS ALAMOS SCIENTISTS

Los Alamos, November 2, 1945

I am grateful to the Executive Committee for this chance to talk to you. I should like to talk tonight—if some of you have long memories perhaps you will regard it as justified—as a fellow scientist, and at least as a fellow worrier about the fix we are in. I do not have anything very radical to say, or anything that will strike most of you with a great flash of enlightenment. I don't have anything to say that will be of an immense encouragement. [...]

I think there are issues which are quite simple and quite deep, and which involve us as a group of scientists—involve us more, perhaps than any other group in the world. I think that it can only help to look a little at what our situation is—at what has happened to us—and that this must give us some honesty, some insight, which will be a source of strength in what may be the not-too-easy days ahead. I would like to take it as deep and serious as I know how, and then perhaps come to more immediate questions in the course of the discussion later. I want anyone who feels like it to ask me a question and if I can't answer it, as will often be the case, I will just have to say so.

What has happened to us—it is really rather major, it is so major that I think in some ways one returns to the greatest developments of the twentieth century, to the discovery of relativity, and to the whole development of atomic theory and its interpretation in terms of complementarity, for analogy. These things, as you know, forced us to re-consider the relations between science and common sense. They forced on us the recognition that the fact that we were in the habit of talking a certain language and

Atomic bombing of Nagasaki, Japan, 1945. Library of Congress.

using certain concepts did not necessarily imply that there was anything in the real world to correspond to these. [...]

But the real impact of the creation of the atomic bomb and atomic weapons—to understand that one has to look further back, look, I think, to the times when physical science was growing in the days of the renaissance, and when the threat that science offered was felt so deeply throughout the Christian world. The analogy is, of course, not perfect. You may even wish to think of the days in the last century when the theories of evolution seemed a threat to the values by which men lived. The analogy is not perfect because there is nothing in atomic weapons—there is certainly nothing that we have done here or in the physics or chemistry that immediately preceded our work here—in which any revolutionary ideas were involved. I don't think that the conceptions of nuclear fission have strained any man's attempts to understand them, and I don't feel that any of us have really learned in a deep sense very much from following this up. It is in a quite different way. It is not an idea—it is a development and a reality—but it has in common with the early days of physical science the fact that the very existence of science is threatened, and its value is threatened. [...]

But when you come right down to it the reason that we did this job is because it was an organic necessity. If you are a scientist you cannot stop such a thing. If you are a scientist you believe that it is good to find out how the world works; that it is good to find out what the realities are; that it is good to turn over to mankind at large the greatest possible power to control the world and to deal with it according to its lights and its values. [...]

It is not possible to be a scientist unless you believe that it is good to learn. It is not good to be a scientist, and it is not possible, unless you think that it is of the highest value to share your knowledge, to share it with anyone who is interested. It is not possible to be a scientist unless you believe that the knowledge of the world, and the power which this gives, is a thing which is of intrinsic value to humanity, and that you are using it to help in the spread of knowledge, and are willing to take the consequences. And, therefore, I think that this resistance which we feel and see all around us to anything which is an attempt to treat science of the future as though it were rather a dangerous thing, a thing that must be watched and managed, is resisted not because of its inconvenience—I think we are in a position where we must be willing to take any inconvenience—but resisted because it is based on a philosophy incompatible with that by which we live, and have learned to live in the past. [...]

I think it is for us to accept it as a very grave crisis, to realize that these atomic weapons which we have started to make are very terrible, that they involve a change, that they are not just a slight modification: to accept this, and to accept with it the necessity for those transformations in the world which will make it possible to integrate these developments into human life. [. . .]

It is clear to me that wars have changed. It is clear to me that if these first bombs—the bomb that was dropped on Nagasaki—that if these can destroy ten square miles, then that is really quite something. It is clear to me that they are going to be very cheap if anyone wants to make them; it is clear to me that this is a situation where a quantitative change, and a change in which the advantage of aggression compared to defense—of attack compared to defense—is shifted, where this quantitative change has all the character of a change in quality, of a change in the nature of the world. I know that whereas wars have become intolerable, and the question would have been raised and would have been pursued after this war, more ardently than after the last, of whether there was not some method by which they could be averted. But I think the advent of the atomic bomb and the facts which will get around that they are not too hard to make—that they will be universal if people wish to make them universal, that they will not constitute a real drain on the economy of any strong nation, and that their power of destruction will grow and is already incomparably greater than that of any other weapon—I think these things create a new situation, so new that there is some danger, even some danger in believing, that what we have is a new argument for arrangements, for hopes, that existed before this development took place. By that I mean that much as I like to hear advocates of a world federation, or advocates of a United Nations organization, who have been talking of these things for years—much as I like to hear them say that here is a new argument, I think that they are in part missing the point, because the point is not that atomic weapons constitute a new argument. There have always been good arguments. The point is that atomic weapons constitute also a field, a new field, and a new opportunity for realizing preconditions. I think when people talk of the fact that this is not only a great peril, but a great hope, this is what they should mean. I do not think they should mean the unknown, though sure, value of industrial and scientific virtues of atomic energy, but rather the simple fact that in this field, because it is a threat, because it is a peril, and because it has certain special characteristics, to which I will return, there exists a possibility of realizing, of beginning to realize, those changes which are needed if there is to be any peace.

I think that we have no hope at all if we yield in our belief in the value of science, in the good that it can be to the world to know about reality, about nature, to attain a gradually greater and greater control of nature, to learn, to teach, to understand. I think that if we lose our faith in this we stop being scientists, we sell out our heritage, we lose what we have most of value for this time of crisis.

But there is another thing: we are not only scientists; we are men, too. We cannot forget our dependence on our fellow men. I mean not only our material dependence, without which no science would be possible, and without which we could not work; I mean also our deep moral dependence, in that the value of science must lie in the world of men, that all our roots lie there. These are the strongest bonds in the world, stronger than those even that bind us to one another, these are the deepest bonds—that bind us to our fellow men.

Source: Oppenheimer, J. Robert. *Letters and Recollections*. Edited by Charles Wiener. Cambridge, MA: Harvard University Press, 1980.

Health and Medicine

Modern Western medicine has applied scientific methods to explore the structure, functions, and diseases of the human body and mind. There are, of course, alternative theories of medicine—Chinese, Indian, and other traditional medicines, homeopathy, and spiritual or religious-inspired medical theories—and many of these are growing in popularity. Most modern medicine practiced today, although it is scientifically based and has recorded significant success, is not perfect, and sometimes harmful therapies or erroneous ideas have persisted, as in Isabella Beeton's recommendation (Document 10) of bloodletting, and even the best efforts have been unable to conquer many diseases, such as cancer and Human Immunodeficiency Virus/Acquired Immunodeficiency Syndrome (HIV/AIDS).

Much new knowledge has been gained by medical science in the modern period. The study of anatomy in eighteenth-century Europe was an area of great interest, even spreading as far as Japan, as the text by Sugita describes (Document 8). The letters to Edward *Jenner* (Document 9) show the important changes in another area, that of vaccination. Some innovations in surgical techniques and antiseptic practices are documented by the description of World War I-era medicine (Document 11). Together, these accounts give further evidence of the ways medicine positively affected everyday life. There are, of course, many areas of major medical achievements in the modern period that are not mentioned in the entries for example: germ theory, antibiotics, anesthetics, imaging technologies, advanced pharmaceuticals, and organ transplants.

One way overall health can be measured is in how long people live on average. In this regard, modern medicine has been very successful, extending the average expected lifespan of 30–35 years in 1700—where it had been for most of human history—to over 70 years in most developed nations and in some countries over 80 years by 2000. The most difficult part of living a long time was surviving birth and childhood, and medical science has been a major factor in reducing infant mortality to less than one percent in many countries. In addition to modern medical knowledge and health care institutions, stable, diverse food supplies, new knowledge in nutrition, and the development of public health systems are also major factors in helping people living longer and healthier lives, although these benefits are not universal.

Another criticism of medical and health care systems is the substantial global disparities in medical care. In much of sub-Saharan Africa, for example, life expectancy is not significantly longer today than in prehistoric times, in part because of complex social, cultural, and economic problems, and in part because of health issues like the HIV/AIDS pandemic (Document 12).

Today, physicians and other health care providers have wiped out diseases like smallpox that at the beginning of the modern era killed millions. They also routinely perform complex, lifesaving surgeries that before modern medicine would have been impossible, and they continue to seek new therapies and cures. Medicine and health care has an important role to play in everyday life—even influencing if, and how long, everyday life goes on.

8. Dutch Anatomy Books in Japan

The scientific principle of learning by experimental observation encountered obstacles in the medical profession, since it was essentially impossible to observe many of the body's internal structures and processes while patients were still alive. Attitudes based on religious beliefs restricted access to the remains of the dead in many cultures, and until well into the modern period, science did not have the cultural force to assert its need for an exception to the cultural norms for treatment of human bodies for study.

Under sakoku—the isolation policy followed by the Japanese government between 1639 and 1853—it was illegal in Japan for Japanese to leave or for foreigners to enter, making the island nation a closed society, although it was not as closed as is sometimes assumed. Trade was allowed, but only with specific nations in specific ports under strict regulations. The Dutch East India Company was the only European nation with any trading rights in Japan, and it was through these limited Dutch contacts that the Japanese were able to learn about European science and other European technologies and ideas.

The following selection, written by Genpaku Sugita, an eighteenth-century Japanese physician, describes the impression of Dutch anatomical texts on the medical profession in Japan. The accuracy of Dutch knowledge is clearly superior in Sugita's mind to the state of Japanese information, which drew largely from Chinese sources. Although at the time disease and its processes were not well understood in Europe, the study of anatomy by Europeans had been flourishing in the seventeenth and eighteenth centuries despite restrictions, and the results of this practical experience impressed Sugita in 1771.

Japan had a large urban, literate population, and Sugita's work is part of the wider Japanese intellectual movement called rangaku, or "Dutch studies," which sought to exploit the access to European intellectual and technical materials through the trading access with the Dutch at the port of Nagasaki. This movement helped lay the foundation not only for the better practice of medicine, but also for Japan's social, cultural, and technological transformation in the later nineteenth century.

March 4, 1771 (the 8th Year of Meiwa Era). The Dissection at Kotsugahara.

Toramatsu, an Eta [the lowest caste in the social system, a sort of untouchable] and a skillful dissector, was expected to perform the task, but he failed to appear on account of a sudden illness. His 90 year old grandfather, a sturdy-looking man, took his place. He said that he had performed a number of dissections ever since his youth. In dissecting the human body, the custom till then was to leave everything to such outcast people. They would cut open the body and point out such organs as the lungs, the liver and the kidneys and the observing doctors simply watched them and came away. All they could say then was: "We actually viewed the inwards of a human body." With no sign tag attached to each organ, all they could do was listen to the dissector's words and nod.

On this occasion too, the old man went on explaining various organs such as the heart, the liver, the gall-bladder and the stomach. Further, he pointed to some other things and said: "I don't know what they are, but they have always been there in all the bodies which I have so far dissected." Checking them later with the Dutch charts, we were able to identify them to be the main arteries and veins and suprarenal glands. The old man also said: "In my past experience of dissection, the doctors present never showed puzzle or asked questions specifically about one thing or another."

Comparing the things we saw with the pictures in the Dutch book Ryotaku and I had with us, we were amazed at their perfect agreement. There was no such divisions either as the six lobes and two auricles of the lungs or the three left lobes and four right lobes of the liver mentioned in old medical books. Also, the positions and the forms of the intestines and the stomach were very different from the traditional descriptions.

The Shogun's official doctors—Yosen Okada and Rissen Fujimoto—had beheld dissections seven or eight times before, but always what they saw were different from what had been taught in the past thousand years, and their puzzle had never been solved. They said they had been making sketches every time they saw something that struck them as strange. On this basis, I suppose, they had written that perhaps the Chinese and the Japanese were different in their internal structures. This I had read.

After the dissection was over, we were tempted to examine the forms of the bones too, and picked up some of the sun bleached bones scattered around the ground. We found that they were nothing like those described in the old books, but were exactly as represented in the Dutch book. We were completely amazed.

Source: Sugita, Genpaku. *Dawn of Western Science in Japan*. Translated by Ryōzō Matsumoto and Eiichi Kiyooka. Tokyo: The Hokuseido Press, 1969.

9. *Vaccination for Smallpox*

Smallpox, *also known as variola in the eighteenth century, was a fearsome disease. It killed an estimated 400,000 Europeans a year in the eighteenth century, with a mortality rate of between 20 and 60 percent, and up to 98 percent in infants and children. Because it was unknown in the New World and Australia where there was virtually no hereditary resistance, smallpox decimated Native American and Australian Aboriginal populations after European contact. It continued to kill millions around the world into the twentieth century. Those who did survive were often left blind or disfigured by scars. However, survivors were also effectively immune to the disease, which eventually led to preventative treatments.*

The procedure called variolation or inoculation (from the Latin word "to graft"), whereby a person would be intentionally infected with active smallpox from another person, had been known in Africa, Asia, and India long before it became part of European medical practice in the eighteenth century. It dramatically decreased the mortality rate, although some patients still died, and there was also the risk of other blood-borne infections with the treatment. When Joseph Marshall, the writer of the two letters reproduced below, refers to "the inoculated smallpox" it is to this less potent infection made by inoculation that he refers.

This entry offers a pair of letters by Marshall, an English physician, to Edward Jenner, *an English physician and scientist who is often credited with popularizing the procedure of vaccination. Jenner began using* cowpox, *a disease similar to smallpox but less virulent, to create cross-immunity. Jenner was the first to scientifically study the use of this type of inoculation, and he tirelessly promoted the use of the new technique, called vaccination (from vaccinia, the Latin name for cowpox) to protect people from infection with smallpox.*

Jenner was successful in showing cross-inoculation worked in practice, in part on the basis of evidence gathered by other physicians like the author of these letters, even though he was working with an imperfect theory of disease and little knowledge of germ theory, microbiology, or immunology, fields later pioneered by the Frenchman Louis Pasteur, *who named his treatments "vaccines" in honor of Jenner's work.*

Smallpox vaccinations have proven so effective that by 1979 the disease had effectively been wiped out, the only human disease known to have been completely eradicated. Children are no longer routinely vaccinated, since there is virtually no threat. The medical science that Jenner promoted has made smallpox, and the suffering and death that it caused, no longer a part of everyday life.

Dear Sir:

My neighbour, Mr. Hicks, having mentioned your wish to be informed of the progress of the inoculation here for the cow-pox, and he also having taken the trouble to transmit to you my minutes of the cases which have fallen under my care, I hope you will pardon the further trouble I now give you in stating the observations I have made upon the subject. When first informed of it, having two children who had not had the smallpox, I determined to inoculate them for the cow-pox whenever I should be so fortunate as to procure matter proper for the purpose. I was, therefore, particularly happy when I was informed that I could procure matter from some of those whom you had inoculated. In the first instance I had no intention of extending the disease further than my own family, but the very extensive influence which the conviction of its efficacy in resisting the smallpox has had upon the minds of the people in general has rendered that intention nugatory, as you will perceive, by the continuation of my cases enclosed in this letter, by which it will appear that since the 22d of March I have inoculated an hundred and seven persons; which, considering the retired situation I resided in, is a very great number. There are also other considerations which, besides that of its influence in resisting the smallpox, appear to have had their weight; the peculiar mildness of the disease, the known safety of it, and its not having in any instance prevented the patient from following his ordinary business. In all the cases under my care there have only occurred two or three which required any application, owing to erysipelatous inflammation on the arm, and they immediately yielded to it. In the remainder the constitutional illness has been slight but sufficiently marked, and considerably less than I ever observed in the same number inoculated with the smallpox. In only one or two of the cases have any other eruptions appeared than those around the spot where the matter was inserted, and those near the infected part. Neither does there appear in the cow-pox to be the least exciting cause to any other disease, which in the smallpox has been frequently observed, the constitution remaining in as full health and vigour after the termination of the disease as before the infection. Another important consideration appears to be the impossibility of the disease being communicated except by actual contact of the matter of the pustule, and consequently the perfect safety of the remaining part of the family, supposing only one or two should wish to be inoculated at the same time.

Upon the whole, it appears evident to me that the cow-pox is a pleasanter, shorter, and infinitely more safe disease than the inoculated smallpox when conducted in the most careful and approved manner; neither is the local affection of the inoculated part, or the constitutional illness, near so violent. I speak with confidence on the subject, having had an opportunity of observing its effects upon a variety of constitutions, from three months old to sixty years; and to which I have paid particular attention. In the cases alluded to here you will observe that the removal from the original source of the matter had made no alteration or change in the nature or appearance of the disease, and that it may be continued, *ad infinitum* (I imagine), from one person to another (if care be observed in taking the matter at a proper period) without any necessity of recurring to the original matter of the cow.

I should be happy if any endeavors of mine could tend further to elucidate the subject, and shall be much gratified in sending you any further observations I may be enabled to make.

I have the pleasure to subscribe myself,

Dear sir, etc.

Joseph H. Marshall

Eastington, Gloucestershire, April 26, 1799.

. . .

Dear Sir:

Since the date of my former letter I have continued to inoculate with the cow-pox virus. Including the cases before enumerated, the number now amounts to four hundred and twenty-three. It would be tedious and useless to detail the progress of the disease in each individual—it is sufficient to observe that I noticed no deviation in any respect from the cases I formerly adduced. The general appearances of the arm exactly corresponded with the account given in your first publication. When they were disposed to become troublesome by erysipelatous inflammation, and application of equal parts of vinegar and water always answered the desired intention. I must not omit to inform you that when the disease had duly acted upon the constitution I have frequently used the vitriolic acid. A portion of a drop applied with the head of a probe or any convenient utensil upon the pustule, suffered to remain about forty seconds, and afterwards washed off with sponge and water, never failed to stop its progress and expedite the formation of a scab.

I have already subjected two hundred and eleven of my patients to the action of the variolous matter, *but every one resisted it*.

The result of my experiments (Which were made with every requisite caution) has fully convinced me that the true cow-pox is a safe and infallible preventive from the smallpox; that in no case which has fallen under my observation has it been in any considerable degree troublesome, much less have I seen any thing like danger; for in no instance were the patients prevented from following their ordinary employments.

In Dr. Woodville's publication on the cow-pox I notice an extraordinary fact. He says that the generality of his patients had pustules. It certainly appears extremely extraordinary that in all my cases there never was but one pustule, which appeared on a patient's elbow on the inoculated arm, and maturated. It appeared exactly like that on the incised part.

The whole of my observations, founded as it appears on an extensive experience, leads me to these obvious conclusions; that those cases which have been or may be adduced against the preventive powers of the cow-pox could not have been those of the true kind, since it must appear to be absolutely impossible that I should have succeeded in such a number of cases without a single exception if such a preventive power did not exist. I cannot entertain a doubt that the inoculated cow-pox must quickly supersede that of the smallpox. If the many important advantages which must result from the new practice are duly considered, we may reasonably infer that the public benefit, the sure test of the real merit of discoveries, will render it generally extensive.

To you, Sir, as the discoverer of this highly beneficial practice, mankind are under the highest obligations. As a private individual I participate in the general feeling; more particularly as you have afforded me an opportunity of noticing the effects of a singular disease, and of viewing the progress of the most curious experiment that ever was recorded in the history of physiology.

I remain, dear sir, etc.

Joseph H. Marshall

Source: Eliot, Charles W., ed. *Scientific Papers: Physiology, Medicine, Surgery, Geology*. The Harvard Classics, Volume 38. New York: P. F. Collier & Son Company, 1910.

10. Mrs. Beeton and Bleeding

Although scientific medicine learned much about the structure and function of the body early in the modern age, effective treatments for many diseases were slower to be discovered. Isabella Beeton was a nineteenth-century English housewife and domestic author who wrote an extremely popular book on household management, one of the last sections of which was medical advice. At a time when a doctor may not always have been either nearby or effective, Beeton offers remedies that combine clinical experience with folk remedies and popular ideas, some of which have since been thoroughly discredited. Some of the treatments described by Beeton for serious conditions also document the limits of the knowledge of popular—and even professional—medicine in the last half of the nineteenth century.

Mrs. Beeton's recommendation to bleed a patient in a fit of apoplexy—a condition most often caused by what is now called a stroke—offers some understanding of the medical problem, but is not an especially effective treatment. Even after the ancient theory of the four bodily humors (blood, phlegm, black bile, and yellow bile) codified by the Roman physician Galen that described disease in terms of the balance or imbalance of the humors lost popularity in the modern age, some physicians continued to bleed patients. Debates over the merits of bleeding continued well into the nineteenth century, although many of the underlying principles had been discredited, and Beeton recommended and prescribed bleeding as an emergency treatment even in 1861, based on what she claimed was reliable medical advice. Other treatments seem to have little to do with modern medicine at all, such as stopping a nosebleed by dropping a key down a child's back.

Another serious disease with a treatment recommended by Beeton that seems odd today is cholera, a life-threatening, highly infectious bacterial dysentery that dehydrates the body and can cause shock and death as quickly as 12–24 hours. Transmitted though contact with infected waste and water, it spread epidemically, killing hundreds of thousands through the nineteenth century. Cholera morbus was also a general term in the nineteenth century for gastrointestinal infections and diarrhea. Beeton's first medical advice is actually a laxative, which would only accelerate the problem. She spends much time trying to offer advice to prevent agitating the bowels and so on, but the real danger of cholera is dehydration causing death. Cleanliness is indeed a good defense, as Beeton says, but modern water and sewage treatment, and in cases of infection, antibiotics, are a much surer cure. Today cholera is still a danger in some places, where public health practices and safe drinking water supplies do not exist. The remedies Beeton describes, whether the best that medicine could do, or traditional treatments, or sincere quackery, nonetheless offer a glimpse into medical practice as conducted in everyday life, rather than theory or research, in the middle of the nineteenth century.

HOW TO BLEED.

2605. In cases of great emergency, such as the strong kind of apoplexy, and when a surgeon cannot possibly be obtained for some considerable time, the life of the patient depends almost entirely upon the fact of his being bled or not. We therefore give instructions how the operation of bleeding is to be performed, but caution the reader only to attempt it in cases of the greatest emergency. Place a handkerchief or piece of tape rather but not too tightly round the arm, about three or four inches above the elbow. This will cause the veins below to swell and become very evident. If this is not sufficient, the hand should be constantly and quickly opened and shut for the same purpose. There will now be seen, passing up the middle of the fore-arm, a vein which, just below the bend of the elbow, sends a branch inwards and outwards, each branch shortly joining another large vein. It is from the *outer* branch—that the person is to be bled. The right arm is the one mostly operated on. The operator should take the lancet in his right hand, between the thumb and first finger, place the thumb of his left hand on the vein below the part where he is going to bleed from, and then gently thrust the tip of the lancet into the vein, and, taking care not to push it too deeply, cut in a gently curved direction, thus and bring it out, point upwards, at about half an inch from the part of the vein into which he had thrust it. The vein must be cut lengthways, and not across. When sufficient blood has been taken away, remove the bandage from above the elbow, and place the thumb of the left hand firmly over the cut, until all the bleeding ceases. A small pad of lint is then to be put over the cut, with a larger pad over it, and the two kept in their places by means of a handkerchief or linen roller bound pretty tightly over them and round the arm. [. . .]

2607. BLEEDING FROM THE NOSE.—Many children, especially those of a sanguineous temperament, are subject to sudden discharges of blood from some part of the body; and as all such fluxes are in general the result of an effort of nature to relieve the system from some overload or pressure, such discharges, unless in excess, and when likely to produce debility, should not be rashly or too abruptly checked. In general, these discharges are confined to the summer or spring months of the year, and follow pains in the head, a sense of drowsiness, languor, or oppression; and, as such symptoms are relieved by the loss of blood, the hemorrhage should, to a certain extent, be encouraged.

When, however, the bleeding is excessive, or returns too frequently, it becomes necessary to apply means to subdue or mitigate the amount. For this purpose the sudden and unexpected application of cold is itself sufficient, in most cases, to arrest the most active hemorrhage. A wet towel laid suddenly on the back, between the shoulders, and placing the child in a recumbent posture, is often sufficient to effect the object; where, however, the effusion resists such simple means, napkins wrung out of cold water must be laid across the forehead and nose, the hands dipped in cold water, and a bottle of hot water applied to the feet. If, in spite of these means, the bleeding continues, a little fine wool or a few folds of lint, tied together by a piece of thread, must be pushed up the nostril from which the blood flows, to act as a plug and pressure on the bleeding vessel. When the discharge has entirely ceased, the plug is to be pulled out by means of the thread. To prevent a repetition of the hemorrhage, the body should be sponged every morning with cold water, and the child put under a course of steel wine, have open-air exercise, and, if possible, salt-water bathing. For children, a key suddenly dropped down the back between the skin and clothes, will often immediately arrest a copious bleeding. [. . .]

2624. THE CHOLERA AND AUTUMNAL COMPLAINTS.—To oppose cholera, there seems no surer or better means than cleanliness, sobriety, and judicious ventilation. Where there is dirt, that is the place for cholera; where windows and doors are kept most jealously shut, there cholera will find easiest entrance; and people who indulge in intemperate diet during the hot days of autumn are actually courting death. To repeat it, cleanliness, sobriety, and free ventilation almost always defy the pestilence; but, in case of attack, immediate recourse should be had to a physician. The faculty say that a large number of lives have been lost, in many seasons, solely from delay in seeking medical assistance. They even assert that, taken early, the cholera is by no means a fatal disorder. The copious use of salt is recommended on very excellent authority. Other autumnal complaints there are, of which diarrhoea is the worst example. They come on with pain, flatulence, sickness, with or without vomiting, followed by loss of appetite, general lassitude, and weakness. If attended to at the first appearance, they may soon be conquered; for which purpose it is necessary to assist nature in throwing off the contents of the bowels, which may be one by means of the following prescription:—Take of calomel 3 grains, rhubarb 8 grains; mix and take it in a little honey or jelly, and repeat the dose three times, at the intervals of four or five hours. The next purpose to be answered is the defence of the lining membrane of the intestines from their acrid contents, which will be best effected by drinking copiously of linseed tea, or of a drink made by pouring boiling water on quince-seeds, which are of a very mucilaginous nature; or, what is still better, full draughts of whey. If the complaint continue after these means have been employed, some astringent or binding medicine will be required, as the subjoined:—Take of prepared chalk 2 drachms, cinnamon-water 7 oz., syrup of poppies 1 oz.; mix, and take 3 tablespoonfuls every four hours. Should this fail to complete the cure, 1/2 oz. of tincture of catechu, or of kino, may be added to it, and then it will seldom fail; or a teaspoonful of the tincture of kino alone, with a little water, every three hours, till the diarrhoea is checked. While any symptoms of derangement are present, particular attention must be paid to the diet, which should be of a soothing, lubricating, and light nature, as instanced in veal or chicken broth, which should contain but little salt. Rice, batter, and bread puddings will be generally relished, and be eaten with advantage; but the stomach is too much impaired to digest food of a more solid nature. Indeed, we should give that organ, together with the bowels, as little trouble as possible, while they are so incapable of acting in their accustomed manner. Much mischief is frequently produced by the absurd practice of taking tincture of rhubarb, which is almost certain of aggravating that species of disorder of which we have now treated; for it is a spirit as strong as brandy, and cannot fail of producing harm upon a surface which is rendered tender by the formation and contact of vitiated bile. But our last advice is, upon the first appearance of such symptoms as are above detailed, have *immediate* recourse to a doctor, where possible.

Source: Beeton, Isabella. *Mrs. Beeton's Book of Household Management: Comprising Information for the Mistress, Housekeeper, Cook, Kitchen-Maid, Butler, Footman, Coachman, Valet, Upper and Under House-Maids, Lady's Maid, Maid-of-all-Work, Laundry-Maid, Nurse and Nurse-Maid, Monthly, Wet, and Sick-Nurses, etc. etc., Also Sanitary, Medical, and Legal Memoranda, with a History of the Origin, Properties, and Uses of All Things Connected with Home Life and Comfort*. London: S. O. Beeton, 1861.

11. *Battlefield Medicine during World War I*

Before and during World War I, called by most at the time the Great War, the modern age had developed means of waging war that were far more efficient at killing people than even a few decades previous. Long-range artillery, landmines, barbed wire, machine guns, poison gas, tanks, trinitrotoluene (TNT), and aircraft were just a few of the new weapons employed. The resulting casualties were shocking.

At the same time, the large numbers of casualties necessitated treatment of those who were wounded but not killed. The same intensity in warfare that drives innovation in technology and strategy can also result in new treatments and better care for the wounded. Battlefield medicine was certainly not a new area of medicine, and it, too, benefited from improvements in practice during the course of the war from 1914 to 1918. Better transportation and evacuation systems, x-rays for finding foreign objects in wounded soldiers' bodies, anesthesia and antiseptic techniques to prevent infection, blood transfusions, and improving surgical techniques all contributed to better care for the wounded. Although the causes of infection were understood, treatments were only preventative, and antibiotic drugs to combat infections were unknown.

This selection, from a volume on the war published in 1918, the year it ended, describes anecdotally some of the new techniques to prevent disease and the sensational surgical procedures performed in British hospitals. The optimistic tone seems rather out of place for the grim stories recounted: shattered jaws, broken bones screwed together, surgeons plucking shrapnel from a man's heart, and an amputated leg riding around London in a taxicab. Soldiers' uniforms were sterilized so when they were shot the pieces of uniform that were pushed into the body by the bullet or shrapnel did not cause infections. While one might be impressed with the resourcefulness and efforts of doctors to do the best they could with the medical knowledge available, altogether they leave an impression of a nightmare reality that was not caused by the medicine, but might have been seen as more acceptable in the context of the horrors of modern life during wartime.

In every one of the belligerent countries there is now a new army, the army of maimed and crippled men. So great is their number—they are to be counted by hundreds of thousands—and so serious is the loss to the efficiency of the respective nations that it is realized that nothing less than heroic measures can minimize the evil both to the community and to the individual sufferer. [. . .]

One of the striking features of the war has been the rapid progress in surgery consequent upon the necessity of saving life and limb. Surgeons have performed operations that were hardly thought possible before the war. New methods have been discovered, new appliances invented, and, indeed, and entirely new chapter has been written in the history of surgery. Soldiers, whose fighting days seemed at an end, have been remade and sent back to the front as fit and strong as when they first joined the colors.

In the old days, as any one who has read history knows, the practice was to amputate as a matter of course. Now every effort is made not to amputate, for surgery in its progress has become conservative in the best sense of the word. Thus, at the Herbert Hospital, Shooter's Hill, London, there have been between three and four thousand operations on wounded soldiers, but of these only about twenty-five have been primary amputations.

Extraordinary operations are being performed every day in cases of bone, muscle, and nerve fracture. The surgeons, discovering that the human body has greater powers of recuperation than they thought, do not hesitate to take a piece of bone from one part of a patient's anatomy and utilize it to repair another that has been destroyed or removed. At another military hospital in London there was, for example, a case of severe injury to the jaw. The surgeon removed a piece of bone about two and one half inches from the tibia (the large shin bone) of the patient and fixed it in the jaw. The man's leg has healed up, and the jaw has improved so much that eating is now a far less painful process. In very many cases a broken bone is rejoined by a steel splint screwed to the bone just as a carpenter screws together two pieces of wood. The steel plate, which is sometimes an inch wide and four or five inches long, remains permanently in the wound, together with the steel screws, without pain or inconvenience. One of the surgeons who has performed many of these operations believes that in time the steel will become dissipated in the system and disappear altogether. As iron is one of the constituents of the blood, the splint does not become a source of danger.

Wonderful successes have also been achieved with injured nerves. At the Hammersmith General Hospital, London, for example, six useless muscles were taken from one side of a patient's wrist and transferred to the other, with the result that the hand, previously paralyzed, could once more be used. In another case the surgeon found four inches of a nerve in an arm gone. He telephoned round to the other London hospitals to inquire whether an amputation was in prospect and learned that a man was to have a leg off that afternoon. He asked that the severed limb should be put at once in a saline bath and brought to him in a taxicab. The patient was already under anaesthetic when the leg, still warm-blooded, arrived. The surgeon promptly transferred four inches of nerve from the amputated leg to the arm of the patient with a perfectly successful result.

But perhaps the most wonderful surgical triumph was that in the case of a man with a shrapnel wound. A piece of metal, about the size of a twenty-five-cent piece and much thicker, had entered the breast and lodged in the region of the heart. It was actually touching the heart and impeding its action. When the opening was made the surgeon thrust his hand right in and pulled out the piece of metal. The soldier made a complete recovery. The triumphs of British, French, and German practitioners would fill volumes.

The bacteriologist has also played an important part in the war. In the earlier period of the war tetanus was playing havoc among the troops, and great work was done in combating its ravages by the famous French physician, Doyen, since dead. More recently an important discovery has been made by Miss Mary Davies, bacteriologist for the Robert Walton Goelet Research Fund, as the result of experiments at a hospital in France. One of the chief causes of infection has been pieces of uniform shot into the body. Miss Davies, who had already gained distinction by inoculating herself with gangrene bacilli to prove the efficacy of Taylor's specific, set to work to discover how soldiers' uniforms could be rendered aseptic. She finally devised a treatment based upon a combination of cresol and soft soap with which the clothing is to be periodically impregnated.

Mr. Lloyd George, the War Minister in England, on receiving Miss Davies's report, ordered that the British soldiers' clothes should be sterilized with her preparation. In addition to its value in reducing the proportion of highly septic wounds the preparation is also welcome as a destroyer of body lice, one of the greatest discomforts of life in the trenches.

Source: Dresser, Horatio W., ed. *The World War.* Volume 15 of *The World's Story: A History of the World in Story Song and Art*, edited by Eva March Tappan. Boston: Houghton Mifflin Company, 1918.

12. Fighting HIV/AIDS in Africa in 2003

In the background of this reading is the contemporary international public health care process. It is a combination of research institutions like universities and hospitals, non-governmental organizations such as the UN's World Health Organization (WHO) and other groups, and governments and governmental organizations like the U.S.'s National Institutes for Health (NIH) and the Centers for Disease Control (CDC). Ideally these groups work together to identify global health threats and crises, conduct medical and health care research, and find treatments and policies—and funding—to deal with them.

Marie Wawer, a medical doctor and researcher from Canada with positions at Columbia University and Johns Hopkins University schools of public health, had been researching HIV transmission in Africa for 15 years in 2003. The following selection, taken from her testimony before Congress on the AIDS crisis in Africa that year, discusses the methods of transmission of HIV so that effective policies could be designed to help prevent the spread of the epidemic. Some researchers had argued that heterosexual transmission was not the primary cause, but needles reused for injections were the likely culprit, although Wawer's research contradicts those conclusions. The U.S. Congress, in deciding what kinds of HIV/AIDS programs to support, would need to understand how the disease is spread to provide support for programs that could most effectively slow its spread.

Of course, there are vast discrepancies in the health care resources available in wealthy, industrialized nations and poorer, developing nations. Like cholera *or* smallpox, *HIV/AIDS has presented a major threat to human health on a global scale. Much attention has been devoted to HIV/AIDS in the developed world, but the burgeoning number of cases in Africa threatens whole populations, like smallpox did a few generations ago. Although medical science has far more sophisticated tools and much greater resources than at the beginning of the modern period, the AIDS pandemic has proven difficult to control, and the everyday lives of millions of people are at stake.*

THE ROLES OF SEXUAL TRANSMISSION AND UNSAFE INJECTIONS IN THE HIV EPIDEMIC IN SUB-SAHARAN AFRICA

Mr. Chairman, Members of the Committee, thank you for this opportunity to testify regarding the very important topic of HIV/AIDS prevention in Africa. Given the AIDS crisis on the African continent, every effort must be made to determine optimal approaches to prevention. [. . .]

WHAT DO THE DATA TELL US ABOUT HIV TRANSMISSION IN AFRICA?

1. The HIV epidemic represents a crisis in the Sub-Saharan region of Africa.

WHO estimates that there are 29.4 million HIV infected persons living in Africa, and that approximately 3.5 million new infections occurred in 2002 (WHO, 2002) This represents a severe humanitarian, social and economic burden.

Although the epidemic has stabilized and abated somewhat in Uganda, we still observe HIV rates of over 10% among adults in towns and cities. Among the 300 Ugandan researchers and health staff who work with me in Rakai, every one has lost family members to the epidemic. We thus urge that every effort be made to curb the spread of HIV.

2. What are the major routes of HIV spread in Africa?

HIV can be spread via unsafe injection practices and blood transfusion. Efforts to reduce such transmission by provision of single use syringes and needles, appropriate sterilization equipment, facilities for the disposal of contaminated injection materials, and high quality HIV screening of potential blood donors, are all highly desirable.

However, data from Africa do not support the hypothesis that unsafe injections represent a common route of HIV transmission in the Sub-Saharan region. Available evidence from a broad range of sources points to heterosexual transmission, followed by mother-to-child transmission, as the major routes of my spread on the continent.

EVIDENCE REGARDING ROUTES OF HIV TRANSMISSION IN AFRICA

To assess the main routes of HIV transmission, we must first examine the epidemiological patterns of infection by age, gender, and reported behaviors, and assess which modes of transmission (unsafe injections, heterosexual and/or mother-to-child) are most plausible.

Age and gender patterns of HIV infection

The data can be summarized as follows:

Rates of HIV infection are low (below 1%) in children aged 5–14, an age at which mother-to-child transmission does not occur and when sexual exposure is unlikely.

Rates of HIV infection increase, often dramatically, during adolescence and young adulthood, reflecting the onset of sexual activity. The increase is usually more rapid among females. Our data and those of others show that girls in many African settings become sexually active at younger ages than boys, and sexual debut frequently occurs with men who are some years older. This places adolescent girls at higher risk than adolescent boys. We reviewed our most recent data on HIV acquisition in Rakai, and again found these patterns: only 1% of new infections occurred among persons aged 15–16, while over 90% occurred in persons aged 17–49, the age range of peak sexual exposure. In women in particular, the rate of new infections dropped to very low levels above age 50.

In the great majority of HIV risk studies, rates of infection are closely associated with reported sexual activity, including numbers of partners. Similar patterns are observed with other STDs, such as HSV-2 (genital herpes).

The age and gender distribution of HIV in Africa does not follow the pattern of receipt of injections (for vaccination and treatment in young children; for treatment in older persons).

HIV acquisition in infants and young children.

Although most infants and young children are exposed to multiple injections (for example, for immunization) the great majority of HIV-positive children in Africa acquire HIV from their infected mothers. In the absence of preventive therapy, approximately 15–20% of HIV infected mothers transmit the virus to the infant in utero or at time of birth, and 10–15% transmit through breast milk.

Early in the recognized epidemic in Kinshasa, Zaire (currently Congo), Mann et al. reported that over a third of early childhood HIV infection was associated with blood transfusion and injections. However, it should be noted that infant testing was still under development in the mid 1980s, and such high rates of non-vertical transmission have not been reported by other researchers or in more recent years. In a study in Kampala, Uganda, 98% of HIV-infected children had an HIV-positive mother (Muller and Moser, 1992). The probable causes of infection in the 2% of HIV+ children who had uninfected mother were transfusion and injections. Researchers in Cote d'Ivoire, Tanzania and Kenya followed a total of over 660 children born to HIV-negative mothers for two years on average, and observed no HIV infections in these children (Sherry et al., Karlsson et al., Ekipni et al.). In a separate study in rural Masaka, Uganda, over 2,500 children aged 5–12 were tested for HIV and only 10 (0.4%) were found to be infected: one of these 10 infections was attributed to transfusion and one to unsafe injections (Kengeya-Kayondo et al.). When 3,941 initially HIV-negative children aged 0–12 were followed in the same district, only one child became HIV-infected over the subsequent year, probably through breast milk (the mother was HIV-positive). The authors concluded that, in this setting, no infections had arisen as a result of injections (Mulder et al).

Biological evidence for modes of transmission

Studies have shown that transmission from an HIV-infected person to a sexual partner is strongly associated with the infected person's HIV viral load (the amount of virus in the blood) (Gray et al., Wawer et al., 2003), and with the presence of genital ulcer.

Comparison of HIV rates with rates of hepatitis C, an infection which is readily spread by injections, shows no common patterns throughout. Africa. For example, South Africa has very high HIV rates but relatively low hepatitis C seroprevalence, whereas the opposite situation occurs in Tanzania (Madhava et al., WHO). However, HIV rates generally mirror those of HSV-2 (genital herpes) which is transmitted sexually, but not through unsafe injections (Wawer et al., 2001).

Unsafe injections

There can be no doubt that unsafe injections represent a public health problem. For example, they have been implicated as major routes of transmission for hepatitis B and hepatitis C (Simonsen et al.); Also, many injections given world wide are unnecessary.

Hollow gauge needles, especially those used for intravenous injections or sample collection, can retain blood. HIV has been recovered from such needles for up to several weeks (Abdola et al). It is less clear whether syringes used for non-intravenous injection (i.e., subcutaneous or intramuscular injections, the types generally administered for immunization and therapy) pose a severe risk of HIV transmission. When syringes used to provide subcutaneous or intramuscular injections to HIV-infected clinic patients were subsequently tested for HIV content using highly sensitive HIV tests, only a small number (<4%) revealed the presence of potentially infectious material (Rich et al.). There is thus likely to be variability in the risk posed by unclean needles, depending on their type, use, and whether blood is left in the needle or syringe.

Although in some studies persons with established HIV infection report receiving more injections than uninfected persons, this may reflect receipt of injections for treatment of HIV-related illness. We recently re-examined our Rakai data and found no association between reported injections and the acquisition of new HIV infection: persons who did not acquire HIV actually reported slightly more injections from all sources (government clinics, medicine shops, traditional healers) than persons who acquired HIV during follow up.

The World Health Organization estimates that approximately 1.4–2.9% (or about 50,000–100,000) cases of HIV are spread annually in Africa through unsafe injections (WHO 2002). However, the risk may be spread unevenly between countries and regions, depending on background HIV rates and injection practices. Clearly, improving injection safety and reducing the number of unnecessary injections would be of public health benefit.

3. CONCLUSIONS

The data indicate that sexual transmission, and in infants, mother-to-child transmission, represent the most common routes of HIV infection in Africa.

However, there are also data that transmission via unsafe injections does occur in Africa, although it is not a main cause of the infection. Given the diversity of the African continent, great differences in medical resources and practices, and in the background rate of HIV infection, it is not possible to arrive at a meaningful summary estimate of the proportion of infections contributed by unsafe injections. The data, however, suggest that it is low and probably below 3% in the great majority of settings.

This should not be a reason for complacency. HIV researchers should reassess existing data to provide greater precision regarding the extent of potential injection-associated transmission, and of the circumstances under which it occurs. Wherever possible, HIV studies should include questions on injection and transfusion practices. Efforts to provide an adequate and long term supply of clean injection equipment, coupled with educational programs to promote needle safety and reduce unnecessary injections, would be of public health benefit.

From the viewpoint of HIV prevention, however, the data argue for continued, concerted efforts to reduce risks of HIV transmission associated with unsafe sex and to improve prevention of mother-to-child transmission.

Source: U.S. Congress. Senate Committee on Health, Education, Labor and Pensions. *AIDS Crisis in Africa: Health Care Transmissions: Hearing before the Committee on Health, Education, Labor and Pensions*. 108th Cong., 1st sess., March 27, 2003.

Language and Literature

One of the things that distinguishes humans from other forms of life is the use of language. Many other species communicate, even in sophisticated ways, but none have the abilities to create languages like humans. Language and literature are centrally important in everyday life. Language is the medium that conveys the meanings of everyday life; without it, we are effectively unable to communicate with each other.

While the use of language does not automatically mean literacy, literacy increased greatly in the modern era, making for more readers than ever before and of a much wider and diverse literature, such as religious texts, novels, poetry, and other genres. Literature and the uses of the written word continue to change as society and technology change—witness the language of instant messaging and the blogosphere as new, emerging styles and genres of writing.

The writer in the modern world was elevated from a patronage-based position of pleasing a sponsor or narrow audience to virtually a social prophet. The English poet Percy Bysshe Shelley (Document 14), typical of his time, sees the poet as an incredibly powerful person in society, and poetry, broadly construed, as one of the cornerstones of civilization. The poet's role is the revelation of beauty, truth, and the way forward for society, even defying social custom and prejudice to reveal knowledge more profound and important than the use of reason and utility could.

Not all saw controversial literature in such edifying terms, and neither were all writers or readers of literature interested in the subtleties of fine poetry. Before violent video games and loud music were corrupting young people, according to Anthony Comstock (Document 15), there was bad literature. Comstock argues for the deleterious impact of inappropriate literature on young and impressionable minds—the same impact Shelley wanted, but Shelley saw it as a tremendously good, even necessary thing. Shelley's defense of poetry extends beyond aesthetic considerations but is ultimately rooted in ideas of beauty and truth. Comstock, a less sophisticated critic of less sophisticated literature, was indifferent to the quality of the dime novel in any aesthetic sense, but is interested in the moral content and example in the sensational stories that were so popular.

While the moral value of literature may be debated, Alexis de Tocqueville (Document 13) and David Crystal (Document 16) address not literature, but language itself and its impact on everyday life. In his tour of the United States in the 1830s, de Tocqueville saw American language as an integral part of America's political, economic, and religious life. Crystal, a contemporary linguist, explains the crisis facing world languages and the dramatic loss of diversity and knowledge that accompanies the extinction of these fundamental ways of seeing and describing the world. All the authors presented here understand language as essential to the everyday life of communities, whether small and illiterate or united only by the texts they share that shape the way they see the world; language matters in everyday life.

13. *Alexis de Tocqueville: Language in Democracy in 1830s America*

Alexis de Tocqueville was sent by the French government to study the American prison system in the 1830s, but his interests were much wider, and he produced a text that has become a landmark of political science, history, and cultural criticism. His analysis of the American democratic system has been widely read for his insights into American life and his prescient predictions of events such as the Civil War *and even the* Cold War.

One can see the influence of eighteenth-century social and political theory on de Tocqueville's thought; he sees a direct connection between the American system of government and virtually every other aspect of American life: religion, economy, politics, art, and even the language that people spoke and how it has changed compared to British English. In this selection taken from Democracy in America, *de Tocqueville considers the effects of the American system on language. He quickly passes over the literary uses of language as being still too tied to English literature. Instead, he focuses on the everyday language of the people.*

He sees democracy exercising a leveling influence on language, making the speech of different classes of people draw closer because of greater fluidity among social groups and greater social mobility. Social origins matter less in America in de Tocqueville's eyes, and the result is a more general and uniform language based in social and political equality.

At the same time, the lack of authority, new uses for older words, and breakdown in a hierarchy of styles creates confusion and linguistic disorder that reflects a certain degree of social disorder, and these are drawbacks to this arrangement, according to de Tocqueville. The France from which de Tocqueville came had entered a period of some stability under a constitutional monarchy after decades of unrest. By the 1830s, when he visited America, the United States had, despite sectionalist tensions, been a stable, functioning democracy with one constitutional republican government since 1789, whereas since the French Revolution *in 1789 France had had nearly a dozen different regimes. Overall, de Tocqueville sees American democracy as dynamic, egalitarian, practical, and changeable, and sees these features of American life directly reflected in the everyday language spoken by Americans.*

American authors may truly be said to live rather in England than in their own country, since they constantly study the English writers and take them every day for their models. But it is not so with the bulk of the population, which is more immediately subjected to the peculiar causes acting upon the United States. It is not, then, to the written, but to the spoken language that attention must be paid if we would detect the changes which the idiom of an aristocratic people may undergo when it becomes the language of a democracy.

Englishmen of education, and more competent judges than I can be of the nicer shades of expression, have frequently assured me that the language of the educated classes in the United States is notably different from that of the educated classes in Great Britain. They complain, not only that the Americans have brought into use a number of new words (the difference and the distance between the two countries might suffice to explain that much), but that these new words are more especially taken from the jargon of parties, the mechanical arts, or the language of trade. In addition to this, they assert that old English words are often used by the Americans in new acceptations; and lastly, that the inhabitants of the United States frequently intermingle phraseology in the strangest manner, and sometimes place words together which are always kept apart in the language of the mother country. These remarks, which were made to me at various times by persons who appeared to be worthy of credit, led me to reflect upon the subject; and my reflections brought me, by theoretical reasoning, to the same point at which my informants had arrived by practical observation.

In aristocracies language must naturally partake of that state of repose in which everything remains. Few new words are coined because few new things are made; and even if new things were made, they would be designated by known words, whose meaning had been determined by tradition. [...]

The constant agitation that prevails in a democratic community tends unceasingly, on the contrary, to change the character of the language, as it does the aspect of affairs. In the midst of this general stir and competition of minds, many new ideas are formed, old ideas are lost, or reappear, or are subdivided into an infinite variety of minor shades. The consequence is that many words must fall into desuetude, and others must be brought into use.

Besides, democratic nations love change for its own sake, and this is seen in their language as much as in their politics. Even when they have no need to change words, they sometimes have the desire.

The genius of a democratic people is not only shown by the great number of words they bring into use, but also by the nature of the ideas these new words represent. Among such a people the majority lays down the law in language as well as in everything else; its prevailing spirit is as manifest in this as in other respects. But the majority is more engaged in business than in study, in political and commercial interests than in philosophical speculation or literary pursuits. Most of the words coined or adopted for its use will bear the mark of these habits; they will mainly serve to express the wants of business, the passions of party, or the details of the public administration. In these departments the language will constantly grow, while it will gradually lose ground in metaphysics and theology.

As to the source from which democratic nations are accustomed to derive their new expressions and the manner in which they coin them, both may easily be described. Men living in democratic countries know but little of the language that was spoken at Athens or at Rome, and they do not care to dive into the lore of antiquity to find the expression that they want. If they sometimes have recourse to learned etymologies, vanity will induce them to search for roots from the dead languages, but erudition does not naturally furnish them its resources. The most ignorant, it sometimes happens, will use them most. The eminently democratic desire to get above their own sphere will often lead them to seek to dignify a vulgar profession by a Greek or Latin name. The lower the calling is and the more remote from learning, the more pompous and erudite is its appellation. Thus the French rope-dancers have transformed themselves into *acrobates* and *funambules*. [. . .]

The most common expedient employed by democratic nations to make an innovation in language consists in giving an unwonted meaning to an expression already in use. This method is very simple, prompt, and convenient; no learning is required to use it correctly and ignorance itself rather facilitates the practice; but that practice is most dangerous to the language. When a democratic people double the meaning of a word in this way, they sometimes render the meaning which it retains as ambiguous as that which it acquires. An author begins by a slight deflection of a known expression from its primitive meaning, and he adapts it, thus modified, as well as he can to his subject. A second writer twists the sense of the expression in another way; a third takes possession of it for another purpose; and as there is no common appeal to the sentence of a permanent tribunal that may definitively settle the meaning of the word, it remains in an unsettled condition. The consequence is that writers hardly ever appear to dwell upon a single thought, but they always seem to aim at a group of ideas, leaving the reader to judge which of them has been hit.

This is a deplorable consequence of democracy. I had rather that the language should be made hideous with words imported from the Chinese, the Tatars, or the Hurons than that the meaning of a word in our own language should become indeterminate. Harmony and uniformity are only secondary beauties in composition: many of these things are conventional, and, strictly speaking, it is possible to do without them; but without clear phraseology there is no good language.

The principle of equality necessarily introduces several other changes into language.

In aristocratic ages, when each nation tends to stand aloof from all others and likes to have a physiognomy of its own, it often happens that several communities which have a common origin become nevertheless strangers to each other; so that, without ceasing to understand the same language, they no longer all speak it in the same manner. In these ages each nation is divided into a certain number of classes, which see but little of each other and do not intermingle. Each of these classes contracts and invariably retains habits of mind peculiar to itself and adopts by choice certain terms which afterwards pass from generation to generation, like their estates. The same idiom then comprises a language of the poor and a language of the rich, a language of the commoner and a language of the nobility, a learned language and a colloquial one. The deeper the divisions and the more impassable the barriers of society become, the more must this be the case. I would lay a wager that among the castes of India there are amazing variations of language, and that there is almost as much difference between the language of a pariah and that of a Brahmin as there is in their dress.

When, on the contrary, men, being no longer restrained by ranks, meet on terms of constant intercourse, when castes are destroyed and the classes of society are recruited from and intermixed with each other, all the words of a language are mingled. Those which are unsuitable to the greater number perish; the remainder form a common store, whence everyone chooses pretty nearly at random. Almost all the different dialects that divided the idioms of European nations are manifestly declining; there is no patois in the New World, and it is disappearing every day from the old countries.

The influence of this revolution in social condition is as much felt in style as it is in language. Not only does everyone use the same words, but a habit springs up of using them without discrimination. The rules which style had set up are almost abolished: the line ceases to be drawn between expressions which seem by their very nature vulgar and others which appear to be refined. Persons springing from different ranks of society carry with them the terms and expressions they are accustomed to use into whatever circumstances they may enter; thus the origin of words is lost like the origin of individuals, and there is as much confusion in language as there is in society.

Source: Tocqueville, Alexis de. *Democracy in America*. Translated by Henry Reeve. Volume 2. New York: J. and H. G. Langley, 1841.

14. Percy Bysshe Shelley: The Power of Poetry

Percy Bysshe Shelley was one of the greatest English poets of the nineteenth century. Like his contemporaries, Lord Byron, *John* Keats, *and others, he led a revival of poetry and helped create the image of the writer and the ideas of poetry that still influence our conceptions of literary art today. Like many members of the late eighteenth- and early nineteenth-century literary movement known as* Romanticism, *Shelley eschewed organized religion and loved nature, the individual genius, the imaginative, the exotic, the sublime, and the inspiring. He saw poetry as one of the highest callings, and central to the structure and meaning of everyday life in society.*

He himself was from a privileged background, but was a social rebel, challenging social norms both in his personal life and in his writing, a role that came to be seen as important to a serious writer. In response to a satirical attack on the value of poetry, Shelley penned A Defence of Poetry *in 1821, from which this selection is taken. A poet himself, Shelley defends poetry by giving it enormous power.*

On the eve of the Industrial Revolution *and the heels of the* Enlightenment, *Shelley defends poetry from attacks on its lack of rationality, utility, and even morality. While acknowledging that rationality and utility supply physical needs and may convince people to act in rational self-interest, which secures a base of civil behavior, poetry, he insists, appeals to motives and needs greater than the base. Morality, he argues, is based in sympathy (an emotional argument typical of Romanticism), and sympathy requires imagination to see oneself in another's place. Poetry feeds the imagination best and thus promotes sympathetic feelings and moral behavior.*

Poetry's use of language gives it a particularly privileged position among the arts, and makes other arts secondary to poetry. Shelley sees language as more intimately connected to thought and imagination than other forms of art. The closer proximity of language and poetic language to the human quest for harmony and unity, for the true and the beautiful, places poetry not only at the root of the arts, but at the root of society. Shelley's argument is that poetic impulses make the everyday life of human society possible.

Because of the insight poets have, even if unconscious, into the essential tendency toward harmony, unity, beauty, and truth at the core of Shelley's understanding of human nature and civilization, poets can, in a spiritual sense, direct the course of humanity. In this sense, Shelley can claim that "poets are the unacknowledged legislators of the world."

Since Shelley's time, other critics, writers, and thinkers have challenged Shelley's ideas and conclusions, although they were very popular in the nineteenth century, and elements of the role of the writer or poet and the nature of literature from Shelley's time continue to influence contemporary ideas. Even if poetry is not the root of civilization, it shows how powerful poetry was believed to be and how intimately Shelley connected literature to everyday life.

Language, color, form, and religious and civil habits of action, are all the instruments and materials of poetry; they may be called poetry by that figure of speech which considers the effect as a synonym of the cause. But poetry in a more restricted sense expresses those arrangements of language, and especially metrical language, which are created by that imperial faculty, whose throne is curtained within the invisible nature of man. And this springs from the nature itself of language, which is a more direct representation of the actions and passions of our internal being, and is susceptible of more various and delicate combinations, than color, form, or motion, and is more plastic and obedient to the control of that faculty of which it is the creation. For language is arbitrarily produced by the imagination, and has relation to thoughts alone; but all other materials, instruments, and conditions of art have relations among each other, which limit and interpose between conception and expression. The former [poetry] is as a mirror which reflects, the latter [other arts] as a cloud which enfeebles, the light of which both are mediums of communication. [...]

The whole objection, however, of the immorality of poetry rests upon a misconception of the manner in which poetry acts to produce the moral improvement of man. Ethical science arranges the elements which poetry has created, and propounds schemes and proposes examples of civil and domestic life; nor is it for want of admirable doctrines that men hate, and despise, and censure, and deceive, and subjugate one another. But poetry acts in another and diviner manner. It awakens and enlarges the mind itself by rendering it the receptacle of a thousand unapprehended combinations of thought. Poetry lifts the veil from the hidden beauty of the world, and makes familiar objects be as if they were not familiar; it reproduces all that it represents, and the impersonations clothed in its Elysian light stand thenceforward in the minds of those who have once contemplated them, as memorials of that gentle and exalted content which extends itself over all thoughts and actions with which it co-exists.

The great secret of morals is love; or a going out of our own nature, and an identification of ourselves with the beautiful which exists in thought, action, or person, not our own. A man, to be greatly good, must imagine intensely and comprehensively; he must put himself in the place of another and of many others; the pains and pleasures of his

Joseph Severn, *Posthumous Portrait of Shelley Writing Prometheus Unbound*, oil on canvas, 1845. Keats-Shelley Memorial House, Rome, Italy / The Bridgeman Art Library.

species must become his own. The great instrument of moral good is the imagination; and poetry administers to the effect by acting upon the cause. Poetry enlarges the circumference of the imagination by replenishing it with thoughts of ever new delight, which have the power of attracting and assimilating to their own nature all other thoughts, and which form new intervals and interstices whose void for ever craves fresh food. Poetry strengthens the faculty which is the organ of the moral nature of man, in the same manner as exercise strengthens a limb. [. . .]

But poets have been challenged to resign the civic crown to reasoners and mechanists, on another plea. It is admitted that the exercise of the imagination is most delightful, but it is alleged that that of reason is more useful. Let us examine, as the grounds of this distinction, what is here meant by utility. Pleasure or good, in a general sense, is that which the consciousness of a sensitive and intelligent being seeks, and in which, when found, it acquiesces. There are two kinds of pleasure, one durable, universal, and permanent; the other transitory and particular. Utility may either express the means of producing the former or the latter. In the former sense, whatever strengthens and purifies the affections, enlarges the imagination, and adds spirit to sense, is useful. But a narrower meaning may be assigned to the word utility, confining it to express that which banishes the importunity of the wants of our animal nature, the surrounding men with security of life, the dispersing the grosser delusions of superstition, and the conciliating such a degree of mutual forbearance among men as may consist with the motives of personal advantage.

Undoubtedly the promoters of utility, in this limited sense, have their appointed office in society. They follow the footsteps of poets, and copy the sketches of their creations into the book of common life. They make space and give time. Their exertions are of the highest value, so long as they confine their administration of the concerns of the inferior powers of our nature within the limits due to the superior ones. But whilst the skeptic destroys gross superstitions, let him spare to deface, as some of the French writers have defaced, the eternal truths charactered upon the imaginations of men. [. . .]

It is impossible to read the compositions of the most celebrated writers of the present day without being startled with the electric life which burns within their words. They measure the circumference and sound the depths of human nature with a comprehensive and all penetrating spirit, and they are themselves perhaps the most sincerely astonished at its manifestations; for it is less their spirit than the spirit of the age. Poets are the hierophants of an unapprehended inspiration; the mirrors of the gigantic shadows which futurity casts upon the present; the words which express what they understand not; the trumpets which sing to battle, and feel not what they inspire; the influence which is moved not, but moves. Poets are the unacknowledged legislators of the world.

Source: Shelley, Percy Bysshe. "A Defence of Poetry." In *Essays, Letters from Abroad, and Fragments*. Edited by Mary Wollstonecraft Shelley. London: Edward Moxon, 1840.

15. *Dangerous Literature*

Anthony Comstock was an anti-vice crusader in New York in the last part of the nineteenth century. He used his position as postal inspector to prevent the dissemination of literature and other materials he considered immoral or improper, including pornography, birth control information, and fraudulent advertising. His efforts against corruption and immorality were informed by a very rigid Victorian sense of moral propriety. Anti-obscenity laws are still sometimes today called Comstock laws. While reviled by civil liberties groups and supported by many religious groups, the importance of Comstock's position here is not the value of his moral positions, but the importance he and so many others attached to literature in the rapidly changing social and moral conditions of the modern world.

The growth of public education and the rise of mass literacy gave rise to new types and styles of literature. Working-class people were becoming generally literate for perhaps the first time in history, and their tastes in literature were met by what were called dime novels in America, penny dreadfuls in England, fait divers *in France, or generally termed boulevard literature. This kind of literature was produced and consumed in mass quantities with greater interest by the publisher in sales and profits and by the readers in amusement or diversion than concern for the moral or aesthetic value of the plentiful stories that were printed on cheap paper and sold on the streets.*

In one regard, Comstock shares the perspective of the dime novelists: he does not care about the aesthetic or literary qualities of the literature he criticizes, although they were typically written hastily with sensational but predictable plots and stock characters. Instead, in this selection from his book Traps for the Young, *he sees literature as a means to encourage young people to criminal, immoral behavior, to cause a breakdown in family and legal authority, and to be the origin of vice and to the detriment of clean living.*

Comstock's objections to the negative effects of mass media, especially on impressionable children, find echoes throughout the twentieth century. Comic books, rock music, violence in film and video games, Internet networking and chat sites: the media have changed but the messages have been similar. In a modern world where movies and recorded music were not yet known, much less video games, Facebook, and whatever comes next, it was reading that was considered decidedly dangerous. Despite Comstock's best efforts, popular literature and its descendants continue to be a part of everyday life for millions, and its effect on aesthetics and morality remains a question that is still debated.

Satan stirred up certain of his willing tools on earth by the promise of a few paltry dollars to improve greatly on the death-dealing quality of the weekly death-traps, and forthwith came a series of new snares of fascinating construction, small and tempting in price, and baited with high-sounding names. These sure-ruin traps comprise a large variety of half-dime novels, five and ten cent story papers, and low-priced pamphlets for boys and girls.

This class includes the silly, insipid tale, the coarse, slangy story in the dialect of the barroom, the blood-and-thunder romance of border life, and the exaggerated details of crimes, real and imaginary. Some have highly colored sensational reports of real crimes, while others, and by far the larger number, deal with most improbable creations of fiction. The unreal far outstrips the real. Crimes are gilded, and lawlessness is painted to resemble valor, making a bid for bandits, brigands, murderers, thieves, and criminals in general. Who would go to the State prison, the gambling saloon, or the brothel to find a suitable companion for the child? Yet a more insidious foe is selected when these stories are allowed to become associates for the child's mind and to shape and direct the thoughts.

The finest fruits of civilization are consumed by these vermin. Nay, these products of corrupt minds are the eggs from which all kinds of villainies are hatched. Put the entire batch of these stories together, and I challenge the publishers and venders to show a single instance where any boy or girl has been elevated in morals, or where any noble or refined instinct has been developed by them.

The leading character in many, if not in the vast majority of these stories, is some boy or girl who possesses usually extraordinary beauty of countenance, the most superb clothing, abundant wealth, the strength of a giant, the agility of a squirrel, the cunning of a fox, the brazen effrontery of the most daring villain, and who is utterly destitute of any regard for the laws of God or man. Such a one is foremost among desperadoes, the companion and beau-ideal of maidens, and the high favorite of some rich person, who by his patronage and endorsement lifts the young villain into lofty positions in society, and provides liberally of his wealth to secure him immunity for his crimes. These stories link the pure maiden with the most foul and loathsome criminals. Many of them favor violation of marriage laws and cheapen female virtue. [...]

A word about bound books.

Recently I purchased a book offered for sale on the railroads, and recommended by the newsboy on a train on the Lake Shore and Michigan Southern Railroad as the "boss book," the "fastest selling book of the day." The web of the story consisted of four murders, three highway robberies, two burglaries, one blackmailing scheme, three attempts to murder women, one attempt to poison a young woman, two conspiracies to ruin a pure girl, one den of counterfeiters in full blast, two gambling halls, one confidence game, one brothel, procurers abducting a young girl for a rich man, three cases of assault and battery, one street fight, two dens of thieves, one forced marriage, two suicides, and oaths, lies, wine-drinking, smoking cigars, et cetera. The character that figured throughout all this was a beautiful young wife, who was the murderess and principal actor in all these horrible and disgusting scenes.

Again, these stories give utterly false and debasing ideas of life. All high moral purposes are made to give way to self-gratification. The great safeguard of human society—reverence to law—is broken down. Disobedience to parents is encouraged. The healthful restraint of parental authority is treated as a species of tyranny which the hero first chafes under, then resists, and lastly ignores.

The boy cheats himself by imagining he is doing a manly thing when he naturally follows a base example. To the child that chafes under home restraint, having taken the initiative step to ignore proper authority, a dangerous and lawless life comes easy.

Again, these stories breed vulgarity, profanity, loose ideas of life, impurity of thought and deed. They render the imagination unclean, destroy domestic peace, desolate homes, cheapen woman's virtue, and make foul-mouthed bullies, cheats, vagabonds, thieves, desperadoes, and libertines. They disparage honest toil, and make real life a drudge and burden. What young man will serve an apprenticeship, working early and late, if his mind is filled with the idea that sudden wealth may be acquired by following the hero of the story? In real life, to begin at the foot of the ladder and work up, step by step, is the rule; but in these stories, inexperienced youth, with no moral character, take the foremost positions, and by trick and device, knife and revolver, bribery and corruption, carry everything before them, lifting themselves in a few short weeks to positions of ease and affluence. Moral courage with such is a thing to be sneered at and despised in many of these stories. If one is asked to drink and refuses, he is set up and twitted till he yields or is compelled to by force. The idea of doing anything from principle is ridiculous in the extreme. As well fill a kerosene-oil lamp with water and expect a brilliant light. And so, in addition to all else, there is early inculcated a distaste for the good, and the piercing blast of ridicule is turned upon the reader to destroy effectually all moral character.

Many critics seem to think it necessary to quote liberally from these authors, to show the dialect or to expose to public contempt the coarse language and worse morals. It is not the writer's purpose to quote these expressions or name these publications. Those who are informed on this subject know what is meant, and others need not know further than the effects.

Source: Comstock, Anthony. *Traps for the Young*. New York: Funk and Wagnalls, 1883.

16. *David Crystal: Dying Languages*

Language is an essential part of being human: all humans have language, and language is an essential part of the human experience. Historically, languages have developed and diverged, and some have died; it is a natural part of human history. However, never have more languages been in danger of disappearing than at the start of the twenty-first century.

David Crystal is a professional linguist who studies both English and world languages, including the disappearance of languages, a phenomenon known as "language death," which occurs when the last known (or even unknown) native speaker of a language dies. The following excerpt is taken from Crystal's 2000 book, Language Death, *in which he documents the processes by which languages are dying around the world, and the consequences. The reasons for language death are complex; most are related to trends specific to the modern world in politics, economics, education, migration, and other areas.*

Whatever the various causes, Crystal documents the disproportionate number of speakers of world languages, and the danger of disappearing that many of the less common languages face. There have been a few well-known "last speakers" in America and Europe, but most endangered languages are in other parts of the world. Aboriginal Australian languages, Native American languages, and Siberian, Pacific Island, South American, and African tribal languages are disappearing at what Crystal calls an alarming rate, with consequences not only for the speakers of those languages, but for all of humanity.

Knowing more than one language gives people a richer and more valuable experience of life. Languages encapsulate unique ways of looking at the world, and the interaction between languages and thus between worldviews adds profoundly to the human experience. He contemplates the losses in terms of lost literatures and lost parts of human experience. Crystal argues that multilingualism is a more common state than monolingualism, and should be seen as the norm. Language is a primary means through which we make and experience everyday life, and when a language disappears, that way of experiencing life—and the possibilities of its interacting with other languages and ways of life—is gone.

We are at a critical point in human linguistic history, and most people don't know.

Language death is real. Does it matter? Should we care? It does, and we should. [...]

Languages are dying as I write. Everyone should be concerned, because it is everyone's loss.

The issue of language loss is itself a source of confusion. People may be aware that languages are dying, but have no idea at what rate. Depending on how they estimate that rate, so their current global guess will be affected: some take a conservative view about the matter; some are radical. Then there is the opposite situation—the fact that not all languages on earth have yet been "discovered," thus allowing an element of growth into the situation. [...]

Beginning with the largest totals: it is evident that a very small number of languages account for a vast proportion of the world's population (thought to have passed 6 billion in mid 1999). The 8 languages over 100 million (Mandarin, Spanish, English, Bengali, Hindi, Portuguese, Russian, Japanese) have nearly 2.4 billion speakers between them; and if we extend this count to include just the top 20 languages, we find a total of 3.2 billion—over half the world's population. If we continued the analysis downwards, we would eventually find that just 4% of the world's languages are spoken by 96% of the population.

Turning this statistic on its head: 96% of the world's languages are spoken by just 4% of the population. That is the perspective within which any discussion of language death must be seen.... [A] quarter of the world's languages are spoken by less than 1,000 people; and well over half by less than 10,000.... If the figure of 20,000 (referred to as a danger-level in some parts of the world) were taken as a universal datum, this would correspond to exactly two-thirds of the world's languages. [W]e are talking about 4,000 languages. Most of these will be found in those parts of the world where languages are most numerous—notably in the equatorial regions everywhere. [...]

As we have already seen, conditions vary so much around the world that it is impossible to generalize from population alone about the rate at which languages die out. That is why there is so much variation in the claims that are currently being made, that "x% of the world's languages are going to die out in the next 100 years"—x here has been anything from 25% (a conservative estimate which correlates with the less than 100 criterion) to 80% or more (a radical estimate which correlates with the less than 100,000 criterion). It is impossible, in our present state of knowledge, to say more about these deductions other than that they are well-informed guesswork. [...]

[A] language contains our history. Through the words and idioms it uses, it provides us with clues about the earlier states of mind of its speakers, and about the kinds of cultural contact they had. There are over 350 living languages listed in the etymological files of the Oxford English Dictionary. Each etymology demonstrates through its presence a point of contact, an index of influence. Words become part of the evidence of social history. George Steiner's comment applies: "Everything forgets. But not a language." With tens of thousands of words, idioms, and metaphors in a language's domestic vocabulary, and large numbers of grammatical constructions available to manipulate these items, it is plain that the potential for linguistic interaction, even between two languages, is immense. And with thousands of languages in the "pool" the capabilities of expression stemming from the human language capacity are almost unimaginable. It is a richness of heritage whose power to facilitate individual expression, in the form of community or personal identity, is virtually unlimited.

Tevfik Esenc, the last remaining speaker of Oubykh, 1984. AP Photo.

Because languages contribute to the sum of human knowledge... identity and history combine to ensure that each language reflects a unique encapsulation and interpretation of human existence, and this gives us yet another reason for caring when languages die. It is a motive that is more self-serving than altruistic, though no less worthy. We should care—because we can learn a great deal from them.

The view that languages other than our own provide us with a means of personal growth, as human beings, is a recurrent theme in literature, at various levels of intellectual profundity. Several proverbial expressions have captured the essential insight. From Slovakia: "With each newly learned language you acquire a new soul." From France: "A man who knows two languages is worth two men." Emerson takes up this theme: "As many languages as he has, as many friends, as many arts and trades, so many times is he a man."

The message is clearly that there is much to be learned and enjoyed in experiencing other languages. And the corollary is that we miss out on this experience if we do not avail ourselves of the opportunity to encounter at least one other language. Everyone who has travelled has felt this limitation, to at least some extent. Here is Emerson again: "No man should travel until he has learned the language of the country he visits. Otherwise he voluntarily makes himself a great baby,—so helpless and so ridiculous." There is a real sense in which a monolingual person, with a monolingual temperament, is disadvantaged, or deprived.

Monolingual people need time to take in this point. And so, before resuming the argument, it is worth a paragraph of digression to stress that there are good grounds for conceiving the natural condition of the human being to be multilingual. The human brain has the natural capacity to learn several languages, and most members of the human race live in settings where they naturally and efficiently use their brains in precisely this way. Half the human race is known to be at least bilingual, and there are probably half as many bilinguals again in those parts of the world where there have been no studies, though cultural contacts are known to be high. People who belong to a predominantly monolingual culture are not used to seeing the world in this way, because their mindset has been established through centuries of being part of a dominant culture, in which other people learn your language and you do not learn theirs. [...]

Humanity gains so much from each fresh expression of itself in a language: "The world is a mosaic of visions. With each language that disappears, a piece of that mosaic is lost." The best way for an educated person to feel the power of this argument, I always think, is to ask what would be missed if—through an imaginary catastrophic language disappearance—we had never had X (where X is any well-known language). What splendours of literature, in particular, would we have never experienced if some event had prematurely ended the development of French, or Spanish, or Russian? What if Norman French had succeeded in displacing Old English after 1066? No Chaucer, Shakespeare, Wordsworth, Dickens now. What if French had never been? No Molière, Hugo, Baudelaire. It has become a cliché, but that does not diminish its truth, to say that everyone would be the poorer.

Source: Crystal, David. *Language Death*. New York: Cambridge University Press, 2000. Reprinted with the permission of Cambridge University Press.

Art

Like many other forms of intellectual life in the modern world, art has undergone tremendous transformations. Many people are confused or bewildered by the work that is credited with being great works of modern art in the twentieth and twenty-first centuries. Of course, not all art has been abstract or non-representational, and there is much twentieth-century art that is more immediately recognizable. In fact, ease of travel, education, public museums, and the printed and electronic reproduction of art have made art more popular and accessible than ever before.

One of the trends at the beginning of the modern era was the rise of public institutions of art. In many European nations, the beginning of the modern age saw both the systematic study of the natural and human worlds, and one of the major focuses was the art of ancient Greece and Rome. This trend also led to the idea that there should be institutions to collect, display, and preserve natural specimens and human artifacts—public museums. Art was just one of the branches of collecting in early museums, and the selection about the Sloane Collection (Document 17) in the middle of the eighteenth century describes where modern museums began. In many European nations, the modern world also saw the establishment of national academies to train artists, primarily through the study of the ideas of beauty in the art of ancient Greece and Rome.

The academic system began to break down in the nineteenth century as new artistic ideas developed. William Gilpin (Document 18) is an early example of the search for explanations of artistic expression that break the academic rules of beauty, harmony, proportion, and perfection. By the early twentieth century, many artists were seeking new ways of seeing and representing the world that were increasingly abstract—but no less serious as art, even if they were not well understood. Indeed many of these artists intentionally sought to provoke and shock as part of their artistic practice. These trends led to a significant shift to non-representational art, art that did not represent anything but itself. Kazimir Malevich's manifesto of 1915 (Document 19) that accompanied his exhibition of non-representational art gives an idea of the innovative artistic ideas of the period.

In recent decades, many artists and thinkers have begun to question the basic assumptions of the modern era about art and the role of the artist, artwork, audience, and even the notion of meaning in art. Vitaly Komar and Alex Melamid (Document 20) are postmodern artists whose work is both within the traditions of art while it poses powerful questions about art itself. (See *Postmodernism* in the Glossary.) One of their ongoing projects, part of a series they call "ecocollaboration," involves teaching Asian elephants—left unemployed by restrictions on logging—to paint, then selling their paintings to raise money for elephant conservation, thus combining environmentalism and art in a unique and irreverent way. Komar and Melamid's parodic ecocollaborations are in a way responding to the artistic revolution that Malevich helped to initiate.

Art in the twentieth and twenty-first centuries has also changed not only in the way in which artists work, but also in the media. While traditional media such as painting, drawing, and sculpting remain popular, new genres have emerged, such as found art, performance art, installation art, video art, and others. Some critics feel that the very idea of art has reached the end of its social usefulness, but art will continue to affect the everyday lives not only of the artists, critics, and patrons, but also of everyone who sees and enjoys it.

17. The Beginnings of the Museum: The Sloane Collection in the Eighteenth Century

Museums often seem like perfectly natural institutions, and yet, the public museum, like the public library, is a uniquely modern institution. Beginning in the early modern period, scholars and aristocrats began amassing collections of artifacts and specimens from natural history. Art and antiquities were also valued and collected by interested individuals, including monarchs. None of these collections were open to the public, and they saw themselves as serving their owners or a select few elites or scholars who may have been invited or permitted to use the materials.

The idea of a general public museum or its related institution, the public art museum, did not really take hold until the eighteenth and nineteenth centuries. The following selection, from an eighteenth-century British periodical, coincidentally also the first to use the term "magazine" in its current usage, describes a visit of the Prince of Wales (Frederick, son of King George II) and his wife, the Princess of Wales, as an excuse to describe the contents of Hans Sloane's collection, which he donated to the British Crown and that subsequently formed the core of the collection of what is now the British Museum. The Sloane Collection as described here included biological specimens from plants and animals; precious stones, jewelry, and geological specimens; numismatic commemorative medals from antiquity and contemporary events; anthropological and archaeological collections from ancient and global cultures; and a library of manuscripts and books. Today the British Museum is one of the largest cultural institutions in the world, with over 13 million objects in its collections.

Museums today see their roles as institutions for education, exhibition, preservation, and study and research of objects of importance and value from human culture or the natural world. Millions of objects are held in museum collections, and hundreds of millions of people visit museums every year. They have become an important part of global culture and centers of intellectual life and are a unique development of the modern world.

AN ACCOUNT OF THE PRINCE AND PRINCESS OF WALES VISITING SIR HANS SLOANE

Dr. Mortimer, Secretary to the Royal Society, conducted their Royal Highnesses into the room where Sir Hans was sitting, being ancient and infirm. The Prince took a chair and sat down by the good old gentleman some time, when he expressed the great esteem and value he had for him personally, and how much the learned world was obliged to him for having collected such a vast library of curious books, and such immense treasures of the valuable and instructive productions of nature and art. Sir Hans's house forms a square of above 100 feet each side, inclosing a court and three front rooms had tables set along the middle, which were spread over with drawers fitted with all sorts of precious stones in their natural beds, or state as they are found in the earth, except the first, that contained stones formed in animals, which are so many diseases of the creature that bears them; as the most beautiful pearls, which are but warts in the shell fish; the bezoars, concretions in the stomach; and stones generated in the kidneys and bladder, of which man woefully knows the effects; but the earth in her bosom generates the verdant emerald, the purple amethist, the golden topaz, the azure saphire, the crimson garnet, the scarlet ruby, the brilliant diamond, the glowing opal, and all the painted varieties that Flora herself might wish to be deck'd with; here the most magnificent vessels of cornelian, onyx, sardonyx, and jasper, delighted the eye, and raised the mind to praise the great creator of all things.

When their Royal highnesses had view'd one room and went into another the scene was shifted, for, when they returned, the same tables were covered for a second course with all sorts of jewels, polish'd and set after the modern fashion; or with gems carv'd or engraved; the stately and instructive remains of antiquity; for the third course the tables were spread with gold and silver ores, with the most precious and remarkable ornaments used in the habits of men, from Siberia to the Cape of Good Hope, from Japan to Peru; and with both ancient and modern coins and medals in gold and silver, the lasting monuments of historical facts, as those of a Prusias, king of Bithynia, who betrayed his allies; of an Alexander, who, mad with ambition, over-ran and invaded his neighbors; of a Caesar, who enslaved his country to satisfy his own pride; of a Titus, the delight of mankind; of a Pope Gregory XIII recording on a silver medal his blind zeal for religion, in perpetuating thereon the massacre of the protestants in France; as did Charles IX, the then reigning king in that country; here may be seen the coins of the king of England, crown'd at Paris; a medal representing France and Spain, striving which should first pay their obeisance to Britannia; others shewing the effect of popular rage, when overmuch oppression by their superiors, as in the case of the DeWitts in Holland; the happy deliverance of Britain, by the arrival of King William; the glorious exploits of a Duke of Marlborough, and the happy arrival of the present illustrious royal family amongst us.

The gallery, 110 feet in length, presented a surprising prospect; the most beautiful corals, crystals, and figured stones; the most brilliant butterflies, and other insects, shells painted with as great variety as the precious stones, and feathers of birds vying with gems; here the remains of the Antediluvian world excited the awful idea of that great catastrophe, so many evident testimonies of the truth of Moses's history; the variety of animals shews us great beauty of all parts of the creation.

Then a noble vista presented itself thro' several rooms filled with books, among these many hundred volumes of dry'd plants; a room full of choice and valuable manuscripts; the noble present sent by the present French king to Sir Hans, of his collections of paintings, medals, statues, palaces, & c. in 25 large atlas volumes; besides other things too many to mention here.

Below stairs some rooms are filled with the curious and venerable antiquities of Egypt, Greece, Hetruria, Rome, Britain, and even America; others with large animals preserved in the skin, the great saloon lined on every side with bottles filled with spirits, containing various animals. The halls are adorned with the horns of divers creatures, as the double horn'd Rhinoceros of Africa, the fossil deer's horns from Ireland nine feet wide; and with weapons of different countries, among which it appears that the Mayalese, and not our most Christian neighbors the French, had the honour of inventing that butcherly weapon the bayonet. Fifty volumes in folio would scarce suffice to contain a detail of this immense museum, consisting of above 200,000 articles.

Their royal highnesses were not wanting in expressing their satisfaction and pleasure, at seeing a collection, which surpas'd all the notions or ideas they had formed from even the most favorable accounts of it. The Prince on this occasion shew'd his great reading and most happy memory; for in such a multiplicity, such a variety of the productions of nature and art; upon any thing being shewn to him he had not seen before, he was ready in recollecting where he had read of it, and upon viewing the ancient and modern medals, he made so many judicious remarks, that he appear'd to be a perfect master of history and chronology; he express'd the great pleasure it gave him to see so magnificent a collection in England, esteeming it an ornament to the nation; and expressed his sentiments how much it must conduce to the benefit of learning, and how great an honour will redound to Britain, to have it established for publick use to the latest posterity.

Source: "An Account of the Prince and Princess of Wales visiting Sir Hans Sloane." *The Gentleman's Magazine*. London, July, 1748.

18. William Gilpin on the Picturesque

William Gilpin was an eighteenth-century English minister and amateur artist as well as an aesthetic philosopher. He spent much time sketching the beauty of the English countryside on walking tours and trying to account for the attractiveness of landscape paintings, which did not fit well with any existing aesthetic theory. The most popular at the time focused on an idea of the beautiful that most often related either to antique Greek and Roman originals and found the beautiful in harmony, proportion, and unity, or on eighteenth-century theories such as Edmund Burke's, *which identified features such as delicacy or smoothness, broadly understood.*

Dissatisfied with these, Gilpin developed a new concept, the "picturesque." In this selection, from a 1794 collection of essays on the topic, he makes a clear distinction between real objects, which may be described as beautiful, and a separate category he establishes for art or representations of objects, which are attractive if they have a different kind of quality called the picturesque.

Gilpin proposes an idea that the picturesque is in a sense the opposite of the beautiful, having roughness in a number of aspects, especially composition and texture, as the defining feature of beauty, in contrast with Burke's idea of smoothness. In the end, Gilpin almost gleefully gives up on determining a logical reason why the picturesque should have such appeal. Gilpin does not care if he cannot find an explanation for why the picturesque is so attractive and compelling: it is sufficient for him to know that it is.

The idea that art can be attractive or compelling without being beautiful in the traditional or classical sense gave a new kind of freedom to artists, whether they painted landscapes or not. Although Gilpin himself did not go so far, his theory is a step toward greater experimentation and allowance for individual expression. The sublime, or awesome power of nature; vigorous, evident brushwork; more energetic, dynamic compositions; and new, less smooth materials like bronze and watercolor gained currency in art. Good art could be provocative, unconventional, and even ugly; nor did it have to be real or rational. Inspiration, emotion, and self-expression became key elements of creativity, and remain central ideas to what the popular understanding of art and the artist are today.

Disputes about beauty might perhaps be involved in less confusion, if a distinction were established, which certainly exists, between such objects as are beautiful, and such as are picturesque—between those, which please the eye in their natural state; and those, which please from some quality, capable of being illustrated in painting. Ideas of beauty vary with the object, and with the eye of the spectator. Those artificial forms appear generally the most beautiful, with which we have been the most conversant. Thus the stone-mason sees beauties in a well-jointed wall, which escape the architect, who surveys the building under a different idea. And thus the painter, who compares his object with the rules of his art, sees it in a different light from the man of general taste, who surveys it only as simply beautiful.

As this difference therefore between the beautiful, and the picturesque appears really to exist, and must depend on some peculiar construction of the object; it may be worth while to examine, what that peculiar construction is. We inquire not into the general sources of beauty, either in nature, or in representation. This would lead into a nice, and scientific discussion, in which it is not our purpose to engage. The question simply is, What is that quality in objects, which particularly marks them as picturesque?

In examining the real object, we shall find, one source of beauty arises from that species of elegance, which we call smoothness, or neatness; for the terms are nearly synonymous. The higher the marble is polished, the brighter the silver is rubbed, and the more the mahogany shines, the more each is considered as an object of beauty: as if the eye delighted in gliding smoothly over a surface.

In the class of larger objects the same idea prevails. In a pile of building we wish to see neatness in every part added to the elegance of the architecture. And if we examine a piece of improved pleasure-ground, every thing rough, and slovenly offends.

Mr. Burke, enumerating the properties of beauty, considers smoothness as one of the most essential. "A very considerable part of the effect of beauty, says he, is owing to this quality: indeed the most considerable: for take any beautiful object, and give it a broken, and rugged surface, and however well-formed it may be in other respects, it pleases no longer. Whereas, let it want ever so many of the other constituents, if it want not this, it becomes more pleasing, than almost all the others without it." How far Mr. Burke may be right in making smoothness the most considerable source of beauty, I rather doubt. A considerable one it certainly is.

Thus then, we suppose, the matter stands with regard to beautiful objects in general. But in picturesque representation it seems somewhat odd, yet we may perhaps find it equally true, that the reverse of this is the case; and that the ideas of neat and smooth, instead of being picturesque, in fact disqualify the object, in which they reside, from any pretentions to picturesque beauty. Nay farther, we do not scruple to assert, that roughness forms the most essential point of difference between the beautiful, and the picturesque; as it seems to be that particular quality, which makes objects chiefly pleasing in painting.—I use the general term roughness; but properly speaking roughness relates only to the surfaces of bodies: when we speak of their delineation, we use the word ruggedness. Both ideas however equally enter into the picturesque; and both are observable in the smaller, as well as in the larger parts of nature—in the outline, and bark of a tree, as in the rude summit, and craggy sides of a mountain. [...]

[R]oughness either real, or apparent, forms an essential difference between the beautiful, and the picturesque; it may be expected, that we should point out the reason of this difference. It is obvious enough, why the painter prefers rough objects to smooth: but it is not so obvious, why the quality of roughness should make an essential difference between the objects of nature, and the objects of artificial representation. [...]

Thus foiled, may we in the true spirit of inquiry, persist; or honestly give up the cause, and own we cannot search out the source of this difference? I am afraid this is the truth, whatever airs of dogmatizing we may assume. Inquiries into principles rarely end in satisfaction. Could we even gain satisfaction in our present question, new doubts would arise. The very first principles of our art would be questioned. [...]

Thus, in our inquiries into first principles, we go on, without end, and without satisfaction. The human understanding is unequal to the search. In philosophy we inquire for them in vain—in physics—in metaphysics—in morals. Even in the polite arts, where the subject, one could imagine, is less recondite, the inquiry, we find, is equally vague. We are puzzled, and bewildered; but not informed. All is uncertainty.

Source: Gilpin, William. *Three Essays on Picturesque Beauty; on Picturesque Travel, and on Sketching Landscape, to Which is Added a Poem, On Landscape Painting*. London: B. Blamire, 1794.

19. *Kazimir Malevich: "The Zero of Form"*

The beginning of the twentieth century saw a flurry of artistic change and innovation. Artists such as Henri Matisse *and Pablo* Picasso *built on the ideas of Impressionists and others and introduced radical changes in the ways art was understood and created. Photography, too, was crucially important, revealing not only how things looked at a particular moment, offering its own qualities as an artistic medium, but also in a sense freeing art from the demand for verisimilitude. Artists quickly seized on this to experiment with styles and ideas. In Paris and Munich, New York and Moscow, young artists gathered, debated, and argued about the new art, about the avant-garde or "leading edge" of what was seen as artistic progress.*

Up until the first decades of the twentieth century, artists had always painted a picture of something else. One of the most important and radical steps in modern art was the shift to non-objective art. For the first time, painters began painting pictures of nothing else—the paintings were not pictures of anything but themselves. One of the pioneers of this dramatic change in art, Kazimir Malevich, was born in 1878 in the Ukraine *to Polish parents and moved to* Moscow *in 1904 to pursue a career in art; he rapidly became a leader of Russian artistic* Modernism.

The following selection is excerpted from Malevich's 1915 manifesto From Cubism and Futurism to Suprematism: The New Painterly Realism, *published in conjunction with the exhibition of paintings in a new style he called "Suprematism." Suprematist paintings are stark, angular, and plain. They show simple, slightly irregular geometric shapes carefully chosen and placed on a white background. Most importantly, they are not simply abstract (a distorted or stylized representation), but truly non-objective.*

Malevich's writing, like his painting, is brash, declamatory, and intentionally provocative. His poor education is revealed in his bad grammar and awkward style. Still, he manages to readily insult and demean other artists and all other artistic styles, especially naturalistic and academic art. Yet there is such an extraordinary enthusiasm for the new—progress and innovation—that it overrides the negativity.

Some may dismiss Malevich's art and manifesto, which he saw as being a first step in the transformation of modern life, as silly or unserious or as not even art, but if he and his fellow artists were serious about anything, they were serious about their art, which still remains iconoclastic and confrontational a century later.

Only when the conscious habit of seeing nature's little nooks, Madonnas, and Venuses in pictures disappears will we witness a purely painterly work of art.

I have transformed myself in the zero of form and have fished myself out of the rubbishy slough of academic art.

I have destroyed the ring of the horizon and got out of the circle of objects, the horizon ring that has imprisoned the artist and the forms of nature.

This accursed ring, by continually revealing novelty after novelty, leads the artist away from the aim of destruction.

And only cowardly consciousness and insolvency of creative power in an artist yield to this deception and establish their art on the forms of nature, afraid of losing the foundation on which the savage and the academy have based their art.

To produce favorite objects and little nooks of nature is just like a thief being enraptured by his shackled legs.

Only dull and impotent artists veil their work with sincerity. Art requires truth, not sincerity.

Objects have vanished like smoke; to attain the new artistic culture, art advances toward creation as an end in itself and toward domination over the forms of nature. [...]

In repeating or tracing the forms of nature, we have nurtured our consciousness with a false conception of art.

The work of the primitives was taken for creation.

The classics also.

If you put the same glass down twenty times, that's also creation.

Art, as the ability to transmit what we see onto a canvas, was considered creation.

Is placing a samovar on a table also really creation?

I think quite differently.

The transmission of real objects onto a canvas is the art of skillful reproduction, that's all.

And between the art of creating and the art of repeating there is a great difference.

To create means to live, forever creating newer and newer things.

And however much we arrange furniture about rooms, we will not extend or create a new form for them.

And however many moonlit landscapes the artist paints, however many grazing cows and pretty sunsets, they will remain the same dear little cows and sunsets. Only in a much worse form.

And in fact, whether an artist is a genius or not is determined by the number of cows he paints.

The artist can be a creator only when the forms in his picture have nothing in common with nature.

For art is the ability to create a construction that derives not from the interrelation of form and color and not on the basis of aesthetic taste in a construction's compositional beauty, but on the basis of weight, speed, and direction of movement.

Forms must be given life and the right to individual existence. [. . .]

An artist is under a vow to be a free creator, but not a free robber.

An artist is given talent in order that he may present to life his share of creation and swell the current of life, so versatile.

Only in absolute creation will he acquire his right.

And this is possible when we free all art of philistine ideas and subject matter and teach our consciousness to see everything in nature not as real objects and forms, but as material, as masses from which forms must be made that have nothing in common with nature.

Then the habit of seeing Madonnas and Venuses in pictures, with fat, flirtatious cupids, will disappear.

Color and texture are of the greatest value in painterly creation—they are the essence of painting; but this essence has always been killed by the subject.

And if the masters of the Renaissance had discovered painterly surface, it would have been much nobler and more valuable than any Madonna or Gioconda [Mona Lisa].

And any hewn pentagon or hexagon would have been a greater work of sculpture than the Venus de Milo or David.

The principle of the savage is to aim to create art that repeats the real forms of nature.

In intending to transmit the living form, they transmitted its corpse in the picture.

The living was turned into a motionless, dead state.

Everything was taken alive and pinned quivering to the canvas, just as insects are pinned in a collection. [. . .]

Suprematist Painting. Kazimir Malecich, 1915. Art Resource, NY.

The efforts of the art authorities to direct art along the path of common sense annulled creation.

And with the most talented people, real form is distortion.

Distortion was driven by the most talented to the point of disappearance, but it did not go outside the bounds of zero.

But I have transformed myself in the zero of form and through zero have reached creation, that is, suprematism, the new painterly realism—nonobjective creation.

Suprematism is the beginning of a new culture: the savage is conquered like the ape.

There is no longer love of little nooks, there is no longer love for which the truth of art was betrayed.

The square is not a subconscious form. It is the creation of intuitive reason.

The face of the new art.

The square is a living, regal infant.

The first step of pure creation in art. Before it there were naïve distortions and copies of nature.

Our world of art has become new, nonobjective, pure.

Everything has disappeared; a mass of material is left from which a new form will be built.

In the art of suprematism, forms will live, like all living forms of nature. These forms announce that man has attained his equilibrium; he has left the level of single reason and reached one of double reason.

(Utilitarian reason and intuitive reason.)

The new painterly realism is a painterly one precisely because it has no realism of mountains, sky, water. . . .

Hitherto there has been a realism of objects, but not of painterly, colored units, which are constructed so that they depend neither on form, nor on color, nor on their position vis-a-vis each other.

Each form is free and individual.

Each form is a world.

Any painterly surface is more alive than any face from which a pair of eyes and a smile protrude.

A face painted in a picture gives a pitiful parody of life, and this allusion is merely a reminder of the living.

But a surface lives; it has been born. A coffin reminds us of the dead; a picture, of the living.

This is why it is strange to look at a red or black painted surface. This is why people snigger and spit at the exhibitions of new trends. Art and its new aim have always been a spittoon.

But cats get used to one place, and it is difficult to house-train them to a new one.

For such people, art is quite unnecessary, as long as their grandmothers and favorite little nooks of lilac groves are painted. [. . .]

I say to all: Abandon love, abandon aestheticism, abandon the baggage of wisdom, for in the new culture, your wisdom is ridiculous and insignificant. I have untied the knots of wisdom and liberated the consciousness of

color!

Hurry up and shed the hardened skin of centuries, so that you can catch up with us more easily.

I have overcome the impossible and made gulfs with my breath. You are caught in the nets of the horizon, like fish!

We, suprematists, throw open the way to you.

Hurry!

For tomorrow you will not recognize us.

Source: From *Russian Art of the Avant-Garde: Theory and Criticism* edited and translated by John E. Bowlt

20. Vitaly Komar and Alex Melamid: If An Elephant Could Paint . . .

Sometimes people look at a work of contemporary *art and say (or at least think), "That looks like a monkey painted it!" In the case of a recent project by artists Vitaly Komar and Alex Melamid, it wasn't a monkey—it was an elephant. The Asian Elephant Art and Conservation Project (AEACP) is both a non-profit environmentalist organization and an ongoing work of art by Komar and Melamid. When environmental concerns led to the banning of teak logging in Southeast Asia—putting logging elephants out of work—the fate of the pachyderms and their handlers became very precarious. Conserving these animals and teaching them to become artists is a typical maneuver for Komar and Melamid, who have a series of (sometimes unrealized) projects they call "ecollaborations," in which they attempt to create artistic collaborations with other species, including dogs, monkeys, beavers, termites, and, most successfully, elephants.*

Komar and Melamid began their careers as dissident artists in the Union of Soviet Socialist Republics. *After having their works literally plowed under by a bulldozer at an unofficial, unsanctioned exhibition in 1974 for developing a new style of painting called "Sotsart" (a parodic combination of Dada, Pop Art, and Socialist Realism, the official artistic style and doctrine of the Soviet Union), they left the Soviet Union in 1977 to criticize not only the Communism they left behind, but the capitalism they found in the West.*

The selection, from the AEACP Web site, shows the elephant art project is serious, yet very much aware of the confrontation it provokes with ideas of art. Are elephant paintings really art? If elephants can paint works that look like human works, are the human works really art and how much value do they have? Are the elephants the artists, or are Komar and Melamid? There is a sense that they are just exploiting an art world that is gullible enough to take this seriously and buy elephant paintings, but the purchasers know what they're doing and even feel they're being ecologically responsible in the process.

If abstract and non-representational art by humans is often considered meaningless and so simple anyone could do it, two postmodern artists have combined a variety of criticisms of contemporary art with global environmentalist concerns in an ongoing postmodern art project that both validates and questions notions of art, artist, audience, creativity, and meaning in art—and connects art with the everyday life not only of people, but elephants, too.

The *Asian Elephant Art & Conservation Project* (AEACP) is a non-profit organization dedicated to aiding people in need and to saving the diminishing number of Asian elephants left on our planet through its work with domesticated elephants. The AEACP raises funds through the sale of artwork created by elephants in order to generate money and create awareness for the people and elephants of Asia.

The AEACP is a continuing work of art by conceptual artists, Komar & Melamid. In its creation, Komar & Melamid brought the idea of teaching elephants how to paint from US zoos to the impoverished countryside of Southeast Asia, where the much needed ban on logging in the late 80's left the remaining few thousand elephants and their caretakers out of work. The extensive logging of the countryside and the explosion of the human population in the area led to the destruction of much of the elephants' natural habitat, leaving them with no wild to return to. Thousands of elephants and their lifelong caretakers were left without financial support and have since been forced to beg for food on crowded city streets. The *Asian Elephant Art & Conservation Project* is designed to help these surviving elephants and the people that care for them. The project is grounded on the basis of art functioning as charity, or art for the betterment of people as a whole.

The idea of art as charity is a largely original concept, although based in a long line of art rhetoric. Back in the 1920's, the Russian theorist, Chuzhak, coined the term, "life building" based upon his studies of Alexander Bogdanov's Organizational Theory of Art, in which Bogdanov theorized that art, as with any human activity, is based upon organization. Art, Bogdanov argued, was simply the organization of colors, lines, shapes, medium, etc. Under this premise, Bogdanov claimed that art of the future would involve the actual organization of people themselves, hopefully for the betterment of those peoples' lives.

During the 60's and 70's these concepts of "life building" were revived in the works of German artist, Joseph Beuys, in what he called, "social sculpture." His works as well as the French Situationists ideas of artistic intervention were based upon the concepts of Russian Constructivism. Komar & Melamid's *Asian Elephant Art & Conservation Project* is a continuation of this body of thought. The marketing and sales of the elephants' work is the pure expression of basic Constructivist theories. The major difference between this project and similar works by artists such as Andy Warhol and Jeff Koons is that the AEACP is not built on a 'business' model, but rather as a full-fledged nonprofit organization designed to better the world in which we live.

The AEACP is not necessarily a vehicle for social change, as Joseph Beuys may have envisioned, but does function as a charity designed to increase peoples' consciousness and to help those individuals in need. Money that is raised by the AEACP is distributed to the people of Southeast Asia, in countries such as Thailand, Cambodia, and Indonesia. The funds raised through the sale of elephant art have real power to improve peoples' lives as well as to improve the welfare of the world's remaining elephants. In order to accomplish our existing mission, we need to expand our realm of influence and activity around the globe. [. . .]

The Asian Elephant Art & Conservation Project (AEACP) promotes and distributes the work of elephant artists to raise funds for elephant conservation. By exhibiting and marketing the paintings internationally, the AEACP aims to increase public awareness of the plight of Asian elephants whose numbers are dwindling at an alarming rate. In recent years, the number of domesticated elephants in Thailand alone has rapidly diminished from 11,000 to only 3,000. Deforestation of the Thai countryside has led to a ban on the logging of teak, an industry that once employed thousands of elephants. Although much needed, the logging ban left these elephants and their life-long owners (mahouts) without a livelihood.

Upon hearing of the situation in Southeast Asia, Komar & Melamid began their first collaboration with an elephant, Renee, at the Toledo Zoo in Ohio in 1995. It was here that Komar & Melamid first developed their method of teaching elephants to paint. Elephants in United States zoos have been painting successfully for two decades. One such painting pachyderm at the Phoenix Zoo named Ruby generated more than $100,000 for the zoo in a single year. After working with elephants in the States, Komar & Melamid then introduced the idea of teaching elephants how to paint to Asia and two years later founded the Asian Elephant Art & Conservation Project.

Komar & Melamid first traveled to Thailand in 1998 and worked with elephants in Lampang, Ayutthaya, Surin, and Phuket. Later that year they gave their first lecture about their elephant art project at the Getty Research Institute in Los Angeles, California. In November 1998, Komar & Melamid opened the world's first elephant art academy in Lampang. To celebrate this event, the Hilton International Hotel in Bangkok hosted the AEACP's first exhibition of elephant art.

In June 1999, Komar & Melamid were asked to represent Russia at the prestigious Venice Biennial and the duo included works by elephant artists Jurhanam, Phitsamai, and Nam Chok—a historic first for elephant artists.

In August 1999, the AEACP established another colony of painting elephants near Ubud in Bali, Indonesia. In conjunction with the Mimi Ferzt Gallery in New York, a selection of elephant paintings created during this period was exhibited at the millennium art show at the Four Seasons in Bali.

In March 2000, a Christie's Auction of elephant art held in New York raised a staggering $75,000 for elephant conservation. One painting was purchased by a collector for $2200.

In 2001, the Sydney Museum of Contemporary Art in Australia raised $27,000 and saw over 42,000 visitors come through its doors for the largest exhibition of elephant art to date.

In the summer of 2002, the AEACP wrapped up another exhibition and online auction of elephant art at the Berkeley Museum of Art in California, which raised an additional $20,000 for this important cause.

The winter of 2002/2003, the AEACP established the first Cambodian elephant art center at the Tamao Wildlife Rescue Center in Phnom Penh, as well as two new centers in Thailand and two in Indonesia, one of which is located on the grounds of the magnificent Borobudur Temple in Central Java.

2003 brought the AEACP and elephant art to the shores of Japan. The Kawamura Memorial Museum of Art just outside of Tokyo held the country's first exhibition of elephant art, even bringing in a Thai elephant for the opening ceremonies. The exhibition was an amazing success, bringing much media attention to the museum. Since the close of the exhibition, two smaller gallery exhibits of elephant art have taken place in and near Tokyo.

The AEACP has received attention and support from around the globe. Komar & Melamid's work with elephants has been featured in the *New York Times*, *The Wall Street Journal*, *The Nation* and *Esquire*, as well as featured on CBS *Sunday Morning*, the *Lehrer NewsHour*, and a substantial segment on *60 Minutes*.

Source: Asian Elephant Art and Conservation Project website (www.elephantart.com). Text by David Ferris. Reprinted with permission.

Part V

MATERIAL LIFE

Material life covers a wide scope of everyday life—the kind of house we live in, the type of food we eat, the variety of clothes we wear, but also the technology we use to work, study, recreate, or just to get about. The stuff of everyday life satisfies our most basic need for shelter and sustenance, but it often does a great deal more than that. Scholars refer to this collectively as "material culture," and just as archaeological objects are important sources for understanding the material life of the distant past, the same is true for the present and the recent, modern past.

This section is divided into subsections on food and drink, houses and furniture, clothing and personal appearance, and technology. The technology subsection is connected to all of the other sections in one way or another; technological changes have driven many of the changes in these aspects of material life. Connections can also readily be drawn between these areas and other aspects of daily life. Florence Nightingale's ideas (Document 7) on cleanliness and health in housing relates to ideas current in medical science, Mary Fulton's discussion of clothing (Document 13) touches on religion and women's roles, Venel's discussion of chocolate (Document 1) is easily linked with growing international trade and European expansion, and Antoinette Linnebur's civic-minded cake recipes (Document 5) reflect an intersection with political life.

Eating and drinking are among the most common everyday human activities, but food and drink have changed fundamentally in the modern world—Isabella Beeton (Document 3) even reflects on this directly in her book on the household. In many respects, food and drink in 1700 was very different from food today. Commodities like cane sugar, chocolate, coffee, tea, and tobacco were becoming widespread but were expensive luxury goods, not staples. Canning, freezing, and refrigeration were unknown, and perishable foods out of season were a technical and logistical impossibility. Food is now global in its sources and influences, a process that has been the result of modern transportation, trade, migration, and the politics of *colonialism* and empire. Table manners, such as described by Arthur Young (Document 2), and recipe transcription, essentially reinvented by Mrs. Beeton, were different, as are the recipes—few people today eat George Washington Pie, much less Toad-in-the-Hole.

Many of the changes in food are technological as well. In food and drink many modern technologies have had far-reaching benefits. Modern agricultural techniques, food safety procedures, and transportation systems have created far greater food security for many—meaning stable, reliable food supplies. Eric Schlosser's muckraking (Document 6) points out that some of the benefits of contemporary technology also have negative aspects. Sometimes food safety systems break down, and there is much about the food we eat—such as the flavoring industry—that we don't know.

Not only the food but also the kitchens and houses in which it is cooked have been altered by developments of the modern period. The addition to domestic architecture over the last 300 years of modern conveniences such as clean running hot and cold water, wastewater sewers, automated climate control, electricity and gas utilities, and other innovations, have fundamentally changed the conditions of material life. Florence Nightingale (Document 7) argued for reforms of private domestic spaces for health reasons. Arthur Train's (Document 9) attempt to predict the future of the twentieth century is surprisingly accurate despite some missteps. The lifestyle of the *Bedouins* of Morocco could hardly be more different. Edmondo De Amicis's visit (Document 8) to Morocco also shows that modern isn't the same everywhere. There are many parts of the modern world where the material culture of industrial societies had not been adopted.

Major trends in modern clothing include the industrialization of the textile industry in the eighteenth and nineteenth centuries, and introduction of synthetic fabrics in the twentieth. Styles of clothing also changed and interacted with other styles from different parts of the modern world. As is the case today, social position was also strongly indicated by clothing: Abigail Adams (Document 10) describes the elaborate dresses of social elites who were still responsible for their own designs, and Leo Deutsch (Document 12) describes being put into prisoner's garb—including having half his head shaved. Some criticize fashion for being impractical, as Florence Nightingale (Document 11) does, and some embrace it, as does Georgia Scott (Document 14) in her discussion of the head wraps of the modern Maya, and Mary Fulton (Document 13) believes her dresses help make her a religious and cultural role model.

The development of technology may seem to be a part of everyday material life that is different from the way that clothing, housing, and food are part of daily life, but technological changes are an important part of what housing looks like; how food is made, packaged, prepared, and even eaten; and what kind of materials are available for clothing and the like. New technologies like steam power, machinery, automobiles, factories, and, more recently, computers have been some of the most defining changes of the modern world, in part because of how they have affected many other aspects of life. Just in terms of material culture, for example, textile machinery and factories altered clothing, while Robert Fulton's (Document 16) steamboats and later gas-powered tractors and trucks, cousins of the automobile (Document 17), changed agriculture and transportation, transforming food and drink. The *Industrial Revolution* is only one part of technological change. The modern world is in the midst of an information revolution as well. Just like Arthur Train (Document 9) tried to imagine in 1938 what 1988 would be like in housing, Jennifer Flynn (Document 18) tries to imagine what the current past will look like from the future. Even the recent past reveals the complexity of contemporary computing technology, which from cell phones to virtual avatars is continuing to change the material reality of everyday life.

Food and Drink

Without food and drink, humans cannot survive, and, obviously, eating and drinking are as old as human life. Yet even as the customs of eating and drinking are different in different times and places around the world, varying with culture, class, climate, and availability of food, there are modern trends in the ways that we eat and drink.

Food is part of everyday life, and is mentioned in most of the other parts of this volume. Preparing and sharing meals is one of the primary activities of domestic groups, and is central to domestic family life and cultural celebrations. Food also finds its way into religious life in fundamental ways, either as a part of ritual, like the Christian *Eucharist* or commemorative feasts, like the Jewish *Passover Seder,* or as in the food offerings to spirits in Japanese *Shinto*.

Growing and trading food for other goods and services is one of the foundations of economic life, and the global trade in food has not only spread certain food products and preparation techniques around the world, but made them central parts of trade. Many of the most popular consumables are grown in parts of the world far from where they are consumed, including coffee, tea, tobacco, and chocolate. Isabella Beeton's recipe (Document 3) for Bengal "chetney" and Gabriel Venel's entry (Document 1) on chocolate in Diderot and d'Alembert's eighteenth-century *Encyclopèdie* both show the increasingly global nature of food in the modern world, as does Samuel G. Wilson's (Document 4) description of tea and tobacco in nineteenth-century *Persia* and Eric Schlosser's critique (Document 6) of the flavoring industry and—yet another uniquely modern phenomenon—the globalization of the fast food industry at the end of the twentieth century.

Mrs. Beeton was the first to write a recipe in the way almost all recipes are presented today, with a list of ingredients and amounts followed by a step-by-step description of preparation. Her menus and recipes, while not especially attractive today, also show the increasing stability of food supplies, changing ideas about what cooking is, and a new kind of book for mass modern life: the cookbook. Antoinette Linnebur (Document 5) shows another way that cooking is connected to everyday life. Using Beeton's format to write recipes, seemingly normal dessert recipes from the nineteenth century connect to a long tradition of politically motivated food. While George *Washington* and the Prince of Wales may have been more honored personages than politicians, it is certainly part of a tradition, now lost, to cook for your candidate.

Modern agricultural and transportation techniques have enabled many people to eat a rich, varied, and appealing diet, including a host of foods out of season and from distant places. At the same time, in other—or even the same—parts of the world, others die for want of food or suffer from malnutrition. None of the entries in this section deal directly with the global inequities of food resources, but famine, like that which underlies Arthur Young's (Document 2) visit to France and Samuel Wilson's description of impoverished Persians, still occurs, and though less common than in the pre-modern past, hunger remains an unfortunate part of modern life.

1. Chocolate: The Food of the Gods

Today chocolate is one of the favorite foods of people around the world; it was also a favorite in the eighteenth century. Known to the Spanish after their contact with Mesoamericans in the sixteenth century, chocolate became a popular luxury item in Europe, steadily gaining popularity throughout the modern period not only for its flavor, but also for its medical properties.

Chocolate, technically speaking, is a food or drink made from the fermented and roasted seeds of the tropical cacao tree, the scientific name of which (theobroma cacao) *means "food of the gods," but its significance is much more than that. It is perhaps the most popular flavor in the world, and chocolate, along with various other food and drink products that began to be imported into Europe in large quantities in the modern era, are linked to important changes in modern culture as well.*

Fashionable, imported drinks such as coffee and chocolate gave rise to public places to consume them, which unlike taverns and other public houses, became places for reading the newspapers, for public political discourse, and for the interaction of a growing intelligentsia, which was enhanced, as compared to bars, by the sobriety of the patrons. Coffee houses and chocolate houses spread across Europe, bringing political and cultural activity with them. The growing demand for cocoa, which can only be grown in tropical environments, like the growth in other commodities like sugar, indigo, coffee, cotton, and tea, either for food or drink or other material needs, also had a significant economic impact on trade patterns.

At the request of Denis Diderot, *one of the French leaders of the* Enlightenment *and one of the editors of the* Encyclopèdie, *Gabriel Venel wrote the entry on chocolate, from which the selection is taken. His article is an interesting combination of anthropology, botany, medicine, and cookery, and he provides everything from the history of chocolate to a wide range of advice and even recipes for how to prepare it. Chocolate was important then, and is important now as the typical dessert, and an important food in many holiday celebrations. Many cannot imagine everyday life without it.*

Chocolate, a type of cake or bar prepared with different ingredients but whose basic element is cocoa. See Cocoa. The beverage made from this bar retains the same name; the cocoa nut originates from the Americas: Spanish travelers established that it was much used in Mexico, when they conquered it around 1520.

Indians, who have enjoyed this beverage since the dawn of time, prepared it in a very simple way: they would roast the cocoa nuts in their clay pots, melt it in warm water and mix the result with some spice, see Spice; for more mannered people, achiote would be added to add some color to the mixture, while atolle would serve to give it more volume. Atolle is a stew made from corn flour, either spiced up by the Mexicans or whose flavor was enhanced by Spanish nuns or ladies, not with spices, but with sugar, cinnamon, scented oils, amber, musk, etc. In these regions, atolle is used in similar ways, for rising rice cream. All these ingredients mixed together give this composition so rough an appearance and so wild a taste, that a Spanish soldier once said that it would be more appropriate to the feeding of pigs than to the relish of humans; and that he would never have gotten used to it, if it were not for the shortage of wine that forced him to such a violent alternative, so that he could alternate pure water with something else.

Spaniards, who learned about this beverage from the Mexicans and were convinced, through their own experience that this beverage, though unrefined, was good for the health, set out to correct its defaults by adding sugar, some ingredients from the Orient, and several local drugs that it is unnecessary to list here, as we only know their name and as, from all these extras, only the vanilla leaf traveled to our regions (similarly, cinnamon was the only ingredient that was universally approved) and proved to resist time as part of the composition of chocolate.

The sweet scent and potent taste it imparts to chocolate have made it highly recommended for it; but time has shown that it could potentially upset one's stomach, and its use has decreased; some people who favor the care of their health to the pleasure of their senses, have stopped using it completely. In Spain and in Italy, chocolate prepared without vanilla has been termed the healthy chocolate; and in our French islands in the Americas, where vanilla is neither rare nor expensive, as it can be in Europe, it is never used, when the consumption of chocolate is as high as in any other part of the world. [. . .]

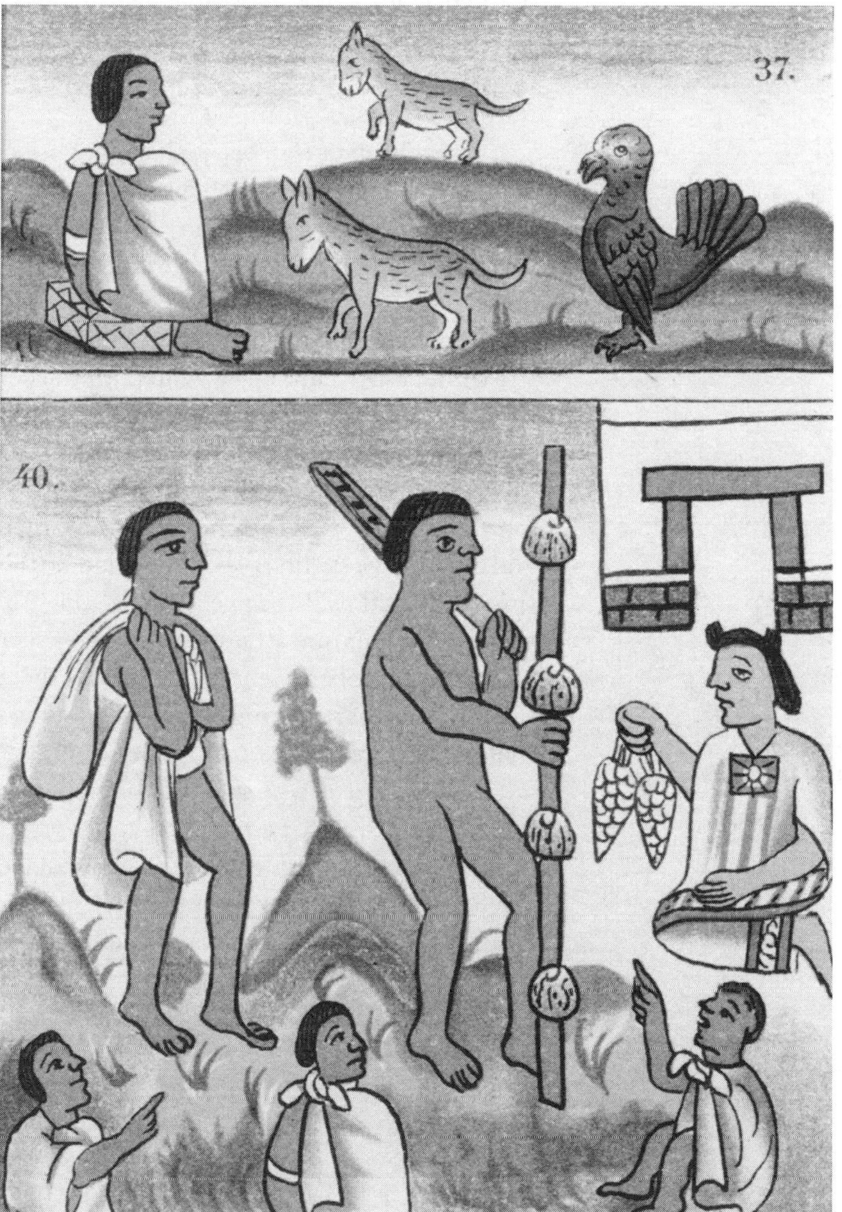

A scene of Aztecs growing cocoa beans from the Florentine codex, c. 1570. The Art Archive / Mireille Vautier.

When the cocoa paste has been well shredded on the stone (see Article Cocoa), sugar can be added once it has been filtered through a silk-cloth sifter; the secret to the true proportion of cocoa and sugar is to put equal quantity of both: one could in fact subtract one quarter out of the dosage of sugar, as it might dry up the paste too much, or render it too sensitive to changes in the air, or endanger it even more to the apparition of worms. But that suppressed quarter of sugar must be used when chocolate, the beverage, is being prepared.

Once sugar is well mixed with the cocoa paste, a very thin powder can be added, made with vanilla seeds and cinnamon sticks finely cut and sifted together; this new mixture shall be mixed on the stone; once every ingredient is well incorporated, the mixture shall be poured into chocolatière pots, the shape of which it will take, and where it will harden. When one loves scents, one could add some amber essence into the pots.

When chocolate is made without vanilla, the proportion of cinnamon is of two dragmes for each pound of cocoa; but if one wants to use vanilla, then the dosage of cinnamon should be cut at least in half. As for vanilla, its measurement is arbitrary: one, two, or three drops, even more, for each pound of cocoa, according to one's whim.

Chocolate chefs, to make it feel like they did use a lot of vanilla, resort to the use of pepper, ginger, etc. There exists some people of declared high taste who would not have it any other way; but, as these spices can but only lead to stomach upsets, wise people would shy away from these excesses, and will pay great attention to never enjoy any chocolate whose composition they have not ensured.

Any chocolate made in this fashion has this quality, that if one is in a hurry to go out, or one travels and lacks the time to melt it in a beverage, one could eat one ounce of the bar, and drink right after it, leaving to the stomach to mix that lunch on the go.

In the Caribbean islands, habits are to make pure cocoa bars, without any other ingredients. See Cocoa. And when one wants to turn his chocolate into a drink, here is how to proceed.

Preparation of chocolate a la French Islands in the Americas: One shreds the cocoa bars in very thin layers with a knife, or rather with a flat grater, when the bats are dry enough and not greasy; when the desired quantity has been shredded, (for example, four filled teaspoonfuls which would amount to one ounce) two or three sprinkles of cinnamon, through a sifter, can be added, as two teaspoonfuls of powdered sugar.

The mixture is then placed in a dish with a fresh egg, that is, both with the yolk and the white; mix well, using a whip until the consistence of liquid honey is reached; then, boiling liquid (water or milk, according to one's whim) can be poured as the stirring continues, so that everything mixes well.

Finally, the dish is put on the stove, or is double-boiled in a caldron filled with boiling water; as soon as the chocolate rises, the dish should be taken away from the heat; and after heavy stirring of the chocolate with the whip, the mixture is poured, in several times, and still well-whipped, in the cups. To heighten the scent, one could add before pouring the mixture a teaspoon of water scented with orange flower, in which one or two drops of amber essences had previously been dissolved.

This way of preparing chocolate has several advantages that are inherent to it, and that makes it preferable to all others.

At first, one can be sure that, if prepared according to the instructions, this chocolate has an exquisite perfume and tastes wonderfully; it is furthermore extremely gentle on your stomach, and leaves no messy residues either in the dish, or in the cups.

Secondly, one may at will prepare it as one fancies, adding more or less sugar and cinnamon, adding or not water scented with orange flower and amber essence; in a word, to make any changes that one would hold for more agreeable.

Thirdly, because nothing was added that could substitute the good qualities of the cocoa nut, the beverage proves to be so neutral that one can enjoy it at any time of the day, however old one might be, in the summer as well as in the winter, without fearing the least problem: whereas chocolate seasoned with vanilla and other sour, spicy ingredients can sometimes be dangerous, especially during the summer for the young and for those with vivacious, dry constitutions. The glass of cool water that one usually drinks before or after the chocolate can only temporarily alleviate the fire that it ignites in the blood and the entrails, once the soothing water has passed along.

Fourthly, this chocolate is so cheap that a cup of it will cost you one sou. If artisans were to learn about this aspect, few would fail to profit from such an easy, gracious, and cheap lunch that needs no other food to accompany it, be it solid or liquid. Nat. hist. of cocoa, see Cocoa.

Source: Venel, Gabriel, "Chocolate." In *La Encyclopèdie*, ed. Denis Diderot and Jean le Rond d'Alembert. Volume 3. Paris: 1751–1777. Trans. Philippe Bonin. Courtesy of Philippe Bonin.

2. French Cuisine and British Cooking

Arthur Young, on his journeys though France just before the French Revolution *in the late eighteenth century, not only made extensive notes on the condition of French agriculture and economy (Economic Life, Document 5), but also, as part of his travel notes, commented on the meals he ate and the manners he observed.*

Stereotypically, English cooking is disparaged and the French are the acknowledged culinary masters of the world. Young, an Englishman in France, offers little to disprove this general perspective. He claims the superiority of a handful of English dishes, but there is a sense that the claim is a formality required by patriotism: who wants boiled mutton and potatoes when you can have French food, and Young is happy to praise French cuisine.

More importantly, he comments at some length on the differences in manners and practices between the English and the French tables. Not only is Young favorably impressed by French food, as indicated by his description of some of the meals he enjoys, but he also comments at some length on the differences in manners and practices between English and French tables. One discovers, for example, that Englishmen would commonly share glasses and not use napkins or table linens, nor have dessert, except among the wealthier classes.

The variety and skill of French cooking, even in rural France in the eighteenth century, shows something of the variety and quality of food available to the traveler in France, and the diet of those who could afford such meals at the time of the French Revolution. It is also important to remember that just prior to the French Revolution there were several failed harvests and several harsh winters; the price of bread spiked and many were hungry or unable to afford food. Even so, Young tells us in his own words about the everyday food and manners of two different but related countries in the first part of the modern *period.*

One of the most amusing circumstances of travelling into other countries is the opportunity of remarking the difference of customs amongst different nations in the common occurrences of life. In the art of living the French have generally been esteemed by the rest of Europe to have made the greatest proficiency, and their manners have been accordingly more imitated and their customs more adopted than those of any other nation. Of their cookery there is but one opinion; for every man in Europe that can afford a great table either keeps a French cook or one instructed in the same manner. That it is far beyond our own I have no doubt in asserting. We have about half a dozen real English dishes that exceed anything, in my opinion, to be met with in France; by English dishes I mean a turbot and lobster sauce—ham and chicken—turtle—a haunch of venison—a turkey and oysters—and after these there is an end of an English table. It is an idle prejudice to class roast beef among them; for there is not better beef in the world than at Paris. Some large pieces were almost constantly on the considerable tables I have dined at. The variety given by their cooks to the same thing is astonishing; they dress a hundred dishes in a hundred different ways, and most of them excellent; and all sorts of vegetables have a savouriness and flavour, from rich sauces, that are absolutely wanted to our greens boiled in water. This variety is not striking in the comparison of a great table in France with another in England; but it is manifest in an instant between the tables of a French and English family of small fortune. The English dinner of a joint of meat and a pudding, as it is called, or pot luck, with a neighbour, is bad luck in England; the same fortune in France gives, by means of cookery only, at least four dishes to one among us, and spreads a small table incomparably better. A regular dessert with us is expected at a considerable table only, or at a moderate one, when a formal entertainment is given; in France it is as essential to the smallest dinner as to the largest; if it consists only of a bunch of dried grapes, or an apple, it will be as regularly served as the soup. I have met with persons in England who imagine the sobriety of a French table carried to such a length that one or two glasses of wine are all that a man can get at dinner; this is an error; your servant mixes the wine and water in what proportion you please; and large bowls of clean glasses are set before the master of the house and some friends of the family at different parts of the table, for serving the richer and rarer sorts of wines, which are drunk in this manner freely enough. The whole nation are scrupulously neat in refusing to drink out of glasses used by other people. At the house of a carpenter or blacksmith a tumbler is set to every cover. This results from the common beverage being wine and water; but if at a large table, as in England, there were porter, beer, cyder, and perry, it would be impossible for three or four tumblers or goblets to stand by every plate; and equally so for the servants to keep such a number separate and distinct. In table-linen they are, I think, cleaner and wiser than the English: that the change may be incessant, it is everywhere coarse. The idea of dining without a napkin seems ridiculous to a Frenchman, but in England we dine at the tables of people of tolerable fortune without them. A journeyman carpenter in France has his napkin as regularly as his fork; and at an inn the fille [girl, hostess] always lays a clean one to every cover that is spread in the kitchen for the lowest order of pedestrian travellers. The expense of linen in England is enormous, from its fineness; surely a great change of that which is coarse would be much more rational. In point of cleanliness I think the merit of the two nations is divided; the French are cleaner in their persons, and the English in their houses; I speak of the mass of the people and not of individuals of considerable fortune.

Source: Young, Arthur. *Travels During the Years 1787, 1788 and 1789 Undertaken More Particularly with a View of Ascertaining the Cultivation, Wealth, Resources, and National Prosperity of the Kingdom of France*. Dublin: R. Cross et al., 1793.

3. *Mrs. Beeton's Recipe for Bubble and Squeak*

Isabella Beeton's Mrs. Beeton's Book of Household Management, *from which the following selection is taken, not only offered advice on how to run a household (Domestic Life,*

Document 2) and treat various maladies (Intellectual Life, Document 10), but also what to cook and how to do it, which accounted for much of its success. Preparing meals was one of the primary responsibilities of the nineteenth-century domestic woman, either directly or through the management of household servants, and rural cooking methods were either being lost or becoming impossible or impractical in industrializing and urbanizing England. In fact, Mrs. Beeton sees modern cooking to be an important mark of civilization.

Beeton was the first to offer recipes in the way they are usually presented today: a list of ingredients followed by step-by-step instructions, and her food and advice became sensationally popular. Her book sold millions of copies, making her one of the best known cooks in Britain and perhaps the first "domestic advice celebrity"—like those who populate cable television today.

The nineteenth century was a time of great European territorial expansion in Africa and Asia. English cooking felt the influence of dishes and foods from China, India, and the Caribbean, although filtered through local sensibilities and availability, and the traditional English diet, heavy on meat, root vegetables, and some fish, remained dominant. Ironically, the recipe for Indian mango chutney contains sour apple (a poor substitute), not mango, which was not available in England.

Other odd dishes include the peculiarly named but traditional English dishes called "Toad-in-the-Hole" and "Bubble and Squeak." This selection concludes with two weeks of suggested menus. At the time, a middle-class English family meal was usually divided into three courses, with the first course being "lighter" with a soup or fish; a meat dish, often with vegetables, for the second; and a sweet or dessert for the third course, if there was one. Nonetheless, even this diet, of mutton neck and beef tongue boiled, offered a variety and stability previously little known, as advances in agriculture and transportation made food supplies increasingly stable and food variety increasingly larger, trends that continue to the present.

Although her recipes are perhaps unappetizing to many today, Beeton helped direct modern cookery and she shows how influences that still matter today, such as cooks as celebrities, how we think about food, and how we learn to cook it, are important parts of food in the modern world.

Man, in his primitive state, lives upon roots and the fruits of the earth, until, by degrees, he is driven to seek for new means, by which his wants may be supplied and enlarged. He then becomes a hunter and a fisher. As his species increases, greater necessities come upon him, when he gradually abandons the roving life of the savage for the more stationary pursuits of the herdsman. These beget still more settled habits, when he begins the practice of agriculture, forms ideas of the rights of property, and has his own, both defined and secured. The forest, the stream, and the sea are now no longer his only resources for food. He sows and he reaps, pastures and breeds cattle, lives on the cultivated produce of his fields, and revels in the luxuries of the dairy; raises flocks for clothing, and assumes, to all intents and purposes, the habits of permanent life and the comfortable condition of a farmer. This is the fourth stage of social progress, up to which the useful or mechanical arts have been incidentally developing themselves, when trade and commerce begin. Through these various phases, only to live has been the great object of mankind; but, by-and-by, comforts are multiplied, and accumulating riches create new wants. The object, then, is not only to live, but to live economically, agreeably, tastefully, and well. Accordingly, the art of cookery commences; and although the fruits of the earth, the fowls of the air, the beasts of the field, and the fish of the sea, are still the only food of mankind, yet these are so prepared, improved, and dressed by skill and ingenuity, that they are the means of immeasurably extending the boundaries of human enjoyments. Everything that is edible, and passes under the hands of the cook, is more or less changed, and assumes new forms. Hence the influence of that functionary is immense upon the happiness of a household. [. . .]

Bengal Recipe for Making Mango Chetney

Ingredients.—1 1/2 lbs. of moist sugar, 3/4 lb. of salt, 1/4 lb. of garlic, 1/4 lb. of onions, 3/4 lb. of powdered ginger, 1/4 lb. of dried chilies, 3/4 lb. of mustard seed, 3/4 lb. of stoned raisins, 2 bottles best vinegar, 30 large unripe sour apples.

Mode.—the sugar must be made into a syrup; the garlic, onion, and ginger be finely pounded in a mortar; the mustard seed be washed in cold vinegar, and dried in the sun; the apples be peeled, cored, and sliced, and boiled in a bottle and a half of the vinegar. When all this is done, and the apples are quite cold, put them into a large pan, and gradually mix the whole of the rest of the ingredients including the remaining half-bottle of vinegar. It must be stirred until the whole is thoroughly blended, and then put into bottle or use. Tie a piece of wet bladder over the mouths of the bottles, after they are well corked. This chetney is very superior to any which can be bought, and one trial will prove it to be delicious.

Note.—This recipe was given by a native to an English lady, who had long been resident in India, and who since her return to her native country, has become well celebrated among her friends for the excellence of this Eastern relish. [. . .]

Bubble-and-Squeak (Cold Meat Cookery).

Ingredients.—A few thin slices of cold boiled beef; butter, cabbage, 1 sliced onion, pepper and salt to taste.

Mode.—Fry the slices of beef gently in a little butter, taking care not to dry them up. Lay them on a flat dish, and cover with fried greens. The greens may be prepared from cabbage sprouts or green savoys. They should be boiled till tender, well drained, minced, and placed, still quite hot, in a frying pan, with butter, a sliced onion, and seasonings of pepper and salt. When the onion is done, it is ready to serve.

Time.—Altogether, 1/2 hour

Average cost, exclusive of the cold beef, 3d.

Seasonable at any time. [. . .]

Toad-in-the-Hole (Cold Meat Cookery).

Ingredients.—6 oz. of flour, 1 pint of milk, 3 eggs, butter, a few slices of cold mutton, pepper and salt to taste, 2 kidneys.

Mode.—Make a smooth batter of flour, milk, and eggs in the above proportion; butter a baking-dish, and pour in the batter. Into this place a few slices of cold mutton, previously well seasoned, and the kidneys, which should be cut into rather small pieces; bake about 1 hour, or rather longer, and send it to the table in the dish it was baked in. Oyster or mushrooms may be substituted for the kidneys, and will be found exceedingly good.

Time.—Rather more than 1 hour

Average cost, exclusive of the cold meat, 8d.

Seasonable at any time. [. . .]

Plain Family Dinners for April.

Sunday.—1. Clear gravy soup. 2. Roast haunch of mutton, sea kale, potatoes. 3. Rhubarb tart, custards in glasses.

Monday.—1. Crimped skate and caper sauce. 2. Boiled knuckle of veal and rice, old mutton, mashed potatoes. 3. Baked plum-pudding.

Tuesday.—1. Vegetable soup. 2. Toad-in-the-hole, made from remains of cold mutton. 3. Stewed rhubarb and baked custard pudding.

Wednesday.—1. Fried soles, anchovy sauce. 2. Boiled beef, carrots, suet dumplings. 3. Lemon pudding.

Thursday.—1. Pea-soup made with liquor that beef was boiled in. 2. Cold beef, mashed potatoes, mutton cutlets, and tomato sauce. 3. Macaroni.

Friday.—1. Bubble-and-squeak, made with remains of cold beef. Roast shoulder of veal stuffed, spinach, potatoes. 2. Boiled batter pudding and sweet sauce.

Saturday.—1. Stewed veal with vegetables, made from the remains of the shoulder. Broiled rump-steaks and oyster sauce. 2. Yeast-dumplings.

Sunday.—1. Boiled salmon and dressed cucumber, anchovy sauce. 2. Roast fore-quarter of lamb, spinach, potatoes, mint sauce. 2 [sic]. Rhubarb tart, cheesecakes.

Monday.—1. Curried salmon, made with remains of salmon, dish of boiled rice. 2. Cold lamb, rumpsteak and kidney pudding, potatoes. 3. Spinach and poached eggs.

Tuesday.—1. Scotch mutton broth with pearl barley. 2. Boiled neck of mutton, caper sauce, suet dumplings, carrots. 3. Baked rice-pudding.

Wednesday.—1. Boiled mackerel and melted butter or fennel sauce, potatoes. 2. Roast fillet of veal, bacon, greens. 3. Fig pudding.

Thursday.—1. Flemish soup. 2. Roast loin of mutton, broccoli, potatoes; veal rolls made from remains of cold veal. 3. Boiled rhubarb pudding.

Friday.—1. Irish stew or haricot, made from cold mutton, minced veal. 2. Half-pay pudding.

Saturday.—1. Rump-steak pie, broiled mutton chops. 2. Baked arrowroot pudding.

Source: Beeton, Isabella. *Mrs. Beeton's Book of Household Management*. London: S. O. Beeton, 1860.

4. Eating in Nineteenth-Century Persia

Even in the modern world, food in the Middle East is largely unfamiliar to those in the West. While popular adaptations of many cuisines have made their way into the popular food of many nations, such as Mexican, Chinese, *and* Indian, *and fusion cuisine, a blending of several national groups of ingredients and styles, is a popular trend in the restaurant industry today, the mention of Persian food will likely draw blank stares.*

Samuel Wilson, a nineteenth-century English traveler and Methodist minister, offers the following description of holiday fare in Persia, *what is today* Iran. *Wilson describes a visit to a rather poor family on the Persian New Year (called Noruz), which coincides with the vernal equinox and has its origins in ancient* Persia *and* Zoroastrianism, *although it is also celebrated as an Islamic holiday in contemporary* Iran.

A number of culinary customs are described, from the content of candy and confections, to the importance of hospitality and tea-drinking, even among the poor, and the popularity of teahouses and tobacco use. The candy and sweets are notably lacking in chocolate, which is the central flavor in virtually all European candy. Although neither tea nor tobacco are native to Iran, they appear at the end of the nineteenth century as central to social practices and institutions, just as they did in Europe. While European nations produced relatively little tobacco and virtually no tea, relying on colonial and imperial trade for these items, Iran produced its own tea and tobacco after these commodities had been introduced by growing global contacts in the eighteenth and nineteenth centuries.

While the specific environment and some of the foods may be uniquely Persian, there are also elements that have commonalities with food and drink in the wider modern world. Although the centrality of food and hospitality to cultural and religious celebrations is not new to modernity, it is, along with the adoption of global commodities and the creation and use of public spaces to consume these things (as in the tea- and tobacco houses) among the marks of the modern world's shifting patterns of everyday eating and drinking.

Here there were set before us some choice sweetmeats. Among the favorite confections is *gaz*. It is made from the juice of the tamarisk-tree and has a delicious flavor, which is increased by being mixed with pistachios. Another favorite is fig-paste, called "ease the throat." This is variously flavored and colored. Among the candies popular in Persia are sugared almond, pomegranate jelly cut in little squares, *khulva,* a taffy of molasses and nuts, rock-candy, and *peshmak,* which is made of sugar and butter, crystallized like snowflakes or thistle-down, and formed into pyramids, cones, and other shapes. A very rich pastry sprinkled with sugar, but without fruit, is much prized. Their cakes, made of rice-flour and nuts, with sheep-tail fat and saffron flavor, are rarely agreeable to foreign taste. Year by year confections are being improved by contact with Tiflis and Constantinople. The best sweetmeats are now made in the houses of the wealthy, and some of their ladies are expert in the art. At Noruz and other festivals great *khonchas* [a large wooden tray carried on the head] of candies are sent in by the clients of the great, and the center of the parlor is occupied by a large display of them. It has lately become the custom to rent a large amount of confections for an occasion, only those being paid for which are eaten, and the rest returned....

New-Year's calls on the poor of Persia revealed a striking contrast. We knocked at the outer door, that the women might have a chance to conceal themselves. Bending low, we stopped down and passed under a long arched way, and entered a little yard with mud-plastered walls. The *cahvakhana* or hall opened into a half-underground room, in one end of which was a poorly made window, covered with oiled paper, its cracks being similarly pasted over to keep out the wind. Its flopping, ill-fitting door was low, while the sill was very high, in order that the shoes may be taken off in the hall and not obstruct the opening and shutting of the door. The rafters overhead were unceiled. The furniture consisted of common carpets *(ghelim)*, a mirror brought with the wedding-outfit, a copper basin and ewer, a small tea-urn and some glasses, and a *kalean* on the lower niches. On the upper niches were a few bottles, and on the once whitened walls had been pasted some cigarette-papers, caricature prints, and verses from the Koran. The host greeted us with a hearty "Welcome! You have done me a great favor." We replied "May your festival be blessed, may your house be blessed!" He answered, "It is a present to you." The other guests rose, placed their right hands first on their hearts, then to their foreheads, and bowed low. We knelt on our knees on calico cushions, the weight of the body resting on the heels. The host, though his circumstances were straitened, was bright in conversation. A small boy dressed like a grown man entered, and we inquired, "Who is this?" "He is your slave," he replied; which meant, "He is my son." A dish of wheat was growing on the window-sill, a symbol of the renewal of the year. A fish was swimming in a pan, which called forth a remark from him that fish always look toward Mecca at Noruz. He placed before us a few candies, some boiled eggs, and pickled grapes. He had the samovar already boiling, and sat down beside it, washed the cups and saucers, and placed tea before us. We did not decline to drink, for the poor man would feel aggrieved. He honored us specially by almost filling our tea-glasses with sugar, though he himself sipped his tea through a small lump which he held between his teeth and retained to sweeten succeeding sups. What does a poor man have besides the things within sight? His goods consist of a few rude dishes of native pottery, a jar or two of pickled herbs and dried vegetables, a flour-bin, some copper pots, and a chest of clothing. With his wages of a dime a day as a laborer or servant his must provide for his Khadija and Ismiel, Husain and Fatima. He thanks God for the blessing of such a family; but how do they live on such a pittance? Most of it goes to buy bread, which, with some salty cheese to give it taste, or a glass of weak tea, constitutes his breakfast; his luncheon is bread and sour milk, garlic or onions or some cheap fruit; for dinner a stew of meat and vegetables, highly seasoned with red peppers and onions—a large quantity for a little meat—makes his bread palatable. Lack of employment or high prices reduce him to bread and water. In winter a few shahis' worth of charcoal lasts the family a long while under the *kurisee*. [...]

The social habit, which is so universally exemplified at Noruz, is a striking trait of the Persian character. One of the social institutions of great attraction is the tea-house. The tea-houses are of various grades. Some are rudely finished, with merely a raised platform which surrounds the sides of the room, and is covered with matting or carpet. Others have an air of comfort imparted to them by divans, mirrors, chandeliers, etc. With tea a half a cent a glass, and one pipeful of tobacco sufficing for a crowd, it is no wonder loafers seek them and business men make appointments in them. The common pipe, cigarettes, and the *kalean* or water-pipe are much used. In the latter the smoke passes through the water and is drawn into the lungs. Lemon-juice and other flavors are sometimes mixed with the water.

The ordinary *kalean* is about two feet high. It consists of a vase capable of holding about a quart of water, a top about the size of a goblet, in which burning charcoal and dampened tobacco are placed, a wooden tube which supports the top on the vase, and a mouthpiece or stem about twenty inches long. The support and stem are turned on the lathe, in various ornamental designs. The vase and bowl are of glass, stone, china, brass, or silver, and are set with turquoise or other jewels, and carved, enameled, and decorated with pictures of the shah, flowers, and similar objects.

Source: Wilson, S. G. *Persian Life and Customs: With Scenes and Incidents of the Residence and Travel in the Land of the Lion and the Sun*. New York: Fleming H. Revell Company, 1899.

5. *Antoinette Linnebur's Political Desserts*

Written by a Missouri woman named Antoinette Linnebur, the recipes in this selection are taken from a handwritten cookbook dating from the late 1900s through the 1920s. Like many recipes of the period, the manuscript lists ingredients, but offers minimum directions, either for how to combine the ingredients or how to bake them. Among recipes in the cookbook for cakes, pies, cookies, pickles, chutneys, sauces, and other food items are recipes for a "Prince of Wales Cake" and a "George Washington Pie." The recipes have no clear connection to the historical figures mentioned, so the names seem odd to the modern reader.

In the first half of the nineteenth century, recipes in England and the United States were named to commemorate important political and military figures. George Washington was one of the most popular figures in American culture, and the George Washington Pie is a patriotic American name, part of the civic cult of Washington that grew in the nineteenth century. The pie itself, like Washington, was quite popular into the twentieth century. Usually it consisted of a denser white cake (called a "pie" because it was baked in a pie pan) with a thick fruit filling, traditionally raspberry, between two layers and sometimes a dusting of powdered sugar. Later, a creamy, custard filling was sometimes used, as in Linnebur's recipe; covered with chocolate, this type became what is now called Boston Cream Pie. The Prince of Wales Cake has its origins relatively late for a patriotic cake or pie, being an early twentieth-century recipe that spread to the United States, apparently more for its flavor than its politics. It was a multi-layer cake of alternating light and dark, spiced layers, often iced with almond frosting or sometimes caramel.

In the second half of the nineteenth century, particularly in the United States, names of foods took on a heightened political connotation, with cakes, pies, cookies, stews, and other foods being named for popular Civil War generals, politicians, or political positions. For example, in the American South one might have found Jefferson Davis Pudding or Secession Biscuits, while in the North, General Philip Sheridan Cake might be served, and Lincoln Cake recipes were republished into the 1890s. The George Washington Pie and the Prince of Wales Cake are more patriotic and commemorative than partisan, originating outside the era of the most politically sensitive recipes, but remaining popular well into the twentieth century.

These political and patriotic recipes were the inventions and work almost exclusively of women. Even if women were denied access to the ballot box, they could express their political allegiances by creating and preparing political recipes in support of their candidates or issues. Perhaps, with the ratification of the Nineteenth Amendment in 1920 granting women the right to vote, it became less imperative to have a "Calvin Coolidge Cookie"—a woman could simply vote for him instead. While the popularity of these cakes may have depended at least as much on their taste as their politics, they reveal interesting facts about cookery in the early twentieth century. At any rate, these recipes show a connection between aspects of daily life not often thought closely related: politics and dessert.

Prince of Wales Cake

Light Part

1 cup of sugar
3 whites of eggs
1/2 cup of butter
1/2 cup of sweet milk

2 cups of flour
2 teaspoons of baking powder

Dark Part
3 yoks [sic] of eggs
1 cup of brown sugar
1/2 cup of sour milk
1/2 cup of butter
1/2 teaspoon soda in
1/2 cup of hot water
1 tablespoon of molasses
1 tablespoon of allspices [sic]
1 cup of raisins
2/3 cup of citron
2/3 cup of figs

Filling
1 pint of sugar & whites of 2 eggs

Cake [for George Washington Pie]

1 cup of sugar
1/2 cup of butter
3 eggs
2 cups of flour
1 1/2 teaspoons of baking powder
flavor to taste

Filling for George Washington Pie

1 1/2 cup of milk
2 tablespoons of corn starch
sugar enough to sweeten to taste & a little vanilla
1 egg

Beat egg and corn starch and a little water together & then put in the boiled milk.

Source: Linnebur, Antoinette. Manuscript cookbook c. 1908–1928. Private collection, used with permission.

6. *Eric Schlosser on Fast Food Flavors*

Modern food culture has become mass food culture. Supermarkets have almost completely eclipsed the farmer's market, and in most places, franchised restaurants have replaced "local joints" and "mom-and-pop" operations that find it hard to compete with the highly marketed, carefully tested and developed products. A global phenomenon, fast food has become one of the most visible symbols of American culture—and American cultural dominance, which is embraced by some and lamented by others.

More than just getting food to the market, creating food that has broad appeal is important, and the fast food corporations, working, as described here, with the flavoring industry, have become very good at it. Nonetheless, a food industry that has to provide food for hundreds of millions of people in the United States, and billions globally, must inevitably be massive in scale. Growing, harvesting, transporting, processing, and packaging the amount of food required to feed us all is a huge business, and is done by huge corporations, in theory with the regulation and inspection of governments for safety.

Eric Schlosser in his recent popular book, Fast Food Nation, *exposed many of the practices and problems in the American fast food industry. In the following selection from* Fast Food Nation, *Schlosser describes part of his own tour of one of the factories of the flavoring industry, businesses where highly trained food flavor specialists called flavorists manipulate thousands of chemicals into specific tastes and odors, then manufacture them and sell them to the producers who make the food we eat and products we use so it all will taste and smell like it does—and so we will buy it. Even Schlosser is happy to snack on some french fries from time to time because they taste good.*

Schlosser writes in the tradition of muckraking journalism, a genre of investigative reporting that takes aim at established institutions, in this case the fast food industry, sometimes in a sensationalist manner. Science, technology, and modern business models have been applied to agriculture and food processing, and often there are stages in the processes that seem unappetizing or even dangerous—and sometimes they are. Overall, what Schlosser manages to reveal is the combination of a variety of modern trends: science, industrialization, mass culture, and large institutions that are instrumental in creating the taste of modern everyday life.

The taste of McDonald's french fries has long been praised by customers, competitors, and even food critics. James Beard loved McDonald's fries. Their distinctive taste does not stem from the type of potatoes that McDonald's buys, the technology that processes them, or the restaurant equipment that fries them. Other chains buy their french fries from the same large processing companies, use Russet Burbanks, and have similar fryers in their restaurant kitchens. The taste of a fast food fry is largely determined by the cooking oil. For decades, McDonald's cooked its French fries in a mixture of about 7 percent soy oil and 93 percent beef tallow. The mix gave the fries their unique flavor—and more saturated beef fat per ounce than a McDonald's hamburger.

Amid a barrage of criticism over the amount of cholesterol in their fries, McDonald's switched to pure vegetable oil in 1990. The switch presented the company with an enormous challenge: how to make fries that subtly taste like beef without cooking them in tallow. A look at the ingredients now used in the preparation of McDonald's french fries suggests how the problem was solved. At the end of the list is a seemingly innocuous, yet oddly mysterious phrase: "natural flavor." The frozen potatoes and the cooking oil at McDonald's both contain "natural flavor." That fact helps to explain not only why the fries taste so good, but also why most fast food—indeed, most of the food Americans eat today—tastes the way it does.

Open your refrigerator, your freezer, your kitchen cupboards, and look at the labels on your food. You'll find "natural flavor" or "artificial flavor" in just about every list of ingredients. The similarities between these two broad categories of flavor are far more significant than their differences. Both are man-made additives that give most processed food its taste. The initial purchase of a food item may be driven by its packaging or appearance, but subsequent purchases are determined mainly by its taste. About 90 percent of the money that Americans spend on food is used to buy processed food. But the canning, freezing, and dehydrating techniques used to process food destroy most of its flavor. Since the end of World War II, a vast industry has arisen in the United States to make processed food palatable. Without this flavor industry, today's fast food industry could not exist. The names of the leading American fast food chains and their best-selling menu items have become famous worldwide, embedded in our popular culture. Few people, however, can name the companies that manufacture fast food's taste.

The flavor industry is highly secretive. Its leading companies will not divulge the precise formulas of flavor compounds or the identities of clients. The secrecy is deemed essential for protecting the reputation of beloved brands. The fast food chains, understandably, would like the public to believe that the flavors of their food somehow originate in their restaurant kitchens, not in distant factories run by other firms.

The New Jersey Turnpike runs through the heart of the flavor industry, an industrial corridor dotted with refineries and chemical plants. International Flavors & Fragrances (IFF), the world's largest flavor company, has a manufacturing facility off Exit 8A in Dayton, New Jersey; Givaudan, the world's second-largest flavor company, has a plant in East Hanover. Haarman & Reimer, the largest German flavor company, has a plant in Teterboro, as does Takasoga, the largest Japanese flavor company. V. Mane Fils, the largest French flavor company, has a plant in Wayne, Bush Boake Allen is in Montvale, and Heavenly Flavors is in Bayonne. Dozens of companies manufacture flavors in New Jersey industrial parks between Teaneck and South Brunswick. Indeed, the area produces about two-thirds of the flavor additives sold in the United States.

The IFF plant in Dayton is a huge pale blue building with a modern office complex attached to the front. It sits in an industrial park, not far from a BASF plastics factory, a Jolly French Toast factory, and a plant that manufactures Liz Claiborne cosmetics. Dozens of tractor-trailers were parked at the IFF loading dock the afternoon I visited, and a thin cloud of steam floated from the chimney. Before entering the plant, I signed a nondisclosure form, promising not to reveal the brand names of products that contain IFF flavors. The place reminded me of Willy Wonka's chocolate factory. Wonderful smells drifted through the hallways, men and women

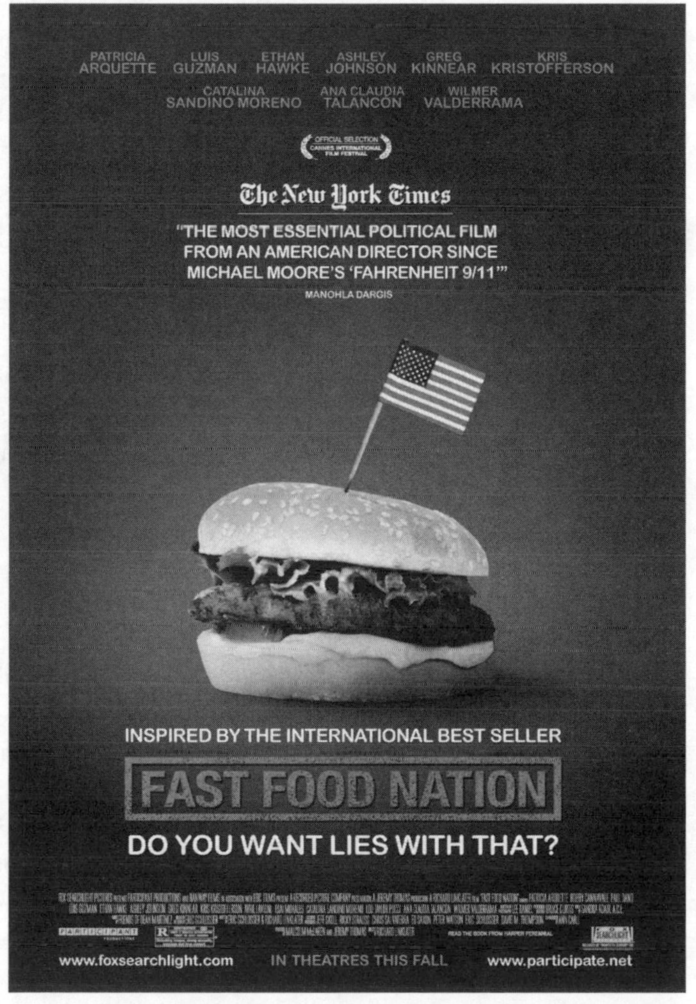

The poster art for Richard Linklater's 2006 film, *Fast Food Nation*. Courtesy of Photofest.

in neat white lab coats cheerfully went about their work, and hundreds of little glass bottles sat on laboratory tables and shelves. The bottles contained powerful but fragile flavor chemicals, shielded from light by the brown glass and the round plastic caps shut tight. The long chemical names on the little white labels were as mystifying to me as medieval Latin. They were the odd-sounding names of things that would be mixed and poured and turned into new substances, like magic potions.

I was not invited to see the manufacturing areas of the IFF plant, where it was thought I might discover trade secrets. Instead, I toured various laboratories and pilot kitchens, where the flavors of well-established brands are tested or adjusted, and where whole new flavors are created. IFF's snack and savory lab is responsible for the flavor of potato chips, corn chips, breads, crackers, breakfast cereals, and pet food. The confectionery lab devises the flavor for ice cream, cookies, candies, toothpastes, mouthwashes, and antacids. Everywhere I looked, I saw famous, widely advertised products sitting on laboratory desks and tables. The beverage lab is full of brightly colored liquids in clear bottles. It comes up with the flavor for popular soft drinks, sport drinks, bottled teas, and wine coolers, for all-natural juice drinks, organic soy drinks, beers, and malt liquors. In one pilot kitchen I saw a dapper chemist, a middle-aged man with an elegant tie beneath his lab coat, carefully preparing a batch of cookies with white frosting and pink-and-white sprinkles. In another pilot kitchen I saw a pizza oven, a grill, a milk-shake machine, and a french fryer identical to those I'd seen behind the counter at countless fast food restaurants.

In addition to being the world's largest flavor company, IFF manufactures the smell of six of the ten best-selling fine perfumes in the United States. It makes the smell of Estee Lauder's Beautiful, Clinique's Happy, Ralph Lauren's Polo, and Calvin Klein's Eternity. It also makes the smell of household products such as deodorant, dishwashing detergent, bath soap, shampoo, furniture polish, and floor wax. All of these aromas are made through the same basic process: the manipulation of volatile chemicals to create a particular smell. The basic science behind the scent of your shaving cream is the same as that governing the flavor of your TV dinner.

Source: Excerpt from *Fast Food Nation: The Dark Side of the All-American Meal* by Eric Schlosser.

Houses and Furniture

How people choose to live determines what kind of housing they choose to build or use. Housing is not only a material aspect, but domestic architecture can be connected to political, domestic, economic, and sometimes religious life. The house, whether it is a temporary structure, free-standing permanent unit, or part of a larger building, is in many ways the home, the center of family and social life.

The individual house is not the only kind of housing in the modern world. Trends toward increasingly urban life and industrialization and highly populous urban centers is a mark of the modern age. Other influences, such as modern building techniques, including reinforced concrete, structural steel, and powered or automated building systems for ventilation, lighting, elevators, and clean and wastewater systems, have helped create new forms of housing, such as the high-rise apartment building. Nonetheless, the single-family house has an enduring popularity, and suburban and exurban areas have continued to grow rapidly in many parts of the world. (See *Exurbs* and *Suburbs* in the Glossary.) Some of these trends are also addressed above in the section on Economic Life.

Florence Nightingale (Document 7) doesn't describe the physical characteristics of the *Victorian* English home, but laments any number of defects she sees toward general health. For complex reasons, including the proximity to so many strangers in the modern city, the home came to be seen as a space created and maintained as a retreat from the outside world, secluded and separated. Typically part of this idea also was the fashion for heavy curtains, closed windows and yards, and layers of privacy, and it is against this that Nightingale reacts for reasons of health and wellness.

At the same time, not all people in the modern era live in such dwellings. The individual privacy desired by the Victorian middle class is a far cry from the *duar* of the inhabitants of the Moroccan interior in the same period. An orderly collection of tents form the communal dwellings of an extended kinship group, and while some attention is paid to privacy, it is not so important. Families have their own tents, but seclusion was not much of a concern or possibility, at least not within the home. Privacy could only be found by leaving the settlement, and the regularity of work for all seems to leave little room for discussion of other matters. Edmondo De Amicis's account (Document 8) of a Moroccan *duar* reveals that, like many other aspects of modern life, there remains significant continuity with pre-modern material life.

In contrast with both of these selections is Arthur Train's description (Document 9) of a dwelling that has never existed. Rather, it was an American prediction of what housing would be like 50 years in the future. This kind of prolepsis (or flash-forward) has been a popular technique in the modern period for writers in science, technology, and other fields far beyond housing. While the technological aspects of life were to have changed radically in Train's future, important other factors have not—the single family, free-standing home with a separate piece of property and suburban location are anticipated to be the norm; despite the changes in technology and materials, there is more in common between the homes Florence Nightingale wants to clean in 1860 and the futuristic home of 1988 than either has with the communal dwellings in Morocco. The material surroundings of a house may not be what transform it into a home, but certainly the material places in which we choose to live say something important about modern life.

7. *Florence Nightingale: A Healthy Victorian House*

In a time when nurses were usually either nuns or prostitutes, an upper-class Englishwoman pursuing a career in nursing was unheard of, not to mention a bit scandalous. Yet this is exactly what Florence Nightingale did in the mid-nineteenth century. A member of an elite and wealthy British family, she used her family connections and social status to promote her interests in hospital administration, public health, and the creation of professional nursing standards. Her experiences as a head of volunteer nurses during the Crimean War *in the 1850s made her a national heroine in Britain. Her name is still a synonym for a compassionate, caring, and competent nurse.*

The "lady with the lamp," as Nightingale became known for her late-night rounds in British military hospitals in the Crimea, took her expertise and ideas from military hospitals to private houses. This isn't that surprising if one considers that at the time hospitalization did not offer any advantages over home care. Hospitals were for the poor or the traveler; most people who fell ill were cared for at home, with regular visits by medical professionals. It often fell to the family and its servants, if they were wealthy, to provide the rest of the care.

Housing standards and domestic architecture were changing in the nineteenth century, as industrialization and urbanization resulted in the rapid growth of cities, with large amounts of new housing both for lower and upper class people in the Western world. As medical and scientific knowledge changed the understanding of disease and its causes, this also led to the creation of sanitary and public health organizations.

Nightingale's main concern in this selection from her landmark 1860 book, Notes on Nursing, *is not the particulars of architecture, but the arrangement of any given housing and furniture for the five features she identifies as important to health: clean air, clean water, drainage, cleanliness, and light. Her recommendations confronted not only many venerable practices, but also, in some sense, contemporary fashions.*

The modern era developed a strong sense of distinction between the public and private, and nineteenth century English fashion created housing and furnishings that reinforced these ideas: heavy curtains and carpets, stuffed furniture, closed windows, and private, concealed interior spaces. Nightingale's recipe of air, light, and cleanliness was a challenge not only to conventional sickbed treatments that sometimes ranged from the magical to the macabre, but also to the ideal house and furnishings, which were given to many of the practices Nightingale opposes. At the same time, the domestic environment was central to the ideal Victorian lifestyle; *it was a private, safe place. That it might be a threat of disease was unconscionable, and Nightingale tried to provide a breath of fresh air that would improve public health, private homes, and everyday lives.*

There are five essential points in securing the health of houses:

1. Pure air.
2. Pure water.
3. Efficient drainage.
4. Cleanliness.
5. Light.

Without these, no house can be healthy. And it will be unhealthy just in proportion as they are deficient.

1. To have pure air, your house must be so constructed as that the outer atmosphere shall find its way with ease to every corner of it. House architects hardly ever consider this. The object in building a house is to obtain the largest interest for the money, not to save doctors' bills to the tenants. But, if tenants should ever become so wise as to refuse to occupy unhealthy constructed houses, and if Insurance Companies should ever come to understand their interest so thoroughly as to pay a Sanitary Surveyor to look after the houses where their clients live, speculative

architects would speedily be brought to their senses. As it is, they build what pays best. And there are always people foolish enough to take the houses they build. And if in the course of time the families die off, as is so often the case, nobody ever thinks of blaming any but Providence for the result. Ill-informed medical men aid in sustaining the delusion, by laying the blame on "current contagions." Badly constructed houses do for the healthy what badly constructed hospitals do for the sick. Once insure that the air in a house is stagnant, and sickness is certain to follow.

2. Pure water is more generally introduced into houses than it used to be, thanks to the exertion of the sanitary reformers. Within the last few years, a large part of London was in the habit of using water polluted by the drainage of its sewers and water closets. This has happily been remedied. But, in many parts of the country, well water of a very impure kind is used for domestic purposes. And when epidemic disease shows itself, persons using such water are almost sure to suffer.
3. It would be curious to ascertain by inspection, how many houses in London are really well drained. Many people would say, surely all or most of them. But many people have no idea in what good drainage consists. They think that a sewer in the street, and a pipe leading to it from the house is good drainage. All the while the sewer may be nothing but a laboratory from which epidemic disease and ill health is being distilled into the house. No house with any untrapped drain pipe communicating immediately with a sewer, whether it be from water closet, sink, or gully-grate, can ever be healthy. An untrapped sink may at any time spread fever to pyaemia among the inmates of the place.

   The ordinary oblong sink is an abomination. That great surface of stone, which is always let wet, is always exhaling into the air. I have known whole houses and hospitals smell of the sink. I have met just as strong a stream of sewer air coming up the back staircase of a grand London house from the sink, as I have ever met at Scutari; and I have see the rooms in that house all ventilated by the open doors, and the passages all unventilated by the closed windows, in order that as much of the sewer air as possible might be conducted into and retained in the bed-rooms. It is wonderful. [...]
4. Without cleanliness, within and without your house, ventilation is comparatively useless. In certain foul districts of London, poor people used to object to open their windows and doors because of the foul smells that came in. Rich people like to have their stables and dunghill near their houses. But does it ever occur to them that with many arrangements of this kind that it would be safer to keep the windows shut than open? You cannot have the air of the house pure with dung-heaps under the windows. These are common all over London. And yet people are surprised that their children, brought up in large "well-aired" nurseries and bed-rooms suffer from children's epidemics. If they studied Nature's law in the matter of children's health, they would not be so surprised.

   There are other ways of have in filth inside a house besides having dirt in heaps. Old papered walls of years' standing, dirty carpets, uncleansed furniture, are just as ready sources of impurity to the air as if there were a dung-heap in the basement. People are so unaccustomed from education and habits to consider how to make a home healthy, that they either never think of it at all, and take every disease as a matter of course, to be "resigned to" when it comes "as from the hand of Providence;" or if they ever entertain the idea of preserving the health of their household as a duty, they are very apt to commit all kinds of "negligences and ignorances" in performing it.

5. A dark house is always an unhealthy house, always an ill-aired house, always a dirty house. Want of light stops growth and promotes scrofula, rickets, &c., among the children.

   People lose their health in a dark house, and if they get ill they cannot get well again in it.

Source: Nightingale, Florence. *Notes on Nursing: What It Is, and What It Is Not*. New York: D. Appleton and Co., 1860.

8. A *Moroccan* Duar

The housing described in this nineteenth-century account of rural Morocco *is scarcely touched by the modern age. One can imagine a similar description from centuries before, as* Edmondo De Amicis, *a peripatetic Italian journalist and writer who published travel notes in 1870 of his journey to* Morocco, *mentions. There is evidence of trade and contact with other groups outside the* duar*—the mirrors, manufactured in* Mediterranean *European cities like* Venice*; shells for drinking from the coast; and other products like guns and saddles. Yet the materials for constructing the dwellings and most of the material culture for everyday life are virtually all local, handmade materials. Most of the* Bedouins, *or semi-nomadic desert-dwellers who lived from the Atlantic coast of North Africa to the Arab Peninsula, have since integrated into local settled populations, but this nineteenth-century account shows the material lives of Bedouins of the Beni-Hassan tribe before that process.*

As in much of human history, groups who live together are connected by bonds of kinship, and extended kinship groups form the basis for society—in this case the whole village or duar. *Still, there is some limited separation and privacy: each nuclear family has its own tent, and within it there are separate sleeping areas for the parents and for the others. Over all, it is a very communal living area and living style. These dwellings do not use modern building materials, and the sensibilities of much of modern everyday life, such as the complex economic specialization, the distinction between private and public, the stricter separation of the individual or at least the nuclear family from larger society, are all lacking or weak. While many modern people would not want to live this way, it remains a viable option for many in some parts of the world. Kinship groups and locally available materials determine housing arrangements for many when other options are too expensive, too far away, or simply too undesirable.*

The simple shelters do not seem that substantial, but in the Moroccan *climate, stouter shelters to protect them from harsh winters or frequent storms are just not necessary. Life is virtually outdoors for the* Moroccans, *their tents being little more than a covering to keep off the sun or rain. The tasks and variations of the daily routine are described by* De Amicis *as being as simple as the housing. Everyday life in the modern world is usually complex, but if* De Amicis *can be believed, not in rural late nineteenth-century* Morocco.

The *duar* is usually a settlement of ten, fifteen or twenty families, connected by some bond of relationship, each family having its own tent. These tents stand in two parallel lines, about thirty feet apart, so that a sort of rectangular space is left in the middle, open at both ends. The tents are almost invariably alike; they are made out of a large piece of black or chocolate-colored material, woven from the fibre of dwarf palms or from goats' or camels' hair; this is stretched over upright stakes or thick reeds, connected by a wooden cross-piece, on which the roof rests, their shape still resembling that of the habitations of the Numidians of the time of Jugurtha, which Sallust compares to overturned ships with their keels in the air. During the autumn and winter the covering is drawn down to the ground and held in place by means of cords and pegs, so as to effectually exclude both wind and rain. In summer a wide aperture is left all around, so that the air may circulate freely, and this is protected by a low hedge of rushes and dried brambles. Owing to these precautions the tent of the *daar* is much cooler in summer and better protected through the rainy season than the same class of Moorish dwellings in the cities, since the latter are without either proper ventilation or glazed windows. The maximum height of a tent is about eight feet, the maximum length about ten. Any which may exceed these dimensions belong to wealthy sheiks, and are extremely rare. A partition made of rushes divides the dwelling in two parts, in one of which the father and mother sleep, and in the other the children and the rest of the family. A few osier mats, a brightly-colored and arabesqued wooden box, containing clothing; a small looking-glass, manufactured in Trieste or Venice; a high tripod, made of canes and covered with a *haïk*, under which the family bathing is done; a couple of stones for grinding wheat; a loom, such as was used in the days of Abraham; a rough tin lantern, a few earthenware jugs, a few goat-skins, a few dishes, a distaff, a saddle, a gun, a big dagger, such is the entire furnishing of one of these dwellings. In one corner a hen gathers in her brood of chickens, a brick oven faces the entrance, and on one side of the tent is a small vegetable garden; beyond are some round holes, faced with stone and cement, in which grain is stored. . . .

The life of the *daar* is of the simplest description. At daybreak every one gets up, says his prayers, the cows are milked, the butter made and the sour milk that is left, drunk; for drinking-cups they use conch and limpet-shells, which they purchase from people living on the coast. Then the men go to their work in the fields, not returning until towards nightfall. The women meanwhile carry wood and water, grind flour, spin the coarse fabrics in which they and their husbands are clothed, twist rope for their tents from the fibre of the dwarf palm; send their husbands' mid-day food to them and prepare the Kuskussú [couscous—a coarsely ground pasta popular in North Africa] for the evening. The Kuskussú is mixed with beans, gourds, onions and other vegetables; sometimes it is sweetened, spiced and dressed with a meat sauce, and on feast days meat is served with it. On the return of the men, supper is eaten, and at sunset everyone goes to bed; but sometimes one of the old men will tell a story after supper, seated in the middle of the family circle. Throughout the night the *daar* is plunged in profound silence and darkness; only a few families will occasionally leave lanterns burning before their tents to guide any wayfarer who may have missed his path.

Source: De Amicis, Edmondo. *Morocco: Its People and Places*. Translated by Maria Hornor Lansdale. 2 vols. Philadelphia: Henry L. Coates and Company, 1897.

9. *Tomorrow—Yesterday:* A 1938 *View of* 1988

In the 1930s, with the rapid changes in the physical reality of modern life; the increasing ability of machines to do work; the wonders of flight; and the invention of radio, television, and a host of labor-saving devices, it is not surprising that people of the time would wonder what would come next. The modern mind has been asking the same question for a long time: what applications or discoveries would the successes of today lead to in the life of tomorrow?

Some of Arthur Train's predictions from this 1938 popular article are impressively accurate, such as cable television and broadband transmissions, garage door openers, burglar alarms, year-round food supplies, household faxes/printers, cell phones as pocket radios with their miniature cameras and microphones, and the profusion of plastic and synthetic household goods—even the importance of a recycling/composting center.

On other accounts, he fails, as in his predictions of beryllium construction materials, molded magnesium furniture, the limits of television, and the abandoning of the car in favor of airplanes for everyday travel. Digital memory he doesn't anticipate, instead opting for tiny reels of photographic film for storing books and other information, and although there is a photoelectric tabulating machine for office use, Train's proto-computer is not emphasized. Predictions of people clothed in three-quarter length rayon smocks using conveniences run on thyratron tubes makes Train's predictions of our past seem more like our own predictions of a Star Trek-inspired future.

Today we still try to predict the future, although the dominant technologies for such predictions in the contemporary world are computer and bio-genetic rather than, as in Train's piece, radio and the aeroplane. Not only for the pleasures of fiction, but also for real economic and social planning, it is important to have a sense of what is changing, and how discoveries or inventions are going to have significant consequences for everyday life.

Like most writers who try to predict what the future will be like, Train got some things right, and most things wrong. What is more important in this selection than keeping score is what the practice of predicting a technologically enhanced utopian future demonstrates. Train's house of 1988 encodes a belief in progress and improvement, a belief in the ability of scientific and technological advances to make everyday life easier and better. Whether that belief is well-founded, only the (real) future will tell.

Our hero, then, John Doe, born in the year of grace 1938, was in bed and asleep at the time our story begins in 1988. (No synthetic substitute for sleep had then been discovered.) Progress in biology, biochemistry, food technology, and related sciences was responsible for the fact that he was considerably heavier and taller than his forefathers, and also that, although half a century old, he was neither too fat nor too thin, and like Uncle Ned had "plenty of wool on the top of his head, the place where the wool ought to be."

The sounds of the city were filtered at the intake-ducts of the air-conditioning apparatus, and such few persistent discords and jangles as did penetrate into the room were deflected toward the ceiling by the walls which slanted gently upward like the glass control windows of radio broadcasting control rooms, where they were absorbed by special insulations. The entering air passed through a dust filter and was freed from other germs by ultra-violet rays. Research into the effects of ionization, barometric pressure, condensation nuclei, and the existence of a metastable state of oxygen had made it possible to supply Mr. Doe's room with air as invigorating as that of the seashore or the mountains. Its chemical composition was nicely calculated to give him a maximum of refreshment at night, while during the day its temperature, humidity, and degree of ionization were automatically varied from time to time in order to avoid the soporific effect of monotony. Incidentally, synthetic air, long considered fantastic, was well on the way toward becoming reality.

Presently, as the radio-controlled clock proclaimed in a soothing voice that it was time to get up (for its direct reading dial showed the hour of seven), the air became sensibly warmer. Heating was provided by the simple process of running the refrigerator mechanism in reverse, although some architects recommended heating coils in the walls or radiant wires in the ceiling.

Although it was dark and rainy outside, the room was gradually flooded with a diffused light. The quantity required was measured out with nice accuracy by the ever watchful photocell, and on sunny days when clouds passed over the sun, the light in the room would remain constant. This light was provided by a gaseous discharge lamp, perhaps employing carbon dioxide, infinitely more efficient than the old-fashioned filament bulbs, and containing as a good a proportion of infrared and ultra-violet rays as that of the brightest summer sun, which were automatically turned on at intervals. [...]

The bathroom into which Mr. Doe stepped for his matutinal shower was a prefabricated affair made like an automobile, all the various appliances such as tub, shower, basin, and toilet forming one integrated unit, with special metallic walls for the outer casing. Three identical bathrooms were grouped with it to form a square in the center of the house, so that a minimum of pluming was required. The old-fashioned system of using thousands of gallons of water to dilute and remove waste, thereby sacrificing its valuable chemical properties, had long ago been superseded by chemical disposal of sewage. The development of new detergents also made it possible to "wash" without water if anyone so desired.

While Doe was slipping into a pair of shorts and light, three-quarter length rayon fabric smock, which, after all, is all that anyone would need in an air-conditioned home, he haphazardly pushed in various buttons controlling the automatic tuning of his television set so that he might see with his own eyes what was going on in different parts of the world. He was a man who liked to spend money on gadgets, and the morning paper had been printed out for him by the facsimile recorder while he slept. It was his habit to leave it on just as people in old days left the radio on, and from the reams of stuff it printed out he would pick what he wanted and throw the rest away. Most of the time, however, he preferred to hear the news rather than read it. [...]

His house was situated at a considerable distance from the city, in an "integrated" neighborhood which had been carefully planned by a city planning board. The houses were grouped about a park, and in addition to the school and library there was a central air-conditioning plant and a community center with a television transmission set, an auditorium whose television receiving

A model of the bus of the future, designed by Norman Bel Geddes for the FUTURAMA exposition in 1939. Flickr (ROGERIOMACHAD).

set boasted color and three-dimensional sound and sight, a trailer camp, all kinds of recreational facilities, the vegetable factory, the poultry factory, and the plant where the garbage was converted into fertilizer.

The house itself was somewhat smaller and had smaller rooms than one would have expected of a man with Mr. Doe's means. The large custom-built house had long ago gone the way of the large custom-built automobile. It was a long, low, flat-roofed building made up of cluster of prefabricated units whose irregular arrangement prevented it from looking monotonous. Unlike the houses of the early part of the century and all preceding eras, whose aim was to give an impression of volume, the whole building was so translucent, neutral, and fragile-looking, so broken into planes by terraces and porches, that it gave the impression of being little more than a part of the out-of-doors which had been etched into the frame with a few strokes of a sharp pointed pencil.

In the construction of the house the use of wood, bricks, and plaster had practically been superseded by panels of beryllium and magnesium alloys; low-grade silicas, or glasslike materials; sheet materials such as asbestos cement, and occasionally plastic which had been developed to a point where its resistance to atmosphere was known. A considerable use was made of moving partitions which made it possible to enclose a small space when privacy was required, and still provide a large space when it was not. The insulation, of "mineral fluff," was of course built into the prefabricated panels.

In the various rooms many of the pieces of furniture were made of plastic molded as a unit, while others were made of magnesium alloy. In place of cushions, spongelike synthetic upholstery was used. Some of the most beautiful hangings were of translucent glass fabric.

Outside a few first edition and beautifully bound volumes with handsome illustrations, Mr. Doe's library contained few books. It consisted chiefly of little drawers filled with thousands of tiny reels of film a few millimeters in width. On his table was a reading machine about the size of a portable typewriter, which projected the tiny photographed pages onto a small screen. Each of these tiny films also carried a sound track, and at his own discretion he could play them on a talking book. Wherever he went Mr. Doe carried a camera hardly bigger than a watch and also a tiny sound-recording device, so that anything he saw or heard during the day he could conveniently remember by mechanical means. The day had not yet arrived (predicted by Sarnoff back in 1936) when each individual would have his own wave-length and by means of a pocket radio could communicate with anybody anywhere. In Doe's office the principle of mechanical aids to memory was developed to a high state of efficiency. All of his records were "remembered," selected and analyzed on photoelectric tabulating machines with far greater efficiency than the human brain could achieve and in much less time.

An inventory of the various objects in Mr. Doe's house would show that the strawboard and fiberboard that lined the walls, the insulation material between them and the outer walls, sometimes the outer wall itself, the synthetic textiles which comprised the clothing of much of the family, and the waterproof materials which protected them if they ever went out in the rain, and all small knick-knacks from ash trays to bottle caps, were made of various types of thermo-plastic resin-derived from such inexpensive raw materials as soy bean, bagasse, sugar cane, straw, wood pulp, sorghum, linseed, flaxseed, cottonseed hulls, oat hulls, nut shell, Jerusalem artichokes, fruit pits, and skim milk.

We have seen how in Mr. Doe's house the electric eye, or photoelectric tube, coupled with the thyratron tube which enables it to act on what it sees, automatically measured the amount of illumination necessary to replace the waning light of day. It also performed the function of a whole corps of servants. It opened the garage door as you drove up, opened the door between the kitchen and the dining room when someone advanced with a tray, opened the door of the refrigerator, and opened and closed windows. But its duties did not end with the fall of day. All night long it was on guard as night watchman, ready to give warning by ringing bells, turning on floodlights, photographing the intruder, paralyzing him with tear gas, and sending for the police.

The roof of the house, as in all houses at that time, was used as a landing field for the family's collection of steep-flight airplanes of assorted sizes, the top storey being used as a garage. Doe didn't bother to use his car very often, and in general it was relegated to trips to the community center and to use by the children, playing the role of the station wagon of the late 30s. Its two cycle motor, smaller, lighter, and more efficient than the old fashioned four-cycle one, could easily drive it along at an average speed of seventy miles an hour on the highly efficient fuels of those days. Such speeds, however, seemed like crawling to Mr. Doe and his friends, who used small steep-flight planes for short hops and giant stratosphere planes for distance flying.

Source: Train, Jr., Arthur, "Keeping Up with the Inventors." *Harper's Monthly Magazine* 176 (March 1938): 363–73.

Clothing and Personal Appearance

Clothing is an integral part of daily life, but the modern era has seen the design and production of clothing move from a labor-intensive and often home-based process to an industrial, highly automated one, with an extraordinary variety of styles and cloths available. The average person in the eighteenth century and into the nineteenth likely wore clothes made at home, often from materials also made by hand or at home. Clothing and other textiles were labor-intensive and valuable. In the eighteenth century, when Abigail Adams was writing (Document 10), virtually all cloth was spun and woven by hand, and clothing was cut and sewn garment by garment. The industrialization of textile production and clothing manufactured in the nineteenth century revolutionized clothing and fashion. Mass production of cloth and the development of sewing machines meant clothing could be made cheaply and quickly in a range of sizes and styles in factories, and this changed fashion. Another major change in the twentieth century has been the creation of synthetic fabrics. Polyester, rayon, nylon, spandex, and blended fabrics are by far the majority of clothing manufactured today. Synthetics make fabric more durable, easier to care for, and cheaper.

Clothing and personal appearance have changed in ways beyond just technology. If the modern world can in part be characterized by an increasing emphasis on individuality and self-control, the growth of self-knowledge and self-discipline, and political and personal freedom, then modern clothing can be seen as reflecting many of those trends.

Clothing and body appearance is often connected with control. In an obvious way, Leo Deutsch's description (Document 12) of being put into prison clothes and leg irons and having his head half-shaved is about having his body out of his control. In other more subtle ways, though, clothing also shows controls, either self-imposed or not. The bound feet of Chinese women (Document 13) controlled their bodies' growth in a way to curtail their being able to walk very far, practically keeping them from active lives outside the home. Western women's corsets and skirts also controlled, shaped, and limited the body, to the consternation of the active and practical nursing advocate Florence Nightingale (Document 11), but at least one American missionary was unconscious of the parallel, or at least approved of it (Document 13). Head coverings, like those described by Georgia Scott (Document 14), could have this element, too, though the Guatemalan women's styles are not obviously controlling. Many Muslim women conceal their bodies, their hair, and sometimes their faces, just as other religious groups advocate modest dress, particular undergarments, or nun's habits.

At the same time, contemporary trends in Western fashion have seen less restrictive clothing, more freedom and casualness in dress, and variation in styles. Tight-lacing whalebone corsets and footbinding are dead practices. Inexpensive mass-manufactured clothing allows more comfortable and more fashionable choices, as well as more exposure of the body, for all social groups, although these choices often are limited by other factors. Clothing combines with other ways of decorating the body, such as hair styles, cosmetics, and jewelry to protect, adorn, dignify, conceal, separate, and identify. Our personal appearance marks us by gender, class, age, profession, culture, and in many other ways. Clothing or other choices that shape our personal appearance in the modern world not only in turn shape how we are seen, but also show how we see ourselves.

10. *Abigail Adams and the Massachusetts Militia: Officers and Gentlewomen in the Eighteenth Century*

The following two excerpts from eighteenth-century documents offer very different descriptions of clothing. The first selection is a 1796 letter by Abigail Adams, wife of John Adams *and later the second First Lady of the United States, to her niece about a ball she attended in England while her husband served as American minister (ambassador) to England. The second selection comprises orders standardizing the military uniforms of officers of the militia of Massachusetts during the American Revolutionary War in 1781. (See* American Revolution *in the Glossary.) It also bears remembering that all the garments mentioned were made by hand; there were no machine-driven textile mills or sewing machines, although industrialization was pioneered in textile industries and the process was beginning in the eighteenth century. Although the cloth used for court dresses and officers' uniforms would be professionally made, most people could not afford such elaborate and expensive clothing, and many spun, wove, and sewed their own textiles and clothing in the home from wool, flax, cotton, or other materials.*

The dresses described for the ball are typical of upper-class formal (or full dress) attire. Sack (or sacque) gowns were popular in evolving form through the eighteenth century, and had a kind of jacket with folds of fabric down the back from the neck to the floor. By Adams' time, the sacque or coat part of the gown split in front to reveal a matching (or contrasting) stomacher and skirt or petticoat. Many of the other details are specific terms describing the types and colors of fabric, ribbons, headpieces, and other trimmings, to which Adams and other women paid great attention. Often these were more expensive than the dress itself—not even including jewelry, and an old dress might be retrimmed, or the trim might be transferred to a new dress for a different effect and a different occasion.

It is clear that Adams thinks it all just a bit above her, but she obviously enjoyed it nonetheless, spending substantial amounts of money for feathers and ribbons and jewelry. While conforming to general trends, it was also important for a fashionable woman to look different or unique, and she had to direct the tailor or seamstress according to her own plans; fashion designers or couturiers who told or advised people on what to wear were a later, nineteenth- and twentieth-century phenomenon. If Adams' letter describes an attempt to look unique, the second excerpt describes an attempt to look alike.

The military uniforms for the Massachusetts officers are described in such detail so they can each have them made properly and still match each other, as was expected for military attire by the eighteenth century. Especially in the cash-strapped colonial armies, soldiers might not have had much of a uniform at all and officers would be responsible for their own uniforms. To insure as much uniformity as possible, specific regulations were issued. Prescribed is a long coat that buttoned closed at the top and opened halfway down, short trousers, waistcoat, neck cloth, and cock'd, or three-cornered hat; notably no mention is made of weapons, stockings, or shoes.

While styles have certainly changed, as well as the methods by which clothing is made, two dominant themes of these selections—individual expression and conformity to express membership in a group—are still important everyday functions of clothing and fashion today.

To amuse you, then, my dear niece, I will give you an account of the dress of the ladies at the ball of Comte d'Adhemar. There was as great a variety of pretty dresses, borrowed wholly from France, as I have ever seen; and amongst the rest, some with sapphire blue satin waists, spangled with silver, and laced down the back and seams with silver stripes; white satin petticoats trimmed with black and blue velvet ribbon; an odd kind of head-dress, which they term the 'Helmet of Minerva.' I did not observe the bird of wisdom, however, nor do I know whether those who wore the dress had any suitable pretensions to it. 'And pray,' say you, 'how were my aunt and cousin dressed?' If it will gratify you to know, you shall hear. Your aunt, then, wore a full dress court cap without the lappets, in which was a wreath of white flowers, and blue sheafs, two black and blue flat feathers (which cost her half a guinea apiece, but that you need not tell of), three pearl pins, bought for Court, and a pair of pearl earrings, the cost of them—no matter what; less than diamonds, however. A sapphire blue demi-saison with a satin stripe, sack and petticoat trimmed with broad black lace; crape flounce, etc. leaves made of blue ribbon, and trimmed with white floss; wreaths of black velvet ribbon spotted with steel beads, which are much in fashion and brought to perfection as to resemble diamonds; white ribbon also in the Vandyke style, made up a trimming, which looks very elegant; and a full dress handkerchief, and a bouquet of roses. 'Full gay, I think, for my aunt.' That is true, Lucy, but nobody is old in Europe. I was seated next the Duchess of Bedford, who had a scarlet satin sack and coat, with a cushion full of diamonds, for hair she had none, and is but seventy-six neither. Well now for your cousin: a small white leghorn hat, bound with pink satin ribbon; a steel buckle and band which turned up at the side, and a confined a large pink bow; a large bow of the same kind of ribbon behind; a wreath of full blown roses around the crown, and another of buds and roses withinside the hat, which, being placed at the back of the hair, brought the roses to the edge; you see it clearly; one red and black feather with two white ones, completed the head-dress. A gown and coat of Chamberi gauze, with a red satin stripe over a pink waist, and coat flounced with crape, trimmed with broad point and pink ribbon; wreaths of roses across the coat, gauze sleeves and ruffles.

...

Orders for the Massachusetts Line

January 5th, 1781.

The Committee of Officers appointed to fix upon the fashion of the Massachusetts uniform, have reported thereupon, and it is a follows:

The color of the coats, waistcoats, linings and buttons, to be agreeable to the General Orders of the 2nd of October, 1779.

The length of the coat, to the upper part of the knee-pan, and to be cut high in the neck. As 3 is to 5, so is the skirt to the waist of the coat; or divide the whole length of the coat into 8 equal parts, take 5 for the waist and 3 for the skirts.

The lappel, at the top of the breast, to be 3 inches wide, and the bottom 2 3/10 inches; the lapel to be as low as the waist, and its wing to button within an inch of the shoulder seam with a small button on the cape. The epaulette to be worn directly on the top of the shoulder joint on the same button with the wing of the lappel. A round and close cuff, three inches wide, with four close worked buttonholes. The cape to be made with a peak behind, and its width in proportion to the lappels. The pocket flaps to be scollopped, four buttonholes, the two inner close worked, the two outer open worked, and to be set on in a curved line from the bottom of the lappel to the button on the hip. The coat to be cut full behind, with a fold on each back skirt, and two close worked buttonholes on each.

Plates from McClellan's *History of American Costume,* illustrated by Sophy Steele, 1904. Elisabeth McClellan, *History of American Costume* (New York, Tudor publishing company, 1917).

Ten open worked buttonholes on the breast of each lappel, with ten large buttons, at equal distance; four large buttons on each cuff, four on each pocket flap, and four on each fold. Those on the cuffs and pocket flaps to be placed agreeable to the buttonholes; and those on the folds, one on the hip, one at the bottom, and two in the centre, at an equal distance with those on the lappel. The coat is to button or hook as low as the fourth buttonhole on the breast, and is to be flaunt at the bottom with a genteel and military air. Four hooks and eyes on the breast as low as the coat is allowed to button. The skirts hook up with a bleu heart at each corner, with such a device as the Field Officers of each Regiment shall direct. The bottoms of the coat to be cut square. The waistcoat to be single-breasted, with twelve buttons and holes on the breast, with pocket flaps, four close worked buttonholes and four buttons, which shall appear below the flaps. The breeches are to be made with a half fall; four buttons on each knee. The small buttons on the waistcoat are to be of the same kind with the large ones on the coat. The number of the Regiment is to be in the centre of the button, with such device as the Field Officers shall direct. The epaulettes to be worn agreeable to his Excellency the Commander-in-Chief's orders of June 18, 1780.

A fashionable military cock'd hat, with a silver button loop, and a small button with the number of the Regiment. To wear a black stock [neck cloth] when on duty and on the parade.

No edging, vellum lace, or indeed any other ornaments which are not mentioned, to be added to the uniform. No officer is to be permitted, at any time, to wear any other uniform than that of his Regiment.

Source: McClellan, Elisabeth. *History of American Costume, 1607–1870*. New York: Tudor Publishing Co., 1937.

11. Florence Nightingale: Unhealthy Dresses

Florence Nightingale was one of the leaders of the reform of nursing in the middle nineteenth century, helping to transform it from a job of dubious morality to a respectable profession for trained, compassionate women. Nightingale was an upper-class British woman with talent, resources, and persistence who changed the practice of medicine with her focus on patients' needs, professionalism, and cleanliness in medical care. In this entry from her 1860 book on nursing (see also Document 7), Nightingale, never afraid to take on conventional wisdom or challenge social norms, lambasts women's fashions of the middle nineteenth century as being absurd and even detrimental to a patient's health.

In the latter half of the nineteenth century, some in Western societies called for fashion reforms, claiming that women's fashionable dresses, with their constricting, body-shaping undergarments and heavy, wide skirts, were unhealthy to the wearers. Nightingale's claim is rather unique: fashionable dress is even unhealthy to those around the wearer. While Nightingale was absolutely correct about the relative impracticality of such skirts and the potential hazards associated with them, whether she was right about the threat to the health of others because of the noise associated with women moving in these dresses is another question.

Some of her advice in this selection, although in principle about the care and comfort of patients, seems at least in part to be separately motivated by dissatisfaction with contemporary fashion; she may have had good reason. After women's skirts had become straight and slender at the beginning of the nineteenth century, they gradually widened as the century went on, requiring ever greater numbers of petticoats, crinolines, and eventually cage crinolines, a dome- or bell-shaped undergarment made of a lattice of spring steel that attached at the waist to the corset and held the skirt in its shape. By 1860, these skirts had become as wide as six feet. While skirt shapes changed again within a few years after Nightingale wrote, many of her criticisms would still pertain to the conflict between the dictates of fashion and the need for practical clothing for women for everyday activities such as nursing.

It is, I think, alarming, peculiarly at this time, when the female ink-bottles are perpetually impressing upon us "woman's" "particular worth and general missionariness," to see that the dress of women is daily more and more unfitting them for any "mission" or usefulness at all. It is equally unfitted for all poetic and all domestic purposes. A man is now a more handy and far less objectionable being in a sick room than a woman. Compelled by her dress, every woman now either shuffles or waddles—only a man can cross the floor of a sick room without shaking it! What is become of woman's light step?—the firm, light, quick step we have been asking for?

Unnecessary noise, then, is the most cruel absence of care which can be inflicted either on sick or well. For, in all these remarks, the sick are only mentioned as suffering in a greater proportion than the well from precisely the same causes.

Unnecessary (although slight) noise injures a sick person much more than necessary noise (of a much greater amount).

All doctrines about mysterious affinities and aversion will be found to resolve themselves very much, if not entirely, into the presence or absence of care in these things.

A nurse who rustles (I am speaking of nurses professional and unprofessional) is the horror of a patient, though perhaps he does not know why.

The fidget of silk and crinoline, the rattling of keys, the creaking of stays and of shoes, will do a patient more harm than all the medicines in the world will do him good.

The noiseless step of a woman, the noiseless drapery of woman, are mere figures of speech in this day. Her skirts (and well if they do not throw down some piece of furniture) will at least brush against every article in the room as she moves.

Fortunate it is if her skirts do not catch fire—and if the nurse does not give herself up to sacrifice together with her patient, to be burnt in her own petticoats. I wish the Registrar-General would tell us the exact number of deaths by burning occasioned by this absurd and hideous custom. But if people will be stupid, let them take measure to protect themselves from their own stupidity—measures which every chemist knows, such as putting alum into starch, which prevents starched articles of dress from blazing up.

I wish, too, that people who wear crinoline could see the indecency of their own dress as other people see it. A respectable elderly woman stooping forward, invested in crinoline, exposes as much of her own person to the patient lying in the room as any opera dancer does on stage. But no one will ever tell her this unpleasant truth.

Source: Nightingale, Florence. *Notes on Nursing: What It Is, and What It Is Not*. New York: D. Appleton and Co., 1860.

12. Leo Deutsch: Prison and Personal Appearance

Condemned by the Russian Imperial government in the late nineteenth century for anti-government terrorist activities to 13 years of labor in Siberia, Leo Deutsch (or Lev Deich) was a socialist and revolutionary. Whatever the merits of his cause or his case, Deutsch's account of being put into the daily attire of a convicted prisoner for the first time is a reminder that going to prison involves an almost total loss of freedom.

Clothing and personal appearance is usually thought of as a mode of self-expression, a way of expressing ourselves, usually informed by a variety of factors, including climate, wealth, gender, age, and culture. In Deustch's case, though, he was deprived of all choice in his appearance. He was given a very specific appearance that was intended to be different from other people, different from any chosen fashion. Not only would this make any runaway prisoners immediately recognizable and so make escape more difficult—even if they did manage to make it out of the leg irons—but it also was intentionally demeaning: no one wears their hair half short, half shaven. The body and personal appearance of Deutsch marks him as an outcast, as a prisoner, as socially unacceptable, and as completely in the control of others.

One of the typical marks of imprisonment in the modern world is enforced uniformity and conformity by means of clothing and personal appearance. The prisoner's personal appearance, including hair and clothing, are taken from his control, making his body's subordination to the state's power physically manifest and nearly complete. In the very last part of the following selection, though, Deutsch mentions that he retains his books. His body and physical appearance are under others' control, but his mind is not.

A fortnight later I was informed that a party of convicts would start for Moscow that evening. I was to accompany them, and accordingly must assume the convict garb. After eighteen years I think of that day with a shudder.

First of all, I was taken into a room where was stored everything necessary to the equipment of a convict under sentence. On the floor lay piles of chains; and clothes, boots, etc., were heaped on shelves. From among them some were selected that were supposed to fit me; and I was then conducted to a second room. Here the right side of my head was shaved, and the hair on the left side cut short. I had seen people in the prison who had been treated in this fashion, and the sight had always made a painful impression on me, as indeed it does on everyone. But when I saw my own face in the glass a cold shudder ran down my spine, and I experienced a sensation of personal degradation to something less than human. I thought of the days—in Russia not so long ago—when criminals were branded with hot irons.

A convict was waiting ready to fasten on my fetters. I was placed on a stool, and had to put my foot on an anvil. The blacksmith fitted an iron ring round each ankle, and welded it together. Every stroke of the hammer made my heart sink, as I realised that a new existence was beginning for me.

The mental depression into which I now fell was soon accompanied by physical discomfort. The fetters at first caused me intolerable pain in walking, and even disturbed my sleep. It also requires considerable practice before one can easily manage to dress and undress. The heavy chains—about 13 lbs. in weight—are not only an encumbrance, but are very painful, as they chafe the skin round the ankles; and the leather lining is but little protection to those unaccustomed to these adornments. Another great torment is the continual clinking of the chains. It is indescribably irritating to the nervous, and reminds the prisoner at every turn that he is a pariah among his kind, "deprived of all rights."

The transformation is completed by the peculiar convict dress, consisting—besides the coarse linen underclothing—of a grey gown made of special material, and a pair of trousers. Prisoners condemned to hard labour wear a square piece of yellow cloth sewn on their gowns. The feet are clad in leathern slippers nicknamed "cats." All these articles of clothing are inconvenient, heavy, and ill-fitting.

I hardly knew myself when I looked in the glass and beheld a fully attired convict. The thought possessed me—"For long years you will have to go about in that hideous disguise." Even the gendarme regarded me with compassion.

"What won't they do to a man?" he said. And I could only try to comfort myself by thinking how many unpleasant things one gets used to, and that time might perhaps accustom one even to this.

My own clothes I gave away to the warders, and any possessions of value—watch, ring, cigarette-case—I sent by post to relations. I kept only my books. I had been given a bag in which to keep a change of linen; and into it I also put a few volumes of Shakespeare, Goethe, Heine...

Source: Deutsch, Leo. *Sixteen Years in Siberia: Some Experiences of a Russian Revolutionist*. Translated by Helen Chisholm. New York: E. P. Dutton, 1904.

13. Bound Virtue: Mary Fulton on Foot Binding in Nineteenth-Century China

In this selection, Mary Fulton, an American Presbyterian missionary to China in the late nineteenth century, tries to impress Chinese women by being not Chinese. One of the major points of difference between the Western Christian woman and her Chinese circle is not only her dress, but also her feet. Since medieval times, Chinese women were believed to be more attractive if they had small feet and a corresponding "lotus gait," so their feet were broken and bound by female relatives to prevent them from growing properly in childhood. This painful process was designed to distend the arch to make feet as short as three inches long, resulting not only in smaller feet, but also in significant pain at best, infection and death at worst. Foot binding was outlawed with the end of the Chinese Imperial period in 1911, for a variety of reasons, including, in part, pressure from Western nations, which saw the practice as unnecessary and cruel.

While bound feet were undoubtedly more painful, much of nineteenth-century Western women's clothing was generally not very comfortable either, including corsets or other extensive, restrictive undergarments that could break women's ribs if pulled too tight; extra layers of outer clothing; high, stiff collars; long sleeves and heavy, full skirts; and tight shoes with heels (see Document 11). Fulton does not perceive these as negative, though, and she conflates her own short finger nails, "pretty and fresh," though cheap, dresses, and well-fitting foreign shoes not simply with being Western, but with her Christian virtues as well. While historically Christians have worn many other things, here the distinctions she makes draw strict parallels between her ethnicity, religion, dress, and personal appearance. Part of her task of converting the Chinese women to Christianity is also converting them to a Western and European style of dress and life. The Chinese women that she describes are also very attached to their long nails, silk gowns, and bound feet as cultural signs of attractiveness, ethnicity, and femininity. Despite the pain and discomfort of women's clothing and appearance in both cultures, women in both use their bodies to define their virtues, and they are attached to it as central parts of their identities and their everyday life.

I am doing what little I can in my small sphere to show an applied Christianity. In the first place, I try always to be neat in dress. This invariably calls out complimentary remarks. The Chinese women at once compare my pretty and fresh, though cheap, dress with their silken (and generally soiled) robes. Then they notice my clean, short finger nails, and contrast them with their long ones,—often a finger in length,—which indicate that they are ladies of leisure. They at once want to know *why* I dress so differently from them. It is an easy step to tell them that God, who made us, has put women into the world for *use*, and not merely to live to adorn our bodies, and that there are many poor suffering children and others who need our help. If we have such long nails and bound feet, we cannot go about to help them.

They all assent to this, and generally there is an inquiry on the part of some one present if she cannot have her feet unbound. Then you should hear the clamor! A dozen will admonish the one who has been so bold as to propose such a thing. Had she lost all her modesty that she wanted to go about like a man? Now you will laugh, but all my arguments are as nothing compared with showing them a well-fitting pretty foreign boot or shoe. I have always thought, since feet are such a momentous question in this land, that we should be very careful to make our own as presentable as possible. To see us start off quickly and gracefully and go through the streets so independently often makes them desirous of imitating us, especially when they see women hobbling along painfully, or being carried on the backs of others.

The same is true of our homes. I try to make mine attractive in its simplicity. I have a weekly prayer meeting here just because I want to show my home to these women who have never seen cleanliness and order in their dark, damp, crowded quarters. I give them, after the meeting, tea and sponge cake, served in pretty cups and plates. Simple as all this is, it lifts them up and out of their sordid surroundings, for the time being, at least, and, I hope, will lead them to make their own houses more homelike. I always urge those coming under my influence to try and be as clean as possible, and I am happy to say that I observe year by year an increasing tendency to the use of foreign soap and handkerchiefs.

Source: Dennis, James S. *Christian Missions and Social Progress: A Sociological Study of Foreign Missions*. New York: Fleming H. Revell Co., 1897.

14. Making Headway: Georgia Scott on Headwraps in Guatemala

Georgia Scott is an African-American who, fascinated by the trend for headwraps among her peers in New York in the 1990s, launched a year-long global trip to investigate headwraps in world cultures. The following selection includes parts of her rationale and her description of her visit to Guatemala in Central America, the last stop on her round-the-world trip.

Scott tries to place the Guatemalan headwraps in historical and global context; she identifies styles that are new and gaining popularity, and styles that are virtually identical to ancient Mayan reliefs. Her descriptions document the variations in styles and expressions among even a single people, the Maya, and the interacting pressure of tradition and the trend toward innovation. Another part of the treatment is simply how compelling and beautiful she finds headwraps, and how each person, each village, each country, and each culture expresses themselves in the type and variety of headwraps they use. Ultimately, the headwraps and headscarves become for Scott a metonym for the richness and diversity of Guatemalan and world cultures, and the variety of dress and body decoration in everyday life.

From July 2000 to July 2001, I traveled around the world with the singular, determined purpose of documenting the world's headwraps and headscarves. [. . .] Headwraps and headscarves are tremendously varied. They can be made of silk, cotton, gauze, muslin, wool, abaca, and many other fabrics. They can be tied, wrapped, pinned, folded, or twisted. They have hundreds of little nuances, from color and texture, to size and shape, to why they're worn and when. In some cultures, they have been wrapped the same way for generations, while other cultures create new styles every season. And they are worn for a variety of reasons. In many countries, such as India, Kenya, Ethiopia, and the United Arab Emirates, they are worn mainly for religious reasons. . . . In some countries headwraps are an integral part of daily life. In Morocco, Mali, and Niger, for example, harsh climate conditions make headwraps a daily necessity, while in other countries, such as Indonesia and Malaysia, traditional headwraps are reserved for special occasions, such as weddings and official state functions. [. . .]

Guatemala City wasn't exactly what I had expected. Maybe I'd done too much partying in the Caribbean, but when I arrived in Guatemala, I didn't sense the raw excitement I'd anticipated in the only Latin American country of my travels. More important[ly], like most cities in Latin America, people in Guatemala City don't wear traditional headwraps.

So I left. I rode north in a dusty, rusty yellow bus to San Pedro Sacatepequez, a Mayan town a few miles from Guatemala City. There, and in seven other Mayan hamlets in the western highlands, I discovered the vibrant celebration of life and tradition I'd come for. In hillside villages with pastel-painted homes and whitewashed churches filled with the scent of incense, I found extended communities of living prisms. Brilliant bursts of bold colors—bright yellow, magenta, green, orange, blue, purple—saturated everything. I was dazzled.

Maya children in Santiago de Atitlán, 2004. Courtesy of Photos.com.

Almost all the textiles, from blankets and tablecloths to shirts, skirts and headwraps, are handwoven with a profusion of bright colors. Reminiscent of the weavings in northern Vietnam and in Indonesia, the colors and decorative motifs in some Mayan garments tell stories about the cultural background of the person wearing them. The vocabulary of colors and textiles varies from village to village. A yellow pineapple could mean health and prosperity in one, but happiness and peace in another.

The Maya of Guatemala are part of the larger Mayan culture that dates back to around 2000 B.C. and stretches through southern Mexico, Belize, Guatemala, and parts of Honduras and El Salvador. [. . .]

I arrived in San Pedro Sacatepequez just as a wedding was about to start. I stood in awe outside the church's wrought iron fence and watched as the bride, her groom, and dozens of guests filed inside. The bride wore a puffy, Western-style white gown and veil. Behind her, a crowd of well-wishers wore a glorious array of colorful traje [village-specific dress]: purple, red and green short-sleeved tops with wide, square necks and equally colorful long wraparound skirts. Tops and skirts were made from strips of thick, handwoven textiles with abstract motifs and floral appliqués. The women had interlaced pastel and neon-colored ribbons, or listons, into the pairs of long braids that hung down their backs, tying the ends in bows as large as grapefruits.

My next stop, Chichicastaenango, was a tourists' playground a few miles further northwest. I arrived on a Saturday morning just as vendors were setting up for the town's biweekly market. Many of the vendors and shoppers came from neighboring villages and wore the traje of their individual communities. All of the women wore knotted, twisted headwraps that circled their heads like halos, leaving the tops of their hair exposed. Some headwraps had thick, six-inch-long tassels and yarn puffs that bounced up and down in the back, sides, and front. Other headwraps were wound with thin ribbon and interlocking cords. Still others were made from streams of four or five separate ribbons all twisted together. Men of Cofridias, or brotherhoods, wore bright red, handwoven tzutes [multipurpose cloths] underneath black hats with the tassels and a large corner of the fabric hanging down their backs. [. . .]

In Santiago Atitlan, the women wear saucer-like wraps called cintas. They wind several yards of narrow, bright red fabric around and around their heads until they have wraps with diameters of nearly a foot wide. They are similar to turbans shown on relief figures from the Itzae ruins of Copan in southern Yucatan, Mexico.

In other parts of Lake Atitlan, I saw the same wide taffeta ribbons I'd seen in San Pedro Sacatepequez. "This style is new but very popular," explained a woman sitting beside me on the boat. "You will see it in many towns. Women don't always have time to weave their headwraps, and some don't like how the turbans hide their hair." Ribbons are bought ready-to-wear and come in a variety of colors that are not village specific. They quickly became popular in several highland communities and are now a recognizable part of a woman's traje, although some women who've adopted the ribbons replace them for more traditional headwraps on special occasions.

I could have stayed in Guatemala for another month without getting bored—with the country's headwraps or its people. But the United States was calling me. Before I left the highlands, I bought a blanket and several scarves. If I couldn't live in their prism, I could at least bring a piece of it home with me.

Source: Scott, Georgia, *Headwraps: A Global Journey*. New York: Public Affairs, 2001. Reprinted by permission of PUBLIC AFFAIRS, a member of Perseus Books Group.

Technology

At the beginning of the modern age, many technologies were similar to those that had been in use for much of human history. Certainly some important changes had taken place in the preceding centuries, such as the use of gunpowder firearms, the printing press, and the three-field system in agriculture, but many of the things that are most readily identifiable as different about the modern era from those that preceded it are technological.

While technological changes in the modern world have been rapid and far-reaching, they can be divided into several different episodes. The *Industrial Revolution*, for example, was driven primarily by technology and is often described in two parts, with the second part in the late nineteenth and twentieth centuries witnessing technological changes of a different kind from those seen in the eighteenth and early nineteenth centuries.

The First Industrial Revolution began in the eighteenth century, and exercised a widespread and significant social impact by the early nineteenth century. It was driven first by water, then by steam engines and pioneered by the machinery developed for the textile industry. John Kennedy's account (Document 15) offers the example of Samuel *Crompton*'s ingenuity, which had wide application and influence resulting in the development of the factory system, despite Crompton's personal misfortune. Transportation innovations were not as immediate, but Robert Fulton's description (Document 16) of his steamboat voyage shows the potential of steamboat and steam-powered engines for railroads that developed rapidly in the nineteenth century.

Other technologies are used to define the Second Industrial Revolution that began in the second half of the nineteenth century and continued well into the twentieth. New techniques led to the development of chemical processes and materials, as well as cheaper production of high-quality steel, which had important consequences for transportation, construction, and manufacturing. The sources of energy also changed, including the use of electricity and the internal combustion engine running on petroleum products instead of steam or falling water. The automobile is one of the most recognizable results of the Second Industrial Revolution; as Paris Fletcher describes (Document 17), it quickly replaced the horse and changed how people moved. Its impact, and that of other vehicles driven by internal combustion engines, has been tremendous in the daily life of the modern world.

The twentieth century saw not only technological innovations that can be classed with the Second Industrial Revolution, but also new kinds of technology, such as nuclear power and practical applications of biological sciences. However, the computer and other communications technology have brought a new kind of technological revolution: the information revolution. The abilities of computing technology to create changes in everyday life are evident to the extent that contemporary life is inconceivable in its current form without the myriad functions performed by microchips. Jennifer Flynn's look back (Document 18) at microchip technology is informative, but appreciably out of date less than 10 years after it was written. Moore's Law, an idea in the microchip industry, is that improvements in design and manufacturing techniques result in a doubling of the transistors, and thus computing power, possible on a chip approximately every two years. This highlights one of the things that is so compelling about technological changes in the modern world: not just the changes themselves, but the exponential rate of change.

Material life is strongly influenced by the available technology, whether modern or otherwise. It is also one of the most obvious areas in which the modern world has changed. The technologies of the first Industrial Revolution were tremendous compared to the pre-modern world, where technologies had advanced, developed, or changed at a comparatively slow pace. The changes of the Second Industrial Revolution and the Information Revolution have far surpassed the changes of the First Industrial Revolution in scope and speed. The modern world has seen drastic changes, numerous inventions, and incredible new technologies that together have repeatedly altered the nature of daily life in the modern world.

15. Samuel Crompton: Innovation and Factories

Samuel Crompton *was an English engineer and inventor who created a device for spinning thread in 1779 that helped remake the textile industry and lead the* Industrial Revolution. *Mass manufacturing and automation have been central to the transition of the modern world from handwork to the vast manufacturing and industrial power of developed nations.*

A friend of Crompton's, John Kennedy, described his life and contributions to the textile industry in an 1830 paper, which is excerpted here. Crompton's biography shows both persistence and great technical ingenuity, but less business acumen. His fate was similar to that of many inventors, who often were not able to capitalize on their creations, and had their ideas bought, stolen, or patented by others who reaped the profits.

The spinning mule Crompton invented was really a combination of two other machines: the spinning jenny, *which enabled the spinning of multiple strands of thread at one time, and the* water frame, *which efficiently spun one thread using water power. The name itself recognizes that Crompton's machine is a hybrid, like a mule is a cross between a horse and a donkey. The combination allowed powered spinning of multiple high-quality threads. The addition of steam power allowed the previously labor-intensive process of spinning thread to be performed very efficiently and largely by machine.*

The new machines were larger than what could be put in one worker's shop or home, and only performed one of the tasks in the production process. Previous production techniques of piecework, being performed in homes or a tradesman's workshop, were designed for one worker to complete all the parts of making a product one at a time and were not easily adapted to the new technologies. The result was the emergence of the factory system: the gathering of machinery and workers to operate it in a large, single manufacturing location called a factory. The factory was an organizational innovation that incorporated many technological innovations, including machinery like Crompton's, on a scale of millions; water and later steam and electrical power; and other new technologies that changed how everyday things were made as well as how and where people worked.

When about sixteen years old he [Samuel Crompton] learnt to spin upon a jenny (of Hargreaves's make), and had occasionally woven the yarn which he had spun. This, being but indifferent work, led him to reflect how it might be improved, and set him to construct the machine which we are about to describe. He was only twenty-one years of age when he commenced this undertaking, which took him five years to effect,—at least before he could bring his improvements to maturity. As he was not a regular mechanic, and possessed only such tools as he purchased with his little earnings acquired by labor at the loom or jenny and as he had also to learn the use of those simple tools, we may be justly surprised that even in five years he succeeded so far as to make his machine practically useful.

He often said that what annoyed him most was that he could not get leave to enjoy his little invention to himself in his garret; for, the product of his machine obtaining a better price than other yearns of those times, a report soon got abroad that he had constructed a new machine for the purpose of improved spinning, and people for the neighborhood, for miles round, came and climbed up at the windows to see him at his work. He erected a screen to prevent this, but the annoyance was so great that he could not proceed advantageously with his ingenious labor; and finally he was induced to lay the whole thing before a number of gentlemen and others, who subscribed a guinea each to look at it. On this as on every other occasion, the late Mr. Pilkinton, of Bolton, gave him his steady and friendly support. These sums amounted to about £50, which enabled him to construct another machine still further improved and of larger dimensions. When relating this little history to Mr. G. A. Lee and myself, Mr. Lee having observed "it is a pity he had not kept the secret to himself," he replied, "that a man had a very insecure tenure of a property which another could carry away with his eyes."....

In 1812 he made a survey of all the cotton districts in England, Scotland, and Ireland, and obtained an estimate of the number of spindles then at work upon his principle, which amounted to between four and five millions. On his return he laid the result of his inquiries before Mr. Lee and myself, with a suggestion that Parliament might grant him something. With these data before him, Mr. Lee, who was a warm friend to genius of every kind, with his usual energy entered fully into his merits, and made an appointment with the late George Duckworth, Esq., of Manchester, who also took a lively interest in the scheme, and gratuitously offered to draw up a memorial to Parliament in behalf of Mr. Crompton. This was signed by most of the principal manufacturers in the kingdom who were acquainted with his merits.... A bill was passed [by Parliament] for a grant of £5000 in full, without fees or charges.

Mr. Crompton was now anxious to place his sons in some business, and fixed upon that of bleaching; but the unfavorable state of the times, the inexperience and mismanagement of his sons, a bad situation, and a misunderstanding with his landlord, which occasioned a tedious lawsuit, conspired in a very short time to put an end to his establishment. His sons then dispersed, and he and his daughter were reduced to poverty. Messrs. Hicks and Rothwell of Bolton, myself, and some others, in that neighborhood and in Manchester, had in 1824 recourse to a second subscription, to purchase a life annuity for him, which produced £63 per annum. The amount raised for this purpose was collected in small sums, from one to ten pounds, some of which were contributed by the Swiss and French spinners, who acknowledged his merits and pitied his misfortunes. At the same time his portrait was engraved for his benefit, and a few impressions were disposed of. He enjoyed this small annuity only two years. He died January 26, 1827, leaving his daughter, his affectionate housekeeper, in poverty.

Source: Kennedy, John. "An Account of Crompton's Life by a Friend." Paper before the Manchester Literary and Philosophical Society, 1830. In *Readings in Modern European History*, edited by James Harvey Robinson and Charles A. Beard. Volume 2, *Europe Since the Congress of Vienna*. Boston: Ginn & Company, 1909.

16. Robert Fulton and Steam Power

Robert Fulton invented and built the first commercially viable steamboat. The following selection includes two of his own accounts of its first voyage up and down the Hudson River between the cities of New York and Albany in 1807. The first is a letter to the editor of a New York newspaper, The American Citizen, *the second is a letter to his friend and supporter Joel Barlow, which is excerpted from a book by Fulton's great-granddaughter. The steam-powered riverboat is just one of the applications of the steam engine, including ocean-going steamships, agricultural equipment, power for manufacturing equipment, and railroad engines, among others.*

While Fulton successfully applied steam power, he was not the inventor of the steam engine; various inventors and engineers had been developing and improving on steam engines through the eighteenth century. Steam power was reliable, efficient, flexible, and portable. It could be adapted to a variety of fuels; anything that can heat water to turn it to steam can be used. The pressure created by steam is then used to create mechanical energy.

In short, the steam engine provided the power for the Industrial Revolution. *Before the design of effective steam engines, the sources of mechanical energy available to power human civilization were limited to muscle—either of humans or animals—and wind and water. Efficiently harnessing wind and water is dependent on having falling water or blowing wind. Both were limited by the location and amount of wind or flowing water. Practical steam power represented a tremendous technological change. Steam provided immense, portable power. No longer did machinery or factories have to be built where there was falling water to power them. No longer did moving people or materials over long distances require waiting for winds to drive sailing ships or maintaining draft animals to pull them. Fulton's steamboat showed how transportation was being revolutionized, but it was just the beginning. Energy became cheap and abundant, and the process of moving and building the modern world with the technology of steam power was begun.*

New York, August 20, [1807]

To the Editor of *The American Citizen*, Sir:

I arrived this afternoon, at four o'clock, [on] the steam boat from Albany. As the success of my experiment gives me great hopes that such boats may be rendered of great importance to my country, to prevent erroneous opinions and give some satisfaction to the friends of useful improvements, you will have the goodness to publish the following statement of facts:

I left New York on Monday at 1 o'clock, and arrived at Clermont, the seat of Chancellor Livingston, at 1 o'clock on Tuesday, time 24 hours; distance, one hundred and ten miles: On Wednesday I departed from the Chancellor's at 9 in the morning, and arrived at Albany at 5 in the afternoon, distance, 40 miles, time, 8 hours; the sum is 150 miles in 32 hours, equal near 5 miles an hour.

On Thursday, at 9 o'clock in the morning, I left Albany, and arrived at the Chancellor's at 6 in the evening; I started from thence at 7, and arrived at New York at 4 in the afternoon; time, 30 hours, space run through 150 miles, equal to 5 miles an hour. Throughout my whole way my going and returning the wind was ahead; no advantage could be derived from my sails—the whole has therefore been performed by the power of the steam engine.

I am, Sir,
Your most obedient,
Robert Fulton

. . .

[Letter to Joel Barlow]

My steamboat voyage to Albany and back has turned out rather more favorably that I had calculated. The distance from New York to Albany is one hundred and fifty miles. I ran it up in thirty-two hours, and down in thirty. I had a light breeze against me the whole way, both going and coming, and the voyage has been performed wholly by the power of the steam engine. I overtook many sloops and schooners, beating to the windward, and parted with them as if they had been at anchor. The power of propelling boats by steam is now fully proved. The morning I left New York there were not perhaps thirty persons in the city who believed that the boat would ever move one mile an hour, or be of the least utility; and while we were putting off from the wharf, which was crowded with spectators, I heard a number of sarcastic remarks. This is the way in which ignorant men compliment what they call philosophers and projectors.

Having employed much time, money, and zeal in accomplishing this work, it gives me, as it will you, great pleasure to see it fully answer my expectations. It will give a cheap and quick conveyance to the merchandise on the Mississippi, Missouri, and other great rivers, which are now laying open their treasures to the enterprise of our countrymen; and although the prospect of personal emolument has been some inducement to me, yet I feel indefinitely more pleasure in reflecting on the immense advantage my country will derive from the invention.

Source: Sutcliffe, Alice Crary. *Robert Fulton and the "Clermont:" The Authoritative Story of Robert Fulton's Early Experiments, Persistent Efforts, and Historic Achievements*. New York: The Century Co., 1909.

17. The Horseless Carriage

In this account by Paris Fletcher, who describes some experiences from his childhood in small-town America, the focus is on the changes to everyday life brought about by that now ubiquitous technology, the automobile. If the factory and steam engine changed how things were made and moved, the auto changed how people moved. These new machines are one of the best expressions of what some scholars call the Second Industrial Revolution, *which was based on technological innovations such as the use of petroleum, chemical engineering, electricity, and steel.*

However, Fletcher is not interested in the new industries that create the cars, but rather he describes in vivid terms many of the changes and challenges of the new technology in practice. The interaction of horses and automobiles could be inconvenient or even dangerous to the animals and their loads and passengers. The transition from horse-powered vehicles to the new automobile causes the appearance of things that are common today: paved roads, road signs, and traffic laws. Other features of everyday life disappear: carriages, hitching posts, watering troughs, and even the horses themselves.

There is a certain amount of nostalgia in the entry; it is written from a backward-looking perspective. The author clearly remembers the difficulties of caring for and using horses for transportation—it was easier to walk than harness and drive a horse. However, at the same time, he is wistfully pleased by recalling what he thinks of as a simpler time. Whether it really was simpler or not, the description nonetheless illustrates how the introduction of a new technology changed everyday life.

This was the era of the horse and buggy. Some of you never knew this era. I suppose this one feature made as much change in the style and pace of living then as any single thing. I have mentioned the freedom it gave small boys to roam the streets. It had a beneficial side effect—people used their legs. Shallow thinkers are wont to ascribe this to rugged virtues of self reliance and virility. The fact of the matter is that when you have to harness a horse instead of pressing the starter button, you favor walking. We had a little Morgan horse who pulled variously a snappy little black runabout with red, hard-rubber tired wheels, a varnished two seater with the proverbial fringe on top, or an ole buckboard with a sag in the middle between the front and rear wheel that almost touched the road. In the barn were two or three old carriages which my grandfather had had, to be drawn by two horses. The most impressive of these was a landaulet with separate passenger compartment enclosed with and separated from the driver by glass panels which moved up and down by means of a broadcloth band. This gave me an early lesson in economics. My father offered it for sale at $50 and was offered $25, then came down to $25, but offers had declined to $10. After a while he sensed that those automobiles were really here to stay, panicked and offered it to anyone who would take it. It was too late. It cost him $10 to have it taken away. The moral is, of course, to constantly review your investment portfolio. The blue chips of yesterday may not always remain blue chips.

There were a few foolhardy souls who gradually essayed that modern contraption, the horseless carriage. If you didn't have to feed 'em it was only fair that you pay the penalty in some other manner and these early adventurers did. It might be as simple as a flat tire—which was really not so simple then, but often it involved a serious accident. Our local butcher lost an eye when his Stanley Steamer exploded. And when an enthusiast made the round trip to Bristol ten miles away without any untoward happening, it was dinner table conversation. People began to wonder whether after all this machine might be here to stay. It seemed to be the more aggressive and least conservative citizens, those who were engaged in the daily risks of their trade—the butcher, the merchant, the contractor, those who were least secure financially,—who first adopted this experiment, all of which figures, I guess. The advent of the automobile posed a peril for horses. When one approached it was standard practice for a horse driven vehicle to pull up by the side of the road and hold a tight rein until the offending vehicle had passed out of sight. There were two reasons for this: the obvious one of soothing the frightened horse, but the other equally valid one that it took that amount of time for the thick dust on the country roads to settle. Frequently the horse couldn't be restrained and the result was a runaway. From the amount of ill will generated by the early drivers, it is really a wonder that automobiles were not legislated off the road before they became accepted.

One consequence of this innovation was the emergence of the first traffic signs. At the Middlebury village limits was a big white sign—"Speed limit 10 miles per hour. Cutout forbidden." Roads began to improve. In a burst of radical legislation, the Middlebury town meeting decided to engage an outside firm to lay down a 400-yard strip of macadam road, the latest thing in hard surface roads. It was a wondrous work when finally finished after about six months—for autos. Horse driven vehicles which were still in the great majority avoided its hard surface like the plague. It must have lasted nearly a year and a half before the pot holes made it probably worse than it had been in its original state. These were the days of water carts sprinkling the dusty village streets, hitching posts, stone horse troughs at key intersections, iron kettles at a spring by the side of a country road. Our pleasures were simple and self-contrived.

Source: Fletcher, Paris. "Reminiscence of Boyhood in Middlebury." Undated typescript. Fletcher Collection. Henry Sheldon Museum of Vermont History. Used with permission.

18. Star Trek *Computer Science: A Look Back at Today*

Computers have become a virtually indispensible part of life in the modern world. They are essential to the manufacturing, communications, and transportation systems that run our everyday life, and the computers run on microchips. Among all the different technological innovations of the twentieth century, the microchip might be the most revolutionary, the most important for its impact on everyday life.

This selection by Jennifer Flynn is an artificial flash back, a look back at the present from an imaginary future perspective—the fictional world of Star Trek. *The article describes the binary system and the chip as a highly sophisticated, extraordinarily miniaturized electrical circuit. While the selection does not discuss particular applications in detail, it does describe the main innovations that make modern computers technologically possible. Without semiconductors and miniaturization of circuitry, computers filled rooms full of vacuum tubes and were reserved for government and research purposes. For example, the first modern general-use electronic computer, called Electronic Numerical Integrator And Computer (ENIAC), was built in 1946 for $500,000 and had around 100,000 diodes, resistors, and capacitors, giving it much less computing power than a contemporary microchip, but it occupied a whole floor in a lab building and weighed around 30 tons. A modern chip can have millions of transistors or circuit features per square millimeter.*

The fact is that the invention of the microchip—based on semiconductor technology—has facilitated a vast array of applications that have transformed everyday life—how we communicate; how we create, store, and share knowledge and information; what we do for fun; and how we work. They run laptops, iPod, ATMs, cell phones, automobiles, and a myriad of other devices.

Obviously the twenty-fourth century, the imaginary viewpoint of this entry, will be much different than Star Trek, *but that doesn't change the fact that the discovery of semiconductors and the invention of the microchip has allowed computers to be what they are today, and will lead them to what they will be tomorrow—whatever that is.*

The microchip was a crucial step forward for the twentieth century PC. With the invention of the microchip, computers could be made smaller, faster, and more powerful for less money. The microchip turned PCs into affordable alternatives to the time-honored (but slower) method of data collection and organization—many of which were still done by hand.

The discovery of semiconductors made the microchip possible. Formed of elements such as silicon and germanium, a semiconductor was a unique electric component: one which did not conduct electricity, yet it did not quite prevent electricity from moving through it. When a small charge of electricity was applied to a semiconductor, it changed from a non-conductor to a conductor of electricity. Computer design engineers now had a controllable conductor of electricity that could be miniaturized, enabling relatively small (desktop) personal computers to be manufactured.

RAM (and many other PC components, including the CPU) was really just a set of complex ON/OFF switches. The data stored in a PC was binary, meaning that it had only two states: 0 and 1. These two states could be represented electronically with tiny ON/OFF switches. Earlier in the twentieth century, computers were constructed with vacuum tubes (devices which controlled the flow of electricity in a vacuum)—but these computers were entirely too large to fit on a desktop (most of them occupied entire rooms). So it wasn't until the semiconductor was invented that a miniaturized "switch" existed, enabling in turn, the miniaturization of the computer itself.

But a PC was more than just a series of ON/OFF switches—most PC components were a combination of several electrical devices: transistors, capacitors, and resistors. Using semiconductors, a single chip of silicon was formed into a complex, integrated circuit—a miniaturized, self-contained collection of electronic components. In a microchip, transistors served as ON/OFF switches (creating the 1s and 0s of a bit). Capacitors held that charge (allowing a bit to keep its value of 0 or 1). Resistors controlled electricity and forced it to flow in one direction, creating logic within the PC—a program could instruct the CPU to do one thing if something were true, another thing if it were not. The resistor forced electricity to flow in a single direction based on the charge of neighboring components, and that direction was then interpreted by the CPU as "Yes" or "No." Such sophistication on a tiny scale made the microchip a giant leap in technology, beyond the purely mechanical storage and logic devices of early computers.

Source: Flynn, Jennifer. *20th Century Computers and How They Worked: The Official Starfleet History of Computers*. Carmel, IN: Alpha Books, 1993.

Part VI
POLITICAL LIFE

Political life is often thought of at the large-scale level, with senators, presidents, kings, and other important people doing important and even historic things. The fact is, whether we like it or not, almost all human interactions, down to the smallest groups, are political—if by political we mean concerned with the acquisition, organization, and exercise of authority or power. The *modern* era has seen dramatic changes in political life, just as it has in virtually every other aspect of everyday life, and several areas of political life are represented here in the following four topical sections: "Social Hierarchy," "Government," "Justice and Legal Systems," and "Warfare."

Sometimes political changes have increased the rights, liberties, and quality of life for many; other times politics have motivated repression, enslavement, or even genocide. The "Social Hierarchy" section primarily describes groups that have been the victim of political oppression, and the injustices perpetrated against them by those with power, including Native American attempts at redress of their grievances from the U.S. government (Document 1), the Armenian genocide (Document 3), and the *Holocaust,* or Shoah (Document 4). On a smaller scale, the selection on textile factory girls (Document 2) reveals that hierarchies do not always have to be institutional and oppressive, national or genocidal—even groups without conventional political power still have political hierarchies.

Governments are perhaps the most obviously political institutions in the modern world, and reflect some of the most important changes in political life. In 1700, most people were the subjects of a monarchical government, in which most political power was centered in one person. Today, most people live under an elected government, where a much larger part of the population shares political power—or at least one that makes that claim. One remarkable feature about the evolution of political life is that many governments that are not democratic seek legitimacy through an illusion of democracy. William Blackstone explains the British parliamentary system in glowing terms (Document 5), while an account of election day in New York in 1896 (Document 6) attempts to illustrate both authentic democracy and corruption, and Nikita Khrushchev extols the values of the Communist Party and the Soviet Union (Document 7).

Another aspect of political life includes the administration of judgment and justice. Often this takes the form of the creation of law, the adjudication of violations of law, and the punishment of lawbreakers. Voltaire's comparison of legal privileges enjoyed by the nobility in England and France in the eighteenth century (Document 8) attacks the injustice of an ancient but unfair system and has some common ground with Gandhi's scathing critique of British colonial domination in India (Document 10), which led to his advocacy of *satyagraha*, a form of nonviolent protest that proved a model for popular resistance to unjust systems. The mechanisms and institutions of justice are discussed in theoretical terms by Alexander Hamilton's essay from the *Federalist Papers* on the proper form of the judicial branch of government (Document 9) and in very practical terms by Sam Gutierrez's diary of a lawbreaker's day in a modern prison (Document 11).

Since Karl von *Clausewitz*'s famous nineteenth-century pronouncement that "War is merely the continuation of policy by other means," war has been seen as a political event. While some dispute Clausewitz's characterization, warfare has undoubtedly been used for political ends by nations in the modern era, and the evolution of warfare is included as an aspect of political life. The nature of warfare has changed since the muskets and bayonets of 1700 have given way to intercontinental ballistic missiles and computerized targeting systems on aircraft and tanks, but the experience of warfare remains a defining experience in the lives of many of those who participate in it—willingly or not—and survive. From the catastrophe of *Napoleon*'s campaign in Russia (Document 12), to the struggles of civilians on the home front in the American Civil War (Document 13), to German submarines in World War I (Document 14), to a Japanese soldier-poet struggling to remember the good times with family (Document 15), to managing the war in Vietnam (Document 16), there is tremendous change, but there is also consistently courage, suffering, a willingness to sacrifice, and the impulse to survive.

In small villages in the "third world," nineteenth-century textile factories, or the top levels of international relations, human interactions have a political dimension. Political life gives societies the rules that determine how we will live together and solve conflicts—peacefully or otherwise. As society becomes ever more global, forms of politics will continue to change, and new models of organization and authority will evolve, but political life will remain inseparable from daily life.

Social Hierarchy

Although many idealists, religious zealots, and social reformers have aspired to totally egalitarian societies, in practice such an arrangement may only be possible in solitude. Nor are social hierarchies inherently bad. In fact, social organization helps us get along, accomplish complex tasks, and order our daily lives. Even the smallest human groups tend to develop hieratic organizations, from school children to the workplace to institutions to nations and to ethnic groups.

Harriet Robinson's description of the hierarchy in the *Lowell system* factories (Document 2) shows how groups organized in the industrial setting that was rapidly growing in the nineteenth century. While the course of industrialization eroded much of the solidarity shared by the mill-girls and management, despite their distinct positions, it marks a generally positive example of how people form groups and work together.

Unfortunately, the use of social power over others has led to profoundly tragic results all too often in the modern world, as is indicated by Henry Morgenthau's horrific account of the Armenian genocide (Document 3), and the quiet desperation of Ignaz Maybaum as he struggles to be a survivor of the *Holocaust* (Document 4). Certainly social oppression, discrimination, and persecution are not unique to the modern world, but the scale of suffering and death caused by the distortion of social power in the twentieth century is unparalleled in history. Only slightly less disturbing is Yellow Buffalo Bull's request for help from the U.S. government (Document 1); one gets a sense that there is little hope for success. The readings in this section call for reflection on how it is that we organize our everyday social lives and what care we must take to assure as just a system as we can.

1. *Yellow Buffalo Bull: A Native American Speaks*

The Ponca *were a small tribe of Native Americans from northern Nebraska. Unlike most Plains tribes, the Ponca were a semi-agricultural people, who grew corn and vegetables instead of relying on buffalo hunting. In the 1880s, the United States government wanted to move the Ponca to Oklahoma in contradiction of its treaty obligations, and the Ponca resisted. Once most of them were forcibly relocated to what is now northern Oklahoma (called at that time the* Indian Territory*), the Ponca tried to make the best of it, but faced difficult circumstances made worse by the neglect of government officials and the deliberate depredations of whites.*

The Ponca sent a delegation, including a Ponca chief, Yellow Buffalo Bull, to Washington, D.C., to seek help. The following selection is from a transcript of the address Yellow Buffalo Bull made to the Acting Commissioner of the Bureau of Indian Affairs. *The letter expresses the hopes of the Ponca for redress of the tribe's grievances with the whites who were harassing them and the Bureau of Indian Affairs agent, who was not helpful.*

In the social hierarchy of the American West, the Native Americans were chronically pushed to the bottom, deprived of land and rights. The letter indicates many of the typical problems Native American groups experienced in the United States. After having been deprived of their land and forcibly relocated, they were plagued by problems, abused by whites, and dependent on an indifferent bureaucracy.

O "Little Grandfather," you who govern the Indians, I will speak to you today about two subjects. I have come to this place because my friend, Mr. Dorsey, sent for me to come and work with him. When I was at the railroad station at Ponca Ind. T. [Indian Territory], just before I started hither, very many of the Poncas followed me that far, and they said that I should have an interview with you. Said they, "When you reach Washington you shall speak to the President about one matter."

The cattle have been trespassing on our reservation from time to time, and that is hard for us to endure. We bought our present reservation for fifty thousand dollars and it is ours. We sold to the railroad company the right of way through our reservation, consisting of one tract fifty feet wide, for one thousand seven hundred dollars. Other white people, not railroad officials, when returning with the stock cars from Oklahoma, shove out the carcasses of the dead cattle upon Ponka land. (They drag them here over a large extent of territory, leaving them to decay, and making all the land smell and covering it with bones, without giving us any damages. Besides, the cattle are brought to the reservation, where they are sold to different persons who take them away in various directions, going at random over our fields and pastures. Thus are our crops injured, and we can not cut hay.)

We begged the agent to help us about this, but he has done nothing. Therefore we Indians consulted together and said, "It is proper to tell this to the President and the Commissioner." So we collected among ourselves two hundred dollars to pay the traveling expenses of some of our men to and from Washington. But since it is difficult to see you without obtaining your consent, they said that I should tell you when I came, as I now have done. The money to pay the railroad fare is our own.

I hope that you will help us, and that you will allow at least two to come and speak about these matters.

The cattle are continually trespassing on our land, therefore all of our people wish to speak about it. We hope that our affairs may be rectified for us.... If you have something to say in reply, I hope that you will decide to pity us, and that you will very soon telegraph to the Ponkas what you have to tell them (I too will send a telegram in order to tell them).

Source: Dorsey, James Owen. *Omaha and Ponka Letters.* Washington, D.C.: Government Printing Office, 1891.

2. Lowell, Massachusetts: The Early Industrial Factory System

As industrialization spread across Europe and North America, changes took place in the social hierarchy of daily life. One of the first and most successful early textile mill towns was Lowell, Massachusetts. The Lowell factories adopted a paternalistic attitude toward the workers, who were predominantly single women from the surrounding countryside. Seeking to avoid many of the negative effects of industrialization already evident in Europe, the Lowell factory system provided factory-owned and monitored housing, encouraged church attendance and cultural activities, and paid high wages. The intent was to provide a clean, moral, and healthy industrial environment where workers would be content. In the early years, it was acclaimed as a great success. While certainly patriarchal, the Lowell system *did offer its workers, especially women, opportunities that previously had not existed for them.*

Harriet Robinson worked in the Lowell mills from age ten in 1834 until she left and married in 1848. She wrote about her experiences in the early days of the industrial textile industry, and it is from her work that the following selection is taken. She describes in detail the social hierarchy in the New England factory town. In the place of traditional social relationships, the factory town developed new patterns of social distinctions, even among the workers themselves, based primarily on one's position within the factory. These new distinctions superseded familial connections, land ownership, education, crafts and trades, religion, and other traditional means of social organization, although certain tendencies remained consistent, such as the higher status of men and American-born people over women and immigrants. The agents and the overseers—exclusively male—were at the highest level, and their wives, too, by virtue of being married to them. The next level, still respectable, comprised the operatives or factory workers, who had ambition and pretensions to upward social movement (primarily through marriage). It is worth noting that the lowest level of the hierarchy, below even the women, was the primarily Irish immigrant laborers and their families.

The system Robinson described in the early days of the mills did not last long. The rapidly developing textile industry and increasing competition made it increasingly difficult to maintain the benevolent aspects of the Lowell system, resulting in greater stratification between labor and management, an increase in the amount and difficulty of the work, and a decrease in wages and cultural programs. The following account gives a vivid description of early industrialization and indicates the changes taking place in social organization, the movement from rural to urban, expanding educational opportunities, nascent labor organization and reform movements, the changing status of women, and the position of immigrant groups, all of which affected the organization of new patterns of industrial social life.

Before 1836 the era of mechanical industry in New England had hardly begun, the industrial life of its people was yet in its infancy, and nearly every article in domestic use that is now made with the help of machinery was then "done by hand." [...]

Their lives had kept pace for so many years with the stage-coach and the canal that they thought, no doubt, if they thought about it at all, that they should crawl along in this way forever. But into this life there came an element that was to open a new era in the activities of the country. This was the genius of mechanical industry, which would build the cotton-factory, set in motion the loom and spinning frame, call together an army of useful people, open wider fields of industry for men and (which was quite important at that time) for women also. [...]

In 1832 the factory population of Lowell was divided into four classes. The agents of the corporations were the aristocrats, not because of their wealth, but on account of the office held, which was one of great responsibility, requiring, as it did, not only some knowledge of business, but also a certain tact in managing, or utilizing the great number of operatives so as to secure the best return for their labor. The agent was also something of an autocrat, and there was no appeal from his decision in matters affecting the industrial interest of those who were employed on his corporation.

The Agents usually lived in large houses, not too near the boarding-houses, surrounded by beautiful garden which seemed like Paradise to some of the home-sick girls, who, as they came from their work in the noisy mill, could look with longing eyes into the sometimes open gate in the high fence, and be reminded afresh of their pleasant country homes. And a glimpse of one handsome woman, the wife of an agent, reading by an astral lamp in the early evening, has always been remembered by one young girl, who looked forward to the time when she, too, might have a parlor of her own, lighted by an astral lamp!

The second class were the overseers, a sort of gentry, ambitious mill-hands who had worked up from the lowest grade of factory labor; and they usually lived in the end-tenements of the blocks, the short connected rows of houses in which the operatives were boarded. However, on one corporation, at least, there was a block devoted exclusively to the overseers, and one of the wives, who had been a factory girl, put on so many airs that the wittiest of her former work-mates fastened the name of "Puckersville" to the whole block where the overseers lived. It was related to one of these

A Lewis Hine photograph of the spooling room in a textile mill in Indian Orchard, Massachusetts, 1916. Library of Congress.

quotidian factory girls, that, with some friends, she once re-visited the room in which she used to work, and to show her genteel friends her ignorance of her old surrounding, she turned to the overseer, who was with the party, and pointing to some wheels and pulleys over her head, she, "What's them things up there?"

The third class were the operatives, and were all spoken of as "girls" or "men;" and the "girls," . . . The working hours of all the girls extended from five o'clock in the morning until seven in the evening, with one-half hour for breakfast and dinner. Even the doffers were forced to be on duty nearly fourteen hours a day, and this was the greatest hardship in the lives of these children, for it was not until 1842 that the hours of labor for children under twelve years of age were limited to ten per day; but the "ten-hour law" itself was not passed until long after some of these little doffers were old enough to appear before the legislative committee on the subject and plead, by their presence, for a reduction of the hours of labor.

At the time the Lowell cotton-mills were started, the factory girl was the lowest among women. In England, and in France particularly, great injustice had been done to her real character; she was represented as subjected to influences that could not fail to destroy her purity and self-respect. In the eyes of the overseer she was but a brute, a slave, to be beaten, pinched, and pushed about. It was to overcome this prejudice that such high wages had been offered to women that they might be induced to become mill-girls, in spite of the opprobrium that still clung to the "degrading occupation." [...]

The fourth class, lords of the spade and the shovel, by whose constant labor the building of the great factories was made possible, and whose children soon became valuable operatives, lived at first on what was called the "Acre," a locality near the present site of the North Grammar schoolhouse. Here, clustered around a small Catholic Church, were hundreds of little shanties, in which they dwelt with their wives and numerous children.

Source: Robinson, Harriet H. *Loom and Spindle, or Life Among the Early Mill Girls*. New York: Thomas Y. Crowell and Co., 1898.

3. The Armenian Genocide of 1915

In the midst of World War I, with the Ottoman Empire *at war with the Russian Empire, the Ottoman Turkish government decided that the Christian minority* Armenians *would likely be sympathetic to the Russians, and in 1915 the Turkish government initiated the mass deportation of Armenians living within Turkey, citing, among other reasons, security concerns.*

As is all too often the case with ethnic and religious minorities, Armenians living under Ottoman rule had been subject to sometimes violent persecution for decades, but the events of 1915 were of a different magnitude altogether. Estimates vary, but between 300,000 and 1,500,000 Armenians died as a result. Many nations and most scholars identify these events as the Armenian Genocide, although some, including the Turkish government, deny both the name and many accounts of the events. Henry Morgenthau Sr. was the U.S. Ambassador to Turkey during these events, and this selection from his account offers a description of some of the tactics and atrocities committed. He collected information from U.S. diplomats and aid agency workers, whom he also helped to organize, and after he returned to the United States in 1916, published this account and worked for the succor of the Armenian population.

Morgenthau's description of cruelty and brutality can be difficult to read. Armenians were systematically forced from their homes and stripped of all their possessions, men were separated and often murdered, sexual assaults and rapes were common, and old men, women, and children were put on forced marches that were intended to result in their deaths.

Genocide was only defined as a concept in 1944, but that didn't prevent such acts from taking place before then. The recognition of genocide has prompted nations to assess their moral and legal responsibilities and powers and promoted the development of international law to provide for intervention, although unfortunately the Armenian genocide was not the only event where a government or ethnic group has tried to eradicate a part of the population in the twentieth century. Among the most well-known are the Nazi's attempt to exterminate the Jews (known as the Holocaust*), the collectivization and purges of Joseph* Stalin *in the* Union of Soviet Socialist Republics *(USSR) in the 1920s and 1930s,* Mao Zedong's Cultural Revolution *in China in the 1960s, the Cambodian killing fields under* Pol Pot *in the 1970s, and Hutu attacks on Tutsis* *in Rwanda and the Serbian ethnic cleansing of Bosnians in the Balkans in the 1990s, among others. Hierarchies based on social, ethnic, and political differences are part of political life. Nonetheless, it is a tragic extreme of social hierarchies when groups resort to exterminating each other.*

I have . . . laid aside any scruples I had as to the propriety of disclosing to my fellow countrymen the facts which I learned while representing them in Turkey. I acquired this knowledge as the servant of the American people, and it is their property as much as it is mine.

The Central Government [of Turkey] now announced its intention of gathering the two million or more Armenians living in the several sections of the empire and transporting them to this desolate and inhospitable region. Had they undertaken such a deportation in good faith it would have represented the height of cruelty and injustice. As a matter of fact, the Turks never had the slightest idea of re-establishing the Armenians in this new country. They knew that the great majority would never reach their destination and that those who did would either die of thirst and starvation, or be murdered by the wild Mohammedan desert tribes. The real purpose of the deportation was robbery and destruction; it really represented a new method of massacre. When the Turkish authorities gave the orders for these deportations, they were merely giving the death warrant to a whole race; they understood this well, and, in their conversations with me, they made no particular attempt to conceal the fact.

All through the spring and summer of 1915 the deportations took place. Of the larger cities, Constantinople, Smyrna, and Aleppo were spared; practically all other places where a single Armenian family lived now became the scenes of these unspeakable tragedies. Scarcely a single Armenian, whatever his education or wealth, or whatever the social class to which he belonged, was exempted from the order. In some villages placards were posted ordering the whole Armenian population to present itself in a public place an appointed time—usually a day or two ahead, and in other places the town crier would go through the streets delivering the order vocally. In still others not the slightest warning was given. The gendarmes would appear before an Armenian house and order all the inmates to follow them. They would take women engaged in their domestic tasks without giving them the chance to change their clothes. The police fell upon them just as the eruption of Vesuvius fell upon Pompeii; women were taken from the wash-tubs, children were snatched out of bed, the bread was left half baked in the oven, the family meal was abandoned partly eaten, the children were taken from the schoolroom, leaving their books open at the daily task, and the men were forced to abandon their ploughs in the fields and their cattle on the mountain side. Even women who had just given birth to children would be forced to leave their beds and join the panic-stricken throng, their sleeping babies in their arms. Such things as they hurriedly snatched up—a shawl, a blanket, perhaps a few scraps of food—were all that they could take of their household belongings. To their frantic questions "Where are we going?" the gendarmes would vouchsafe only one reply: "To the interior."

In some cases the refugees were given a few hours, in exceptional instances a few days, to dispose of their property and household effects. But the proceeding, of course, amounted simply to robbery. They could sell only to Turks, and since both buyers and sellers knew that they had only a day or two to market the accumulations of a lifetime, the prices obtained represented a small fraction of their value. Sewing machines would bring one or two dollars—a cow would go for a dollar, a houseful of furniture would be sold for a pittance. In many cases Armenians were prohibited from selling or Turks from buying even at these ridiculous prices; under pretense that the Government intended to sell their effects to pay the creditors whom they would inevitably leave behind, their household furniture would be placed in stores or heaped up in public places, where it was usually pillaged by Turkish men and women. The government officials would also inform the Armenians that, since their deportation was only temporary, the intention being to bring them back after the war was over, they would not be permitted to sell their houses. Scarcely had the former possessors left the village, when Mohammedan *mohad*—immigrants from other parts of Turkey—would be moved into the Armenian quarters. Similarly all their valuables—money, rings, watches, and jewellery—would be taken to the police stations for "safe keeping," pending their return, and then parcelled out among the Turks. Yet these robberies gave the refugees little anguish, for far more terrible and agonizing scenes were taking place under their eyes. The systematic extermination of the men continued; such males as the persecutions which I have already described had left were now violently dealt with. Before the caravans were started, it became the regular practice to separate the young men from the families, tie them together in groups of four, lead them to the outskirts, and shoot them. Public hangings without trial—the only offense being that the victims were Armenians—were taking place constantly. The gendarmes showed a particular desire to annihilate the educated and the influential. From American consuls and missionaries I was constantly receiving reports of such executions, and many of the events which they described will never fade from my memory. At Angora all Armenian men from fifteen to seventy were arrested, bound together in groups of four, and sent on the road in the direction of Caesarea. When they had travelled five or six hours and had reached a secluded valley, a mob of Turkish peasants fell upon them with clubs, hammers, axes, scythes, spades, and saws. Such instruments not only caused more agonizing deaths than guns and pistols, but, as the Turks themselves boasted, they were more economical, since they did not involve the waste of powder and shell. In this way they exterminated the whole male population of Angora, including all its men of wealth and breeding, and their bodies, horribly mutilated, were left in the valley, where they were devoured by wild beasts. After completing this destruction, the peasants and gendarmes gathered in the local tavern, comparing notes and boasting of the number of "giaours" that each had slain. In Trebizond the men were placed in boats and sent out on the Black Sea; gendarmes would follow them in boats, shoot them down, and throw their bodies into the water.

When the signal was given for the caravans to move, therefore, they almost invariably consisted of women, children, and old men. Anyone who could possibly have protected them from the fate that awaited them had been destroyed. Not infrequently the prefect of the city, as the mass started on its way, would wish them a derisive "pleasant journey." Before the caravan moved the women were sometimes offered the alternative of becoming Mohammedans. Even though they accepted the new faith, which few of them did, their earthly troubles did not end. The converts were started, the individuals bore some resemblance to human beings; in a few hours, however, the dust of the road plastered their faces and clothes, the mud caked their lower members, and the slowly advancing mobs, frequently bent with fatigue and crazed by the brutality of their "protectors," resembled some new and strange animal species. Yet for the better part of six months, from April to October, 1915, practically all the highways in Asia Minor were crowded with these unearthly bands of exiles. They could be seen winding in and out of every valley and climbing up the sides of nearly every mountain—moving on and on, they scarcely knew whither, except that every road led to death. Village after village and town after town was evacuated of its Armenian population, under the distressing circumstances already detailed. In these six months, as far as can be ascertained, about 1,200,000 people started on this journey to the Syrian desert.

"Pray for us," they would say as they left their homes—the homes in which their ancestors had lived for 2,500 years. "We shall not see you in this world again, but sometime we shall meet. Pray for us!"

Source: Morgenthau, Henry. *Ambassador Morgenthau's Story*. New York: Doubleday and Page, 1918.

4. *Ignaz Maybaum: The Third* Churban—*Jewish Life after the Holocaust*

The Holocaust, or Shoah, as it is called in Hebrew, is one of the defining events of the twentieth century in Western culture, and perhaps of the modern world. During the 1930s and early 1940s an estimated 6,000,000 Jews were put to death by the Nazi government of Germany or their allies or sympathizers. A long history of anti-Semitism *in Europe helped created an environment where unthinkable horrors were perpetrated, where, as in the case of the Armenian genocide (see Document 3), the consequences of a distorted social hierarchy shifted in totalitarian Nazi Germany from the oppression of certain social groups to systematic persecution, and eventually to the grimly named "Final Solution"—the extermination of all Jews. Aside from Jews, political opponents, prisoners of war, clergy and religious, Slavs and gypsies, the disabled, and others designated as racially impure or otherwise undesirable were arrested, imprisoned, forced to work, and often simply executed, adding another 2–4 million to the total number of lives taken. Holocaust survivors have documented their experiences in detail, describing their daily life inside Nazi concentration camps.*

This selection is not about living through the Holocaust, but living after it. Ignaz Maybaum, a Jewish rabbi and theologian, did not personally live through the camp experience. Originally from Vienna, Austria, he had become one of the chief rabbis in Berlin, Germany, by the late 1930s. He eventually fled Germany in 1939 with his wife and children. His mother and sisters were not able to leave and he never saw them again—they died in Nazi concentration camps. Maybaum speaks of the Holocaust as if it were a churban, *or destruction, a term that often refers to the destruction of the First and Second Temples in Jerusalem, historically the most sacred place in the world to Jews. The events of the Second World War (1939–1945) and the Holocaust broke the faith of some Jews, but the virtual eradication of Jews in Eastern Europe points for Maybaum to the need for Jews to rediscover and remake their faith and their fate as a religious people.*

Whether or not Maybaum is right about the religious response to the Shoah, there is no doubt that he struggles to come to some kind of explanation as to how to continue daily social life in the wake of such a cataclysm. He laments and praises the dead, seeks to comprehend their suffering in religious terms, and seeks to use that consolation to find the courage to go on. While many Holocaust survivors and contemporary Jews take issue with Maybaum's theological approach and his controversial position that the Shoah was in some sense a punishment of the Jews for the sins of the rest of the world, there remains the clear impression that for Maybaum, things have changed forever for the survivors of the Holocaust, for the future of all Jews, religious or not, and for the daily lives of not only the survivors, but for those who still live where the victims once did—a part of their community was destroyed, too.

While Henry Morgenthau reported the genocide of Armenians *from the outside, Maybaum deals with the Shoah from the inside. What can he do or say to allow him to cope with the loss of family and friends, home and homeland, culture and traditions—the destruction of virtually all of his everyday life.*

In the year 586 before the Common Era the first Temple was destroyed. In the year 70 of the Common Era the second Temple was destroyed. In our history books we speak of the first churban and of the second churban. The third churban took place in the years 1933 to 1945. Six and half million Jews were murdered.

We are the survivors of the third churban. Whatever else we are is of no importance in comparison with this crucial fact of our life.

We may be happy or unhappy, well-to-do or poor, we may be rich still with memories of the past or stripped bare of tradition like children of the Displaced Persons camps who know only that they are of Jewish origin because it was for this they suffered persecution. We may be deeply rooted in the civilization of our surroundings or we may be newcomers making ourselves known as foreigners with the first few words we utter. All these are minor differences amongst us Jews of this generation. There is a common badge which we all wear and which makes us a band of brothers and sisters singled out by God. We are survivors of the third churban.

Dumbfounded and in agony we ask, What actually happened? The historian will try to explain what happened. He will show in detail how a sick civilisation collapsed and how this collapse involved the end of East European Jewry and the utter dissolution of continental Western Jewry. Perhaps it was residue from the Middle Ages, still present in our own age, which poisoned the body of the European continent. A corpse can poison a living organism. Perhaps it was the rise of new generations which were only outwardly civilized and were in fact barbarians. These barbarians wanted to break out from what they felt to be the prison of civilization. Perhaps the feudal civilization of the Middle Ages, strengthened by the legions of Prussia, revolted against the protestant civilization of the free democracies of the West.

The historian will analyse the past events of our time and offer us his findings. The historian is a retrospective prophet. He may do his best, but the way into the future remains full of risks. The biblical prophet looks back into the past like the historian but also gives guidance for the future. He speaks of the Judgment Day of God cleansing the land.

No man can be called righteous before God. But one thing can certainly be said of the six and a half million Jews who died. They were not the creators of, nor were they accountable for, that old, sick civilization which was destroyed. They stand visibly for all the innocent who must die with the guilty when God's Judgment Day destroys the Wicked City. Even in their death, these six and a half million Jews fulfilled their holy mission.

We who have survived the Judgment Day ask what is our consolation, what is our duty, and what is our hope for the future. Our own blood has been spilled; parents, brothers, sisters, friends have been foully murdered. Those who must live without consolation are embittered, and those who are embittered cannot build up new life.

There is only one consolation. We shall find it in our way to God. Only God can 'wipe away the tears from all the faces, and the scandalous shame done to his people, and he will extinguish it from off all the earth' (Isaiah 25:8). We, the survivors, must find our way to this God or we must drag on without consolation and therefore without the ability to live, still remaining the living victims of the catastrophe. Jewry has a religious future or none at all.

Those who survived and think and act as if their old background still exists will be condemned to walk through life as ghosts of a dead past. To be a survivor must mean something else. When a man loses everything, he is alone. Being alone, he has nothing unless he can progress to a new future. The good tidings of the Prophet of Consolation are not concerned with political or cultural prospects; the good tidings foretell that the people will stand again before God as in the great days of the past. The prophet says: 'Behold your God' (Isaiah 40:9).

The Day of Judgment which has destroyed a past has its meaning for the future. We who have not been devoured by the wrath of judgment have one duty as survivors: we must change.

What is left in us from that past about which God has passed judgment must become changed. No one among us must remain merely the nineteenth century Jew. God wants us to change. A man is not a man when he is a type.

East European Jewry was the heart of Jewry, from which the life blood streamed to all its members. It was absolutely united with Western Jewry. East European Jewry looked to the West always. It had itself migrated from the West in the eleventh and twelfth century. We had no political union connecting East European Jewry and Western Jewry. We did not need one. We were an historic unit closely knit together by the power of religion. This historic unit has been destroyed in the third churban. Jerusalem has been destroyed. The past from which we all come, whether Central or Eastern Europe was our home, is a religious past.

We shall have a future if it is a religious future. We must build Jerusalem again. This we cannot do if we remain what we were. We must not remain simply contemporaries of that catastrophe which devoured six and a half million Jews and left us alive. God sat in His judgment seat, and our old ideals and ideologies have been condemned. Whether we are Orthodox or Liberals or belong to the Reform Movement, whether we are Zionists or non-Zionists, we must not remain after the Day of Judgment what we were before.

Source: Maybaum, Ignaz. *The Face of God After Auschwitz*. Amsterdam: Polak and Van Gennep, 1965. Reprinted from Nicolas de Lange, ed. *Ignaz Maybaum: A Reader*. New York: Berghahn Books, 2001.

Government

Government is perhaps what most people think of when they think of political life. Changes in the dominant forms of government and the theoretical and philosophical underpinnings of those systems have been one of the most important phenomena in political life in the modern period. At the beginning of the modern period, political power was largely a function of the accident of birth. The opportunities to govern if one was not perceived as born to that right were limited. Short of mass violence, most of the governed in such societies had little say about the policies that affected them. This situation changed in the modern period, when societies came to see the legitimacy of government in the consent of the governed. Whether by bloody revolution or protracted political evolution, most modern states shifted real political control to a more or less large voting public, although both the right to vote and the real power of the voting public has been limited in most places and times.

William Blackstone (Document 5) describes the *Parliament* of England as an effective compromise between different political stakeholders in the eighteenth century. The extension of the franchise (or voting rights) to most adult males by the end of the nineteenth century becomes the setting for Ernest Ingersoll's description of an election day in New York in 1896 (Document 6). If Blackstone looks at the system from an institutional point of view, Ingersoll looks at republican democracy from the point of view of individuals within it; political functionaries, individual voters, even the children who cannot vote, but who participate in the social activities of election day. With political power at stake, sophisticated political organizations, called political machines, evolved to use, bend, or even break the rules to help assure victory.

Representative democracy is not the only model of government in modern political life. Nikita Khrushchev, who was first secretary of the Soviet Communist Party from 1953 to 1964, offers a summary of the Communist system (Document 7), which originated with the philosophy of Karl *Marx* in the middle nineteenth century, was the ideology of the former *Union of Soviet Socialist Republics*, and remains that of the People's Republic of China today. While theoretically it puts power in the hands of the working masses and takes power from all other social classes, in practice it has been rather different.

5. Sir William Blackstone on Modern Parliamentary Democracy

Sir William Blackstone (1723–1780) was an eighteenth-century English jurist whose Commentaries on the Laws of England *are still the primary reference work for English common law. The following selection is Blackstone's account of the relationship of different parts of the government in the British system. He describes three groups as checks on each other: the king, the lords (nobility and church leaders), and the people. The similarity of the idea to the "checks and balances" of the United States Constitution is evident, although the details of the system are different in several important respects. First, there is no strict distinction between branches of government—all the elements in the British system participate in the legislative function. The members of* Parliament, *although elected locally, do not directly represent the areas from which they come, as in the Senate or House of Representatives in the United States. Another noteworthy difference is the establishment of a state religion; the* Church of England *is a part of the state and has its own representatives (bishops and archbishops) in Parliament, the national legislature.*

While not apparently radical to us today, this limitation of monarchical and parliamentary powers was only achieved in England by much discord. The seventeenth century had seen conflict between Parliament and the king culminate in the English Civil War, *the execution of* Charles I, *the creation of the Commonwealth, and the* Glorious Revolution *of 1688. In short, the century preceding Blackstone's birth had been a turbulent one in English political history. Blackstone is strongly in favor of the arrangement, wherein the nobility, the church, the sovereign, and the people are all represented and cooperate within one institution. He goes to some length to blur the distinction between the pure* democracy *of an idealized ancient Greek world and the representative democratic body of Parliament in the British* parliamentary system. *Blackstone is quick to praise the status quo, in part because it had produced stability following decades of revolution and conflict. The same basic system continues in Britain today. The king or queen is no longer a true political force, but still ceremonially functions to open and close Parliament and approves all new laws. The House of Lords remains, although the real focus of power in the modern democratic United Kingdom is the House of Commons.*

Blackstone's England gave real political power to a much broader part of the population than nearly anywhere else in the world, although property qualifications and other restriction continued well into the nineteenth century for men, and women were not fully enfranchised until 1928. The creation of representative governments, whether republics or—as in Britain—limited monarchies, was a marked change from the vestigial feudalism *and absolute* monarchy *or aristocracy that had dominated European political systems in the pre-modern periods. British Parliamentary democracy preceded the establishment of such states in America and France in the eighteenth century, Latin America and other European nations in the nineteenth century, and many other countries around the world in the twentieth century. Although not a perfect system, the one described in Blackstone's account represents the beginnings of one of the most important trends in government in the modern world.*

The constituent parts of a Parliament are the next objects of our inquiry. And these are the king's majesty, sitting there in his royal political capacity, and the three estates of the realm,—the lords spiritual, the lords temporal (who sit together with the king, in one House), and the Commons, who sit by themselves in another. And the king and these three estates, together, form the great corporation or body politic of the kingdom, of which the king is said to be *caput, principium, et finis*. For upon their coming together the king meets them, either in person or by representations; without which there can be no beginning of a Parliament; and he also has alone the power of dissolving them.

It is highly necessary for preserving the balance of the constitution, that the executive power should be a branch, though not the whole, of the legislature... The crown cannot begin of itself any alterations in the present established law; but it may approve or disapprove of the alterations suggested and consented to by the two Houses. The legislative therefore cannot abridge the executive power of any rights which it now has by law, without its own consent, since the law must perpetually stand as it now does, unless all the powers agree to alter it.

And herein indeed consists the true excellence of the English government, that all parts of it form a mutual check upon each other. In the legislature, the people are a check upon the nobility, and the nobility a check upon the people, by the mutual privilege of rejecting what the other has resolved; while the king is a check upon both, which preserves the executive power from encroachments. And this very executive power is again checked and kept within due bounds by the two Houses, through the privilege they have of inquiring into, impeaching, and punishing the conduct, not indeed of the king, which would destroy his constitutional independence; but—which is more beneficial to the public—of his evil and pernicious counselors. Thus every branch of our civil polity supports and is supported, regulates and is regulated, by the rest. [. . .]

The spiritual lords consist of two archbishops and twenty-four bishops; and, at the dissolution of the monasteries by Henry VIII, consisted likewise of twenty-six mitered abbots and two priors: a very considerable body, and in those times equal in number to the temporal nobility. [. . .]

The lords temporal consist of all the peers of the realm (the bishops not being in strictness held to be such, but merely lords of Parliament) by whatever title of nobility distinguished—dukes, marquises, earls, viscounts, or barons; of which dignities we shall speak more hereafter. Some of these sit by descent, as do all ancient peers; some by creation, as do all new-made ones; others, since the union with Scotland, by election, which is the case of the sixteen peers who represent the body of the Scots nobility. There number is indefinite, and may be increased at will by the power of the crown; and once, in the reign of Queen Anne, there was an instance of creating no less than twelve together. [. . .]

The Commons consist of all such men of any property in the kingdom as have not seats in the House of Lords, every one of which has a voice in Parliament, either personally or by his representatives. In a free State every man, who is supposed a free agent, ought to be, in some measure, his own governor; and therefore a branch at least of the legislative power should reside in the whole body of the people. And this power, when the territories of the State are small and its citizens easily known, should be exercised by the people in their aggregate or collective capacity, as was wisely ordained in the petty republics of Greece and the first rudiments of the Roman State. But this will be highly inconvenient when the public territory is extended to any considerable degree, and the number of citizens is increased. [. . .]

In so large a state as ours it is therefore very wisely contrived that the people should do that by their representatives which it is impracticable to perform in person;—representatives chosen by a number of minute and separate districts, wherein all the voters are, or easily may be, distinguished. The counties are therefore represented by knights, elected by the proprietors of lands; the cities and boroughs are represented by citizens and burgesses, chosen by the mercantile part or supposed trading interest of the nation, much in the same manner as the burghers in the diet of Sweden are chosen by the corporate towns, Stockholm sending four, as London does with us, other cities two, and some only one. The number of English representatives is 513, and of Scots 45: in all 558. And every member, though chosen by one particular district, when elected and returned serves for the whole realm.... And therefore he is not bound, like a deputy in the United Provinces, to consult with, or take the advice of, his constituents upon any particular point, unless he himself thinks it proper or prudent so to do.

These are the constituent parts of a Parliament: the king, the lords spiritual and temporal, and the Commons. Parts, of which each is so necessary, that the consent of all three is required to make any new law that shall bind the subject. Whatever is enacted for law for one, or by two only, of the three is no statute, and to it no regard is due, unless in matters relating to their own privileges.

Source: Blackstone, Sir William. *Commentaries on the Laws of England.* London, 1756. Reprinted from James Harvey Robinson, and Charles A. Beard, eds. *Readings in Modern European History.* Volume 1: *The Eighteenth Century: The French Revolution and the Napoleonic Period.* Boston: Ginn & Company, 1909.

6. *Honest Democracy, Honest Corruption: Election Day in New York in 1896*

Elections are a central element in modern political life. There is no modern substitute for the legitimacy conferred by winning the support of the people who will be governed—or at least appearing to do so. Political parties develop complex, sophisticated organizations to acquire and keep power through electoral politics. In practice, elections can be messy, even corrupt affairs, with virtual armies of volunteers and operatives on all sides holding nothing back to give their candidate the best possible chance to win. Sometimes, of course, that also includes breaking the rules.

The following account by Ernest Ingersoll looks at the daily experience of an election in nineteenth-century urban America. The local party organizations reached into every ward, even down into every block, with a hierarchical and systematic approach. The efficiency of these party organizations earned them the nickname of political machines. *Machines functioned to win elections and amass power not so much by violence or intimidation (although they were used as well), but through offers of favors and assistance in return for votes. Before government-run social welfare programs, political machines often fulfilled this function by finding patronage jobs; subsidizing rent, food, or medical care for families in need; helping immigrants negotiate municipal bureaucracies; and providing other services. At the same time, they were also corrupt, and served as fronts for illegal activities such as graft, fraud, racketeering, embezzling, and other crimes.*

The following selection describes an election in New York in 1896. The Democratic Party machine in New York City centered at Tammany Hall, *a name synonymous with corrupt politics and the center of power in New York political life for over a century. Author Ernest Ingersoll is careful to describe in detail the integrity of the election procedure and officials to assure the readers of the legitimacy of the process, perhaps in contrast to the dirty politics of years past. Ingersoll makes clear the differences in education, sophistication, and position within a political hierarchy in his description of the machine members and operatives. He also points out the equality of social classes at the polls: workingman or lawyer, it's one man, one vote. Of course, equality had its clear limits; the only voters were men. Women were legally barred from voting in New York until 1917.*

Ingersoll's article illustrates how elections affected everyday life, how the whole community was involved, how the election equalized and discriminated, how the political machine worked and was combated, and how street-level electioneering was managed. Corrupt or not, elections like the one described here were an integral part of the experience of government and political life.

Election Day morning is the earliest of the year. The polls open at six o'clock—long before daylight in that late and cloudy month of November. At three the policemen who are to serve at the polls (nearly three thousand of them on the last occasion) are aroused and sent to breakfast. An hour later they reassemble, are paraded before the desks of the station-houses, instructed, and despatched to their polls, taking with them all the ballot-boxes, ballots, and other furniture, for the safety of which they are held responsible. [...]

Before the polls open the small closets or "booths" in which the voters prepare their ballots, and which are built of canvas stretched upon light frames, hinged together so as to be collapsible, are unfolded and set up, one being provided for each fifty voters on the list. The ballot boxes, which have two glass sides and a solid cover perforated by a narrow slit, are opened, proved to be empty, relocked by the chairman of the Board of Inspectors, and then arranged upon tables. Outside of all is set up a "guard-rail," as a legal rather than an actual barrier to the approach within it of unprivileged persons. The ballot clerks set in order their ballots ready to be dealt out, while the poll clerks open their registry books containing the names of men supposed to be electors, and prepare to record each vote. Finally, any watchers present take their places within the rail, where they may scrutinize every proceeding. To the intelligence, vigilance, and courageous protests of these watchers all over the city the handsome result against misrule in 1894, and the freedom from illegal election methods, were very largely due, and they will be a regular institution hereafter.

On the stroke of six the poll is declared open, and the voting immediately begins, the name and address of each applicant being called out by the inspector as soon as the voter presents himself. If he is reported as properly registered, and no one challenges his right, the ballots are given him, their number is recorded by the clerks and every one else interested, and he retires to a booth to select in secret the ticket or tickets he wishes to vote. This done, he returns, hands his ballots to the inspectors, so folded that no one can see their purport, the fact that he has voted is proclaimed and recorded, and he leaves the inclosure. If challenged, he "swears in" his vote, or refuses to do so, according as he is willing or not to take the responsibility of an oath. [...]

Meanwhile the great city is waking up. This is a legal holiday, but the smaller provision stores open up for a few hours... Toward the polling places come groups of strong, active, but rather seedy men, talking the polyglot slang of the school of the curbstone. One, better dressed, cleaner shaved, strides briskly around the corner, and is instantly attended to. He shakes hands with everybody, calling each by his Christian name—or a part of it, for time is precious this morning. Now and then he throws his arm about the neck of a henchman, and whispers a sentence or two in his ear, whereupon the recipient of the favor hurries away. This [ward captain] is the leader of the district on one side, or perhaps an alderman, or maybe even a candidate, and these others are his

George Caleb Bingham, *The County Election*, 1851–52. Art Resource, NY.

"workers," who share his chances, hopeful of recognition if he succeeds, failing which they will desert to the opposition, and possibly "squeal," or betray damaging secrets against him. He is now making a round of the polls in his district to be sure that his representatives are on duty near by. [...]

To many who are more or less visible all day there this is the most important occasion of the year. To be sure, it may be worth a few dollars to them, directly or indirectly; but plainly they look further than this... It is these men who make the voting-places picturesque. In rough garb and with lordly swagger, they sandwich themselves between neat and dignified lawyers, merchants, and clergymen, proudly sensible of their equality at the polls. Sometimes the motley line reaches out of doors and down the street. [...]

In the afternoon the brisk captain, who has been dodging all day from poll to poll, obtains an approximate list of those on his side who have not yet voted, and despatches workers to "bring them out." They search their haunts, and presently return with recruits. Some of these delinquents have simply been tardy, others are sick or lame or blind, and gently conducted to the polls, perhaps in a carriage, placed in the line, and carefully assisted to the ballot box. The attention he gets on election day is a genuine comfort to many a poor devil kicked about all the rest of the year. Now and then a henchman seizes a captain and whispers something portentously in his ear. A moment later he hurries off, looking very important, and soon reappears with a companion, who is sent on alone, while he himself stays back at the corner. This means that some voter has been ascertained to be out of town or sick abed, and that a willing and thrifty stranger has come to vote (illegally) in his name. This is only one of many tricks election officers must guard against toward the end of the day, and sometimes a cost of no small courage; for whiskey emboldens the roughest workers to "stand on his head" any one who interferes with them. [...]

The moment the polls close the liquor-saloons open, but the excessive drunkenness and brawling common in former years are not now seen. Five o'clock editions of the newspapers are issued, but have little to tell, for everywhere the clerks are still busily counting the votes. The streets overflow with boys who hardly wait for the earliest darkness to institute their picturesque part of the day's doings. The New York citizen begins to break election-day laws as soon as he can toddle about the block. Bonfires are strictly prohibited, yet thousands of them redden the air and set all the windows aglow before seven o'clock. [...]

But the fun of the street, which is now beginning, is not for that band of reporters at headquarters, not for those other bands of writers in the newspaper offices down-town, who, with almost superhuman diligence and endurance, are tabulating and putting into type and commenting upon these returns for delectation of the public next morning.

The tenement-house districts have been alive with people since sundown, dancing about the fires. They have learned long ago the outlines of the result, and those on the successful side are rejoicing in their tumultuous way, sure of the support of all the boys. [. . .]

The greatest of the indoor jollifications is that at Tammany Hall. Early in the evening the spacious auditorium becomes packed with tribesmen, a brass band is stationed in the gallery, the wives and daughters of prominent braves appear in the boxes, and the big and little sachems, wiskinskies, and all the rest, gather about a mythical council fire on the stage. A member with a stentorophonic voice reads telegrams from the district leaders and police headquarters, against a storm of cheerful yells and witticisms when the news is favorable, and of hoots and cat-calls when it is not.

Source: Ingersoll, Ernest. "Election Day in New York." *The Century Magazine* 53:1 (November 1896).

7. *Nikita Khrushchev on Communism and Freedom*

The political language of the modern era begins primarily in the Enlightenment *with ideas such as liberty, equality,* democracy, *self-determination, and government of the people. These ideas—which replaced the monarchical,* divine-right *language that preceded them—may be under attack today by some postmodern political theorists who see the political structure that evolved from them as oppressing minorities and other marginalized groups. (See* Monarchy *and* Postmodernism *in the Glossary.) At the same time, the compelling attraction of liberal freedoms has led to the use of such language to bolster many political systems. Along with the United States, the* Union of Soviet Socialist Republics *(USSR) dominated world politics from World War II until the USSR's dissolution in 1991.*

The Soviet Union, born from the collapse of the Russian Empire in 1917, was one of the most brutal and repressive governments of the twentieth century. Joseph Stalin, *its leader from 1929 to 1953, surpassed even Adolph* Hitler *of Nazi Germany in the number of people killed by the government he led. Nikita Khrushchev, the author of the following selection, followed Stalin as leader of the Soviet Union. Once in power, he repudiated many of Stalin's actions, but the Soviet Union remained in many respects an unfree place.*

The platform of the Soviet Communist Party, excerpted from the 22nd Party Congress held in 1961, offers a Marxist view of history and repeats the guarantees of progress, freedom, and liberty enjoyed by the Soviet people. Written at the height of the Cold War *between the United States and the USSR, it claims that* Russian Revolution *of October 1917 initiated a new era in history and the imminent achievement of utopian* communism.

The Marxist philosophy that underlay the political system of Communism *took whole social classes—not individuals—as the fundamental constituents of the political system. (See Karl* Marx *in the Glossary.) As a result, the will of the working class as a whole, as determined by its political manifestation, the Communist Party, was more important than the will of any particular person or other group, and trumped individual rights. While the political tensions of the Cold War led the United States government to infringe on some of its citizens' rights as well, the political life of the Soviet Union was authoritarian. The state provided for the basic needs of individuals through housing, health care, education, employment, and pensions, but despite the fact that Soviet citizens were theoretically guaranteed* Enlightenment *liberties like freedom of speech, assembly, conscience, and self-determination, in practice individual rights were significantly restricted. Most churches were closed. All press and media were owned and controlled by the state. Only one political party existed, and elections were to demonstrate political unanimity, not to make political choices. People were not allowed to leave the country, and foreigners were carefully monitored. Soviet society was a closed society, controlled from the top down. Nonetheless, the rhetoric of freedom and liberty that has been a dominant part of the modern model of political legitimacy was still a central part of Soviet political life.*

I. THE HISTORICAL NECESSITY OF THE TRANSITION FROM CAPITALISM TO SOCIALISM

The epoch-making turn of mankind from capitalism to socialism, initiated by the October Revolution, is a natural result of the development of society. Marxism-Leninism discovered the objective laws of social development and revealed the contradictions inherent in capitalism, the inevitability of their bringing about a revolutionary explosion and of the transition of society to communism.

The working class, which is the most consistent revolutionary class, is the chief motive force of the revolutionary transformation of the world. In the course of class struggles it becomes organized, sets up its trade unions and political parties, and wages an economic, political and theoretical struggle against capitalism. In fulfilling its historic mission as the revolutionary re-maker of the old society and creator of a new system, the working class becomes the exponent, not only of its own class interests, but of the interests of all working people. It is the natural leader of all forces fighting against capitalism.

[...]

II. THE HISTORIC SIGNIFICANCE OF THE OCTOBER REVOLUTION AND OF THE VICTORY OF SOCIALISM IN THE U.S.S.R.

The Great October Revolution breached the imperialist front in Russia, one of the world's largest countries, firmly established the dictatorship of the proletariat and created a new type of state the Soviet socialist state, and a new type of democracy—democracy for the working people. [...]

The October Revolution undermined the economic basis of a system of exploitation and social injustice. Soviet power nationalized industry, the railways, banks, and the land. It abolished the landlord system and fulfilled the peasants' age-long dream of land.

The October Revolution smashed the chains of national oppression; it proclaimed and put into effect the right of nations to self-determination, up to and including the right to secede. The Revolution completely abolished the social-estate and class privileges of the exploiters. For the first time in history, it emancipated women and granted them the same rights as men.

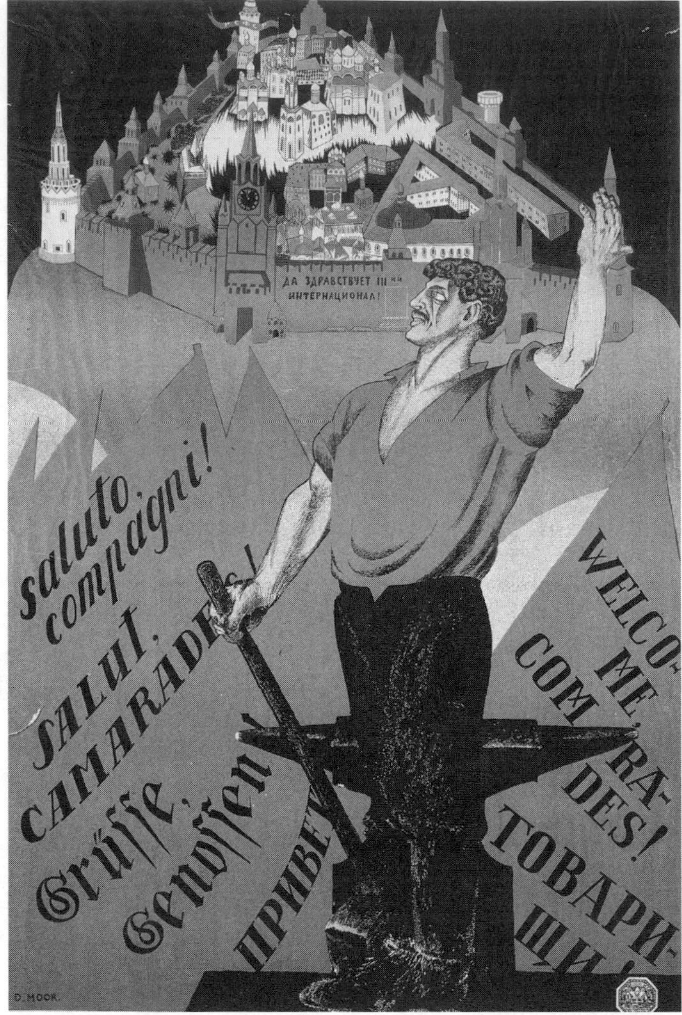

Russian poster by D. Moor created during the Russian Revolution appealing to foreign workers to join. The Art Archive / Musée des 2 Guerres Mondiales Paris / Gianni Dagli Orti.

The socialist revolution in Russia shook the entire structure of world capitalism to its very foundations; the world split into two opposing systems.

For the first time there emerged in the international arena a state which put forward the great slogan of peace and began carrying through new principles in relations between peoples and countries. Mankind acquired a reliable bulwark in its struggle against wars of conquest, for peace and the security of the peoples. [. . .]

The entire life of socialist society is based on the principle of broad democracy. Working people take an active part, through the Soviets, trade unions, and other mass organizations, in managing the affairs of the state and in solving problems of economic and cultural advancement. Socialist democracy includes both political freedoms—freedom of speech, of the press and of assembly, the right to elect and to be elected, and also social rights—the right to work, to rest and leisure, to free education and free medical services, to material security in old age and in case of illness or disability; equality of citizens of all races and nationalities; equal rights for women and men in all spheres of political, economic and cultural activity. Socialist democracy, unlike bourgeois democracy, does not merely proclaim the rights of the people, but guarantees that they are really implemented. Soviet society ensures the real liberty of the individual. The highest manifestation of this liberty is man's emancipation from exploitation, which is what primarily constitutes genuine social justice. [. . .]

COMMUNISM—THE BRIGHT FUTURE OF ALL MANKIND

The building of a communist society has become an immediate practical task for the Soviet people. The gradual development of socialism into communism is an objective law; it has been prepared by the development of Soviet socialist society throughout the preceding period.

WHAT IS COMMUNISM?

Communism is a classless social system with one form of public ownership of the means of production and full social equality of all members of society; under it, the all-round development of people will be accompanied by the growth of the productive forces through continuous progress in science and technology; all the springs of co-operative wealth will flow more abundantly, and the great principle "From each according to his ability, to each according to his needs" will be implemented. Communism is a highly organized society of free, socially conscious working people in which public self-government will be established, a society in which labor for the good of society will become the prime vital requirement of everyone, a necessity recognized by one and all, and the ability of each person will be employed to the greatest benefit of the people.

A high degree of communist consciousness, industry, discipline, and devotion to the public interest are qualities typifying the man of communist society.

Communism ensures the continuous development of social production and rising labor productivity through rapid scientific and technological progress; it equips man with the best and most powerful machines, greatly increases his power over nature and enables him to control its elemental forces to an ever greater extent. The social economy reaches the highest stage of planned organization, and the most effective and rational use is made of the material wealth and labor reserves to meet the growing requirements of the members of society.

Under communism there will be no classes, and the socio-economic and cultural distinctions, and differences in living conditions, between town and countryside will disappear; the countryside will rise to the level of the town in the development of the productive forces and the nature of work, the forms of production relations, living conditions and the well-being of the population. With the victory of communism mental and physical labor will merge organically in the production activity of people. The intelligentsia will no longer be a distinct social stratum. Workers by hand will have risen in cultural and technological standards to the level of workers by brain. [...]

The C.P.S.U. [Communist Party of the Soviet Union] being a party of scientific communism, proposes and fulfils the tasks of communist construction in step with the preparation and maturing of the material and spiritual prerequisites, considering that it would be wrong to jump over necessary stages of development, and that it would be equally wrong to halt at an achieved level and thus check progress. The building of communism must be carried out by successive stages.

Source: Khrushchev, Nikita. "Report of the Central Committee of the Communist Party of the Soviet Union to the 22nd Congress of the C.P.S.U." In *The Road to Communism: Documents of the 22nd Congress of the Communist Party of the Soviet Union*. Moscow: Foreign Language Publishing House, 1961.

Justice and Legal Systems

At the beginning of the modern era, ideas of individual liberty and self-government spread, resulting in the creation of new systems of law and justice. Voltaire, writing in the decades before the start of the *French Revolution* in 1789 (Document 8), used his acerbic pen to critique a French system of law that heavily favored the nobility and gave them power to judge and tax at their discretion, or even their whim. In the *Federalist Papers*, Alexander Hamilton (Document 9) signals a new and typically modern approach: the rule of law. Hamilton's ultimate concern is to keep government limited by assuring the judiciary is independent, impartial, and enabled to prevent abuses and infringements on the people's liberties. Central concepts in legal systems today, human rights and civil liberties were enshrined in legal reforms and the justice systems created in the modern period.

At the same time, most European states, and other industrializing nations as well, including the United States and Japan, acquired control of large imperial territories in Asia, Africa, America, and Australia. While most of these nations were progressively extending privileges to their own people, they also deprived vast numbers of other people of the same rights they were granting to their own citizens. Mohandas Gandhi's call for the expulsion of the British from India (Document 10) was a direct result of racial and imperial policies that contradicted Britain's own domestic political arrangements. Unfortunately, even after the withdrawal of most imperial powers, the rule of law has failed to take firm hold in many former colonies. On the other hand, Gandhi's idea of *satyagraha*, or love-force, has become the inspiration for the practice of non-violent protest, a new and powerful method of achieving justice when legal systems cannot or will not provide it.

While Gandhi, Voltaire, and Hamilton offer particular views on the arrangement of legal institutions and the pursuit of just political systems in the modern world, Sam Gutierrez's diary (Document 11) gives the perspective of a person inside the penal system in the United States. All of these figures, like Gutierrez, found themselves at various points in their lives in trouble with legal and justice systems: Voltaire repeatedly avoided politically motivated imprisonment by fleeing several countries; Hamilton risked imprisonment or execution when he and the other colonists rebelled against Great Britain; and Gandhi, like Gutierrez, spent significant time in prison, but this is not the only point of contact between them. The daily experience of a prisoner is inextricably linked to the systems that imprison him. Gutierrez does not focus on what he did, or the justice of his sentence, but to imprison him, or anyone, as a just act requires the kind of just systems that the modern world, with exceptions, of course, has sought to establish.

8. Voltaire on the Abuses of the Eighteenth-Century French Aristocracy

Voltaire, the pseudonym of the eighteenth-century French philosopher, Deist, *and political thinker Francois-Marie Arouet, lived most of his life in Geneva, Switzerland, because he had been expelled from most other European countries for criticizing their governments. He was one of the foremost minds of the* Enlightenment *and a harsh critic of governmental abuse, tyranny, hypocrisy, and organized religion.*

In this selection, from his well-known Philosophical Letters, *republished in English in 1778 as* Letters on the English, *his target is the legal privileges of the French nobility, who as a class retained many of the rights they had under the medieval system of* feudalism. *He does so by contrast with the English nobility, who still had some power, but, by the time Voltaire wrote, nothing like the power still exercised by the French nobility. In later eighteenth-century Britain, real political authority, as indicated by William Blackstone (Document 5), had mostly shifted to the House of Commons in the English* Parliament.

Among the rights and privileges Voltaire attacks is the French nobles' continuing close connection to their land and control over territories; their right to hunt anywhere in their fiefdoms, even on another's property; their right to act as judge and jury in legal matters in their dominions; their right to levy their own taxes; and their exemption from paying taxes themselves to the French king.

Yet it is not the nobles' rights themselves that rouses Voltaire's ire, but the inequality of social groups and the relationship of the nobility to the law. The Enlightenment strongly advocated for the equal rights of individuals, liberty, and the rule of law. A legal system that placed the will of the king or a class of aristocrats above the law and gave them arbitrary powers to tax, judge, hunt, or anything else struck the Enlightenment mind as fundamentally unfair and in need of reform. Voltaire, who was not a proponent of general democracy, *applauds the English system, which makes everyone, even the nobility, subject to the law and puts the power to tax and make laws in the hands of the people's representatives, the House of Commons. He also notes the practical advantages in the greater prosperity and industriousness of the English, who do not have to fear their success being simply taken by a greedy local aristocrat.*

The French Revolution *would sweep away the old aristocracy and its privileges in 1789, behead the king in 1791, and slip into a Reign of Terror before the French state was eventually taken over by* Napoleon, *who restored many of the aristocratic privileges in building the French Empire. Regardless of the vicissitudes of history, the shift from an ideal of justice in which different social groups have fundamentally different relationships to the law to one where the rule of law is seen as paramount to a just legal system is an essential part of the evolution of political life in the modern age.*

Since only peers are, properly speaking, noble in England, there would be no such thing, in strictness of law, as nobility in that island, had not the kings created new barons from time to time, and preserved the body of peers, once a terror to them, to oppose them to the Commons, since become so formidable.

Moreover, these new peers who compose the upper House receive nothing but their titles from the king, and very few of them have estates in those places whence they take their titles. One is Duke of D_____, though he has not a foot of land in Dorsetshire; and another is earl of a village, though he scarce knows where it is situated. The peers have power, but it is only in the Parliament House.

Francois Marie Arouet de Voltaire. Courtesy of Photos.com.

There is no such thing here in England as the power enjoyed by the French lords to judge in all matters, civil and criminal; or their right or privilege of hunting in the grounds of a citizen, who at the same time is not permitted to fire a gun in his own field.

No one is exempted in this country from paying certain taxes, because he is a nobleman or a priest. All imposts and taxes are fixed by the House of Commons, whose power is greater than that of the peers, though inferior to it in dignity. The spiritual as well as temporal lords have the right to reject a money bill brought in by the Commons, but they are not allowed to alter anything in it, and must either pass or throw it out without amendment. When the bill has passed the lords and is signed by the king, then the whole nation pays, every man in proportion to his revenue or estate, not according to his title, which would be absurd. There is no such thing as an arbitrary subsidy or poll tax, but a real tax on the lands, the value of which was determined in the reign of the famous King William III.

The land tax continues still upon the same footing, though the revenue of the lands is increased. Thus no one is tyrannized over, and everyone is in comfortable circumstances. The feet of the peasants are not bruised by wooden shoes; they eat white bread, are well clothed, and are not afraid of increasing their stock of cattle, nor of tiling their houses, from any apprehensions that their taxes will be raised the year following. The annual income of the estates of a great many commoners in England amounts to no less than two thousand livres: and yet these do not think it beneath them to plow the lands to which they owe their wealth, and on which they enjoy their liberty.

Source: Voltaire [Francois-Marie Arouet, pseud.]. *Philosophical Letters*. Paris. 1734. Reprinted in James Harvey Robinson and Charles A. Beard, eds. *Readings in Modern European History*. Volume 1: *The Eighteenth Century: The French Revolution and the Napoleonic Period*. Boston: Ginn & Company, 1909.

9. Alexander Hamilton: The Judiciary in a Federal Republic

The Federalist Papers *comprised a series of 85 articles explaining the merits of the proposed United States Constitution and first published in New York newspapers and later collected into a book due to their popularity. They were all published under the pseudonym "Publius," a name that invokes one of the founders of the ancient Roman Republic, although there were three real authors: Alexander Hamilton, one of the founders of the United States, who served as the first secretary of the Treasury; John Jay, the first chief justice of the Supreme Court; and James Madison, the Father of the Constitution and fourth president of the United States. While scholars have debated the importance of the* Federalist Papers *in securing ratification of the Constitution, they remain central documents in understanding the intentions and ideas of those who actually wrote the U.S. Constitution.*

The paper from which the following selection comes, "Federalist 78," is among the most famous. It deals in part with the powers of the judicial branch of the proposed federal government. Hamilton explains and supports the idea of judicial review, or the power of the courts to review laws and declare them unconstitutional, by the clever argument that the Constitution represents the people's will, and when the courts rule the legislature's acts unconstitutional, they are not above the Constitution, but protecting the people from the overreaching of the government.

Hamilton also insists that the judiciary is the weakest of the three branches, and he argues for the independence of the judiciary, claiming that it does not have the power of the legislative or executive branches, and its independence will insure it is a more effective check on the others and will secure the courts' interest in impartially applying and interpreting the law. In the U.S. Constitution, federal judges are chosen by the president, confirmed by the Senate, and appointed for life, which has the advantage of insulating them from political considerations as well as the danger of preventing their being responsible to the people for their judgments. In recent years, critics of various courts' decisions have decried judicial activism and claimed federal courts are acting outside of their legitimate authority and contrary to Hamilton's and the framers' intent. Hamilton considers the possibility of this happening, although he does not call it judicial activism, but dismisses it, claiming the best defense against it is the system the Constitution proposes of permanent, independent judges, whose interest is unclouded by politics and who are impeachable only for bad conduct, not unpopular decisions.

The Federalist No. 78
The Judiciary Department
Independent Journal
Saturday, June 14, 1788
To the People of the State of New York:

WE PROCEED now to an examination of the judiciary department of the proposed government. [...]

Whoever attentively considers the different departments of power must perceive, that, in a government in which they are separated from each other, the judiciary, from the nature of its functions, will always be the least dangerous to the political rights of the Constitution; because it will be least in a capacity to annoy or injure them. The Executive not only dispenses the honors, but holds the sword of the community. The legislature not only commands the purse, but prescribes the rules by which the duties and rights of every citizen are to be regulated. The judiciary, on the contrary, has no influence over either the sword or the purse; no direction either of the strength or of the wealth of the society; and can take no active resolution whatever. It may truly be said to have neither FORCE nor WILL, but merely judgment; and must ultimately depend upon the aid of the executive arm even for the efficacy of its judgments.

This simple view of the matter suggests several important consequences. It proves incontestably, that the judiciary is beyond comparison the weakest of the three departments of power; that it can never attack with success either of the other two; and that all possible care is requisite to enable it to defend itself against their attacks. It equally proves, that though individual oppression may now and then proceed from the courts of justice, the general liberty of the people can never be endangered from that quarter; I mean so long as the judiciary remains truly distinct from both the legislature and the Executive. For I agree [with Montesquieu] that "there is no liberty, if the power of judging be not separated from the legislative and executive powers." And it proves, in the last place, that as liberty can have nothing to fear from the judiciary alone, but would have every thing to fear from its union with either of the other departments; that as all the effects of such a union must ensue from a dependence of the former on the latter, notwithstanding a nominal and apparent separation; that as, from the natural feebleness of the judiciary, it is in continual jeopardy of being overpowered, awed, or influenced by its co-ordinate branches; and that as nothing can contribute so much to its firmness and independence as permanency in office, this quality may therefore be justly regarded as an indispensable ingredient in its constitution, and, in a great measure, as the citadel of the public justice and the public security.

Some perplexity respecting the rights of the courts to pronounce legislative acts void, because contrary to the Constitution, has arisen from an imagination that the doctrine would imply a superiority of the judiciary to the legislative power. It is urged that the authority which can declare the acts of another void, must necessarily be superior

Alexander Hamilton addressing three judges with others looking on in the courtroom. Library of Congress.

to the one whose acts may be declared void. As this doctrine is of great importance in all the American constitutions, a brief discussion of the ground on which it rests cannot be unacceptable. [. . .]

No legislative act, therefore, contrary to the Constitution, can be valid. To deny this, would be to affirm, that the deputy is greater than his principal; that the servant is above his master; that the representatives of the people are superior to the people themselves; that men acting by virtue of powers, may do not only what their powers do not authorize, but what they forbid.

Nor does this conclusion by any means suppose a superiority of the judicial to the legislative power. It only supposes that the power of the people is superior to both; and that where the will of the legislature, declared in its statutes, stands in opposition to that of the people, declared in the Constitution, the judges ought to be governed by the latter rather than the former. They ought to regulate their decisions by the fundamental laws, rather than by those which are not fundamental.

It can be of no weight to say that the courts, on the pretense of a repugnancy, may substitute their own pleasure to the constitutional intentions of the legislature. This might as well happen in the case of two contradictory statutes; or it might as well happen in every adjudication upon any single statute. The courts must declare the sense of the law; and if they should be disposed to exercise WILL instead of JUDGMENT, the consequence would equally be the substitution of their pleasure to that of the legislative body. The observation, if it prove any thing, would prove that there ought to be no judges distinct from that body.

If, then, the courts of justice are to be considered as the bulwarks of a limited Constitution against legislative encroachments, this consideration will afford a strong argument for the permanent tenure of judicial offices, since nothing will contribute so much as this to that independent spirit in the judges which must be essential to the faithful performance of so arduous a duty.

That inflexible and uniform adherence to the rights of the Constitution, and of individuals, which we perceive to be indispensable in the courts of justice, can certainly not be expected from judges who hold their offices by a temporary commission. Periodical appointments, however regulated, or by whomsoever made, would, in some way or other, be fatal to their necessary independence. If the power of making them was committed either to the Executive or legislature, there would be danger of an improper complaisance to the branch which possessed it; if to both, there would be an unwillingness to hazard the displeasure of either; if to the people, or to persons chosen by them for the special purpose, there would be too great a disposition to consult popularity, to justify a reliance that nothing would be consulted but the Constitution and the laws.

Upon the whole, there can be no room to doubt that the convention acted wisely in copying from the models of those constitutions which have established *good behavior* as the tenure of their judicial offices, in point of duration; and that so far from being blamable on this account, their plan would have been inexcusably defective, if it had wanted this important feature of good government. The experience of Great Britain affords an illustrious comment on the excellence of the institution.

PUBLIUS

Source: [Hamilton, Alexander, John Jay, and James Madison], *The Federalist: A Collection of Essays in Favour of the New Constitution*. New York: J. and A. M'Lean, 1788.

10. Mohandas K. Gandhi on Colonialism and Nonviolence

Beginning in the early modern period, European nations began exerting control over non-European territories, a phenomenon often called colonialism. *Some colonies were settled by European emigrants, who largely displaced the native inhabitants, such as in North America or Australia. In other places, Europeans ruled in fact or in name over the native populations. The idea of the "white man's burden," as the English author Rudyard* Kipling *named it, was the responsibility of European nations to bring progress and civilization—whether wanted or not—to the cultures of America, Africa, and Asia, which were often thought of as barbarian or savage. Racism, repression, and exploitation were common in colonial states. Colonial control also often meant arranging a favorable economic relationship for the colonizers, exploiting the resources of the colony and importing finished goods to colonial markets while also competing with other European nations for geopolitical power and influence.*

The system of colonial domination began to break down in the twentieth century, a process accelerated by the First and Second World Wars, which put extreme pressure on European colonial powers. One of the largest colonies in the world was British India, and here the movement against British colonial domination was led by Mohandas Gandhi, *who rose to global prominence as an unconventional spiritual and political leader. Trained as a British lawyer and civil servant, Gandhi evolved a powerful pacifist philosophy, and pioneered the use of what is often now called civil disobedience or non-violent resistance along with several other famous thinkers and popular leaders of the twentieth century, including* Leo Tolstoy, *the Russian writer, and* Martin Luther King, *Jr., the leader of the American* Civil Rights Movement.

The following selection is from the conclusion of Gandhi's first important book, Indian Home Rule, *published in 1908. It predates his most famous period of activism in the 1920s, 1930s, and 1940s, but it offers a sharp critique of European civilization and advocates for Indian Home Rule, or self-government, and thus independence from British rule. India eventually did achieve its independence in 1947, a year before Gandhi was assassinated.*

Scholars, governments, and cultures are still dealing with the consequences of European colonialism, and endemic social issues and geopolitical inequities of the post-colonial era are often hard to separate from causes related to the colonial past. (See Postcolonialism *in the Glossary.) While the debate goes on, there is no doubt that colonial expansion and contraction affected the lives of millions in the modern age, and Gandhi offers a powerful non-Western and non-violent voice on the subject.*

If the English vacated India, bag and baggage, it must not be supposed that she would be widowed, it is possible that those who are forced to observe peace under their pressure would fight after their withdrawal. There can be no advantage in suppressing an eruption; it must have its vent. If, therefore, before we can remain at peace, we must fight amongst ourselves, it is better that we do so. There is no occasion for a third party to protect the weak. It is this so called protection which has unnerved us. Such protection can only make the weak weaker. Unless we realize this, we cannot have Home Rule. I would paraphrase the thought of an English divine and say that anarchy under Home Rule were better than orderly foreign rule. Only, the meaning that the learned divine attached to Home Rule is different from Indian Home Rule according to my conception. We have to learn, and to teach others, that we do not want the tyranny of either English rule or Indian rule. [. . .]

To them [the English] I would respectfully say: "I admit you are my rulers. It is not necessary to debate the question whether, you hold India by the sword or by my consent. I have no objection to your remaining in my country, but although you are the rulers, you will have to remain as servants of the people. It is not we who have to do as you wish, but it is you who have to do as we wish. You may keep the riches that you have drained away from this land, but you may not drain riches henceforth. Your function will be, if you so wish, to police India; you must abandon the idea of deriving any commercial benefit from us. We hold the civilization that you support to be the reverse of civilization. We consider our civilization to be far superior to yours. If you realize this truth, it will be to your advantage and, if you do not, according to your own proverb, you should only live in our country in the same manner as we do. You must not do anything that is contrary to our religions. It is your duty as rulers that for the sake of the Hindus you should eschew beef, and for the sake of Mohammedans you should avoid bacon and ham. We have hitherto said nothing because we have been cowed down, but you need not consider that you have not hurt our feelings by your conduct. We are not expressing our sentiments either through base selfishness or fear, but because it is our duty now to speak out boldly. We consider your schools and law courts to be useless. We want our own ancient schools and courts to be restored. The common language of India is not English but Hindi. You should, therefore, learn it. We can hold communication with you only in our national language.

"We cannot tolerate the idea of your spending money on railways and the military. We see no occasion for either. You may fear Russia; we do not. When she comes we shall look after her. If you are with us, we may then receive her jointly. We do not need any European cloth. We shall manage with articles produced and manufactured at home. You may not keep one eye on Manchester and the other on India. We can work together only if our interests are identical.

"This has not been said to you in arrogance. You have great military resources. Your naval power is matchless. If we wanted to fight with you on your own ground, we should be unable to do so, but if the above submissions are not acceptable to you, we cease to play the part of the ruled. You may, if you like, cut us to pieces. You may shatter us at the cannon's mouth. If you act contrary to our will, we shall not help you; and without our help, we know that you cannot move one step forward.

"It is likely that you will laugh at all this in the intoxication of your power. We may not be able to disillusion you at once, but if there be any manliness in us, you will see shortly that your intoxication is suicidal and that your laugh at our expense is an aberration of intellect. We believe that at heart you belong to a religious nation. We are living in a land which is the source of religions. How we came together need not be considered, but we can make mutual good use of our relations.

"You, English, who have come to India are not good specimens of the English nation, nor can we, almost half-Anglicized Indians, be considered good specimens of the real Indian nation. If the English nation were to know all you have done, it would oppose many of your actions. The mass of the Indians have had few dealings with you. If you will abandon your so-called civilization and search into your own scriptures, you will find that our demands are just. Only on condition of our demands being fully satisfied may you remain in India; and if you remain under those conditions, we shall learn several things from you and you will learn many from us. So doing we shall benefit each other and the world. But that will happen only when the root of our relationship is sunk in a religious soil." [...]

Let each do his duty. If I do my duty, that is, serve myself, I shall be able to serve others. Before I leave you, I will take the liberty of repeating:

1. Real home-rule is self-rule or self-control.
2. The way to it is passive resistance: that is soul-force or love-force.
3. In order to exert this force, Swadeshi [use of goods made in India only] in every sense is necessary.
4. What we want to do should be done, not because we object to the English or because or we want to retaliate but because it is our duty to do so.

Thus, supposing that the English remove the salt-tax, restore our money, give the highest posts to Indians, withdraw the English troops, we shall certainly not use their machine-made goods, nor use the English language, nor many of their industries. It is worth noting that these things are in their nature, harmful; hence we do not want them. I bear no enmity towards the English but I do towards their civilization.

In my opinion, we have used the term "Swaraj" [Home Rule] without understanding its real significance. I have endeavored to explain it as I understand it, and my conscience testifies that my life henceforth is dedicated to its attainment.

Source: Gandhi, Mohandas K. *Indian Home Rule.* 1908. Madras: Ganesh, 1919.

11. Sam Gutierrez: Behind Bars in the United States

Every society must have a way to deal with members who break its rules. In the modern era, societies have developed complex institutions of police, courts, and prisons. The following selection is taken from a recent account made by an inmate in Stateville Prison in Illinois, Simon "Sam" Gutierrez, and edited by a leading prison scholar, Norval Morris.

Gutierrez's account shows in a frank way a glimpse of a type of daily life in a part of the modern world about which many people do not often think—that of the incarcerated. With systematic security, interest in rehabilitation of prisoners, and provisions for health and wellness, life in Stateville Prison is a completely different from the early modern prison or medieval dungeon. However, contemporary prison life is by no means pleasant; rather, it is boring, dangerous, and demeaning. Almost every aspect of Sam's life is regimented, controlled, and observed, not only by guards, but also by other prisoners. Even with constant company and surveillance, Gutierrez seems isolated. There is an interesting distance between Sam and the other prisoners, even his cellmate, Tyrone. They seem to interact with each other as little as possible—remarkably little, given that they share a 6' × 9' cell with no privacy.

Although we never learn what crime he committed to get into prison, Gutierrez is held in a maximum security facility that is somewhat unique because it is modeled on a Panopticon, *a style of prison invented by the English philosopher Jeremy* Bentham *in the nineteenth century, which created a circular roundhouse of several levels of cells with a central control tower. This arrangement allows maximum surveillance with minimum knowledge by the prisoners of when they are being watched, so the idea is that they must always act as if they are being watched and control themselves. The twentieth-century French philosopher Michel* Foucault *took the Panopticon as a metaphor for modern society, where individuals are coerced into controlling themselves in ways they can neither control nor fully understand. In Foucault's view, the modern world is a form of self-imposed prison for everyone. Whatever one thinks of Foucault's philosophy, Sam Gutierrez documents how even in an actual prison the attempt to totally control fails as the rules and regulations of everyday life there are constantly subverted and challenged. Drugs, sex, gangs, corruption—all are forbidden but remain ineradicable elements of everyday prison life.*

ONE DAY IN THE LIFE OF #12345

Before I start on the diary, let me say this: if you expect the usual prison tale of constant violence, brutal guards, gang rapes, daily escape efforts, turmoil, and fearsome adventures, you will be deeply disappointed. Prison life is really nothing like what the press, television, and movies suggest. It is not a daily round of threats, fights, plots, and "shanks" (prison-made knives)—though you have to be constantly careful to avoid situations or behavior that might lead to violence. A sense of impending danger is always with you; you must be careful to move around people rather than against or through them, but with care and reasonable sense you can move safely enough. For me, and many like me in prison, violence is not the major problem; the major problem is monotony. It is the dull sameness of prison life, its idleness and boredom, that grinds me down. Nothing matters; everything is inconsequential other than when you will be free and how to make time pass until then. But boredom, time-slowing boredom, interrupted by occasional bursts of fear and anger, is the governing reality of life in prison.

So, here is my diary for yesterday:

5:30 A.M.:

I was awakened by the wake-up call for the kitchen detail. I am not on that detail, but the banging on the bars of the cell near me, to awaken a prisoner who is on the kitchen detail, wakes me every morning. I knew I could doze for the next half hour, half awake but careful not to think about where I was. I heard Tyrone stirring in the bunk beneath mine, but today he did not, as he often does, celebrate the new day with a loud and odorous fart.

As F House came to life, the noise began—radios, TVs, shouting from cell to cell—and so it would go on till night, with an occasional scream of rage or fear through the night.

Tyrone and I did our best to keep out of each other's way in the space of nine feet by six in our cell while we used our toilet and washed and dressed and pulled up the blankets on our steel bunks. We change our outer clothes sometimes twice a week, sometimes once a week, and our socks and underwear every other day. If you have money, or influence, or a friend in the laundry, you can do better than this. Our dress in summer is blue jeans and a blue shirt or a white T-shirt; in winter we wear blue jeans, a blue shirt, and one of those heavy, lined, blue jackets. Our sartorial flourish is our sneakers, with Nike outranking Reebok and so on down the line; they cost a lot, but in this place they are worth it. [...]

8:05 A.M.:

All the cells throughout the prison, ours included, were locked for "Morning Count." I laid down on my bunk and turned the radio on. Our cell is #304. The guard came by and looked into our cell, making a mark on a pad he was carrying, and walked on. You could hear him shout in front of each cell, "302, 303,...305," telling those inside to look up and be recognized as alive and not dummies. He didn't call out in front of our cell; he saw and knew us; he didn't have to speak to us, and we didn't have to reply. Our cell is different from some of the others in that we have not put up a "curtain"—some material across the bars—to achieve some privacy. We prefer to leave the cell open; it's too much trouble putting the curtain up and taking it down. These curtains are not allowed, but they are tolerated—there is much like this in Stateville. Disciplinary "tickets" are occasionally written but not routinely.

The count, usually four times a day but sometimes more, is a slow process. The early morning count and the last count around 11:30 P.M. do not interfere with the routine of the prison, since all prisoners are then locked in their cells and the count is easier to take. The other counts present more difficulty. Nothing goes on in the prison until the count is reported from every cell house and from everywhere that prisoners are supposed to be, nothing until the numbers reported reconcile exactly with the numbers that are supposed to be there. It can go on for a long time. It is the central ritual of prison life. [...]

5:00 P.M.:

I watched the local news. It was depressing, much of it about the activities of people who are on their way here. I lay on my bunk, half listening to the news, half daydreaming of freedom. Like most other prisoners, I devote much of my waking thought, and all my dream time, to being out of prison.

5:25 P.M.:

The loudspeaker blared again, "Three and four galleries, get ready for chow." The food is often worse in the evening than at lunch, but it is better to go than to stay in what is by now the thundering noise of F House, with TVs and radios blaring and, it seems to me, every prisoner shouting to another prisoner and nobody listening.

The evening meal was a less-adequate replica of lunch, with more bread and less pasta; but the pushing and shoving was also less, and the gangs were less active.

7:00 P.M.:

The evening count—it also went smoothly. Most everyone was by now back in the cell houses, and there were fewer places—schoolroom, gym, yard, industry, barbershop, kitchen, and so on—to be counted. [...]

Well, that was my diary for yesterday. Let me comment a bit on it.

I am not sure whether the average prisoner is safer physically in prison than on the streets, where most of us come from. In Stateville, we are less likely to be shot and killed but possibly slightly more likely to be knifed or injured seriously in a fight. Fights are not uncommon but they are always followed up by the prison authorities, and an effort is made to punish those responsible. There are regular and intermittent shakedowns of all the cells and other areas for shanks and other contraband. It is a violent place, but most prisoners do their time without being victimized physically unless they are looking to prove something to themselves or unless they get into trouble with betting, or hooch, or drugs, or with the gangs. Those who adhere to the main tenets of the prison culture—never "rat" on another prisoner, always keep your distance from staff, "do your own time"—have the best chance of avoiding violence.

I hope this diary is of use to you; it fails to capture the constant unhappiness of prison life and the constant sense of danger—you are never for a moment happy, except sometimes briefly on visitors days, and that is a bitter happiness. The letter misses the relentless, slow-moving routine, the dull repetitiveness, the tension mixed with occasional flashes of fear and rage; it misses the consuming stupidity of living this way. I am sorry; it is not easy. Probably prison was easier to describe many years ago when prison guards saw themselves as punishers, inflicting pain on prisoners, and prisoners joined together to resist them. Now, in prisons like Stateville, purposes are unclear, education is largely a token, idleness takes the place of work and industry, and keeping peace and safety between prisoner and prisoner is the prevailing aim. Anyhow, that is how it appears to this prisoner.

Let me know when you will next visit me; I hope soon.

Sincerely,

Prisoner #12345

Source: Gutierrez, Simon, and Norval Morris. "A Day in the Life of Prisoner #12345." In *The Oxford History of the Prison*, edited by Norval Morris and David J. Rothman. New York: Oxford University Press, 1997. By permission of Oxford University Press, Inc.

Warfare

Warfare has retained its central role in modern political life despite the objections of various groups and individuals. The political goals linked to the waging of war have been both domestic and international. Domestically, war has been used to quell the dissent of certain groups and garner support from the general populace. Internationally, war has brought about the redistribution of political power and the redrawing of state boundaries.

Yet, the effects of warfare on daily life have been more easily recognizable in the suffering that comes with it. Soldiers have always faced the obvious dangers of battle that can lead to injury or death. In the modern era, however, advances in technology have also increased the ability of humans to wage war on an ever deadlier scale. The muzzle-loading firearms and cannons of earlier centuries turned into the machine guns and nuclear weapons of the twentieth and twenty-first centuries. Advances in aircraft and submarine technology expanded the field of warfare into the skies and under the water.

On the other hand, advances in medical technology have also worked to mitigate the effects of deadlier weapons with developments like antibiotics and modern surgical techniques. Today's military hospitals are far better equipped to help war casualties than the medical facilities that preceded them.

The dangers of warfare as seen in the following selections encompass much more than those stemming from a soldier's foe. Climate could be a deadly enemy, as the troops under *Napoleon* found out during their 1812 campaign in Russia (Document 12). Even exposure to less extreme weather conditions also had the capacity to slowly wear a soldier down until he was no longer able to function. While thinking about food could be a comfort during wartime, as it was to the World War II Japanese soldier Shōichi Ishikawa (Document 15), such thoughts could be torture to those severely deprived of nutrition. Under such conditions, disease posed a serious threat, especially given that personal hygiene often had to be ignored during wartime, a fact noted by World War I German submarine commander Georg-Günther von Forstner (Document 14).

Despite the dangers and privations faced by soldiers during warfare, the belief that one is doing good has often served as a morale booster during difficult times. Von Forstner focused not on the dangers and difficulties of chasing down enemy vessels but on the service he was providing to his countrymen at home with each ship he took out of action. During the *Vietnam War,* American serviceman Kevin Fitzsimmons (Document 16) found meaning in the idea that he was there to help the Vietnamese people ultimately live better, freer lives.

War brings hardships not only for the troops engaged in battle but also commonly for the civilian populace living in the war zone and for those on the home fronts. Virginia Clayton and her household (Document 13) had to do without basic goods during the American *Civil War,* a shortage linked to the blockade of southern ports by the Union. The Vietnamese typist working in Fitzsimmons's office experienced warfare even more directly, as a civilian casualty caught in the crossfire (Document #16).

War changes daily life even beyond hardship and suffering. Clayton's account also indicates how the economy changed, as crops grown for local consumption replaced those produced for the larger market. Given that many wars required large numbers of the male population to leave for an extended period of time, the women who remained on the home front often had to assume control of the business endeavors that their absent husbands had run, producing not only a change in the economy but also one in gender roles. This change could often lead to greater economic independence for women formally entering the workforce. Women gained greater social independence during these times as well, a transformation that could arise relatively quickly. Some of these changes in gender roles could be seen in the propaganda from World War II, for example, with the image of Rosie the Riveter.

12. *Warfare and Weather: Napoleon's Retreat from Moscow*

By 1812, Europe had experienced two decades of warfare brought about by various countries forming coalitions intended to prevent French expansion. Yet, none proved capable of stopping the French forces, now under the control of Napoleon *Bonaparte. Feeling invincible and attempting to further enhance his dominance in Europe, Napoleon hoped to bring his often less than reliable ally, Russia, under control through a military campaign. Believing he would again succeed by using the method of quick attack, Napoleon launched an assault on Russia in June 1812.*

Instead of standing and fighting the French, however, the Russian army began a process of repeated retreats east into the Russian interior. Napoleon's troops followed, finally engaging the Russian forces in battle at Borodino. Yet, Napoleon did not achieve a conclusive victory, and the Russian troops continued their retreat. Upon entering Moscow in September, Napoleon hoped to find suitable quarters and supplies there for the quickly approaching winter. Instead, he found little of use, a situation worsened by a fire set the following day that caused additional damage to the city. After some deliberation, Napoleon decided to retreat west. Yet, by the time his troops left Moscow, the vast distances that had to be covered meant the troops undoubtedly would have to face the Russian winter.

As valet and companion to Napoleon, Louis Constant Wairy provides a first-hand account of the French army's miserable retreat out of Russia. Here the account begins with an army so depleted of men that it no longer made sense to have so many senior officers, so generals took up the rank of captain instead. In a time before war became industrialized and when the cavalry still formed an indispensable arm of the military, the lack of horses posed another large problem. Constant indicates that even Napoleon had to give up his own horses to help transport artillery.

Constant provides an especially harrowing account of the crossing of the Beresina River. Ill-equipped for such an undertaking and under pressure from the Russian forces attempting to catch up with them, the French troops constructed a makeshift bridge over the river to allow men and artillery to cross. Yet, the method proved of limited success because the bridge broke under the strain. The French quickly constructed an even more basic bridge, but it had no railings to prevent men from falling off. In the panic of trying to outrun the Russians, both man and beast perished at the hands of others trying to cross, who, in their haste, pushed unlucky victims to their deaths in the icy waters of the Beresina. Although Constant portrays Napoleon favorably, the account serves as an indication of the emperor's miscalculation regarding the ferocity of the frigid Russian winter.

Horses were lacking for the artillery, and at this critical moment the artillery was the safeguard of the army. The Emperor gave orders that his horses should be taken; he estimated that the loss of even one cannon or artillery wagon would be incalculable; the artillery was confided to a corps composed entirely of officers; it amounted to about five hundred men. It affected His Majesty to see these brave officers become soldiers once more, putting their hands to the pieces like simple cannoneers, and going back through devotion to the lessons of the school. The Emperor called this his *sacred squadron!* For the same reason which made the officers become soldiers, the other superior commanders descended from their rank without disturbing themselves about the designation of their grade. Generals of division Grouchy and Sébastiani resumed the rank of simple captains.

Near Borozino we were arrested by loud shouting; we thought ourselves cut off by the Russian army; I saw the Emperor turn pale; this was a thunderbolt; several lancers were dispatched as quickly as possible; we saw them return waving their flags; His Majesty comprehended the signals, and long before we could have been reassured by the cuirassiers, he said: "*I bet that it is Victor*"; so accurately present to his mind were even the possible positions of each corps of the army. Marshal Victor was, in fact, awaiting our passage with keen impatience. It seemed that his army had received some vague tidings of our misfortunes, and was, therefore, prepared to give the Emperor an enthusiastic welcome. His soldiers, still fresh and vigorous, at least in comparison with the rest of the army, could not believe their eyes when they saw us in such a miserable condition; the shouts of *Long live the Emperor!* resounded none the less on that account.

But when the rear portion of the army began to defile before them, another impression was produced. A great confusion ensued. All those in the Marshal's army who recognized any of their companions left their ranks and ran toward them, offering bread and clothes; they were frightened by the voracity with which these wretches ate; many embraced each other weeping. One of the brave and kindly officers of the Marshal took off his own uniform to give it to a poor soldier whose ragged garments exposed him naked to the cold, putting on his own back a tattered old infantry coat, because he was more capable of resisting the rigors of the weather. If excessive misery withers the soul, on the other hand it sometimes expands it to the highest point, as one may see. Many of the most wretched blew their brains out in despair. In that act, the last which nature indicates to put an end to wretchedness, there was a resignation and coolness that made one shudder. Those who thus assailed their own lives were not seeking death so much as a term to insupportable sufferings, and in this disastrous campaign I saw what vanities are physical force and human courage where that moral force which is born of a determined will is non-existent.

The Emperor marched between the army of Marshal Victor and that of Marshal Oudinot. It was frightful to see these moving masses sometimes halting progressively, the advance corps first, then those that followed, then the last; when Marshal Oudinot, who was ahead, suspended his march for some unknown reason, there would be a movement of general uneasiness, then alarming speeches would begin, and, as men who have seen everything, both true and false tidings easily found credit; the fright would last until the front of the army began to move on, when a degree of confidence was restored.

By five o'clock in the evening of the 25th some trestles had been fixed above the stream, constructed of wooden beams taken from Polish cabins. It was rumored in the army that the bridge would be finished during the night. The Emperor was much annoyed when the army deceived itself in this way, because he knew that people grow much more quickly discouraged when they have indulged in vain hopes; for this reason he took great care to have the rear of the army made acquainted with the slightest incidents, so as never to leave the soldiers under so cruel an illusion. The trestles gave way at a little past five o'clock. They were not strong enough. It was necessary to wait until the next day, and the army relapsed into its dismal conjectures. It was plain that next day it would have to sustain the enemy's fire; but there was no room for choice. At the end of that night of anguish and sufferings of every sort, the first trestles were driven down into the river. People do not comprehend that the soldiers had stood up to their lips in water full of floating ice, summoning every force with which nature had endowed them, and all the remaining courage born of energy and devotion in order to drive piles several feet deep in to a miry river bed; struggling against the most horrible fatigues; pushing away with their hands enormous masses of ice which would have knocked them down and submerged them by their weight; fighting, in a word, and fighting unto death with cold, the greatest enemy of life. Well, that is what our French pontonniers did. Several of them were either dragged down by the currents or suffocated by the cold. That is a glory, it seems to me, which outweighs many another. [. . .]

Before the bridge was finished, some four hundred men were partially transported from the other side of the river on two miserable rafts which they could with difficulty steer against the current. From the shore, we saw them greatly shaken by the great pieces of ice which clogged the river. These masses would come to the very edge of the raft; meeting an obstacle, they would stop for a while and then be drawn underneath those feeble planks and produce horrible shocks. Our soldiers would stop the largest ones with their bayonets and make them deviate insensibly beyond the rafts. [. . .]

When the artillery and the baggage were crossing, the bridge was so thronged that it broke. Then ensued that retrograde movement which crowded back in horrible confusion the whole multitude of stragglers who were advancing, like driven cattle, behind the artillery. Another bridge had been hastily constructed, as if in sad prevision of the breaking of the first one; but the second one was narrow and unprotected at the sides. However, it was a makeshift which at first glance seemed very precious in such an appalling calamity; but what miseries ensued! The laggards flocked thither in droves. As the artillery, the baggage,—in a word, the entire material of the army—had been in advance on the first bridge, when it broke, and by the sudden recoil which took place the catastrophe became known, then those who had been behind were the first to gain the other bridge. But it was necessary that the artillery should cross first. It pressed forward then with impetuosity toward the only way of salvation which was left. Here the pen refuses to describe the scene of horrors that took place. It was literally over a road of crushed bodies that the wagons of every sort reached the bridge. On this occasion one saw what hardness, what systematic ferocity even, can be imparted to the soul by the instinct of self-preservation. There were some of the stragglers, the craziest of any, who wounded and even killed with bayonet thrusts the unfortunate horses who did not obey the whip of their drivers. Several wagons had to abandoned in consequence of this odious proceeding.

I have said that the bridge had no ledges at the sides. Crowds of poor wretches who were trying to cross it were seen to fall into the stream and be sucked under the masses of ice. Others tried to cling to the miserable planks of the bridge, and would remain hanging over the abyss until their hands, crushed by the wheels of the wagons, would let go their hold; then they went to rejoin their comrades and were engulfed by the waters. Whole artillery wagons, horses and drivers alike, were plunged into the stream.

Source: Wairy, Louis Constant. *Memoirs of Constant, First Valet de Chambre of the Emperor, on the Private Life of Napoleon, His Family and His Court.* Translated by Elizabeth Gilbert Martin. New York: C. Scribner's Sons, 1895.

13. A Southern Plantation Wife during the American Civil War

War not only causes hardships for the men who go off to fight but also for those who stay behind, including their wives. This was true in the case of Victoria Clayton, who remained on her family's Alabama plantation when her husband went off to fight for the Confederacy *in the* Civil War. *As often happens during times of war, provisions that had once been easily obtainable became scarce. Such hardships proved especially true for the Confederacy because Union ships blockaded the South's ports. Hence, cotton could not be shipped out for sale, and other goods, such as the coffee and white sugar that Clayton mentions, could not be imported. Instead of buying silk gowns, local women made homespun clothes out of cotton. This need meant the learning of new skills like weaving and the reorientation of the plantation from producing cotton for the market to growing an assortment of crops needed to fulfill basic needs at home.*

Not surprisingly, with so many men off at war, their wives often filled the void by playing much more active roles in the running of affairs, such as Clayton did on her family's plantation. Although she corresponded with her husband upon occasion to ask for advice, it was Clayton who now performed inspections of the plantation or oversaw repairs on a local bridge. Although many women's husbands returned from fighting to take up such roles again after their terms in the army were over or when the war finally ended, the massive casualties of the Civil War meant that many would not. Furthermore, while Clayton may have been able to manage the transition more effectively than some of the poor women she employed to weave cloth, who did not have slaves to help them, her text also alludes to the potentially negative side of this situation. Conflict could erupt closer to home if the slaves were not properly controlled.

Clayton does not portray the war years as completely bad; she reminisces about the accomplishments achieved by pulling together and the pride gained from aiding the war effort. She fondly remembers working with Joe and the relationship they had, not noting a contradiction between the love her family felt for him and his status as their slave. Although not uncommon in war memoirs, these positive feelings were perhaps made stronger in Clayton by the fact that this world she knew and the institution of slavery *that underpinned it would be swept away at the end of the Civil War.*

While my husband was at the front doing active service, suffering fatigue, privations, and the many ills attendant on a soldier's life, I was at home struggling to keep the family comfortable.

We were blockaded on every side, could get nothing from without, so had to make everything at home; and having been heretofore only an agricultural people, it became necessary for every home to be supplied with spinning wheels and the old-fashioned loom, in order to manufacture clothing for members of the family. This was no small undertaking. I knew nothing about spinning and weaving cloth. I had to learn myself, and then to teach the negroes. Fortunately for me, most of the negroes knew how to spin thread, the first step towards clothmaking. Our work was hard and continuous. To this we did not object, but our hearts sorrowed for our loved ones in the field. [. . .]

There was no white person on the plantation beside myself and children, the oldest of whom was attending school in Eufaula, as our Clayton schools were closed, and my time was so occupied that it was impossible for me to teach my children. Four small children and myself constituted the white family at home.

I entrusted the planting and cultivation of the various crops to old Joe. He had been my husband's nurse in infancy, and we always loved and trusted him. I kept a gentle saddle horse, and occasionally accompanied by Joe, would ride over the entire plantation on a tour of inspection. Each night, when the day's work was done, Joe came in to make a report of everything that had been done on the plantation that day. When Mr. Clayton was where he could receive my letters, I wrote him a letter every night before retiring, and in this way he, being kept informed about the work at home, could write and make suggestions about various things to help me manage successfully.

We made good crops every year, but after the second year we planted provision crops entirely, except enough cotton for home use.

All the coloring matter for cloth had to be gathered from the forest. We would get roots and herbs and experiment with them until we found the color desired, or a near approach to it. We also found out what would dye cotton and what woolen fabrics. We had about one hundred head of sheep; and the wool yielded by these sheep and the cotton grown in the fields furnished us the material for our looms. After much hard work and experience we learned to make very comfortable clothing, some of our cloth being really pretty.

Our ladies would attend services in the church of God, dressed in their home-spun goods, and felt well pleased with their appearances; indeed, better pleased than if they had been dressed in silk of the finest fabric.

We made good warm flannels and other articles of apparel for our soldiers, and every woman learned to knit socks and stockings for her household, and many of the former were sent to the army.

In these dark days the Southern matron, when she sat down at night feeling that the day's work was over, took her knitting in her hands as a pastime, instead of the fancy work which ladies so frequently indulge in now.

I kept one woman at the loom weaving, and several spinning all the time, but found that I could not get sufficient cloth made at home; consequently I gave employment to many a poor woman whose husband was far away. Many a time have I gone ten miles in the country with my buggy filled with thread, to get one of these ladies to weave a piece of cloth for me, and then in return for her labor sent her syrup, sugar, or any of our home produce she wished.

We always planted and raised large crops of wheat, rice, sugar cane, and potatoes. In fact, we grew almost everything that would make food for man or beast. Our land is particularly blest in this respect. I venture to say there is no land under the sun that will grow a greater variety of products than the land in these Southern states.

Being blockaded, we were obliged to put our ingenuity to work to meet the demands on us as heads of families. Some things we could not raise; for instance, the accustomed necessary luxury of every home—coffee. So we went to work to hunt up a substitute. Various articles were tried, but the best of all was the sweet potato. The potatoes were peeled, sliced, and cut into pieces as large as a coffee bean, dried, and then roasted just as we prepared coffee. This substitute, mixed with genuine coffee, makes a very palatable drink for breakfast. . . .

Another accustomed luxury of which we were deprived was white sugar. We had, however, a good substitute with which we soon became satisfied; our home-made brown sugar, from the sugar cane. It had the redeeming quality of being pure. . . .

We made gallons of wine from the scuppernong [a large native American grape] and other grapes every year. One year I remember particularly. Sheets were spread under the long scuppernong arbors, little negro boys put on top to throw the grapes down, and grown men underneath to gather them in baskets as they fell. When brought to the house they measured thirty-two bushels, and made one hundred and twenty gallons of wine. I did not make so large a quantity from the other varieties of grapes. This wine was kept in the cellar and used for the common benefit. When the negroes would get caught out in the rain, and come to the house wet, they did not hesitate to say, "Mistus, please give me a little wine to keep cold away"; and they always received it. There never was any ill result from the use of domestic wine. We were a temperate family and the use was invariably beneficial.

Closed in as we were on every side, with nearly every white man of proper age and health enlisted in the army, with the country filled with white women, children, and old, infirm men, with thousands of slaves to be controlled, and caused through their systematic labor to feed and clothe the people at home, and to provide for our army, I often wonder, as I contemplate those by-gone days of labor and sorrow, and recall how peacefully we moved on and accomplished what we did.

We were required to give one-tenth of all that was raised, to the government. There being no educated white person on the plantation except myself, it was necessary that I should attend to the gathering and measuring of every crop and the delivery of the tenth to the government authorities. This one-tenth we gave cheerfully and often wished we had more to give.

My duties, as will be seen, were numerous and often laborious; the family on the increase continually, and every one added increased labor and responsibility. And this was the case with the typical Southern woman.

Source: Clayton, Victoria V. *White and Black under the Old Regime*. Milwaukee: The Young Churchman Co., 1899.

14. Modern War at Sea: A German U-Boat during World War I

Submarines first entered the fleets of the world as more than experimental vessels in the late nineteenth century and became crucial to naval warfare during the First World War of 1914–1918. As the Allies attempted a blockade to keep goods from entering German ports, Germany responded by engaging its submarines, or U-boats, to sink ships transporting goods to Allied ports. The torpedoing of neutral ships in addition to those of the Allies eventually incited the United States to enter the war against Germany in 1917.

Georg-Günther von Forstner's journal chronicles his exploits as a commander of one of Germany's U-boats during the early stages of World War I. He focuses on the innovativeness of submarine technology when describing the cutting-edge machinery housed in the limited space of the vessel's hull. The curiosity and concern about the effects of long-term submersion on the crew also reveals the relative newness of submarine warfare, although by this point the technology was reliable enough that it was mainly a matter of having enough time before diving to pull in fresh air. Yet, this technological advance still could not remedy basic privations the crew would have to face while on a mission, such as limited opportunities for bathing.

Von Forstner provides a good sense of how the U-boat commander proceeded to hunt for targets. Since the difference between a neutral and an Allied ship could be difficult to ascertain, largely due to the latter's attempt to disguise itself, a great deal of time needed to be spent on a detailed review of a vessel's documentation. Just stopping a ship, however, could prove difficult; as von Forstner indicates, it could attempt to run. Yet von Forstner did not hesitate to use force when necessary. He focused not on the suffering of the enemy, but on the service he was providing for those at home, whom he helped with every additional ship he torpedoed.

A submarine conceals within its small compass the most concentrated technical disposition known in the art of mechanical construction, especially so in the spaces reserved for the steering gear of the boat and for the manipulation of its weapons.

The life on board becomes such a matter of habit that we can peacefully sleep at great depths under the sea, while the noise is distinctly heard of the propellers of the enemy's ships, hunting for us overhead; for water is an excellent sound conductor, and conveys from a long distance the approach of a steamer. We are often asked, "How can you breathe under water?" The health of our crew is the best proof that this is possible. We possessed as fellow passengers a dozen guinea pigs, the gift of a kindly and anxious friend, who had been told these little creatures were very sensitive to the ill effects of a vitiated atmosphere. They flourished in our midst and proved amusing companions.

It is essential before a U-boat submerges to drive out the exhausted air through powerful ventilating machines, and to suck in the purest air obtainable; but often in war time one is obliged to dive with the emanations of cooking, machine oil, and the breath of the crew still permeating the atmosphere, for it is of the utmost importance to the success of a submarine attack that the enemy should not detect our presence; therefore, it is impossible at such short notice to clear the air within the boat. These conditions, however, are bearable, although one must be constantly on the watch to supply in time fresh ventilation. [. . .]

When everything is in readiness, the crew is given a short leave on land, to go and take the much coveted hot bath. This is the most important ceremony before and after a cruise, especially when the men return, for when they have remained unwashed for weeks, soaked with machine oil, and saturated with salt spray, their first thought is—a hot bath. At sea, we must be very sparing of our fresh-water supply, and its use for washing must be carefully restricted.

The commander usually spends the eve of his departure in the circle of his comrades, but it is a solemn moment for him as soon as he sails from his native shore. He becomes responsible for every action which is taken, and for many weeks no orders reach him from his superiors. He is unable to ask any one's advice, or to consult with his inferiors, and he stands alone in the solitude of his higher rank. Even the common sailor is conscious of the seriousness of the task ahead and of the adventures which may occur below seas. No loud farewells, no jolly hand, no beckoning girls are there to bid us Godspeed. Quietly and silently do we take our departure. Neither wife nor child, nor our nearest and dearest, know whither we go, if we remain in home waters, or if we go forth to encounter the foe. We can bid no one farewell. It is through the absence of news that they know that we are gone, and no one is aware, except the special high officer in this department of the Admiralty who gives the commander his orders, on what errand we are bound or when we shall return, for the slightest indiscretion might forfeit the success of our mission.

Before dawn, on the day of our departure, the last pieces of equipment and of armament are put on board, and the machinery is once more tested; then, at the appointed hour, the chief engineer informs the commander that everything is ready. A shrill whistle bids the crew cast loose the moorings, and at the sound of the signal bell the boat begins to move. As we glide rapidly out of port, we exchange by mutual signs a few last greetings with our less favored comrades on the decks of the ships we leave behind, who no doubt also long to go forth and meet the enemy. [...]

In this manner, on a fine March morning, we steered our course to the English coast, to take active part in the commercial war. Gently the waves splashed around the prow and glided over the lower deck. Our duty was to examine every merchantman we met with the object of destroying those of the enemy. The essential thing was to ascertain the nationality of the ships we stopped. On the following morning, we were given several opportunities to fulfill our task.

It is well known that the English merchantmen were ordered by their Government to fly a neutral flag, so as to avoid being captured by our warships. We all remember how, on one of her earlier trips through the war zone, the gigantic "Lusitania" received a wireless message to conceal the Union Jack and to fly the Stars and Stripes of the United States, but destiny after all overtook her at a later date.

All of us U-boat commanders were told not to trust to the nationality of any flag we saw, and to stop every steamer on our path and to examine her papers thoroughly. Even these might be falsified, and we must therefore judge for ourselves, according to the appearance of the crew and the way in which the ship was built, whether she were in reality a neutral. Of course many neutrals had to suffer from the deceptions practiced by the English, and although their colors were painted on their sides and they were lighted at night by electricity, yet this device could also be copied. Therefore, we were obliged to detain and examine all the ships we encountered, greatly to the inconvenience of the innocent ones.

I will describe the manner in which a warship undertakes the search of a merchantman: Through flag signals the merchantman is bidden to stop immediately; if he does not obey, the warship makes his orders more imperative by firing blank shot as a warning. If then the merchantman tries to escape, the warship is justified in hitting the runaway. On the other hand, if the steamer or sailboat obeys the summons, then the warship puts out a boat with an armed prize crew and an officer to look over the ship's papers. These consist in certificates of nationality, of the sailing port, and port of destination, and they contain a bill of lading as to the nature of the cargo, also the names of the crew and a passenger list if it is a passenger steamer. If the ship is a neutral and her papers are satisfactory, she is allowed to proceed, whereas an enemy's ship is either captured or sunk. If a neutral ship carries contraband of war, this is either confiscated or destroyed, but if it exceeds half the total cargo, then this ship is also condemned.

It is nearly impossible for a submarine to send a prize crew on board a big ship, therefore neutral States have given their captains the order to go in a ship's boat and deliver their papers themselves on board the submarine; but they often annoyed us by a long parley and delay, and it was always with a feeling of disappointment that we were obliged to leave inactive our cannons and torpedoes, the crew sadly exclaiming, "After all, they were only neutrals!"

One sunny afternoon, we were in the act of examining the papers of a Dutch steamer that we had stopped in the neighborhood of the Meuse Lightship, when we perceived on the horizon another steamer coming rapidly towards us, and we judged by its outline that it was of English construction. The steamer we were examining proved to be unobjectionable in every respect, and sailing only between neutral ports, so we dismissed it, and just as it was departing, the English steamer, evidently apprehending our presence, turned about in great haste in hope to escape from us, and steered with full steam ahead towards the English shores, to seek the protection of the ships on the watch patrolling the English coast.

The English captain well knew what fate awaited him if he fell into the hands of a wicked German U-boat. Mighty clouds of smoke rose from her funnels, giving evidence of the active endeavors of the stokers in the boiler-room to bring the engines up to their highest speed, and before we had time to give signal to stop, the steamer was in flight.

Meanwhile we had also put on all steam in pursuit, and drove our engines to their utmost capacity. The English ship was going at a great pace, and we had many knots to cover before we could catch up with her to impose our commands, for she paid no heed to the international flag-signal we had hoisted—"Stop at once or we fire!"—and she was striving her uttermost to reach a zone of safety. Our prow plunged into the surging seas, and showered boat and crew alike with silvery, sparkling foam. The engineers were being urged to their greatest power, and the whir of the propeller proved that below, at the motor valves, each man was doing his very best. Anxiously, we measured the distance that still separated us from our prey. Was it diminishing? Or would they get away from us before our guns could take effect? Joyfully we saw the interval lessening between us, and before long our first warning shot, across her bow, raised a high, threatening column of water. But still the Englishman hoped to escape from us, and the thick smoke belching from the funnels showed that the stokers were shoveling more and more coal into the glowing furnace; they well knew what risk they had to run.

Even after two well-aimed shots were discharged from the steel mouths of our cannons, right and left on either side of the fugitive, which must have warned the captain that the next shot would undoubtedly strike the stern, he was still resolved neither to stop nor surrender.

Nothing now remained for us but to use our last means to enforce our will. With a whistling sound, a shell flew from the muzzle of our cannon and a few seconds later fell with a loud crash in a cloud of smoke on the rear deck of the steamer. This produced the desired effect.

Immediately the steamer stopped and informed us by three quick blasts from the steam whistle (the international signal) that the engines would be reversed and the ship stopped. The captain had given up his wild race.

Huge white clouds from the uselessly accumulated steam rose from the funnels, and to our signal, "Abandon the ship at once," the Englishman replied with a heavy heart by hoisting a white and red striped pennon, the preconcerted international sign that our order had been understood and was being obeyed.

This small striped pennon has a deep significance: it means that a captain accepts this most painful necessity knowing that his dear old boat will soon lie at the bottom of the sea; truly a difficult decision for the captain of a proud ship to make. The crew were by this time reconciled to their fate and, as we drew near to parley with the captain, the life boats were launched; the men tossed in their belongings and, jumping in, took their places at the oars. It need hardly be said that we, on the other hand, were pleased with our capture. I have often shaken hands with the gunner who had fired the last deadly shot, for we waste no emotion over our adversary's fate. With every enemy's ship sent to the bottom, one hope of the hated foe is annihilated. We simply pay off our account against their criminal wish to starve all our people, our women, and our children, as they are unable to beat us in open fight with polished steel. Ought we not therefore rejoice in our justifiable satisfaction?

Source: Forstner, Georg-Günther von. *The Journal of Submarine Commander von Forstner.* Translated by Mrs. Russell Codman. Introduced by John Hays Hammond, Jr. Boston and New York: Houghton Mifflin, 1917.

15. A Japanese Soldier's Poem, 1944

In July 1944, a Japanese solider named Shōichi Ishikawa wrote a poem that he sent to his family. Although short in length, it expresses both personal and national goals. For himself, Ishikawa hoped to return to his home. The poem expresses this by referencing a kine, or mallet. Ishikawa means the mallet commonly used in preparing the traditional New Year's dish by pounding rice into a dough-like form called mochi. With this reference the poem evokes the warmth of home, the visiting of family on a holiday, and the abundance of food during such celebrations, all things soldiers in the field daydreamed about.

For Japan, Ishikawa hoped for victory. This is likely another reason why Ishikawa chose to place the events of the poem around New Year's, although he wrote it at the height of summer. By 1944, Japan suffered from declining fortunes in the war. Although it is unclear during which part of July Ishikawa composed the poem, by the middle of the month the prime minister and head of the army, Hideki Tojo, *was forced to resign after the devastating loss of Saipan, events that shook Japan's morale. Ishikawa set the poem at New Year's to indicate not only a time for celebration with family, but also a new beginning, a chance for Japan to turn its fortunes around.*

Listening to the sound of the beating mallet
Welcoming in this year of total victory
Thinking of home, I gaze at the moon
From my oil-drum bath

Source: Poem by Ishikawa Shōichi. Private collection. Translated by Stephen Snyder. Courtesy of Yukitoshi Ishikawa and Stephen Snyder.

16. An American Serviceman's Letters from Vietnam, 1969

In June 1969, Kevin Fitzsimmons, a volunteer from Long Island, New York, began his tour of duty in Vietnam. Linked to a larger policy aimed at containing Communism *during the* Cold War, *U.S. involvement grew slowly, but eventually ballooned under President Lyndon* Johnson's *administration into active engagement, as both the deployment of troops to Vietnam and American casualties increased. Protest from Americans over engagement in Vietnam also grew, and the United States finally withdrew in 1973. For his part, Fitzsimmons served in Long Binh, near Saigon, working in one of the base offices.*

Instead of flying bullets and burning villages, Fitzsimmons's letters provide a glimpse of another side of the Vietnam War: *filing papers, shopping, and chatting with others. Yet, the more dangerous side of war is not absent either. Fitzsimmons tells his wife about the recent attack on his base to temper whatever she might hear through official news channels and to prevent her from worrying. Yet, even though the attack clearly unsettled him, the account also indicates how such events themselves partially became a normal part of life in a war zone, something not to be played up too much.*

The following excerpt also underlines the various ways in which Fitzsimmons kept his morale up. News from home was a major boost. Even reading a local paper that discussed the various events going on in New York City gave Fitzsimmons a way to stay connected. In addition to Fitzsimmons's religious beliefs, his morale was also boosted by his empathy for the people he saw around him on a daily basis and the desire to help them. This provides a notable contrast to the mood of general disillusionment with American involvement in Vietnam for which the period is more commonly remembered.

18 August, 1969

Dear Teresa,

Today I received your two loving letters of 9th and 10th. Really darling, you are such a good writer... What a treat. All those thoughtful things you sent me. The one item I'm a little hesitant about using is the fan. After all, it is pink. It was a lovely thought, though. Speaking about fans, yesterday they were selling them in a PX so I bought one. It's quite large for a table model and works by pushing buttons on the base of the stand. There are 3 speeds and you can choose oscillation or not, whatever you wish. It cost $19.50 but I think it was well worth it as when I leave here I should be able to get $15 for it. You have an excellent skill in choosing tobacco. It's just wonderful! xxx How much did you pay for it? I hope not too much. I am thoroughly enjoying smoking it. Thank you for the Village Voice, it reminds you of all the different things happening in this big city. I will eagerly look forward to getting my copy in the mail every so often thru the subscriptions you mailed in. xxxx The colander, Molly Frank catalog, candy and everything else is so nice to get. I feel it's like Christmas in August. It makes me exceedingly happy...

...By now darling, you have probably read in the papers that Long Binh was hit by the VC. They did make an advance on our bunker line but they were beaten back. Also, they let loose with from 40–60 rockets. They were 104 mm size. Your father can explain how large that is. One landed up by the showers but no one got hurt. I was safely in a bunker but the noise and flash was quite nerve wracking. In Security Guard Co, which is the next company over, one landed in the road in front of the mess hall and tore up the railing and knocked out 2 jeeps that were parked 10 feet away. I tell you darling, God is with the men, at least in my area for 2 men were sitting in a latrine and a rocket hit the ground and exploded 2 feet from the building. They weren't hurt, which is a miracle for they were awfully close to the exploding rocket. Needless to say,

I didn't sleep too well last night. Hearing these rockets coming in and exploding is an experience one is not likely to forget. I just hope and pray this was the end of it. I love you so much! xxxx I don't want to cause you more worry than is necessary. I decided to tell you the above because I knew that back in the U.S. they would play it up bigger than it was.

As far as the electrical outlet problem goes, I purchased an extension cord and have it coming over to the head of my bed. I use it to plug in my razor, fan and my tape recorder wherein I listen to your beautiful voice... try and keep happy, darling. xx Please don't worry, someone is watching over me and I'll be safe.

Love always,
Kevin

...

[no date]

Darling,

...The past two days I've been filing personnel records and counting what kind of paperwork was processed when and in what quantity for the last 6 months. It's not hard but it sure is boring. When it starts getting to me I get up and walk out of the office and chew the fat with other soldiers or some Vietnamese office workers who are mostly women. It's very interesting to talk to them through broken English and mispronounced words. They seem to be very gentle and kind. I'm interested in their mode of thought and their ideas on different subjects, the war included. It's also very sad to see people just trying to live their lives and be frustrated and caught up in the war. The typist in my office, a Miss Try-Mong-Lan (Dream Flower) is half Chinese and half Vietnamese. She lives in Choulon, the Chinese part of Saigon, and during Tet she was caught in a crossfire between VC and U.S. troops. She was shot in the leg though luckily it was just a flesh wound. She's all right now. Anyway, she is 25 and says she will never marry because with the war she is afraid her husband would be caught in a battle and be killed and she would be all alone with children. For the Vietnamese there is little security for life, limb or property. I am anxious for the war to be over not only for us and the U.S. troops but also for the Vietnamese people... Maybe I'm getting too sentimental but when you talk to the people you feel a lot of sympathy. Heavens help these people if the VC win! I guess these are some of the reasons why I offered to teach our typist some English. On my part, of course, there is also curiosity. After a while, as you get to know them, race disappears and you see them as individuals, like you and me, trying to get along as best we can. I hope when the war ends this govt. will spend money to rebuild this country. I think if the war protestors could get over here and see things the way they are and meet the people face to face they would quickly change their tune... well, it's sleep time. So I'll leave you on this sentence. You will forever occupy my entire heart.

Love,
Kevin

Source: Letters from Kevin Fitzsimmons, August 18, 1969 and undated, private collection. Courtesy of Kevin Fitzsimmons.

Part VII
RECREATIONAL LIFE

Not all our time is taken up with work, education, and other obligations. Humans recreate, and the patterns of recreation in the modern world have been different than in previous periods. Professional sports, a central cultural element in many modern nations, were virtually unknown before the modern period. Not only sports. Music, theatre, dance, and travel are enjoyed by millions around the world in forms and fashions beyond the imagining of earlier generations.

Games are nothing new, and neither are sports, but the organized leagues and teams of contemporary sports are a modern phenomenon. While often played just for fun and competition, sports and games tend to reflect the values of the people who are playing and watching. Some sports are typical of certain social groups or classes, and eschewed by others. While, in many places, sport is a unifying cultural element, it can also be divisive: the modern Olympics, based on the ancient Greek games, represent some of the best impulses of global sports—an international forum to bring together competitors from around the world (Document 2). On the other hand, Jackie Robinson's description (Document 3) of being the first African-American player in American major league baseball shows some of the ugliness of racial bigotry. Much earlier, in the eighteenth century, Benjamin Franklin wanted chess to show us the path to a moral life (Document 1), and he helped introduce this ancient game, which continues to be tremendously popular around the world, to the North American continent.

Another popular recreational activity is travel. More people travel for leisure now than ever before in history. Modern tourism's roots are found in the Grand Tour, an extended trip through Continental Europe for upper-class Englishmen and other Northern Europeans to complete their educations, although as the selections from James Boswell's letters (Document 5) indicate there was more than French food and Roman antiquities on the minds of some. Olaudah Equiano's account (Document 4) of his journey through Europe as a slave provides another perspective on travel. While travel has expanded dramatically and become easier and more popular, the nature of travel has changed. S. L. Bensusan (Document 6) relishes the increasingly difficult task of travel to a place where tourists do not go, while, as Deborah McLaren's selection points out (Document 7), travel and tourism has become so popular that some see it as a threat to ecological stability and the survival of local cultures.

People need not go far from home to enjoy music and dance, however, and these are other popular recreational activities. Music and dance can inspire and unite people, as the entries about the Omaha Corn Dance (Document 8) and the words to eighteenth-century political tunes (Document 9) indicate. At the same time, these activities can be shocking or taboo, as in a reviewer's description of a near-riot at the premiere of a Modernist ballet (Document 11) or Holland Weeks's implication (Document 10) of divine judgment for dancing at a ball.

Often these recreational activities can be connected to other facets of life: the religious implications of dance, the political use of music, and the economic consequences of sports are just a few examples. Whether for these reasons or simply for pleasure, listening to music, traveling to faraway places, or playing games are just some of the things that people do every day to relax and enjoy themselves. The modern world has continually created new and varied kinds of entertainments that have become part of recreational life.

Games and Sports

Throughout history, when people have leisure time, they have often played games. Some of the games of the modern period are similar to those from earlier periods, but, as in most aspects of modern life, new forms of games and sports have developed in response to changes in social structures, economic patterns, media and technology, and other influences.

One important change is the emergence of mass spectatorship. In fact, following games and sports either in person or by media has become a more popular pastime than actually playing them. Large audiences for sports events have made professional sports a possibility. Team sports, while not unique to the modern world, are also far more common today than they were before 1700. The result is the typical model of modern sport: professional team sports played with codified rules and organized leagues or associations have evolved or spread around the world, and clubs and teams representing institutions or geographic areas receive the loyalty of devoted fans. Successful players become celebrities, and events such as the World Cup in soccer or the Super Bowl in American football are significant cultural events.

No modern sporting event, however, rivals the Olympic Games. The modern revival of the Olympic Games, as described by the Games' founder Pierre de Coubertin (Document 2), was conceived as a forum for amateur athletics and a symbol of international cooperation and sporting competition. Billions of people worldwide focus every four years on the Olympic spectacle.

While the Olympics have generally been, as Pierre de Coubertin envisioned, a force for international unity and cooperation, games and sports can also reflect our divisions. When Jackie Robinson became the first African-American in American major league baseball in 1947, the event was a landmark in eradicating racial divisions in the United States, but his account of his reception in the Major Leagues (Document 3) also gives evidence of the depth of those divisions and the power of sport to bridge them.

Not all sports are team sports, and not all games are athletic. Board games, games of chance, card games, and computer games are played by millions and may require some combination of luck and mental skill, but minimal physical athleticism. Chess, for example, is a game popular the world over that occupies the mind. Not new to the modern age, it has remained popular. Benjamin Franklin was an avid chess player and his essay on the morals of the game (Document 1) implies that recreational activities can be instructive about other aspects of daily life. Chess may have been around for thousands of years, and the Olympics and baseball appear as if they will remain popular for the foreseeable future, but new forms of sports and games are constantly evolving, while others all but disappear. Few people play whist (an eighteenth- and nineteenth-century card game) anymore, and no one had ever tried snowboarding a generation ago. New or old, games and sports are undoubtedly part of modern life.

1. Benjamin Franklin: Chess, Morals, and Modern Life

Benjamin Franklin (1706–1790) is famous for many reasons; he is known as a politician and inventor, an educator and diplomat, a womanizer and wit. He was also, like many in his time and throughout the modern period, an avid chess player. Chess is not a modern game; it originated in India or China and had taken a form recognizable as modern chess in Persia *in the sixth century. Brought to Europe in the middle ages, the vizier became the queen, elephants became bishops, and chariots were rooks.*

Unlike many other games, it is relatively simple in its rules, offers profound complexity and virtually infinite variations, and involves no element of chance or luck. It inhabits culture from the children's whimsy of Lewis Carroll *and Harry* Potter *to the modernist iconoclasts* Marcel Duchamp *and Vladimir* Nabokov. *Matches had repercussions for international politics in the* Cold War. *In Franklin's day, a mechanical chess-playing automaton dressed as a Turk (actually a compelling illusion) fascinated the crowned heads of Europe, even beating* Napoleon, *while in recent years Garry* Kasparov's *matches against IBM's Deep Blue were front-page news around the world.*

Franklin's commentary expands the importance of chess beyond a merely amusing and compelling pastime to a game that can be a powerful metaphor for life. Chess, for Franklin, is to be taken seriously and the lessons it can teach are both important and worthwhile. He explains the relationship between chess and daily life, and the virtues it teaches—foresight, circumspection, and caution, but also hope and perseverance—and he also offers advice on how to play fairly in a social setting, with the same rules implicit for other social interactions.

The gamesmanship that Franklin decries is still a part of chess, however. While some players or commentators see chess as metaphorically violent or brutal, and many have despised and even tried to suppress the game, the practical and optimistic Franklin, in a view typical of the eighteenth century, sees in the game not a paradigm of battle, but a way to improve the individual and a means to create a more civil and rational society.

Whether or not one finds Franklin's morals persuasive, chess continues to be popular despite the changes since his time. While hundreds of other games have come and gone, chess has proven remarkably enduring—there are more people playing chess today than ever before in history. Far from being defeated by the computer age, tens of millions of games are played on the Internet each year and the ancient game of chess remains an integral part of everyday life.

THE MORALS OF CHESS

Playing at Chess, is the most ancient and universal game known among men; for its original is beyond the memory of history, and it has, for numberless ages, been the amusement of all the civilized nations of Asia, the Persians, the Indians, and the Chinese. Europe has had it above a thousand years; the Spaniards have spread it over their part of America, and it begins lately to make its appearance in these States. It is so interesting in itself, as not to need the view of gain to induce engaging in it; and thence it is never played for money. Those, therefore, who have leisure for such diversions, cannot find one that is more innocent; and the following piece, written with a view to correct (among a few young friends) some little improprieties in the practice of it, shews at the same time that it may, in its effects on the mind, be not merely innocent, but advantageous, to the vanquished as well as to the victor.

The Game of Chess is not merely an idle amusement; several very valuable qualities of the mind, useful in the course of human life, are to be acquired and strengthened by it, so as to become habits ready on all occasions; for life is a kind of Chess, in which we have often points to gain, and competitors or adversaries to contend with, and in which there is a vast variety of good and ill events, that are, in some degree, the effect of prudence, or the want of it. By playing at Chess then, we may learn:

1st: Foresight, which looks a little into futurity, and considers the consequences that may attend an action; for it is continually occurring to the player, "If I move this Piece, what will be the advantage or disadvantage of my new situation? What use can my adversary make of it to annoy me? What other moves can I make to support it, and to defend myself from his attacks?"

2nd: Circumspection, which surveys the whole Chess-board, or scene of action:—the relation of the several Pieces, and their situations; the dangers they are repeatedly exposed to; the several possibilities of their aiding each other; the probabilities that the adversary may make this or that move, and the attack this or that Piece; and what different means can be used to avoid his stroke, or turn its consequences against him.

3rd: Caution, not to make our moves too hastily. This habit is best acquired by observing strictly the laws of the game; such as, if you touch a piece you must move it somewhere; if you set it down, you must let it stand.

Therefore, it would be the better way to observe these rules, as the game becomes thereby more the image of human life, and particularly of war; in which if you have incautiously put yourself into a bad and dangerous position, you cannot obtain your enemy's leave to withdraw your troops, and place them more securely, but you must abide by all the consequences of your rashness.

And, lastly, we learn chess by the habit of not being discouraged by present bad appearances in the state of our affairs; the habit of hoping for a favourable chance, and that of preserving in the search of resources. The game is so full of events, there is such a variety of turns in it, the fortune of it is so subject to vicissitudes, and one so frequently, after contemplation, discovers the means of extricating one's self from a supposed insurmountable difficulty, that one is encouraged to continue the contest to the last, in hopes of victory from our skill; or, at least, from the negligence of our adversary: and whoever considers, what in Chess he often sees instances of, that success is apt to produce presumption and its consequent inattention, by which more is afterwards lost than was gained by the preceding advantage, while misfortunes produce more care and attention, by which the loss may be recovered, will learn not to be too much discouraged by any present successes of his adversary, nor to despair of final good fortune upon every little check he receives in the pursuit of it.

That we may therefore, be induced more frequently to choose this beneficial amusement in preference of others, which are not attended with the same advantages, every circumstance that may increase the pleasure of it should be regarded; and every action or word that is unfair, disrespectful, or that in any way may give uneasiness, should be avoided, as contrary to the immediate intention of both the parties, which is, to pass the time agreeably.

1st: Therefore, if it is agreed to play according to the strict rules, then those rules are to be strictly observed by both parties; and should not be insisted upon for one side, while deviated from by the other: for this is not equitable.

2nd: if it is agreed not to observe the rules exactly, but one party demands indulgences, he should then be as willing to allow them to the other.

3rd: No false move should ever be made to extricate yourself out of a difficulty, or to gain an advantage; for there can be no pleasure in playing with a man once detected in such unfair practice.

4th: If your adversary is long in playing, you ought not to hurry him, or express any uneasiness at his delay; not even by looking at your watch, or taking up a book to read: you should not sing, nor whistle, nor make a tapping with your feet on the floor, or with your fingers on the table, nor do anything that may distract his attention: for all these things displease, and they do not prove your skill in playing, but your craftiness and your rudeness.

5th: You ought not to endeavour to amuse and deceive your adversary by pretending to have made bad moves; and saying you have now lost the game, in order to make him secure and careless, and inattentive to your schemes; for this is fraud and deceit, not skill in the game of Chess.

6th: You must not, when you have gained a victory, use any triumphing or insulting expressions, nor show too much of the pleasure you feel; but endeavour to console your adversary, and make him less dissatisfied with himself by every kind and civil expression that may be used with truth; such as, you understand the game better than I, but you are a little inattentive, or, you play too fast; or, you had the best of the game, but something happened to divert your thoughts, and that turned it in my favour.

7th: If you are a spectator, while others play, observe the most perfect silence: for if you give advice, you offend both the parties: him against whom you give it, because it may cause him to lose the game: him in whose favour you give it, because, though it be good, and he follow it, he loses the pleasure he might have had, if you had permitted him to think till it occurred to himself. Even after a move or moves, you must not, by replacing the Pieces, show how they might have been placed better; for that displeases, and might occasion disputes or doubts about their true situation.

All talking to the players lessens or diverts their attention; and is, therefore, unpleasing; nor should you give the least hint to either party, by any kind of noise or motion; if you do, you are unworthy to be a spectator.

If you desire to exercise or show your judgment, do it in playing your own game, when you have an opportunity, not in criticizing or meddling with, or counseling the play of others.

Lastly, if the game is not to be played rigorously, according to the rules before mentioned, then moderate your desire of victory over your adversary, and be pleased with one over yourself.

Snatch not eagerly at every advantage offered by his unskillfulness or inattention; but point out to him kindly, that by such a move he places or leaves a Piece en prise unsupported; that by another, he will put his King into a dangerous situation, &c.

By this general civility (so opposite to the unfairness before forbidden) you may happen indeed to lose the game; but you will win what is better, his esteem, his respect, and his affection; together with the silent approbation and the good will of the spectators.

Source: Franklin, Benjamin. "The Morals of Chess." *Columbian Magazine*, 1786.

2. Pierre de Coubertin on the First Modern Olympics, 1896

The original Olympic Games were held in ancient Greece beginning in 776 B.C. *and running until the fourth century* A.D.*; their revival in the late nineteenth century has made them a staple of international sports for over 100 years. While the modern Olympics have become a tremendously successful institution, they do not compare with the ancient games, which lasted for over 1,200 years. The following selection by Pierre de Coubertin, a Frenchman who was instrumental in organizing the revival of the Olympic Games, describes the first modern games held in Athens in 1896.*

Many of the features he describes are still familiar around the world as important parts of the Olympics today, such as the opening and closing ceremonies, the bestowing of medals, and the absence of other prizes. The games also saw the inauguration of the Marathon. *Although there were only a few hundred athletes compared to today's thousands, it was the largest international sporting event ever held at the time, and has become a central part of global sports culture. Nonetheless, the Olympic Games have not been without controversy. The truly amateur nature of the athletes is more or less gone, various groups of nations have boycotted games for political purposes, and several games have been marred by ugly incidents, such as Adolph Hitler's racism at the 1936 Berlin games, the hostage crisis and death of Israeli athletes at Munich in 1972, and the persistent temptation of athletes to cheat by taking drugs.*

Overall, though, the ideal of a spirit of international friendship and competition has persisted, much like the vision of de Coubertin. From their origins in 1896, the modern Olympics have only grown. Women's events were added in 1900, and a separate winter Olympics were added in 1924. Today, hundreds of countries send thousands of athletes to games that are watched by billions; the modern Olympics are unquestionably an important part of sports in modern life.

The Olympic Games which recently took place at Athens were modern in character, not alone because of their programs, which substituted bicycles for chariot races, and fencing for the brutalities of pugilism, but because in their origin and regulations they were international and universal, and consequently adapted to the conditions in which athletics have developed at the present day. The ancient games had an exclusively Hellenic [Greek] character; they were always held in the same place, and Greek blood was a necessary condition of admission to them. It is true that strangers were in time tolerated; but their presence at Olympia was a tribute paid to the superiority of Greek civilization than a right exercise in the name of racial equality. With the modern games it is quite otherwise. Their creation is the work of "Barbarians." It is due to the delegates of the athletic associations of all countries assembled in Paris in 1894. It was there agreed that every county should celebrate the Olympic games in turn. The first place belonged by right to Greece; it was accorded by unanimous vote; and in order to emphasize the permanence of the institution, its wide bearings, and its essentially cosmopolitan character, an international committee was appointed, the members of which were to represent the various nations, European and American, with whom athletics are held in honor. The presidency of this committee falls to the country in which the next games are to be held. [. . .]

Easter Monday, April 6, the streets of Athens wore a look of extraordinary animation. All the public buildings were draped in bunting; multicolored streamers floated in the wind; green wreaths decked the house-fronts. Everywhere were the two letters "O.A.," the Greek initials of the Olympic games, and the two dates, B.C. 776, A.D. 1896, indicating their ancient past and their present renascence. At two o'clock in the afternoon the crowd began to throng the Stadion and to take possession of the seats. It was a joyous and motley concourse. The skirts and braided jackets of the palikars contrasted with the somber and ugly European habiliments. The women used large paper fans to shield them from the sun, parasols, which would have obstructed the view, being prohibited. The king and queen drove up a little before three o'clock, followed by Princess Marie, their daughter, and her fiancé, Grand Duke George of Russia.

An audience watching a fencing match during the original Olympic games in Greece, 1896. Library of Congress.

The crown prince, taking his stand in the arena, facing the king, then made a short speech, in which he touched upon the origin of the enterprise, and the obstacles surmounted in bringing it to fruition. Addressing the king, he asked him to proclaim the opening of the Olympic games, and king, rising, declared them opened. It was a thrilling moment. Fifteen hundred and two years before, the Emperor Theodosius had suppressed the Olympic games, thinking, no doubt, that in abolishing this hated survival of paganism he was furthering the cause of progress; and here was a Christian monarch, amid the applause of an assemblage composed almost exclusively of Christians, announcing the formal annulment of the imperial decree. [. . .]

The Greeks are novices in the matter of athletic sports, and had not looked for much success in their own country. One event only seemed likely to be theirs from its very nature—the long-distance run from Marathon. [. . .] A young peasant named Loues, from the village of Marousi, was the winner in two hours and fifty five minutes. He reached his goal fresh and in fine form. He was followed by two other Greeks. . . . When Loues came in to the Stadion, the crowd, which numbered sixty thousand persons, rose to its feet like one man, swayed by extraordinary excitement. [. . .]

Every night while the games were in progress the streets of Athens were illuminated. There were torch-light processions, bands played the different national hymns, and the students of the university got up ovations under the windows of the foreign athletic crews, and harangued them in the noble tongue of Demosthenes. [. . .]

There were nocturnal festivities on the Acropolis, where the Parthenon was illuminated with colored lights, and at the Piraeus, where the vessels were hung with Japanese lanterns. Unluckily, the weather changed, and the sea was so high on the day appointed for the boat-races, that the project was abandoned. The distribution of prizes was likewise postponed for twenty-four hours. It came off with much solemnity, on the morning of April 15, in the Stadion. The sun shone again, and sparkled on the officers' uniforms. [. . .]

The prizes were an olive branch from the very spot, at Olympia, where stood the ancient Altis, a diploma drawn by a Greek artist, and a silver medal . . . On one side of the medal is the Acropolis, with the Parthenon and the Propylaea; on the other a colossal head of the Olympian Zeus . . .

After the distribution of prizes, the athletes formed for the traditional procession around the Stadion. Loues, the victor of the Marathon, came first, bearing the Greek flag. Then the Americas, the Hungarians, the French, the Germans. The ceremony, moreover, was made more memorable by a charming incident. One of the contestants, Mr. Robertson, an Oxford student, recited an ode which he had composed, in ancient Greek and in the Pindaric mode, in honor of the games. Music had opened them, and Poetry was present at their close; and thus was the bond once more renewed which in the past united the muses with feats of physical strength, the mind with the well-trained body. [. . .]

Should the institution prosper,—as I am persuaded, all civilized nations aiding, that it will,—it may be a potent, if indirect factor in securing universal peace. Wars break out because nations misunderstand each other. We shall not have peace until the prejudices which now separate the individual races shall have been outlived. To attain this end, what better means than to bring the youth of all countries periodically together for amicable trials of muscular strength and agility? The Olympic games, with the ancients, controlled athletics and promoted peace. It is not visionary to look to them for similar benefactions in the future.

Source: Coubertin, Pierre de. "The Olympic Games of 1896." *The Century Magazine* 53:1 (November 1896).

3. *Race, Baseball, and Jackie Robinson*

Baseball was being played in the United States by the 1840s after being invented, according to legend, by Abner Doubleday *in 1839. As early as the 1870s, baseball was called America's* National Pastime *and was the most popular sport in the United States. In the modern era, baseball has played a central role in American society. Like team sports in many other places, American baseball served not only as an entertainment, but also as a means of identity, unifying people, and creating common experiences in a mass culture.*

However, baseball also divided. The racial segregation of baseball echoed the segregation of the United States, and the integration of baseball became a bellwether for the Civil Rights Movement and the end of institutional racial discrimination. Professional basketball and football had integrated earlier, but because of baseball's greater popularity and higher status in the national consciousness, it was a greater barrier.

Through the Second World War, major league baseball in the United States was played only by white men. Separate Negro Leagues *had been established for African-American players, who were not allowed to play with whites. That situation changed when Jackie Robinson took the field for the Brooklyn Dodgers against the Boston Braves in April, 1947. Jackie Robinson gave his own account of these events in his 1972 autobiography,* I Never Had It Made: The Jackie Robinson Story, *from which the following selection is taken.*

Although by nature a proud man who was always willing to stand up for his rights and his dignity, Robinson was unable to do so when he entered the major leagues. The non-violent resistance that Robinson demonstrated—not reacting to insults, threats, and even violence against him on and off the baseball field—anticipated the broader non-violent protests that gave so much power to the Civil Rights Movements in the 1950s and 1960s.

The breaking of the color barrier in major league baseball by Jackie Robinson was not only an event in sports, but an important event in the culture of everyday life in a racially segregated society. Of course, Robinson did not fully integrate baseball, nor did his play end racism or stop racial injustice. He succeeded brilliantly at baseball, and his success made possible important changes in sports and society. Some of the language in the following selection is strong, even objectionable, but Robinson was certainly called many names, and the story of how he was treated is inseparable from the story of sports and everyday life in the United States in the twentieth century.

"So there's more than just playing," he [Branch Rickey] said. "I wish it meant only hits, runs, and errors—only the things they put in the box score. Because you know—yes, you would know, Robinson, that a baseball box score is a democratic thing. It doesn't tell how big you are, what church you attend, what color you are, or how your father voted in the last election. It just tells what kind of baseball player you were on that particular day."

I interrupted. "But it's the box score that really counts—that and that alone, isn't it?"

"It's all that ought to count," he replied. "But it isn't. Maybe one of these days it will be all that counts. That is one of the reasons I've got you here, Robinson. If you're a good enough man, we can make this a start in the right direction. But let me tell you, it's going to take an awful lot of courage."

The next few minutes were tough. Branch Rickey had to make absolutely sure that I knew what I would face. Beanballs would be thrown at me. I would be called the

PRESENTATION OF A CHAMPION BAT TO THE "RED STOCKING" BASE-BALL CLUB, CINCINNATI, OHIO, ON ITS RETURN HOME.—[SKETCHED BY J. A. GERVIS.]

Members of the Red Stocking baseball team and distinguished guests standing around a "champion" baseball bat, 27 feet in length, presented to the team after amassing a 21–0 record, 1869. Library of Congress.

kind of names which would hurt and infuriate any man. I would be physically attacked. Could I take all of this and control my temper, remain steadfastly loyal to our ultimate aim? [. . .]

On the morning of April 9, 1947, just before an exhibition game, reporters in the press box received a single sheet of paper with a one-line announcement. It read: "Brooklyn announces the purchase of the contract of Jack Roosevelt Robinson from Montreal. Signed, Branch Rickey." [. . .]

Early in the season, the Philadelphia Phillies came to Ebbets Field for a three-game series. I was still in my slump and events of the opening game certainly didn't help. Starting to the plate in the first inning, I could scarcely believe my ears. Almost as if it had been synchronized by some master conductor, hate poured forth from the Phillies dugout.

"Hey, nigger, why don't you go back to the cotton field where you belong?"
"They're waiting for you in the jungles, black boy!"
"Hey, snowflake, which one of those white boys' wives are you dating tonight?"

"We don't want you here, nigger!"
"Go back to the bushes!"

Those insults and taunts were only samples of the torrent of abuse which poured out from the Phillies dugout that April day. I have to admit that this day of all the unpleasant days in my life, brought me nearer to cracking up than I ever had been.... I felt tortured and I tried just to play ball and ignore the insults. But it was really getting to me. What did the Phillies want from me? What, indeed, did Mr. Rickey expect of me? I was, after all, a human being. What was I doing here turning the other cheek as though I weren't a man?

Source: Robinson, Jackie, as told to Alfred Duckett, *"I Never Had It Made": The Jackie Robinson Story*. New York: G. P. Putnam's Sons, 1972.

Travel

Travel before the modern age was often difficult and only undertaken with a serious purpose. Reasons for travel might be emigration, war, trade, education, or religious pilgrimage. The idea of tourism, travel for amusement and recreation, is a modern idea, enhanced by the increasing ease and decreasing costs of travelling long distances. Not all modern travel is touristic, of course. Olaudah Equiano's story (Document 4) tells of his capture as a slave and then recounts his seeing Europe through African eyes. Although he later traveled widely to make a living, he also enjoyed the new experiences of travel. James Boswell (Document 5) was an Englishman of privilege in the eighteenth century, an era when many such young men were sent to complete their education by a trip to the European Continent. So popular was this route that it came to be known as the Grand Tour, and was nearly obligatory for young aristocrats, later followed by many from the middle classes, seeking similar educational and recreational benefits. The Grand Tour of the nineteenth century then might be rather like studying abroad or backpacking through Europe for modern students, many of whom follow the same routes and see the same sights as their eighteenth-century predecessors, although few travelers today hike or ride a donkey across the Alps anymore, the only way to do it in Boswell's day.

The sheer number of people traveling has made tourism a large industry. As tourism grew in popularity, responses to the consequences of tourism have emerged. S. L. Bensusan (Document 6) describes with pleasure the difficulties and isolation of his trip to Marrakesh, where there are no trains and no other tourists, and, consequently, no tourist industry or the perceived artifice that accompanies it. Another, more recent response to tourism is ecotourism, which focuses on visiting places with natural sights to see, rather than man-made or historical ones. Deborah McLaren's critique (Document 7) as well as *ecotourism* itself brings an awareness of the negative effects tourism can have on the ecology and the economies of tourists' destinations.

The effect of tourism's role in the daily lives of so many is much different than the relatively few young British gentlemen in the eighteenth century. From college kids with backpacks to retirees seeing the world in their golden years, travel has become an immensely popular hobby and part of everyday recreational life.

4. Olaudah Equiano: An African Point of View on Travel

Olaudah Equiano, also known as Gustavus Vassa, was born around 1745 in Africa, in what is present-day Nigeria. He was captured and sold into slavery as a child, but he avoided the harshness of life as a plantation slave in the Caribbean or British American colonies that was the fate of most slaves, instead laboring as a slave on British naval and commercial sailing ships. He eventually bought his freedom, became literate, and embarked on a career as a sailor, servant, explorer, merchant, and abolitionist. He also eventually became a Christian, married an Englishwoman, and wrote an autobiography, which proved very popular, especially in the English abolitionist movement.

Although included in this section on recreational life, Equiano's travels were not undertaken for strictly recreational purposes. His first travels were a result of being kidnapped and transported, barely surviving the Middle Passage, *on a slave ship bound for the Caribbean. After he was sold to a sea captain, he sailed where his masters sailed, and had no choice in the matter, even being taken into battle.*

Even after he purchased his freedom, travel for Equiano was employment, not recreation. Certainly he chose the life he did in part because he enjoyed the adventure, stimulation, risk of exploration, travel, and going to unknown places. Of course, that is part of the appeal of travel even today for tourists. For Equiano, though, the risks and adventures were considerably greater. He visited many places and nearly died any number of times, being shipwrecked, kidnapped, nearly frozen, and caught in a volcanic eruption—his adventures are too many to include them all here.

The following excerpt from his autobiography recounts several different parts of his life, from his first encounters with some European technology and customs, to his first sight of snow and to his impressions of Italy, all formed from a very different perspective than that of James Boswell, who toured Italy in the same period (see Document 5).

Some of Equiano's comments on his capture by slave traders seem calculated to appeal to the entirely white audience for the book. For example, one might wonder if he is playing on racial stereotypes as he describes his wonder at the magic of a sailing ship. Indeed, some scholars have questioned the authenticity of Equiano's story of his origins and account of the Middle Passage. *Regardless, the text is one of the earliest slave narratives and one of the few texts published by an African in the eighteenth century. Equiano's career of slavery, adventure, and travel offer interest and insight into the beginning of the modern period.*

The first object which saluted my eyes when I arrived on the coast was the sea, and a slave-ship, which was then riding at anchor, and waiting for its cargo. These filled me with astonishment, which was soon converted into terror, which I am yet at a loss to describe, nor the then feelings of my mind.... I was now persuaded that I had gotten into a world of bad spirits, and that they were going to kill me. Their complexions too differing so much from ours, their long hair, and the language they spoke, which was very different from any I had ever heard, united to confirm me in this belief. Indeed, such were the horrors of my views and fears at the moment, that, if ten thousand worlds had been my own, I would have freely parted with them all to have exchanged my condition with that of the meanest slave in my own country.

In a little time after, amongst the poor chained men, I found some of my own nation, which in a small degree gave ease to my mind. I inquired of these what was to be done with us? They gave me to understand we were to be carried to these white people's country to work for them. I then was a little revived, and thought, if it were no worse than working, my situation was not so desperate: but still I feared I should be put to death, the white people looked and acted, as I thought, in so savage a manner; for I had never seen among any people such instances of brutal cruelty; and this not only shewn towards us blacks, but also to some of the whites themselves. One white man in particular I saw, when we were permitted to be on deck, flogged so unmercifully with a large rope near the foremast, that he died in consequence of it; and they tossed him over the side as they would have done a brute. This made me fear these people the more; and I expected nothing less than to be treated in the same manner. I could not help expressing my fears and apprehensions to some of my countrymen: I asked them if these people had no country, but lived in this hollow place the ship? They told me they did not, but came from a distant one. "Then," said I, "How comes it in all our country we never heard of them?" They told me, because they lived so very far off. I then asked where were their women? Had they any like themselves! I was told they had: "And why," said I, "do we not see them?" They answered, because they were left behind. I asked how the vessel could go? they told me they could not tell; but that there were cloths put upon the masts by the help of the ropes I saw, and then the vessel went on; and the white men had some spell or magic they put in the water when they liked in order to stop the vessel. I was exceedingly amazed at this account, and really thought they were spirits. [. . .]

At last, when the ship we were in had got in all her cargo, they made ready with many fearful noises, and we were all put under deck, so that we could not see how they managed the vessel. But this disappointment was the least of my sorrow. The stench of the hold while we were on the coast was so intolerably loathsome, that it was dangerous to remain there for any time, and some of us had been permitted to stay on the deck for the fresh air; but now that the whole ship's cargo were confined together, it became absolutely pestilential. The closeness of the place, and the heat of the climate, added to the number in the ship, which was so crowded that each had scarcely room to turn himself, almost suffocated us. This produced copious perspirations, so that the air soon became unfit for respiration, from a variety of loathsome smells, and brought on a sickness among the slaves, of which many died, thus falling victims to the improvident avarice, as I may call it, of their purchasers. This wretched situation was again aggravated by the galling of the chains, now become insupportable; and the filth of the necessary tubs, into which

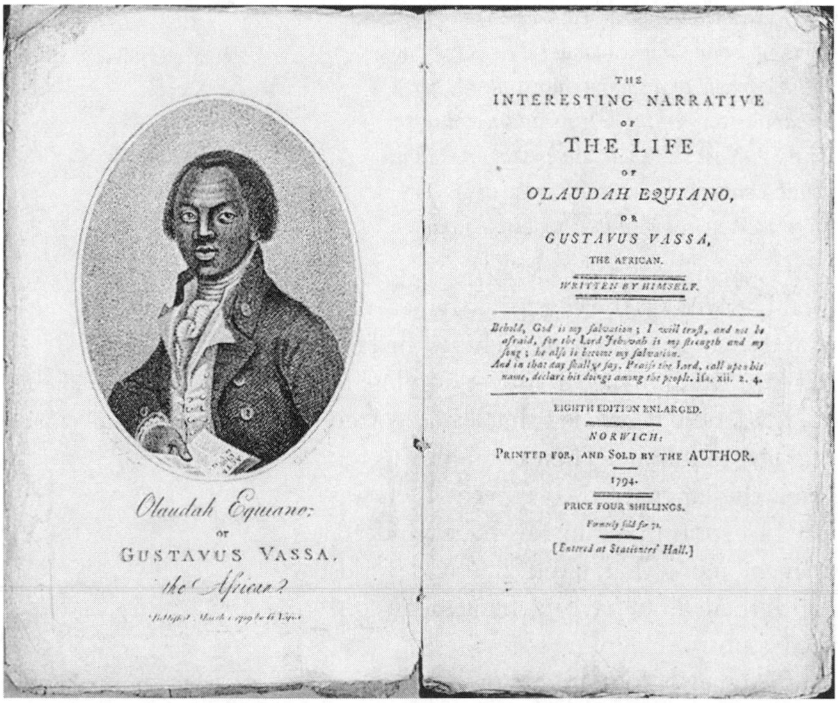

Frontispiece and title page from *The Interesting Narrative of the Life of Olaudah Equiano*, 1794. Courtesy Eon Images.

the children often fell, and were almost suffocated. The shrieks of the women, and the groans of the dying, rendered the whole a scene of horror almost inconceiveable.

It was about the beginning of the spring 1757 when I arrived in England, and I was near twelve years of age at that time. I was very much struck with the buildings and the pavement of the streets in Falmouth; and, indeed, any object I saw filled me with new surprise. One morning, when I got upon deck, I saw it covered all over with the snow that fell over-night: as I had never seen anything of the kind before, I thought it was salt; so I immediately ran down to the mate, and desired him, as well as I could, to come and see how somebody in the night had thrown salt all over the deck. He, knowing what it was, desired me to bring some of it down to him: accordingly I took up a handful of it, which I found very cold indeed; and when I brought it to him he desired me to taste it. I did so, and I was surprised beyond measure. I then asked him what it was? He told me it was snow: but I could not in any wise understand him. He asked me if we had no such thing in my country? and I told him, No. I then asked him the use of it, and who made it; he told me a great man in the heavens, called God: but here again I was to all intents and purposes at a loss to understand him; and the more so, when a little after I saw the air filled with it, in a heavy shower, which fell down on the same day. After this I went to church; and having never been at such a place before, I was again amazed at seeing and hearing the service. I asked all I could about it; and they gave me to understand it was worshipping God, who made us and all things. I was still at a great loss, and soon got into an endless field of inquiries, as well as I was able to speak and ask about things. . . . [I] was amazed at their not sacrificing, or making any offerings, and eating with unwashed hands, and touching the dead. I likewise could not help remarking the particular slenderness of their women, which I did not at first like; and I thought they were not so modest and shamefaced as the African women. [. . .]

I thought it best, therefore, to try the sea again in quest of more money, as I had been bred to it, and had hitherto found the profession of it successful. I had also a very great desire to see Turkey, and I now determined to gratify it. Accordingly, in the month of May, 1768, I told the Doctor of my wish to go to sea again, to which he made no opposition; and we parted on friendly terms. [. . .]

We sailed from England in July following, and our voyage was extremely pleasant. We went to Villa Franca, Nice, and Leghorn; and in all these places I was charmed with the richness and beauty of the countries, and struck with the elegant buildings with which they abound. We had always in them plenty of extraordinary good wines and rich fruits, which I was very fond of; and I had frequent occasions of gratifying both my taste and curiosity; for my captain always lodged on shore in those places,

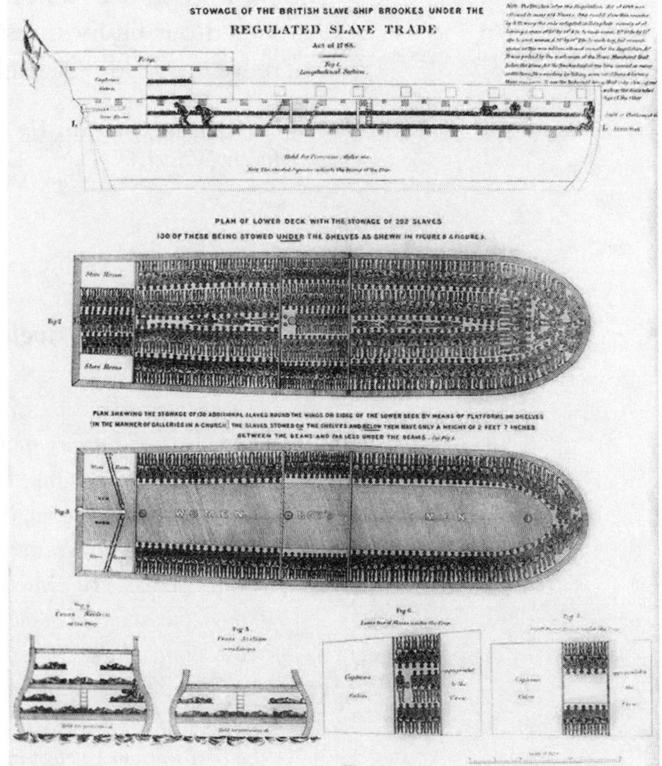

Stowage of the British slave ship *Brookes* under the Regulated Slave Trade Act of 1788. Plan shows that over 400 slaves could be transported by being closely packed on the lower deck of the ship. Courtesy of Eon Images.

which afforded me opportunities to see the country around. I also learned navigation of the mate, which I was very fond of. When we left Italy, we had delightful sailing among the Archipelago islands, and from thence to Smyrna in Turkey. This is a very ancient city; the houses are built of stone, and most of them have graves adjoining to them; so that they sometimes present the appearance of church-yards. Provisions are very plentiful in this city, and good wine less than a penny a pint. The grapes, pomegranates, and many other fruits, were also the richest and largest I ever saw or tasted. The natives are well-looking and strong made, and treated me always with great civility. [. . .]

Our next voyage was to the Mediterranean. The ship was again got ready, and we sailed in September for Genoa. This is one of the finest cities I ever saw; some of the edifices were of beautiful marble, and made a most noble appearance; and many had very curious fountains before them. The churches were rich and magnificent, and curiously adorned both in the inside and out. But all this grandeur was, in my eyes, disgraced by the galley-slaves, whose condition, both there and in other parts of Italy, is truly piteous and wretched. After we had staid there some weeks, during which we bought many different things we wanted, and got them very cheap, we sailed to Naples, a charming city, and remarkably clean. The bay is the most beautiful I ever saw; the moles for shipping are excellent. I thought it extraordinary to see grand operas acted here on Sunday nights, and even attended by their Majesties. While we remained here, there happened an eruption of Mount Vesuvius, of which I had a perfect view. It was extremely awful; and we were so near that the ashes from it used to be thick on our deck. After we had transacted our business at Naples, we sailed with a fair wind once more for Smyrna, where we arrived in December.

Source: Equiano, Olaudah. *The Interesting Narrative of the Life of Olaudah Equiano or Gustavus Vassa, the African, Written by Himself*. London, 1789.

5. *James Boswell: The Grand Tour in the Eighteenth Century*

Before the modern era, travel for the sake of education was uncommon. By the beginning of the eighteenth century, though, young men from England, other parts of northern Europe, and even from the United States, were being sent to Continental Europe on what came to be known as the Grand Tour, an extended trip that usually included France, Switzerland, Italy, and perhaps Germany and the Low Countries and that could last several months to several years. The Grand Tour was restricted by the expense of travel to only elites, although this changed in the nineteenth century as rail travel made tourism a rapidly growing recreational choice.

The following selection includes excerpts from the journals and letters to friends in England of James Boswell that were written during his stay in Rome in 1765. Boswell is one of the best-known English memoirists and travel writers of the eighteenth century. His letters and journals are known for their wit as well as their frank treatment of his sexual activities, an element that plays a part here.

On their journeys, those on the Grand Tour would complete their educations, refining their knowledge of Continental manners and customs, languages, and fashion; calling on the famous and elites of the places they visited; and touring the sights, which focused on the works of the Renaissance and classical antiquity in Italy. Boswell's case was not different; after visiting the French philosophes Voltaire and Jean-Jacques Rousseau, *he made his way to Italy, and his journal entries in Rome evidence his appreciation of the Eternal City's sights and the proper responses to the art and antiquities he was being shown. At the same time, his letter reveals that his activities were not limited to art and thus resulted in an outbreak of venereal disease. Whether punctuated by sexual misadventures or not, the Grand Tour is taken by many to be a direct predecessor of modern tourism, and stands at the beginning of a uniquely modern type of travel.*

Course in Antiquities and Arts in Rome, 1765.

MONDAY 25 MARCH. Mr. Morison, a Scottish antiquary, began to show me the most remarkable sights of Rome. We went out in the morning, as we intended to do every day.

[...] Then we went to the Capitoline hill. We climbed on the roof of the modern Senate, from which Mr. Morison pointed out ancient Rome on its seven hills. He showed me a little map of it, and read me a clear summary of the growth of this famous city to its present extent.

TUESDAY 26 MARCH. We viewed the celebrated Forum. I experienced sublime and melancholy emotions as I thought of all the great affairs which had taken place there, and saw the place now all it ruins, with the wretched huts of carpenters and other artisans occupying the site of that rostrum from which Cicero had flung forth stunning eloquence. I saw there the remains of the magnificent portico that once adorned the Forum, whose three remaining column give us a superb idea of what it was.... We entered the former Colosseum, which certainly presents a vast and sublime idea of the grandeur of the ancient Romans. It is hard to tell whether the astonishing massiveness or the exquisite taste of this superb building should be more admired. A hermit has a little apartment inside. We passed through his hermitage to climb to where the seats and corridors of the theatre once were; Mr. Morison gave me a clear picture of all this. It was shocking to discover several portions of this theatre full of dung. It is rented to people who use it in this fashion.

WEDNESDAY 27 MARCH. We went out in the afternoon.... We climbed the Palatine hill, where the magnificent Palace of the emperors stood. Since it has suffered many changes, we must believe that the ruins we now see date from the time of Domitian.... We much classical gaiety enjoyed, notwithstanding of our direct opposition of sentiment on every important subject. He is an exception to all general rules, and his constant felicity shakes my solid speculations on human woe. He has an elasticity of mind that nothing can crush.

...

[Letter from Boswell to John Johnston]

Monigo, 19 July 1765

MY DEAR JOHNSTON... I intended to have left Rome before the middle of May, but I formed a great intimacy with Lord Mountstuart, who kept me on from week to week and at last insisted with me to accompany him in the rest of his tour of Italy. He removed the objections which I made on my father's account by assuring me that he

Piranesi, Giovanni Battista, *Veduta di Roma: The Colosseum*, eighteenth century. Bildarchiv Preussischer Kulturbesitz / Art Resource, NY.

would take care to have my conduct represented to him in such a manner that instead of being offended he should be highly satisfied with me. You may be sure this made me very happy, and on the fourteenth of June I set out with pride and pleasure as the distinguished friend of an amiable young nobleman, son to the favourite of our Sovereign. I promised myself a sure interest for life, and I felt my heart warm with affection to a branch of the royal house of Stuart. [. . .]

We are now at his seat in the country, where fine air, regular living, and moderate amusement keep us in a state like what you have proved in your simple summer days at Shaw. This is a new strong proof to me that a man ought never to despair; for after all my tossings in the variety of life, after all my dismal days of horrid gloom, I am now clear as when my mind was rural, young, and undisturbed except one day in seven. And yet, Johnston, I have reason to be unhappy, for my conduct of late has not been that of a sage. At Rome I ran about among the prostitutes till I was interrupted by that distemper which scourges vice in this world. When I got to Venice I had still some small remains of disease, but strange, gay ideas which I had formed of the Venetian courtesans turned my head, and away I went to an opera dancer and took Lord Mountstuart with me. We both had her; and we both found ourselves taken in for the punishment which I had met with at Rome. Pretty doings! Our evil has been recompensed but moderately but we are as much to blame as if we had suffered most sadly. I have blamed myself so much, and repented so sincerely, that I am now no more distressed. Besides I do assure you the climate of Italy affects me much. It inflamed my hot desires, and now it keeps my blood so warm that I have all day long such spirits as a man has after having taken a cheerful glass....

I leave this in a day or two, and after going with my Lord as far as Verona, I shall separate from him and go to Parma, where I have an amiable French acquaintance, a man of knowledge and taste and sensibility to whom I was recommended by M. Rousseau. I may perhaps [spend] a little time at the Court of Parma and then go straight to Florence, and after seeing the curiosities there, jaunt through the rest of Tuscany, embark at Leghorn and sail to Genoa, where I shall embark for France. You must know I (have) been longer in Italy than my father intended and have spent £440 since the month of January. I hope my worthy father will not be uneasy; for I am determined (to) do what he inclines as far as may lie in my power.

I think, Johnston, you have here a pretty full account of me. Let me add that my regard and affection for you is just as when we walked upon Arthur Seat, and that I will convince you of when we meet. I am uneasy to think that I am not yet master of myself, but I always hope to be better. Remember me kindly to all friends, and pray write soon. Adieu, my dear friend. I am ever yours,

James Boswell.

Source: Boswell, James. *Boswell on the Grand Tour: Italy, Corsica and France, 1765–1766*. Edited by Frank Brady and Frederick A. Pottle. New York: McGraw Hill, 1955. Quoted by permission of the Editorial Committee of the Yale Editions of the Private Papers of James Boswell.

6. On the Road to Marrakesh

Driven in large part by the spread of railroads and steamships, the number of people who could manage the lowered cost, reduced time, and decreased difficulties of recreational travel grew tremendously, and the tourist industry developed in the nineteenth century to provide transportation, accommodations, and other services to the masses of new tourists.

The growth of tourism made some feel as though travel had been deprived of some of its adventure. S. L. Bensusan is among these. Writing at the turn of the twentieth century, Bensusan describes the lure of getting to someplace exotic and special, away from other tourists with their guidebooks and photographic equipment. He laments the typical seeing of standard sights, which he claims results in really seeing very little. Whether his disdain for the typical tourist is justified or not, what his commentary makes clear is that tourism was becoming a sufficiently popular pastime and industry to be criticized for its scale.

Of course, Bensusan remains a tourist, even if he chooses to ride a mule to Marrakesh instead of taking a train to someplace more popular. Although he mentions the trash and the dirt, his impressions are sentimental and decidedly those of a tourist; he mentions the major sites and some local color, although it remains quite clear that his experience there is one of a stranger, and his understanding of the culture of the Maghreb is limited.

His motivations, however, are still alive and well today, and though the typical tourist has a guidebook uploaded to her Blackberry and a digital camera with built-in Global Positioning System, the impulse to see what others have not seen, to go where others cannot or will not go, to do what others have not done, still stimulates many travelers.

IN RED MARRAKESH

There are certain cities that cannot be approached for the first time by any sympathetic traveler without a sense of solemnity and reverence that is not far removed from awe. Athens, Rome, Constantinople, Damascus, and Jerusalem may be cited as examples; each in its turn has filled me with great wonder and deep joy. But all of these are to be reached nowadays by the railway, that great modern purge of sensibility. Even Jerusalem is not exempt. A single line stretches from Jaffa by the sea to the very gates of the Holy City, playing hide-and-seek among the mountains of Judea by the way, because the Turk was too poor to tunnel a direct path.

In Morocco, on the other hand, the railway is still unknown. He who seeks any of the country's inland cities must take horse or mule, camel or donkey, or, as a last resource, be content with a staff to aid him, and walk. Whether he fare to Fez, the city of Mulan Idrees, in which an old writer assures us, "all the beauties of the earth are united"; or to Mequinez, where great Mulai Ismail kept a stream of human blood flowing constantly from his palace that all might know he ruled; or to Red Marrakesh, which Yusuf ibn Tachfin built nine hundred years ago,—his own exertion must convoy him. There must be days and nights of scant fare and small comfort, with all those hundred and one happenings of the road that make for pleasant memories. So far as I have been able to gather in the nine years that have passed since I first visited Morocco, one road is like another road, unless you have the Moghrebbin Arabic at your command and can go off the beaten track in Moorish dress....

For the rank and file of us the Government roads and the harmless necessary soldier must suffice, until the Gordian knot of Morocco's future has been untied or cut. Then perhaps, as a result of French pacific penetration, flying railway trains loaded with tourists, guide-book in hand and camera at the ready, will pierce the secret places of the land, and men will speak of "doing" Morocco, as they "do" other countries in their rush across the world, seeing all the stereotyped sights and appreciating none. For the present, by Allah's grace, matters are quite otherwise.

Marrakesh unfolded its beauties to us slowly and one by one as we pushed horses and mules into a canter over the level plains of Hillreeli. Forests of date-palm took definite shape; certain mosques, those of Sidi ben Yusuf and Bab Dukala, stood out clearly before us without the aid of glasses, but the Library mosque dominated the landscape by reason of the Kutubia tower by its side. The Atlas Mountains came out of the clouds and revealed the snows that would soon melt and set every southern river aflood, and then the town began to show limits to the east and west where, at first, there was nothing but haze....

I had little thought to spare for such matters as we rode into Marrakesh for the first time. The spell of the city was overmastering. It is certainly the most African city in Morocco to-day, almost the last survivor of the changes that began in the latter half of the nineteenth century, and have brought the Dark Continent from end to end within the sphere of European influence. Fez and Mequinez are cities of fair men, while here on every side one recognized the influence of the Soudan and the country beyond the great desert. Not only have the wives and concubines brought from beyond the great sand sea darkened the skin of the present generation of the Marrakshis, but they have given to most if not all a suggestion of relationship to the Negro races that is not to be seen in any other Moorish city I have visited. It is not a suggestion of fanaticism or intolerance. By the action as well as their appearance one knew most of the passers for friends rather than enemies. They would gratify their curiosity at our expense as we gratified ours at theirs, convinced that all Europeans are harmless, uncivilized folk from a far land, where people smoke tobacco, drink wine, suffer their women-folk to go unveiled, and live without the True Faith....

ROUND ABOUT MARRAKESH

The charm of Marrakesh comes slowly to the traveler, but it stays with him always, and colours his impressions of such other cities as may attract his wandering footsteps. So soon as he has left the plains behind on his way to the coast, the town's defects are relegated to the background of the picture his memory paints. He forgets the dirty lanes that serve for roads, the heaps of refuse at every corner, the pariah curs that howled or snapped at his horse's heels when he rode abroad, the roughness and discomfort of the accommodation, the poverty and disease that everywhere went hand in hand around him.

But he remembers and always will remember the city in its picturesque aspects. How can he forget Moorish hospitality, so lavishly exercised in patios where the hands of architect and gardener meet—those delightful gatherings of friends whose surroundings are recalled when he sees, even in the world of the West—

Groups under the dreaming garden trees,
And the full moon, and the white evening star.

He will never forget the Kutubia tower flanking the mosque of the Library, with its three glittering balls that are solid gold, if you care to believe the Moors (and who should know better!), though the European authorities declare they are but gilded copper. He will hear, across all intervening sea and lands, the sonorous voices of the three blind mueddins who call True Believers to prayer from the adjacent minarets.

Source: Bensusan, S. L. *Morocco*. Painted by A. S. Forrest. London: Adam and Charles Black, 1904.

7. *Ecology Meets Tourism*

With the growth of interest in environmentalism and consciousness of the Earth's finite resources, a new variety of travel emerged in the late twentieth century: ecotourism, *or tourism that has as its object not the usual sights and cities and ruins, but sites of ecological importance, such as coral reefs, rain forests, and the like. Of course, these types of tourism, as all others, have an impact on the places where increasingly large numbers of persons want to go. Even though many poorer countries see clear economic benefits from comparatively wealthy foreigners visiting—and spending their money—and are eager to encourage tourism, either ecotourism or the more traditional types, success often brings unintended consequences.*

In the following excerpt, Deborah McLaren does not target the ecotourist; her main objections are to the tourism industry and the underlying cultural structures that allow and even promote tourism that, in developing tourist destinations and services, does not act responsibly toward local economies, indigenous groups and cultures, and environmental conditions.

Growing out of her own experiences as a tourist, McLaren's position reflects a re-examination by some of the assumptions about travel and recreation in the late twentieth century. McLaren argues that ecotourism reflects an interest in nature that is not met by contemporary daily life, so many travelers have shifted tourism priorities to outdoors and nature-oriented activities. However, travelers' interest is not just in nature. Earlier in the modern period, tourists were not especially concerned about the social and environmental impact of their tourism. For McLaren and those who share her view, tourism has significant consequences in many other areas: ecology, economics, anthropology, even geopolitics. She calls for a change that will preserve indigenous and local cultures and values, enhance local ecological stability, and provide sustainable economic models, without preventing travel itself. The agenda is ambitious, but whether or not one agrees with her re-evaluation of touristic priorities, McLaren's ecotourist is a new kind of traveler with a new set of sensibilities for the modern age.

My participation as a tourist propelled me into a process of critical analysis and a conscious effort to support change within the tourism industry. From this perspective, my goal is to demonstrate how traditional tourism, especially in countries in the global South (so-called developing countries in the Southern Hemisphere), basically follows a consumption-oriented Western model. The overwhelming growth of tourism has been destructive to both ecology and people in host countries. [...]

A desperate need exists for information and tools to create change. I've learned to look past immediate tourism issues for root causes—to world economics, the media and technologies, development models, corporate control, the continuation of colonization, racism, and other forms of injustice. My exploration of tourism issues has been difficult, alarming, and wonderful and has led me to look for ways to change, challenge, and sometimes completely denounce the industry. [...]

Tourism is inherently about our earth. Vacations at lakeside camps, at ski resorts, and in national parks reflect the need for human beings to spend time in nature. The global tourism industry obviously has an enormous impact on the environment and in most cases sells nature as part of the tourist product. We cannot simply buy into the eco-jargon. What we need is an overview of tourism that acknowledges that "green" travel, or ecotravel, is a mere part of the larger impact of the industry and that we urgently need to look at the broad issues related to tourism's impacts upon the earth.

Traditional tourism is experiencing increasing resistance. Some of it has simply been to "greenwash" tourism and promote it as a sustainable development strategy or as "cultural heritage" that enshrines past culture and negates current culture. Since the 1970s, however, local people have joined with ecumenical groups, Indigenous Peoples, women's groups, grassroots groups, environmentalists, and even tourists to challenge and denounce the negative impacts of global tourism and seek alternatives in an international "responsible tourism" movement. Growing numbers of organizations outside of but reliant upon the travel industry are also rethinking their roles in tourism and creating strategies for change. Some of these groups are organizing solidarity tours to pressure governments and support each other at the grassroots level; others are linking with each other on social justice issues.

Thousands of communities around the world are attempting some form of tourism development. Many people in communities where abrupt transformations are taking place have little information about the forces changing their lives. What is apparent, though, is that most of these communities are going through almost entirely the same process: fairly well-defined cycles of expectation and disappointment. Yet tourism continues to grow haphazardly, often to the detriment of local people, communities, and the environment, with little long-term, integrated planning.

The effects of travel and tourism development are usually studied in bits and pieces. For instance, environmentalists typically scrutinize the negative effects of tourism development upon natural resources and focus primarily on conservation issues. Economists concentrate upon business, employment, trade, and financial issues. Anthropologists document changing tribal cultures, some on the verge of vanishing. In the United States, we tend to study the global South as a separate entity, although we have recently come to learn that its survival is directly tied to the survival of the industrialized nations of the North. We must begin to explore the overlapping issues of tourism development and its effects upon the earth and society through a more integrated approach. Tourists are becoming increasingly concerned about the impact of their travel and the control of the giant tourism industry, and they are looking for information and tools to assist them in becoming more responsible travelers and bringing about change within the industry.

But should we work to change tourism, or should we stop traveling altogether? Concepts for alternative tourism as well as for alternatives to tourism reflect the growing awareness of the importance of cultural preservation, ecological protection, and decentralized political and economic decision making. These factors are critical, especially as the era of exploitive free trade and globalization of the economy intensifies. In the struggle to return control of tourism to the local community, we must increasingly scrutinize our motives for traveling, decide whether we have the "right" as consumers to buy other cultures and environments, and support responsible tourism. We must analyze "green" strategies such as ecotourism and sustainable tourism to determine whether we are simply being "greenwashed." In an age when the media dominates and shapes our views of the world, we must utilize tourism as a means to communicate with one another. In fact, we have no better way to understand the global crisis that we face than through people-to-people communication. Through firsthand, one-on-one meetings with people we encounter in our travels, we discover universal themes of human culture. We become more aware that no matter where we live, we are all confronting similar situations. Even nature travel is in many ways a reconnection between post-industrialized society and Mother Earth.

The issue of growth in the travel industry—how much, how fast, what kind—is crucial to the future of communities, local lifestyles and cultures, and the natural environment. A variety of instabilities and inequities are associated with the expansion of tourism. If the social costs of infinite growth (human consequences of ecological pollution, centralized concentration of power, inequitable income distribution) are as high as they appear to be, our current social systems cannot support such growth indefinitely. Tourism remains a passive luxury for thousands of travelers. This situation must change. [. . .]

Where will tourists be traveling in the next century? Will there be any places left to "discover"? Or will our search for unspoiled environments and cultures be in vain, as they become replaced by manufactured cultures on reconstructed islands of paradise? If the megamall, theme park, and cruise ship are any indication of our future, "super-tourists," who can afford it, may pay to visit the last pristine places on the planet, to view the history of the Indigenous Peoples and organic agriculture, admire what used to be rain forests, and watch "virtual" cultural entertainment. Perhaps they will visit private, enclosed biospheres or even the moon. Of course, there will be plenty of souvenirs for them to buy.

Source: McLaren, Deborah. *Rethinking Tourism and Ecotravel.* Bloomfield, CT: Kumarian Press, 2003. Used with permission.

Music and Dance

Music and dance are popular recreational activities. In the age of mp3 players and digital downloads, it is easy to forget that before the modern era, music was most often made by people who wanted to hear it, and could not be recorded or preserved. When people wanted music, they made it, just as when people wanted to dance, they danced. The ability of music and dance to inspire and entertain, to convince and to celebrate, to attract and to unify, has been used for many reasons in the modern era. Not all groups in the modern world see music and dance as simply a pastime. For some, such as the Omaha (Document 8), dance is a sacred activity that celebrates life and encourages the divine world to look favorably on the dancers. On the other hand, some groups refuse to dance or condemn dancing, as Holland Weeks does in his letter (Document 10) to his siblings, telling them of a young girl who is dying after dancing at a ball.

Not all music and dancing have religious connotations, of course. Music and dance can also be more deliberately aesthetic, as in ballet or symphonic music, or sometimes they have a political dimension, or other underlying purposes as well. The eighteenth-century songs from France and Ireland (Document 9) are expressions of political sentiment as well as entertaining tunes. The music and dance of the early twentieth century ballet *Le Sacre du Printemps* proved to be so radical and, though deeply influential on twentieth century performing arts, provoked a shocked response from the audience (Document 11). This shouldn't be surprising. While the forms and styles of music and dance have changed, and the ease with which they are enjoyed is greater, the power of music and dance to move us remains evident from religion, to politics, to youthful rebellion. Music and dance are a part of everyday modern life.

8. *Descriptions of Native American Dances*

Corn was an important staple crop for Native Americans from Canada into Mexico. The rituals performed for a good harvest, described in part by the songs and dances described here, come from several North American tribes, including the Omaha and Pawnee of the plains, and the Osage, who had been pushed westward into the plains from the Ohio and Mississippi valleys by the expansion of the United States. These groups engaged both in hunting and agriculture. Even into the beginning of the modern period, agriculture was intensive labor without a sure reward. The consequences of failure could mean privation. This was of course true not only of Native American agriculture, but of virtually all agriculture before modern techniques and transportation systems made for higher yields with less labor and the ability to move large amounts of food to areas with poor harvests from those with better ones.

The following descriptions were written by Alice Fletcher from her own late nineteenth- and early twentieth-century observations of Native American dances, then adapted for use by children's groups to perform. While today the re-enacting of sacred dances of Native American tribes by groups of children might be seen by some as disrespectful, the text still gives an effective description of the detailed actions and words of Native American music and dance.

While for some recreating the dances might be a summer-camp amusement, dances such as the corn dance are more than simply recreation. They are part of sacred rituals performed to assure the success of crops, on which the very lives of the performers might depend. At the same time, they were no doubt fun for the original dancers, providing a way for the community to come together and celebrate a new growing season. They are serious music and dance, but beautiful to behold, even if the outside observer does not understand the full ritual significance of the actions, and all the more so for the original participants who would see the significance of each movement, gesture, and word. They were an important part of the everyday life of the tribes who performed them.

THE LIFE OF THE CORN
A DRAMA
IN
FIVE DANCES

INTRODUCTION.—These Dances in their purport and music are taken from the sacred rituals of the Omaha, the Osage and the Pawnee tribes. The richness and beauty of symbolism in the original language suffer a loss of native naivete in their English interpretation.

Among the Omaha tribe when the time came for planting, four kernels from a red ear of corn were given to each family by the keeper of this sacred rite. These four red kernels were mixed with the ordinary seed corn, that it might be vivified by them and made to yield an ample harvest. Red is the symbolic color of life. In this ceremony is preserved a trace of the far-away time when all the precious seed corn was in the care of priestly keepers. The ceremony of giving out the four red kernels served to turn the thoughts of the people from a dependence solely on their own labor in cultivating corn to the life-giving power of Wakon'da dwelling within the maize.

In the Omaha Ritual Song of twenty-six stanzas which preceded the distribution of the four red kernels, the Corn speaks. It tells of its roots reaching in the four directions (where dwell the messengers that bring life), of the growth of its jointed stalk, of the unfolding of its leaves, of the changing color of the silk and of the tassel, of the ripening of the fruit, of the bidding of the people to come, to pluck and to eat.

The music of this Ritual Song is simple. It is here given with a very brief paraphrase of the words of the Ritual Song.

DANCE I

INTRODUCTORY Note.—This ceremonial dance touches upon the mystery of the giving of life that life may be maintained; an exchange that links together the different forms of life and enhances the joy of living.

Properties.—Thin green mantles; yellow plumes like the corn tassel; bone clips; as many of these articles as there are dancers.

Directions.—This dance belongs to both sexes and a number of each should take part, if that is possible. Should there be trees near the open space where the dance takes place, one-half of the dancers, closely wrapped in their green mantles, should be grouped at one side among the trees and the other half similarly placed at the other side. In the center of the space a single dancer stands facing the rear, wrapped about the head and body with the green mantle, leaving only the face exposed.

All being in readiness, the central figure turns slowly, lifts a draped arm and says slowly and impressively:

"Harken! The Corn speaks!"

The group of dancers on the right then sing softly the first line only of the Ritual Song in which the Corn speaks. The group of dancers on the left repeat the same line like an echo of the first group. Both groups of dancers now begin to move slowly and in rhythm with the following song toward the figure standing in the center of the space, singing, as they move, the Ritual Song from the beginning:

Ritual Song No. 1

Fourfold deep lie my roots within the land;
Clad in green, bearing fruit, Lo! here I stand!
Pluck and eat, life for life, behold, I give!
Shout with joy, dance and sing with all that live.

At the words "Lo! here I stand!" the company of dancers should all be standing in a semi-circle. As the words in the third line, "Behold, I give!" are sung, the draped arms should be slightly extended forward as in a presentation. The fourth line requires some dramatic action, but it should be restrained rather than free. The arms, still draped with the green mantles, should be raised a little as the words "Shout with joy" are sung, and

San Buenaventura's Day Corn Dance, performed by the two moieties, first the Turquoise, then the Pumpkin, in front of the church and campo santo. Two of the three Koshare clowns who were present can be seen just in front of the chorus. Library of Congress.

during the singing of the remainder of the line swayed from side to side in rhythm with the song, always with a reserve in the movements, because of the mystery mentioned in the words of the song, that life is maintained by the giving of life. A pause of about two beats should follow this Ritual Song.

As "Ho-o! Ho-o!" the opening of the next song, is given, every dancer should suddenly turn half-way round, give a movement of the head such as would cause the mantle to fall back and leave the head with the corn tassel exposed; the ends of the mantle should be gathered in the hands so that the mantle can wave with the dance as the following song is sung:

Song No. 2

Ho-o! Ho-o!
Dance we singing,
Promise bringing
Of the wealth of summer fair;
Hearts beat lightly,
Skies shine brightly,
Youth and Hope are ev'rywhere.
Refrain: Ho-o! Ho-o! Ho! Ho! Ho!

As each "Ho-o!" of the refrain is sung, the dancers should whirl like merry sprites, twine and untwine their green mantles about their forms until the song begins again. Then they should all skip off with springing, rhythmic steps in open Indian file, letting their mantles float and wave about them as they wind in and out over the camp ground carrying "Youth and Hope ev'rywhere." Every time the refrain is reached, the dancers should stop and whirl, then as the song begins again move off in line, dancing as before. When they are ready to stop (that can only be done during the singing and whirling of the refrain), each dancer should whirl from the line and keep up that movement, singing "Ho!" until his or her tent is reached.

Source: Fletcher, Alice C. *Indian Games and Dances with Native Songs: Arranged from American Indian Ceremonials and Sports*. New York: C. C. Birchard and Co., 1915.

9. Political Music: "The Marseillaise" and "The Wearin' O' the Green"

The two songs in this selection are both from the eighteenth century and originate in important political movements. The Marseillaise *was the marching song of volunteers from the southern French city of Marseille, who marched to Paris in 1792 to support the* French Revolution. *Although banned at various points in French history because of its revolutionary content, it is the national anthem of France today (although the lyrics were later officially changed to something less overtly bloody). The song has a stirring, martial marching melody, and it shows how music can be turned to political ends. The translation of the lyrics given here is not precisely literal, and it is designed to fit the music, rather than be a word-for-word meaning. For example, the original uses the words "citoyens," for citizens, which contrasted after the French Revolution with the population's previous status as "subjects" of the king. The refrain actually speaks of watering the fields with the enemies' "impure blood," but it was, after all, a battle song.*

The Wearin' O' the Green *is another popular eighteenth-century political tune that originated in Ireland. Political (and religious) connotations to colors are still popular even today in Ireland and elsewhere. In Ireland, orange is associated with Protestantism and English rule, and green is the color of Catholicism and Irish independence. In the late eighteenth century, when Ireland was under English rule, a movement to lift the restrictions on Irish Catholics, which included laws prohibiting Catholics from owning land, operating schools, or serving as a lawyer, juror, soldier, or in any public office, took the Shamrock as its token. (See* Roman Catholic Church *in the Glossary.)*

Influenced by and allied with the French Revolutionary government, whose anthem was The Marseillaise, *they shifted into a non-sectarian liberal revolutionary party intent on establishing a free Irish state on the French model. Following an unsuccessful rebellion in 1798, wearing a shamrock, a revolutionary insignia, became a crime punishable by hanging, and the song reflects the rhetoric both of political liberation and emergent nationalism. Sectarian (that is based on a religious sect) violence rather than simply separatist (interested in separating Ireland from the British crown, regardless of faith) violence followed the failure of the rebellion through most of the nineteenth century. As a note, James Napper Tandy was an Irish rebel leader in exile after 1798, and* caubeen *is an Irish Gaelic word for a traditional peasant hat resembling a beret.*

The Marseillaise (1792) by Claude Joseph Rouget de Lisle

Ye sons of freedom, wake to glory!
Hark! hark! what myriads bid you rise!
Your children, wives, and grandsires hoary
Behold their tears and hear their cries!
Shall hateful tyrants, mischief breeding,
With hireling hosts, a ruffian band,
Affright and desolate the land.
While peace and liberty lie bleeding?
To arms! to arms! ye brave!
The avenging sword unsheathe;
March on! march on! all hearts resolved
On victory or death.

Now, now the dangerous storm is rolling,
Which treacherous kings confederate raise;
The dogs of war, let loose, are howling.
And lo! our walls and cities blaze;
And shall we basely view the ruin,
While lawless force with guilty stride,
Spreads desolation far and wide.
With crime and blood his hands imbruing.
To arms! to arms! ye brave!
The avenging sword unsheathe;
March on! march on! all hearts resolved
On victory or death.

With luxury and pride surrounded,
The vile insatiate despots dare,
Their thirst of gold and power unbounded,
To mete and vend the light and air!
Like beasts of burden they would lead us,
Like gods, would bid their slaves adore;
But man is man, and who is more?
Then shall they longer lash and goad us?
To arms! to arms! ye brave!
The avenging sword unsheathe;
March on! march on! all hearts resolved
On victory or death.

O Liberty! can man resign thee,
Once having felt thy generous flame?
Can dungeons, bolts, or bars confine thee,
Or whips thy noble spirit tame?
Too long the world has wept, bewailing
That falsehood's dagger tyrants wield,
But freedom is our sword and shield,
And all their arts are unavailing.
To arms! to arms! ye brave!
The avenging sword unsheathe;
March on! march on! all hearts resolved
On victory or death.

The Wearin' O' the Green (1798)

Oh, Paddy dear! an' did ye hear the news that's goin' round?
The shamrock is by law forbid to grow on Irish ground!
No more St. Patrick's Day we'll keep, his color can't be seen,
For there's a cruel law agin' the wearin' o' the green!
I met with Napper Tandy, and he took me by the hand,
And he said, "How's poor Ould Ireland, and how does she stand?"
She's the most disthressful country that iver yet was seen,
For they're hangin' men and women there for wearin' o' the green.

An' if the color we must wear is England's cruel red,
Let it remind us of the blood that Ireland has shed;
Then pull the shamrock from your hat, and throw it on the sod,—
And never fear, 'twill take root there, tho' under foot 'tis trod!
When law can stop the blades of grass from growin' as they grow,
And when the leaves in summer-time their color dare not show,
Then I will change the color, too, I wear in my caubeen,
But till that day, plaze God, I'll stick to wearin' o' the green.

Source: Tappan, Eva March, ed. *The World's Story: A History of the World in Story Song and Art*. Volume 5: *Italy, France, Spain and Portugal* and Volume 10: *England, Scotland, Ireland and Wales*. Boston: Houghton Mifflin Company, 1914.

10. *Dancing to Death:* A *Cautionary Tale,* 1802

While dancing is a custom in cultures around the world, not all groups engage in or approve of dancing. The more austere Protestant Christianity of the Puritans and other English nonconformist groups who settled in New England often rejected dancing as a practice that was at best foolish and at worst sinful—as some religious groups continue to do today. The author of the following selection, Holland Weeks, was an active minister in Connecticut and Vermont, and pastor of the First Church in Waterbury, Connecticut, when he wrote this letter to his siblings in 1802. Weeks gives a great deal of advice in his letter and backs it up with a vivid didactic story of a girl who falls ill with consumption, known today as tuberculosis, after attending a ball. Essentially, she dances herself to death as a cautionary tale. The moral of the story is clear: dancing leads to no good.

Medically, of course, there is nothing in Weeks's description to show that the poor girl actually contracted tuberculosis from going to the ball, dancing, or anything else. She could just as easily have become infected at church. Rather than a medical case, though, Weeks presents her disease as divine punishment for her dissolute behavior—dancing at a ball was seen as vanity and a social stimulation of sexual attraction. He implies that God's justice and mercy are evident in her living long enough to repent of her ways and tell others to avoid the vice for which she will pay with her life.

This kind of didactic tale was a common educational technique and literary genre in the eighteenth and early nineteenth centuries; good children are rewarded for their virtue, and those who are not so virtuous have a far less pleasant fate. A greedy girl sticks her hand in boiling jam and is permanently disfigured; a boy who doesn't want to go to school hides in the woods and is eaten by wolves, a vain girl is disfigured by smallpox. *Although many would disagree with Weeks, his description of the vice of dancing is, like the virtue of dancing, a part of daily life.*

Waterbury, Sept. 14th, 1802.

To my younger brothers and sisters.

Dear and beloved; [...]

I have [...]* advice to give you. And that is, to read your bibles and other good books. Frequent your closets every day. Always attend public worship. Love one another. Speak no angry, boisterous words and harsh words to one another. Be profoundly dutiful, respectful, and obedient to our aged grandmother and to our honored Parents. Behave with a modest respect towards all superiors; Improve every opportunity to obtain instruction in good manners and religion. Spend your time always to some good purpose. Avoid those foolish amusements which serve more to corrupt than improve and reform the youthful mind. I will relate to you the case of a young girl in Waterbury who now lies at the point of death with the consumption. She attended a ball last spring and was immediately confined to her bed. She must now be called to the bar of God in consequence of that very act. She might have died in her impenitent state. But God we trust has been pleased to have mercy on her soul. She appears to be remarkably resigned. She says, "a death bed is pleasant." But she looks upon the practice of attending balls as an awful thing. She says, "if young people will go, the Lord will not go with them": and this is one thing which makes it appear awful to her. And she says that if young people felt as they ought they would have no desire to go. I hope you will kindly receive this admonition. Write to me as soon as you can.

Your affectionate brother Holland.

* damaged manuscript, word missing

Source: Holland Weeks to his siblings, September 14, 1802. Weeks Family Papers. Henry Sheldon Museum, Middlebury, Vermont. Used with permission.

11. *Rite of Scandal: Shocked Reaction to Igor Stravinsky's* The Rite of Spring

Ballet had developed in Europe into a style of formal, refined concert dance that was popular among the elites of Europe and increasingly around the world throughout the modern period. Although ballet became less popular in Western Europe in the nineteenth century, it especially flourished in Russia. The Russian impresario Sergei Diaghilev *brought his company of the* Ballets Russes, *or Russian Ballet, to Paris in 1909, and quickly developed a reputation for exotic, stimulating, and interesting ballet and opera. Diaghilev and his company helped fuel a revival of interest in ballet, and made the seventeenth-century courtly dance into an art form relevant and influential in the twentieth century. However, nothing had really prepared audiences for the radical artistic* Modernism *of Igor Stravinsky's music and Vaslav* Nijinsky's *choreography, and the Ballet Russes took the high society of Paris by storm in 1913, when a new ballet,* Le Sacre du Printemps (The Rite of Spring), *debuted.*

The setting of Le Sacre du Printemps *is spring in prehistoric Russia: an exotic, faraway place to the Parisian audience. The plot is very simple: in the first act, the tribes play springtime games with primitive religious overtones. The second act becomes more sinister when a maiden is chosen, and must dance herself to death to appease the vernal deities. Unlike the graceful, elongated movements and harmonious music of most ballet, the dancers stomped and squatted and struck awkward poses to pulsing, irregular, and dissonant music.*

Both the music and the dance heralded a new age in art: the Modern. *The new forms and sounds, incomprehensible to many, provoked a raucous reaction in the theater during the performance, countered by those who embraced the innovative and daring style. The result was a scandalous event, a near-riot in a fashionable theater, and exactly what the producers wanted; the kind of event that creates publicity and interest that money can't buy.*

Gustave de Pawlowski, the critic wrote this review of the first performance, coined the phrase "Massacre du Printemps." He grasps but does not altogether like the primitivism of the ballet on stage, and harshly treats the audience for being just as uncivilized as the show.

More than making money, the work of Stravinsky and Nijinsky was central to the development of twentieth-century music and dance, influencing such figures as Martha Graham, *Aaron* Copland, *and many others. The Ballets Russes in many ways revived ballet and created avenues for exploration of new dance styles and new musical innovations, changing and anticipating much of how these art forms were a part of daily life in the twentieth century.*

Where on earth, then, were these pigs brought up?

That is the kindest sentence among plenty of others which came to mind throughout this memorable and elegant occasion.

It puts in a nutshell the astonishment which we should feel in witnessing the stupid and intentional nastiness of what is euphemistically called "the Paris elite" in the presence of any truly new and bold innovation. This same audience, which for years has never protested the most dull vaudevilles, the butt ends of operettas served up to them every day with an English sauce to cover,... this same public pretends to suffer intolerably when an artist, captivated by something exotic, attempts to wrest from this feeling something new, to entertain or even interest [us] with hitherto unknown lines and movements.

Real snobbery, according to Thackeray, consists, whatever one may think, not in daring but in reaction. It accepts only those old audacities experienced a hundred times and admitted by caste. True audacity belongs to the lonely artists. Therefore, while the dances from Prince Igor were enjoyed for the hundredth time with attention and respect, since their primitive naïvetés are photographed in history and geography text books, Le Sacre du Printemps was greeted with horror because it showed earlier customs than those pictured in the particular history text books consulted by these cosmopolitan people. It is true the majority of the audience present could not have understood the title of the work. The men though it would deal with bloody beatings, and the women assumed it would concern the latest fashion promoted by a novelty shop.

Thus it was only by cupping our ears in the middle of an indescribable racket that we could painfully grasp an approximate idea of this new work, which was drowned out equally by its defender and its adversaries. We respect to the limit the rights of the defendant in a court of assizes; but it seems that artists who put forth their cases in the theater do not enjoy the right to the same consideration. It is enough to make you wild.

All of this does not mean, I hasten to add, that this new work is above all criticism. Far from it. The authors and the interpreters have brought off an improbable tour-de-force by staging in two acts these primitive gestures, unthinking, childish frenzies of primitive tribes awakening to the mysteries of life; but a work of art, I have already observed this once before, should not be based only upon the vulgar or the ugly.... If one uses ugliness in art it should be used only as a point of comparison. There would be nothing wrong, for example, with showing us the impoverished gestures of primitive tribes in Le Sacre du Printemps as long as this demonstration was short, incidental, and did not last two full acts. [...]

The authors of Le Sacre du Printemps have used nothing but onomatopoeia. Their personal style does not assert itself enough. We are shown a certain kind of prehistoric naturalism in a setting where we are not accustomed to expect it, a slice of life hewn out of an auroch [an extinct type of wild cow]. The experiment, from the artistic point of view, is not without real interest: it offers us something new at a time when the artistic world seems no longer to know novelty.

Moreover, even if the general idea behind this work seems to us a bit weak, it is true nevertheless that through the meticulous direction and through the coordination of the gestures with the music, a kind of strange and new stylization results, a style which I should probably call the style of reflexive movements, or, if you prefer, of automaticity.

I am sure you have experiences at a travelling circus that kind of giddiness which is produces by the cacophony of different orchestras and the absurdity of contradictory gestures which you notice in all the attractions.... [I]t is an intense hurly-burly but one that gives you, strangely, a general impression of harmony. We derived the same kind of feeling from the jerky gestures of prehistoric automatons, from the spontaneous and irrational poses in Le Sacre du Printemps, and all that, in spite of the dissonances, give the impression of animal automaticity, of very precisely stylized convulsive reflexes clearly outlined. And was it not the intention of the authors to convey to us exactly this impression of animality, of instinctive reflexes?

Whatever their intention was, never has an attempt been so thoroughly misunderstood. It was not a "Sacre" but a "Massacre du Printemps," and the fact is, to say the least, scandalous. [...]

The audience thinks it is showing its good taste in revolting. Such an attitude surpasses snobbery—it is the vicious hatred of art.

But we must console ourselves with the thought that everybody shows his admiration as he is able: the toad slobbers when the sun is too hot, the distinguished ladies shake their feather boas, their escorts make dangerous signs of congestions, the crowd makes its own animal cries.

And this, for the clear-sighted artists, is, in fact, the prettiest concert of praise he could hope for. For everyone expresses himself according to his own nature, and the comparison, you must admit, serves the interpreters to advantage, even when the author puts savages on the stage.

Source: Pawlowski, Gustave de. "Au Theatre des Champs-Elysees: Le Sacre du Printemps, ballet de deux actes de M. Igor Stravinsky" [At the Champs-Elysees Theater: The Rite of Spring, a ballet by Igor Stravinsky]. Comoedia, VIII/2068 (May 31, 1913). Translated by Truman Bullard. Courtesy of Truman Bullard.

Part VIII
RELIGIOUS LIFE

Religious life is a central part of life for many in the modern world. Religious affiliation is often a major part of the identities of both individuals and groups, combining with geographical, ethnic, familial, and other factors to fundamentally shape how people and groups see themselves and the world. This can be either positive or, unfortunately, negative. Religions are often major motivators and promoters of charity, reconciliation, and peace, but religious beliefs can also create intolerance and serious, sometimes intractable, conflicts.

The patterns of religious life and practice have changed in the modern period. One major change is the evolution of religious freedom. Along with the evolution of other human and political rights, freedom of conscience has come to be seen as a basic right in many places in the modern world. At the same time, there have been and still are places where the practice of religion is restricted or repressed by religious governments, anti-religious governments, or other religious groups. For example, in 1700, there was no place in the English-speaking world where Roman Catholics could legally celebrate the Mass; today there is nowhere in the English-speaking world where the same ritual is illegal. The repression of Jews was far worse, culminating in the *Holocaust* that took millions of Jewish lives, and even today various Muslim communities are negotiating difficult circumstances in the midst of complex global situations.

Another important occurrence is the increasing movement and communication of people that has brought more people from different places into contact with each other than ever before, and one of the things they share or bring to the contact is their religious life. Consequently, this volume has a section titled "Religions in Contact," which is intended to help document the ways in which religions have interacted in the modern world, from missionaries in North America (Document 1), to philosophers in Japan (Document 3) and the tensions among Christianity, Judaism, and a rationalist modern *Deism* (Document 2). The importance of contact between religions is central to modern religious life.

Other basic ways of looking at modern religions and religious life include their forms of worship, belief systems, and their understanding of death and the afterlife. Of course, none of these elements is easily divorced from the others in the practice of a religion: forms of worship reflect aspects of the belief system. The differences between

Catholics and Protestants that Henry Hills (see Document 4) highlights in his pamphlet are essentially doctrinal, but they result in substantial differences in religious worship. It is impossible to imagine the hajj taking on the form that Sir Richard Francis Burton (Document 5) describes without the belief system of Islam being as it is. Russian Orthodox (Document 6) and Jewish belief systems are also described (Document 7). Pope Paul VI's confirmation (Document 10) of the prohibitions of artificial birth control and extramarital sex essentially as extensions of the celebration of marriage has very specific consequences for religious practice: the teaching he sets out regulates a form that is just one part of a larger system of beliefs. Other selections describe the Cult of the Supreme Being in Revolutionary France (Document 8) and the practice of modern *Shinto* in Japan (Document 9).

How religions react to death is a part of belief, and funerary practices and the attitudes toward death that they reveal are themselves often a form of worship and a part of a larger belief system about the nature of the person and the world from a particular religious point of view. The tombstones of New Englanders (Document 13) mark and identify the remains of the dead, memorialize the individual, and express hopes for his or her salvation in a Protestant Christian context, while the unique funerals of the Indian Zoroastrian Parsis (Document 12) show less concern for the body and an overriding interest in community and reverence for earth, fire, and water. (See *Zoroastrianism* in the Glossary.) Louis de Jaucourt's entry on "Death" in the eighteenth-century *Encyclopédie* (Document 11) takes a rationalist, scientific view of death as a natural process. Around the modern world, more so than perhaps at any other time, religious life is diverse, vibrant, and complex.

Religions in Contact

Encounters between people of different faiths are certainly not unique to the modern world. The movements of people caused by migration, trade, military conflicts, and even enslavement have brought differing religions into interaction. Accelerated transportation and communications, *colonialism* and global trade, and a variety of other trends in the modern world have made contact between religions an increasingly important part of modern religious life.

One important trend has been the missionary activities of predominantly Christian Europeans as they spread across the globe in the modern period. This brought them into contact with many different religious traditions in Asia, Africa, and the Americas, including those Fr. Francisco Hildago describes in Texas (Document 1). Other changes in religious life made for new kinds of contacts; not all religious contacts are between new groups. The modern world has produced some devoutly empirical thinkers like the American Thomas Paine (Document 2), who derided revealed religion as superstitious and often hypocritical. Christians and Jews had long been living in proximity, with the Christians in many cases oppressing the Jews, and Paine lambastes them both, but evidences his own biases in the process.

Not all religious contact produces conflicts, however, as Ueda Shizuteru's thought from the Kyoto School of philosophy and theology shows (Document 3). Centered at Kyoto University in Japan in the twentieth century, the ideas of the Kyoto School integrate elements of Christianity and *Buddhism*. The result is neither wholly Christian nor Buddhist, but a new perspective on religious belief and in some cases a new form and practice unique to the modern world. Whether through proselytizing, synthesizing, criticizing, simply coexisting, or some other form of contact, religious life exists in the modern world in the context of faiths in contact with other faiths.

1. Fr. Francisco Hidalgo: Spanish Missionaries in Eighteenth-Century Texas

One of the central issues of interaction between the indigenous inhabitants of the Americas and the Europeans and Africans who conquered or colonized in America is the meeting of religious traditions. The Spanish were especially adept at using religious missions as ways to extend influence over the large areas of America that they claimed.

The Spanish brought with them strategies and technologies that allowed them to both impress and offer protection to the Indians who accepted Christianity, although disease was a problem in the missions, as with much European-Native American contact, and many Native Americans who moved to the Spanish missions suffered because of a lack of immunity to European diseases.

In this selection, Fr. Francisco Hidalgo, a Spanish missionary priest of the Roman Catholic Church *working in the early eighteenth century, reports to his superiors on the life and religious practices of the Native American inhabitants and the interaction of Roman Catholic Christianity and the indigenous religious traditions in what is now eastern Texas. Fr. Hidalgo's observations are interesting on a number of levels: first, they provide an important documentary account of Tejas religious practice; the Tejas themselves had no written language and created no records of their own practices and beliefs. At the same time, Fr. Hidalgo's own religious point of view can also be detected. While he sees the indigenous cult to be superstitious and in need of eradication, he seems genuine in his own faith and in his concern for the souls of the Tejas, who seem generally to view Christianity in similar terms, resisting conversion and believing it is bad for them—even bringing death.*

The ways that both Fr. Hidalgo himself and the Tejas people negotiate the tensions that arise as a result of this contact between their different religious traditions are in some ways typical. Some on each side reject the other religion, and even when some of the Tejas adopt the Christianity of the Franciscan priests, they remain unwilling to wholly abandon their native religious practices.

Eventually most of the inhabitants did become Roman Catholic, but the relationship between Christian evangelization and Native American religious traditions was—and in some places remains—a central part of daily religious life when Europeans came into contact with Native Americans.

[To Friar Isidro Cassos]
November 20, 1710

...In the pueblo [village] of San Francisco de los Texas a priest went to a house near where I was to baptize an Indian. At the door he found a Tesusan Indian dancing in a circle of live coals without getting burned. The priest, in the name of God, forbade the Indian to come out of the circle. The Tesusan Indian strove to come out to keep the priest from baptizing the sick Indian, but he could not in spite of everything he did....

I have heard it said on many occasions that the fire the Tejas Indians have in their houses was brought from the house of their high priest, whom they call *chenesí*. If the fire goes out they start immediately for the house of the priest to get new fire. It never goes out in the house of sacrifice. The Indians say they have two children from God whom they call in their language *coneneses* "the little ones."...The Indians go at night to say their prayers. Their priest assumes the voices of the two children and asks for what he needs for their use. He threatens that if they do not do as they are told they will be punished suddenly with snake bites. They make many prayers in their language to the two *coneseses* and when they have finished and start out at the door they bleat like goats that are following close after the herd. Once Father Fray Antonio Bordoi went into the house of sacrifice to see the *coneneses* to find out what they were. The priest objected and declared that he would certainly die. But the father went in and found a little box with packages. But he did not see any children. Into the fire which the Indians keep burning in their houses they throw a great amount of fat, offering it to the "Great Captain." After their crops are matured all the Indians gather in the house and *patio* of their captain to hold their feasts. Those who are to dance come out of a house near the captain's. It is a little straw hut they build for the occasion. Twelve old men come out of it to dance, all having tufts or plumes. They advance singing in a strange tongue which the people do not understand. These twelve old men stay in the little straw hut as long as the feast lasts. There they go through their ceremonies, say their prayers, and drink a tea [*cacina*] like that commonly used in Florida. This I saw. Every evening these same twelve old men come to the *patio* of the captain's house, singing these same songs in a strange tongue. One follows exactly behind the other and immediately form a circle. There they hold three dances during these days and there are no more during the rest of the year. The Indians have the doors of all their houses toward the east. I heard them tell the soldiers on this occasion they did this because it never blows from that side, I do not understand the mystery. When they kill a deer they never cut it up until the priest of the pueblo arrives. He cuts it up. The Indians had rather lose it than to cut it open before their priest arrives. He cuts it up, selects the portion belonging to his priestly office, and it is sent to him. The same thing is done in the case of their crops of corn and beans. Each one and each family gives a portion of everything to the high priest.

Frey Francisco Hidalgo

...

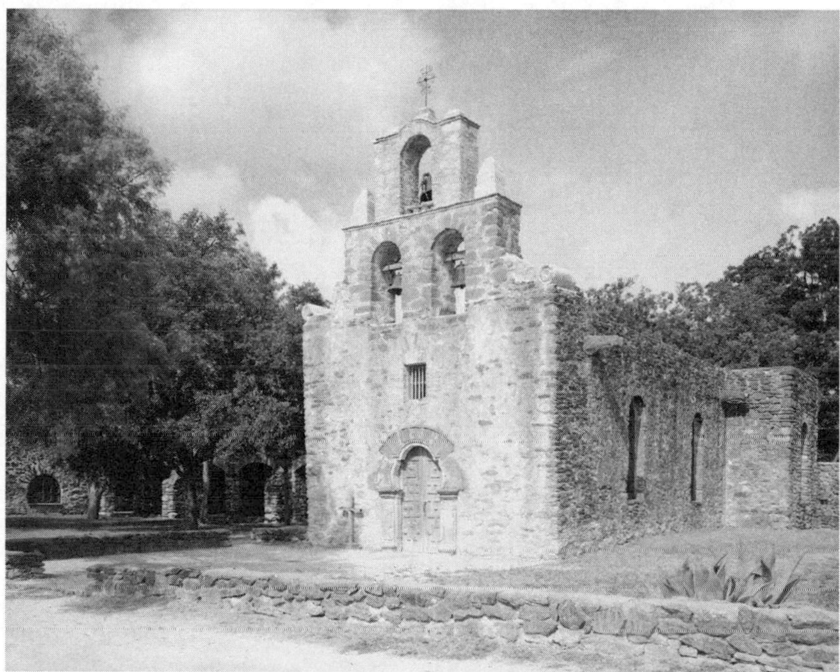

The old church at the Mission San Francisco de la Espada, San Antonio, Texas. Library of Congress.

[To Viceroy Baltasar de Zúñiga y Guzmán]
November 4, 1716
Most Excellent Sir,
[...]

[O]n June 28 of the present year, 1716, we reached the boundaries of the country of the Tejas where, having exchanged all the customary courtesies and after a warm welcome to our Spaniards by the said Indians, an account of everything and of the establishment of the missions was given to that superior government.

It now remains for me to give an account of our experience and of the information I have acquired as to the condition of the said country. And, because these are so important, your Excellency will be good enough to consider them, so that when everything is taken into consideration, a good ending may be forecast.

This nation of the Asinai, whom we call Tejas or Texias, contains many tribes. It extends as far as Rio del Misuri [Missouri River], according to the reports of the Indians from the north and west. It contains many settlements, some large and some small. On the northern border, reckoning from that court and looking in the direction above mentioned, the four missions for the different tribes are located. [...]

The whole nation is idolatrous—as is at present recognized. They have houses of worship and a perpetual fire which they never let die out. They are very perverted and in their dances they have the Indian braves or the Indian women who get drunk on peyote or frixolillo, which they make for the occasion, and the people believe everything these persons tell them they have seen. They have idols large and small. They believe in the devil and offer sacrifices to him believing that he is the true god. In the pictures they make of him they paint him with horns and a face of fire and with other features that prove their great deception.

The old convent at the Mission Senora de la Purisima Concepcion, San Antonio, Texas. Library of Congress.

We have not succeeded in getting them to put their houses close to the church, although they promised at first to do so. Therefore, there is no Christian doctrine imparted to them, first, because of the great repugnance they have for Christianity, and, second, because of the great distance there is between their houses and because of other motives and reasons they have. Their repugnance to baptism from past times is well known, for they have formed the belief that the water kills them. Some of those who have been baptized have died, both adults and children. They do not wish for fire to be taken from their houses because they believe that someone in the house will die. [...]

They bury their dead, after bathing them, interring with them the trophies they have captured, with the deer skins they possess, and with all the gifts their relatives supply. They place there something of everything they have to eat as well as buffalo hides. They bury the scalps so that their enemies may go along to serve them in the other life. They place there provisions for the journey and other possessions to serve for clothing.

Frey Francisco Hildago

Source: Hatcher, Mattie Austin. "Description of the Tejas or Asinai Indians, 1691–1722." *Southwestern Historical Quarterly Online* 31, no. 1 (1927): 50–62. http://www.tsha.utexas.edu/publications/journals/shq/online/v031/n1/article_7.html.

2. Thomas Paine: Enlightened Intolerance

Thomas Paine (1737–1809) was an English-born intellectual, revolutionary, inventor, radical, and pamphleteer who was passionately committed to liberal values and Enlightenment *ideals. Among his ideas were progressive income taxes, abolition of* slavery, *guaranteed minimum incomes, and many other ideas radical for his era, and even ours. After immigrating to America in 1774, he began promoting American independence. He is perhaps best known today for his 1776 pamphlet* Common Sense, *which dramatically solidified support in America for declaring independence from Britain. As a* Deist *who believed in an unknowable and non-interfering God, he despised revealed, organized religion as dangerous superstition and an impediment to social progress and liberty, claiming, "My own mind is my own Church." In this he was hardly alone: widespread sectarianism,* anti-Semitism, *and anti-clericalism (especially in the English speaking world) were facts of life in the eighteenth century.*

His poem "The Monk and the Jew" displays both the clever satirical wit valued among Enlightenment thinkers, and attacks some of their favorite targets: social and religious attitudes formed outside of enlightened reason. Paine evidences a sharply prejudiced attitude toward Christianity in general and the Roman Catholic Church *in particular, as well as an anti-Semitism that marred some of the most open minds of the age, including those of Voltaire and Immanuel Kant. Though the Monk comes across as a heartless and doctrinaire hypocrite who refuses to help his neighbor as Christ commanded, the Jew is an ugly caricature of speech and personality, willing to lie, cheat, and deceive to get what he wants. While Paine makes a valid point about Christian anti-Semitism and religious intolerance, one can only conclude that Paine himself was little more tolerant of others' beliefs than those he sought to satirize.*

The Monk and the Jew

An unbelieving Jew one day
Was skating o'er the icy way,
Which being brittle let him in,
Just deep enough to catch his chin;
And in that woeful plight he hung,
With only power to move his tongue.
A brother skater near at hand,
A Papist born in foreign land,

With hasty strokes directly flew
To save poor Mordecai the Jew—
"But first," quoth he, "I must enjoin
That you renounce your faith for mine;
There's no entreaties else will do,
'Tis heresy to help a Jew—"

"Forswear mine fait! No! Cot forbid!
Dat would be very base indeed,
Come never mind such tings as deeze,
Tink, tink, how fery hard it freeze.
More coot you do, more coot you be,
Vat signifies your faith to me?
Come tink agen, how cold and vet,
And help me out von little bit."

"By holy mass, 'tis hard, I own,
To see a man both Hang and drown,
And can't relieve him from his plight
Because he is an Israelite;
The Church refuses all assistance,
Beyond a certain pale and distance;
And all the service I can lend
Is praying for your soul, my friend."

"Pray for my soul, ha! ha! you make me laugh.
You petter help me out py half:
Mine soul I farrant vill take care,
To pray for her own self, my tear:
So tink a little now for me,
'Tis I am in the hole not she."

"The Church forbids it, friend, and saith
That all shall die who had no faith."
"Vell, if I must pelieve, I must,
But help me out von little first."
"No, not an inch without Amen
That seals the whole"—"Vell, hear me den,
I here renounce for coot and all
De race of Jews both great and small;
'Tis de verst trade peneath the sun,
Or vurst religion; dat's all von.
Dey cheat, and get deir living py't,
Amd lie, and swear the lie is right.
I'll co to mass as soon as ever
I get to toder side the river.
So help me out, dow Christian friend,
Dat I may do as I *intend*."

"Perhaps you do intend to cheat,
If once you get upon your feet."
"No, no, I do intend to be
A *Christian*, such as one as *dee*."
For, thought the Jew, he is as much

A Christian man as I am such.
The bigot Papist joyful hearted
To hear the heretic converted,
Replied to the *designing* Jew,

"This was a happy fall for you:
You'd better die a Christian now,
For if you live you'll break your vow."
Then said no more, but in a trice
Popp'd Mordecai beneath the ice.

Source: Paine, Thomas. *The Life and Writings of Thomas Paine*. Edited by Daniel Edwin Wheeler. Volume 10. New York: Vincent Parke and Co., 1908.

3. *Philosophy and Theology in Twentieth-Century Japan: The Kyoto School*

The Kyoto school is not a literal school, but is the name given to a group of Japanese philosophers and thinkers of several generations at Kyoto University, who began in the first half of the twentieth century to integrate Western philosophical and theological traditions with different strains of Buddhism. *Most members of the Kyoto school were practicing Buddhists, and some had even lived and trained as Buddhist monks. Buddhism was treated both as a religious practice and as an object of study in the Western tradition, and the results have been compelling scholarship on the Western academic model that offers insight into Buddhist and Christian traditions. However, the work did not stop there; for example, one member of the Kyoto school, Hisamatsu Shin'ichi, went beyond the bounds of academic study and started a new religious movement with students that focused on scholarship as service and the unity of religious practice.*

The following selection is from a work by Ueda Shizuteru, who studied at Kyoto University and Marburg University in Germany. It seeks points of contact between the German medieval Christian mystic Meister Eckhart (1260–1328) and the teachings of Zen Buddhism *on the idea of "nothingness." Although the discussion gets rather abstract, the conclusions which Shizuteru draws are ideas that are not wholly consistent either with Christian theology or Zen teaching, but something new that tries to incorporate them both. In this sense, it is a good illustration of the idea of the Kyoto school and an interesting example of religions in contact in the modern world.*

According to Meister Eckhart, God gives birth to his Son in the solitary soul. "The Father begets me as his Son, as his very same Son. Whatever God works is one. Thus he begets me as his Son without any distinction." The "birth of God in the soul," spoken of here in the language of the Christian doctrine of the Trinity, is the leap to realization of his own authentic life that man experiences in "solitariness" with the surrender of ego. "The Father begets me as his Son without any distinction." This means that the absolute event of salvation touches each and every individual in its full originality, without first passing through a mediator. This being the case, Eckhart stands very close to Mahayana Buddhism, the philosophical-religious base of Zen

Buddhism. According to Mahayana teaching, the very same awakening to the very same truth transforms each and every individual into the very same Buddha—that is, it makes of each individual the same "Awakened One" that it made of the historical Buddha, Gautama.

So far the similarity is only of a general nature. A more deep-reaching spiritual kinship appears when Eckhart speaks of a "breakthrough to the nothingness of the godhead." "The soul is not content with being a Son of God." "The soul wants to penetrate to the simple ground of God, to the silent desert where not a trace of distinction is to be seen, neither Father nor Son nor Holy Spirit." By carrying out in radical fashion his neoplatonically laden understanding of "being one," Eckhart transfers the essence or ground of god back beyond the divine God to the simply modeless, formless, unthinkable, and unspeakable purity that he calls, in distinction to God, "godhead" and that he describes as a nothingness. [...]

God is divine in turning towards his creatures: for in his essence, beyond the opposition of God and creatures, he is a nothingness pure and simple.... For Eckhart, the nothingness of the godhead is, in a non-objective manner, the soul's very own ground. Hence the soul, in order to return to its original ground, must break through God and out into the nothingness of the godhead.... Here is true freedom, freedom without God, a "godlessness" wherein the nothingness of the godhead, and thus the essence of God, is present. Eckhart's thought draws him here beyond the opposition of theism and atheism, beyond the opposition of personalism and impersonalism. [...]

In Zen Buddhism this same coincidence is at stake—except that there negation and affirmation are effected more radically than they are in Eckhart. The radicalness of Zen is evident from the fact that it speaks of nothingness pure and simple, while Eckhart speaks of nothingness of the godhead. [...]

Eckhart advances a radical de-imaging of the soul which is consummated in and as a ceaseless "letting go." This "letting go" accord his teaching with its extremely dynamic quality, corresponding to the dynamic of the Zen coincidence of negation and affirmation—except that in Zen, where we see a radical execution of the Mahayana Buddhist thinking on relatedness, the scope of this coincidence is wider than it is in Eckhart. [...]

In the history of Buddhism, it has been Zen that has given this coincidence a fresh, existential concreteness to cut through the layers of speculations surrounding it. This Zen has achieved by having the concepts of absolute nothingness and the self interpenetrate one another. In a word, we are presented with a nothingness-self—or, one might say, a nothingness viewed as a someone rather than a something. [...]

In general, philosophy and Zen—crudely put, thinking and non-thinking—stand opposed to one another. This tension, however, became something creative... through Zen and philosophy bringing one another into question. In the light of Zen, philosophy was made into a question about the origination of principles. In the light of philosophy, Zen was made into a question about the possibility of the project of building a world and possibility of cultivating a logic.

Source: Ueda Shizuteru. "'Nothingness' in Meister Eckhart and Zen Buddhism." In *The Buddha Eye: An Anthology of the Kyoto School*. Translated by James W. Heig, edited by Frederick Frank. New York: Crossroad, 1982.

Forms of Worship

Sometimes what a believer does is more important than what he or she says or believes. Almost all organized religions have some kind of organized worship activities, whether in churches, temples, synagogues, mosques, or other places. Sometimes these forms of worship can be a cause of great conflict between religions, or there can be internal disputes over forms of rites and rituals as serious as any over doctrine. The dissent of the sixteenth-century *Protestant Reformation* over liturgy and worship as much as theology, which is reflected below in Henry Hills' pamphlet (Document 4), led to decades of wars in Europe, and is still disputed among Christians today.

The emphasis in this section is not on disputes, however. Forms of worship here are less strictly construed, and extend to actions undertaken for religious reasons outside of formal rituals. Thus, not only is the attendance at church on Easter described by Henri Troyat (Document 6) a form of worship but also his description of the family's feast and celebrations afterward. The centrality of the family in the celebration is just as important to the celebration of Easter as their liturgical observations, just as it is to the family of Rafael Uzan (Document 7) in his family's preparations for *Passover*. Of course, forms of worship can also be highly formalized rituals, as the extended description of the culmination of the *hajj* for Richard Burton (Document 5) as an impostor shows. Whether formal or informal; communal, familial, or individual; public or private; the variety of worship in the modern world reflects the importance of diversity of religious life.

4. Reformation Rhetoric: Catholic Pamphleteer Henry Hills

Henry Hills was a Catholic pamphleteer in Protestant England at the end of the seventeenth century. At first, the following selection might seem a little confusing: although Hills' pamphlet is defending the positions of the Roman Catholic Church, *it begins with a series of positive assertions that represent Protestant positions on a series of issues that were in contention between Catholics and various Protestant groups during the* Protestant Reformation *and* Catholic Reformation, *offering a rhetorical challenge to provide support for these positions (which Protestant pamphleteers were in turn happy to provide). The religious environment in which Hills was writing was a volatile one, to say the least.*

Although the United States draws much of its legal and cultural heritage from England, one of the freedoms Americans enjoy is the free exercise of religion and the prohibition of the establishment of a state religion. This is not exactly the case in England, where, though broad religious freedom is a fact today, Henry VIII (r. 1509–1547) established the Church of England *in 1534, and the monarch, as head of the state, was simultaneously the head of the state church, a position Queen Elizabeth II retains to this day.*

Many of the issues Hills raises relate directly to the Mass, *the Roman Catholic worship service. Catholics believe that the bread and wine becomes transubstantiated into the body and blood of Christ (see* Transubstantiation *in the Glossary), called the* Eucharist, *through the ritual of the Mass. Protestant groups developed different beliefs about the Eucharist according to group or denomination. Some, like the Church of England, believe in consubstantiation, that bread and wine remains bread and wine but becomes simultaneously also Christ's body and blood; other believe that the nature of the bread and wine depends on the believer's attitude; still others believe that it is simply a symbol or that all Eucharistic practice is idolatrous worship of bread and wine rather than of God. While the Eucharist and many of the other points of contention that Hills mentions may seem unimportant to those outside the Christian tradition, they were at the center of intense religious disputes at the beginning of the* modern *era.*

While the intense divisions in Christianity of the sixteenth-century Protestant Reformation and Catholic Reformation have persisted through the Modern period, the disputes became more simply religious and cultural, and less political and military. With some notable exceptions, by the eighteenth century, Catholics and Protestants generally stopped killing each other just for being Catholics and Protestants. Other reasons, such as ethnic conflicts and nationalism, imperial ambitions, class antagonisms, and other loyalties either ameliorated religious tensions or subsumed religious animosities into other disputes. Regardless, Christian religious beliefs, whether Catholic or Protestant, continued to play a central role in the daily lives of many in the modern world of Europe and far beyond.

A Request To Protestants, To produce Plain Scriptures directly authorizing these their Tenets.

I. Scripture is clear, in all necessaries, to every Sober Enquirer
II. The Secular Prince hath all Spiritual Jurisdiction and Authority, immediately, from and under God.
III. Justification by Faith alone (viz. a Persuasion that we are justified) is a wholesome Doctrin.
IV. The Substance of Bread and Wine remains after, what it was before Sacerdotal Consecration.
V. Our Lord's Presence in or with the Eucharist is merely gracious and influential; and, if more, only to the Faithful.
VI. Adoration of the Eucharist (i.e. of our Saviour under the Species of Bread and Wine) is Idolatry.
VII. All Christians, whenever they communicate [receive Communion], are Oblig'd to receive in both Kinds.
VIII. Chastity, deliberately vow'd, may be, inoffensively, violated.
IX. All Christian Excellencies are commended.
X. Every Soul, as soon as expired, is convey'd to Heaven or Hell.
XI. Desiring the Intercessions of the Blessed, is more Superstitious, and derogatory to our Lord's Mediatorship, than entreating the Prayers of Holy Men Militant.
XII. Honouring the Cross, the Reliques and Representations of our Lord and his Saints, with that degree of Reverence we do the Gospels, (commonly kiss'd and sworn by) Altar, and other Sacred Utensils, is Idolatry.
XIII. The Pope is Antichrist.
XIV. Every Prayer us'd in Divine Office, must be in a language vulgar, and intelligible to every Auditor.
XV. A Company of Christians, voluntarily separating from all other Christian Societies, condemning their Doctrins and Rites, destitute also of any visible Correspondence with them in the Eucharist, in any Religious Assemblies or Solemn Devotions can, notwithstanding this perverse, entire, and manifest

separation, be a mystical member of Christ, in Catholic Unity, and a Charitable part of the Catholic Church.

XVI. The whole clergy of the Catholic Church may apostatize from Fundamental Truth and Holiness; whilst part of a National Laity may preserve both, discover the Clergies Defection, and depriving them, heap to Themselves Teachers of their own sending and instruction.

Source: Hills, Henry. "A Request to Protestants. . . ." London, 1667.

5. *Sir Richard Francis Burton: A Non-Muslim's Pilgrimage to Mecca*

One of the Four (sometimes Five) Pillars of Islam *is the* hajj, *or pilgrimage to* Mecca, *to be made, if possible, at least once in a Muslim's life. The other Pillars are prayer, zakat or charitable giving, fasting during the holy month of Ramadan, and sometimes as a fifth (or rather first), a declaration of faith in Allah and his prophet Muhammad. The following nineteenth-century account of the hajj pilgrimage and completion of the prescribed rituals comes from an interesting source: Sir Richard Francis Burton, an English officer, adventurer, linguist, and translator who was not himself Muslim at all. In 1853, he disguised himself as an Indian-born Afghan and undertook the hajj as if he was Muslim. Had he been discovered, he most likely would have been executed.*

A certain European and Christian bias is evident in Burton's passages, and he is quite willing to criticize on a number of levels: he calls Indian architecture barbarian, derides the interpolation of his guide boy's prayers with cursing at groups who get in their way, highlights the need to force one's way violently through the crowd, and points out the conflicts within Islam, whether on national and ethnic grounds or religious differences (such as Sunnism *and* Shi'ism*).*

While his presence demonstrates a certain level of indifference to Muslim religious sensibilities, at the same time, Burton has a complex relationship to what he is doing. He is not unsympathetic to his fellow pilgrims, and seems genuinely interested in the rituals and practices of the pilgrimage, although he does not assign the same values to them that his fellow pilgrims do. Burton's account offers a perspective that is both necessarily that of an outsider, but it is also given from an inside point of view impossible for a total outsider to have. Burton provides a detailed account of the culmination of the hajj that explains to his non-Muslim audience what a Muslim describing the same experience might have taken for granted. Regardless of what one thinks of what Burton did, he offers a vivid and informative account of an act of worship central to the religious beliefs and everyday life of millions.

There at last it lay, the bourn of my long and weary Pilgrimage, realising the plans and hopes of many and many a year. The mirage medium of Fancy invested the huge catafalque amid its gloomy pall with peculiar charms. There were no giant fragments of hoar antiquity as in Egypt, no remains of graceful and harmonious beauty as in Greece and Italy, no barbarous gorgeousness as in the buildings of India; yet the view was strange, unique—and how few have looked upon the celebrated shrine! I may truly say that, of all the worshippers who clung weeping to the curtain, or who pressed their beating hearts to the stone, none felt for the moment a deeper emotion than did the Haji, from the far north. It was as if the poetical legends of the Arab spoke truth, and that the waving wings of angels, not the sweet breeze of morning, were agitating and swelling the black covering of the shrine. But, to confess humbling truth, theirs was the high feeling of religious enthusiasm, mine was the ecstasy of gratified pride.

Few Moslems contemplate for the first time the Ka'abah, without fear and awe: there is a popular jest against new comers, that they generally inquire the direction of prayer. This being the Kiblah, or fronting place, Moslems pray all around it; a circumstance which of course cannot take place in any spot of Al-Islam but the Harim [Haram—the mosque in Mecca]. The boy Mohammed, therefore, left me for a few minutes to myself; but presently he warned me that it was time to begin. Advancing, we entered through the Bab Benu Shaybah, the "Gate of the Sons of the Shaybah" (old woman). There we raised our hands, repeated the Labbayk, the Takbir, and Tahlil; after which we uttered certain supplications, and drew our hands down our faces. Then we proceeded to the Shafe'is' place of worship—the open pavement between the Makam Ibrahim and the well Zemzem—where we performed the usual two-bow prayer in honour of the Mosque. This was followed by a cup of holy water and a present to the Sakkas, or carriers, who for the consideration distributed, in my name, a large earthen vaseful to poor pilgrims. [. . .]

Then commenced the ceremony of Tamif or circumambulation, our route being the Malaf—the low oval of polished granite immediately surrounding the Ka'abah. I repeated, after my Mutawwif, or cicerone [guide], "In the Name of Allah, and Allah is omnipotent! I purpose to circuit seven circuits unto Almighty Allah, glorified and exalted!" This is technically called the Niyat (intention) of Tawaf. Then we began the prayer, "O Allah (I do this), in Thy Belief, and in Verification of Thy Book, and in Faithfulness to Thy Covenant, and in Perseverance of the Example of the Apostle Mohammed—may Allah bless Him and preserve!" till we reached the place Al-Multazem, between the corner of the Black Stone arid the Ka'abah door. Here we ejaculated, "O Allah, Thou hast Rights, so pardon my transgressing them!" Opposite the door we repeated, "O Allah, verily the House is Thy House, and the Sanctuary Thy Sanctuary and the Safeguard Thy Safeguard, and this is the Place of him who flies to Thee from (hell) Fire!" At the little building called Makam Ibrahim we said, "O Allah, verily this is the Place of Abraham, who took Refuge with and fled to Thee from the Fire! O deny my Flesh and Blood, my Skin and Bones to the (eternal) Flames!" As we paced slowly round the north or Irak corner of the Ka'abah we exclaimed, "O Allah, verily I take Refuge with Thee from Polytheism, and Disobedience, and Hypocrisy and evil Conversation, and evil Thoughts concerning Family and Property and Progeny!" When fronting the Mizab, or spout, we repeated the words, "O Allah, verily I beg of Thee Faith which shall not decline, and a Certainty which shall not perish and the good Aid of Thy Prophet Mohammed—may Allah bless Him and preserve! O Allah, shadow me in Thy Shadow on that Day when there is no Shade but Thy Shadow and cause me to drink from the Cup of Thine Apostle Mohammed—may Allah bless Him and preserve!—that pleasant Draught after which is no Thrist to all Eternity O Lord of Honour and Glory!" Turning the west corner, or the Rukn al-Shami, we exclaimed, "O Allah, make it an acceptable Pilgrimage, and a Forgiveness of Sins, and a laudable Endeavour, and a pleasant Action (in Thy sight), and a store which perisheth not, O Thou Glorious! O Thou Pardoner!" This was repeated thrice, till we arrived at the Yamani, or south corner, where, the crowd being less importunate, we touched the wall with the right hand, after the example of the Prophet, and kissed the finger-tips. Finally between the south angle and that of the Black Stone, where our circuit would be completed, we said, "O Allah, verily I take Refuge with Thee from Infidelity and I take Refuge with Thee from Want, and from the Tortures of the Tomb, and from the Troubles of Life and Death. And I fly to Thee from Ignominy in this World and the next, and I implore Thy Pardon for the Present and for the Future. O Lord, grant to me in this Life Prosperity, and in the next Life Prosperity, and save me from the Punishment of Fire!"

Moslems worshipping the shrines sacred to Islam, Mecca, ca. 1885. Library of Congress.

Thus finished a Shaut, or single course round the house. Of these we performed the first three at the pace called Harwalah, very similar to the French pas gymnastique, or Tarammul, that is to say "moving the shoulders as if walking in sand." The four latter are performed in Tarammul, slowly and leisurely; the reverse of the Sai, or running. These seven Ashwat, or courses, are called collectively one Usbu. The Moslem origin of this custom is too well known to require mention. After each Tautah or circuit, we, being unable to kiss or even to touch the Black Stone, fronted towards it, raised our hands to our ears, exclaimed, "In the Name of Allah, and Allah is omnipotent!" kissed our fingers, and resumed the ceremony of circumambulation, as before, with "Allah, in Thy Belief," &c.

At the conclusion of the Tawaf it was deemed advisable to attempt to kiss the stone. For a time I stood looking in despair at the swarming crowd of Badawi and other pilgrims that besieged it. But the boy Mohammed was equal to the occasion. During our circuit he had displayed a fiery zeal against heresy and schism, by foully abusing every Persian in his path; and the inopportune introduction of hard words into his prayers made the latter a strange patchwork; as 'Ave Maria purissima,—arrah, don't ye be letting the pig at the pot,—sanctissima," and so forth. He might, for instance, be repeating "And I take Refuge with Thee from Ignominy in this World," when "O thou rejected one, son of the rejected!" would be the interpolation addressed to some long-bearded Khorasani,—"And in that to come"—"O hog and brother of a hoggess" And so he continued till I wondered that none dared to turn and rend him. After vainly addressing the pilgrims, of whom nothing could be seen but a mosaic of occupits and shoulder-blades, the boy Mohammed collected about half a dozen stalwart Meccans, with whose assistance, by sheer strength, we wedged our way into the thin and light-legged crowd. The Badawin turned round upon us like wild-cats, but they had no daggers. The season being autumn, they had not swelled themselves with milk for six months; and they had become such living mummies, that I could have managed single-handed half a dozen of them. After thus reaching the stone, despite popular indignation testified by impatient shouts, we monopolised the use of it for at least ten minutes. Whilst kissing it and rubbing hands and forehead upon it I narrowly observed it, and came away persuaded that it is an aerolite. It is curious that almost all travellers agree upon one point, namely, that the stone is volcanic. [. . .]

Nineteenth-century illustration, "The Kaaba in Mecca." Courtesy of Eon Images.

Having kissed the stone we fought our way through the crowd to the place called Al-Multazem. Here we pressed our stomachs, chests, and right cheeks to the Ka'abah, raising our arms high above our heads and exclaiming, "O Allah! O Lord of the Ancient House, free my Neck from Hell-fire, and preserve me from every ill Deed, and make me contented with that daily bread which Thou hast given to me, and bless me in all Thou hast granted!" Then came the Istighfar, or begging of pardon: "I beg Pardon of Allah the most high, who, there is no other God but He, the Living, the Eternal, and unto Him I repent myself!" After which we blessed the Prophet, and then asked for ourselves all that our souls most desired.

After embracing the Multazem, we repaired to the Shafeis' place of prayer near the Makam Ibrahim,and there recited two prostrations, technically called Sunnat-al-Tuwaf, or the (Apostle's) practice of circumambulation. The chapter repeated in the first was "Say thou, O Infidels," in the second, "Say thou He is the one God." We then went to the door of the building in which is Zemzem: there I was condemned to another nauseous draught, and was deluged with two or three skinfuls of water dashed over my head en douche. This ablution causes sins to fall from the spirit like dust. During the potation we prayed, "O Allah, verily I beg of Thee plentiful daily Bread, and profitable Learning, and the healing of every Disease!" Then we returned towards the Black Stone, stood far away opposite, because unable to touch it, ejaculated the Takbir, the Tahlil, and the Hamdilah; and thoroughly worn out with scorched feet and a burning head,—both extremities, it must be remembered, were bare, and various delays had detained us till ten A.M.,—I left the Mosque.

Source: Burton, Richard Francis. *Personal Narrative of a Pilgrimage to Al-Medinah and Meccah*. New York: G. P. Putnam & Co., 1856.

6. *Orthodox Christian Easter in Pre-Revolutionary Moscow*

The most important religious celebration of the year for Christians is Easter, when they believe Jesus Christ rose from the dead three days after his crucifixion. In pre-Revolutionary Russia, an officially Orthodox Christian state and traditionally Orthodox Christian *culture, the celebration as described here by Henri Troyat was a major holiday that extended far beyond the doors of the churches. Like many religious observations, the celebration included a communal meal with specific dishes, including paskha, a pyramid shaped cheesecake with dried fruit, and kulich, a round sweet bread with icing. Gifts are also exchanged, social calls are made to family and friends, and greetings are offered to complete strangers. Russians do not greet each other with "Happy Easter!" but instead say "Christ is Risen!" and the polite response is "Indeed, He is Risen!" All these are ritual parts of the celebration that make the holiday something that penetrates almost every aspect of life.*

The following selection is from a work of fiction in which John Russell, an Englishman, visits Moscow under the protection of the Zubov family, a business connection of his father's. The plot is an excuse to demonstrate daily life in Moscow, cobbled together from Troyat's own memory and his parents' and others' stories.

The account gives a vivid impression and accurate details, even if as a whole it is rather romanticized and idealized. Troyat, born Lev Aslanovich Tarasov in Russia in 1911, was a Russian émigré and exile; he fled Russia as a child and never returned to his own country. His family left in fear of the Russian Revolution *in 1917, and although Troyat became a prolific and prize-winning writer in France, he could only have had vague memories of celebrating Easter in Moscow.*

After the Revolution of 1917, the officially atheist Soviet Union replaced the officially Orthodox Russian Empire and such celebrations of Easter were suppressed. After the fall of the Union of Soviet Socialist Republics, *these celebrations came back quickly, and many of the traditions described here are once again central parts of Russian religious life.*

For midnight mass the Zubovs and Russell went to the Kremlin. The crowd was so dense within the old crenellated walls that they were unable to get into the Cathedral of the Assumption. Although Alexander Vassilievitch had explained and described the ceremony to him beforehand, Russell was filled with wonder at the ocean of heads that rippled among the reefs of the churches and the palaces. The domes shone far above them in a dark wet mist. But on this evening the stars had come down to earth, for each of the faithful held a wax taper in his hand—a light for every face. The flames flickered in the wind. All classes of the population were represented among those gathered together. Some carried colored eggs and paskha wrapped in paper. Alexander Vassilievitch vanished and soon came back with tapers which he gave to his wife, son-in-law, daughters, son and guest. Russell hunted in his pocket for matches. Tatiana Sergeyevna stopped him. Was he going to commit sacrilege? His neighbor on the left, a robust tradesman, wearing boots and wrapped in a long blue tunic, gave him his own lighted candle. The flame had to pass in this way from one to another like faith in Jesus Christ. The wax sputtered and then burned brightly.

"Thank you," said Russell.

And as his neighbor looked at him with surprise, he pulled himself together and murmured: "Spasibo!"

Tatiana Sergeyevna, and then Helen, came to light their candles from the same bright source, which Russell shielded with his hand. Soon all the members of the Zubov family were lit from below like the icons. Helen's eyes shone like diamonds. A gilded line emphasized the curve of her cheek. Her lips were smiling with happiness. Everyone around her had a joyful air. People were not praying; they were whispering and jostling with feverish impatience, as they awaited permission to give free expression to their gladness. Distant singing flowed out through the cathedral doors. A misty glimmer floated above the entrance. All the candelabra were lit inside. Russell's candle softened in his grasp. Suddenly Helen cried "Look!"

The religious processions emerged simultaneously from all the Kremlin's churches. Banners, tapers and golden chasubles formed long and scintillating rivers. Each procession moved forward through the crowd with a thousand flickering flames. Priests, deacons and the congregation were seeking Christ outside the sepulcher in the marvelous certainty of His resurrection. The choir's powerful singing rose so high and carried so far that it must have been heard at the ends of the earth. A star with a fluorescent train leapt into the sky, followed by another. Suddenly everything was lit up. Fireworks! Golden rain fell upon the domes, catherine wheels whirled at the top of the towers, and fiery letters—X.B.—quivered on the palace façades [X.B. are the Cyrillic letters that abbreviate "Khristos voskrese!"—"Christ is risen!"]. Under this torrent of light the whole Kremlin—its domes, crosses, battlements and columns—quivered like a magic vessel, ready to break from its moorings and make off into the darkness. The earth vibrated beneath Russell's feet. An enormous and melodious sound fell upon his ears. Light silver and heavy bronze, Ivan Veliky's bells were giving the signal for Christian rejoicing and all the city's bells replied. Deafened by this uproar, Russell was astonished to see his neighbor, the tradesman, turn to him a face that was overwhelmed with thankfulness:

"Khristos voskrese!" said the man.

And Russell felt the touch of a perfumed beard on his cheek. In his confusion he recalled Alexander Vassilievitch's advice and stammered:

"Voistinu voskrese! [Indeed He is risen!]"

Having exchanged the triple kiss with this stranger, he turned to the Zubovs, and every member of the family repeated the gesture. Russell repeated: Khristos voskrese, offered his lips and opened his arms. His heart was overflowing with Christian love. As he brushed Helen's smooth cool cheek with his lips, he felt like an angel amongst angels. All around them people were embracing, congratulating one another and offering each other eggs.

Russian Orthodox Patriarch Alexy II holds Easter service at the Christ the Savior Cathedral in Moscow, 2001. AP / Wide World Photos.

"I am so hungry!" said Alexander Vassilievitch.

That same night, at the Zubovs' home, there was a gigantic supper for many guests. The servants, each of whom had received a little gift (paskha, kulich, cheap jewelry), all had merry faces. Russell was much amused by the custom of "egg fights" among those at table. Each took a colored hard-boiled egg and, grasping it in his hand, lightly struck the egg held by his neighbor. The one whose egg was broken was out of the game, and the winner at once faced a new adversary, and so on. The experts chose by preference the eggs with pointed ends and held them closely in their hands to lessen the area of impact. At the end of the fight, the host announced the winner, who put his victorious egg aside in anticipation of a further trial and broke another on the edge of his plate for immediate consumption. Pink, yellow or green marbling, due to the coloring matter having penetrated the shell, sometimes marked the plump white surfaces of the shelled eggs. They were salted and munched rapturously. Even those who had taken great care not to observe Lent gave the impression of not having satisfied their hunger for seven weeks.

The eggs gave way to hot and cold zakuski [appetizers]. And the hot and cold zakuski gave place to the traditional sucking-pig, with its crisp crackling, its half-closed eyes, and a colored egg in its half-open mouth. Glasses of vodka, zubrovka and pertzovka [flavored vodkas] were the punctuation marks in this long gastronomic sentence. By turns, toasts were drunk to the lady of the house, the host, to the present and absent, to Britain, to Russia, to women in general and pretty women in particular. The paskha, in the shape of a truncated pyramid, white and packed with preserved fruits, flavored with vanilla, the cylindrical kulich with its topping of melted sugar, received the praise of the connoisseurs. Supper ended at four in the morning.

The next day Russell was awakened by the melodious ringing of a thousand bells which echoed the good news across the city.

Source: Troyat, Henri. *Daily Life in Russia under the Last Tsar.* New York: Macmillan and Co., 1962.

7. *Preparing for Passover: A Jewish Family in Tunisia in the Twentieth Century*

This selection is taken from an account by Rafael Uzan, whose childhood nickname was Fallu, of the preparations of his family for Passover, *one of the major holidays of the Jewish calendar. Passover celebrates the biblical story of the angel of death "passing over" the homes of the Israelites that were marked with the blood of an unblemished lamb and killing the firstborn of all others in Egypt, a plague that finally prompted the pharaoh to release the Israelites from* slavery.

Uzan grew up in Nabeul, a small town on the Tunisian coast, but immigrated to Israel in the 1950s like many North African Jews. At the time Uzan is writing, there seems to be peaceful coexistence between the minority Jewish population and the majority Muslims, although there are clear indicators that this has not always been the case. Uzan and his family were Sephardic Jews, *or Jews who trace their origins or ritual practices to the Iberian (Spanish) peninsula, from which they spread to North Africa, other Mediterranean locations, and colonial America. Sephardic Jews contrast with* Ashkenazi Jews, *who can be traced to Germanic Central Europe and who gradually spread eastward, with large numbers also later emigrating to North America. Some of the elements Uzan mentions are specific to North African and Sephardic traditions, but many of the preparations for the Passover celebration are common to Jewish communities around the world.*

Strict observance of Jewish custom requires that meat be slaughtered and inspected by the rabbi, and during Passover not a trace of leaven could remain in a house, and the thorough cleaning and extensive period of preparation also have the effect of enhancing the celebration of the holiday. In addition, the ritual slaughter of a sheep, marking the door with its blood, and the Seder meal, which Fallu looks forward to with great enthusiasm, are essential parts of the biblical and ritual observance of Passover.

Jews have been minority communities virtually everywhere they have lived since the destruction of the Second Temple in 70 A.D. and the Jewish Diaspora from the second century until the creation of Israel as a state in 1948. Sometimes oppressed, less often not, they have persevered and preserved their ancient rituals in circumstances of varying difficulty, and the observance of Passover is still a part of everyday Jewish life.

Passover preparations got under way the very moment Purim [another Jewish holiday] flickered out. As only four weeks separate Passover from Purim there was much to be done if we wanted to celebrate our feast of freedom properly and even children had to pitch in. School was closed so that our classrooms could be taken over by a crowd of matzoh bakers, men working in shifts day and night, preparing the mountains of matzohs needed to feed the Jews of Nabeul for a week. Small portions of unleavened dough were flattened out with sticks; patterns were punched through the thin discs with the help of ten fingers, miraculously transforming lifeless lumps of dough into large flowers and crisp wagon wheels. The oven did the rest. Boys employed alongside the men would be running all over the place carrying flour and firewood, while women and grown-up girls, unclean for reasons that are obvious, had to stay away. As those hand-fashioned matzohs were naturally expensive, our committee would distribute them to the needy free of charge; my father, however, always made a point of paying for our rations. It was not the price of the matzohs, though, that was his greatest worry. The house had to be whitewashed inside and out; new shoes and clothes bought for the entire family; plenty of eggs and vegetables for the traditional dishes. What is more, without the slaughter of a sheep Passover was unthinkable. [...]

[O]nce our room had received its new coat of blue lime, Passover cleaning could begin in earnest. The short weeks still separating us from the Seder night were spent scouring, scraping and washing to make sure not the tiniest bread crumb, a speck of flour or anything else likely to ferment had been overlooked in our household. It is by refraining from contact with bread or other leavened food and drink that we try to relive the hardships our fathers suffered on their passage from slavery to freedom, from Egypt to the other side of the Red Sea over three thousand years ago. Rightly fearing that the Pharaoh would have second thoughts and pursue the builders of his towns into the desert, our people left in great haste. They had not even waited for their dough to rise, taking wafer-thin bread called matzoh with them on their flight. I have never understood why eating matzohs is considered a hardship. Those we crunched every year for eight days in honor of the Exodus were so delicious that our Moslem neighbors liked them better than any other of our holiday specialties, gratefully accepting every morsel we could spare.

For the moment, though, much remained to be done before we could recline at the Seder table eating matzohs. Anything movable in the house was taken apart for a thorough cleaning. Doors and shutters were taken off their hinges; all clothes, curtains and blankets were washed. My mother and her neighbors spent their days in the courtyard amid the soapy steam of linens boiling in copper vats, amicably chattering over the noise of water buckets rattling up and down the cistern. Patient and unruffled throughout the year, my mother became frantic during Passover cleaning. [...]

The next morning was slaughter day at my grandfather's house. Grazing on whatever there is to graze upon in a bare yard, our beautiful fat sheep had been there for some time in company of three or four others belonging to my uncles. It was a dark little yard, shadowed on all sides by a wall taller than the house itself, a thick, crumbly white wall full of holes. Goat cheese, I called it.

The old family fortress, wall and house, had been built by my grandfather's grandfather—the one they said had come from Italy. The fortunes of our family had long since dwindled and my grandparents, seeing their children stare at the naked walls with hunger in their eves, had often wished the stones would turn to bread. . . . I loved the old house. Having known no true hunger in my childhood I liked the walls just as they were, hill of holes and crevices. [. . .]

It was bright morning and in one more day it would be Passover eve. Rabbi Shushan, the slaughterer, was standing in my grandfather's yard, sharpening his knife. He did so for a long time, drawing the blade back and forth, back and forth over his stone until the blade was sharp enough to kill a sheep with one single, swift stroke through the throat. [. . .] My grandmother, praying for a happy Passover, was kissing the mezuzah as he gave the blade a last test on his fingernail. One slit—the blood gushed out and everybody tensed, breathlessly looking at the rabbi as he pulled the bowels out of the carcass. One blemish on the stomach, a blue spot on the liver, a tear in the intestine and our beautiful sheep would be declared unclean, barely good enough to be sold to a Moslem at half price. Only after Rabbi Shushan had blown up the lungs through the windpipe and had found them whole would he at last smack his bloody hand on the sheep's hind legs—his way of saying that the meat was fit for Passover.

With broad smiles, men's blessings, women's ululations, one sheep after the other passed the test. Proud that I could stand the sight of blood without crying, I plunged my hand into the red stream, then, held up by my grandfather, planted it over the gate, beside his own broad, furrowed print. Everybody was singing and joking, the men busily stripping skins, the women cutting meat and scraping the bowels that would be made into spicy sausages and other stuffed delicacies. [. . .] Apart from teeth and hooves, not a morsel of the animal was thrown away. The meat, of course, was cooked or roasted, including the skin covering the head. The bones went into soups and stews. And if the sheep had been a ram, its horns were destined to become a shofar, to sound in the new year in the fall. The hide, smeared with salt and lime, was nailed to the door where it was left to dry skin side up until after the holiday, when, well rinsed in the sea, it would make me a soft and springy new bed.

Around noon on that busy day before the eve of Passover my mother and I went back to our own house where Nisria, the mother of my three little Moslem friends, was already waiting to buy our hametz. "God bless you, Nisria, what would we do without you?" My mother kissed our neighbor on both checks, then helped her carry over to her cave whatever was still left of our winter provisions: dried couscous, beans, flour—in short any food forbidden to us on Passover. Nisria was well versed in the game; making believe this was a true transaction, she paid us two sous for the whole bargain and left. But my mother did not have to worry: once the holiday was over Nisria would return everything untouched. Not a bean, a lentil or grain of couscous would be missing. On the contrary, Nisria would always add freshly baked bread for the whole family, a sudden taste of heaven when you have gone without it for a week. How avidly we always fell upon her bread and how thankful she was for our matzohs.

For the rest of the day and far into the night my mother was completely absorbed in her cooking. She and her four neighbors squatting on low stools behind the charcoal burning in their tripods were cutting vegetables, chopping meat, swapping recipes and spices to the sound of bubbling stews and brass pestles, lustily pounding sesame seeds and cinnamon. Munching lettuce leaves and carrot chunks, I flitted about among the pots, pestles and women, fanning fires to burn brighter and faces to cool off. [...]

I ran off... to help my mother find hiding places for the bread, I said. Custom requires that we conceal ten small pieces of bread in our home on the night before Passover.

Getting up in the morning our first thought was again for the bread. Carefully counting, we collected the ten pieces from under the bed, the drawer, and from behind the water jug to burn them in the yard. Our neighbors were doing likewise and after we had all checked and re-checked the premises, convincing ourselves nothing leavened had been overlooked, we broke into loud congratulations.

"Happy holiday, happy holiday—next year in Jerusalem!" The women embraced as the sabruta, their high-pitched, warbling howl of joy echoed from one yard to the other. Surprising us with some last-minute shopping and the astonishing announcement, coming from him, that "You can't eat money, can you? Passover comes but once a year..." My father put a big bag of almonds in my mother's hands. Then shops bolted their doors though it was still early in the day, and while the Jews got into their new clothes Bab Salah Street lay empty in the sun, lazily stretching out in her own festive dress of freshly painted lime. Nothing more for me to do than wait, I thought, as I sat in the shelter of three big red hands that had barely had the time to dry, one just on top of me over the gate, and one on each side of the doorpost. Not even Mahmood, Kasham and Abdel Fader, my three Arab friends, were out in the street; nobody to play with but the mewing cats. Driven half crazy by the vapors of stewing lamb floating from every window, the cats came at me with trembling, upturned tails, furiously rubbing their heads against my legs.

"Patience, patience," I told them, waiting more ardently for the first stars to show up and Passover to begin...

Source: Awret, Irene. "Preparing for Passover in North Africa." In *The Life of Judaism*, edited by Harvey E. Goldberg. © 2001 by the Regents of the University of California. Published by the University of California Press. Reprinted with permission.

Systems of Belief

Different religious groups have systems of belief that are articulated to various degrees of specificity to offer adherents instruction in descriptions of the nature of the world, as well as moral issues and descriptions of the right way to live and worship. Belief systems may come from sacred texts or religious leaders. Some religious groups rely on personal experience for the formation of beliefs. Other ways of seeing parallels and distinctions are possible as well, of course, and the selections included in this section offer only a few examples of different systems.

In the wake of the *French Revolution* of the 1790s, the *Roman Catholic Church*, which had been the established church of the monarchical French royal state, was stripped of power and property. In its place, some revolutionaries, such as Louis de Saint-Just (Document 8), advocated establishing a wholly new religion devoted to a Supreme Being who was not the Christian God. The idea of a non-intervening, *Deist* god appealed to many who saw Christian religious belief systems as mystical, superstitious, hierarchical, and incompatible with liberty and rationality. Nonetheless, it shared the idea of a state-sanctioned, monotheistic religion. (See *Monotheism* in the glossary.)

Shinto in Japan also was state-sanctioned (Document 9), especially in the late nineteenth century, but differs from Western religions in many important aspects. It does not have a hierarchical priesthood or a single deity; instead, its animist beliefs center on revering ancestors and spirits, called kami, who may represent abstract ideas, guard clans, and inhabit everything from natural objects like rocks or trees, to foods. (See *Animism* in the Glossary.) Shinto builds shrines to individual kami; these shrines may vary in size from a small altar in a home to a large temple with extensive grounds.

The belief system of Shinto in Japan is much less structured than was Pope Paul VI's Catholic Church in the mid-twentieth century. Shinto does not have a well-developed moral theology, although behavior is still strongly regulated by tradition. On the other hand, Pope Paul VI's description (Document 10) of artificial birth control and extramarital sexual activity is an example of moral features of a belief system, even if some adherents to that system do not practice it. These differing belief systems are just a few examples of the extraordinary diversity of religious practices in modern life.

8. Revolutionary France: The Cult of the Supreme Being

Louis de Saint-Just (1767–1794) was a French revolutionary whose writings advocate the pervasive social and religious reforms the leaders of the Revolutionary government sought to implement after the overthrow and execution of Louis XVI in 1793. A close compatriot of Maximilien Robespierre *(1758–1794), under whose authority the Revolution became known as the Terror, Saint-Just was arrested with Robespierre and himself guillotined on July 28, 1794, or "10 Thermidor An II" in the Revolutionary calendar.*

Saint-Just's recommendations were to position new French Republican (a term used here to contrast with monarchical and unconnected to American political parties) ideals in the place of all the aspects of life formerly dominated by a religion seen as being complicit in the oppression of the French people and supporting the claims of a divine-right monarch to absolute authority. It is not coincidental that Saint-Just demands together the redistribution of land, reform of education, institution of new forms of worship, and the revision of the calendar. The Roman Catholic Church *was one of the largest landholders in France, had created and run the educational system, and was the official state religion whose rituals and forms of worship marked everything from birth, death, and marriage to the coronation of the king; its calendar, based on the year since the birth of Christ and on the cycle of saints' feasts and religious holidays, largely determined the patterns of everyday life.*

Aside from confiscating Church property and schools, the program of education that Saint-Just proposed adapted the most current theories of education and instruction of the day to create natural, disciplined Republican citizens. The new Republican forms of worship were also rooted in eighteenth-century ideas that were primarily Deist, *a religious philosophy that argued a Supreme Being existed, but was to be understood by reason rather than revelation, was not immanent or present in the world, did not perform miracles or intercede in response to prayer, and was best worshipped in new, non-sectarian temples rather than by sacrifice or obedience in churches. The* French Revolution *also instituted an elegant, symmetrical decimal calendar with names derived from nature, holidays named for the working classes, and a 10-day week, 10-hour days, 100-minute hours, and 100-second minutes.*

The French Revolution's rhetoric of liberty and equality did not mean for Saint-Just that the state was to relinquish its authority, however, but rather that the new state would implement its new ideals of egalitarianism, education, and civil religion in much the same ways that Saint-Just saw the Catholic Church having done under the previous regime. For Saint-Just and other revolutionaries, the reordering of religious life was virtually identical to the reordering of social and political life.

I challenge you to establish liberty so long as it remains possible to arouse the unfortunate classes against the new order of things, and I defy you to do away with poverty altogether unless each one has his own land.... When you find large landowners you find many poor people. Nothing can be done in a country where agriculture is carried out on a large scale. Man was not made for the workshop, the hospital, or the poorhouse. All that is horrible. Men must live in independence, each with his own wife and his robust and healthy children. We must have neither rich nor poor.

The poor man is superior to government and the powers of the world; he should address them as a master. We must have a system which puts all these principles in practice and assures comfort to the entire people. Opulence is a crime: it consists in supporting fewer children, whether one's own or adopted, than one has thousands of francs of income. [...]

Children shall belong to their mother, provided she has suckled them herself, until they are five years old; after that they shall belong to the republic until death. The mother who does not suckle her children ceases to be a mother in the eyes of the country. Child and citizen belong to the country, and a common instruction is essential. Children shall be brought up in the love of silence and scorn for fine talkers. They shall be trained in laconic speech. Games shall be prohibited in which they declaim, and they shall be habituated to the simple truth.

The boys shall be educated, from the age of five to sixteen, by the country; from five to ten they shall learn to read, write, and swim. No one shall strike or caress a child. They shall be taught what is good and left to nature. He who strikes a child shall be banished. The children shall eat together and shall live on roots, fruit, vegetables, milk, cheese, bread, and water. The teachers of children from five to ten years old shall not be less than sixty years of age.... The education of children from ten to sixteen shall be military and agricultural.

Every man twenty-one years of age shall publicly state in the temples who are his friends. This declaration shall be renewed each year during the month of Ventose [from the word for "wind," roughly March]. If a man deserts his friend, he is bound to explain his motives before the people in the temples; if he refuses, he shall be banished. Friends shall not put their contracts into writing, nor shall they oppose one another at law. If a man commits a crime, his friends shall be banished. Friends shall dig the grave of a deceased friend and prepare for the obsequies, and with the children of the deceased they shall scatter flowers on the grave. He who says that he does not believe in friendship, or who has no friends, shall be banished. A man convicted of ingratitude shall be banished.

The French people recognize the existence of the Supreme Being and the immortality of the soul. The first day of every month is consecrated to the Eternal. Incense shall burn day and night in the temples and shall be tended in turn for twenty-four hours by the men who have reached the age of sixty. The temples shall never be closed. The French people devote their fortunes and their children to the Eternal. The immortal souls of all those who have died for the fatherland, who have been good citizens, who have cherished their father and mother and never abandoned them, are in the bosom of the Eternal.

The first day of the month Germinal [from the word for "sprout," roughly April] the republic shall celebrate the festival of the Divinity, of nature, and of the People; the first day of the month Floréal [from the word for "bloom," roughly May], the festival of the Divinity, of love, and of husband and wife, etc.

Every year on the first day of Floréal the people of each commune shall select, from among the inhabitants of the commune, and in the temple, a young man rich and virtuous and without deformity, at least twenty-one years of age and not over thirty, who shall in turn select and marry a poor maiden, in everlasting memory of human equality.

Source: Saint-Just, Louis de. "Selections from the *Republican Institutions of Saint-Just*." In *Readings in Modern European History*, edited by James Harvey Robinson and Charles A. Beard. Volume 1: *The Eighteenth Century: The French Revolution and the Napoleonic Period*. Boston: Ginn & Company, 1909.

9. The Emergence of Modern Japanese Shinto

Milton Terry was an American Protestant minister and Asianist, at the time called an orientalist, who visited Japan and compiled his experiences of the practice of Shinto *in the late nineteenth century into a book for an American Protestant audience who knew little of the indigenous Japanese religion. The impression that Terry gives of the timelessness of the Shinto cult is only partially justified. The Shinto that Terry describes has its origins in the ancient practices of Japanese religious life, influenced by* Buddhism *and Confucianism imported from China, but is itself a manifestation of modern influences on religious life, rather than a true relic of ancient Japan.*

Terry was writing in the wake of the Meiji Restoration *in 1868, which had created a strong Imperial power in Japan and supplanted the power of the* shoguns, *or feudal lords. At the same time, late nineteenth-century Japan, closed to foreign influences for hundreds of years, had been forced by Western powers, such as the United States, into trading relationships. In response, Japan rapidly undertook radical social and technological reforms. The Meiji emperors sought to use a national version of Shinto to support their rule and bolster their authority in a period of significant cultural change.*

Shinto remains the dominant religion of Japan today, and many of its citizens practice this ancient faith. It lacks many of the features commonly found in other world religions, such as formalized doctrines, a priesthood or ritual class, or a central religious authority or power structure. Nonetheless, it is a powerful cultural influence and an integral part of Japanese daily life.

From what we have now stated it is to be seen that reverence and worship of the ancestors of the Japanese, and the recognition of the Mikado's [Emperor's] divinity as the incarnation and earthly representation of the celestial gods, constitute the essence of the Shinto cult. All the Japanese are offsprings of the gods, but the imperial "Sovran Grandchild" of Amaterasu, the Sun-Goddess, is pre-eminently divine and worshipful. The first Mikado, however, was not the real son of Amaterasu, according to the mythic tradition of the prehistoric time, but her nephew, the son of Oshi-ho-mi-mi, whom she adopted as her son. But the title of "Sovran Grandchild," having been applied first to the founder of the Mikado's dynasty, came in time to be the common title of all the Mikado's successors. The imperial worship, accordingly, represents the most conspicuous national form of the Shinto cult.

9. The Great Sanctuaries. The Mikado's palace would, accordingly, be the most holy shrine of the national worship, the private and exclusive sanctuary of the imperial ancestors. But the most notable shrine of the Sun-Goddess is not now the residence of the Mikado. On account of some great calamity that occurred far back in prehistoric times, her worship was removed to a separate temple, and was finally established in the province of Isè, in which the temples, called the "Two great divine Palaces," are the resort of thousands of pilgrims every year, and, though not the most ancient, are regarded as first among all the Shinto temples in the land. These two divine palaces, or temples, called Geku and Nallot, are about three miles apart, and stand in the midst of groves of aged cryptomeria trees. They are approached through archways (called torii, or toriui) of simple construction. The Geku temple is an irregular oblong structure, 247 feet wide at the front, but only 235 feet wide in the rear; while the side to the right of the entrance is 339 feet, and that on the left is 335. Within this large enclosure are others of similar structure, all made of the wood of cryptomeria trees, and left unpainted and without ornamentation. The various buildings of the temples are thus fashioned after the manner of the simple, huts, or dwellings of the earliest inhabitants of these islands. Some of the buildings are covered with thatched roofs and have their walls and doors made of rough matting. [. . .]

11. The Ancestor Worship. We have already observed that ancestor worship is the basis of the Shinto cult. This kind of worship is also conspicuous among the Chinese, and is held by many writers to have been the original cult of all civilized races and peoples. It began, they tell us, with a belief in ghosts, and at the first there was no clear distinction between ghosts and gods. The departed spirit was thought of as abiding near the place where the dead body was deposited, and the earliest shrines would therefore be the graves or tombs of the dead. Later thought would beget the idea that the invisible spirits were present to witness the acts and share the joys and sorrows of the living. And this fundamental idea would, of course, develop into many diverse conceptions and practices among the different tribes. [. . .]

[T]he Shinto ancestor-worship [may be described] under its three forms of Domestic, Communal, and State cults. In every case it is a worship of the dead, but the individual, whether he be the most obscure servant, the influential citizen, the commanding chieftain, or even the Mikado, is but a part and parcel of the body politic. There is a most remarkable unity of popular and national life. Government and religion are virtually identical, and there is no distinction between religion and morality. Obedience and conformity to the rules of family life, and to the customs of society and the requirements of the State—these are the simple sum-total of Shinto law and gospel. The individual must always stand ready to be sacrificed for the good of the community or of the State. Everything is to be regarded as public, and must serve the public weal. There is no such thing as privacy, and oddities have no respectable standing. Tradition and custom seem to constitute the essence of religion as well as of family, communal, and more public life.

An elderly woman cleanses herself at a Shinto shrine in Japan. Courtesy of Photos.com.

There is no code of moral law; there is nothing in the worship that is fairly comparable to what we understand by dogma, creed, or Church. Strictly speaking, this system has no heaven or hell, no deep sense of sin, and no concept of mediatorial redemption from sin and evil. The dead—all the dead of all the ages—are conceived as somehow living in the unseen vacancy around, above, below; they are present at the worship; they haunt the tombs; they are interested in the life and works of their descendants; they visit their former homes and attend the family worship there; their happiness, in fact, depends upon the honor and worship which their living descendants pay them; and also the happiness and prosperity of the living is believed to depend upon their sense of filial duty and proper reverence toward the dead. Furthermore, all the dead are supposed to become gods and attain to supernatural power. But there is no one Supreme Deity; no central throne of God; no paradise of heavenly blessedness. So far as any ideas of this kind obtain among the people, they may be regarded as later conceptions introduced by missionaries or adherents of other religious systems. But the cult implies beyond question a belief in some kind of future life. The Yomi, or Hades, of Shinto mythology, into which Izanagi went to seek his lost sister, was conceived as hideous and polluted land, and even the realm of the unseen heavenly deities was never longed for by the devotees of Shinto.

12. Elements of Animism. The ancestor-worship of Shinto can not be disassociated altogether from the elements of Animism which appear in the names and titles of certain deities, and also in the fact that there are "evil gods" and demons who are capable of working mischief and calamity in the family, the community, and the State. How these evil deities originated is matter of myth, legend, and speculation. Bad men would naturally be supposed to carry their evil character with them into the unseen world of the dead, and to have the same power to work harm among the living as the good spirits have to bestow benefits. But human spirits would hardly be supposed to become deities of the wind, and the thunder, and the waves, and the mountains; of the trees, and the fire, and the sun, and the moon, and the autumn, and the food of men. Here the old mythology of the Ko-ji-ki comes in to tell us of a prehistoric and cosmical origin of evils.

[...] These evil gods afterwards multiplied, and may be supposed to be the authors of all the demons, goblins, and mischievous spirits of evil that disturb the world and its inhabitants. But there are also good spirits innumerable that animate all moving things. The winds and the waters, the songs of birds and the hum of the bees, the growing plants and trees, are all instinct with a sort of conscious life, and the spirits that live and move in them are to be recognized and reverenced by prayers and offerings.

The spirits of dead ancestors and the powerful spirits of the winds and the storms and the growths of nature may or may not have been supposed to have concert of action understood between them. The Japanese mind seems never to have elaborated any formal philosophy of this life or any specific theories of the life to come.

Source: Terry, Milton S. *The Shinto Cult: A Christian Study of the Ancient Religion of Japan*. Cincinnati, OH: Jennings and Graham, 1910.

10. *Pope Paul VI's* On Human Life

Regulating sexual activity and families has long been a function of complex social, moral, and religious beliefs, but evading such norms is just as old a practice. Among the changes of the twentieth century in the industrialized world were expansions in the social positions of women, alterations in family life, and the development of effective means of preventing conception and regulating birth.

Although the religious and moral aspect is important, regulation of family sizes and population has not only been a religious issue; governments and other groups, seeing social and economic consequences to demographic trends, have intervened in a variety of ways. Some governments have employed natalist policies to grow families and population. For example, in the 1930s, the Soviet Union awarded medals to "Heroic Mothers" who had large numbers of children. Some governments have enforced anti-natalist laws to control population, such as China's current policies of forced sterilizations or abortions and a limit of one child per family.

Religious groups have also been mixed in their attitudes. Many Christian denominations, which had almost universally opposed artificial birth control and abortion, changed their positions on these issues in the twentieth century on a variety of grounds. Some observers expected the Roman Catholic Church *to officially do the same in the 1960s, but Pope Paul VI, the head of the Church, did exactly the opposite on July 25, 1968, when he issued an encyclical (i.e., papal letter) titled* Humanae Vitae *(On Human Life), from which the following selection is taken.*

Paul VI describes the unique characteristics of married love and argues that sexual activity is appropriate only in the context of marriage and then when it is naturally both unitive and procreative, thereby forbidding the use of artificial birth control. In practice, Paul VI's view is not shared by many, including many Catholics. Critics may accuse the Catholic Church of being rigid, patriarchal, or out of touch, while supporters may claim Paul VI's predictions of social ills, such as increased poverty, disease, gender inequalities, and familial instabilities resulting from what he sees as immoral practices, prove him right. Whether this document and others like it show the continuing need for religious voices to help direct people in their daily lives, or serve as an example of the irrelevance of organized religious moral teaching, it nonetheless offers a significant religious perspective on a uniquely modern problem of everyday life.

HUMANAE VITAE
ENCYCLICAL OF POPE PAUL VI
ON THE REGULATION OF BIRTH
JULY 25, 1968

To His Venerable Brothers the Patriarchs, Archbishops, Bishops and other Local Ordinaries in Peace and Communion with the Apostolic See, to the Clergy and Faithful of the Whole Catholic World, and to All Men of Good Will.

Honored Brothers and Dear Sons, Health and Apostolic Benediction.

The transmission of human life is a most serious role in which married people collaborate freely and responsibly with God the Creator. It has always been a source of great joy to them, even though it sometimes entails many difficulties and hardships.

The fulfillment of this duty has always posed problems to the conscience of married people, but the recent course of human society and the concomitant changes have provoked new questions. The Church cannot ignore these questions, for they concern matters intimately connected with the life and happiness of human beings. [. . .]

NEW QUESTIONS

3. This new state of things gives rise to new questions. Granted the conditions of life today and taking into account the relevance of married love to the harmony and mutual fidelity of husband and wife, would it not be right to review the moral norms in force till now, especially when it is felt that these can be observed only with the gravest difficulty, sometimes only by heroic effort?

Moreover, if one were to apply here the so called principle of totality, could it not be accepted that the intention to have a less prolific but more rationally planned family might transform an action which renders natural processes infertile into a licit and provident control of birth? Could it not be admitted, in other words, that procreative finality applies to the totality of married life rather than to each single act? A further question is whether, because people are more conscious today of their responsibilities, the time has not come when the transmission of life should be regulated by their intelligence and will rather than through the specific rhythms of their own bodies. [. . .]

MARRIED LOVE

9. In the light of these facts the characteristic features and exigencies of married love are clearly indicated, and it is of the highest importance to evaluate them exactly.

This love is above all fully human, a compound of sense and spirit. It is not, then, merely a question of natural instinct or emotional drive. It is also, and above all, an act of the free will, whose trust is such that it is meant not only to survive the joys and sorrows of daily life, but also to grow, so that husband and wife become in a way one heart and one soul, and together attain their human fulfillment.

It is a love which is total—that very special form of personal friendship in which husband and wife generously share everything, allowing no unreasonable exceptions and not thinking solely of their own convenience. Whoever really loves his partner loves not only for what he receives, but loves that partner for the partner's own sake, content to be able to enrich the other with the gift of himself.

Married love is also faithful and exclusive of all other, and this until death. This is how husband and wife understood it on the day on which, fully aware of what they were doing, they freely vowed themselves to one another in marriage. Though this fidelity of husband and wife sometimes presents difficulties, no one has the right to assert that it is impossible; it is, on the contrary, always honorable and meritorious. The example of countless married couples proves not only that fidelity is in accord with the nature of marriage, but also that it is the source of profound and enduring happiness.

Finally, this love is fecund. It is not confined wholly to the loving interchange of husband and wife; it also contrives to go beyond this to bring new life into being. "Marriage and conjugal love are by their nature ordained toward the procreation and education of children. Children are really the supreme gift of marriage and contribute in the highest degree to their parents' welfare." [...]

OBSERVING THE NATURAL LAW

11. The sexual activity, in which husband and wife are intimately and chastely united with one another, through which human life is transmitted, is, as the recent Council recalled, "noble and worthy." It does not, moreover, cease to be legitimate even when, for reasons independent of their will, it is foreseen to be infertile. For its natural adaptation to the expression and strengthening of the union of husband and wife is not thereby suppressed. The fact is, as experience shows, that new life is not the result of each and every act of sexual intercourse. God has wisely ordered laws of nature and the incidence of fertility in such a way that successive births are already naturally spaced through the inherent operation of these laws. The Church, nevertheless, in urging men to the observance of the precepts of the natural law, which it interprets by its constant doctrine, teaches that each and every marital act must of necessity retain its intrinsic relationship to the procreation of human life. [...]

UNION AND PROCREATION

12. This particular doctrine, often expounded by the magisterium [collective teaching authority] of the Church, is based on the inseparable connection, established by God, which man on his own initiative may not break, between the unitive significance and the procreative significance which are both inherent to the marriage act.

The reason is that the fundamental nature of the marriage act, while uniting husband and wife in the closest intimacy, also renders them capable of generating new life—and this as a result of laws written into the actual nature of man and of woman. And if each of these essential qualities, the unitive and the procreative, is preserved, the use of marriage fully retains its sense of true mutual love and its ordination to the supreme responsibility of parenthood to which man is called. We believe that our contemporaries are particularly capable of seeing that this teaching is in harmony with human reason.

Source: Paul VI, Pope, *Humanae Vitae* [On human life]. © Libreria Editrice Vaticana, 1968. Reprinted with permission.

Death and Afterlife

How people deal with death, and what they believe happens after death, are usually informed by their religious perspectives. Whether the person lives on in some form, undergoes some kind of transformation, or simply ceases to exist is a matter of opinion often conditioned by religious beliefs or lack thereof. Not all religions have a well-developed theology of death, while others have complex descriptions of the fate of the person after life ends.

The selections in this section illustrate a variety of approaches taken by different religious traditions. Louis de Jaucourt (Document 11), an eighteenth-century Deist and rationalist, carefully avoids any anti-Christian statements in the *Encyclopédie*, one of the first attempted compendiums of human knowledge, but published in France, which at the time was an officially Christian country with a strict censor. Instead, he focuses almost entirely on assuaging fears of death by assuring his audience that the process is usually peaceful and relatively painless. The Parsi (Document 12), a group who settled in India after leaving Persia, have a very unusual way of dealing with the physical remains of the dead that comes directly from the tenets of their faith, known as *Zoroastrianism*. The tombstone engravings of New England Puritans and other Protestant non-conformists (Document 13) show a typical Christian approach. Their dead were buried in the earth and commemorated on tombstones, some of which included elaborate epitaphs that reveal things about what these communities valued and believed.

Even though both groups believed in a final judgment and salvation, burial in earth and separation of remains from other members of the community would be unthinkable to a Parsi, just as allowing bodies to be consumed by carrion birds as the Parsis do would be extremely disrespectful to a Congregationalist preacher. Jaucourt is quiet on the question of the treatment of bodies, although it seems it would not be of special importance to him. Of course, fundamental differences in practice do not always correspond to fundamental differences in belief, but they do add to the richness of this aspect of modern religious life.

11. Louis de Jaucourt: "Death" in the Encyclopédie

Taken from the landmark Encyclopédie *of Denis Diderot and Jean le Rond* d'Alembert, *one of the first attempts to gather together and organize all of human knowledge, the following selection from the* Encyclopédie *entry "Death" by an eighteenth-century French nobleman, Louis de Jaucourt, takes great pains to reflect on death as a natural process, and avoids any theological discussions. Writing in the spirit of the* Enlightenment, *a movement in the eighteenth century that emphasized rational, non-religious knowledge and an increasingly scientific approach to the study not only of the natural world, but of the social world as well, Jaucourt emphasizes what he thinks can be known about death, rather than the things that cannot. As empirical knowledge of the fate of the human after death was not available to him, he relied on other sources of information that he could verify. To Jaucourt, death is best approached as the investigation of natural phenomena, and examining the physiology of death is both more interesting and useful than the condition of an invisible, unmeasurable soul.*

While religions often soothe the fear of death with the consolation of continued life after death, Jaucourt has the same goal—to cope with the fear of death—but his approach is very different. Fear of death he associates with ignorance of the actual process of a typical death and the fear of pain. He argues that most people die in calm and peace without pain, and death should not arouse fear—it only does so because of cultural habit and education.

Rather than commenting at all on the fate of the person after death, Jaucourt avoids angering the religious authorities of his time. Instead, he draws on the most recent medical research to explain death as a natural step in the context of the growth and decline of the human organism from its origins in the womb to its fullest development to its decline and eventually the "destruction of the vital organs." Life itself, Jaucourt says, is not an absolute, but a quantifiable, measurable thing, with a greater difference between the quantity of life in a person in full vigor and someone at the point of death than that in the very old or ill and the dead.

Death: destruction of the vital organs so that they cannot be revived. Birth is but a step towards this destruction. [...]

At the moment the foetus is formed, bodily life does not yet exist or is almost nothing, as one of the greatest geniuses of the Academy of Sciences (Buffon) has observed. Little by little, life increases and extends; it acquires substance as the body grows, develops and gains strength; as soon as it begins to decline, the quantity of life diminishes; finally, when it becomes bent, dry and collapses, life withers, contracts and is reduced almost to nothing. We begin to live by degrees, and we finish dying like we begin to live. All the causes of decline continually act on our material being and bring it little by little to dissolution. Death, this striking change of state, which is so feared, is in nature only the last nuance of a previous being; this necessary phase of our bodies' withering away is brought about like all the others that preceded it. Life starts to be extinguished long before it goes out completely; and in fact, there is perhaps a greater distance from old age to youth than from decrepitude to death; for we should not consider life here as an absolute, but as a quantity that can increase, diminish and finally arrive at its necessary destruction. [...]

The true philosophy, he says, is to see things as they really are. Our inner feelings would agree with this philosophy, if they were not perverted by the illusions of our imagination and by the unfortunate habit we have adopted of forging mental phantoms of pleasure and pain. Things are only pleasant or frightening from far away, but to be convinced of this, we need the wisdom and the courage to look at them close up. If we ask city doctors and ministers of the church, who are used to observing the actions of the dying, and who have heard their last words, they will agree that with the exception of a small number of chronically sick people, whose agitation, caused by convulsive movements, seems to indicate that they are suffering, in all other cases, people die peacefully and painlessly. And even those terrible agonies frighten the people present more than they torment the sick person; for how many people have we not seen who, after having survived this last extremity, have lost all memory of what had happened and what they felt: they had truly ceased to be for themselves at the time, since they had to wipe from the number of their days all those they spent in that state, of which they no longer had any idea. [...]

When the scythe of fate is raised to cut off our days, we do not see it, we do not feel it strike—the scythe, did I say? A poetic illusion! Death is not armed with a sharp instrument, no violence comes with it, we finish living by imperceptible degrees. The exhaustion of our forces nullifies all feeling and excites only a vague sensation in us that we feel when we give ourselves up to a vague reverie. From a distance, we fear this state, since we project ourselves into it, but when it arrives we have been weakened by the gradual steps leading up to it, and the decisive moment comes without our suspecting it and without our thinking about it. This is how most human beings die, and among the small number who remain conscious until their last breath, there is perhaps not a single one who does not, at the same time, still retain hope and who does not persuade himself that he will return to life. For the happiness of mankind, nature has made this feeling stronger than reason; and if we did not awaken terror by the sad attentions and mournful ceremonies that precede death in society, we would not see it coming. [. . .]

An individual who had been cut off early on from relations with other people, and who had no way of understanding his origins, would believe not only that he had not been born, but even that his life would have no end. . . . A savage who saw none of his own kind die, would believe he was immortal. So we only fear death so much because of habit, education and prejudice.

But the greatest alarm reigns mainly in people who have lived in the world, in our cities, and whose education has made them more sensitive than others, since the common people, especially in the countryside, look on death without fear; death is the end of the sadness and the calamities of the poor. Death, said Cato, can never be premature for a consul, regrettable or dishonourable for a good man or unhappy for a wise man. [. . .]

It seems we pay a greater tribute of pain when we come into the world than when we leave it: in the first case, the baby cries, in the second, the old man sighs. At least it is true that we leave this world as we come into it, without knowing it. Death and love are consumed by the same means, by exhalation. We reproduce ourselves when it is from love that we die; when we become nothing (I am only speaking about the body, so let no one accuse me of materialism) it is by the shears of Atropos [a Greek goddess, one of the three Fates, who cut the thread of human life with her scissors]. Let us thank nature, which has granted the liveliest pleasures to the reproduction of our species, and almost always takes the edge off the sensation of pain, in the moments when it cannot keep us alive.

Death is thus not as terrible as we think. From far off we are poor judges of it; it is a spectre that strikes us with terror from a distance and that disappears when we come closer to it. We only form false ideas about it; we look at it not only as the greatest misfortune, but also as an evil accompanied by the most horrible anguish. We even try to increase its dire image in our imagination, and to increase our fears by reasoning about the nature of its pains. But nothing is more ill founded; since what can produce or give rise to it? Shall we say that pain resides in the soul or in the body? The pain of the soul can only be produced by thinking, and the pain of the body is always in proportion to the body's strength or weakness. In the instant of natural death, the body is weaker than ever, so it can only feel very little pain, if it even feels any.

Men fear death like children fear the dark, and only because their imaginations have been alarmed by ghosts that are as empty as they are frightening. All the ceremony of last farewells, the tears of our friends, mourning and the ceremony of the funeral, the convulsions of the body approaching dissolution—this is what tends to frighten us.

Source: Jaucourt, Louis de, "Death [Mort]." In *La Encyclopédie*, edited by Denis Diderot and Jean le Rond d'Alembert. Vol. 10. Paris: 1751–1777, 716, s.v. "Mort." Translated by Malcolm Eden. Courtesy of Malcolm Eden.

12. Towers of Silence: Parsi Funerary Practices

The dominant religions in India are Hinduism, Islam, and Buddhism, *with some Christianity and a few Zoroastrian Parsis as well. The Parsis are a very small religious minority that has survived on the Indian subcontinent since medieval times, preserving their ethnic and religious identity through great effort. The Parsis still cluster today around the city of Bombay, as they did in the nineteenth century when Monier Monier-Williams, the author of the following account, was writing.*

Monier-Williams was born in India to English parents, and became a professor of Sanskrit at Oxford. He was an important Indian scholar, and in this selection he describes his encounter with the funerary practices and religious beliefs of the Zoroastrian sect in Bombay for an English audience whom he would expect to know little or nothing of Zo- roastrianism. *Zoroastrians follow the teachings of the ancient Persian prophet Zoroaster, who taught a monotheistic, dualist religion that worships one deity called Ahura Mazda. Zoroastrians have a special reverence for fire and the sun, which represent the divine creative energy.*

Different groups and cultures have different funerary practices, but this nineteenth-century account shows how one particular group dealt with the remains of its dead and the beliefs about the relationship of the body to the world after death. To the Parsi, the dead are seen as unclean, both ritually and physically, once the process of putrefaction begins. This is consistent with the ancient caste system and majority Hindi religious view in India, where handling the bodies of the dead is considered an undesirable and unclean task.

Rather than burying or burning, which Parsis feared would be disrespectful to the sanctity of the elements of fire and earth, Parsis built a series of large funerary structures called the "Towers of Silence," and they placed the remains of the deceased members of their community on the top in the open, exposed to weather and scavengers until nothing but bones remained—a rapid process thanks to the vultures Monier-Williams describes. The bones were then collected and placed inside the Towers of Silence with the bones of all other deceased Parsis.

The towers and practice still exist today, but the vultures are mostly gone, so solar panels have been installed to speed the decomposition process—an innovation that combines the ancient practice with current technology in the practice of modern religious life.

The Parsis are descendants of the ancient Persians who were expelled from Persia by the Muhammadan conquerors, and who first settle at Surat about 1,100 years ago. According to the last census they do not number more than 70,000 souls, of whom about 50,000 are found in the city of Bombay, the remaining 20,000 in different parts of India, but chiefly in Gujarāt and the Bombay Presidency....

Their religion, as delivered in its original purity by their prophet Zoroaster, and as propounded in the Zand-Avasta, is monotheistic, or, perhaps, rather pantheistic, in spite of its philosophical dualism and the apparent worship of fire and the elements, regarded as visible representations of the Deity. Its morality is summed up in three precepts of two words each—"good thoughts," "good words," "good deeds"; of which the Parsi is constantly reminded by the triple coil of his white cotton girdle....

A man must be born a Brahman or Parsi; no power can convert him into either one or the other. One notable peculiarity, however, distinguishes Parsiism. Nothing similar to its funeral rites prevails among other nations; though the practice of exposing bodies on the tops of rocks is said to prevail among the Buddhists of Bhotan.

The Dakhmas, or Parsi Towers of Silence, are erected in a garden, on the highest point of Malabar Hill—a beautiful rising ground on the north side of Back Bay, noted for the bungalows and compounds of the European and wealthier inhabitants of Bombay, scattered in every direction over its surface.

The garden is approached by a well-constructed private road, all access to which, except to Parsis, is barred by strong iron gates. Thanks to the omnipotent Sir Jamsetjee, no obstacles impeded my advance. The massive gates flew open before me as if by magic. I drove rapidly through a park-like enclosure, and found the courteous Secretary of the Parsi Panchayat, Mr. Nusserwanjee Byramjee, awaiting my arrival at the entrance to the garden. He took me at once to the highest point in the consecrated ground, and we stood together on the terrace of the longest of the three *Sagris*, or Houses of Prayer, which overlook the five Towers of Silence. This principal Sagri contains the sacred fire, which, once kindled and consecrated by solemn ceremonial, is fed day and night with incense and fragrant sandal and never extinguished. The view from this spot can scarcely be surpassed by any in the world. . . .

But what are those five circular structures which appear at intervals rising mysteriously out of the foliage? They are masses of solid masonry, massive enough to last for centuries, built of the hardest black granite, and covered with white chunam, the purity and smoothness of which are disfigured by patches of black fungus-like incrustations. Towers they scarcely deserved to be called; for the height of each is quite out of proportion to its diameter. The largest of the five, built with such solid granite that the cost of erection was three lacs [groups of 100,000] of rupees, seemed 50 or 60 feet in diameter and not more than 25 feet in height. The oldest and smallest of the five was constructed 200 years ago, when the Parsis first settled in Bombay, and is now only used by the Modi family, whose forefathers built it, and here the bones of many kindred generations are commingled. The next oldest was erected in 1756, and the other three during the succeeding century. A sixth tower stands quite apart from the others. It is square in shape, and only used for persons who have suffered death for heinous crimes. The bones of convicted criminals are never allowed to mingle with those of the rest of the community.

But the strangest feature in these strange, unsightly structures, so incongruously intermixed with graceful cypresses and palms, exquisite shrubs, and gorgeous flowers, remains to be described. Though wholly destitute of ornament, and even of the simplest moulding, the parapet of each tower possesses an extraordinary coping, which instantly attracts and fascinates the gaze. It is a coping formed, not of dead stone, but of living vultures. These birds, on the occasion of my visit, had settled themselves side by side in perfect order and in a complete circle around the parapets of the towers, with their heads pointed inwards, and so lazily did they sit there and so motionless was their whole mien that, except for the colour, they might have been carved out of the stonework. So much for the external aspects of the celebrated Towers of Silence. After they have been consecrated by solemn ceremonies no one, except the corpse-bearers, is allowed to enter; nor is any one, not even a Parsi High Priest, permitted to approach within 30 feet of the immediate precincts. An exact model of the interior was, however, shown to me. . . .

While I was engaged with the Secretary in examining the model, a sudden stir among the vultures made us raise our heads. At least a hundred birds, collected round one of the towers, began to show symptoms of excitement, while others swooped down from neighbouring trees. The cause of this sudden abandonment of their previous apathy soon revealed itself. A funeral was seen to be approaching. However distant the house of a deceased person, and whether he be rich or poor, high or low in rank, his body is always carried to the towers by the official corpse-bearers, called *Nasa-salar*, who form a distinct class, the mourners walking behind. As the bearers are supposed to contract impurity in the discharge of their duty, they are forced to live quite apart from the rest of the community, and are, therefore, highly paid. . . .

The tower selected for the present funeral was one in which other members of the same family had before been laid. The two bearers speedily unlocked the door, reverently conveyed the body of the child into the interior, and, unseen by any one, laid it uncovered in one of the open stone receptacles nearest the central well. In two minutes they re-appeared with the empty bier and white cloth. But scarcely had they closed the door when a dozen vultures swooped down upon the body, and were rapidly followed by flights of others. In five minutes more we saw the satiated birds fly back and lazily settle down again upon the parapet. They had left nothing behind but a skeleton. Meanwhile the bearers were seen to enter a building shaped like a huge barrel. There, as the Secretary informed me, they changed their clothes and washed themselves. Shortly afterwards we saw them come out and deposit their cast-off funeral garments on a stone-receptacle near at hand. Not a thread leaves the garden, lest it should carry defilement into the city. Perfectly new garments are supplied at each funeral. In a fortnight, or at most four weeks, the same bearers return, and with gloved hands and implements resembling tongs place the dry skeleton in the central well. There the bones find their last resting-place, and there the dust of whole generations of Parsis commingling is left undisturbed for centuries.

The revolting sight of the gorged vultures made me turn my back to the towers with ill-concealed abhorrence. I asked the Secretary how it was possible to become reconciled to such a usage. His reply was nearly in the following words:—"Our Prophet Zoroaster, who lived 6,000 years ago, taught us to regard the elements as symbols of the Deity. Earth, fire, water, he said, ought never, under any circumstances, to be defiled by contact with putrefying flesh. Naked, he said, we came into the world, and naked we ought to leave it. But the decaying particles of our bodies should be dissipated as rapidly as possible, and in such a way that neither Mother Earth nor the beings she supports should be contaminated in the slightest degree. In fact our Prophet was the greatest of health officers, and, following his sanitary laws, we build our towers on the tops of hills, above all human habitations. We spare no expense in constructing them of the hardest materials, and we expose our putrescent bodies in open stone receptacles, resting on 14 feet of solid granite, not necessarily to be consumed by vultures, but to be dissipated in the speediest possible manner, and without the possibility of polluting the earth or contaminating a single living being dwelling thereon. God, indeed, sends the vultures, and, as a matter of fact, these birds do their appointed work much more expeditiously than millions of insects would do if we committed our bodies to the ground. In a sanitary point of view nothing can be more perfect than our plan. Even the rain water which washes our skeletons is conducted by channels into purifying charcoal. Here in these five towers rest the bones of all the Parsis that have lived in Bombay for the last 200 years. We form a united body in life, and we are united in death. Even our leader,

Sir Jamsetjee, likes to feel that when he dies he will be reduced to perfect equality with the poorest and humblest of the Parsi community."

When the Secretary had finished his defence of the Towers of Silence, I could not help thinking that however much such a system may shock our European feelings and ideas, yet our own method of internment, if regarded from a Parsi point of view, may possibly be equally revolting to Parsi sensibilities.

Source: Monier-Williams, Monier. *Modern India and the Indians: Being a Series of Impressions, Notes, and Essays*. London: Trubner and Company, 1878.

13. *Colonial Yankee Tombstone Epitaphs*

It is the norm in many cultures and religious groups to bury the dead and mark the grave with a monument of some sort. This practice recognizes the individuality of the deceased, and serves to remind the family and larger community of those who have died. Such funeral monuments, when carved in stone, have the advantage of being more durable than many other types of records. Not only can they serve to document the names, lives, and relationships between people, but styles, shapes, locations, and inscriptions can offer insights into the lives and the attitudes toward death and the afterlife of the groups that erected the monuments.

The tombstones transcribed in this selection come from the graveyard in Groton, Massachusetts, a New England town founded in the middle of the seventeenth century. The Groton Old Burying Ground has stones dated as early as 1704, but those that make up this selection date to the latter half of the eighteenth century.

Then, as now, monuments reflected the wealth and status of the deceased. Some of the inscriptions give extensive details of prominent members of the community, such as the pastor of one of the churches, or the colonel, judge, and assemblyman. These epitaphs not only list the social standing and achievements of the dead, but also carefully enumerate their personal virtues, including, of course, the practice of Christian religion and the hope of Christian salvation. However, the longest epitaphs for the most important people are not necessarily the most effective or interesting. Others relate with much greater poignancy the death of small children, or the ravages of smallpox in a family, or the dangers of childbirth, where a woman and her child might both die, leaving a husband without wife or child.

Often New England tombstones were decorated with small sculptural motifs, which are indicated in brackets. Some of these are clearly religious, such as angelic cherub heads, or winged skulls, called Death's Heads, which have been variously interpreted, sometimes as a dour Puritan reminder of mortality, or as a more hopeful symbol of the transience of death. An hourglass indicates the swift passage of time. The phrase "Memento Mori" is Latin and means "Remember [your] mortality." In the eighteenth century world where disease or even pregnancy could easily be mortal, the inscriptions serve as records of everyday life, but also as records of the importance of religion and the consolation of belief in the afterlife for the Christians of Groton.

Underneath This Stone Lies the Body of The
Revd Caleb Trowbridge, late Pastor of the Church
of Christ in Groton, born of reputable Parents in the Town
of Newton, educated at Harvard College in Cambridge

New-England; of such natural and acquir'd Endowments as render'd him an Ornament and a Blessing in the several Relations which he sustain'd: he was a good steward over the House of God, and discharg'd the Duties of his Pastoral relation with Prudence and impartiality, Diligence and Fidelity, He was a tender and loving Husband, an affectionate and kind Parent; an agreeable and faithful friend; and a Useful Member of Society: he was much belovd and respected while he liv'd, and dyed greatly lamented, the 9th day of septr AD, 1760, in the 69th year of his Age and 46st of his Ministry, and is we trust receiving the reward of his Labours in the Kingdom of his Lord: and in Honour to his Memory his loving People have erected this Monument over his Grave.
Blessed are the Dead that die in the Lord for they rest from their Labour and their works do follow them.
The Memory of ye Just is Blessed

. . .

Memento [hour glass] Mori
[Death's head]
Here lies ye Body of Simeon Ames ye son
of Mr. Samuel and Mrs. Hannah Ames. A hopeful & promising young man, but cruel
death that regards none snatched him out
of the world in the Bloom of Life, and
early frustrated the fond hopes of
his indulgent Parents, and the
raised Expectation of his
acquaintance, he was much beloved
in his Life and greatly Lamented
in his death he died of the small pox
decemeber ye 10th A D 1760 Aged
19 years 5 months and 6 days
Remember thy Creator in the days of thy
youth for thus saith the Lord I Love them
that Love me and those that seek me shall find me.

. . .

[Cherub's Head]
Memento Mori
Here lies the
Body of Joseph
Davis, son of Mr.
Benjn. Davis & Mrs.
Sarah his wife, he
died Febr. 13th 1761
In ye 16th year of his age
Likeways Elizabeth there
Daughter died Febr. 27th 1762.
In ye 12 month of her age.

. . .

Old New England cemetery under a canopy of fall foliage in late October. © Paula Stephens / Dreamstime.com.

Memento Mori
[Cherub's Head]
here lies the
Body of Mr. Josiah
Boyden, who depar-
ted this Life Octr.
17th 1772. in ye 72d
year of his age.
Also 8 of his Children 5
sons & 3 daughters all
lyeing near this place

. . .

Here lies the
Body of Joseph
Stone son of Mr.
Nathaniel Stone
& Mrs. Sybel his
wife who died
Novr. 10th 1772.
Aged 2 years.

. . .

Memento mori
[Cherub]
Here lies Buried ye
Body of Mrs.
Prudence Warren
wife of Mr. Abijah

Warren; she depar-
ted this Life Febr.
1st 1773. Aged 23
Years. Likeways a
little babe still born
10 days before she died.

. . .

Here lye the remains of Colln. William
Lawrence, who departed this Life May 19th
A.D. 1764. Anno Aetatis 67.
he was a Gentleman who in military life rose
from the rank of Capn. Lieut. to the command of
a Regiment. In the year 1739, he was made a Justice
of the peace afterwards Quorum unus; a special
Justice of the court of common Pleas for the County
of Middlesex, and a standing Justice of the Court.
he for many years represented the Town of Groton
with the Districts of Pepperrell and Shirley in the
general Assembly of this Province. In all his public
betrustments he acquitted himself with fidelity
and honour. In private life his behavior was
becoming his Christian profession. He was remarkably industrious in the improvement of time, Just in his
dealings, a good neighbor, a faithful friend, patient
of injuries and ready to forgive them, gratefull to
Benefactors, very ready in affording assistance to
the widow and fatherless, and mercifull to all proper
Objects of pity. He was a strict observer of the
Lord's Day, a constant and serious attender on
the public exercises of Religin, a devout worship-
er of God in his family.
Blessed are the dead who dye in the Lord.
Here also lies the Body of Mrs. Susanna
Lawrence Relict of the above named Colln.
William Lawrence
She was a woman of Piety and good Sense,
An industrious, Prudent wife; and indulgent
parent, a good Neighbour, a faithfull Friend,
A hater of Hypocrisy and Guile; a lover of
Hospitality, Patiet under Affliction and Resigned to
The will of Heaven in death by which she
was called out of the world to Receive the
Rewards of a faithfull Servant on the 10th of
Sept. & in the 80th year of her Age. AD: 1771.

Source: Green, Samuel A. *Epitaphs from the Old Burying Ground in Groton, Massachusetts*. Boston: Little, Brown, & Company, 1878.

GLOSSARY OF INDIVIDUALS AND TERMS

Compiled by John Wagner and Mariah Gumpert.

See the Appendix for biographical information on the authors of documents included in this volume.

Adams, John (1735–1826). The second president of the United States, serving from 1797 to 1801. Adams was also one of the Founding Fathers of the American Republic, serving as a delegate from Massachusetts in the Continental Congresses of the 1770s, where he was a leading advocate of American independence and a member of the committee charged with drafting the Declaration of Independence. He was also congressional commissioner to France (1778–79), one of the American commissioners who negotiated the Treaty of Paris (1782) ending the Revolutionary War, minister to Great Britain (1785–88), and first vice president of the United States. (1789–97). He was a friend and, for a time, political opponent of Thomas Jefferson, and the father of John Quincy Adams, the sixth president of the United States. His correspondence with Jefferson and with his wife, Abigail Adams, is an important source for American politics and society in the Revolutionary and Early National periods.

American Civil War. *See* Civil War (American).

American Revolution (1775–1783). The American Revolution was a late eighteenth-century movement by which the 13 English colonies in North America sought and won their independence from Britain. After more than a decade of political dispute, the colonies formally declared their independence in July 1776, proclaiming themselves the United States of America. The resulting American Revolutionary War, or War for American Independence, culminated in American military victory at the Battle of Yorktown in 1781 and British recognition of the new American Republic in the Treaty of Paris in 1783.

Animism. A belief system that attributes souls or spirits to animals, plants, geographical features, and other natural phenomena and objects.

Anti-Semitism. Anti-Semitism is prejudice, hostility, or discrimination directed toward Jews as a religious, racial, or ethnic group.

Apprentice System. A system of training skilled craft workers by attaching them to an experienced craftsman for a certain term of service, thereby allowing them to learn their craft on the job. The apprenticeship system was developed in the late Middle Ages by guilds and town governments.

Arcadia. Named for a region of southern Greece, Arcadia (*l'Acadie*) was a French colony in eastern Canada that comprised all or part of the present-day Canadian provinces of Nova Scotia, New Brunswick, and Prince Edward Island, and the American state of Maine. In 1713, Britain assumed control of the colony under the terms of the Treaty of Utrecht. In the 1750s, many French Arcadians, suspected of disloyalty by the British, were expelled from the colony, with a large number eventually settling in Louisiana. Also called Acadia.

Armenia/Armenians. An ancient kingdom lying between the Black and Caspian Seas. In the sixteenth century, Ottoman Turkey and Persia extinguished Armenian independence by dividing the country between them; in the twentieth century, much of the formerly Persian-controlled portion became a Soviet republic. In 1915 during World War I, the Turkish government, suspecting the Armenians within Turkey of being pro-Russian, began a severe repression that is estimated to have led to the deaths of more than a million Armenians and has become known as the Armenian Genocide. In 1991, the Soviet Republic of Armenia became an independent state.

Ashkenazi Jews. The Ashkenazi ("Germanic Jews") are descended from central and northern European Jews who spoke Yiddish and originated in communities in western Germany. In the middle ages, many moved eastward to establish new communities across eastern Europe and into Russia. *See also* Sephardic Jews.

Ashura, Day of. The tenth day of Muharram, the first month of the Islamic calendar. For the Shiite Muslim, Ashura is a day of mourning for Husayn ibn Ali, the grandson of the prophet Muhammad, who was killed in battle on 10 Muhurram in A.D. 680. For Sunni Muslims, Ashura is a day when fasting is recommended but not required.

Baby Boom. This term refers to the sharp increase in birth rates experienced by the United States and other countries in the years following World War II. "Baby Boomer" describes someone born between 1946 and 1964.

Ballets Russes. French for the "Russian Ballets," the *Ballets Russes* is the name of a ballet troupe founded in Paris by Russian impresario Serge Diaghilev in 1909. The combination of talent from the Russian Imperial Ballets in St. Petersburg and the innovative, avant-garde collaborations with Russian and Western composers, artists, and choreographers made the *Ballet Russes* a sensation in Paris and elsewhere and greatly influenced the overall development of ballet in the twentieth century.

Bedouins. Arab nomads who live in small groups in the desert regions running from the Atlantic coast of Saharan North Africa in the west to the deserts of Arabia in the east. Since the 1960s, many Bedouins have left their traditional nomadic lifestyle to settle in the cities of North Africa and the Middle East.

Bentham, Jeremy (1748–1832). An English philosopher, social reformer, and advocate of utilitarianism, an ethical philosophy that measures the moral worth of an action by its utility, or the overall benefit it provides for society as a whole. *See also* Panopticon.

Bonaparte, Napoleon. *See* Napoleon.

Boyar. A member of the feudal aristocracy of Russia and other eastern European societies from the tenth through the seventeenth centuries.

Boy Scouts. An organization of boys who are part of a youth movement begun in 1907 by Robert Baden-Powell, a British military officer whose program is designed to build character, citizenship, and physical fitness. The Scouting movement has expanded around the world, and today also includes Scouting organizations for girls.

British East India Company. Established in 1600 as an English joint-stock trading company with special trade privileges in India and East Asia, the British East India Company had by the nineteenth century acquired political and military control of India and other British colonies in Asia. Nationalized in 1858, following the Indian Sepoy Mutiny of 1857, the company saw oversight of all its dominions transferred to the British government.

Buddhism. Buddhism is a religious philosophy that developed in India in the fifth century B.C. from the teachings of Siddhartha Gautama, who is known as Gautama Buddha or simply "the Buddha." The fourth largest religion in the world today behind Christianity, Islam, and Hinduism, Buddhism has divided into two major branches: Mahayana Buddhism, practiced in China, Vietnam, Korea, Tibet, and Japan, and Theravada Buddhism, practiced in Sri Lanka, Thailand, Myanmar, Laos, Cambodia, and other parts of southern Asia. *See also* Zen Buddhism.

Bureau of Indian Affairs (BIA). Established in 1824 as the Office of Indian Affairs, the Bureau of Indian Affairs is a federal agency that oversees the U.S. government's relations with Native Americans. Acquiring its present name in 1947, the BIA, now part of the Department of the Interior, today supervises millions of acres of land held in trust for Native American tribes.

Burke, Edmund (1729–1797). An eighteenth-century Irish politician and author, Burke was one of the leading political theorists of his time. He was a strong supporter of the American colonies during the American Revolution and, as appeared in his most influential work, *Reflections on the Revolution in France* (1790), a strong opponent of the French Revolution. Burke is today regarded as the father of Anglo-American conservatism.

Byron, George Gordon [Lord Byron] (1788–1824). An eighteenth-century English poet, who, with John Keats and Percy Bysshe Shelley, is considered a leader of the Romantic movement. Byron greatly influenced many later English and American poets, and he lent his name to a new type of dark, flawed, but still attractive "Byronic" hero. He died while fighting in the Greek War of Independence against the Ottoman Turks. *See also* Keats, John.

Canton System. A system of trade regulation employed by the government of China between 1760 and 1842. Designed to control and limit the extent of European trade and influence in China, the Canton system restricted British trade to the harbor of Canton, where specially designated Chinese merchants acted as middlemen between British traders and Chinese citizens, with whom the British were forbidden to trade directly. The system collapsed in 1842 following the Chinese defeat in the First Opium War.

Capitalism. An economic and social system in which the means of production are, in most cases, privately owned and operated and not under the control or direction of the state. In a capitalist system, the rights of the individual in property and labor are recognized and prices, wages, incomes, production, distribution, and other economic factors are determined by the operation of the market, not by governmental action. From roughly the fifteenth to the seventeenth centuries, capitalism gradually replaced feudalism as the dominant economic system in the West.

Carroll, Lewis (1832–1898). Lewis Carroll is the pen name for the Reverend Charles Lutwidge Dodgson, a mathematician and Anglican clergyman who is best known as the author of *Alice's Adventures in Wonderland* and nonsense poems such as "The Hunting of the Snark." Noted for their whimsical word play and inventive fantasy these works have been enjoyed by both adults and children and have heavily influenced later writers.

Catholic Reformation. The Catholic Reformation is the name given to the period of reform and revival that occurred in the Roman Catholic Church in the sixteenth and seventeenth centuries roughly parallel to the Protestant Reformation. Important events included the Council of Trent (1545–1563), the reform of the liturgy and clerical training, the emergence of new spiritual movements and devotional life, the founding and reformation of religious orders such as the Jesuits, educational and missionary activity, and the defining and clarification of what constituted official Catholic doctrine and practice. Also known as the Counter Reformation. *See also* Protestant Reformation.

Charles I (1600–1649). King of England, Scotland, and Ireland from 1625 to 1649. An advocate of the divine right of kings, Charles fought the forces of Parliament during the English Civil War in the 1640s. Upon his defeat, Charles was tried, convicted, and executed for treason in 1649, when the English monarchy was abolished until the restoration of his son, Charles II, in 1660. *See also* Divine Right; English Civil War.

Chipewyan. The Chipewyan are a Native American people living in the artic regions of Canada around Hudson Bay. They are not, despite the similarity in the names, related to the Chippewa, or Ojibwa people, who live in southern Canada and the northern United States.

Cholera. An infectious disease caused by the bacterium *Vibrio cholerae*. Potentially fatal within hours, transmission of cholera in humans is caused by contaminated food, water, or waste. Thought to be endemic to India, cholera spread via trade routes to Russia and then into Europe. Severe epidemics of cholera in various parts of the world in the nineteenth and early twentieth centuries caused many deaths, although with modern sanitation practices cholera is no longer considered a serious health threat in Europe and North America.

Chop (of tea). A certain number of chests all carrying tea of the same manufacture and quality.

Church of England. The official state Church in England, also known as the Anglican Church. The monarch of England has been head of the Church since 1534, when Henry VIII separated the Church in England from the Roman Catholic Church. The English Church subsequently persecuted Roman Catholics and other religious groups such as the Puritans and adopted many of the doctrines and practices of continental Protestant churches. *See also* Protestant Reformation.

Civil War (American) (1861–1865). Also known as the War Between the States, the American Civil War was a four-year conflict fought between the United States of America and the Confederate States of America, a group of 11 southern slave states that had seceded (i.e., withdrawn) from the United States following the 1860 election of Abraham Lincoln as president. The Confederacy was defeated by 1865, and the states that had comprised it eventually returned to full membership in the United States. In addition, slavery was outlawed, and the repercussions of the war still effect American life. *See also* Confederacy.

Clausewitz, Karl von (1780–1831). A nineteenth-century Prussian soldier, historian, and military theorist best known for his military treatise *Vom Kriege (On War)*, which was based upon his participation in the French Revolutionary and Napoleonic Wars and his extensive research into other wars in history. The first to apply a philosophical approach to military thinking, Clausewitz revolutionized military administration and organization in the nineteenth century.

Cold War. The political, military, and ideological conflict between the two superpowers, the United States and the Soviet Union, that emerged after the end of World War II in the mid-1940s. Marked by proxy wars in places like Afghanistan and Vietnam, a nuclear arms race, and geopolitical maneuvering, the Cold War never became a hot war, or open, full-scale military conflict. The collapse of the Soviet Union in the early 1990s ended the Cold War.

Colonialism. Colonialism is the subjugation by a nation of usually non-contiguous lands and peoples outside its borders, or the ideology used to support such colonial domination. Colonizing powers generally control and exploit the resources and institutions of the colony, and may govern or replace the native population. In the nineteenth and early twentieth centuries, much of Africa, Australia, and Asia was under the colonial dominance of one or another European power.

Communism. An economic and social system that seeks to create a classless and stateless society through communal ownership of the means of production and the elimination of free markets and private property. Based on the writings and theories of Karl Marx and others, communism is one of the philosophies and ideologies that comprise the broader socialist movement. While promising equality in a stateless and classless world society, most communist states have been unfree and authoritarian. The governing philosophy of the Soviet Union and its satellites until the 1990s, communism today is still the official philosophy of the People's Republic of China and various other states. *See also* Capitalism; Marx, Karl.

Comte, Auguste (1798–1857). A nineteenth-century French thinker best known for developing positivism, a philosophical theory that only scientific knowledge is authentic, or positive knowledge. In developing a positivist science of society he coined the term "sociology."

Confederacy/Confederate States of America (CSA). A group of 11 southern slave states that seceded (i.e., withdrew) from the United States following the election of Abraham Lincoln as president in 1860 and formed the Confederate States of America in 1861. Never recognized by the United States or any other country as an independent nation, the Confederacy was composed of South Carolina, Georgia, Alabama, Mississippi, Florida, Louisiana, Texas, Virginia, North Carolina, Tennessee, and Arkansas. The CSA fought the American Civil War between 1861 and 1865, lost, and was dissolved with the end of the war. Its constituent states returned to the United States. *See also* Civil War (American).

Coolidge, Calvin (1872–1933). The thirtieth president of the United States, serving from 1923 to 1929. He was elected vice president in 1920 under Warren G. Harding, whom he succeeded as president when Harding died of a heart attack. He won the presidential election in a landslide in 1924. Popular and Republican, Coolidge's pro-business approach to the office of president coincided with the stable, economically booming years of the 1920s.

Copland, Aaron (1900–1990). Copland was an American composer of concert and film music. He is best known for integrating modern and folk music into a distinctly American style of musical composition in works such as *Appalachian Spring* and *Fanfare for the Common Man*. As a composer, score writer, and conductor, Copland was one of the foremost figures in twentieth century music.

Counter-Reformation. *See* Catholic Reformation.

Cowpox. A disease of the skin caused by a virus that was used in the late eighteenth century to devise a vaccine for a far deadlier but related disease, smallpox.

Crimean War (1853–1856). Fought between Russia and an alliance comprising Britain, France, Piedmont, and the Ottoman Empire, the Crimean War occurred mainly on Russia's Crimean Peninsula in the Black Sea. Despite the first wartime use of railroads and telegraphs, the war was poorly conducted on both sides and prompted military reforms in its aftermath.

Crompton, Samuel (1753–1827). An English inventor and pioneer of the spinning industry who is best known as the inventor of the spinning mule, a device that combined the water frame with the spinning jenny and allowed for the creation of a large amount of high quality textiles in a short amount of time.

Cultural Revolution (1966–1976). A decade-long political and social campaign initiated by Mao Zedong in 1966 in the People's Republic of China. The campaign, which led to intense political factionalism, social chaos, and economic disruption in China, also resulted in mass deportations, the destruction of cultural artifacts and traditions, and the deaths of a million Chinese. *See also* Mao Zedong.

d'Alembert, Jean le Rond (1717–1783). A French Enlightenment mathematician, physicist, and philosopher who was coeditor of the *Encyclopédie* with Denis Diderot. *See also* Diderot, Denis; Enlightenment.

Davis, Jefferson (1808–1889). An American politician and slaveholder who served as first and only president of the Confederate States of America from 1861 to 1865. After the war, he published *The Rise and Fall of the Confederate Government* in 1881 and completed *A Short History of the Confederate States of America* shortly before his death. *See also* Civil War (American); Confederacy/Confederate States of America.

Decolonization. Decolonization refers to the ending of colonialism, and specifically to the shift from colonial rule to autonomy of most of the various colonial possessions of Western powers in Africa and Asia during the years following the end of World War II in 1945. *See also* Colonialism.

Deist/Deism. A religious philosophy that bases belief in the existence and nature of God on reason, rather than, like Christianity, Islam, and Judaism, upon divine revelation through sacred scriptures. Deists generally reject the supernatural, believing that God does not intervene in human affairs. Often associated with Enlightenment thought, Deism was influential in Britain and America in the eighteenth century. *See also* Enlightenment.

Democracy. From the Greek meaning "rule of the people," democracy is a form of government usually characterized by competitive elections, freedom of speech and press, civilian control of the military, the rule of law, and adherence to the philosophical principle of equal rights. In a representative democracy, such as the United States, the people elect representatives to act on their behalf for a certain term; in a direct democracy, such as Athens in the fifth century B.C., sovereignty is lodged in an assembly comprising all citizens of the state who choose to participate in public affairs. *See also* Monarchy, Theocracy.

Diaghilev, Sergei (1872–1929). A Russian art critic, art patron, ballet impresario, and founder of the *Ballets Russes*, the ballet company from which emerged many of the most famous dancers and choreographers of the twentieth century. Diaghilev's most famous collaboration was with composer Igor Stravinsky, from whom he commissioned *The Firebird* (1910), *Petrushka* (1911), and *The Rite of Spring* (1913). After the Russian Revolution of 1917, Diaghilev stayed away from Russia, and the new Soviet regime condemned him as an example of bourgeois decadence and Soviet art historians ignored him for more than 60 years. *See also* Ballets Russes; Modernism; Russian Revolution; Stravinsky, Igor.

Diderot, Denis (1713–1784). An eighteenth-century French Enlightenment author and philosopher who was editor, with Jean le Rond d'Alembert, of the *Encyclopédie*. *See also* d'Alembert, Jean le Rond; *Encyclopédie;* Enlightenment.

Divine Right. A political and religious idea holding that a monarch derives his right to rule from the will of God, and not from any temporal authority, including the will of his subjects or previous law. It thus conflicts with democratic and constitutionalist ideas. In England, divine right ideas were associated with the early seventeenth-century Stuart kings, James I and his son Charles I. *See also* Charles I; Monarchy.

Domesticity. In the nineteenth century, domesticity was the dominant belief of the upper and middle classes in the United States and Europe that the ideal woman was delicate, virtuous, and submissive to male authority in society. The private home was regarded as the proper sphere of women and parenting their proper role. The ideal of feminine domesticity waned in the early twentieth century with the rise of feminism and the movement for women's voting rights, but then revived in a more modern form in the United States in the 1950s, when the stay-at-home mother with children and working father were seen as the ideal family.

Dorsey, James Owen (1848–1895). An American ethnologist and missionary known primarily for his ethnographic and linguistic studies of the Siouan tribes of the Great Plains.

Doubleday, Abner (1819–1893). A nineteenth-century American military officer and Union Civil War general. Although recent research has thrown much doubt on the story, Doubleday is best known as the inventor of baseball, a game he is said to have devised in a cow pasture near Cooperstown, New York, in 1839.

Dualism. A moral or spiritual belief that accepts the existence of two fundamental concepts, which often are equal but opposed to each other, such as harmony and conflict, or good and evil.

Duchamp, Marcel (18870–1968). A French Surrealist and Dadaist artist whose work and philosophy of art strongly influenced the development of art in the twentieth century. His later career was as a chess master. Among his most famous works are *Nude Descending a Staircase* and his readymade sculptures, especially *Fountain*—which was a urinal.

Ecotourism. Ecotourism is a form of tourism that has become increasingly popular in the late twentieth and early twenty-first centuries. It generally focuses on volunteerism, personal growth, and learning new ways to live ecologically sound lives and typically involves environmentally sustainable travel to destinations where plants, animals, and current culture are primary attractions.

Edict of Fontainebleau (1685). Issued in 1685 by King Louis XIV of France, the Edict of Fontainebleau revoked the 1598 Edict of Nantes, which had granted French Protestants, known as Huguenots, freedom of worship. The Edict of Fontainebleau formalized Louis's policy of persecuting Huguenots. *See also* Edict of Nantes.

Edict of Nantes (1598). Issued in 1598 by King Henry IV of France, the Edict of Nantes, in an effort to end the French wars of religion, granted freedom of conscience to French Protestants, known as Huguenots. Protestants were offered amnesty and restoration of their civil rights. The Edict of Nantes was revoked in 1685. *See also* Edict of Fontainebleau.

Edwardian. A term used in Britain (and to some extent in the United States) to describe the political and social trends of the period 1901 to 1910, the reign of King

Edward VII. Often extended to the start of World War I in 1914, the period was one of important changes, such as workers and women's movements, but also the height of British imperial power and great cultural opulence.

Einstein, Albert (1879–1955). A twentieth-century German theoretical physicist best known for his theory of relativity and many other advancements in theoretical physics. He is perhaps the most recognized scientist of the last century, and the winner of the 1921 Nobel Prize in Physics.

***Encyclopédie*.** A highly influential encyclopedia published in France between 1751 and 1772, with later updates to 1780. Edited by the French *philosophes* Denis Diderot and Jean le Rond d'Alembert, the *Encyclopédie* was designed to be a compendium of human knowledge; it eventually comprised 35 volumes and over 71,000 articles and 3,000 illustrations. Part of its great influence rested on the fact that it was written in French, the European language of diplomacy and government, and on its effective presentation and espousal of Enlightenment ideals. *See also* d'Alembert, Jean le Rond; Diderot, Denis; Enlightenment; *Philosophes*.

English Civil War (1642–1651). A series of seventeenth-century English military conflicts fought between the forces of Parliament and those of the king. The first two wars ended with the execution of King Charles I in 1649. The war ended the monopoly of the Church of England and established, following the Glorious Revolution of 1688, the principle that the king could not rule without the consent of Parliament. *See also* Charles I; Glorious Revolution; Parliament.

Enlightenment. An eighteenth-century European intellectual movement that advocated human reason as the primary basis of authority, and questioned the authority of such institutions as the Church and the aristocracy. Centered in France, Britain, and Germany, the Enlightenment influenced political, social, and religious thought in all of Europe. *See also Philosophes*.

Estates General. A French legislative assembly comprising the three classes or estates of the realm—nobility, clergy, and commoners. The estates general, which had to be summoned by the king, met infrequently from the fifteenth through the seventeenth centuries and not at all in the eighteenth century until it was summoned in 1789, just prior to the French Revolution. *See also* French Revolution.

Ethnography. A twentieth century academic discipline that undertakes the study, based on fieldwork, of human social phenomena.

Eucharist. Derived from a Greek word meaning "thanksgiving," the Eucharist is one of the most common forms of Christian worship. The ritual is believed by most Christians to have been instituted by Jesus during the Last Supper with his disciples on the eve of his crucifixion. Almost every Christian denomination celebrates Eucharist in some form, though the meaning and significance of the rite varies by denomination. *See also* Mass; Roman Catholic Church; Transubstantiation.

Exurbs. A semi-rural region lying beyond the suburbs of a city. *See also* Suburbs.

Feminism. A number of social, cultural, and political movements, theories, and philosophies, emerging particularly in the nineteenth and twentieth centuries which are concerned with gender inequalities and rights for women.

Feudalism. A political and social system, prominent in Europe from the early Middle Ages to the fifteenth century that was based upon the giving of a grant of land by a ruler or noble to a knight or lesser noble in return for military service. In the later Middle Ages, services given by vassals could be legal, political, economic, or domestic, as well as military.

Forty-niner. Name given to one who participated in the California gold rush of 1849.

Foucault, Michel (1926–1984). A French philosopher, historian, critic, and sociologist best known for his critical studies of various social institutions, especially psychiatry, medicine, and the prison system, as well as for his work on the history of human sexuality.

French and Indian War (1754–1763). The North American phase of an Anglo-French conflict that was known in Europe as the Seven Years War. The American war is so-named because it pitted British forces and colonists against the French and their Indian allies. The war resulted in the British conquest of all of North America east of the Mississippi River.

French Revolution (1789–1799). A period of political and social upheaval in France at the end of the eighteenth century. Inspired by Enlightenment ideals, the French Revolution led to the overthrow of the French monarchy, and the suppression of the privileges of the aristocracy and the Catholic Church. Various attempts at establishing a French republic ensued. Marked by war abroad and civil chaos and the Terror within, the Revolutionary period ended with the rise of Napoleon to power. *See also* Enlightenment; Napoleon; Robespierre, Maximilien.

Gautama. *See* Buddhism.

Glorious Revolution (1688). The name given to the overthrow of King James II and his supplanting on the thrones of England, Scotland, and Ireland by his Dutch son-in-law William of Orange and his daughter Mary, who thereafter ruled jointly as William III and Mary II. The Glorious Revolution secured a Protestant succession and established the principle that the monarch must rule with the consent of Parliament. *See also* Divine Right; English Civil War.

Graham, Martha (1894–1991). An American dancer and choreographer who is considered an originator of modern dance and one of the most influential dancers of the twentieth century. Her dance company produced a host of well-known performers, and she taught dance and movement to a variety of actors and performers well into her 80s.

Greeley, Horace (1811–1872). A nineteenth-century American newspaper editor and political reformer who is best known for his opposition to slavery and his advocacy of other reform movements. His newspaper, the *New York Tribune,* was one of the most influential publications in the United States from the 1840s to the 1870s.

Guild. An association of craftspeople producing a particular product. Guilds were especially prevalent in medieval Europe, where they controlled prices, wages, labor, and training. *See also* Apprentice System.

Hajj. The pilgrimage to Mecca in Arabia made annually by thousands of Muslims. The hajj is one of the Pillars of Islam and must be carried out at least once in a lifetime by every able-bodied Muslim able to afford the trip. *See also* Pillars of Islam.

Hametz/Chametz. In Jewish dietary tradition, hametz is food made from one of the five species of grain—wheat, barley, rye, oats, and spelt—in which leavening or fermentation induced by the presence of water has taken place. Traditionally, all hametz must be removed from Jewish homes for the celebration of Passover.

Harem. A harem is a separate portion of a polygynous household designated for women and that is strictly forbidden to outside men. The idea originated in the Islamic Middle East and came to the attention of the West through the Ottoman Empire, the sultan of which maintained a large harem of wives and concubines in his palace. *See also* Ottoman Empire; Polygamy.

Hinduism. A polytheistic religion originating in India in the second millennium B.C., Hinduism is the third largest religion in the world after Christianity and Islam, with the majority of its adherents in India and South Asia. It is also the oldest continually practiced religion on earth., Hinduism has no single founder and is today an amalgam of various beliefs and traditions. *See also* Buddhism.

Hitler, Adolf (1889–1945). Leader of the German National Socialist (Nazi) Party and chancellor and dictator of Germany from 1933 to 1945. Hitler's aggressive foreign policy initiated World War II in Europe, and his anti-Semitism and racially-charged nationalism led to the deaths of six million Jews and millions of others who were considered opponents of the regime or otherwise undesirable. *See also* Anti-Semitism; Holocaust.

Holocaust. A term used to describe the killing of some six million European Jews during World War II as part of a deliberate plan of extermination carried out by the German National Socialist (Nazi) regime of Adolph Hitler and its allies. The Hebrew term for the Holocaust is Shoah, which means "calamity." Although the Nazis also murdered members of many other groups, many scholars do not include them within the Holocaust, which is defined strictly as a genocide of the Jews. *See also* Hitler, Adolf.

House of Commons. *See* Parliament.

House of Lords. *See* Parliament.

Huguenot. The name given to members of the Protestant Reformed Church of France from the sixteenth to the eighteenth centuries. In the seventeenth century, many Huguenots left France to settle in England, Ireland, Germany, and the Americas. *See also* Edict of Fontainebleau; Edict of Nantes.

Imperialism. The extension of a nation's power over another nation by establishing economic, political, and cultural control, either by direct, territorial conquest or more informal means. Imperialism also describes the ideology of the superiority of imperialist powers that legitimates the subordination and domination of foreign peoples. Modern European imperialism reached its zenith in the nineteenth century, when European states competed with one another to increase their prestige and extend their control across wide areas of Africa and Asia.

Indian Territory. This describes U.S. land set aside by the Indian Intercourse Act of 1834 for the use of Native Americans. The Indian Territory served as a destination for tribes, such as the Cherokee, who were removed from their ancestral lands by the government policy of Indian removal. By the late nineteenth century, the Indian Territory had been reduced to the land comprising the present-day state of Oklahoma, and then, with the organization of the Oklahoma Territory in 1890, to just the eastern half of the Territory. The Indian Territory was extinguished when Oklahoma was admitted to the Union in 1907.

Industrial Revolution. A period beginning in the eighteenth century characterized by the application of power-driven machinery to manufacturing, transportation, and agriculture, accompanied by widespread social, cultural, economic, and political changes. The movement began in earnest in Europe in the mid-eighteenth century, particularly in Britain, and then spread in the nineteenth and twentieth centuries to the United States and elsewhere and still continues today in some parts of the world. *See also* Capitalism.

Invisible Hand. A metaphor coined by Scottish economist Adam Smith. In his *The Wealth of Nations* and other writings, Smith argued that in a free market an individual pursuing his own self-interest also tends to promote the good of the entire community; the individual is led, as if by an "invisible hand," to take actions leading to unintended ends that will benefit the whole of society.

Iranian Revolution (1979). A 1979 revolution that replaced the Iranian monarchy under Shah Mohammad Reza Pahlavi of the Pahlavi Dynasty with an Islamic republic led by Ayatollah Ruhollah Khomeini, who had returned to Iran from exile in France to lead the revolutionary movement. *See also* Mohammad Reza Pahlavi; Pahlavi Dynasty.

Jay, John (1745–1829). An American statesman, diplomat, and jurist who coauthored the *Federalist Papers* with Alexander Hamilton and James Madison and who served as first chief justice of the United States Supreme Court from 1789 to 1795. During the American Revolution, he was American minister to Spain and France and helped negotiate the Treaty of Paris with Britain, which ended the American Revolutionary War. *See also* American Revolution; Hamilton, Alexander; Madison, James.

Jenner, Edward (1749–1823). A nineteenth-century English scientist and doctor who discovered and introduced the use of the smallpox vaccine.

Jim Crow Laws. State and local laws passed and enforced between 1876 and 1965, mainly in southern states of the United States, which mandated "separate but equal" facilities and accommodations for whites and blacks, upheld by the U.S. Supreme Court's 1896 decision in *Plessy v. Ferguson*. Named for "Jump Jim Crow," a song-and-dance caricature of African Americans, these laws almost invariably led to inferior treatment for African Americans. The U.S. Supreme Court's 1954 decision in *Brown v. Board of Education* struck down segregated schools, while most other Jim Crow laws were overturned by the Voting Rights Act of 1965.

Johnson, Lyndon B. (1908–1973). The 36th president of the United States. A Democrat from Texas, Johnson was vice president under President John Kennedy, and assumed office following Kennedy's assassination in 1963. Elected in his own right in 1964, Johnson pursued an ambitious social agenda he called the Great Society. In foreign policy, Johnson escalated American military involvement in the Vietnam War, which led to increasing anti-war unrest in the United States. *See also* Vietnam War.

Kaaba. A cube-shaped building that predates Islam located within the Masjid al-Haram Mosque in Mecca that is the holiest of Muslim sites. Muslim pilgrims who come to Mecca for their Hajj make a ritual circumambulation around the Kaaba and Muslims throughout the world turn in the direction of the Kaaba to make their daily prayers. The eastern corner of the Kaaba contains a black stone generally thought to be an ancient meteorite. *See also* Hajj; Masjid al-Haram; Mecca.

Kami. *See* Shinto.

Kasparov, Garry (1963–). A Russian chess grandmaster and the youngest person to ever win the World Chess Championship, which he captured in 1985 at the age of 22. In 1997, Kasparov famously lost a match to the IBM computer, Deep Blue.

Keats, John (1795–1821). A nineteenth-century English poet, who, with his friends Shelley and Byron, was a leader of the English Romantic movement. Although much criticized during his life, his poetry greatly influenced later poets, such as Tennyson. His most famous works are his odes, such as "Ode to Psyche," "Ode on a Grecian Urn," "Ode to a Nightingale," "Ode on Melancholy," and "To Autumn." *See also* Byron, George Gordon.

King, Martin Luther, Jr. (1929–1968). American clergyman, orator, and one of the leaders of the American Civil Rights Movement in the 1950s and 1960s. King helped organize the 1963 March on Washington, where he delivered his famous "I Have a Dream" speech, He raised public awareness of the Civil Rights Movement. In 1964, King became the youngest person to receive the Nobel Peace Prize for his efforts to end segregation and racial discrimination through civil disobedience and nonviolent protest. He was assassinated in Memphis in 1968.

Kipling, Rudyard (1865–1936). An Indian-born British author and poet who, through such works as *The Jungle Book* (1894), *Just So Stories* (1902), "The White Man's Burden" (1899) and "Gunga Din" (1890), became one of the most popular writers of the late nineteenth and early twentieth centuries. A talented and prolific writer, the militarism and imperialism present in many of his works have also made him controversial. He won the Nobel Prize for Literature in 1907. *See also* Imperialism.

Kitaro, Nishida (1870–1945). A prominent twentieth-century Japanese philosopher and founder of the Kyoto School of Philosophy.

Kremlin. A fortress complex in central Moscow that dates in its current form to the fifteenth century and includes palaces, cathedrals, and an enclosing wall and towers. The complex serves as the official residence of the president of Russia and the seat of its government. The term "the Kremlin" is often used as a shorthand for the Russian (and previously the Soviet) government. *See also* Union of Soviet Socialist Republics (USSR).

Laissez-faire. Laissez-faire, from a French phrase meaning "to let be," is an economic policy that favors minimal intervention by the state in the form of regulation and taxation that goes beyond what is thought necessary to maintain liberty, order, and security. Laissez-faire economics responded to the interventionism of eighteenth century mercantilism and were popular through the nineteenth century, though most modern governments exert a significant amount of economic control. *See also* Capitalism, Mercantilism.

Livre/Sous. French units of currency used until the introduction of the franc in 1795.

Lorestan. A province and historical territory of western Iran that is centered in the Zagros Mountains with its capital at Khorramabad. Lorestan, which means "land of the Lurs," is one of the oldest settled regions of Iran. The Lurs, who inhabit much of southwestern Iran, speak Lori, an Iranian language closely related to Persian.

Lowell System. A textile factory system employed in the early nineteenth century in the New England textile mills of Francis Cabot Lowell. To avoid the poverty and disorder that plagued English mill towns, Lowell closely supervised both the living and working conditions of his employees, who were mainly young, unmarried women. The Lowell system stressed cleanliness, encouraged church attendance, enforced strict curfews, paid good wages, and provided good food in well-maintained employee boardinghouses. Increasing competition led to the breakdown of Lowell's system.

Madison, James (1751–1836). Fourth president of the United States, serving from 1809 to 1817, and leading the country through the War of 1812. Madison was also one of the chief architects of the United States Constitution, one of the authors of the *Federalist Papers*, and a founder of the Democratic-Republican Party. He is considered the "Father of the Bill of Rights," the first ten amendments to the Constitution, of which he was the primary author.

Magisterium. A Latin term from the Roman Catholic Church that refers to the teaching authority of the Church exercised by Pope and bishops. *See also* Roman Catholic Church.

Mahayana Buddhism. *See* Buddhism.

Mao Zedong (1893–1976). Chinese political and military leader who led the Communist Party to victory in the Chinese Civil War and who led the People's Republic of China from 1949 until his death. To maintain his grip on power, Mao initiated the period of political and social upheaval known as the Cultural Revolution in 1966. *See also* Cultural Revolution.

Marathon. A long-distance running event of 42 kilometers (just over 26 miles). Its name comes from the legend of Pheidippides, a Greek soldier who in 490 B.C. ran the entire distance from the battlefield to Athens to announce, before collapsing and dying of exhaustion, that the Greeks had defeated the Persians at the Battle of Marathon.

"The Marseillaise." A marching song composed in 1792 by Claude Joseph Rouget de Lisle that became the anthem of the French Revolution and is today the national anthem of France. Its name comes from the fact that it was first sung in the streets of Paris by military volunteers from the city of Marseille. *See also* French Revolution.

Marx, Karl (1818–1883). A nineteenth-century German philosopher, political economist, and revolutionary, who, in such works as *The Communist Manifesto* (1848), argued that capitalism would be destroyed and eventually replaced by communism. *See also* Capitalism; Communism.

Masjid al-Haram. Arabic for "The Sacred Mosque," the Masjid al-Haram is the largest mosque in the world and the object of the hajj pilgrimage. Located in the city of Mecca, it surrounds the Kaaba, the holiest place on earth to Muslims. *See also* Hajj; Kaaba; Mecca.

Mass. The Eucharistic celebration of the Roman Catholic Church. *See also* Eucharist; Roman Catholic Church; Transubstantiation.

Matisse, Henri (1869–1954). A twentieth-century French artist, known primarily as a painter, whose skill at drawing and expressive use of color made him one of the leading figures in modern art. Some of his better-known works include *Woman with a Hat* (1905), *Madras Rouge* (1907), and *La Danse* (1909). A leader of the Fauvist movement, which emphasized strong color and artistic technique, Matisse later in life worked with paper cutouts, such as the famous *Jazz* series.

Matzoh. A cracker-like flatbread made of plain white flour and water that is the substitute for leavened breads during the Jewish holiday of Passover. *See also* Passover.

Mecca. A city in western Saudi Arabia and the holiest city in Islam, being the birthplace of Muhammad (570–632), the founder of Islam, and the location of the most sacred site in Islam, the Masjid al-Haram, the Sacred Mosque of Mecca. The fifth of the Five Pillars of Islam calls upon each able-bodied Muslim who can afford it to make a pilgrimage (hajj) to Mecca at least once in a lifetime. *See also* Hajj; Medina; Pillars of Islam.

Medina. A city in western Saudi Arabia and, after Mecca, the second holiest city in Islam. It is the burial place of Muhammad, the founder of Islam, and the city to which he emigrated in 622 when he and his followers faced growing opposition and persecution in Mecca. *See also* Mecca.

Meiji Restoration. A political revolution occurring in Japan in the late 1860s whereby the shogunate, a hereditary military dictatorship that had ruled Japan since 1600, was overthrown and political power was theoretically restored to the emperor. The new government used its authority to industrialize and militarize Japan, which by the Russo-Japanese War of 1904–1905 had become a recognized world power. *See also* Russo-Japanese War.

Mercantilism. An economic theory which holds that the economic strength of a nation depends upon its share of finite global economic value. Mercantilism calls for the government to play an interventionist and protectionist role in the economy by extensive regulation, tariffs, and taxes, especially on imported items. Mercantilism was the dominant economic theory in Europe from the sixteenth to the eighteenth centuries.

Middle Passage. The Middle Passage was the leg of the eighteenth-century trans-Atlantic triangle trade from West Africa to the Americas. The cargo was usually enslaved Africans, and the conditions maintained aboard the ships that transported slaves were horrendous. More than 600 slaves could be shackled together below decks and fed only one meal a day on a voyage that could last months. Many died of disease or starvation before the ship ever reached its destination. *See also* Triangle Trade.

Miscegenation. Marriage, cohabitation, or sexual relations between persons of different races. The term was often applied to the passage of statutes—so-called anti-miscegenation laws—which banned racial intermarriage or sexual contact. The term usually has a negative connation and is often considered offensive.

Modern. Historians use the term "Modern" generally to describe the period beginning in the eighteenth century and running to the present; however, the term also is used to refer to the late nineteenth and twentieth centuries only or even to only portions of the latter. *See also* Modernity.

Modernism. A term that describes a series of late nineteenth- and early twentieth-century cultural movements in art, literature, music, architecture, and the applied arts. *See also* Postmodernism.

Modernity. Of or related to the Modern period and the cultural phenomena that comprise it. *See also* Modern.

Mohammad Reza Pahlavi (1919–1980). Shah of Iran from 1941 to 1979 and last monarch of the Pahlavi Dynasty. An ally of the United States, the shah was overthrown by the 1979 Iranian Revolution, which resulted in the establishment of an Islamic Republic in Iran. The shah lost support because of his pro-Western policies, his recognition of Israel, and his suppression of internal dissent. *See also* Iranian Revolution; Pahlavi Dynasty; Reza Shah Pahlavi.

Monarchy. Form of government in which the head of state is (usually) a single individual who exercises power for life and passes his office to children or another member of the family. In the early Modern period, European monarchs exercised extensive powers, but by the twentieth century most remaining monarchs were constitutional rulers who served as head of state but exercised little or no political power. *See also* Republicanism.

Monotheism. Belief in the existence of only one deity. Judaism, Christianity, and Islam are monotheistic religions. *See also* Pantheism.

Mughal Empire. Imperial Muslim state that, during its height in the seventeenth centuries, ruled most of the Indian subcontinent. The empire declined rapidly after about

1725, but the last Mughal ruler was not deposed until 1857, when he was exiled by the British in the aftermath of the Sepoy Mutiny.

Nabokov, Vladimir (1899–1977). A Russian-American novelist and short story writer who is best known for his 1955 novel *Lolita*.

Napoleon (1769–1821). Born Napoleon Bonaparte on the Mediterranean island of Corsica, Napoleon was a French Revolutionary military and political leader who ruled France as First Consul from 1799 to 1802 and as Emperor Napoleon I from 1802 until his abdication in 1814, and then again briefly in 1815. Through his military victories, he redrew the political map of Europe and extended French influence and the ideals of the French Revolution throughout Europe. Napoleon is also credited with reforming the French legal code. After his failed campaign against Russia in 1812 and his final defeat at Waterloo in 1815, he was exiled by the British to the Atlantic island of St. Helena, where he died in 1821. *See also* French Revolution.

Natural Law. An ethical theory that posits the existence of a set of moral norms which can be defined by the rational observation of the nature of the world and human beings and therefore in effect everywhere. Originating in pre-modern religious and philosophical thought, its influence is evident in the Enlightenment and modern ideas of human rights.

Nijinsky, Vaslav (1890–1950). A Russian ballet dancer and choreographer who worked for the Ballets Russes, Nijinsky is considered one of the best male dancers and one of the most innovative choreographers of the twentieth century. His choreography and performances include the ballets *L'après-midi d'un faune (The Afternoon of a Faun)* (1912) and *Le Sacre du Printemps (The Rite of Spring)*, with music by Igor Stravinsky (1913). His work in *The Rite of Spring* was so nontraditional that it caused a riot among the audience when it premiered in Paris. *See also* Diaghilev, Serge; Ballets Russes.

Nirvana. A term used by the Buddha, the founder of Buddhism, to describe the state of perfect peace of mind. *See also* Buddhism.

Opium Wars. Two wars, fought from 1839 to 1842 and 1856 to 1860, between China and Britain, which resulted from ongoing trade disputes between the two nations and the British practice of smuggling opium from India into China in defiance of Chinese drug laws. Defeated in both wars, China was forced to accept the opium trade, to open several of its ports to foreign trade, and to cede Hong Kong to Britain.

Orthodox Christianity. A Christian religious tradition that traces its origins and rites to the original Christian communities of the eastern Mediterranean or areas evangelized by them, such as the Greek Orthodox Church or the Russian Orthodox Church. The Orthodox Churches separated from the Roman Catholic Church of the West in the eleventh century over political and doctrinal issues. *See also* Roman Catholic Church.

Ottoman Empire. An Islamic Turkish empire that during its height in the sixteenth and seventeenth centuries ruled the Balkans, the Eastern Mediterranean, and much of the Middle East to the Caspian Sea and the Persian Gulf., The Ottoman Empire declined during the nineteenth century and finally collapsed after World War I, during which the Empire supported the Central Powers, and the Republic of Turkey was proclaimed in 1923.

Pahlavi Dynasty. A twentieth-century dynasty that ruled Iran from 1925 to 1979. The founder of the dynasty was Reza Shah Pahlavi, an Iranian army officer who overthrew the reigning Qajar Dynasty in 1925. His son, Mohammad Reza Pahlavi, succeeded him in 1941 when Reza Shah Pahlavi was overthrown and exiled by an Anglo-Soviet invasion launched when the shah was feared to be pro-German. The dynasty came to an end in 1979 when Mohammad Reza Pahlavi was overthrown by the Iranian Revolution. *See also* Iranian Revolution; Mohammad Reza Pahlavi; Reza Shah Pahlavi.

Panopticon. A type of prison building designed by English philosopher Jeremy Bentham in 1785. The structure is designed to allow guards to watch all the prisoners without the prisoners knowing whether or not they are being observed, thus influencing the prisoners to behave as if they are under observation at all times. Never built, many modern prisons are modified versions of Bentham's panopticon design. *See also* Bentham, Jeremy.

Pantheism. Belief in the equivalence of the Universe, Nature, and God and that God is to be found in all things. *See also* Monotheism.

Parliament. A legislative body, especially one patterned on the British Parliament and system of government. In Britain, Parliament comprises two houses, the House of Commons, elected by the people and today the real seat of political power, and the House of Lords, consisting of titled hereditary members or members appointed by the government for their lives only. *See also* Parliamentary System.

Parliamentary System. A form of representative government distinguished by no clear separation of powers between the executive and legislative branches of the government, unlike the situation pertaining in a presidential republic like the United States. Parliamentary systems usually have a clear differentiation between the head of government (usually a prime minister or premier) and the head of state (an elected president or a hereditary monarch). Britain has one of the oldest and best-known parliamentary systems of government. *See also* Parliament; Republicanism.

Passover. An annual Jewish religious observance commemorating the flight of the Jews under Moses from bondage in Egypt as described in the biblical Book of Exodus. The name derives from the story in Exodus about the Angel of Death passing over the Jewish households marked with the blood of a lamb as it came bringing the tenth plague, the slaying of every first-born male in Egypt.

Pasteur, Louis (1822–1895). A nineteenth-century French chemist and microbiologist whose experiments confirmed the germ theory of disease and created the first vaccine for rabies. One of the founders of microbiology, Pasteur is also known for inventing a method to destroy harmful microbes in milk and wine, a process now known as "pasteurization."

Penicillin. An antibiotic drug used in the treatment of various bacterial infections that was discovered by Sir Alexander Fleming in 1928 and developed for medical use by Howard Walter Florey.

Persia. The ancient and traditional name of modern-day Iran, which was the heart of the ancient Persian Empire in the sixth to the fourth centuries B.C.

Peter the Great (1672–1725). Czar of Russia from 1682 until his death—he ruled jointly with his half-brother Ivan V until 1696. Peter pursued a policy of Westernization and military expansion that transformed Russia into a major European power. In 1703, he founded a new capital at St. Petersburg. *See also* St. Petersburg.

Philosophe. From French for "philosopher," one of a loose group of eighteenth-century Enlightenment intellectuals who advocated a new approach to society that encouraged reason, knowledge, and education, and criticized political and religious authority and some forms of social injustice. The *philosophes* Denis Diderot and Jean le Rond d'Alembert edited the *Encyclopédie* (1751–1772), which represented their belief that everything could be known, classified, and understood by humans. *See also* d'Alembert, Jean le Rond; Diderot, Denis; *Encyclopédie;* Enlightenment.

Picasso, Pablo (1881–1973). A Spanish painter and sculptor who was one of the most famous artists of the twentieth century. He is best known as a founder of the Cubist movement and for a prolific body of work encompassing a wide variety of artistic styles. His most famous works include *Les Demoiselles d'Avignon* (1907), which foreshadowed the Cubist style, and *Guernica* (1937), which depicts the German bombing of the Spanish town of Guernica during the Spanish Civil War of the 1930s.

Picul. English word for a traditional Chinese measurement of weight.

Pillars of Islam. The five obligations of every Muslim. The five pillars are (1) Shahadah, a profession of faith; (2) Salat, the saying of ritual prayer five times per day; (3) Sawm, fasting during Ramadan; (4) Zakat, charity given to family, friends, and the needy; and (5) Hajj, pilgrimage to Mecca. To Sunni Muslims, these practices are essential; Shi'a Muslim ritual practices largely coincide with the Pillars. *See also* Hajj; Shiism; Sunnism.

Poe, Edgar Allan (1809–1849). A nineteenth-century American poet, short story writer, editor, and literary critic, who is best known for his poems and his tales of mystery and the macabre. Considered part of the American Romantic movement, Poe is credited as being the inventor of the detective-fiction genre. Among his best-known works are the poem "The Raven," and the stories "The Pit and the Pendulum," "The Tell-tale Heart," and "The Murders in the Rue Morgue."

Political Machine. An unofficial system of political organization based on control of government patronage and the work of supporters who further the ends of the organization in return for government jobs, favors, and contracts. Such organizations often controlled the politics of major American cities in the late nineteenth and early twentieth centuries. *See also* Tammany Hall.

Pol Pot (1925–1998). Leader of the Cambodian Communist movement known as the Khmer Rouge and prime minister of Cambodia from 1976 to 1979. While in power, Pol Pot adopted a policy of agrarian collectivization and forced labor projects. This practice, when combined with frequent executions of political and ideological opponents, led to the deaths of an estimated 750,000 to 1.7 million people.

Polygamy. A form of marriage in which a person has more than one spouse.

Ponca. A Native American tribe living mainly in northern Nebraska and Oklahoma. The tribe numbered only about 200 individuals when it was visited by the Lewis and Clark expedition in 1804.

Positivism. A philosophy that declares the only authentic knowledge to be scientific knowledge, which can only be gained from affirmation of theories through strict application of the scientific method. Positivism was developed by Auguste Comte in the mid-nineteenth century, and, in various versions, became one of the dominant strains of British and American philosophy in the twentieth century. *See also* Comte, Auguste.

Postcolonialism. A set of theories and concepts in philosophy, literature, the arts, and political science that deal with the cultural legacy of imperial or colonial rule. *See also* Colonialism; Decolonization; Imperialism.

Postmodernism. A wide-ranging set of ideas, theories, and developments in philosophy, art, literature, architecture, and culture that are generally characterized as either emerging from, reacting to, or superseding the ideas and characteristics of Modernism. *See also* Modernism.

Pound/Shilling/Penny. Units of British currency. Prior to 1971, the pound was worth 20 shillings and the shilling worth 12 pence, making the pound worth 240 pence. In 1971, a pound was declared to be worth 100 pence.

Protestant Reformation. A European religious reform movement of the sixteenth century that resulted in the emergence of various new Protestant Christian denominations that rejected the authority of the pope and adopted various new doctrines and practices not approved by the Roman Catholic Church. Among the leaders of the Reformation were Martin Luther, John Calvin, and Ulrich Zwingli. *See also* Catholic Reformation, Roman Catholic Church.

Prussia. A Germanic kingdom with its capital at Berlin that in the nineteenth century became the core and driving force for unification of the modern Germany, with the King of Prussia becoming the emperor of Germany in 1871.

Pueblo. A traditional Native American village or settlement of the American Southwest, sometimes characterized by adobe dwellings.

Qanat. A type of underground irrigation system which dates to ancient times, qanats are designed to supply water to communities in hot, arid climates from distant, subterranean sources. Use of the system spread from the Middle East to North Africa, Spain, Italy and elsewhere, following the Muslim conquests of the seventh century.

Quit-rent. A type of land tax. Under feudalism in the Middle Ages, payment of a quit-rent freed the holder of the land from performing service obligations otherwise due to the feudal lord. British colonial governments often imposed quit-rents on landholders from the eighteenth into the twentieth century. *See also* Feudalism.

Reformation. *See* Catholic Reformation; Protestant Reformation.

Republicanism. A political ideology that emphasizes the belief that the citizens of a state are the source of political power or sovereignty and that a legitimate government represents the will or consent of the people. Republicanism has become increasingly common and popular in the modern period.

Reza Shah Pahlavi (1878–1944). Shah of Iran from 1925 to 1941, and founder of the Pahlavi Dynasty. An Iranian military officer, he overthrew the ruling Qajar Dynasty in 1925 and established an authoritarian regime that was secular, militaristic, and anti-communist. His many economic and political reforms helped to modernize the country, but also generated much opposition. He was forced to abdicate in favor of his son, Mohammad Reza Pahlavi, in 1941, when fears that he was pro-German prompted Britain and the Soviet Union to invade Iran. *See also* Iranian Revolution; Mohammad Reza Pahlavi; Pahlavi Dynasty.

Robespierre, Maximilien (1758–1794). A French Revolutionary and politician, Robespierre became the de facto leader of the Revolutionary government in 1793 and began the elimination of perceived enemies of the Revolution, ordering thousands arrested and guillotined without trial. This period, known as the Reign of Terror, ended with Robespierre's own arrest and execution by guillotine in 1794. *See also* French Revolution.

Roman Catholic Church. The Church led by the Pope or Bishop of Rome, who, through apostolic succession, traces his authority back to the biblical commission given by Jesus to St. Peter, whom Catholics consider to be the first pope, at the founding of Christianity. The Church's main mission is to preach the Gospel of Christ and administer the sacraments, such as the Eucharist, and it also runs numerous charitable and social programs and ministries throughout the world. In the sixteenth century, reformers such as Martin Luther questioned various Roman Catholic doctrines and practices, which led to the eventual development of Protestantism. *See also* Catholic Reformation; Magisterium; Mass; Orthodox Christianity; Protestant Reformation.

Romanticism. A cultural movement arising in late eighteenth- and early nineteenth-century Europe that emphasized individuality and imagination. Responding to the rationalism of the Enlightenment and the technologies of the Industrial Revolution, Romanticism was most strongly embodied in the visual arts, music, and literature. The complex movement stressed aesthetic experience and strong emotion over reason and social norms and brought a new appreciation to folk art, the exotic, and the inspiration provided by the natural world.

Roosevelt, Theodore (1858–1919). An American statesman, conservationist, and author. The 26th president of the United States, Roosevelt, a Republican and Progressive, served from 1901 to 1909. He became president of the New York City Police Commissioners Board in 1895, and he organized volunteer cavalry regiment, dubbed the "Rough Riders," during the Spanish-American War in 1898. He was elected vice president under William McKinley in 1900, assumed office upon McKinley's assassination in 1901, and won a term in his own right in 1904. He was known for his outgoing, energetic personality, his role in the building of the Panama Canal, his conservationism, and his mediation during the Russo-Japanese War, for which he won a Nobel Peace Prize. *See also* Russo-Japanese War.

Rousseau, Jean-Jacques (1712–1778). A French Enlightenment political philosopher and writer, whose political and social theories greatly influenced the French Revolution and inspired the Romantic movement. His novel, *Julie, or the New Heloise,* was one of the best-selling works of fiction of the eighteenth century. *See also* Enlightenment; French Revolution; Romanticism.

Russian Revolution (1917). A series of political, social, and economic upheavals that occurred in Russia during the year 1917 and led to the overthrow of Czar Nicholas II and the end of the Russian Empire. The Bolshevik faction of the Communist party—under the leadership of Vladimir Lenin—subsequently seized power. The Bolsheviks, who eventually became the Communist Party of the Soviet Union, founded the Union of Soviet Socialist Republics (USSR) in 1922 and governed until the collapse of the USSR in 1991. *See also* Communism; Stalin, Joseph; Union of Soviet Socialist Republics.

Russo-Japanese War (1904–1905). A war between the Russian and Japanese Empires that arose from the conflicting imperial ambitions of each in East Asia. A total victory for Japan, the war was the first modern instance of an Asian nation defeating a European nation, and it raised Japan to the rank of a world power. The war was ended by the 1905 Treaty of Portsmouth, which was mediated by President Theodore Roosevelt of the United States, who won a Nobel Peace Prize for his efforts.

St. Petersburg. Former capital city of Russia, St. Petersburg was a completely new city founded by Czar Peter the Great in 1703 at a site in northeastern Russia along the Neva River with access to the Baltic Sea. The city was the capital of Russia until 1918, when it was supplanted by Moscow. Renamed Petrograd in 1914 and Leningrad in 1924, the city resumed the name St. Petersburg upon the collapse of the Soviet Union in 1991. *See also* Peter the Great; Union of Soviet Socialist Republics (USSR).

Satyagraha. A practical philosophy of nonviolent resistance developed in the early twentieth century by Indian nationalist leader Mohandas K. Gandhi. Gandhi employed *satyagraha* in his campaigns for racial justice in South Africa and his campaigns for independence from Britain in India. *Satyagraha* also strongly influenced the thinking of American civil rights leader Martin Luther King, Jr. *See also* King, Martin Luther, Jr.

Scientific Management. *See* Taylorism.

Secession. The act of withdrawing from an organization, union, or political entity. In American history, the term "secession" refers to the attempted withdrawal from the United States of 11 southern states in 1860 and 1861 to form the Confederate States of America, which led to the American Civil War. *See also* Civil War (American); Confederacy/Confederate States of America.

Seder. A Jewish ritual meal held on the first night of Passover. *See also* Passover.

Selamlik. The portion of a Turkish palace or house reserved for men.

Sephardic Jews. The Sephardi ("Spanish Jews") are Jews descended from communities originating in the Iberian Peninsula, North Africa, and the Middle East. *See also* Ashkenazi Jews.

Sharia. The body of Islamic religious law.

Sheridan, Philip (1831–1888). A Union Army general during the American Civil War, who rose rapidly through the ranks through his leadership, skill, and close association with General Ulysses S. Grant. *See also* Civil War (American); Confederacy/Confederate States of America.

Shiism (Shi'a Islam). The second largest denomination of Islam, comprising roughly 15 percent of all Muslims worldwide. The major point of contention between Shiites and Sunnis (members of the majority Muslim denomination) involves the disputed succession to the political authority of Muhammad, the founder of Islam. Shiites are the majority today in Iran, Iraq, Bahrain, and large minorities in several other countries. *See also* Ashura, Day of; Sunnism.

Shinto. The native religion and formerly the state religion of Japan. An animistic belief system that attributes souls to animals, plants, and natural phenomena, Shinto is a polytheistic religion that involves the worship of numerous spirits, known as *kami*, which can be associated with a particular place or natural object, such as the sun or a mountain. *See also* Animism.

Shoah. *See* Holocaust.

Shogun. Title given to the leader of the feudal military dictatorship that ruled Japan from 1600 to 1868. The Meiji Restoration ended the rule of the shoguns. *See also* Meiji Restoration.

Slavery. A socio-economic institution in which certain persons are forced into involuntary servitude. The term "chattel slavery" describes persons who are treated as the personal property of another person or group. Slavery has existed in human societies since ancient times, being, for instance, a vital part of the economy of ancient Rome. Africans were brought to the Americas as slaves beginning in the sixteenth century, and slavery based on race continued in the United States until 1865, when it was abolished following the Civil War. Today slavery is illegal almost everywhere in the world, but is still practiced secretly in some places, particularly in West Africa. *See also* Civil War (American).

Smallpox. An acute infectious disease unique to humans that is caused by either of two variants of the same virus, *Variola major* and *Variola minor*. The disease was first named "smallpox" in the fifteenth century to distinguish it from syphilis, the so-called "great pox." Smallpox was a leading cause of death in Europe in the eighteenth century and it is believed that smallpox was one of the chief Old World diseases responsible for the deaths of a large percentage of Native Americans following initial contact with Europeans. With the development of vaccines starting in the late eighteenth century, smallpox was eventually eradicated in the twentieth century, with the last death due to the disease occurring in 1978. *See also* Cowpox.

Soviet. In pre-Revolutionary Russia, a soviet was a local workers' council, which were first formed about 1905. After the Russian Revolution of 1917, the soviet became, at least theoretically, the basic unit of political organization in the Union of Soviet Socialist Republics (USSR), and the term became shorthand for something relating to the USSR. *See also* Russian Revolution; Union of Soviet Socialist Republics.

Spinning Jenny. A multiple-spool spinning wheel invented in the 1760s by British inventor James Hargreaves. The device significantly reduced the amount of human work required to produce yarn.

Sprawl. *See* Urban Sprawl.

Stalin, Joseph (1878–1953). General Secretary of the Communist Party of the Soviet Union and de facto ruler of the USSR from the mid-1920s to his death in 1953. He manipulated communist ideas to establish an authoritarian regime known as Stalinism, which was characterized by extensive propaganda to create a cult of personality around Stalin himself as absolute dictator and the employment of secret police to create terror and stifle political dissent. His programs of rapid industrialization, forced deportation and labor, manufactured famine, and collectivization of agriculture made his personal power absolute and the Soviet Union an industrial and political superpower but at the cost of millions of lives. *See also* Cold War; Communism; Russian Revolution; Union of Soviet Socialists Republics.

Stravinsky, Igor (1882–1971). A Russian composer, pianist, and conductor who is considered one of the most important composers of the twentieth century. Stravinsky achieved international fame with three ballets commissioned by Sergei Diaghilev's *Ballets Russe*. *L'Oiseau de feu (The Firebird)* (1910), *Petrushka* (1911/1947), and *Le sacre du printemps (The Rite of Spring)* (1913). The last of these was so innovative, it provoked a riot among the audience at its premier, but it also heavily influenced the work of many modernist composers.

Suburbs. Primarily residential communities on the outskirts of large cities or towns. *See also* Exurb; Urban Sprawl.

Sunnism. The largest denomination of Islam, comprising almost 85 percent of all Muslims worldwide. The major point of contention between Sunnis and Shiites (members of the second largest Muslim denomination) involves the disputed succession to the political authority of Muhammad, the founder of Islam. Sunnis are the majority through most of North Africa and the Middle East, as well as in parts of Southeast Asia, such as Indonesia. *See also* Shiism.

Swaraj. Meaning, in general, "self-government" or "home-rule," the term swaraj usually refers in particular to a concept for Indian independence from foreign rule put forward in the 1910s by Mohandas Gandhi. As explained by Gandhi, swaraj is a form of decentralized self-government that flows from individuals to the greater community; it envisions a type of direct democracy that is classless and stateless and thus rejects a hierarchical centralized government and class system, such as were imposed on India by Britain prior to 1947. The modern Indian government is generally not considered a model of Gandhi's swaraj ideal.

Syncretism. The attempt to reconcile and integrate disparate or contradictory religious or philosophical beliefs, often while melding practices of various schools of thought.

Tael. The English name for a Chinese system of weight measures. Tael weighing standards tended to vary by region and type of trade.

Taille. A direct tax on land or wealth imposed by the pre-Revolutionary French royal government. Privileged groups were exempted from the tax, disproportionately burdening peasants and non-nobles. The taille was abolished at the start of the French Revolution in 1789. *See also* French Revolution.

Tammany Hall. The Democratic Party political machine that largely controlled New York City politics from the 1850s to the 1930s. The political machine arose from the Tammany Society, which was founded in May 1789. Named for a local Native American leader, the Society adopted many Native American words and customs, calling its hall a wigwam and its leader the Grand Sachem. In 1830, the Society established its headquarters in a building called Tammany Hall, and thereafter the names of the building and the group were synonymous. *See also* Political machine.

Taylor, Frederick Winslow. *See* Taylorism.

Taylorism. Also known as "Scientific Management," Taylorism is a theory of management that applies scientific models to analyze and synthesize work processes to improve labor productivity. The core ideas of the theory were developed by Frederick Winslow Taylor (1856–1915) in the 1880s and 1890s and first published in *Shop Management* (1905) and *The Principles of Scientific Management* (1911). Taylor believed that decisions should be based on precise procedures developed after careful study of individuals at work rather than on tradition or basic rules of thumb.

Tenement. An apartment house or multi-unit dwelling that meets only minimum standards of sanitation, safety, and comfort and that is usually located in a large city.

Theocracy. A form of government in which sovereignty is believed to be in a god or deity. Laws are usually considered divine commands. Power is usually vested in an individual who claims personal divinity or the hierarchy of a religious group.

Theravada Buddhism. *See* Buddhism.

Tojo, Hideki (1884–1948). A general in the Imperial Japanese Army, Tojo was prime minister of Japan during World War II, from October 1941 to July 1944. After the war, the International Military Tribunal for the Far East tried and convicted Tojo for war crimes. He was sentenced to death and executed in 1948.

Tolstoy, Leo (1828–1910). A Russian writer and philosopher who is best known for his novels *War and Peace* and *Anna Karenina,* both masterful depictions of nineteenth-century Russian life and considered to be among the greatest novels of all time. Later in his life he also developed ideas of nonviolent resistance that inspired Mohandas Gandhi and Martin Luther King, Jr. *See also* Gandhi, Mohandas; King, Martin Luther, Jr.

Transubstantiation. The doctrine of the Eucharist taught by the Roman Catholic and Orthodox Christian Churches. Transubstantiation means that during the Mass or Divine Liturgy the bread and wine are changed by God, through the priest, into the actual body and blood of Christ. In the sixteenth century, Protestant denominations developed different teachings on the Eucharist. *See also* Eucharist; Mass; Roman Catholic Church.

Triangle Trade. A historical term used to describe an ongoing trade between three ports or regions. The best-known example of such trade is the three-cornered trans-Atlantic connection that existed in the eighteenth century between Europe, West Africa, and the European colonies in the West Indies and on the east coast of North America. The westward leg of this trade, running from Africa to America, was the infamous "Middle Passage," on which traders carried as cargo newly captured or purchased Africans to be sold into slavery in the Americas. *See also* Middle Passage.

Ukraine. An eastern European region that in the nineteenth century was incorporated into the Russian Empire and in 1922 became part of the Union of Soviet Socialist Republics (USSR). Following the break-up of the USSR in 1991, Ukraine became an independent state with a capitalist free market economy. *See also* Union of Soviet Socialist Republics.

Union of Soviet Socialist Republics (USSR). The largest country in the world, the USSR was founded in 1922 from the remains of the Russian Empire. Dominated by the majority ethnic Russians and governed by the Communist Party of the Soviet Union, it eventually comprised 15 national republics. An ally of Britain and America during World War II when it was invaded by Nazi Germany, the Soviet Union became one of two superpowers in the post-war period and the Cold War era. The USSR collapsed in 1991. *See also* Cold War; Russian Revolution; Stalin, Joseph.

Urban Sprawl. The spreading of a city and its low-density suburbs and exurbs over rural land at the edge of the city, a growth pattern that was characteristic of many American cities in the twentieth century. Because of the effect of such growth on the environment, communities, and the health of residents, the term has a generally negative connotation. *See also* Exurbs; Suburbs.

Victorian. A term describing British and general Western culture during the reign of Queen Victoria in Britain (1837–1901). Despite the dramatic changes of the period, Victorian society was dominated by conservative, middle-class tastes and morals. *See also* Edwardian.

Viet Cong (VC). A guerilla force of Vietnamese Communists supported by the North Vietnamese Army who fought against the government of South Vietnam and the United States during the Vietnam War. They were called Viet Cong (meaning Vietnamese Communists) by the U.S.-backed government of South Vietnamese President Ngo Dinh Diem and simply "VC" by the U.S. troops who fought them in the 1960s and 1970s. *See also* Communism; Vietnam War.

Vietnam War. A war between the Soviet- and Chinese-supported Communist Democratic Republic of Vietnam (North Vietnam) and the United States-supported Republic of Vietnam (South Vietnam), which lasted from 1959 to 1975. Although U.S. advisors had been present in Vietnam since the 1950s, significant numbers of U.S. ground forces did not engage in combat until 1965. The United States withdrew from Vietnam in 1973 after the loss of almost 60,000 men, and South Vietnam, fighting on without American support, fell to the North within two years, thus creating the current unified Socialist Republic of Vietnam. *See also* Johnson, Lyndon J.; Viet Cong.

Washington, George (1732–1799). Foremost of the American Founding Fathers, commander of the Continental Army during the American Revolution, and first president of the United States, serving from 1789 to 1797.

Water Frame. The name given to the spinning frame, a device that increases the production of yarn for textiles, when water power is employed to drive it. Application of one to the other is credited to the English inventor Richard Arkwright, who patented and exploited the technology in the 1770s.

Zen Buddhism. A school of Mahayana Buddhism that originated in China and that has spread gradually eastward into Japan and Korea. *See also* Buddhism.

Zionism. The international political movement formally organized in the nineteenth century to support the recreation of a homeland for the Jewish people in Palestine, which it achieved with the founding of the modern-day state of Israel in 1948. The movement continues today primarily as a support for Israel.

Zoroastrianism/Mazdayasna. An ancient Persian religion and philosophy based on the teachings of the prophet Zoroaster, who is traditionally though to have lived in the sixth century B.C.

APPENDIX: BIOGRAPHIES OF DOCUMENT AUTHORS

Compiled by John Wagner and Mariah Gumpert.

Adams, Abigail (1744–1818): Born Abigail Smith, Abigail Adams was the wife of the second president of the United States, John Adams and the mother of the sixth U.S. president, John Quincy Adams; she was thus the second First Lady of the United States, even though that term was not coined until well after her death. She is best known for the many letters that she exchanged with her husband while she was at home in Massachusetts and he was in Philadelphia serving in the Continental Congress. John Adams frequently sought his wife's advice on matters both personal and political, and their letters are filled with intellectual discussions on politics, government, society, and gender. The letters are important sources of information on life during the American Revolution and the Early National period.

Aurangzeb (1618–1707): Also known by his Imperial title Alamgir I (Conqueror of the Universe), Aurangzeb was ruler of the Mughal Empire from 1658 until his death in 1707. The son of Shah Jehan, Aurangzeb, through his conquests, brought the Mughal state to its greatest territorial extent, but his constant campaigns left the empire dangerously overextended and by his death large portions of the empire had been lost. A devout Sunni Muslim, he abandoned the religious toleration of his predecessors and attempted to impose Sharia (Islamic law) throughout the empire. During his reign, many Hindu temples were destroyed and replaced by mosques and the hated jizya tax, imposed only on non-Muslims, was reinstated. Considered the last of the strong Mughal rulers, Aurangzeb's empire fell into decline after his death.

Baden-Powell, Robert, 1st Baron Baden-Powell (1857–1941): A lieutenant-general in the British Army and founder of the Scouting movement. He served in India and Africa between 1876 and 1910, being particularly known for his part in the defense of Mafeking during the Second Boer War in 1899. Because his several books on military reconnaissance and scout training, written during his years in Africa, were also read by boys, he later wrote *Scouting for Boys* (1908) especially for a young readership. The book offered activities for boys that centered around camping, observation, woodcraft, chivalry, lifesaving, and patriotism. Baden-Powell tested many of these ideas on a camping trip to Brownsea Island that he organized for 20 boys in August 1907, an event that is now considered the start of the worldwide Scouting movement.

Beeton, Isabella Mary (1836–1865): The author of *Mrs. Beeton's Book of Household Management* (1861), a best-selling guidebook on how to run a Victorian household. The book, which sold millions of copies within a few years of its publication, offers advice on fashion, childcare, animal husbandry, poisons, the management of servants, and cooking. Of the book's more than 1,100 pages, some 900 contain recipes, accounting for the volume's popular title, *Mrs. Beeton's Cookbook,* and for the author's status as one of the most famous cookery writers in English history. Beeton was only 21 when she began writing the volume, and only 28 when she died of complications following childbirth.

Bensusan, Samuel Levy (1872–1958): British journalist and author who wrote numerous works on travel and art, such as *Morocco* (1904), *Wild-Life Stories: Stores from a Home County* (1907), *On the Tramp in Wales: The Record of a Springtime Pilgrimage in Search of Agricultural Knowledge and Seasonable Recreation* (1929); *Tales from the Saxon Shore* (1939), and *Back of Beyond: A Countryman's Pre-War Commonplace Book* (1946).

Blackstone, Sir William (1723–1780): An eighteenth-century English jurist who produced the most famous and influential treatise on English common law, *Commentaries on the Laws of England,* which was published in four volumes between 1765 and 1769. In 1743, Blackstone became a barrister—a type of common law lawyer—and practiced before the courts until 1758, when he became the first holder of the Vinerian Professorship of Common Law at Oxford University, a position he retained until 1766. Blackstone also wrote treatises on Magna Carta and on the Charter of the Forests. Blackstone's *Commentaries* are still taken by U.S. courts as the definitive source on pre-Revolutionary common law and the framers of the U.S. Constitution drew many of their terms and phrases from Blackstone's works.

Boswell, James (1740–1795): An eighteenth-century Scottish writer, lawyer, and diarist of a noble family who is best known as the biographer of the English writer Samuel Johnson. He is also known for his voluminous journals, only discovered in the 1920s, which provide detailed and frank descriptions of long periods of his life. The journals include extensive notes on the Grand Tour of Europe that he took as a young man and his later tour of Scotland with Dr. Johnson. His journals also record meetings and conversations with eminent contemporaries David Garrick, Edmund Burke, Joshua Reynolds, and Oliver Goldsmith.

Bruegmann, Robert: An historian of architecture, landscape, and the built environment who teaches in the School of Architecture and the Program in Urban Policy and Planning at the University of Illinois at Chicago. His best-known work is *Sprawl: A Compact History,* published by the University of Chicago Press in 2005.

Bump, Lottie M.: A Salisbury, Vermont, farm wife, who kept a diary of life on her family farm in 1868. The diary entries detail early morning temperatures and daily domestic affairs on the farm. She also notes the activities of her husband Samuel, her health, the birth of her first child, and the comings and goings of family and friends.

Burton, Sir Richard Francis (1821–1890): A nineteenth-century English explorer, writer, soldier, linguist, and translator who is best known for his travels in Asia and Africa and his extraordinary knowledge of languages (it was claimed he spoke 29) and cultures. His most famous undertakings include traveling in disguise as a Muslim pilgrim to Mecca, making an unexpurgated English translation of *The Book of One Thousand Nights and A Night* (more commonly known as *The Arabian Nights*), making a translation of the Indian erotic text the *Kama Sutra*, and journeying into the African interior with the first party of white men to seek the source of the Nile. He was also a prolific author and wrote numerous books and scholarly articles about such subjects as travel, fencing, and ethnography.

Clayton, Victoria Virginia: Born Victoria Hunter, she married Henry DeLamar Clayton around 1849 in Clayton, Alabama, where he had a law practice. Henry Clayton was a judge, member of the Alabama Legislature, Confederate major general, and president of the University of Alabama from 1886 to his death in 1889. Two of Clayton's sons, Henry DeLamar Clayton and Bertram Tracy Clayton, became United States congressmen. In 1899, Victoria Clayton published her recollections of life during the Civil War in a memoir entitled *White and Black under the Old Regime*.

Comstock, Anthony (1844–1915): A nineteenth-century U.S. postal inspector best known for his firm advocacy of Victorian notions of morality. In 1873, he founded the New York Society for the Suppression of Vice, an organization dedicated to the regulation of public morality. He also successfully lobbied the U.S. Congress to pass the Comstock Law (1873), which made it illegal to deliver through the mail or transport any obscene, lewd, or lascivious material or any material promoting or pertaining to birth control. Comstock aroused the ire of civil liberties groups and his name eventually became a by-word for the prohibitions he supported.

Coubertin, Pierre de (1863–1937): Pierre de Frédy, Baron de Coubertin, was a French teacher and historian, who is best known as the founder of the International Olympic Committee (IOC), for which he served as first general secretary. After the success of the first Olympic Games in Athens in 1896, de Coubertin became president of the IOC, a post he held until 1924.

Crystal, David (1941–): A twentieth-century British linguist and author whose academic interests include English language learning and teaching, forensic linguistics, and language death. Born in Ireland and raised in Wales, he grew up fluent in both Welsh and English, a fact that influenced his approach to language education. He has edited many reference works on language and linguistics and is the author of *The Stories of English* (2004), a history of the English language. He is currently honorary professor and part-time lecturer of linguistics at the University of Bangor.

De Amicis, Edmondo (1846–1908): An Italian novelist, journalist, poet, and short story and travel writer who is best known for his 1886 children's novel *Cuore (Heart)*, which had been widely published and translated. Among his other well-known works are *La vita militaire* (1868), *Novelle* (1872), *Poesie* (1880), and *La carozza di tutti* (1899).

Delano, Alonzo (c. 1809–1874): A writer and humorist who is best known for his books and letters describing life in California in the first years following the discovery of gold there in 184. Delano journeyed to California in the spring of 1849, and published his account of that journey in 1854 as *Life on the Plains and Among the Diggings*. Delano set up as a merchant supplying the miners in the various California boomtowns. He eventually gravitated to San Francisco where he established a business in 1850. After prospering there, he moved eventually to Grass Valley, which was in the heart of the northern California gold mining district. In Grass Valley, he became a banker, Wells Fargo agent, and, eventually, city treasurer. His sketches of California life appeared, under his nickname, "The Old Block," in *Pen-Knife Sketches; or, Chips of the Old Block* (1853) and *Old Block's Sketch Book* (1856).

Deutsch, Leo (1855–1941): Born Lev Deich, but known as Leo Deutsch, he was a Russian Marxist revolutionary and founding member of the Menshevik Party prior to the Russian Revolution of 1917. Arrested and convicted of terrorism in 1884 by the czarist regime, he was sentenced to hard labor in a Siberian prison camp, from which he escaped in 1901. He returned to Russia during the 1905 revolution, but was again arrested and sentenced to Siberia, but once again escaped, this time to London. He returned to Russia in 1917, where he edited a revolutionary newspaper and eventually wrote his memoirs.

Diderot, Denis (1713–1784): An eighteenth-century French Enlightenment philosopher and writer who was editor, with Jean le Rond d'Alembert, of the *Encyclopédie*. *See also* d'Alembert, Jean le Rond; *Encyclopédie;* Enlightenment.

Douglass, Frederick (c. 1817–1895): One of the most prominent figures in African American history, Frederick Douglass was an editor, orator, author, statesman, reformer, and leader of the abolitionist movement. Born a slave in Maryland, Douglass learned to read and write from the wife of one of his masters and then through his own efforts. After several failed attempts, Douglass escaped from his master in 1838. His best-known work is his autobiography, *Narrative of the Life of Frederick Douglass, an American Slave, Written by Himself*, published in 1845. Douglass was the editor of various antislavery newspapers, including *The North Star,* and a popular lecturer in both the United States and Europe, becoming a forceful proponent of the equality of all people.

Equiano, Olaudah (c. 1745–1797): Also known as Gustavus Vassa, Equiano was a former slave who became the most prominent African activist in the effort to abolish the slave trade throughout the British Empire. He wrote an autobiography entitled *The Interesting Narrative of the Life of Olaudah Equiano or Gustavus Vassa, the African, Written by Himself* (1789), which depicted the horrors of slavery and helped influence British lawmakers to abolish the slave trade in 1807. During his life, Equiano worked as a seaman, merchant, and explorer in South America, the Caribbean, the Arctic, the Americas, and Britain.

Fletcher, Alice Cunningham (1838–1923): An American ethnologist of the nineteenth and early twentieth centuries who studied the remains of Indian civilizations of the Ohio and Mississippi river valleys and who worked and lived among the Omaha people as a representative of the Peabody Museum of Archaeology and Ethnology at Harvard University. Her publications include *Indian Education and Civilization* (1888), a special report to the U.S. Bureau of Education; *Indian Story and Song from North America* (1900); and *The Omaha Tribe* (1911), which was co-authored with Francis La Flesche, an Omaha Indian.

Flynn, Jennifer: The author of various volumes on computers and computing, including the Star Trek Series volume *20th Century Computers and How They Worked* (1993), which provides a visual tour of computer technology from the vantage point of a twenty-fourth-century Starfleet Academy course in computer history.

Franklin, Benjamin (1706–1790): An eighteenth-century American author, printer, politician, scientist, inventor, and diplomat, as well as one of the principal Founding Fathers of the United States. Besides conducting experiments with electricity, Franklin invented the lightning rod, bifocals, and the Franklin stove. A newspaper editor, printer, and merchant in Philadelphia, he formed the first lending library in the American colonies and the first fire department in Pennsylvania, founded the University of Pennsylvania, and grew wealthy publishing the *Pennsylvania Gazette* and *Poor Richard's Almanack*. He was also a member of the committee that drafted the Declaration of Independence in 1776, American minister to France from 1776 to 1785, and a delegate to the Constitutional Convention in 1787.

Frederick II, the Great (1712–1786): King of Prussia from 1740 to 1786 and a proponent of "enlightened absolutism," a form of despotism in which the ruler was influenced by Enlightenment principles. He reorganized the Prussian army and expanded Prussian territory, winning military renown for himself and his kingdom, for which he won recognition as a European power. A correspondent of Voltaire and a patron of artists and philosophers, Frederick modernized the Prussian bureaucracy and civil service, established public education, and promoted religious toleration.

Friedan, Betty (1921–2006): An American feminist and writer best known for her influential 1963 book, *The Feminine Mystique*, which effectively criticized the popularly held notion that women could find fulfillment only as wives, mothers, and homemakers. The book is often credited with launching the so-called Second Wave of the feminist movement, which reached its peak in the late 1960s and 1970s. Friedan was a cofounder of the National Organization for Women (NOW), serving as its first president from 1966 to 1970.

Fulton, Mary (d. 1926): Born in Ashland, Ohio, Mary Fulton was a medical missionary for the Philadelphia branch of the Presbyterian Church. She spent more than 20 years in China teaching school and providing medical care. One of her pupils was Sun Yat-Sen, the first president of the Republic of China. Fulton also served as director of a hospital and formed a school for nurses in China.

Fulton, Robert (1765–1815): A nineteenth-century American engineer and inventor who is credited with developing the first commercially successful steamboat, which began carrying passengers on the Hudson River in 1807. He also experimented with submarine torpedoes and torpedo boats, and he designed what is considered the first practical submarine.

Gandhi, Mohandas K. (1869–1948): The political and spiritual leader of the Indian independence movement. His philosophy of *Satyagraha*, which called for active, nonviolent resistance to evil, led to the independence of India in 1947 and inspired other civil rights and independence movements worldwide, including the Civil Rights Movement in the United States, where Gandhi's philosophy influenced Martin Luther King, Jr. Gandhi first employed civil disobedience in the struggle for civil rights for the Indian community in South Africa, where he lived from 1893 to 1915. Returning to India, he assumed leadership of the Indian National Congress and led nationwide campaigns for the alleviation of poverty, the liberation of women, the brotherhood of all religious and ethnic groups, an end to untouchability and caste discrimination, economic self-sufficiency, and, above all, for *Swaraj*, the independence of India from foreign domination. He was assassinated in 1948.

Gilpin, William (1724–1804): An eighteenth-century English artist, author, clergyman, and schoolmaster who is best known as one of the chief originators of the idea of the picturesque. He first defined the term in his popular 1768 work, *Essay on Prints*, and thereafter began to more widely expound his principles of picturesque beauty, which were based largely on his knowledge of landscape painting. In 1782, he published *Observations on the River Wye and Several Parts of South Wales, etc. Relative Chiefly to Picturesque Beauty; Made in the Summer of the Year 1770*, which included reproductions of some of his own sketches. This volume was followed in the next decade by several similar works on various areas of Britain.

Gutierrez, Simon "Sam": A prisoner at Stateville Prison in Illinois who, at the behest of noted criminal justice scholar Norval Morris, kept a detailed diary of a single day of prison routine that effectively captured what it was like to be incarcerated in the United States in the late twentieth century. The diary was included as a chapter in Morris's 1995 publication, *The Oxford History of the Prison*. *See also* Morris, Norval.

Halid, Halil (d. 1934): A Turkish writer, politician, and diplomat, who taught Turkish literature at Cambridge University. He was the author of some notable and controversial books on late Ottoman political thought that were published in English in the early years of the twentieth century.

Hamilton, Alexander (c. 1755–1804): An eighteenth-century American military officer, politician, lawyer, and political theorist, as well as an important framer of the U.S. Constitution and first secretary of the Treasury. He was the anonymous author, under the pseudonym "Publius," of 51 of the 85 *Federalist Papers*, a series of articles published in 1787–1788 that advocated ratification of the U.S. Constitution. A New York delegate to the 1787 Constitutional Convention and one of the founders of the Federalist Party in the 1790s, Hamilton favored a strong central government and as secretary of the Treasury under President George Washington pushed Congress to adopt an expansive view of federal powers under the Constitution, a policy that led to the funding of the national debt, federal assumption of state debts, and creation of a national bank. Hamilton was killed in a duel with his political rival Aaron Burr.

Hidalgo, Francisco (1659–1726): A Franciscan missionary priest working in Spanish Texas in the early eighteenth century who was the strongest and most persistent advocate for expansion of Spanish missionary activity from the Rio Grande region into East Texas. Thanks to Father Hidalgo's efforts a new mission was established under his charge in East Texas at Nuestro Padre San Francisco de los Tejas in 1716. He remained at the mission until East Texas was abandoned by the Spanish in 1719. Hidalgo then resided at San Antonio de Valero Mission in San Antonio, where he remained until 1725, when he resigned and petitioned unsuccessfully to preach among the Apaches. He died in 1726 at the age of 67.

Hills, Henry (d. c. 1689): A late seventeenth-century English writer of pro-Catholic pamphlets and printer to King Charles II of England. He became Master of the Stationer's Company under the Catholic Monarch James II in about 1685, but was forced into exile when James himself was deposed and exiled in 1688.

Ingersoll, Ernest (1852–1946): American writer, lecturer, and naturalist, who wrote many magazine articles and guide books, primarily on scientific subjects. He studied at Oberlin College and then at Harvard University, where he was a student of the Swiss-American zoologist Louis Agassiz.

Jaucourt, Louis de (1704–1779): A French aristocrat who was the most prolific contributor to the *Encyclopédie;* he was the author of about 18,000 entries, or nearly one-quarter of the work. Being independently wealthy, he sought no payment for his work, which focused mainly on such subjects as physiology, chemistry, botany, and pathology, but also covered some topics in political history and philosophy. His entries were rarely as overtly political as those of some other contributors, such as Voltaire and *Encyclopédie* editor Denis Diderot, but those covering historical topics reveal a deeply held anti-clericalism and an abhorrence of slavery.

Kennedy, John (1769–1855): An English cotton spinner and inventor who devised several important improvements for the spinning of yarns, including the invention of the jack frame. He was an active member of the Manchester Literary and Philosophical Society and presented to the Society a number of papers on the history of English industrialization, including "On the Rise and Progress of the Cotton Trade" (1815), "Observations on the Influence of Machinery on the Working Classes" (1826), and "A Memoir of Samuel Crompton" (1830).

Khrushchev, Nikita (1894–1971): Successor to Joseph Stalin as first secretary of the Communist Party of the Soviet Union, serving from 1953 to 1964, and chairman of the Soviet Council of Ministers from 1958 to 1964. He was the face of the Soviet Union during the midst of the Cold War in the 1950s and early 1960s, and became infamous for his difficult and boorish behavior on trips to the West, especially during his 1959 tour of the United States, when he tried unsuccessfully to visit Disneyland, and his 1960 appearance at the United Nations. In 1964 he was forced to retire in favor of Leonid Brezhnev.

Kingsley, Mary (1862–1900): A nineteenth-century English writer and explorer who greatly influenced European ideas about Africa and the treatment and education of Africans. Her criticisms of European missionaries for attempting to change the living habits of African peoples incurred the displeasure of the Church of England, and her defense of African traditions and practices, including polygamy, shocked her Victorian audience. However, her two books, *Travels in West Africa* (1897) and *West African Studies* (1899), were widely read and made her famous.

Komar, Vitaly (1943–): A twentieth-century Russian artist, who collaborated from 1965 to 2004 with fellow Russian artist Alex Melamid on various artistic projects including a series of "ecocollaborations," the best known of which is the Asian Elephant Project, which sells paintings made by Asian elephants to raise money for the protection and maintenance of the elephants. In 1978, Komar and Melamid left the Soviet Union, where their iconoclastic art had led to their arrest and to the destruction of their work, and settled in New York. In 1981, they became the first Russians to receive a National Endowment for the Arts grant.

Malevich, Kasimir (1878–1935): A twentieth-century Russian painter and art theoretician who pioneered nonrepresentational art, one of the most important innovations in modern art. Malevich was a leading member of the Russian avant-garde and invented Suprematist art. He supported the Russian Revolution, but his views on art and his criticism of more traditional forms eventually caused him to fall out of favor with the Soviet authorities, though he is now recognized as a seminal figure in Modernism.

Marshall, Joseph Head (d. c. 1815): An English physician who was among the first to learn the technique of vaccination from Edward Jenner, the first European to use cowpox inoculations to create immunity to smallpox. Marshall introduced the vaccination to British soldiers and civilians in the Mediterranean during the Napoleonic Wars. Marshall later worked as a British secret agent in Napoleonic France and disappeared there in about 1815.

Maybaum, Ignaz (1897–1976): One of the most prominent Jewish theologians of the post-Holocaust period, Maybaum is best known for his controversial statement that the Holocaust was God's punishment of the Jews for the sins and misdeeds of the rest of the world. Born in Vienna, Maybaum became a rabbi in Bingen, Frankfurt, and then Berlin, but fled Germany with his wife and children in 1939 at the start of World War II. His mother and sisters remained in Germany and died in Nazi concentration camps. In 1939, he became rabbi of Edgware Reform Synagogue in London, and, in 1956, he co-founded Leo Baeck College in London, a school for the training of Reform and Liberal rabbis.

McLaren, Deborah (1959–): An international leader in the movement toward responsible tourism. Her 2003 book *Rethinking Tourism and Ecotravel* grew out of a typical tourist vacation to Jamaica in the 1980s.McLaren also came to question the validity of the popularized notion of ecotourism—an idea created with good intentions, but that has been marketed indiscriminately and is often in conflict with local people and the very wilderness and wildlife it promotes.

Melamid, Alex (1945–): A twentieth-century Russian artist who collaborated from 1965 to 2004 with fellow Russian artist Vitaly Komar on various artistic projects including a series of "ecocollaborations," the best known of which is the Asian Elephant Project, which sells paintings made by Asian elephants to raise money for the protection and maintenance of the elephants. In 1978, Melamid and Komar left the Soviet Union, where their iconoclastic art had led to their arrest and to the destruction of their work, and settled in New York. In 1981, they became the first Russians to receive a National Endowment for the Arts grant.

Melrose, William (1817–1863): Member of a nineteenth-century British tea trading family who was sent to China in 1842 as a tea buyer. He stayed in China until 1855 and his letters, published in 1973 in *William Melrose in China, 1845–1855: The Letters of a Scottish Tea Merchant*, provide a vivid description of European trade in China in the years between the two Opium Wars.

Monier-Williams, Sir Monier (1819–1899): A nineteenth-century British scholar of Asian languages who compiled a widely used Sanskrit-English dictionary. Born in Bombay, India, he taught Asian languages at the East India Company College from 1844 to 1858. Monier-Williams won appointment as the second holder of the Boden Chair of Sanskrit at Oxford University in 1860. He founded Oxford's Indian Institute in 1883.

Montesquieu, Charles-Louis de Secondat, Baron de (1689–1755): An eighteenth-century French Enlightenment social commentator and political thinker who is best known for his articulation of the theory of separation of powers, which heavily influenced the framers of the U.S. Constitution. His publications include the landmark *De l'Esprit des Lois* (*The Spirit of the Laws*, 1748), as well as *Lettres persanes* (*Persian Letters*, 1721), a satire of contemporary French society, and *Considérations sur les causes de la grandeur des Romains et de leur décadence* (*Considerations on the Causes of the Grandeur and Decadence of the Romans*, 1734).

Moore, Amasa (1801–1865): Born in New York, Amasa Moore was the sixth child and third son of Pliny Moore. He entered Middlebury College in Vermont in 1817 and married Charlotte Mooers in 1826.

Morgenthau, Henry, Sr. (1856–1946): Author and U.S. ambassador to the Ottoman Empire for the Wilson Administration from 1913 to 1916 during the first years of World War I. His memoirs of his tenure as ambassador, *Ambassador Morgenthau's Story* (1918), provide a detailed description of the events that later became known as the Armenain Genocide. In 1919, he accompanied Wilson to the Paris peace conference and then headed a U.S. government fact-finding mission to Poland, which resulted in publication of the *Morgenthau Report* criticizing the treatment of Polish Jews.

Morris, Norval (1923–2004): An influential twentieth-century criminal justice writer and theorist who served as dean of the University of Chicago Law School from 1975 to 1978. He was also a founding director of the University of Chicago Law School's Center for Studies in Criminal Justice and a professor of law and criminology. His publications included *Machonochie's Gentlemen: The Story of Norfolk Island and the Roots of Modern Prison Reform* (2003), *The Oxford History of the Prison* (1995) with David Rothman, *The Brothel Boy and Other Parables of the Law* (1992), *Between Prison and Probation: Intermediate Punishments in a Rational Sentencing System* (1990) with Michael Tonry, and *Madness and the Criminal Law* (1982). *See also* Gutierrez, Simon.

Nightingale, Florence (1820–1910): A nineteenth-century English writer, statistician, and pioneer of the modern nursing profession. She is most famous for her nursing activities during the Crimean War in the early 1850s, when she became known as "the lady with the lamp," from a London *Times* article describing her moving among the wounded in the hospital wards with a little lamp in her hand. Although suffering from a fever she contracted in the Crimea, Nightingale was instrumental in the establishment of the Royal Commission on the Health of the Army in 1857. Although, as a woman, she could not sit on the Commission, she wrote its 1,000-page report, which included detailed statistical summaries, and she was vital to the implementation of its recommendations. The report led to a major overhaul of army military care, and to the establishment of an Army Medical School and a comprehensive system of medical records.

Oppenheimer, J. Robert (1904–1967): Known as the father of the atomic bomb, Oppenheimer was a twentieth-century American physicist who directed the Manhattan Project, the American World War II effort to development atomic weapons at a secret laboratory in Los Alamos, New Mexico. After the war, Oppenheimer was chief advisor to the United States Atomic Energy Commission and used that position to lobby for international control of atomic energy and against the nuclear arms race with the Soviet Union. His outspoken opinions, delivered during the Communist scare of the 1950s, outraged many politicians and scientists and, as a result, his security clearance was revoked during a much-publicized hearing in 1954.

Paine, Thomas (1737–1809): An eighteenth-century American pamphleteer, radical, intellectual, and revolutionary who is best known as the author of *Common Sense* (1776), a pamphlet that strongly advocated American independence, and *The American Crisis*, a series of pamphlets published in the late 1770s that denounced British Loyalists and supported the revolutionary cause. Paine emigrated to the American colonies from Britain in 1774. His *Rights of Man* (1791) greatly influenced the French Revolution and he was elected to the French National Assembly in 1792, even though he spoke no French. He then fell into disfavor with Maximilien Robespierre and his faction and was arrested and imprisoned in Paris in 1793, although he was released in the following year. He was widely criticized for his book *The Age of Reason* (1793–1794), which promoted deism and attacked Christianity. He returned to the United States in 1802.

Paul VI, Pope (1897–1978): Head of the Roman Catholic Church from 1963 until his death, Paul VI is known for his issuance in 1968 of the encyclical *Humanae Vitae* reaffirming the Catholic Church's opposition to the use of artificial birth control. Born Giovanni Montini in the Italian province of Brescia, he was papal secretary of state under Pope Pius XII from 1944 and archbishop of Milan from 1954. In 1963, he succeeded Pope John XXIII, who had convened the Second Vatican Council; as pope, Paul VI presided over most of the sessions of the council and oversaw the implementation of its decrees.

Razavi, William Mohammad (1973–): An American writer, Razavi was born in Tehran, Iran. His father, Seyed Abolhassan Razavi, was a colonel in the Imperial Iranian Army, who, after being forced into early retirement, brought his family to the United States in 1976. William Razavi grew up in Texas where he graduated from Trinity University in 1995. He earned an MFA in Playwriting from Brandeis University in 1997. His play *Making Up For Lost Time* was workshopped at the American Repertory Theatre in Cambridge, Massachusetts, and was nominated for an ATAC Globe award in San Antonio, Texas. He directed a production of his most recent play, *The Complete Fragments of Menander: Some Assembly Required*, at the San Antonio Museum of Art in 2008. Razavi returned to Iran for the first time in 20 years in 1996 and has returned frequently since, including a lengthy stay in 2004–2005. In 2002, his maternal grandmother, administering the charitable legacy of his grandfather, Mohammad Ali Salessi, suggested the construction of a new high school for girls in the Razavi hometown of Aligudarz in Lorestan. Ground was broken later that year and in 2005 the Mohammad William Razavi High School opened its doors. Razavi became an American citizen in 2008.

Riis, Jacob (1849–1914): A Danish-American muckraking journalist, photographer, and social reformer who is best known for his writings and photographic essays exposing the poverty and dangerous, unhealthful living conditions of the poor in New York City at the turn of the twentieth century. Riis' most important work, *How the Other Half Lives: Studies Among the Tenements of New York* (1890), helped bring about the creation of model tenements that improved living conditions for some New Yorkers. Despite his strong sense of social justice, Riis reveals in his writings an equally strong sexism and bias against certain ethnic groups, whom he tends to describe in stereotypes.

Robinson, Harriet Hanson (1825–1911): Best known as the author of *Loom and Spindle, or Life Among the Early Mill Girls* (1898), her account of life as a young female worker in the textile mills of Lowell, Massachusetts, from 1835 until her marriage in 1848. Her father died when she was only six, leaving her mother with four young children to support. To help her mother, Harriet began working in the mill when she was 10. Her husband, William Robinson, published an anti-slavery newspaper. After his death, Mrs. Robinson became a strong supporter of voting rights for women.

Robinson, Jack Roosevelt "Jackie" (1919–1972): Jackie Robinson ended 80 years of racial segregation in baseball by becoming the first African American to play for a major league team in the modern era when he joined the Brooklyn Dodgers in 1947. During the season, Robinson suffered continuous harassment from fans and players. He was named Rookie of the Year in 1947 and National League MVP in 1949. He was inducted into the Hall of Fame in 1962. After his retirement, he became a political activist and a strong supporter of such civil rights leaders as Martin Luther King, Jr., and Malcolm X.

Sacre-Coeur, Sr. Marie-Andre du (1899–?): Born Jeanne Dorge, Sister Marie-Andre du Sacre-Coeur was a French White Sister who, while serving as a nurse, teacher, social worker, and missionary in French West Africa, began vigorously denouncing the oppression suffered by African women in their marriages and families. She lobbied for legislation improving the status of women, especially as regards to dowries and marriage arrangements, and also addressed the United Nations on the subject. Her major works include *La Femme Noire en Afrique Occidentale* (*The Black Woman in West Africa*, 1939) and *The House Stands Firm: Family Life in West Africa* (1962).

Saint-Just, Louis de (1767–1794): A French revolutionary leader who was closely associated with Maximilien Robespierre, with whom he served on the Committee of Public Safety during the French Reign of Terror. He supported the execution of the king, the reform of the calendar, the redistribution of land, and the replacement of Catholic orthodoxy with the deistic Cult of the Supreme Being. He and Robespierre both fell from power in 1794 and were guillotined on the same day.

Schlosser, Eric (1959–): A twentieth-century American author and investigative journalist who is known for his bestselling book, *Fast Food Nation: The Dark Side of the All American Meal* (2001), an exposé of the unsanitary and discriminatory practices of the American fast food industry. His work has also been published in *Atlantic Monthly*, *Vanity Fair*, *The Nation*, and *The New Yorker*. He won the National Magazine Award for reporting on his two-part series "Reefer Madness" and "Marijuana and the Law," which was published in *Atlantic Monthly* in 1994.

Scott, Georgia: An American author, travel consultant, and cultural coach who provides clients with information on current international hot topics, country briefings, and help with overseas relocations and foreign assignments. She is the author of *Headwraps: A Global Journey* (2003) as well as the forthcoming *Globetripper's Travel Guide* and various other travel books.

Secondat, Charles-Louis de, Baron de Montesquieu: *See* Montesquieu.

Sezikawa Hidehiko: Professor at Tokyo Keizai University and Senior Fellow and former Director of the Hakuhodo Institute for Life and Living (HILL), a think tank associated with Hakuhodo, one of Japan's largest advertising agencies. A member of the Japanese Baby Boom generation, his research employs Hakuhodo's approach of sei-katsu-sha, a holistic approach to advertising and marketing that focuses on the whole person, rather than just their consumer behaviors.

Sharp, Henry S.: An anthropologist noted for his work in the late twentieth century among the Chipewyan people of northern Canada. His doctoral dissertation, completed at Drake University in 1973, was entitled "The Kinship Systems of the Black Lake Chipewyan." His most important publications on the Chipewyan are *Chipewyan Marriage* (1979) and *The Transformation of Bigfoot: Maleness, Power, and Belief Among the Chipewyan* (1988).

Shelley, Percy Bysshe (1792–1822): A nineteenth-century English Romantic poet who is today considered one of the finest lyric poets in English literature. His best-known works include "Ozymandias," "Ode to the West Wind," "To a Skylark," and "The Masque of Anarchy." Idealistic and unconventional, he was much criticized during his lifetime, but he became a major influence on poets and writers of the later nineteenth century, including Robert Browning; Alfred, Lord Tennyson; William Butler Yeats; and Karl Marx. He was the husband of novelist Mary Shelley and a close associate of the poets John Keats and Lord Byron. He spent his later years traveling in Italy, where he was drowned while sailing in 1822 a month before his 30th birthday.

Shinzutera Ueda (1926–): A twentieth-century Japanese philosopher specializing in the philosophy of religion. The son of a Buddhist priest, he studied philosophy at Kyoto University under Keiji Nishitani, who oriented his studies toward medieval mystics. He then went to Germany and obtained a doctorate at the University of Marburg. He then returned to Kyoto University to teach philosophy of religion. Later he specialized in the thought of Kitaro Nishida. A practitioner of zen, he is considered a third generation member of Kyoto School.

Smith, Adam (1723–1790): An eighteenth-century Scottish political economist and moral philosopher who is best known for his two treatises *The Theory of Moral Sentiments* (1759) and *An Inquiry into the Nature and Causes of the Wealth of Nations*, usually known as *The Wealth of Nations* (1776). The latter was one of the earliest systematic studies of the historical development of industry and commerce in Europe, as well as a detailed criticism of the doctrine and practice of mercantilism. Smith believed that rational self-interest and competition could lead to the economic betterment of society. Smith's work helped create the modern discipline of economics and provided one of the best-known rationales for free trade and capitalism.

Sugita, Genpaku (1733–1817): A eighteenth-century Japanese scholar best known for assembling a team to translate a Dutch book of anatomy into the *Kaitai Shinsho (New Book of Anatomy)*, a massive undertaking that was finally published in 1774. Sugita undertook the work after an autopsy that he attended indicated the superiority of Western drawings of human organs over those available in Chinese handbooks of anatomy. He was also the author of *Rangaku Kotohajime (Beginning of Dutch Studies).*

Terry, Milton S. (1840–1914): An American Protestant minister and Orientalist who visited Japan at the turn of the twentieth century and wrote a book entitled *The Shinto Cult: A Christian Study of the Ancient Religion of Japan*, which offered American Protestant audiences his observations on the practice of Shinto, the indigenous Japanese religion, in the late nineteenth century.

Tocqueville, Alexis de (1805–1859): A nineteenth-century French writer, historian, and political thinker who is best known for his two-volume work, *Democracy in America* (1835, 1840), a widely read commentary on the state of American politics and society in the 1830s. Based on Tocqueville's travels in America, his book is today considered one of the earliest works in sociology. Tocqueville's other major work is *The Old Regime and the Revolution* (1856), which, like *Democracy in America*, traces the effects of the rising equality of social conditions on the individual and the state in Western societies.

Train, Arthur, Jr. (1902–1981): A twentieth-century American writer, Arthur Train, Jr., was the son of Arthur C. Train, an attorney and well-known author of legal thrillers. He studied at Oxford and was a lieutenant commander in the Navy at the end of World War II. He became a translator, a frequent contributor to *Reader's Digest* and other periodicals, and the author of two books, *The Story of Everyday Things* (1941) and *Spoken Like a Frenchman* (1966).

Troyat, Henri (1911–2007): A twentieth-century Russian author, historian, novelist, and biographer working in France who published more than 100 works, among the best known of which are his biographies of Anton Chekhov, Catherine the Great, Rasputin, Ivan the Terrible, and Leo Tolstoy. Born Lev Aslanovich Tarasov in Moscow to Armenian parents, his family settled in Paris in 1920 after fleeing Russia to escape the 1917 Russian Revolution.

Uzan, Rafael: A twentieth-century Jewish artist best known for his published reminiscence of life as a Jewish child in the Tunisian coastal village of Nabeul, which appeared in 1984 as *Days of Honey: The Tunisian Boyhood of Rafael Uzan* by Irene Awret. Like many other North African Jews, Uzan moved with his family to Israel in the 1950s.

Voltaire (1694–1774): The pen name for François-Marie Arouet, an eighteenth-century French Enlightenment writer, essayist, philosopher, and *Deist* who was known across Europe for his wit and his liberal views. His ideas, which included support for freedom of religion, greatly influenced the thinking of supporters of both the American and French Revolutions. His works include *Lettres philosophiques sur les Anglais* (1733), which was revised as *Letters on the English* in 1778; *Candide* (1759); *Dictionnaire philosophique* (1764), which criticized French political institutions, the Bible, and the Roman Catholic Church; and numerous articles in Denis Diderot's *Encyclopédie*. An extremely prolific writer, he also authored plays, poetry, essays, novels, pamphlets, historical and scientific books, and more than 20,000 letters.

Von Forstner, Georg-Günther: The captain of German U-boat 28 during World War I. His journal detailing the events of his command in 1915 was printed in German in 1916, with an English translation appearing as *The Journal of Submarine Commander von Forstner* in 1917.

Wairy, Louis Constant (1778–1845): Head valet to Emperor Napoleon I of France and author of the *Memoirs of Constant*, which provide significant information on the person and private life of Napoleon.

Wawer, Maria J.: Professor of clinical population and family health at the Mailman School of Public Health, Columbia University. She received her doctorate from the University of Toronto in 1979. Her research activities focus on HIV, associated infections, and reproductive health in Uganda. In 1988, collaboration with colleagues at the Uganda Virus Research Institute in Entebbe, Makerere University in Kampala, and at Johns Hopkins, she established the Rakai Health Sciences Program, which has become one of the largest HIV research, prevention, and care programs in Africa.

Weber, Friedrich Christian (d. c. 1739): A diplomat who represented English interests at the court of Czar Peter the Great of Russia in the late 1710s. Like King George I, who became ruler of Britain in 1714 and who appointed him to his post, Weber was born in the German state of Hanover. Weber is best known for his written account of his time in Russia, which was translated into English and published in 1722–1723 as *The Present State of Russia*.

Weeks, Holland (c. 1768–1843): An early nineteenth-century Congregationalist minister who led churches in Vermont, Connecticut, Massachusetts, and New York. He was pastor of First Church in Waterbury, Connecticut, in the early 1800s, and then pastored a church in Abingdon, Massachusetts, from 1815 to 1820 before moving to a church in Henderson, New York, in 1821.

Wills, Nathan Parker (1806–1867): An American author and editor who published the works of such notable writers as Harriet Jacobs and Edgar Allan Poe. He founded the short-lived *American Monthly Magazine* in 1829 and was foreign editor and correspondent for the *New York Mirror* in the 1830s. In 1844, he co-founded another newspaper, the *Evening Mirror,* in which he published "The Raven," the great poem of his friend Poe on January 29, 1845. He also published many of Poe's contributions to the so-called "Longfellow War," a long literary feud between Poe and the admirers of Henry Wadsworth Longfellow, whom Poe felt was an overrated plagiarist. In 1846, Wills became editor of the *National Press*, which he renamed the *Home Journal,* and in which he promoted the work of various women poets, including Frances Sargent Osgood, Anne Lynch Botta, Grace Greenwood, and Julia Ward Howe.

Wilson, Samuel G. (d. 1916): A Presbyterian missionary stationed for 15 years in Persia, where he served for a time as principal of a missionary school and was also in charge of Armenian relief work during World War I. His experiences in Persia in the late nineteenth and early twentieth centuries resulted in two publications, *Persian Life and Customs* and *Persia: Western Missions*.

Young, Arthur (1741–1820): The greatest and most prolific of English agricultural writers, Young is also known as a keen observer of eighteenth-century politics and society. He conducted various agricultural experiments on his farm in Essex, which he described in *A Course of Experimental Agriculture* (1770). In the late 1760s, he undertook a series of journeys through Britain that resulted in three books of observations: *Six Weeks' Tour through the Southern Counties of England and Wales*, *A Six Months' Tour through the North of England,* and *Farmer's Tour through the East of England*. He traveled through Ireland in 1776, and published *Tour in Ireland* in 1780. In the late 1780s, he undertook several tours of France, which resulted in the two-volume *Travels in France* (1792), which is a valuable account of social conditions in that country on the eve of the French Revolution. In 1793, Young was appointed secretary of the British Board of Agriculture. Young is also known as a pioneering statistician; his *Political Arithmetic* and his various accounts of English tours produced important estimates of English national income.

BIBLIOGRAPHY

SOURCES

"Account of the Prince and Princess of Wales visiting Sir Hans Sloane, An." *The Gentleman's Magazine*. London, July, 1748.

Amasa Moore Papers. College Archives, Special Collections, Middlebury College.

Awret, Irene. "Preparing for Passover in North Africa." In *The Life of Judaism*, edited by Harvey E. Goldberg. Berkeley: University of California Press, 2001.

Baden-Powell, Sir Robert. "The Most Impressive Sight I Ever Saw: The Royal Rally of Boy Scouts at Windsor." *The Strand Magazine*, January 1914.

Barnard, Henry, ed. *Memoirs of Eminent Teachers and Educators with Contributions to the History of Education in Germany*. Rev. ed. Hartford, CT: Brown & Gross, 1878.

Beeton, Isabella. Mrs. *Beeton's Book of Household Management: Comprising Information for the Mistress, Housekeeper, Cook, Kitchen-Maid, Butler, Footman, Coachman, Valet, Upper and Under House-Maids, Lady's Maid, Maid-of-all-Work, Laundry-Maid, Nurse and Nurse-Maid, Monthly, Wet, and Sick-Nurses, etc. etc., Also Sanitary, Medical, and Legal Memoranda, with a History of the Origin, Properties, and Uses of All Things Connected with Home Life and Comfort*. London: S. O. Beeton, 1861.

Bensusan, S. L. *Morocco*. Painted by A. S. Forrest. London: Adam and Charles Black, 1904.

Blackstone, Sir William. *Commentaries on the Laws of England*. London, 1756. Reprinted from James Harvey Robinson, and Charles A. Beard, eds. *Readings in Modern European History*. Vol. 1: *The Eighteenth Century: The French Revolution and the Napoleonic Period*. Boston: Ginn & Company, 1909.

Boswell, James. *Boswell on the Grand Tour: Italy Corsica and France, 1765–1766*. Edited by Frank Brady and Frederick A. Pottle. New York: McGraw Hill, 1955.

Bowlt, John, ed. and trans. *Russian Art of the Avant-Garde: Theory and Criticism*. London: Thames and Hudson, 1988.

Breugmann, Robert. *Sprawl: A Compact History*. Chicago: University of Chicago Press, 2006.

Bump, Lottie. "Diary of Lottie Bump." Unpublished typescript. The Henry Sheldon Museum of Vermont History, Middlebury, Vermont.

Burton, Richard Francis. *Personal Narrative of a Pilgrimage to Al-Medinah and Meccah*. New York: G. P. Putnam & Co., 1856.

Clayton, Victoria V. *White and Black under the Old Regime*. Milwaukee: The Young Churchman Co., 1899.

Comstock, Anthony. *Traps for the Young*. New York: Funk and Wagnalls, 1883.

Coubertin, Pierre de. "The Olympic Games of 1896." *The Century Magazine* 53:1 (November 1896).

Crystal, David. *Language Death*. New York: Cambridge University Press, 2000.

De Amicis, Edmondo. *Morocco: Its People and Places*. Translated by Maria Hornor Lansdale. 2 vols. Philadelphia: Henry L. Coates and Company, 1897.

Delano, Alonzo. *Life on the Plains and Among the Diggings: Being Scenes and Adventures of an Overland Journey to California: With Particular Incidents of the Route, Mistakes, and Sufferings of the Emigrants, the Indian Tribes, the Present and the Future of the Great West*. Auburn, NY: Miller, Orton & Mulligan, 1854.

Dennis, James S. *Christian Missions and Social Progress: A Sociological Study of Foreign Missions*. New York: Fleming H. Revell Co., 1897.

Deutsch, Leo. *Sixteen Years in Siberia: Some Experiences of a Russian Revolutionist*. Translated by Helen Chisholm. New York: E. P. Dutton, 1904.

Dorsey, James Owen. *Omaha and Ponka Letters*. Washington, DC: Government Printing Office, 1891.

Douglass, Frederick. *Narrative of the Life of Frederick Douglass, an American Slave, Written by Himself*. Boston: The Anti-Slavery Office, 1845.

Dresser, Horatio W., ed. *The World War*. Vol. 15 of *The World's Story: A History of the World in Story Song and Art*, edited by Eva March Tappan. Boston: Houghton Mifflin Company, 1918.

Eliot, Charles W., ed. *Scientific Papers: Physiology, Medicine, Surgery, Geology*. The Harvard Classics, vol. 38. New York: P. F. Collier & Son Company, 1910.

Elliot, Sir Henry Miers. *The History of India, as Told by Its Own Historians: The Muhammadan Period*. Edited by John Dowson. Vol. 7. London: Trubner, 1867–1877.

Equiano, Olaudah. *The Interesting Narrative of the Life of Olaudah Equiano or Gustavus Vassa, the African, Written by Himself*. London, 1789.

"Extracts from a Parliamentary Report on Child Labor." In *Readings in Modern European History*, edited by James Harvey Robinson and Charles A. Beard. Vol. 2: *Europe Since the Congress of Vienna*. Boston: Ginn and Company, 1909.

Fitzsimmons, Kevin. Papers. Private collection.

Ferris, David. Asian Elephant Art and Conservation Project website, www.elephantart.com.

Fletcher, Alice C. *Indian Games and Dances with Native Songs: Arranged From American Indian Ceremonials and Sports*. New York: C. C. Birchard and Co., 1915.

Fletcher, Paris. Papers. The Henry Sheldon Museum of Vermont History. Middlebury, Vermont.

Flynn, Jennifer. *20th Century Computers and How They Worked: The Official Starfleet History of Computers*. Carmel, IN: Alpha Books, 1993.

Force, Peter, ed. *American Archives: Containing a Documentary History of the English Colonies of North America from the King's Message to Parliament of March 4, 1774, to the Declaration of Independence by the United States*. Vol. 1. Washington, DC, 1837.

Forstner, Georg-Günther von. *The Journal of Submarine Commander von Forstner*. Translated by Mrs. Russell Codman. Introduced by John Hays Hammond, Jr. Boston and New York: Houghton Mifflin, 1917.

Franklin, Benjamin. "The Morals of Chess." *Columbian Magazine*, 1786.

Friedan, Betty. *The Feminine Mystique*. New York: W. W. Norton and Co., 1963.

Gandhi, Mohandas K. *Indian Home Rule*. Madras, India: Ganesh, 1919.

Gilpin, William. *Three Essays on Picturesque Beauty; on Picturesque Travel, and on Sketching Landscape, to Which is Added a Poem, On Landscape Painting*. London: B. Blamire, 1794.

Green, Samuel A. *Epitaphs from the Old Burying Ground in Groton, Massachusetts*. Boston: Little, Brown, & Company, 1878.

Gutierrez, Simon, and Norval Morris. "A Day in the Life of Prisoner #12345." In *The Oxford History of the Prison*, edited by Norval Morris and David J. Rothman. New York: Oxford University Press, 1997.

Halid, Halil. *Diary of a Turk*. London: Charles and Black, 1903.

[Hamilton, Alexander, John Jay, and James Madison]. *The Federalist: A Collection of Essays in Favour of the New Constitution*. New York. J. and A. M'Lean, 1788.

Hatcher, Mattie Austin. "Description of the Tejas or Asinai Indians, 1691–1722," *Southwestern Historical Quarterly Online* 31, no. 1 (1927): 50–62. http://www.tsha.utexas.edu/publications/journals/shq/online/v031/n1/article_7.html

Hills, Henry. "A Request to Protestants. . . ." London, 1667.

Ingersoll, Ernest. "Election Day in New York." *The Century Magazine* 53:1 (November 1896).

Ishikawa Shōichi. Unpublished manuscript, c. 1944. Private collection.

Jaucourt, Louis de. "Death [Mort]." In *La Encyclopédie*, edited by Denis Diderot and Jean le Rond d'Alembert. Vol. 10. Paris: Briasson, 1751–1777. Translated by Malcolm Eden.

——. "Wife [Femme]." In *La Encyclopédie*, edited by Denis Diderot and Jean le Rond d'Alembert. Vol. 6. Paris: Briasson, 1751–1777. Translated by Naomi Andrews.

Kennedy, John. "An Account of Crompton's Life by a Friend." Paper before the Manchester Literary and Philosophical Society, 1830. In *Readings in Modern European History*, edited by James Harvey Robinson and Charles A. Beard. Vol. 2, *Europe Since the Congress of Vienna*. Boston: Ginn & Company, 1909.

Khanin, Vladimir. *Documents on Ukrainian-Jewish Identity and Emigration, 1944–1990*. New York: Routledge, 2002.

Khrushchev, Nikita. "Report of the Central Committee of the Communist Party of the Soviet Union to the 22nd Congress of the C.P.S.U." In *The Road to Communism: Documents of the 22nd Congress of the Communist Party of the Soviet Union*. Moscow: Foreign Language Publishing House, 1961.

Kingsley, Mary H. *Travels in West Africa: Congo Français, Corisco and Cameroons*. London: Macmillan and Company, Ltd., 1897.

Linnebur, Antoinette. Manuscript cookbook c. 1908–1928. Private collection.

Maybaum, Ignaz. *The Face of God after Auschwitz*. Amsterdam: Polak and Van Gennep, 1965. Reprinted from Nicolas de Lange, ed. *Ignaz Maybaum: A Reader*. New York: Berghahn Books, 2001.

McClellan, Elisabeth. *History of American Costume, 1607–1870*. New York: Tudor Publishing Co., 1937.

McCreery, John L. *Japanese Consumer Behavior: From Worker Bees to Wary Shoppers: An Anthropologist Reads Research by the Hakuhodo Institute of Life and Living*. Honolulu: University of Hawai'i Press, 2000.

McLaren, Deborah. *Rethinking Travel and Ecotravel*. Bloomfield, CT: Kumarian Press, 2003.

Melrose, William. *William Melrose in China, 1845–1855: The Letters of a Scottish Tea Merchant*. Edited by Hoh-cheung Mui and Lorna H. Mui. Edinburgh: T. and A. Constable, 1973.

Monier-Williams, Monier. *Modern India and the Indians: Being a Series of Impressions, Notes, and Essays*. London: Trubner and Company, 1878.

Moore, Amasa. Papers. Middlebury College, Middlebury, Vermont.

Morgenthau, Henry. *Ambassador Morgenthau's Story*. New York: Doubleday and Page, 1918.

Nightingale, Florence. *Notes on Nursing: What It Is, and What It Is Not*. New York: D. Appleton and Co., 1860.

Oppenheimer, J. Robert. *Letters and Recollections*. Edited by Charles Wiener. Cambridge, MA: Harvard University Press, 1980.

Paine, Thomas. *The Life and Writings of Thomas Paine*. Edited by Daniel Edwin Wheeler. Vol. 10. New York: Vincent Parke and Co., 1908.

Paul VI, Pope. *Humanae Vitae* [On human life]. Rome: Typis Polyglottis Vaticanis, 1968.

Pawlowski, Gustave de. "Au Theatre des Champs-Elysees: Le Sacre du Printemps, ballet de deux actes de M. Igor Stravinsky" [At the Champs-Elysees Theater: Rite of Spring, a ballet by Igor Stravinsky]. *Comoedia*, VIII/2068 (May 31, 1913). Translated by Truman Bullard.

Razavi, William M. "Turban Cowboy." Unpublished manuscript, 2007.

Riis, Jacob. *How the Other Half Lives*. New York: Charles Scribner's Sons, 1890.

Robinson, Harriet H. *Loom and Spindle, or Life Among the Early Mill Girls*. New York: Thomas Y. Crowell and Co., 1898.

Robinson, Jackie, as told to Alfred Duckett. "*I Never Had It Made*." New York: G.P. Putnam's Sons, 1972.

Robinson, James Harvey, and Charles A. Beard, eds. *Readings in Modern European History*. 2 vols. Boston: Ginn & Company, 1909.

Sacre Coeur, Sister Marie-Andre du. *The House Stands Firm: Family Life in West Africa*. Translated by Alba I. Zizzamia. Milwaukee: The Bruce Publishing Company, 1962.

Saint-Just, Louis de. "Selections from the *Republican Institutions of Saint-Just*." In *Readings in Modern European History*, edited by James Harvey Robinson and Charles A. Beard. Vol. 1: *The Eighteenth Century: The French Revolution and the Napoleonic Period*. Boston: Ginn & Company, 1909.

Schlosser, Eric. *Fast Food Nation: The Dark Side of the All-American Meal*. Boston: Houghton-Mifflin, 2001.

Scott, Georgia. *Headwraps: A Global Journey*. New York: Public Affairs, 2001.

Secondat, Charles de, Baron de Montesquieu. *The Spirit of Laws*. Translated by Thomas Nugent. London: J. Nourse and P. Vaillant, 1750.

Sekizawa Hidehiko. *See* McCreery, John L.

Sharp, Henry. "Old Age Among the Chipewyan." In *Other Ways of Growing Old: Anthropological Perspectives*, edited by Pamela T. Amoss and Stevan Harrell. Stanford, CA: Stanford University Press, 1981.

Shelley, Percy Bysshe. "A Defence of Poetry." In *Essays, Letters from Abroad, and Fragments*. Edited by Mary Wollstonecraft Shelley. London: Edward Moxon, 1840.

Smith, Adam. *An Inquiry into the Nature and Causes of the Wealth of Nations*. London: W. Strahan and T. Cadell, 1776.

Sugita, Genpaku. *Dawn of Western Science in Japan*. Translated by Ryōzō Matsumoto and Eiichi Kiyooka. Tokyo: The Hokuseido Press, 1969.

Sutcliffe, Alice Crary. *Robert Fulton and the "Clermont:" The Authoritative Story of Robert Fulton's Early Experiments, Persistent Efforts, and Historic Achievements*. New York: The Century Co., 1909.

Tappan, Eva March, ed. *The World's Story: A History of the World in Story Song and Art*. 15 vols. Boston: Houghton Mifflin Company, 1914.

Terry, Milton S. *The Shinto Cult: A Christian Study of the Ancient Religion of Japan*. Cincinnati, OH: Jennings and Graham, 1910.

Thompson, Clarence Bertrand, ed. *Scientific Management: A Collection of the More Significant Articles Describing the Taylor System of Management*. Cambridge, MA: Harvard University Press, 1914.

Tocqueville, Alexis de. *Democracy in America*. Translated by Henry Reeve. Vol. 2. New York: J. and H. G. Langley, 1841.

Train, Arthur Jr. "Keeping Up with the Inventors." *Harper's Monthly Magazine* 176 (March 1938): 363–73.

Troyat, Henri. *Daily Life in Russia under the Last Tsar*. New York: Macmillan and Co., 1962.

Ueda Shizuteru. "'Nothingness' in Meister Eckhart and Zen Buddhism." In *The Buddha Eye: An Anthology of the Kyoto School*. Translated by James W. Heig, edited by Frederick Frank. New York: Crossroad, 1982.

U.S. Congress. Senate. Committee on Health, Education, Labor and Pensions. *AIDS Crisis in Africa: Health Care Transmissions: Hearing before the Committee on Health, Education, Labor and Pensions*. 108th Cong., 1st sess., March 27, 2003.

Venel, Gabriel. "Chocolate [Chocolat]." In *La Encyclopédie*, edited by Denis Diderot and Jean le Rond d'Alembert. Vol. 3. Paris: 1751–1777. Translated by Philippe Bonin.

Voltaire [Francois-Marie Arouet, pseud.]. *Philosophical Letters*, 1734. Paris. 1778. Reprinted in James Harvey Robinson and Charles A. Beard, eds. *Readings in Modern European History*. Vol. 1: *The Eighteenth Century: The French Revolution and the Napoleonic Period*. Boston: Ginn & Company, 1909.

Wairy, Louis Constant. *Memoirs of Constant, First Valet de Chambre of the Emperor, on the Private Life of Napoleon, His Family and His Court*. Translated by Elizabeth Gilbert Martin. New York: C. Scribner's Sons, 1895.

Weber, Christian. *The Present State of Russia in Two Volumes . . . with a Description of Petersbourg and Cronslot, And Several other Pieces relating to the Affairs of Russia*. London: W. Taylor, W. and J. Innys, and J. Osborn, 1723.

Weeks, Holland. Papers. The Henry Sheldon Museum of Vermont History, Middlebury, Vermont.

Willis, N. Parker. *Rural Letters and Other Records of Thought at Leisure Written in the Intervals of More Hurried Literary Labor*. New York: Baker and Scribner, 1849.

Wilson, S. G. *Persian Life and Customs: With Scenes and Incidents of the Residence and Travel in the Land of the Lion and the Sun*. New York: Fleming H. Revell Company, 1899.

Young, Arthur. *Travels during the Years 1787, 1788 and 1789 Undertaken more Particularly with a View of Ascertaining the Cultivation, Wealth, Resources, and National Prosperity of the Kingdom of France*. Dublin: R. Cross et al., 1793.

SECONDARY INFORMATION RESOURCES

Alexander, June Granatir. *Daily Life in Immigrant America, 1870–1920*. Westport, CT: Greenwood Press, 2007.

Anderson, James M. *Daily Life during the French Revolution*. Westport, CT: Greenwood Press, 2007.

Atkin, Nicholas. *Daily Lives of Civilians in Wartime Twentieth-Century Europe*. Westport, CT: Greenwood Press, 2008.

Bergquist, James M. *Daily Life in Immigrant America, 1820–1870*. Westport, CT: Greenwood Press, 2007.

Black, Brian. *Nature and the Environment in Nineteenth-Century American Life*. Westport, CT: Greenwood Press, 2006.

——. *Nature and the Environment in Twentieth-Century American Life*. Westport, CT: Greenwood Press, 2006.

Bourque, Stephen A. *Post-Cold War*. American Soldiers' Lives Series. Westport, CT: Greenwood Press, 2008.

Bucher, Greta. *Daily Life in Imperial Russia*. Westport, CT: Greenwood Press, 2008.

Burns, William E. *Science and Technology in Colonial America*. Westport, CT: Greenwood Press, 2005.

Cimbala, Paul A. *The Civil War*. American Soldiers' Lives Series. Westport, CT: Greenwood Press, 2008.

Cumo, Christopher. *Science and Technology in 20th-Century American Life*. Westport, CT: Greenwood Press, 2007.

Eaton, Katherine B. *Daily Life in the Soviet Union*. Westport, CT: Greenwood Press, 2004.

Edwards, Paul M. *The Korean War*. American Soldiers' Lives Series. Westport, CT: Greenwood Press, 2006.

Fixico, Donald. *Daily Life of Native Americans in the Twentieth Century*. Westport, CT: Greenwood Press, 2006.

Frey, Linda S., and Marsha L. Frey. *Daily Lives of Civilians in Wartime Europe, 1618–1900*. Westport, CT: Greenwood Press, 2007.

Heidler, David S., and Jeanne T. Heidler. *Daily Life in the Early American Republic, 1790–1820: Creating a New Nation*. Westport, CT: Greenwood Press, 2004.

———. *Daily Life of Civilians in Wartime Early America: From the Colonial Era to the Civil War*. Westport, CT: Greenwood Press, 2007.

———. *Daily Lives of Civilians in Wartime Modern America: From the Indian Wars to the Vietnam War*. Westport, CT: Greenwood Press, 2007.

Heyman, Neil M. *Daily Life during World War I*. Westport, CT: Greenwood Press, 2002.

Husband, Julie, and Jim O'Laughlin. *Daily Life in the Industrial United States, 1870–1900*. Westport, CT: Greenwood Press, 2004.

Jones, Mary Ellen. *Daily Life on the Nineteenth Century American Frontier*. Westport, CT: Greenwood Press, 1998.

Kaledin, Eugenia. *Daily Life in the United States, 1940–1959: Shifting Worlds*. Westport, CT: Greenwood Press, 2000.

Keene, Jennifer D. *World War I*. American Soldiers' Lives Series. Westport, CT: Greenwood Press, 2006.

Kyvig, David E. *Daily Life in the United States, 1920–1939: Decades of Pain and Promise*. Westport, CT: Greenwood Press, 2001.

Laband, John. *Daily Lives of Civilians in Wartime Africa: From Slavery Days to Rwandan Genocide*. Westport, CT: Greenwood Press, 2006.

Lone, Stewart. *Daily Lives of Civilians in Wartime Asia: From the Taiping Rebellion to the Vietnam War*. Westport, CT: Greenwood Press, 2007.

Marty, Myron A. *Daily Life in the United States, 1960–1990: Decades of Discord*. Westport, CT: Greenwood Press, 1997.

Miller, Randall M. *The Greenwood Encyclopedia of Daily Life in America*. 4 vols. Westport, CT: Greenwood Press, 2008.

Mitchell, Sally. *Daily Life in Victorian England*. Westport, CT: Greenwood Press, 1996.

Nash, Alice, and Strobel Christoph. *Daily Life of Native Americans from Post-Columbian through Nineteenth-Century America*. Westport, CT: Greenwood Press, 2006.

Neimeyer, Charles P. *The Revolutionary War*. American Soldiers' Lives Series. Westport, CT: Greenwood Press, 2007.

Olsen, Kirstin. *Daily Life in 18th-Century England*. Westport, CT: Greenwood Press, 1999.

Pabis, George S. *Daily Life along the Mississippi*. Westport, CT: Greenwood Press, 2007.

Perez, Louis G. *Daily Life in Early Modern Japan*. Westport, CT: Greenwood Press, 2001.

Piehler, G. Kurt. *World War II*. American Soldiers' Lives Series. Westport, CT: Greenwood Press, 2007.

Soumerai, Eve Nussbaum, and Carol D. Schulz. *Daily Life during the Holocaust*. Westport, CT: Greenwood Press, 1998.

Timmons, Todd. *Science and Technology in Nineteenth-Century America*. Westport, CT: Greenwood Press, 2005.

Volo, Dorothy Denneen, and James M. Volo. *Daily Life during the American Revolution*. Westport, CT: Greenwood Press, 2003.

——. *Daily Life in Civil War America*. Westport, CT: Greenwood Press, 1998.

——. *Daily Life in the Age of Sail*. Westport, CT: Greenwood Press, 2001.

Westheider, James E. *The Vietnam War*. American Soldiers' Lives Series. Westport, CT: Greenwood Press, 2007.

INDEX

ABOUT THE EDITORS

LAWRENCE MORRIS, General Editor, is Assistant Professor of English at Albright College. He received his PhD from Harvard University and has taught English literature and history at a variety of institutions including Harvard, University of Wisconsin–Green Bay, and Fitzwilliam College (Cambridge University). Morris is currently writing about the relationship between truth and literary fiction in the religious writing of the medieval British Isles.

DAVID M. BORGMEYER, Volume Editor, holds a PhD in Slavic Languages and Literatures from the University of Southern California and is Adjunct Assistant Professor in the School for Professional Studies, St. Louis University; Senior Lecturer at Fontbonne University; and Adjunct Faculty at Webster University. His research focuses on Russian Modernism.

REBECCA AYAKO BENNETTE, Volume Editor, is Assistant Professor of History at Middlebury College. She received her PhD from Harvard University with a specialty in modern German history. Her publications have focused on religion, gender, and nationalism. She has been recognized for distinction in teaching.